Mastering Adobe Captivate 8

Create responsive demonstrations, simulations, and quizzes for multiscreen delivery with Adobe Captivate

Damien Bruyndonckx

BIRMINGHAM - MUMBAI

Mastering Adobe Captivate 8

First published: August 2012

Second edition: February 2014

Third edition: April 2015

Production reference: 1060415

Published by Packt Publishing Ltd.
Livery Place
35 Livery Street
Birmingham B3 2PB, UK.

ISBN 978-1-78439-830-9

www.packtpub.com

Cover image by Céline Frère

Credits

Author
Damien Bruyndonckx

Project Coordinator
Mary Alex

Reviewers
Karen Drummey

Ruhul Islam Laskar

Proofreaders
Simran Bhogal

Kevin McGowan

Commissioning Editor
Nadeem N. Bagban

Indexer
Rekha Nair

Acquisition Editor
Harsha Bharwani

Production Coordinator
Arvindkumar Gupta

Content Development Editor
Rohit Kumar Singh

Cover Work
Arvindkumar Gupta

Technical Editors
Mrunmayee Patil

Shruti Rawool

Copy Editor
Roshni Banerjee

Foreword

In today's world, the use of devices across all areas of work, home, and travel has become a way of life. Users look at eLearning in the same way as they look at other sources of information, be it news, entertainment, or e-mail. Organizations, schools, and universities worldwide design learning strategies around changes in learner behavior. Also, the pace of transition from pure classroom training to blended or pure eLearning has never been faster. However, the budgets allocated to developing and delivering this content have not grown.

As we evolve through this phase to create more effective and engaging learning content, there is a need to maximize the utility of the tools available and use them productively to achieve our goals of content creation. The need to produce high-quality content without compromising the time taken to create it remains the paramount requirement.

Over the years, Adobe Captivate has established itself as the leading eLearning-authoring tool. Using Adobe Captivate, you'll be able to create everything in eLearning with little or no programming and deploy it across a variety of formats and locations. Adobe Captivate 8's responsive learning capability has been a game changer in eLearning.

To take the first step toward mastering Adobe Captivate, I recommend this wonderful book by Damien Bruyndonckx. Damien takes you through Adobe Captivate with an easy-to-understand, yet comprehensive, description of its features. The wealth of information and resources that Damien has acquired over the years of being an eLearning expert is now easily accessible in one book. Damien is well known in the Adobe community for his deep knowledge of our tools.

If you are an eLearning professional looking to upskill yourself or are aspiring to become one, this book will ensure that you gain expertise with Adobe Captivate and achieve your professional goals.

Happy learning!

Akshay Bharadwaj
Senior product manager
Adobe Captivate

About the Author

Damien Bruyndonckx has an interest in teaching that dates back to his original training as an elementary school teacher. He began his career in 1998, teaching French as a foreign language in two elementary public schools in Louisiana, USA. In 2001, he came back to Belgium, his home country, and began to work as an IT trainer. He soon acquired the title of Adobe Certified Instructor on various Adobe products, which allowed him to work for a large number of customers and Adobe-authorized training centers across Europe. In 2009, he went back to teaching in a school. He now works at IHECS (`http://www.ihecs.be`), a higher education school of communications, based in Brussels, where he teaches multimedia and serves as the eLearning coordinator of the school. Thanks to his work at IHECS, Damien became an Adobe Education Leader in November 2011. He also has his own company that provides Adobe Training and eLearning consultancy. Damien is the author of *Adobe Captivate 7 for Mobile Learning*, published in August 2013, and *Mastering Adobe Captivate 7*, published in February 2014, both by Packt Publishing. You will find him speaking at various Captivate and eLearning-related events around the world. He lives in Thuin, Belgium, with his girlfriend and his two children. Damien is a music lover and occasionally works as a sound and lighting technician in the entertainment industry. You can contact him on Twitter at `@damienbkx` and via his website at `http://www.dbr-training.eu`.

Acknowledgments

If you go to the "About Adobe Captivate" menu item, you will have a chance to see the names of the members of the Adobe Captivate product team. These are the men and women who work very hard on a daily basis to create the piece of software you are about to learn. Last October, I had a chance to meet some of them in Las Vegas during the Adobe Learning Summit. For the first time, I found out who the men and women behind Captivate were. I had a great time chatting and hanging around with them. In addition to being the greatest world-class professionals in their respective fields, they are a group of bright individuals with a great vision of what education should be. They have a real passion for the software product they build. I would like to dedicate this book to the entire Adobe Captivate product team in India. By giving us Captivate, you've made a tremendous contribution to education and changed the lives of thousands of people all around the world (including me).

I also want to thank the editorial team at Packt Publishing for helping me be an author for the fourth time. Special thanks to my long-time partner Harsha Bharwani (Harsha, this is the third book we've done together; can you imagine that?) and to Rohit Kumar Singh for the smooth ride all along this project.

Finally, I want to thank those who share my life on a daily basis. They have to cope with my very long working hours as I write these books. Their love and support played a prominent role in the making of this work. A special thanks to my sweet Céline for taking the most beautiful cover image in the world and for being part of my life for the past 6 years.

It is now time for you to jump headfirst into *Mastering Adobe Captivate 8*. I want to thank you for buying this book. I wish you a great reading experience and, above all, a lot of fun with Adobe Captivate.

About the Reviewers

Karen Drummey has been a learning and online marketing professional for over 25 years. She specializes in instructional design, presentations, and websites. She has worked in corporate, nonprofit environments as well as freelanced to share her expertise with small businesses, real estate, healthcare, and meteorology industries. Her course—"Where's the Power? What's the Point?"—teaches people how to create engaging presentations even if they don't have a designer's eye.

Ruhul Islam Laskar is a learning specialist by profession and technical evangelist by passion. He started his career as a system administrator. His interest in sharing knowledge soon made him a trainer. He holds industry experience in learning design and organizational development and has worked with different multinationals on training implementation. He believes, "Training that enlightens the audience and content that excites the learner are essential factors for educational excellence". His interests lie in the latest authoring tools and delivery platforms to produce creative content for effective learning. In his leisure time, he practices still photography, likes to trek, and contributes to social learning.

www.PacktPub.com

Support files, eBooks, discount offers, and more

For support files and downloads related to your book, please visit www.PacktPub.com.

Did you know that Packt offers eBook versions of every book published, with PDF and ePub files available? You can upgrade to the eBook version at www.PacktPub.com and as a print book customer, you are entitled to a discount on the eBook copy. Get in touch with us at service@packtpub.com for more details.

At www.PacktPub.com, you can also read a collection of free technical articles, sign up for a range of free newsletters and receive exclusive discounts and offers on Packt books and eBooks.

https://www2.packtpub.com/books/subscription/packtlib

Do you need instant solutions to your IT questions? PacktLib is Packt's online digital book library. Here, you can search, access, and read Packt's entire library of books.

Why subscribe?

- Fully searchable across every book published by Packt
- Copy and paste, print, and bookmark content
- On demand and accessible via a web browser

Free access for Packt account holders

If you have an account with Packt at www.PacktPub.com, you can use this to access PacktLib today and view 9 entirely free books. Simply use your login credentials for immediate access.

Table of Contents

Preface   **xiii**

Chapter 1: Getting Started with Adobe Captivate 8   **1**

Obtaining Captivate   **2**
The Captivate perpetual license   2
The Captivate subscription   3
Captivate in Technical Communication Suite   4
The first look at a typical production workflow   **4**
Step zero – the preproduction phase   4
Step one – capturing the slide   5
Step two – the editing phase   5
Step three – the publishing phase   5
Touring the Captivate interface   **6**
Using the advanced interface mode   10
Working with panels   12
Creating a new workspace   13
  Extra credit   15
Renaming and deleting custom workspaces   15
Workspaces in normal mode   16
Exploring the sample applications   **17**
Experiencing the Encoder demonstration   17
Experiencing the Encoder simulation   20
Experiencing the Driving in Belgium sample application   21
Experiencing the Going Mobile responsive application   22
Experiencing the Encoder Video Demo   24
Discussing the sample apps scenario   **27**
Summary   **27**

Meet the community   **28**
  Dr. Pooja Jaisingh   28
  Bio   28
  Contact details   28
Chapter 2: Capturing the Slides   **29**
  Choosing the right resolution for the project   **30**
    Describing the problem   30
    Resizing the project after the initial shooting   31
    Downsizing the application during shooting   31
    Using the panning feature of Captivate   32
    Using the Scalable HTML Content feature   33
    Using a Responsive Project   33
    Conclusion   33
  Recording the first project   **34**
    Preparing the application to record   34
    Rehearsing the scenario   36
    Resetting the application   37
    Recording the movie   37
      Enabling access to assistive devices (Mac users only)   38
      Preparing Captivate to record the sequence   38
      And... action!   40
    Previewing the rushes   41
  The inner working of the Captivate capture engine   **41**
    Understanding the FMR mode   43
  Controlling Captivate during the shooting session   **45**
  Exploring the preferences   **47**
    Exploring the automatic recording modes   47
    Exploring the recording settings   50
    The Video Demo preferences pane   50
  Recording the other versions of the project   **51**
    Previewing the second rushes   54
  Recording with System Audio   **55**
  The Video Demo recording mode   **58**
  Automatic and manual panning   **61**
  Responsive capture   **63**
  Rescaling a project   **67**
  Summary   **68**
  Meet the community   **69**
    Anita Horsley   69
    Contact details   69

Chapter 3: Working with Standard Objects — 71

Preparing your work — 72
Working with the Properties panel — 72
Exploring the objects of Captivate — 76
  Using the Text Caption object — 76
    Modifying the content of a Text Caption — 76
    Creating new Text Captions — 78
    Formatting a Text Caption — 80
  The Highlight Box object — 83
  Working with the mouse — 86
    Understanding the mouse movements — 86
    Formatting the mouse object — 89
  Working with images — 92
    Inserting a slide from another project — 92
    Inserting an image on a slide — 93
    Using the image editing tools — 94
    Inserting a picture slide — 95
    Extra credit – working with characters — 96
  Working with Text Animations — 98
    Duplicating slides — 100
    Converting a Typing object into a Text Animation object — 101
  Working with Smart Shapes — 103
    Drawing a simple Smart Shape — 103
    Drawing additional Smart Shapes — 104
    Creating and saving your own Smart Shapes — 106
    Using Smart Shapes as Highlight Boxes — 110
    Adding text inside Smart Shapes — 112
  The Equation editor — 114
Working with Text Effects — 116
Summary — 120
Meet the community — 120
  Lieve Weymeis — 120
  Contact details — 121

Chapter 4: Working with Multimedia — 123

Editing a Full Motion Recording — 124
Inserting external animations into the project — 126
  Importing Flash animations — 126
  Importing HTML5 animations — 129
Working with video — 133
Working with audio — 136
  Adding audio to the objects — 137
Adding background music to the entire project — 139

Adding audio to the slides   **142**

Recording narration with Captivate   143

Setting up the sound system   143

Recording the narration   145

Importing an external sound clip   148

Using Text-to-Speech to generate narration   150

Installing the Captivate speech agents   150

Working with the Slide Notes panel   150

Converting text to speech   152

Using the Speech Management window   154

Editing a sound clip in Captivate   **156**

Using the Advanced Audio Management window   **159**

Adding Closed Captions to the slides   **160**

Viewing the Closed Captions   163

Closed captioning a video file   164

Extra credit – adding Closed Captions   167

Summary   **168**

Meet the community   **168**

Allen Partridge   169

Contact details   169

Chapter 5: Working with the Timeline and Other Useful Tools   **171**

Preparing your work   **172**

Working with the Library   **172**

Importing external assets into the library   174

Reusing library items   177

Importing objects from another library   178

Deleting unused assets from the library   178

Laying out the objects on the slides   **180**

Using Smart Guides   180

Grouping objects   181

Using the Align toolbar   183

Selecting multiple objects   184

Extra credit – aligning and distributing the remaining objects   186

Putting it all together   187

Working with the Timeline   **189**

Using the Timeline to select objects   189

Using the Timeline to lock and unlock objects   190

Using the Timeline to show and hide objects   192

Using the Timeline to change the stacking order of the objects   192

Using the Timeline to set the timing of the objects 193
Tips and tricks for great syncing 195
Extra credit – adjusting the timing of the other slides 202
Adding effects to objects **203**
Combining effects 205
Extra credit – adding effects to images 206
Finishing touches 207
Summary **208**
Meet the community **209**
Kevin Siegel 209
Contact details 209

Chapter 6: Working with Interactive Objects **211**
Preparing your work **212**
Working with Buttons **212**
Formatting Buttons 214
Using Smart Shapes as Buttons 216
Branching with Buttons 219
Discovering the Rollover objects **221**
Working with Rollover Captions 221
Working with Rollover Smart Shapes 223
Working with Rollover Images 226
Working with Rollover Slidelets 228
Inserting and formatting a Rollover Slidelet 228
Inserting objects in a Rollover Slidelet 231
Working with the Drag and Drop interaction **233**
Using the Drag and Drop interaction wizard 234
Using the Drag and Drop panel 237
Using the Drag and Drop interaction for branching and navigation 238
Creating a simulation **242**
Hiding the Mouse object 243
Replacing the video file and the project title 244
Using Find and Replace 245
Working with Click Boxes 247
Branching with Click Boxes 249
Extra credit – adding the remaining Click Boxes 252
Working with Text Entry Boxes 252
Finishing touches 256
Summary **258**
Meet the community **258**
Joe Ganci 259
Contact details 259

Chapter 7: Working with Styles, Master Slides, Themes, and Templates   261

Working with the Swatch Manager	**262**
Importing custom Swatches to the Swatches panel	264
Using custom colors	264
Extra credit – importing custom swatches	266
Working with Styles	**267**
Managing Styles with the Properties panel	267
Resetting a style	268
Creating new Styles	269
Applying Styles	269
Modifying a Style	270
Applying styles automatically	270
Working with the Object Style Manager	275
Renaming styles	275
Exporting a style	277
Importing a style	278
Creating a style in the Object Style Manager	279
Extra credit – exporting and importing styles	281
Working with Themes	**282**
Applying a Theme to an existing project	282
The elements of a Theme	284
The Master Slides	284
Styles	288
Creating a custom Theme	**289**
Customizing the Master Slides of the Theme	290
Customizing the Main Master Slide	291
Adding a Master Slide to the Theme	292
Adding Placeholders to the Master Slides	294
Applying the Master Slides to the Slides of the Project	295
Modifying a Master Slide	296
Adding Styles to the Theme	298
Styling the titles	298
Extra credit – styling the remaining objects	300
Saving the styles in the Theme	301
Extra credit – applying the Theme to another project	301
Working with Templates	**302**
Creating a Template	302
Adding Placeholder Slides	304
Adding the last slides	305
Saving the Template	306
Creating a new Captivate project from a Template	306
Summary	**308**

Meet the community — **309**
Richard John Jenkins — 309
Contact details — 309

Chapter 8: Producing a Video Demo — **311**
The Video Demo interface — **312**
The postproduction phase of a Video Demo project — **313**
Adding objects to a Video Demo project — 314
Inserting images in a Video Demo project — 314
Inserting objects in a Video Demo project — 315
Removing unwanted popups — 316
Adding Pan & Zoom animation — 317
Adding Transitions — 319
Publishing a Video Demo project — **321**
Publishing to YouTube — 323
Summary — **324**
Meet the community — **325**
Michael Lund — 325
Contact details — 325

Chapter 9: Creating a Responsive Project — **327**
About Responsive Projects — **328**
Viewport size versus screen size — 329
Understanding breakpoints — 330
Setting up a Responsive Project — **332**
Adjusting the breakpoints — 333
Adjusting the slide height — 334
Applying a responsive theme — 336
Testing a Responsive Project — **339**
Testing in the authoring environment — 339
Testing in a browser — 340
Testing with Adobe Edge Inspect — 341
Installing Adobe Edge Inspect — 341
Testing a Captivate project on your mobile devices — 342
Adding content in a Responsive Project — **345**
Understanding the view hierarchy — 346
Extra credit – adding text content in a Responsive Project — 347
Relinking views — 348
Extra credit – relinking text content — 352
Excluding content from views — 352
Excluding content from other views — 353
Sizing and positioning content in a Responsive Project — **358**
Making images responsive — 359
Creating responsive text — 362

Pixel and percent positioning	365
Using Percent Relative positioning	368
Using Smart Position	369
Extra credit – smart positioning the other objects	373
Summary	**374**
Meet the community	**375**
Josh Cavalier	375
Contact details	375
Chapter 10: Working with Quizzes	**377**
Introducing the quiz	**378**
Creating Question Slides	**380**
Inserting the first Question Slide	380
Using the Multiple Choice question	384
Understanding the basic question properties	385
Working with Partial Scoring	387
Branching with Question Slides	388
Finalizing the Question Slide	389
Using Smart Shapes as feedback messages	390
Importing Question Slides from a GIFT file	391
Working with Matching questions	392
Working with Short Answer questions	394
Working with True/False questions	396
Adding the remaining Question Slides	398
Working with Fill-In-The-Blank questions	398
Working with Hotspot questions	400
Working with Sequence questions	402
Creating surveys with Likert questions	403
Previewing the quiz	**405**
Creating a Pretest	**406**
Exploring the Quiz Preferences	**408**
Setting the passing score of a quiz	411
Working with Question Pools	**414**
Creating a Question Pool	414
Inserting questions in a Question Pool	416
Inserting random Question Slides in the main project	417
Styling the elements of the Question Slides	**419**
Reporting scores to an LMS	**421**
Understanding SCORM, AICC, and Tin Can	422
Enabling reporting in Captivate	423
Reporting options at the interaction level	423
Setting up project-level reporting options	431
Creating a SCORM manifest file	434

Summary	**436**
Meet the community	**436**
Rod Ward	436
Tristan Ward	437
Contact details	437
Chapter 11: Using Captivate with Other Applications	**439**
Integrating Captivate with PowerPoint	**440**
Converting an existing presentation to Captivate	440
Viewing the presentation in PowerPoint	441
Creating a Captivate project from a PowerPoint presentation	441
Round Tripping between Captivate and PowerPoint	446
Updating a linked PowerPoint presentation	448
Inserting a PowerPoint slide in a Captivate project	450
Localizing a Captivate project using Microsoft Word	**454**
Importing a Photoshop file into Captivate	**457**
Round Tripping between Captivate and Photoshop	463
Editing audio with Adobe Audition	**464**
Exporting to Flash Professional	**468**
Exporting the project to XML	**471**
Summary	**472**
Meet the community	**472**
Jim Leichliter	473
Contact details	473
Chapter 12: Working with Variables, Advanced Actions,	
and Widgets	**475**
Working with variables	**476**
System and User Variables	477
Exploring System Variables	477
Generating text dynamically	479
Extra credit – generating a Quiz Results slide for the Pretest	481
Using User Variables	482
Creating a User Variable	482
Capturing values with Text Entry Boxes	483
Using user-defined variables to dynamically generate text	484
Working with Advanced Actions	**485**
Using Standard Actions	486
Automatically turning on Closed Captions with Advanced Actions	486
Extra credit – turning Closed Captions off	489
Using Conditional Actions	490
Creating the necessary variables	491
Assigning a score to each possible answer	493
Giving names to objects	495

Conditionally showing and hiding objects 497
Using a Conditional Action to implement branching with the Pretest 503
Using Shared Actions 506
Importing the necessary slides 506
Creating the necessary variables and naming the objects 507
Creating the Shared Action 509
Saving the Shared Action 511
Using and reusing the Shared Action 512
Geolocation in Adobe Captivate **516**
Inserting an extra slide 516
Detecting the location of the learner 517
Creating a custom Geolocation variable 518
Altering the content based on the learner's location 520
Working with Smart Learning Interactions **521**
Working with the Accordion Interaction 522
Working with the Web Object Interaction 525
Extra credit – working with the Award of Excellence Interaction 527
Summary **528**
Meet the community **528**
Rick Zanotti 529
Contact details 529
Chapter 13: Finishing Touches and Publishing **531**
Finishing touches **532**
Checking the spelling 532
Exploring the Start and End preferences 536
Using the project metadata and accessibility 538
Exploring other project preferences 542
Exporting project preferences 543
Customizing the project Skin 545
Customizing the Playback Controls bar 546
Working with Borders 550
Adding a Table of Contents 552
Applying the same Skin to other projects 557
Publishing a Captivate project **560**
Publishing to Flash 561
Using the Scalable HTML content option 564
Publishing to HTML5 564
Using the HTML5 Tracker panel 565
Publishing the project in HTML5 566
Publishing a Responsive Project 568
Using Mobile Palette 568
Publishing a Responsive Project 570

Publishing an eLearning-enabled project   571
  Hiding and showing slides   571
  Publishing the SCORM package in HTML5   572
  Extra credit – publishing the Flash version of the SCORM package   573
Working with the Multi SCO packager   574
  Creating a SCORM package from the Video Demo project   574
  Creating a single-course package from multiple SCOs   576
Publishing to PDF   579
Publishing as a standalone application   580
Publishing as an .mp4 video file   582
  Publishing to YouTube   583
Publishing to Microsoft Word   585
  Extra credit – publishing to Word   586
Publishing for devices   **586**
Summary   **592**
Meet the community   **593**
  Kirsten Rourke   593
  Contact details   593
Index   **595**

Preface

Adobe Captivate is the industry-leading solution for authoring highly interactive eLearning content that can be delivered on any device. With Adobe Captivate, you can capture onscreen action, enhance eLearning projects, insert SCORM and Tin Can-compliant quizzes, optimize content for multiscreen delivery, and publish the work in various formats (including Adobe Flash and HTML5) for easy deployment on virtually any desktop or mobile device.

Mastering Adobe Captivate 8 is a comprehensive step-by-step learning guide to creating SCORM-compliant demonstrations, simulations, and quizzes that can be experienced on any device. The sample projects demonstrate virtually every feature of Adobe Captivate, giving you the expertise you need to create and deploy your own professional quality eLearning courses.

This book will guide you through the creation of eLearning projects, including a Demonstration, a Simulation, a Video Demo, a Responsive Project, and a SCORM-compliant Quiz.

What this book covers

Chapter 1, *Getting Started with Adobe Captivate 8*, introduces Captivate as an eLearning solution. It drives you through the tool icons and panels of the Captivate interface. At the end of this chapter, we will discuss the finished sample applications that we will build during the course of this book.

Chapter 2, *Capturing the Slides*, introduces the Captivate screen capture engine that allows you to capture the slides of your projects. You will also learn how to choose the right size for the projects you have to make.

Chapter 3, Working with Standard Objects, teaches you how to use the standard objects of Captivate to enhance the slides captured in the previous chapter. The standard objects discussed in this chapter include Text Captions, Highlight Boxes, Images, and Mouse Movements.

Chapter 4, Working with Multimedia, teaches you how to include and edit various types of multimedia elements in your eLearning projects. The tools covered in this chapter include the insertion of video and audio files in the project, the Captivate Text-To-Speech engine, and Close Captioning of the audio narration.

Chapter 5, Working with the Timeline and Other Useful Tools, covers various tools and features (such as the Alignment tools and Smart Guides) used to lay the objects out in the physical space of the slide. The use of the Timeline panel to synchronize the components of the project is also discussed in detail.

Chapter 6, Working with Interactive Objects, introduces the objects that bring interactivity to the project. These objects include the Rollover objects, the Drag and Drop interaction, Click Box, Text Entry Box and Button. These objects will be used to convert a demonstration into a simulation and to discuss Branching.

Chapter 7, Working with Styles, Master Slides, Themes, and Templates, focuses on the cosmetic aspects of your projects. You will learn how to ensure visual consistency both within a given project and across projects using Styles, Master Slides, Themes, and Templates.

Chapter 8, Producing a Video Demo, introduces the concept of Video Demo. This chapter covers the specifics of that type of project as compared to the regular Captivate projects used in previous chapters.

Chapter 9, Creating a Responsive Project, discusses the new Responsive project features of Captivate in detail. You will learn how to optimize your eLearning content for multiple desktop, tablet, and phone devices using responsive design techniques. You will also learn how to test a responsive project on your mobile devices using Adobe Edge Inspect.

Chapter 10, Working with Quizzes, discusses the powerful Quizzing engine of Captivate. You will import questions into your Captivate project using various techniques, review each and every question type of Captivate one by one, and integrate them into question pools to generate random quizzes. In the second part of this chapter, you will see how these interactions can be reported to a SCORM- or Tin Can-compliant LMS to easily track your student's performance.

Chapter 11, Using Captivate with Other Applications, explores the relationship between Captivate and other Adobe and third-party applications. First, you will convert a PowerPoint presentation into a Captivate project. You will then export some Captivate data to Microsoft Word in order to localize a Captivate project. You will also import an Adobe Photoshop file, edit audio with Adobe Audition, and export the project to Adobe Flash.

Chapter 12, Working with Variables, Advanced Actions, and Widgets, unleashes the true power of Captivate and explores Variables, Advanced Actions, Widgets, and Smart Learning Interactions. These features will help you design and develop highly interactive eLearning content that offers a unique experience to each and every learner.

Chapter 13, Finishing Touches and Publishing, explains the final steps of publishing. You will make your projects ready for publishing by modifying project-level options and preferences. One of these options is the Skin Editor that lets you customize the playback controls and the table of contents of your projects. In the second part of this chapter, you will make your projects available to the outside world by publishing them in various formats including Adobe Flash, HTML5, video, and PDF.

What you need for this book

You need the latest version of Adobe Captivate 8 (available as a free 30-day trial version on the Adobe website) to complete the exercises in this book. Some exercises require the free Captivate 8.0.1 update patch available on the Adobe website, and some exercises require Adobe eLearning assets and Text-To-Speech voice agents. Both of them are available for free on the Adobe website.

Other requirements are as follows:

- Adobe Media Encoder CS 6 (AME CS6 is part of the Captivate 8 download)
- A modern web browser with the latest version of the Flash Player installed
- Microsoft PowerPoint 2003 or higher (optional)
- Microsoft Word 2003 or higher (optional)
- Adobe Photoshop CS6 or higher (optional)
- Adobe Flash CS6 or higher (optional)
- Adobe Audition CS6 or higher (optional)

Who this book is for

This book is for you if you are:

- A teacher wanting to produce high quality eLearning content for your students

- An instructional designer, eLearning developer, or human resources manager who wants to implement eLearning in your company

- Using a SCORM- or Tin Can-compliant LMS and want to produce eLearning content and track the performances of your students

- A webmaster in need of a fun and interactive way to produce an FAQ or a support site

- A brand owner in need of great training and support material for your products.

- Interested in eLearning

A basic knowledge of your operating system (Mac or Windows) is all it takes to be the author of the next generation of eLearning content.

Conventions

In this book, you will find a number of text styles that distinguish between different kinds of information. Here are some examples of these styles and an explanation of their meaning.

Code words in text, database table names, folder names, filenames, file extensions, pathnames, dummy URLs, user input, and Twitter handles are shown as follows: "Video Demo projects use the `.cpvc` file extension and have a specific user interface."

New terms and **important words** are shown in bold. Words that you see on the screen, for example, in menus or dialog boxes, appear in the text like this: "In the **Preview** dropdown, choose the **Play Slide** option."

Warnings or important notes appear in a box like this.

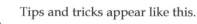

Tips and tricks appear like this.

Reader feedback

Feedback from our readers is always welcome. Let us know what you think about this book—what you liked or disliked. Reader feedback is important for us as it helps us develop titles that you will really get the most out of.

To send us general feedback, simply e-mail feedback@packtpub.com, and mention the book's title in the subject of your message.

If there is a topic that you have expertise in and you are interested in either writing or contributing to a book, see our author guide at www.packtpub.com/authors.

Customer support

Now that you are the proud owner of a Packt book, we have a number of things to help you to get the most from your purchase.

Downloading the example code

You can download the example code files from your account at http://www.packtpub.com for all the Packt Publishing books you have purchased. If you purchased this book elsewhere, you can visit http://www.packtpub.com/support and register to have the files e-mailed directly to you.

Downloading the color images of this book

We also provide you with a PDF file that has color images of the screenshots/diagrams used in this book. The color images will help you better understand the changes in the output. You can download this file from http://www.packtpub.com/sites/default/files/downloads/8309OT_ColoredImages.pdf.

Errata

Although we have taken every care to ensure the accuracy of our content, mistakes do happen. If you find a mistake in one of our books—maybe a mistake in the text or the code—we would be grateful if you could report this to us. By doing so, you can save other readers from frustration and help us improve subsequent versions of this book. If you find any errata, please report them by visiting http://www.packtpub.com/submit-errata, selecting your book, clicking on the **Errata Submission Form** link, and entering the details of your errata. Once your errata are verified, your submission will be accepted and the errata will be uploaded to our website or added to any list of existing errata under the Errata section of that title.

To view the previously submitted errata, go to https://www.packtpub.com/books/content/support and enter the name of the book in the search field. The required information will appear under the **Errata** section.

Piracy

Piracy of copyrighted material on the Internet is an ongoing problem across all media. At Packt, we take the protection of our copyright and licenses very seriously. If you come across any illegal copies of our works in any form on the Internet, please provide us with the location address or website name immediately so that we can pursue a remedy.

Please contact us at copyright@packtpub.com with a link to the suspected pirated material.

We appreciate your help in protecting our authors and our ability to bring you valuable content.

Questions

If you have a problem with any aspect of this book, you can contact us at questions@packtpub.com, and we will do our best to address the problem.

1
Getting Started with Adobe Captivate 8

Since its introduction in 2004, Captivate has always been the leading solution for authoring eLearning content. In the beginning, it was a very simple screen-capture utility called FlashCam. In 2002, a company named eHelp acquired FlashCam and turned it into a fully-fledged eLearning authoring tool called RoboDemo. In 2004, another company called Macromedia acquired eHelp, changed the name of the product once again, and **Macromedia Captivate** was born. A few months later, Adobe acquired Macromedia and, consequently, Macromedia Captivate became **Adobe Captivate**.

As the years passed, Adobe released Captivate 2, 3, and 4—adding tools, objects, and features along the way. One of the most significant events in the Captivate history took place in July 2010, when Adobe released Captivate 5. For that release, Adobe engineers rewrote the code of the entire application from the ground up. As a result, Captivate 5 was the first version to be available on both Mac OS and Windows. Version 6 was another milestone for Captivate as it was the first version to propose an HTML5 publishing mechanism. Prior to Captivate 6, the main publishing option was Adobe Flash.

As of today, the latest version of Captivate is Version 8. Captivate 8 introduces a revolutionary new feature called **Responsive Projects**. Responsive Projects allow you to rearrange the content of your eLearning projects for the desktop, the tablet, and for smartphone, making mobile learning a whole lot easier and powerful. Other new features introduced in Captivate 8 include an improved HTML5 publishing mechanism, support for geolocation and gestures on mobile devices, a brand new user interface, and tons of other (not so) small enhancements.

With all this power sitting one click away, it is easy to overcharge your projects with lots of complicated audiovisual effects and sophisticated interactions that can ultimately drive the learner away from the primary objective of every Captivate project: teaching.

While working with Captivate, one should never forget that Captivate is an eLearning authoring tool. At the most basic level, it simply means that you, the developer of the project, and your audience are united by a very special kind of relationship: a student-teacher relationship. Therefore, from now on—and for the rest of the book—you will not be called *the developer* or the *programmer*, but *the teacher*. The ones who will view your finished applications will not be the *users* or the *visitors*, but will be called *the learners* or *the students*. You will see that it changes everything.

In this chapter, you will:

- Discover the available options to obtain Captivate
- Discover the general steps of the Captivate production process
- Tour the all new Captivate 8 interface
- Work with panels and workspaces
- View the finished sample applications

Obtaining Captivate

Before you can start working with Captivate, it is necessary to download and install the software. In this section, you will discover the three ways by which Adobe makes Captivate available to you.

The Captivate perpetual license

This is the old-fashioned way of obtaining the software. You buy Captivate and get a serial number to activate your installation. Once activated, Captivate will be permanently available on your computer, even when you don't need it. With this option, you get all the core functionalities of Captivate and you can start working on your eLearning projects right away! This book works flawlessly with the Captivate perpetual license.

 See the Captivate page on the Adobe website at `http://www.adobe.com/products/captivate.html`.

You can download and use this version of Captivate free of charge for 30 days. It should be more than enough for you to go through the exercises of this book. However, once the trial period is over, you will not have access to Captivate unless you convert your trial to a licensed version. This can be a perpetual or a subscription license.

 Download your Captivate 30-day trial from `http://www.adobe.com/go/trycaptivate/`.

The Captivate subscription

With this licensing model, you subscribe to Captivate on a monthly basis. It means that you pay a certain amount of money each month to keep using Captivate. The main benefit of the subscription model is that you automatically get all the updates as they are released. The subscription model is the best way to ensure that you always have the latest version of Captivate installed on your system. Note that the subscription is just another licensing model, and the software is identical to the perpetual licensing model.

More information on the Captivate subscription model can be found at `http://www.adobe.com/products/captivate/buying-guide-subscriptions.html`.

Although the Captivate subscription model is very similar to the way Adobe Creative Cloud works, Captivate is—at the time of writing—not a part of the Creative Cloud.

Captivate and the Creative Cloud

If you already have a Creative Cloud subscription, you'll need another subscription for Captivate.

Captivate in Technical Communication Suite

Technical Communication Suite (TCS) is yet another bundle of applications from Adobe. It is designed to create technical content such as help files and user guides. TCS includes applications such as Adobe RoboHelp, Adobe FrameMaker, Adobe Acrobat Professional, and of course, Adobe Captivate.

For more information on TCS, visit `http://www.adobe.com/ products/technicalcommunicationsuite.html`.

The first look at a typical production workflow

Producing content with Captivate is a three-step process—or, to be exact, a four-step process. However, only three of the four steps take place in Captivate. That's why I like to refer to the first step as "step zero"!

Step zero – the preproduction phase

This is the only step of the process that does not involve working with the Captivate application. Depending on the project you are planning, it can last from a few minutes to a few months. This step is probably the most important of the entire process as it is where you actually create the scenarios and the storyboards of your teaching project. This is where you develop the pedagogical approach that will drive the entire project. What will you teach the students? In what order will you introduce the topics? How and when will you assess the students' knowledge? These are some of the very important questions you should answer before opening Captivate for the first time. Step zero is where the teacher's skills fully express themselves.

Blog post - Scenario-based training

Make sure you read this series of posts on the official Adobe Captivate Blog. Dr. Pooja Jaisingh, Adobe eLearning evangelist, shares her experience in creating scenario-based training. These posts clearly stress the importance of "step zero" and give you a first high-level approach to the Captivate production process. The first post of the series can be found at `http://blogs.adobe.com/captivate/2012/03/ my-experience-with-creating-a-scenario-based-course- part-1.html`.

Step one – capturing the slide

If your project involves teaching computer-related skills, you will use one of the most popular Captivate features: the ability to record any action you perform onscreen. You will simply use your mouse to perform actions on your computer. Behind the scenes, Captivate will be watching and recording any action you do using a sophisticated screen capture engine based on screenshots. This first step can be compared to shooting a movie. The goal is to acquire the needed images, actions, and sequences. In the movie industry, the raw material that comes out of the shooting is called "the rushes". It is not uncommon for a movie director to discard lots of rushes along the way so that only the very best sequences are part of the final release. Step one of the process will be covered in *Chapter 2*, *Capturing the Slides*.

Sometimes, the Captivate project you will be working on will not be based on screenshots. In such a case, you will create the slides entirely within Captivate or import them from Microsoft PowerPoint. Importing PowerPoint slides in Captivate will be covered in *Chapter 11*, *Using Captivate with Other Applications*.

Step two – the editing phase

This step is the most time-consuming of the entire process. This is where your project will slowly take shape. In this step, you will arrange the final sequence of actions, record narrations, add objects to the slides (such as Text Captions and Buttons), arrange those objects in the timeline, add title and ending slides, develop the advanced interactions, and so on. At the end of this step, the project should be ready for publication.

Step three – the publishing phase

Step three is used to make your project available to the learners, and this is where Captivate really is awesome! Captivate lets you publish your project in the popular Adobe Flash format. This is great since it makes the deployment of your eLearning courses very easy: only the Flash player is needed. The very same Flash player that is used to read Flash-enabled websites or YouTube videos is all you need to play back your published Captivate projects. The major caveat of this publishing format is that it is not supported on mobile devices.

To address this issue, Captivate can also publish in HTML5, which makes the project available to web and mobile devices, without the need for any extra third-party plugins. You can also publish in both Flash and HTML5, and let Captivate decide what format will be served to your learners depending on the device they use to access the course.

Captivate can also publish the project as a standalone application (.exe on Windows and .app on Macintosh) or as video files that can be easily uploaded to YouTube and viewed on a tablet or smartphone.

Step three will be covered in detail in *Chapter 13, Finishing Touches and Publishing*.

Blog post

Make sure you read this wonderful blog post by Allen Partridge, *The How & Why of iPads, HTML5 & Mobile Devices in eLearning, Training & Education* at http://blogs.adobe.com/captivate/2011/11/ the-how-why-of-ipads-html5-mobile-devices-in- elearning-training-education.html.

Touring the Captivate interface

In this book, we shall cover the three steps of the process requiring the use of Captivate. You will discover that Captivate has specific tools to handle each of the three steps. Actually, each step requires so many options, tools, and features that Captivate has a very large numbers of icons, panels, dialog boxes, and controls available.

You will now discover this new interface using the following steps:

1. Open Captivate.
2. If needed, click on the **Recent** tab situated at the top of the Welcome screen.
3. Click on the **Browse** button situated at the bottom of the **Recent** tab of the Welcome screen.
4. Open the final/encoderDemo_800.cptx file situated in the exercise folder.

Your screen should look similar to the following screenshot:

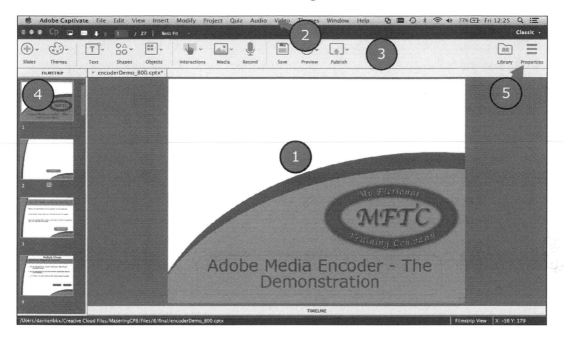

The default Captivate user interface looks very simple and clean. The main area is covered by the stage (**1**). The stage is where you will lay out the objects that make up each slide of the project.

At the very top of the screen is the **Menu bar** (**2**). The menu bar gives you access to every single feature of Captivate.

Below the menu bar is the main set of icons of Captivate 8 (**3**). These icons are primarily used to insert new slides and new objects into the project, but it also contains important tools for operations such as previewing, publishing, and saving. On the Captivate forum, this bar has been nicknamed the **Big Buttons Bar** (or **BBB**).

On the left-hand side of the screen is the **Filmstrip (4)** panel. It shows the sequence of slides that make up your Captivate project. The primary use of the **Filmstrip** panel is to enable navigation between the slides of the project, but it can also be used to perform basic operations on the slides such as reordering or deleting slides.

5. At the far right-hand side of the Big Buttons Bar, click on the **Properties** button (**5**).

This action reveals the **Properties** panel. The **Properties** panel is one of the most important panels of Captivate. It is used to control and adjust all the properties pertaining to the selected object.

6. Click on the **Properties** button of the Big Buttons Bar one more time to hide the **Properties** panel.

7. Click on the **Library** button located just next to the **Properties** button to open the **Library** panel.

The **Library** panel is another key component of Captivate. It maintains a list of all the assets (such as images, audio clips, animations, and so on.) present in the project.

8. Click on the **Library** button of the Big Buttons Bar to close the **Library**.

9. Click on the **Timeline** panel that appears at the very bottom of the screen to reveal the **Timeline** panel.

The **Timeline** panel is used to arrange the objects of the slide in time. This panel is also used to set up the stacking order of the objects. It is, of course, possible to open many panels at the same time.

10. Click on the **Properties** button of the Big Buttons Bar to reopen the **Properties** panel.

Both the **Timeline** and the **Properties** panel should now be open.

The **Properties, Library,** and **Timeline** panels are among the most important panels of Captivate. This is why they are only one mouse click away on the default user interface. However, Captivate contains a lot more of these panels giving you access to a myriad of interesting tools. To get the most out of Captivate, you should know how to turn them on and off.

11. Open the **Window** menu of Captivate.

The **Window** menu displays a list of all the panels available in Adobe Captivate.

12. Click on **Slide Notes** to open the **Slide Notes** panel.

The **Slide Notes** panel appears at the bottom of the screen next to the **Timeline** panel as depicted in the following screenshot:

SLIDE NOTES	TIMELINE
▣ ▤ ▣◄ ▣⬚ Text-to-Speech Closed Captioning Filter Notes ▼ ✚ ━	

Let's now open one more panel.

13. Use the **Window | HTML5 Tracker** menu item to open the **HTML5 Tracker** panel.

The **HTML5 Tracker** panel lists the features and objects of the project that are not supported in the HTML5 output. Note that this panel is floating on top of the interface. This is very different from the **Slide Notes** panel you opened earlier that was attached (docked) at the bottom of the interface.

Each panel of Captivate is either docked or floating. Also note that in Captivate 8, it is—by default—not possible to dock a floating panel or to undock a docked panel.

The interface is now very different from what it was when you first opened Captivate.

14. Quit the Captivate application without saving the changes made to the open file.

15. Reopen Captivate.

When Captivate reopens, you should see the **Recent** tab of the Welcome screen by default with a thumbnail showing the last open project(s).

16. Double-click on the **encoderDemo_800** thumbnail to reopen the project.

When the project reopens, notice that the default Captivate interface is displayed even though many more panels were open when you exited Captivate a few minutes ago.

Thanks to these little experiments, you have been exposed to some important basic concepts about the Captivate interface. Before moving on, let's summarize what you have learnt so far:

- The Captivate interface is composed of panels laid out around the main editing area called the stage.
- By default, most of the panels are hidden, making the default interface simple and clean.

- Some panels of Captivate are not immediately available on the default interface. You must use the **Window** menu to turn these panels on and off.

- When you close and restart Captivate, the interface setup is not maintained across sessions.

Using the advanced interface mode

If you are used to other Adobe tools, such as Photoshop, InDesign, or Illustrator, this behavior probably looks very strange and annoying. Hopefully, there is a way to make the Captivate interface behave similarly to the interface of other popular Adobe tools. This is called the **advanced interface mode**.

1. Use the **Adobe Captivate | Preferences** menu item (for Mac) or the **Edit | Preferences** menu item (for Windows) to open the **Preferences** dialog box of Captivate.

2. In the **General Settings** category of the **Preferences** dialog box, select the **Enable custom workspaces / panel undocking** option as shown in the following screenshot:

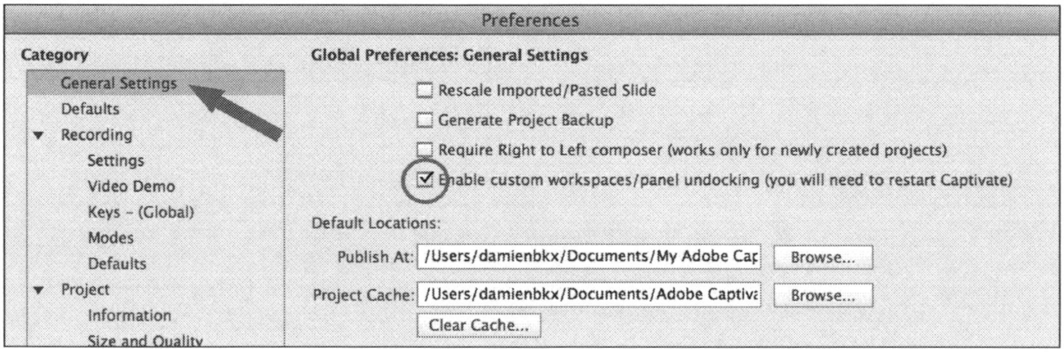

3. Click on **OK** to validate the new option and close the **Preferences** dialog.

4. As indicated in the **Preferences** dialog box, restart Adobe Captivate to enable the new option. Make sure you don't save the possible changes made to the file.

5. When Captivate restarts, double-click on the **encoderDemo_800** thumbnail on the **Recent** tab of the Welcome screen.

Note that the **Properties** and **Library** buttons of the Big Buttons Bar are not displayed anymore.

6. Go to **Window | Properties** to reopen the **Properties** panel.

7. Use the same procedure to reopen the **Library** and **Slide Notes** panels.

8. Return to the **Window** menu one last time to turn the **HTML5 Tracker** panel on.

9. At the bottom of the interface, click on the **Timeline** button to reveal the **Timeline** panel.

The interface should now look pretty much the same as when you first left Captivate earlier in this chapter.

10. Restart Captivate one more time. Make sure that you don't save the possible changes made to the project.

11. When Captivate restarts, reopen the project by clicking on the **encoderDemo_800** thumbnail on the **Recent** tab of the Welcome screen.

The panel layout should have been maintained, as shown in the following screenshot:

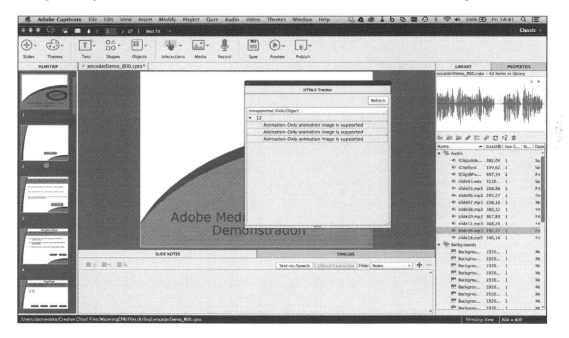

In the next section, you will take a closer look at those panels, but let's first make a quick summary of what has been covered in this section:

- To make the Captivate interface behave like the interface of other Adobe tools, you must switch to the advanced interface mode.

- To do so, select **Enable custom workspaces/panel undocking** in the **Preferences** window of Captivate. It is necessary to restart Captivate for this change to take effect.

Working with panels

You already know that Captivate contains a lot of panels and that those panels can be turned on and off using the **Window** menu. Now, in advanced interface mode, the Captivate interface offers even more flexibility. In this section, you will learn how to move the panels around in order to create a unique custom panel arrangement.

1. Place your mouse on the black area at the top of the floating **HTML5 Tracker** panel.
2. Drag the panel to the right and drop it on **Properties** and **Library** situated at the top of the **Properties** and **Library** panels panel.

When a panel is moved above a possible docking location, a blue bar appears on the screen. Releasing the mouse at that moment docks the panel at the location highlighted by the blue bar.

This action should dock the **HTML5 Tracker** panel with the **Properties** and **Library** panels, as shown in the following screenshot:

LIBRARY	PROPERTIES	HTML5 Tracker
		Refresh
Unsupported Slide/Object		
▼ 12		
Animation–Only animation image is supported		
Animation–Only animation image is supported		
Animation–Only animation image is supported		

This first manipulation illustrates how to dock the panels that are initially floating on the interface. You will do the opposite manipulation to illustrate the fact that a docked panel can be turned into a floating panel:

3. Place your mouse on top of the **Library** mention situated on the right hand side of the screen.

4. Drag the **Library** panel out of the **Library** / **Properties** / **HTML5 Tracker** group and drop it on top of the stage.

You have now arranged the panels in a truly unique way. Such an arrangement of panels is called a **workspace**.

Creating a new workspace

The advanced interface mode of Captivate allows you to come up with unique (custom) workspaces. Depending on the project you are working on, the size of your computer screen, your working habits, and so on, you might want to quickly switch between the workspaces you came up with. In this section, you will first learn how to reset the default workspace. You will then create and save a brand new custom workspace.

The default workspace that is applied when you first open Captivate is called the **Classic** workspace as indicated in the top-right corner of the Captivate interface.

1. Click on the **Classic** button at the top-right corner of the screen.

2. Choose **Reset Classic** in the drop-down menu as shown in the following screenshot.

After this operation, the Captivate interface reverts to what it looked like when you first opened the application at the beginning of this chapter.

This default **Classic** workspace is an excellent starting point for defining a custom workspace.

3. Use the **Window | Quiz Properties** menu item to turn the **Quiz** panel on.

4. In the **Filmstrip** panel, select the fourth slide of the project.

By default, the **Quiz** panel appears on the right hand side of the screen. When a question slide (such as slide 4) is selected, the **Quiz** panel shows the quiz-specific properties applied to that particular question. Take some time to examine the properties present in this panel, and don't worry if you don't understand them all. You will have a detailed overview of the Quiz feature in *Chapter 10, Working with Quizzes*.

5. Use the **Window | Properties** menu item to turn the **Properties** panel on.

6. Drag the **Properties** panel out of the **Properties/Quiz** group and drop on it on top of the **Filmstrip** panel in order to dock the **Properties** panel with the **Filmstrip** panel.

After this last manipulation, your screen should look like the following screenshot:

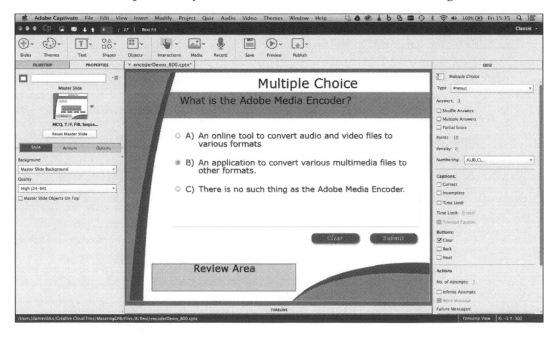

This particular workspace is very practical when you work with the Quiz feature of Captivate, so you will now save this panel layout as a new workspace.

7. Click on the same **Classic** button you used earlier at the top right corner of the screen.

8. Choose **New Workspace** from the drop-down menu.

9. In the **New Workspace** dialog, name your new workspace Quizzing and click on **OK**.

Note that a **Quizzing** button now replaces the old **Classic** button. You can now use this button to switch between the Classic workspace of Captivate and your very own custom Quizzing workspace!

10. Click on the **Quizzing** button at the top right corner of the screen.

11. Click on **Classic** in the drop-down menu to reapply the default **Classic** workspace.

12. Click on the **Classic** button and reapply the **Quizzing** workspace.

This demonstrates how you can quickly switch between the workspaces you have saved.

Extra credit

You know all the tools you need to know in order to create custom workspaces. I suggest you now take some time to experiment with these tools on your own. Try turning panels on and off using the **Window** menu. Of course, feel free to examine the other panels of Captivate, such as the **Question Pool** or **Project Info** panels. When you feel like you came up with a great workspace, save it under your name.

Renaming and deleting custom workspaces

If you need to rename or delete a custom workspace, execute the following steps:

1. Go to **Window | Workspace | Manage Workspace**.

Note that navigating to **Window | Workspace** displays the very same drop-down menu as the workspace switcher button situated at the top right corner of the screen.

2. In the **Manage Workspace** dialog, choose the workspace to delete/rename.

Note that the default **Classic** workspace is not listed. It means that this default workspace cannot be renamed or deleted.

3. Click on the **Rename** or **Delete** button. In this example, click on the **OK** button to close the box without any changes.

4. Open the workspace switcher one last time to reapply the **Classic** workspace before moving on to the next topic.

Updating a workspace

There is no menu item to update an existing workspace. If you want to update an existing workspace, use the **New Workspace** menu item and give the new workspace the name of the existing workspace you want to update.

Workspaces in normal mode

You can return to the normal interface mode using the following steps:

1. Use the **Adobe Captivate | Preferences** menu item (for Mac) or the **Edit | Preferences** menu item (for Windows) to reopen the **Preferences** of Captivate.

2. In the **General Settings** category of the **Preferences** dialog box, deselect the **Enable custom workspaces/panel undocking**.

3. Restart Captivate without saving the changes made to the open project.

4. When Captivate reopens, double-click on the **encoderDemo_800.cptx** thumbnail to reopen the project.

Confirm that the **Properties** and **Library** buttons are back at the right-hand side of the Big Buttons Bar. This indicates that you are back in normal interface mode.

5. Click on the workspace switcher button at the top-right corner of the Captivate interface. It should currently read **Classic**.

In normal interface mode (that is, when the **Enable custom workspaces/panel undocking** option of the **Preferences** category is not selected), only the **Classic** workspace can be applied or reset. If you want to use your custom Quizzing workspace that you created earlier, you first need to return to advanced interface mode and to restart Captivate.

Before moving on to the next topic, these are the key points to keep in mind when creating custom workspaces:

- It is necessary to set Captivate in advanced interface mode to be able to dock and undock panels and to create new workspaces.

- Use the **Window | Workspace | New Workspace** menu item to save the current panel layout as a new workspace.

- Use the **Window | Workspace | Manage Workspace** menu item to rename or delete your custom workspaces.

- To update an existing workspace, use the **New Workspace** command and give the new workspace the same name as the workspace you want to update.

- The default Classic workspace of Captivate cannot be deleted or renamed.

- In normal interface mode, only the default Classic workspace is available.

Exploring the sample applications

Now that you know a bit more about the Captivate interface, let's take a look at the sample applications you will build during the course of this book. These applications have been designed to showcase almost every single feature of Captivate. Use them as a reference if there is something unclear during one of the exercises.

Experiencing the Encoder demonstration

The first application that you will explore is a typical Captivate project. It uses the screen capture engine of Captivate to create a screenshots-based movie.

1. Use the **File | Open** menu item to open the `encoderDemo_800.cptx` file situated in the `final` folder of the exercises you downloaded from the Web.

2. Click on the **Preview** icon of the Big Buttons Bar.

3. From the drop-down list, choose the **Project** item to preview the entire project.

Captivate generates a temporary Flash file and opens it in the floating **Preview** pane. Follow the onscreen instructions to go through the project. This puts you in the same situation as a learner viewing this eLearning content for the first time.

The project begins with a short welcome video followed by a pretest of three questions. The pretest is made to check if the learner really needs to take this particular training. Learners that fail the pretest must take the course, while those who pass can skip the course if they want to. To fully understand this feature, it is necessary to take the course twice. Try to answer the questions of the pretest correctly the first time and incorrectly the second time to see how you experience the project in both situations.

The second part of this first sample application (after the pretest) is known as a **demonstration**. As the name suggests, a demonstration is used to demonstrate something to the learner. Consequently, the learner is passive and simply watches whatever is going on on the screen. In a demonstration, the mouse object is shown. It moves and clicks automatically.

This particular demonstration features some of the most popular Captivate objects such as Text Captions and Highlight Boxes. You have also experienced sound in the Captivate demonstration as well as the closed captions.

4. When finished, close the **Preview** pane.

5. Take some time to take a closer look at the **Preview** icon in the following screenshot:

This is one of the icons you'll use the most during the course of this book. It has seven options to control which part of the project you want to preview and how you want to preview it. Note that each of these options is associated with a keyboard shortcut that depends on the system you work on (Mac or Windows). Place your mouse on top of each of the items in the list to see the associated shortcut in a tooltip.

> **Previewing a responsive project**
>
> When in a responsive project, the preview options do not behave exactly as described in the following list. The responsive projects will be covered in *Chapter 9, Creating a Responsive Project*.

Let's now describe the options of the **Preview** icon in detail:

- **Play Slide**: This option plays the current slide in the Captivate Interface. It is the only preview option that does not open the default web browser or a floating preview pane. Consequently, this preview option is not able to render all the features of Captivate. Previewing a single slide is a good option to quickly test the timing of the objects.

- **Project**: This option generates a temporary Flash file and plays the entire project in the Preview pane.

- **From this Slide**: This option generates a temporary Flash file, so every single feature of Captivate is supported in this preview mode. Captivate opens the Preview pane and plays the project from the currently selected slide to the end.

- **Next 5 Slides**: This is a great option to quickly test a specific sequence of the project. Captivate opens the Preview pane to play a temporary Flash file containing five slides, starting from the currently selected slide.

- **In Browser**: Using this preview option, you will see the project in a context very close to the one that will be used by your learners. Captivate generates a temporary Flash file as well as a temporary HTML file. It then plays the entire project in the default browser.

- **HTML5 in Browser**: When using this option, the project is published in HTML5, JavaScript, CSS, and images. It is then played in the default web browser. Note that some features and objects of Captivate are not supported in the HTML5 output. If you plan on publishing your project in HTML5, make sure you use this preview option to ensure that the features, animations, and objects you use in your project are supported in HTML5.

- **In Adobe Edge Inspect**: This is one of the coolest new features of Captivate 8! It is very useful for testing and previewing your responsive projects. It allows you to connect your mobile devices (iOS, Android, or Kindle Fire) to your web browser (Google Chrome only) in order to view your project right on your devices. This feature will be covered in *Chapter 9, Creating a Responsive Project*.

Floating and Modal panels

In Captivate, a panel can be floating or docked. When a panel floats, the tools and switches situated on other panels are still active. But when the **Preview** panel is open, only the buttons of that panel are active, while the tools of the other panels are not active anymore. The Preview pane is said to be a **Modal** floating panel because it disables every tool situated on other panels. Also, note that the Preview panel cannot be docked.

Experiencing the Encoder simulation

You will now open another sample application. Actually, it is not a real *other* application, but another version of the Encoder demonstration you experienced in the previous topic:

1. Use the **File | Open** menu item and open the `encoderSim_800.cptx` file situated in the `final` folder of the exercises.

2. Once the file is open, click on the **Preview** icon of the Big Buttons Bar and choose the **In Browser** option.

3. The project opens in the default web browser and starts to play automatically.

When the project reaches slide 5, it stops and waits for you to interact with the movie. This is the main difference between a demonstration and a simulation.

In Captivate, a **simulation** is a project in which the learner is active. In a simulation, the mouse object is hidden, as learners use their own mouse to click around the screen in order to progress toward the end of the movie. The very fact that the students are active implies a whole new level of complexity; the learners can perform either the right or the wrong action. In each case, the course must react accordingly. This concept is known as **branching**, that is, each student experiences the application based on his/her own actions.

4. Follow the onscreen instructions and try to perform the right actions. The application has been set to give you two chances to perform each action correctly.

5. When you are through, close the browser and return to Captivate.

In order to experience the branching concept hands on, preview the entire project again but, this time, give yourself a break and perform the wrong actions at each and every step of the simulation (don't worry, it is not graded!). You will see that the application reacts differently and shows you things that were not shown when the right actions were performed! That's branching in action!

This second sample application features pretty much the same Captivate objects as the demonstration you experienced earlier. Only the mouse had to be replaced by interactive objects. Three of those interactive objects have the ability to stop the course and wait for the learner to interact. All these interactive objects can implement the branching concept. Using these objects will be covered in *Chapter 6, Working with Interactive Objects*.

Both the Encoder demonstration and simulation are based on screenshots. To create these sample applications, the first two steps of the production process described earlier have been used.

- In step one (the capture step), the actions have been actually performed in the real Adobe Media Encoder; they were recorded by Captivate behind the scenes.

- In step two (the postproduction step), the course has been edited in Captivate. Sound and closed captions were added, video was imported, the title and ending slides were created, timing was adjusted, and so on. I even imported a slide created in Microsoft PowerPoint!

- Step three (the publishing step) has not (yet) been performed on these files.

Experiencing the Driving in Belgium sample application

You will now preview the third sample application.

1. Use the **File | Open** menu item and open the `drivingInBe.cptx` file situated in the `final` folder of the exercises.

2. Once the file is open, click on the **Preview** icon of the Big Buttons Bar and choose the **In Browser** option.

3. Take the course in the web browser as a regular student would.

When done, return to Captivate and use the **Preview** icon again to preview the entire project a second time. Answer the questions differently from the first time. You will have yet another experience of the branching concept.

This third sample application is very different from the projects you have experienced so far. It is not really a demonstration or a simulation. It is none of it and a bit of both at the same time. As you can see, the borderline between a demonstration and a simulation is sometimes very difficult to spot!

When it comes to sound, this movie makes use of the Text-to-Speech engine of Captivate. Text-to-Speech is a great alternative to quickly create the sound clips you need, but the quality of the speech is not as good as when a real human being speaks in front of a good old microphone!

This application is not based on screenshots and does not teach software-related skills. Instead, each slide has been created one by one, right in Captivate.

This application is also much more sophisticated than the Encoder applications. Advanced actions and variables are used throughout the project to power the dynamic features such as the name of the student appearing in a text caption. It also features the certificate interaction on the last slide (only if you pass the quiz!) and uses the built-in collection of characters to spice up the training with a human touch! But the most impressive feature of this particular project is probably the **Quiz**, one of the brightest and most popular Captivate tools.

The project contains eight question slides. Six of these are stored in a **Question pool**. Each time the project is viewed, one question is shown to the student and a second one is randomly chosen from the question pool. That's why you did not experience the exact same quiz as the first time, when you previewed the application the second time.

Experiencing the Going Mobile responsive application

The Going Mobile project is a new responsive project. Responsive projects have been introduced in Captivate 8.

1. Use the **File | Open** menu item and open the `goingMobile.cptx` file situated in the `final` folder of the exercises.

As soon as the project opens in Captivate, you should notice the extra ruler at the top of the stage. This extra ruler lets you switch between the three views of a responsive project as shown in the following screenshot:

2. Click on the tablet icon (**2**) to switch to the **Tablet** view.
3. Click on the mobile phone icon (**3**) to switch to the **Mobile** view.
4. Finally, click on the desktop icon (**1**) to return to the **Primary** view.

Voila! You have the basic idea behind the new responsive project features. It allows you to reposition and reformat each object in each of the three views, effectively optimizing your eLearning content for each type of mobile device.

5. Click on the **Preview** icon of the Big Buttons Bar.

Note that the **Preview** icon does not provide as many preview options when in a responsive project. This is because a responsive project can only be published in HTML5. All the Flash-based previewing options are therefore not available.

6. Click on the **Project** option to preview the whole project.

Unlike when in a regular Captivate project, when in a responsive project, navigating to **Preview | Project** opens the default web browser. Once the preview opens in the browser, use the buttons and the slider situated on top of the project (as shown in the following screenshot) to test the three views:

Note how each object is resized and repositioned as you move the slider. The project is able to adapt itself to the available viewport width and this is what responsive is all about!

7. Follow the onscreen instructions as if you were a learner taking the course for the first time. When you are done, close the browser and return to Captivate.

These special previewing features are excellent to let you quickly test the responsiveness of your project during the development phase, but they have one major disadvantage. Because you preview the project using the default browser of your desktop or laptop computer, you can't actually experience the mobile situation to its full extent.

The ultimate test drive for such a project is to view it on a mobile device using a touchscreen and tap actions. If you have such a device available, the final version of this project can be viewed online.

8. Use your tablet and/or your smartphone to browse the following URL: `http://courses.dbr-training.eu/8/goingmobile`.

9. Make sure you go through the entire project using each of the devices you have. As you do so, notice the differences and the similarities between the desktop, tablet, and mobile experiences.

The responsiveness of the project is based on the available viewport width, not on the detection of an actual device. For example, when using a tablet in landscape mode, the project will most probably use the primary layout—even though you are using a tablet. If you have a big smartphone (also known as a phablet), the tablet layout will be used instead of the mobile layout.

This is an interesting and complex topic that will be covered in more detail in *Chapter 9, Creating a Responsive Project.*

Experiencing the Encoder Video Demo

Video Demo mode is a special recording mode of Captivate that is used to produce `.mp4` video files. These files can easily be uploaded to online services such as YouTube, Vimeo, or Daily Motion for playback on any device (including iPad, iPhone, and other Internet-enabled mobile devices).

1. Use the **File | Open** menu item and open the `encoderVideo.cpvc` file situated in the `final` folder of the exercises.

First, note that a Video Demo project does not use the same `.cptx` file extension as a regular Captivate project. It uses the `.cpvc` file extension instead. This is the first indication that this project is not going to behave as the other ones you have experienced so far. In addition to a specific file extension, Video Demo projects also have their own Captivate interface, as shown in the following screenshot:

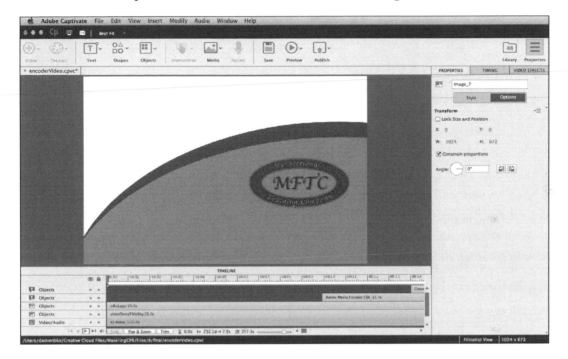

In the preceding screenshot, note the absence of the **Filmstrip** panel. A Video Demo project is not based on slides. Actually, it is a single big video file, so the **Filmstrip** panel makes no sense in a Video Demo project.

In a video file, interactions are not possible. The file can only be experienced from start to finish in the order defined by the teacher. In other words, it is said that a video file proposes a linear experience to the learner while branch-aware interactive projects propose a nonlinear experience. Therefore, interactive objects as well as quizzes and branching are not available in a Video Demo project.

2. Take some time to inspect the rest of the interface. Try to spot the other differences between the regular Captivate interface and the interface used for Video Demos.

3. When you are ready, click on the **Preview** icon.

Surprise! Only two options are available in the **Preview** icon!

4. In the **Preview** dropdown, choose the **Play Slide** option.

5. Watch the whole movie as if you were viewing it on YouTube!

6. Use the **File | Close All** menu item and close every open file. If prompted to save the changes, make sure you do *not* save the changes to these files.

After viewing these sample applications, you should have a pretty good idea of the tools and general capabilities of Captivate. Before moving on, let's summarize what you have learned from these movies:

- Captivate is able to capture the actions you do on your computer and turn them into slides using a sophisticated capture engine based on screenshots.

- A **demonstration** is a project in which the learner is passive and simply watches the onscreen action.

- A **simulation** is a project in which the user is active.

- Sound and video can be imported in Captivate. The application also features a Text-to-Speech engine and closed captioning.

- Question slides can be created in Captivate. These question slides can be stored in question pools to create random quizzes.

- Other objects that can be included in a Captivate project include text captions, the highlight boxes, and so on.

- Captivate contains interactive objects. Three of these interactive objects are able to stop the playhead and wait for the user to interact with the course.

- A responsive project contains three different views to let you optimize your eLearning content for multi-screen delivery. The responsive project feature is a new capability of Captivate 8.

- A Video Demo is not based on screenshots, but is a big video file instead.
- Video Demo projects use the `.cpvc` file extension and have a specific user interface.

Discussing the sample apps scenario

In the exercise folder you downloaded from the Web, you'll find the scenarios of these sample apps in PDF format in the `scenarios` folder. Take some time to read those documents and to compare them to the finished applications.

When working with Captivate, the scenario is a very important document. Its goal is to guide you during the whole production process. Thanks to the scenario, you'll always have the big picture of the entire project in mind. The scenario will also help you stay within the scope of your project.

That being said, the scenario can, and probably will, evolve during the production process. And this is a good thing! Every teacher knows that his/her own understanding of a given topic increases and changes while teaching it. What is true in a classroom is also true in a Captivate project. After all, working in Captivate is all about teaching and, consequently, your scenario is nothing more than a guide.

Summary

In this chapter, you have been introduced to the four steps of a typical Captivate production process. You toured the application interface and learned how to customize it to fit your needs. Thanks to the advanced interface mode and to the workspace feature, you have been able to save your customized interface as a new workspace in order to reapply your custom panel layout anytime you want to.

Finally, you have been walked through the sample applications you will develop in this book, which gave you the first high-level overview of Captivate's rich set of features.

In the next chapter, you will concentrate on the first step of the Captivate production process: the capture step. You will learn various techniques used to capture the slides and you will discover the inner working of Captivate's capture engine. You will also learn about tips and tricks that will help you take a first critical decision—choosing the right size for your project.

 To see and experience more Captivate applications, visit `http://www.adobe.com/products/captivate/showcase.html`.

Meet the community

The title of the book you are reading is *Mastering Adobe Captivate 8*. In order to truly "master" a piece of software, I'm convinced that one must be introduced to the community that supports it.

At the end of each chapter is a *Meet the community* section that will introduce you to a key member of the community. By the end of the book, you'll have known the names, blog addresses, twitter handles of some of the most influential members of the Captivate and eLearning community. I hope these resources will jump start your own Captivate career and, who knows, your own involvement in the community.

Dr. Pooja Jaisingh

In this first *Meet the community* section, I'd like to introduce you to Dr Pooja Jaisingh. Pooja is one of the Adobe eLearning evangelists. In particular, she is one of the main contributors to the official Adobe Captivate blog and to the Captivate page on Facebook. Pooja also organizes free Captivate trainings and webinars. See the schedule of these free trainings at `http://www.adobe.com/cfusion/event/index.cfm?event=list&loc=en_us&type=&product=Captivate`.

Thanks to Pooja, I had a chance to teach an amazing Captivate class in Seoul, South Korea, in June 2014. This was my first experience in Asia and I'll never forget it! Thank you Pooja!

Bio

Pooja Jaisingh has worked for more than 14 years as a teacher trainer, eLearning instructional designer, and, currently, is a senior eLearning evangelist with Adobe Systems. Pooja's core strengths are communication and innovation. In all her roles, she has promoted eLearning as a mode of delivery and has created a host of eLearning courses. In her current role, she conducts numerous seminars and workshops, educating training folks on the features of Adobe Systems' eLearning products. She regularly blogs, initiating creative discussions on multiple opportunities in eLearning. She holds a master's degree in Education and Economics and a Doctorate in Educational Technology.

Contact details

- **Blog**: `http://blogs.adobe.com/captivate`
- **Twitter**: `@poojajaisingh`
- **Facebook**: `http://www.facebook.com/adobecaptivate`

2
Capturing the Slides

Now that you have a better understanding of the features of Captivate, it is time to explore the first step of the production process: capturing the slides. You will use this step when you need to teach software-related skills, such as the manipulation of an application, or to demonstrate how a website works.

This step can be compared to the filming of a movie. When filming a movie, the director wants to capture all the images, sequences, and shots he needs. In the movie industry, this raw material is called the **rushes**. When the filming is complete, the director goes back to the studio to start the postproduction process. It is during the postproduction step of the process that the final movie takes shape. Only the best rushes make their way to the movie theater while the others are discarded along the way. That being said, the postproduction phase can only be successful if the filming provides enough good quality material to create a great movie.

The same basic idea applies to Captivate. When capturing the slide, you should always keep in mind that the postproduction phase will follow. Therefore, the goal of the capture phase is to create enough quality slides to ensure the success of the next phase of the process.

At the end of this chapter, you will be far from the final result you want to achieve, but you will have enough quality slides to start editing your projects.

In this chapter, you will:

- Learn how to choose the right size/resolution for the project
- Tour the recording preferences and the recording modes
- Record demonstrations and simulations
- Record System Audio

- Discuss and use the Full Motion Recording
- Discuss and experience the Video Demo recording mode
- Use Manual Panning
- Resize a project

If you are ready, it's almost time to turn the camera on and start the real action!

Choosing the right resolution for the project

Choosing the right resolution for capturing the slides is the first critical decision you have to make. You have to make it right because the size of the captured slides will play a critical role in the quality of the final movie.

Describing the problem

A typical Captivate project, such as the Encoder demonstration you experienced in *Chapter 1*, *Getting Started with Adobe Captivate 8*, involves taking screenshots of an actual piece of software. At the end of the process, the project will typically be published in Flash or HTML5 and placed on a web page. Most of the time, that web page displays many other page elements (such as logos, headers, footers, navigation bars, and so on) in addition to incorporating your Captivate movie. This can lead to a very delicate situation, as shown in the following image:

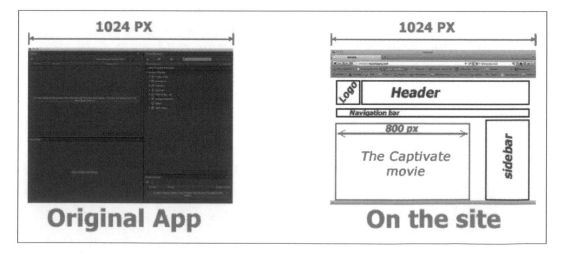

The preceding image shows the application you need to capture on the left. Let's pretend this application requires a minimal width of 1024 pixels to be displayed without horizontal scrollbars. On the right-hand side of the image is the wireframe of the web page you must put your finished movie on. The page has been designed to fit a 1024-pixel-wide screen and has to display lots of elements in addition to the Captivate content. To cope with the design requirement of the web page, your project should not be wider than 800 pixels.

So here is your problem: you have to find a way to fit 1024 pixels into 800 pixels! Several approaches are available to address this situation. Each of these approaches has its pros and cons, and we will go through a brief review of each.

Resizing the project after the initial shooting

The first approach is a two-step process. The first step is to record the project with a width of 1024 pixels, and the second step is to use the Rescale Project feature of Captivate to downsize the project to 800 pixels.

By recording with a screen width of 1024 pixels, the application is captured in its intended size, matching the student's experience of the application.

The main disadvantage of this approach is that it requires resizing the Captivate project. In Captivate, the resize operation is a one-way destructive operation. It always has a cost in terms of image quality. Surprisingly, the resize operation can result in a larger file size, even if the new resolution is smaller than the original one. Also, if the new resolution is smaller, the screenshots will be smaller as well and the information they contain might become very difficult to read.

Here are a few things you need to keep in mind when resizing a project:

- It is always better to downsize a project than to make it bigger.
- Always keep a backup copy of the project in its original resolution. Remember that the resize operation is a one-way destructive operation. Your backup copy is the only way to rollback the resize operation in case something goes wrong!

Downsizing the application during shooting

The second approach is to downsize the application to record during the capture in order to fit the requirements of the project. In this example, it means the application would be 800 pixels wide instead of 1024 pixels during the capture.

As far as Captivate is concerned, this is the easiest solution, as no destructive or complex resize operation is needed. But for the captured application, this situation is not ideal. Remember that the application you capture requires a minimal width of 1024 pixels. So, by downsizing it to a width of 800 pixels, it does not have enough room to display all its components and generates horizontal scrollbars. These scrollbars and their associated scrolling actions (if any) will be captured and will appear in the resulting Captivate animation. Also, scrollbars sometimes hide important information from the screen, and therefore, from your students.

Using the panning feature of Captivate

In the movie industry, panning refers to moving the camera while filming. In Captivate, it means that you can move the recording area while capturing the slides.

This approach tries to cope with both the requirements of the application to record and the requirements of the movie to be produced.

The idea is to leave the application at its intended width of 1024 pixels, and—at the same time—define a capture area that is 800 pixels wide. During the recording, the smaller capture area can be moved over the bigger application, as shown in the following image:

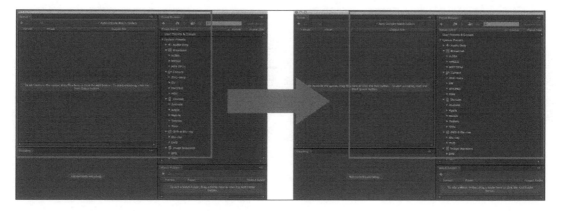

In the preceding screenshot, the capture area is the red rectangle. In other words, Captivate only captures what is inside the red rectangle. As you can see, the capture area does not always cover the same part of the application during the recording.

This approach is a good compromise, but it has two major disadvantages. Moving the recording area while filming increases the file size of your final movie. But more importantly, using this approach, your learner never sees the application entirely, which could compromise the quality of the learning process.

Using the Scalable HTML Content feature

The Scalable HTML Content feature makes the published movie fluid, so it fits the screen it is viewed on (even as the screen is resized!).

For example, say you shoot and publish your movie at a size of 1024 pixels, but the movie is viewed on a website where the maximal resolution can only be 800 pixels. In such a case, the Scalable HTML Content feature scales the movie down to 800 pixels so it fits in the available space.

This approach is quick and easy to implement, but it has a major flaw: you lose control over how your content will be actually experienced. Only a small percentage of your learners (those who have the exact same screen as yours) will see the course as you designed it. The other learners will see the course either bigger (which means possibly pixelized) or smaller (which probably means too small to be comfortable).

This option will be covered in *Chapter 13, Finishing Touches and Publishing*.

Using a Responsive Project

Captivate 8 introduces one more solution to this problem. By using a responsive project, you can rearrange the layout and the content of your course to make it fit various screen sizes.

The main advantage of this approach is that you can control almost every aspect of your project on virtually any screen size. On the other hand, the projects built using this solution can only be published in HTML5, so only the objects supported in HTML5 can be used in such projects. Also, creating a responsive project takes a bit more time and requires using special tools and features of Captivate.

Building a responsive project is covered in *Chapter 9, Creating a Responsive Project*.

Conclusion

None of these approaches is perfect, but you'll have to choose one anyway. The best approach depends on the project, on your learners, and on your personal taste. Here are some general guidelines to help you make the best choice:

- The size of the capture area must match the size of the application to capture whenever possible.

- If you need to resize the project, take a bigger project and make it smaller to help maintain the best possible image quality. Also, make sure you keep a backup copy of the project at its original size.

- Use panning only if you really need it.

- When panning, move the camera (the red capture area) only when necessary, and move it slowly enough to help the students build a mental picture of the entire application.

- If you use the Scalable HTML Content feature, make sure you test your work on an array of different screens and devices to ensure the best possible student experience in the majority of the scenarios.

- Responsive projects can only be published in HTML5. They also require some more work and the use of special tools.

Finally, never forget that you are teaching. Your learners don't care about your sizing concerns; they just want to learn something. If the chosen approach compromises the quality of the learning process, then it is the wrong approach!

About screen sizes

For more information about the screen sizes in use today, visit `http://www.websitedimensions.com/`.

Recording the first project

It is time to have a first hands-on experience of an actual recording session. Recording a Captivate project is a five-step process:

1. Preparing the application to record.
2. Rehearsing the scenario.
3. Resetting the application.
4. Recording the movie.
5. Previewing the rushes.

Let's review these steps one by one.

Preparing the application to record

For this exercise, the application you will record is Adobe Media Encoder CS6. This application is used to convert video and audio files in a wide range of formats. **Adobe Media Encoder (AME)** is included in the standard Captivate package; if you have Captivate (even the trial version), you also have AME.

First, you will reset the Captivate workspace and open AME by performing the following steps:

1. Open Captivate. If Captivate is already open, close all open files.

2. If needed, reset the Classic workspace using the **Window | Workspace | Reset 'Classic'** menu item.

3. Open AME. On Mac, it is situated in the `/Applications/Adobe Media Encoder CS6` folder. On Windows, a shortcut to AME should be available in the **Start** menu.

When AME opens, make sure it looks like the following screenshot:

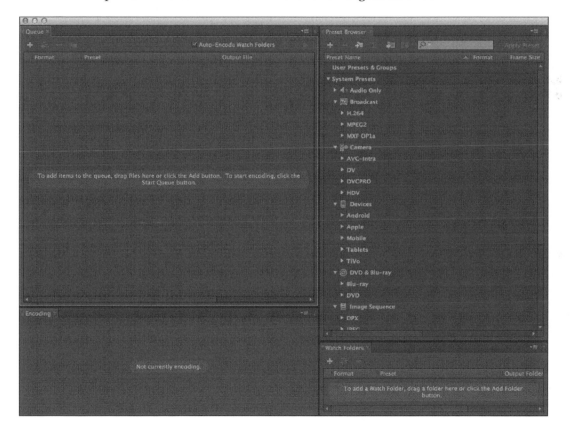

This exercise and the screenshots are based on Adobe Media Encoder CS6, which is the version installed with Captivate 8, but it also works with Adobe Media Encoder CC. In Version CC 2014, it is not possible to convert a file to the .flv format. Therefore, the exercise will not work if you use Adobe Media Encoder CC 2014.

Rehearsing the scenario

The goal of this Captivate project is to teach students how to use AME to convert a QuickTime movie (with a .mov extension) to Flash video (with a .flv extension). This scenario follows the exact same steps as those used in the demonstration and simulation you experienced in the previous chapter. Make sure the audio system of your computer is turned on before rehearsing the following scenario. Here are the steps:

1. Go to the Adobe Media Encoder application.
2. In the top-left corner of the application, click on the + icon.
3. Browse to the videos/MOV folder of the exercise files and load the demo_en.mov QuickTime movie into AME.
4. Open the **Format** drop-down list and choose the .flv format.

If the .flv format is not available in your version of Adobe Media Encoder, use the H.264 format instead. You will then create an .mp4 file instead of an .flv file.

5. Open the **Preset** drop-down list and apply the last 4 x 3 preset (the one before the last in the list).
6. Click on the preset name to open the **Export Settings** dialog.
7. If needed, open the **Video** tab situated in the lower right area of the **Export Settings** dialog.
8. Scroll down the **Video** tab until you see the **Resize Video** section.
9. Make sure the Maintain Aspect Ratio icon (the chain icon) is active, and change the width of the video to 400 pixels. Normally, the new height of the video is automatically set to **300** pixels.
10. Click on the **OK** button to validate the new export settings.
11. Click on the Start Queue button (the green play icon) to start the actual encoding.

The encoding process begins. In the **Encoding** panel at the bottom of the screen, a yellow bar shows the progress of this operation. When the operation is complete, the system plays a brief chime sound effect.

Make sure you master these steps, and make sure AME behaves as expected before continuing. If you need more practice, feel free to rehearse this scenario a few more times before the recording. After all, on a real movie set, even the most famous actors rehearse their scenes many times before the director finally decides to turn the camera on.

Resetting the application

When you are ready to record the sequence, don't forget to reset AME to its original state. The best way to do it is to perform the following steps:

1. Close and restart AME.
2. When the application reopens, make sure it looks like the previous image again.

Also, delete the `.flv` file(s) generated during the rehearsal(s) by performing the following steps:

3. Open the **Finder** (Mac) or the **Windows Explorer** (Windows) and browse to the `videos/MOV` folder of the exercises.
4. Delete every `.flv` file present in this folder.

On a real movie set, this is the job of the script girl!

Recording the movie

You know the scenario and Adobe Media Encoder is ready to be captured. Let's head back to Captivate and start the actual recording process.

Enabling access to assistive devices (Mac users only)

If you work on Mac, there is one system option to change before Captivate can record the project. Use the following steps to make your Mac ready to record:

1. The first time you create a new software simulation with Captivate, a dialog box appears on the screen asking you if you want to allow Captivate to access the assistive devices.

2. Click on **Open System Preferences** to open the **System Preferences** application.

3. If needed, click on the lock icon at the bottom-left corner of the **System Preference** application and authenticate as an administrator.

4. Select the **Captivate** option to grant Captivate access to the assistive devices.

Without this step, Mac OS does not broadcast the events that Captivate uses to capture user interactivity (clicking on a button, typing a text entry, and so on).

Preparing Captivate to record the sequence

For this first practice recording, you will use the default options of Captivate to record the sequence using the following steps:

1. Close every open file so that the Captivate Welcome screen is displayed.

2. On the **New** tab of the Welcome screen, double-click on the **Software Simulation** thumbnail. You can also use the **File | Record new Software Simulation** menu item to achieve the same result.

The Captivate interface disappears and a red rectangle is displayed on the screen. This red rectangle is the recording area.

3. In the recording window, choose **Application** to record an application.

4. In the **Select the window to record** drop-down list, choose to record the **Adobe Media Encoder CS6** application.

The **Adobe Media Encoder** application opens and the red recording area snaps to the application window.

5. In the **Snap to** section of the box, choose to record at **Custom Size**.

6. Choose the **1024 x 768** size from the drop-down list. The red recording area and AME are both resized to the chosen size.

7. Leave the remaining options at their default settings.

8. The recording window should look like the following screenshot:

In the preceding screenshot, notice the **Demo** checkbox in the lower part of the window. Make sure this checkbox is the only one selected.

 Mac users, the **System Audio** checkbox might be unavailable on your system. This problem will be addressed later in this chapter.

The stage is set and the actors are in place. Everyone is waiting for the director's signal to get started!

And... action!

The signal is the red **Record** button at the bottom of the recording window. Once you click on it, all your actions are recorded by Captivate until you stop the capture:

 If you have a problem while doing this exercise, refer to the `Chapter02/final/encoderDemo_1_1024.cptx` file of your exercises folder.

1. Click on the red **Record** button at the bottom of the recording window. After a short countdown, you'll be in recording mode.

2. In the **Adobe Media Encoder** window, perform the actions as written in the scenario you rehearsed earlier in this chapter.

During the recording, pay close attention to the following things:

- Each time you click, you should hear a camera shutter sound
- When you type in the **Width** field, you should hear keystrokes
- After clicking on the **Start Queue** button, AME displays a yellowish progress bar in the bottom-left panel
- When the encoding process is finished, the application plays a brief chimes sound effect

Also, make sure you perform the actions slowly to allow Captivate enough time to capture all the needed images and actions.

3. After completing all the steps, hit the *End* key (Windows) or use the *cmd + enter* shortcut (Mac) to stop the recording and generate the slides in Captivate.

 Shortcuts on Mac

On some Mac models, it is necessary to add the *fn* key to the mix. In this instance, some Mac models require the *cmd + fn + enter* shortcut to stop the recording.

4. When the project has finished loading in Captivate, save it as `Chapter02/encoderDemo_1_1024.cptx`.

5. Close the **Adobe Media Encoder** application.

The recording phase of the project is now finished. If you don't get it right the first time, don't worry, you can simply discard your sequence and start over. On a real movie set, even the most famous actors are granted many chances to do it right.

Previewing the rushes

The project should be open in Captivate. To launch the preview, you will use the same icon as in *Chapter 1*, *Getting Started with Adobe Captivate 8* as explained in the following steps:

1. Click on the **Preview** icon of the Big Buttons Bar. From the drop-down list, choose **Project** to preview the entire project (you can also use the *F4* shortcut key to do the same thing).

2. Captivate generates the slides in a temporary Flash file and opens the **Preview** pane.

Captivate has already generated lots of objects on the slides. Remember that in the recording window, the **Demo** mode was selected by default. The **Demo** mode automatically adds Text Captions, Highlight Boxes, and Mouse movements to the slides.

Of course, some of the content of the Text Captions must be corrected; the size and position of the Highlight Boxes must be fine-tuned; and the overall rhythm of the project is probably too fast, but this is an acceptable starting point.

The main problem of these rushes is how the movie ends. While previewing the project, you probably noticed that the yellowish progress bar has not been captured by Captivate.

In order to understand why Captivate did not capture this yellowish progress bar, it is necessary to further dive into the inner working of the Captivate capture engine.

3. Close the **Preview** pane when done.

The inner working of the Captivate capture engine

The Captivate capture engine is based on static screenshots. Going back to the Adobe Media Encoder project, let's review what exactly happened when you clicked your mouse during the capture using the following steps:

1. Return to the Chapter02/encoderDemo_1_1024.cptx file.

2. Make sure that the first slide is selected in the **Filmstrip** panel.

The first slide shows the initial state of the application. When recording, you used your mouse to click on the Add Source icon of AME. When you clicked on this icon, Captivate launched a sequence of actions behind the scenes:

- Captivate recorded the position of the mouse at the time of the click (using x and y coordinates).

- Adobe Media Encoder executed the action.

- When Adobe Media Encoder completed its action, Captivate took a second static screenshot to capture the new state of the application. This second screenshot is used as the background image of slide 2.

You then used your mouse a second time to double-click on the demo_en.mov file. When this second click occurred, Captivate launched the same sequence of actions and took a third static screenshot to use as the background image of slide 3.

When the movie plays, the static screenshot of the first slide (a .bmp image) is displayed. When the mouse has to move, Captivate recreates a movement from the top-left corner of the slide to the position of the click as recorded during the filming. Just after the click, Captivate displays the static (.bmp) screenshot of the second slide.

When it is time to move the mouse on the second slide, Captivate recreates a movement from where the click occurred on the first slide to the location of the click on the second slide as recorded during the filming. Right after the second click, Captivate displays the third static screenshot. This process repeats itself till the end of the movie.

It may sound very simple and logical, but the way this process works has lots of implications, as mentioned in the following list:

- Only the starting and ending points of the mouse movements are recorded by Captivate. During playback, a movement is recreated between these points.

- The actual mouse movements made during the recording between two clicks are therefore not recorded.

- The animations displayed by the Captured application (in this case, the yellowish progress bar) are not captured.

- The Timeline of the generated movie is independent of the time that has passed during filming.

This system creates a very lightweight animation: a bunch of images and a few coordinates are enough to reproduce an entire movie.

However, this system is limited. Some mouse actions, such as drag-and-drop and scrolling actions, cannot be reproduced that way. These actions require an actual frame-by-frame video recording to be played back correctly. In Captivate, such a frame-by-frame sequence is known as **Full Motion Recording (FMR)**.

Understanding the FMR mode

To make sure you understand this concept, let's take a look at some of the preferences of Captivate:

1. In Captivate, use the **Edit | Preferences** (Windows) or **Adobe Captivate | Preferences** (Mac) menu item to open the **Preferences** window.

2. Once the **Preferences** window opens, click on **Settings** under the **Recording** group, as shown in the following screenshot:

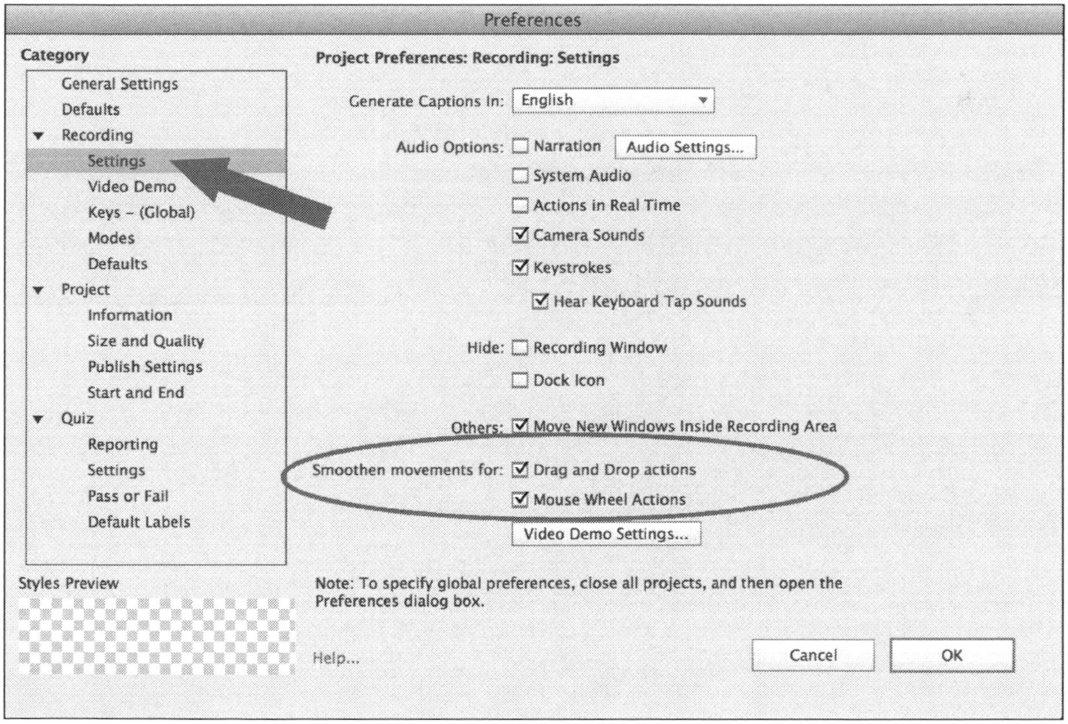

At the end of the **Preferences** window, there are two options that help you control the FMR behavior of Captivate: **Smoothen movements for Drag and Drop actions** and **Smoothen movements for Mouse Wheel Actions**. These two options should be selected by default.

3. Make sure these two options are selected and close the **Preferences** window.

4. In the **Filmstrip** panel, take a close look at the icons situated beneath each of the slide's thumbnail.

While most of the slides display the icon of a mouse, one slide should display the icon of a video camera. This is shown in the following screenshot:

As shown in the preceding screenshot, slide 9 is where the scrolling movement on the **Video** tab of AME occurs.

 The actual slide number may vary depending on how your particular recording session went.

Because the **Smoothen movements for Drag and Drop actions** and **Smoothen movements for Mouse Wheel Actions** options were turned on, Captivate has detected this scrolling movement and has automatically switched to the FMR mode when capturing that particular slide.

One of the limitations of FMR is that it does not allow any kind of interaction. During the playback, the learners cannot perform such scrolling movement themselves.

The FMR mode will also help you capture the yellowish progress bar at the end of the project. The only problem is that the yellowish progress bar is not linked to any scrolling or drag-and-drop action. Fortunately, there is another way to control the FMR mode.

Controlling Captivate during the shooting session

Controlling Captivate during the recording session is quite a challenge for your operating system (Mac or Windows). Even though both Windows and Mac OS are multitasking operating systems (it means they can handle multiple applications running at the same time), there can only be one active application at any given time. The active application is the one you currently interact with, and therefore, is the one that currently listens to the keyboard, the mouse, and other input devices.

When recording with Captivate, there are two active applications: the application you capture and Captivate itself. You should be able to interact with both these applications, so they both share the same mouse and the same keyboard at the same time. That is a very unusual situation to deal with for an operating system.

By default, the mouse and the keyboard send their data to the application you record, except for a few keys and shortcuts that are wired to Captivate. Let's take a deeper look at this system using the following steps:

1. Use the **Adobe Captivate | Preferences** (Mac) or **Edit | Preferences** (Windows) menu item to open the **Preferences** window of Captivate.

2. In the left column of the **Preferences** window, open the **Keys - (Global)** category.

This part of the **Preferences** dialog lists all the keys and shortcuts that allow you to interact with Captivate during the recording, as shown in the following screenshot:

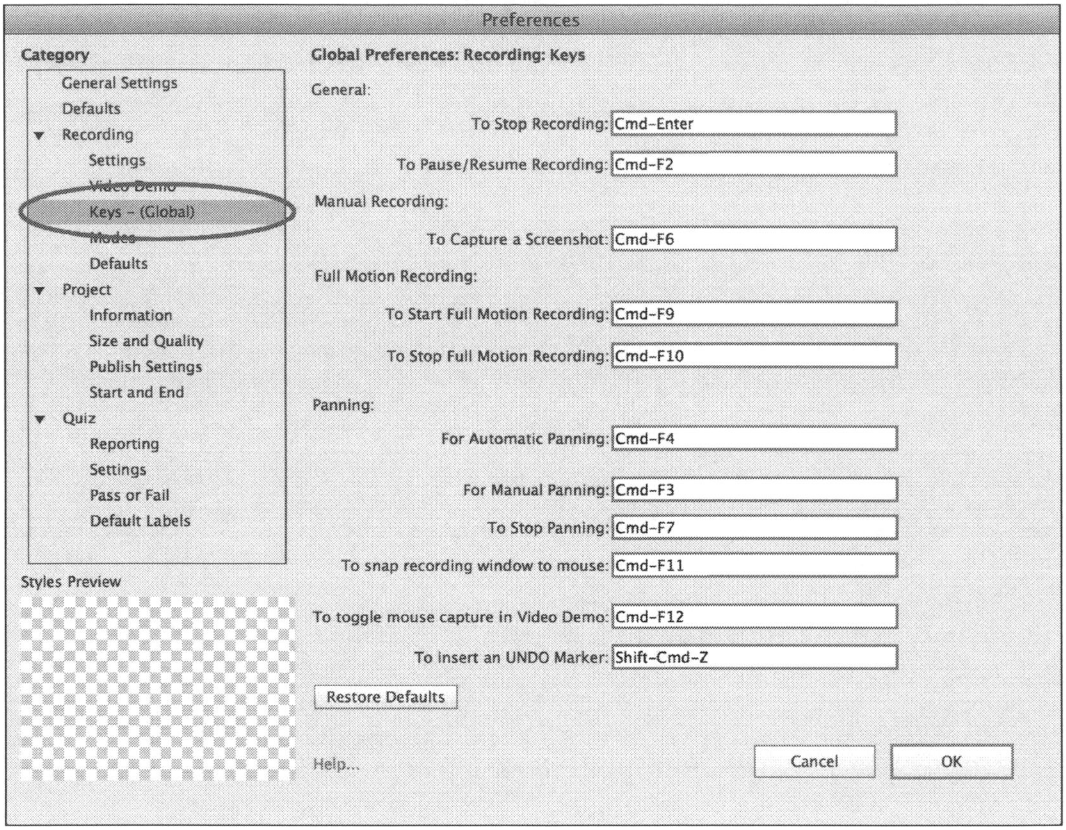

> The preceding screenshot has been taken on a Mac. If you work with Windows, the dialog box will be exactly the same with the exception of the shortcuts that are a bit different on Windows.

Remember that all the other keys as well as the mouse are wired to the application you capture.

3. Take some time to review the available keys and shortcuts.

Of special interest are the keyboard shortcuts you can use to manually start and stop a FMR. Also, notice that you can use a keyboard shortcut (*Print Screen* on Windows or *cmd + F6* on Mac) to manually take extra screenshots if needed. Finally, the *End* (Windows) or *cmd + enter* (Mac) shortcut is used to stop the recording.

In some situations, you may need to change these recording keys.

4. Click on the field where the key used to stop recording is defined (*End* on Windows or *cmd + enter* on the Mac).

5. Type the *Ctrl + E* shortcut on your keyboard. The *Ctrl + E* shortcut is now assigned to the stop recording action.

6. At the bottom of the window, click on the **Restore Defaults** button to return to the default settings.

7. Leave the **Preferences** window open.

You will now take some time to inspect the remaining preferences of Captivate.

Exploring the preferences

In this section, you will explore the remaining recording preferences of Captivate. You will start by exploring the automatic recording modes.

Exploring the automatic recording modes

In the previous section, your first recording experience was based on the default preferences of Captivate. In order to take full control of the situation, you will explore and fine-tune the automatic recording modes before having a second try. Perform the following steps to explore the automatic recording modes:

1. On the left-hand side of the **Preferences** window, click on the **Modes** category under the **Recording** section.

2. At the top of the **Preferences** window, make sure the **Mode** drop-down list is set to **Demonstration**, as shown in the following screenshot:

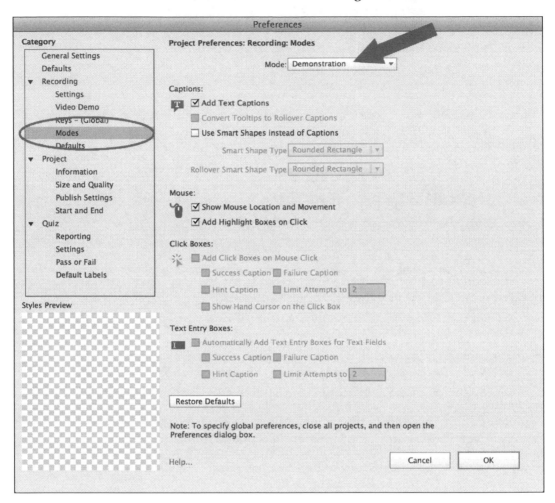

The **Preferences** window currently displays the settings of the **Demonstration** recording mode you used during your first capture session. As expected, this recording mode adds Text Captions to the slides. It also shows the mouse and adds a Highlight Box each time the mouse is clicked during the capture. These settings reflect what you have seen when previewing the rushes of the first movie.

3. At the top of the **Preferences** window, open the **Modes** drop-down list.

4. Choose the **Assessment Simulation** option.

The **Assessment Simulation** mode is the second automatic recording mode of Captivate. As discussed earlier, a simulation is a project in which the user is active, so the **Show Mouse Location and Movement** option is, logically, not selected. Instead, each time a mouse click occurs during the filming, a Click Box is automatically added to the slide.

The Click Box is one of the interactive objects of Captivate. It can pause the course and wait for the learner to click on the same location as clicked during the capture. Because the **Failure Caption** option is selected, a failure notice will be displayed if the learner does not click on the right spot.

If you use the keyboard during the recording process, Captivate generates a Text Entry Box. The Text Entry Box is another interactive object of Captivate that stops the playhead and waits for the student to interact with the course.

5. Open the **Modes** drop-down list again.

6. In the list, choose the **Training Simulation** mode.

The **Training Simulation** mode is very similar to the **Assessment Simulation** mode. The only difference is the **Hint Caption** option that is selected for both the Click Box object and the Text Entry Box object. A Hint Caption is a piece of text that is displayed when the student passes the mouse over the hit area of the Click Box / Text Entry Box.

7. Open the **Modes** drop-down list one last time.

8. In the drop-down list, choose the **Custom** mode.

Surprise! When choosing the **Custom** mode, no option is selected by default. In fact, the Custom mode is yours to create, so let's go!

9. In the **Caption** section, select the **Add Text Captions** box.

10. In the **Click Boxes** section, select the **Add Click Boxes on Mouse Click** option. Also, select the **Failure Caption** and **Hint Caption** boxes.

11. Finally, in the **Text Entry Boxes** section, select the **Automatically Add Text Entry Boxes for Text Fields** option with a **Failure Caption** and a **Hint Caption**.

Depending on the recording mode, Text Captions, Failure Captions, and/or Hint Captions will be added to the slides.

Exploring the recording settings

Let's now focus on the **Recording: Settings** category of the **Preferences** window:

1. Open the **Recording: Settings** category by clicking on **Settings** under the **Recording** category in the left-hand side column of the **Preferences** window.

The first available option at the top of the recording settings preference pane is the **Generate Captions In** drop-down list. Use it to choose the language used by Captivate to generate the various types of captions.

Other options available on this pane include the following:

- When the **Actions in Real Time** checkbox is selected, the recording is played back at the same speed as the actions performed during the recording.

- The **Camera Sounds** click box is used to turn the camera shutter sound on or off during the recording. Make sure this option is selected.

- The **Keystrokes** and **Hear Keyboard Tap Sounds** options are responsible for recording the keystrokes and for the keystrokes sound during the filming. It is best to leave these options selected.

- The **Move New Windows Inside Recording Area** option is used during the capture when the application you record opens a new window or a dialog box. It prevents the new window from opening outside or partially outside of the recording area. This option should be selected at all times.

- (For Windows only). The **Hide System Tray Icon** and **Hide Task Icon** checkboxes are great when you record fullscreen. When turned on, they hide the Captivate button from the taskbar and the Captivate icon from the notification area.

- (For Mac only). The **Hide Dock Icon** checkbox is used to remove the Captivate icon from Dock during the filming. This option is very useful when recording fullscreen.

The Video Demo preferences pane

To finish off with the **Recording** preferences, you will now explore one last **Preferences** pane:

1. Click on the **Video Demo** category to open the **Video Demo** preferences pane.

The **Video Demo** preferences pane shows options to control and optimize the conversion of a FMR into a Flash or HTML5 video. Normally, the default options should work fine in almost every situation, so there is no need to change anything on this page right now.

2. Click on **OK** to close the **Preferences** window and save the changes.

Now that you have a better idea of the available preferences, it is time to have a second try at recording your project.

Recording the other versions of the project

It is now time to start another recording session. For this second experience, you will pursue the following objectives:

- You will generate both the demonstration and simulation versions of the project in a single recording session.
- At the end of the project, you will use an FMR to capture the yellowish bar showing the progress of the encoding process.

Before turning on the camera for the second time, here are some additional tips and tricks for successful capture:

- Use the automatic recording modes whenever possible.
- If you have to record fullscreen, reset your desktop to its default appearance, that is, remove your custom wallpaper, and turn off any custom color scheme, or mouse pointer sets. Your computer should look like any computer.
- Turn off your screensaver.
- Turn on the sound so that you can hear the camera shutter and the keystrokes. This will help you have better control over the recording process.
- If you are not sure whether or not Captivate took a given screenshot, don't hesitate to take one manually using the *Print Screen* key (Windows) or the *cmd + F6* shortcut (Mac). During the editing phase that follows, it is much easier to delete an extra slide than to generate a missing slide.
- Perform the actions slowly, especially the text typing actions and the actions that require a FMR. You'll be able to set up the timing of each slide with great precision during the editing phase.
- Rehearse your scripts before recording.

With these tips and tricks in mind, let's concentrate on the actual recording. Your first concern is to reset the stage by performing the following steps:

1. Reopen AME. When the application appears, make sure it looks like the screenshot in the *Preparing the application to record* section earlier in this chapter.

2. Delete all the .flv files situated in the videos/MOV folder of the exercise files you downloaded from the Internet.

3. Return to Captivate and close every open file, if needed.

4. Use the **File | Record new Software Simulation** menu item or the **Software Simulation** thumbnail situated on the **New** tab of the Welcome screen to create a new project. The main Captivate interface disappears and the red recording area is displayed.

5. In the recording window, choose **Application** to record Adobe Media Encoder CS6. The red recording area snaps to the **Adobe Media Encoder** window.

6. Use a **Custom Size** of **1024 x 768** pixels to record your application.

7. In the recording modes section of the recording window, select all four automatic recording modes (**Demo**, **Assessment**, **Training**, and **Custom**).

8. Leave the other options at their current value.

9. Make sure your recording window looks like the following screenshot:

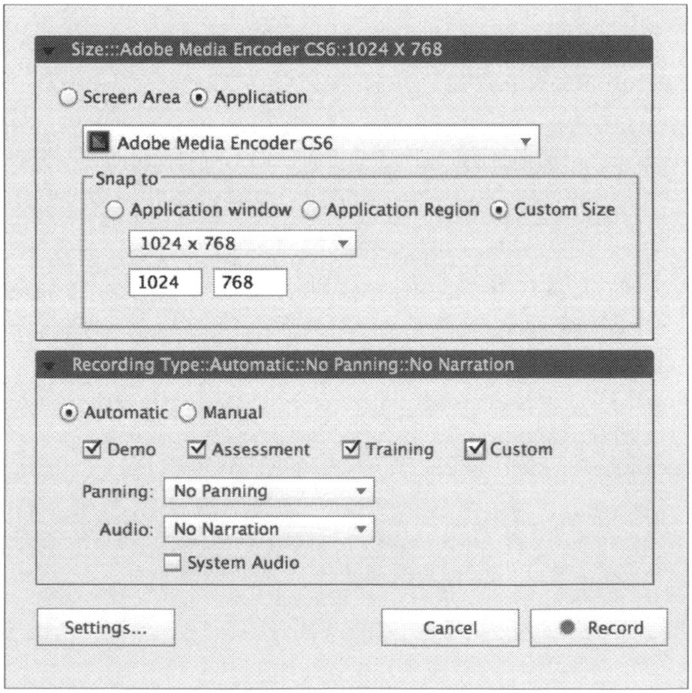

10. When you are ready, click on the red **Record** button. After a short countdown, you'll be back in the recording mode.

11. In Adobe Media Encoder, perform the actions as rehearsed earlier in this chapter. Behind the scenes, Captivate is recording!

You should hear a camera shutter sound each time you click and a keystroke sound each time you use the keyboard. Notice that, even though two applications are currently active, the mouse and the keyboard are interacting with AME, not with Captivate.

12. Just before clicking on the Start Queue button (the Play icon), click on the *Print Screen* (Windows) or *cmd + F6* (Mac) buttons to take an extra screenshot manually.

This extra screenshot is necessary to correctly capture the yellowish bar with a FMR. A camera shutter sound lets you know that an extra screenshot has indeed been captured.

Mac users, if you don't hear the camera shutter sound, remember that some Mac models require that you add the *fn* key to the mix. The shortcut to take an extra screenshot might therefore be *cmd + fn + F6*.

You will now turn the FMR on and click on the Start Queue button.

13. Use either the *F9* (Windows) or *cmd + F9* (Mac) shortcut to turn FMR on.

14. Click on the Start Queue button of AME to start the actual encoding of the video.

15. When the encoding is finished, use either the *F10* (Windows) or *cmd + F10* (Mac) shortcut to stop FMR.

16. Finally, use the *End* key (Windows) or the *cmd + enter* shortcut (Mac) to stop the recording.

Captivate generates the slides. When that process is over, Captivate has a nice surprise for you!

Alternative way to stop a Captivate recording

In addition to the keyboard shortcuts discussed previously, you can also use your mouse to stop a Captivate recording. On Windows systems, click on the Captivate taskbar icon at the bottom of the screen. On Mac systems, the same icon is situated in the notification area at the top right-hand corner of the screen.

Previewing the second rushes

The nice surprise is that Captivate has generated four versions of the same project. This is due to the four checkboxes that you selected at the end of the recording window just before pressing the **Record** button:

- The `untitled_demo1.cptx` file was generated based on the **Demo** mode. Save it in your exercises folder as `Chapter02/encoderDemo_1024.cptx`.

- The `untitled_assessment1.cptx` file was generated based on the **Assessment Simulation** mode. Save it in your exercises folder as `Chapter02/encoderAssessment_1024.cptx`.

- The `untitled_training1.cptx` file was generated based on the **Training Simulation** mode. Save it in your exercises folder as `Chapter02/encoderTraining_1024.cptx`.

- The `untitled_custom.cptx` file was generated with the settings of your very own **Custom** mode. Save it in your exercises folder as `Chapter02/encoderCustom_1024.cptx`.

Now that these files are saved, you will preview them one by one:

1. Select the `Chapter02/encoderDemo_1024.cptx` file.

2. Use the **Preview | Project** icon of the Big Buttons Bar to preview the entire project.

Captivate generates the slides and opens the **Preview** pane.

 If you did not succeed in producing great recordings, you can use the files situated in the `Chapter02/final` folder of the exercises.

The **Demo** version of the project is very similar to the one you shot earlier in this chapter. The only major difference is the yellowish progress bar that has been correctly captured by FMR.

3. When the preview is finished, close the **Preview** pane.

4. Select the `Chapter02/encoderAssessment_1024.cptx` file.

5. Use the **Preview | Project** icon to preview the entire project.

As described in the **Assessment Simulation** recording mode, the mouse pointer and the Text Captions have not been added to this version of the project. After a short while, the project pauses. If you don't do anything, nothing happens as Captivate is waiting for you to click on the right spot. If you click on the right icon, the project moves on to the next slide and pauses again waiting for your second action. If you do not perform the right action, a red Failure Caption is displayed.

6. When you complete the entire project, close the **Preview** pane.

7. Return to the `Chapter02/encoderTraining_1024.cptx` file.

8. Once again, use the **Preview | Project** icon of the Big Buttons Bar to preview the entire project.

As expected, this version of the project is very similar to the previous one. The only difference is the orange Hint Caption that is displayed when the mouse is over the hit area of the Click Boxes or Text Entry Boxes. This Hint Caption can provide some useful information on the action to be performed by the student.

9. When you are through the entire project, close the **Preview** pane.

10. Go to the `Chapter02/encoderCustom_1024.cptx` file.

11. Use the **Preview** icon one more time to preview the entire project.

Your **Custom** recording mode has added Text Captions, Click Boxes, and Text Entry Boxes to the slides, effectively providing an entirely new customized experience.

Of course, none of these four versions of the project are final in any way. There is a lot of work to be done before these projects can be published. That being said, the automatic recording modes of Captivate have successfully provided enough raw material of good quality to get you started. Remember, this is exactly what you should expect from the capture step of the process.

Recording with System Audio

System Audio is the sound effects that originate from the application you capture or from your operating system. In the AME example, it is the chimes sound effect that is played when the encoding is finished. In this exercise, you will once again capture the sequence of actions described in the scenario; this time, Captivate will record the System Audio in addition to screenshots and mouse movements.

First, you should reset your applications to their original state:

1. Close AME if it is still open.
2. Reopen AME.

By restarting AME, you effectively reset the application to its default state.

3. Delete every .flv file that is situated in the video/MOV folder of the exercises.

The second step is to get Captivate ready for the capture session.

4. Return to Captivate, and use the **File | Close All** menu item to close all open files (if any).
5. Use the **File | Record New Software Simulation** menu item or the **Software Simulation** thumbnail situated on the **New** tab of the welcome screen to create a new project.
6. In the recording window, choose **Application** to record the Adobe Media Encoder application. The red recording area snaps to the AME window.
7. Use **Custom Size** of **1024 x 768** pixels to shoot your application.
8. In the recording modes section of the recording window, make sure the **Demo** mode is the only one selected.
9. Also, select the **System Audio** checkbox.

System Audio on Mac

If you are on a Mac, the **System Audio** checkbox is not available. Actually, you need to install the Soundflower system extension and configure your audio system accordingly before being able to use the System Audio feature of Captivate. The procedure is explained in the knowledge base article at http://helpx.adobe.com/captivate/kb/system-audio-disabled.html.

On Windows, System Audio should work right out of the box!

System Audio requires at least Windows Vista to work. It does not work on Windows XP!

Once System Audio has been correctly set up, the recording window should look like the following screenshot:

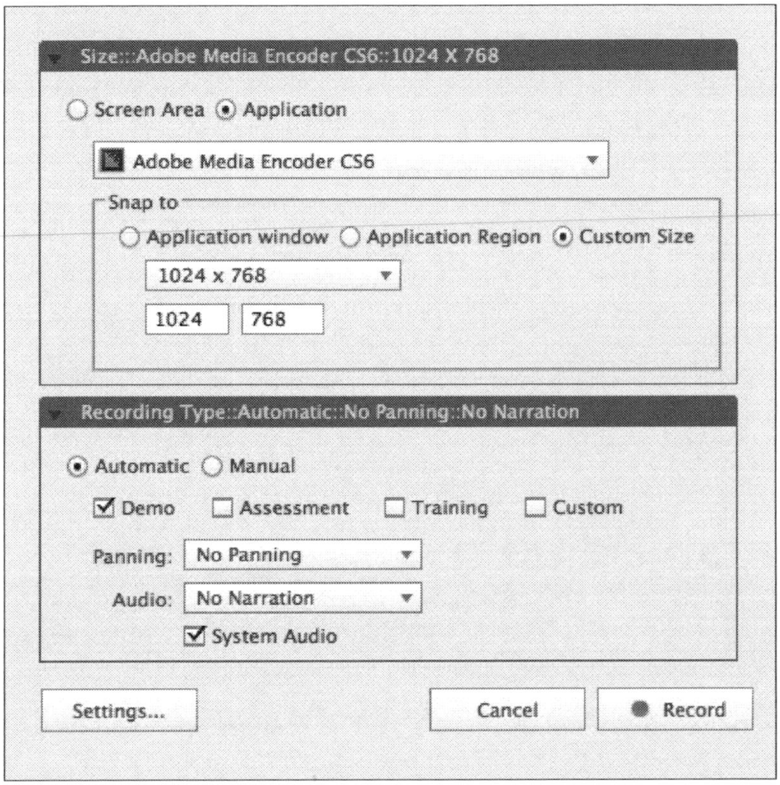

10. When you are ready, click on the red **Record** button. After a short countdown, you'll be back in recording mode.

11. In Adobe Media Encoder, perform the actions as rehearsed earlier in this chapter. Behind the scenes, Captivate is recording!

Notice that you do not hear the camera shutter sounds and the keystrokes sounds anymore. When System Audio is activated, these sounds are automatically disabled, because—obviously—they don't need to be recorded.

12. Just before clicking on the Start Queue button (the Play icon), press the *Print Screen* (Windows) or *cmd + F6* (Mac) shortcut to take an extra screenshot manually.

13. Use the *F9* (Windows) or *cmd + F9* (Mac) shortcut to turn FMR on.

14. Click on the Start Queue button of AME to start the actual encoding the video.

15. When the encoding is finished, use the *F10* (Windows) or *cmd + F10* (Mac) shortcut to stop FMR.

16. Finally, use the *End* key (Windows) or the *cmd + enter* shortcut (Mac) to stop the recording.

17. When Captivate has finished generating all the slides, save this file in the exercises folder as `Chapter02/encoderDemo_sysAudio_1024.cptx`.

As usual, let's now preview the rushes of this new recording session.

18. Use the **Preview | Project** icon of the Big Buttons Bar to preview the entire project.

This version of the project is, again, very similar to the demonstrations you have seen earlier. However, you should notice one significant difference. At the end of the project, when the encoding process is completely finished, you should hear the chimes sound of AME that has been captured thanks to the System Audio feature of Captivate!

The Video Demo recording mode

The Video Demo recording mode was introduced as a new feature of Captivate 6. It allows you to create a video file by shooting the onscreen actions. A Video Demo recording project is actually a big Full Motion Recording.

A Video Demo project is very different from the other projects you have worked on so far. Because a Video Demo project can only be published as an `.mp4` video file, no interactive objects are possible in such a project. In other words, it can only be a demonstration. Because a Video Demo project is based on a single big video file, there is no slide and no **Filmstrip** panel in a Video Demo project. This makes Video Demo projects particularly suitable for upload to an online video hosting service such as YouTube, Vimeo, or Daily Motion.

In the next exercise, you will create a Video Demo version of Encoder Demonstration. The first operation to do is to reset your system:

 If you have a problem while doing this exercise, refer to the `Chapter02/final/encoderVideo.cpvc` file of your exercises folder.

1. Restart the Adobe Media Encoder application.

2. Delete all the `.flv` files present in the `videos/MOV` folder of the exercise files.

Now that your system is ready, let's create a Video Demo project.

3. Use the **File | Record new Video Demo** menu item to start a new Video Demo project.

This option is also available on the **New** tab of the welcome screen of Captivate when no file is open.

4. In the drop-down list at the top of the recording window, choose to record the Adobe Media Encoder application.

5. In the **Snap to** section, choose to record at **Custom Size** of **1024 x 768** pixels.

Most of the time, a narration is added to such a project. If you have a microphone available, you'll record your voice in addition to the onscreen action. If you don't have a microphone available, just read through these steps. Audio can also be added later in the process if needed.

6. If a microphone is available, open the **Audio** drop-down list and choose your microphone (or the audio interface the mic is plugged in) in the list of entries.

7. Make sure the other options are at their default settings. The recording window should now look like the following screenshot:

As demonstrated in the preceding screenshot and in the `Chapter02/final/encoderVideo.cpvc` file of your exercises folder, it is possible to record both the narration and the System Audio.

8. Click on the red **Record** button to start the recording.

If it is the first time you are recording sound with your Captivate installation, you'll have to calibrate the sensitivity of your microphone.

9. [Optional]. In the **Calibrate Audio Input** dialog, click on the **Auto Calibrate** button. Speak normally in the microphone until the **Input level OK** message appears on the screen. Click on **OK** to validate the sensitivity settings and to discard the box.

10. After a short countdown, the recording begins.

11. In Adobe Media Encoder, perform the actions as rehearsed earlier in this chapter. If you have a microphone, speak as you go through the steps of the scenario.

12. When done, hit the *End* key (Windows) or the *cmd + enter* shortcut (Mac).

Captivate finalizes the video capture. When the finalization process is finished, your entire video is played back. Enjoy the show!

13. When the video has finished playing, click on the **Edit** button in the bottom right corner of the screen.

By clicking on the **Edit** button, you leave the preview mode of the Video Demo project and enter the editing mode. Note how the interface of a Video Demo project is different from the interface of a standard Captivate project.

14. Save your file as `Chapter02/encoderVideo.cpvc`.

Notice that a Video Demo project does not use the standard `.cptx` file extension, but uses the `.cpvc` file extension instead. The **Video Demo** recording mode will be covered in more detail in *Chapter 8, Producing a Video Demo*.

Automatic and manual panning

In the movie industry, panning refers to moving the camera during filming. In Captivate, the camera is the red recording area. When panning is turned on in Captivate, it simply means that the red recording area can be moved during the recording. This enables you to capture a bigger application with a smaller recording area.

Earlier in this chapter, we had a discussion on how to solve the project-sizing problem. Panning was one of the possible approaches. Let's take a closer look at it.

 If you have a problem while doing this exercise, refer to the `Chapter02/final/encoderDemo_panning.cptx` file of your exercises folder.

1. Restart AME to reset the user interface.

2. Delete all the `.flv` files present in the `videos/MOV` folder of the exercise.

3. Return to Captivate and use the **File | Record New Software Simulation** menu item or the corresponding thumbnail of the **New** tab of the Welcome screen to start a new project.

The Captivate interface disappears, and the red recording area shows up.

4. In the recording window, choose to record a **Screen Area** (and not an **Application** as before). Give the area **Custom Size** of **800 x 600** pixels.

Normally, the size of the **Adobe Media Encoder** application should still be **1024 x 768** pixels from the previous filming sessions.

5. Move the red recording area such that its top-left corner corresponds to the top-left corner of the **Adobe Media Encoder** application window.

In this configuration, the size of AME does not match the size of the red recording area. The recording area should be smaller than AME.

6. In the bottom part of the recording window, make sure the **Demo** mode is the only one selected.

7. In the **Panning** drop-down list, choose **Manual Panning**.

8. If necessary, set the **Audio** dropdown to **No Narration** and deselect the **System Audio** checkbox.

Your computer screen should look like the following screenshot:

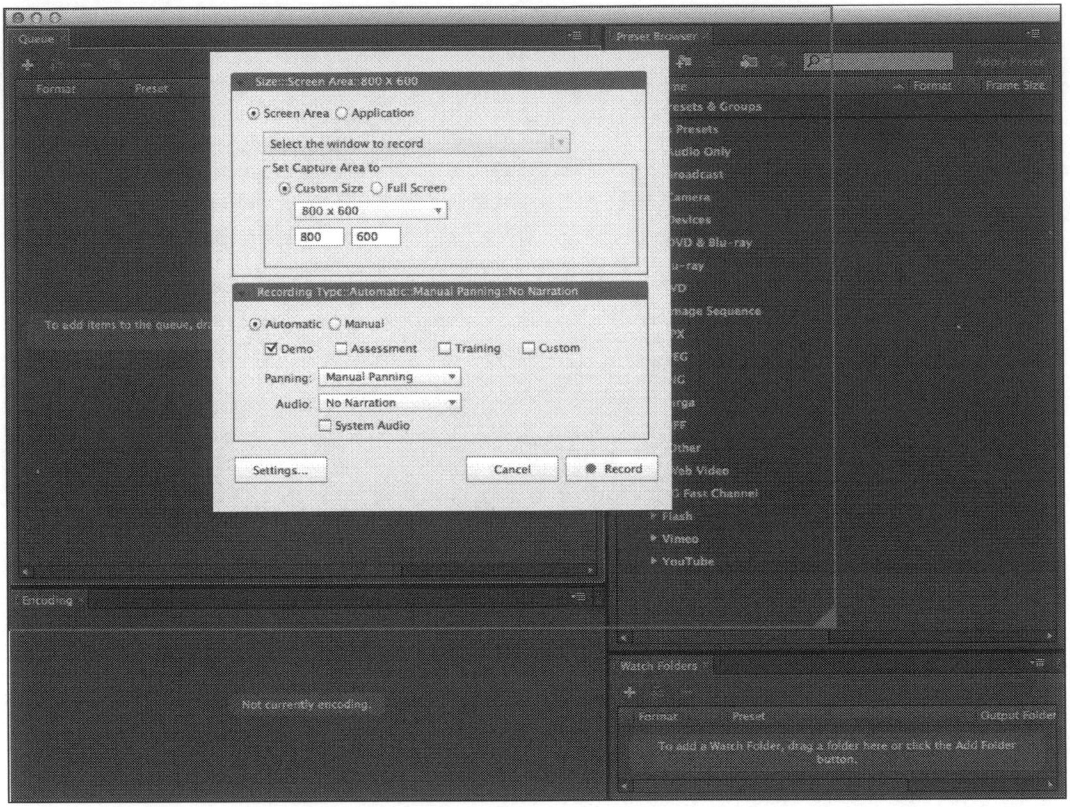

9. When ready, click on the red **Record** button to switch to the recording mode.

10. After the countdown, perform the first few steps of the scenario in the **Adobe Media Encoder** application.

11. When the **Export Settings** window opens, place your mouse above the red line of the recording area until the mouse turns into a grabbing hand. Then, slowly move the red recording area until it covers more or less the lower right section of the **Export Settings** window.

12. In AME, modify the size of the video as defined in the scenario.

13. When the **Export Settings** dialog closes after you click on the **OK** button, move the red recording area back to its original position.

14. Just before clicking on the Start Queue button (the Play icon), press the *Print Screen* (Windows) or *cmd + F6* (Mac) shortcut to take an extra screenshot manually.

15. Use the *F9* (Windows) or *cmd + F9* (Mac) shortcut to turn FMR on.

16. Click on the Start Queue button of AME to start the actual encoding the video.

17. When the encoding is finished, use the *F10* (Windows) or *cmd + F10* (Mac) shortcut to stop the FMR.

18. Finally, use the *End* key (Windows) or the *cmd + Enter* shortcut (Mac) to stop the recording.

19. When Captivate has finished generating all the slides, save this file. When the movie is finished, close the **Preview** pane, and save the file as Chapter02/ encoderDemo_panning.cptx.

Back in Captivate, take a look at the **Filmstrip** panel. Beneath some of the slides thumbnails, you should see the camera icon indicating that there are some FMR slides in the project. FMR is used to reproduce the panning movements made during the capture.

In this example, you have used manual panning. When using automatic panning, Captivate places the mouse at the center of the red recording area. During filming, the red recording area automatically follows any mouse movement. Automatic panning produces a lot of unnecessary movements and, consequently, a lot of extra FMR slides.

Responsive capture

Responsive projects are the groundbreaking new feature of Adobe Captivate 8. It allows you to adapt the content and the layout of your Captivate project for the desktop, the tablet and the smartphone. When published in HTML5, all three versions of the project are part of the same package. At runtime, the system decides which version of the project is displayed depending on the device used by the learner.

When it comes to screen capture, responsive projects allow you to capture static screenshots and to rearrange those screenshots in the different views. The exact procedure is as follows:

1. Restart AME to reset the user interface.

2. Delete all the .flv files present in the videos/MOV folder of the exercise.

3. Return to Captivate and close any open files, so that you see the Welcome screen.

4. Double-click on the **Responsive Project** thumbnail on the **New** tab of the Welcome screen. You can also use the **File | New Project | Responsive Project** menu item.

This action creates a new responsive project. For this first experiment with responsive projects, you will use the default settings of Captivate. At the top of the stage, you should see an extra ruler with three breakpoints: one for the desktop computer, one for the tablet, and the third one for mobile devices.

By default, these three breakpoints are positioned as follows:

- The **Primary** breakpoint is placed at **1024** pixels
- The **Tablet** breakpoint is located at **768** pixels
- The **Mobile** breakpoint is located at **360** pixels

You can see these values by passing your mouse on the breakpoints as illustrated in the following screenshot:

If you want to see the default height of the project, there is one more thing to do:

5. Select the **View Device Height** checkbox on the right-hand side of the breakpoints ruler (see the arrow in the preceding screenshot).

Notice that the default height of the stage when in the **Primary** breakpoint is **627** pixels. This means that the default dimension of the stage in the **Primary** view is **1024 x 627** pixels.

Use the following steps to add slides into this responsive project using the capture engine of Captivate:

6. Click on the **Slides** icon, which is the very first icon of the Big Buttons Bar.

7. Choose the **Software Simulation** option in the drop-down menu.

8. Click on the **OK** button at the end of the **Record Additional Slides** dialog to insert the new slides after the first (and only) slide of the project.

The Captivate interface disappears and the red recording area shows up.

9. In the drop-down list at the top of the recording window, choose to record the **Adobe Media Encoder** application.

10. Make sure the **Snap to** window checkbox is selected to have the red recording area snap to the AME window.

11. Make sure the **Demo** mode is selected on the **Mode** drop-down menu.

12. If needed, reset the **Panning** dropdown to **No Panning** and the **Audio** dropdown to **No Narration**.

Unlike your previous recording experiences, you cannot choose the recording size. This is because the project already exists and already has a size of 1024 x 627 pixels. Therefore, the red recording area already has the same size as the project. Your screen should now look like the following screenshot:

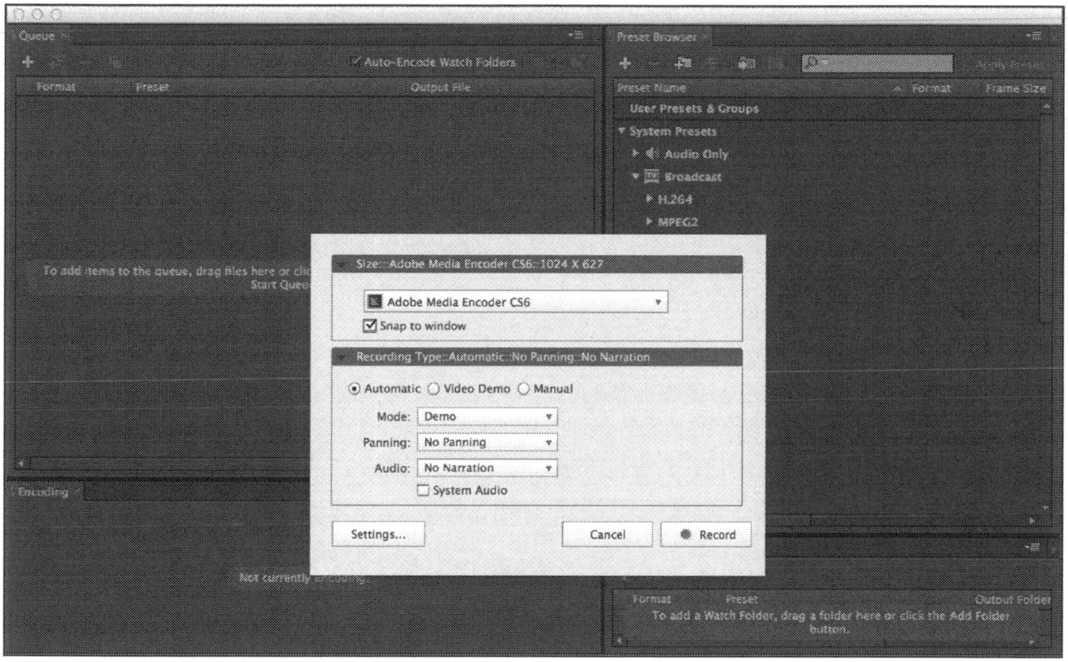

You are now ready for your first responsive capture!

13. Click on the red **Record** button. After a short countdown, you'll be back in the recording mode.

14. In Adobe Media Encoder, perform the actions as rehearsed earlier in this chapter. Behind the scenes, Captivate is recording!

15. Just before clicking on the Start Queue button (the Play icon), press the *Print Screen* (Windows) or *cmd + F6* (Mac) shortcut to take an extra screenshot manually.

16. Use the *F9* (Windows) or *cmd + F9* (Mac) shortcut to turn FMR on.

17. Click on the Start Queue button of AME to start the actual encoding of the video.

18. When the encoding is finished, use the *F10* (Windows) or *cmd + F10* (Mac) shortcut to stop the FMR.

19. Finally, use the *End* key (Windows) or the *cmd + Enter* shortcut (Mac) to stop the recording.

20. When Captivate has finished generating all the slides, save this file in the exercises folder as `Chapter02/encoderDemo_responsive.cptx`.

So far, so good! The story is almost exactly the same as before. But this project is a bit special. Because it is a responsive project, it has three different views in which the captured screenshots can be arranged.

21. Use the **Filmstrip** panel to select the second slide of the project.

22. Use the breakpoint switcher at the top of the stage to switch to **Tablet** view.

When in **Tablet** view, note that the captured image is bigger than the stage. You cannot resize the captured image, even in a responsive project, but you can move the stage on top of the image in order to choose which part of the screenshot is displayed.

23. Place your mouse in an empty area of the stage and move the stage around so it shows another part of the captured screenshot.

24. Use the breakpoint switcher to switch to **Mobile** view.

25. When in **Mobile** view, experiment with moving the stage around to choose which part of the captured image is displayed.

Note that Captivate automatically places the captured background image so that the spot where you clicked during the capture is displayed. This does not prevent you from checking all the slides in all three views to control and choose which part of the captured image is displayed on smaller screens. You will now save the file and preview it in a web browser.

26. Use the **Preview | Project** icon of the Big Buttons Bar to preview the entire project. Because you are in a responsive project, this option plays the demonstration in the default web browser.

27. When in the browser, feel free to use the slider at the top of the preview to test the responsiveness of the project.

28. When done, close the browser and return to Captivate.

While there is a lot more to learn about the new responsive projects of Captivate, you will now move on to the next section of the book. You will cover this topic in much more detail in *Chapter 9, Creating a Responsive Project*.

Rescaling a project

This chapter opened with a discussion on choosing the right size for the project. This discussion led to four possible approaches to manage the size difference between the application to capture and the course to produce.

The first approach was to shoot big and then downsize. The first step of this approach was done when you used a resolution of 1024 x 768 pixels to record your very first sequence. You will now take care of the second step: resizing the movie to 800 x 600 pixels:

 Remember that resizing a project is a one-way operation that always results in data and quality loss. If another solution that does not require resizing the project is available, go for it! If a resize operation cannot be avoided, always keep a backup copy of your project at its original size.

1. In Captivate, open the `Chapter02/encoderDemo_1024.cptx` file.

 If you did not successfully save this file earlier in this chapter, you can use the one saved in the `Chapter02/final` folder.

If you have a problem while doing this exercise, refer to the `Chapter02/final/encoderDemo_800.cptx` file of your exercises folder.

2. Use the **File | Save As** menu item to save the file as `Chapter02/encoderDemo_800.cptx`.

3. When the project is saved, use the **Modify | Rescale project** menu item to open the **Rescale Project** dialog.

This window is divided into three parts. The top part allows you to define the new size of the project. It is the only part available at the moment.

4. Make sure the **Maintain Aspect Ration** box is selected.

5. Reduce the **Width** of the project from **1024** to 800 pixels. The new **Height** of **600** pixels should be calculated automatically.

Since the new size is smaller than the original size, the lower right part of the box becomes available. It is titled: **If new size is smaller**. The lower left part of the box is still inactive. It would activate if the new size of the project were larger than the original size.

6. Take some time to review the available options, but leave the default unchanged. When ready, click on **Finish**.

7. A dialog box informs you that resizing a project cannot be undone. Click on **OK** to confirm you want to resize the project anyway.

8. Captivate resizes each slide, one by one.

9. Save the file when the resize process is complete.

Although Captivate does a great job resizing all the objects on the slides, I still recommend going though each slide to ensure the size conversion was successful for every object on every slide.

Summary

In this chapter, you have completed the first step of the Captivate production process: capturing the slides. Throughout this chapter, your main concern was to manage the size of the project as compared to the size of the application to capture.

Several approaches are possible to address this size issue. While experiencing each of these approaches you uncovered three important features of Captivate: Full Motion Recording, Panning, and responsive capture.

You also discovered that Captivate has four automatic recording modes: **Demonstration**, **Assessment Simulation**, **Training Simulation**, and a **Custom** mode that is yours to create. Each of these automatic recording modes adds Text Captions and other objects to the slides.

The **Video Demo** recording mode is entirely dedicated to producing linear, noninteractive .mp4 video files. These can be easily uploaded to online video hosting services such as YouTube, Vimeo, and DailyMotion.

The System Audio feature allows you to capture sound effects originating from the applications or from the system in addition to the screenshots and the onscreen action.

Of course, the recordings made in this chapter are by no means final products, but that was not your goal anyway. These projects now have to go through the editing phase to reach their final aspect.

In the next chapter, you will begin the editing phase of your work. The editing phase is the most time-consuming phase of the entire process. There are so many options and tools to discover that one chapter will not be enough to cover it all. Consequently, the editing phase will span almost all the remaining chapters of this book!

Meet the community

In this section, I'd like to introduce you to Anita Horsley, one of the most active members of the Captivate community and an awesome Captivate Certified Instructor. She has authored the video series *Fast Track to Adobe Captivate 6*, *Packt Publishing* (see `http://www.packtpub.com/fast-track-to-adobe-captivate-6/video`). She has also been a reviewer for two of my Captivate books. We finally met in October 2014 during the Adobe learning summit in Las Vegas. I was completely jetlagged by the trip, but Anita was kind enough to offer me a gigantic cup of coffee!

Anita Horsley

During Anita Horsley's tenure as a firefighter, she initiated, developed, and managed the health and safety program. At the Oregon State Fire Marshal, she founded the eLearning track as well as implemented and coordinated the eLearning team and the internal training. She managed the learning management system and chaired the Oregon State Captivate User Group. She is the founder and President of CALEX Learning Consultants, LLC, and an independent consultant. In addition, she is an Adobe Captivate instructor and eLearning developer. She presents webinars for Adobe and ASTD and at conferences nationally. She has authored the video tutorial series *Fast Track To Adobe Captivate 6*, *Packt Publishing*. She also has a blog named *Crazy About Captivate* that provides tips and tricks on Adobe Captivate. She holds a Master's degree and is an Adobe Certified Expert in Captivate.

Contact details

- **Web**: `http://calex-llc.com`
- **Blog**: `http://captivatecrazy.blogspot.com`
- **Twitter**: `@captivatecrazy`
- **LinkedIn**: `http://www.linkedin.com/in/anitahorsley`
- **Google +**: `https://plus.google.com/u/0/+CALEXLearningConsultantsLLCCharleston/posts`
- **Facebook**: `https://www.facebook.com/CALEXLearningConsultantsLLC`

3
Working with Standard Objects

When the filming is complete, the director takes the rushes and heads towards the postproduction studio to begin the most time-consuming phase of the process. While in the studio, the director arranges the sequences shot during the filming in the correct order, adds sound effects, arranges transitions, fine-tunes visual and special effects, adds subtitles, and re-records narration, among other actions. When the director leaves the postproduction studio, the motion picture is complete and ready for publishing.

The same basic principle applies to your Captivate projects. During the postproduction phase, you will revisit each slide one by one to arrange, reorder, synchronize, add, modify, align, delete, and so on. To help you turn your rushes into a great eLearning experience, Captivate provides an extensive array of tools, features, and objects. In the next few chapters, you will take a deep look at each of them one by one.

The first thing you can do to enhance your projects is to add objects on top of the slides. This particular chapter introduces the most standard and basic objects of Captivate. It also focuses on the general workflow of dealing with such objects.

In this chapter, you will:

- Learn how use the Properties panel
- Work with text objects
- Work with highlight boxes
- Work with images, characters, and equations
- Work with Smart Shapes
- Add basic formatting to all these objects
- Experiment with text effects

Preparing your work

Before getting started, you will make Captivate ready by opening the required files using the following steps:

1. Open or restart Captivate.

2. Use the **File** | **Open** menu item to open the Chapter03/encoderDemo_800. cptx file situated in your exercises folder.

3. Open the Chapter03/drivingInBe.cptx project in your exercises folder.

If you are using the default interface mode (as described in *Chapter 1, Getting Started with Adobe Captivate 8*), restarting Captivate should reset your workspace to the default interface. If you are using the advanced interface mode, be aware that the screenshots of this book as well as the step-by-step instructions have been made using the default interface. The procedure to switch back to the default interface mode is described in *Chapter 1, Getting Started with Adobe Captivate 8*.

 To ensure maximum accuracy between the files you work with and the exercises described in this book, make sure you use the files from the Chapter03 folder and not the ones you created in the previous chapter. During the exercises, feel free to experiment with the files. You'll have a fresh set of files to work with at the beginning of each chapter.

Working with the Properties panel

The **Properties** panel is one of the most important and most widely used panels of Captivate. In this section, you will take some time to inspect the **Properties** panel in more detail. For this exercise, you will use the Chapter03/encoderDemo_800.cptx file.

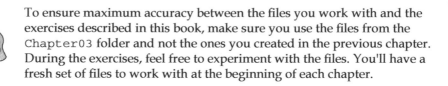 The Chapter03/final folder contains the completed projects as they are supposed to be at the end of this chapter. If you are confused by any exercise, use these projects as references.

In Captivate 8, the **Properties** panel is hidden by default, so your first task is to turn it on using the following steps:

1. Click on the **Properties** icon situated at the right-hand side of the Big Buttons Bar to open the **Properties** panel.

2. Click on the same icon a second time to toggle the **Properties** panel back off.

3. In the **Filmstrip** panel, double-click on any slide. This also opens the **Properties** panel.

In Captivate, double-clicking on an object opens the **Properties** panel of the object that has been double-clicked.

The **Properties** and **Library** icons of the Big Buttons Bar are used to toggle the corresponding panels on and off. Make sure the **Properties** panel is visible before moving on with this exercise.

> **Panels in advanced interface mode**
>
> Remember that in advanced interface mode, the **Properties** and **Library** icons are not present on the Big Buttons Bar. Use the **Window** menu to turn these panels on and off.

The **Properties** panel is a dynamic panel. It means that its content changes depending on the selected object. Let's experiment with this.

4. On the **Filmstrip** panel, click on the first slide to make it the active slide.

After clicking on the first slide, the **Properties** panel should look like the following screenshot. The icon (marked as **1**) at the top of the **Properties** panel, as well as a blue outline in the **Filmstrip** panel around slide 1, tell you that the slide is the currently selected object.

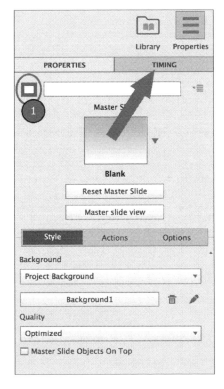

Take some time to examine the available properties and options in the **Properties** panel.

The **Properties** panel is actually a group of two panels: the **Properties** and the **Timing** panels.

5. At the very top of the rightmost column, click on **Timing** to make it the active panel (see the arrow in the preceding screenshot).

6. Take some time to examine the properties of the **Timing** panel. When done, return to the **Properties** panel.

The **Properties** panel itself is divided into three different tabs: the **Styles**, **Actions**, and **Options** tabs.

7. Take some time to examine the content of each of the tabs of the **Properties** panel.

The selected slide contains three objects: **Text Caption**, the **Mouse** object, and a blue **Highlight Box** next to the mouse pointer. These three objects have been automatically generated by the demo recording mode used during the capture.

8. Click on the **Text Caption** object of slide 1 to make it the active object.

Now that **Text Caption** is selected, the **Properties** panel shows the properties relevant to an object of the type Text Caption.

9. Click on **Timing** to make it the active panel.

Note that the options present in the **Timing** panel are not exactly the same as when the slide was selected.

10. Return to the **Properties** panel by clicking on the **Properties** button at the top of the right column.

The **Properties** panel of a Text Caption only contains two tabs: the **Style** and **Options** tabs.

11. Take some time to examine the **Style** tab of the **Properties** panel when a Text Caption is selected on the stage.

12. At the bottom of the **Style** tab, open the **Shadow and Reflection** section by clicking on the disclosure triangle.

13. When done, take some time to examine the properties situated in the **Options** tab of the **Properties** panel.

14. While still on slide 1, select the blue **Highlight Box** next to the mouse pointer.

Because all three objects share the same area of the slide, selecting the **Highlight Box** might be tricky. To make the selection easier, you can reveal the **Timeline** panel by clicking on the **Timeline** button at the bottom of the screen and selecting the blue **Highlight Box** from the **Timeline** panel.

With the blue **Highlight Box** as the selected object, the **Properties** panel now displays the properties relevant to an object of the type Highlight Box.

15. Take a close look at the available properties in each of the tabs of the **Properties** panel.

Notice that the **Options** tabs as well as the **Timing** panel contain the very same options and properties as when the **Text Caption** object was selected; only the **Style** tab of the **Properties** panel is different.

To work with the **Properties** panel, remember the following points:

- In normal interface mode, the **Properties** panel is not displayed by default. Use the **Properties** button on the right-hand side of the Big Buttons Bar to toggle its visibility on and off. In advanced interface mode, use the **Window** menu.

- You can also double-click on any object to open the **Properties** panel of that particular object. This object can be a slide in the **Filmstrip** panel or any object present on a slide.

- By clicking on the **Properties** button of the Big Buttons Bar, you actually reveal both the **Properties** and the **Timing** panels.

- The **Properties** and the **Timing** panels are both *dynamic* panels. It means they show the properties relevant to the *active* object. Consequently, selecting another object updates the content of these panels.

- The **Properties** panel is further divided into tabs whose number depends on the selected object.

- Usually, the **Style** tab is specific to the selected object, while the **Options** tab is more or less the same for all the objects.

Now that you know how the **Properties** panel works, you will learn about the basic objects of Captivate.

Exploring the objects of Captivate

Captivate offers more than a dozen objects. In this section, you will learn about the standard non interactive objects of Captivate. You will learn about the more complex objects later in this book. The first object you will focus on is the Text Caption object.

Using the Text Caption object

Text Caption is the most basic object in Captivate. It is typically used to display text to learners. In its most basic form, Text Caption is a text item that appears and disappears from the screen according to its position on the **Timeline** panel.

The Demonstration auto-recording mode you used during the filming already added many Text Captions on your slides. Some of these might be just right, but most of them—if not all of them—need some extra work.

Modifying the content of a Text Caption

There are two editing modes available when working with Text Captions:

- First, you can consider Text Caption as an *object*. In this case, eight white squares appear around the Text Caption (**1**). These white squares are the *handles* used to resize the Text Caption. In this mode, you can move Text Caption around and resize it, but you cannot edit the text inside Text Caption.

- To edit the text you must be in text-editing mode. In text-editing mode, the eight white handles disappear and a blinking cursor (**2**) appears in Text Caption, as shown in the following screenshot:

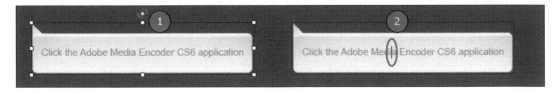

In the next exercise, you will modify the content of some Text Captions:

1. In the `encoderDemo_800.cptx` file, click on the Text Caption of slide 1 to make it the active object.

2. Double-click on the Text Caption object or press the *F2* shortcut key to switch to text-editing mode.

The eight white handles disappear and a blinking cursor appears on Text Caption:

3. Triple-click on Text Caption to select all its current content.

4. In Text Caption, type `The Mouse will now click on the Add files icon.`

5. Hit the *Esc* key to toggle the Text Caption back to the original mode.

Now take some time to practice that by updating the content of the remaining Text Captions of the project according to the following table. You may need to resize Text Captions appropriately:

Slide number	Content of Text Caption
Slide 2	`The mouse will now double-click on the demo_en.mov video file.`
Slide 3	`The mouse will now click on the Format drop-down menu.`
Slide 4	`The mouse will now click on the FLV menu item.`
Slide 5	`The mouse will now click on the Preset drop-down menu.`
Slide 6	`The mouse will now click on the WEB - 640x480, 4x3... preset.`
Slide 7	`The mouse will now click on the preset's name to open the Export Settings dialog.`
Slide 10	`The mouse will now click on the current Width of the video.`
Slide 11	`Enter the desired width (in this case 400 pixels) and hit the ENTER key.`
Slide 12	`The mouse will now click on the OK button to validate the changes and close the Export Settings dialog.`

These simple edits already make the project much easier to understand for the learners.

6. Save the file (*Ctrl* + *S* on Windows or *command* + *S* on Mac).

7. Use the **Preview | Project** icon of the Big Buttons Bar to test the entire project.

Of course, you still have to fine-tune the formatting and the timing of the objects, but the content of Text Captions should be correct.

8. Close the **Preview** pane when finished.

Next, you will learn how to add new Text Captions to the project.

Creating new Text Captions

So far, you have modified Text Captions that were automatically generated during the filming. You will now create and modify brand new Text Captions.

1. Use the **Filmstrip** panel to return to slide 1.

Slide 1 already contains one Text Caption. You will now add a second one.

2. Click on the **Text** icon of the Big Buttons Bar and select the **Text Caption** item.

By default, the new Text Caption appears in the middle of the slide in text-editing mode.

3. Type `Welcome to the Adobe Media Encoder` in the new Text Caption.

4. Hit the *Esc* key to leave the text-editing mode. The new Text Caption should still be selected.

In this particular project, the default formatting of a new Text Caption is not suitable for easy reading.

5. With the Text Caption still selected, turn your attention to the **Style** tab of the **Properties** panel. Note that the **Caption Type** drop-down list is set to **Transparent**.

6. Open the **Caption Type** dropdown and choose **Halo Blue** in the list of available Text Caption types.

You will now add a new Text Caption on slide 4, using a keyboard shortcut instead of the **Text** icon of the Big Buttons Bar.

7. Use the **Filmstrip** panel to select slide 4.

8. Use *command* + *Shift* + *C* (for Mac) or *Ctrl* + *Shift* + *C* (for Windows) to create a new Text Caption on slide 4. By default, the new Text Caption appears in the middle of the slide in text-editing mode.

9. Type the following lines: `The H.264 options generate a .mp4 video file The MP3 option is for sound only!`

10. Hit the *Esc* key to leave the text-editing mode while keeping the Text Caption selected.

11. In the **Properties** panel, go to the **Style** tab and change the **Caption Type** to **Halo Blue**.

This exercise shows you two different ways of inserting a new Text Caption into the project:

- By using the **Text | Text Caption** menu item on the Big Buttons Bar
- By using the *Ctrl* + *Shift* + *C* (for Windows) or *command* + *Shift* + *C* (for Mac) shortcut keys

Extra credit – adding Text Captions

Add the remaining Text Captions in the project according to the following table. Make sure you apply the **Halo Blue Caption Type** to each new text caption:

Slide	Text Caption	Final amount of Text Captions on the slide.
Slide 5	The Adobe Media Encoder contains a list of presets to help you make the right choice.	3
	The conversion settings will be different depending on the intended purpose of your video file.	
Slide 7	The chosen preset needs some adjustments to perfectly match your needs.	2
Slide 8	The chosen preset already adjusted most of these options correctly.	3
	Only the size of the generated video must be changed.	
Slide 12	Notice that AME has automatically calculated the new height of the video.	3
	This is because the Maintain aspect ratio icon is currently selected.	
Slide 13	By modifying an existing preset, you actually created a new one.	2
	The mouse will now click on the Process Queue icon.	
Slide 14	The encoding panel contains information about how the conversion is progressing.	1
Slide 15	All done!	1

Formatting a Text Caption

Captivate offers many tools and features to format a Text Caption object. Most of them are available in the various tabs of the **Properties** panel.

Resizing and moving Text Captions

In Captivate, resizing and moving an object is very easy and can be done in two different ways: using the white handles or using the **Options** section of the **Properties** panel. The steps are as follows:

1. While still in the encoderDemo_800.cptx file, use the **Filmstrip** panel to select slide 1.

2. Click on the **Welcome to the Adobe Media Encoder** Text Caption to make it the active object.

3. Open the **Options** tab of the **Properties** panel.

The **Options** tab contains the properties that control the size and the position of the selected object. **W** indicates the width of the object, while **H** stands for the height. Both dimensions are expressed in pixels (actual values may differ from the ones shown in the following screenshot):

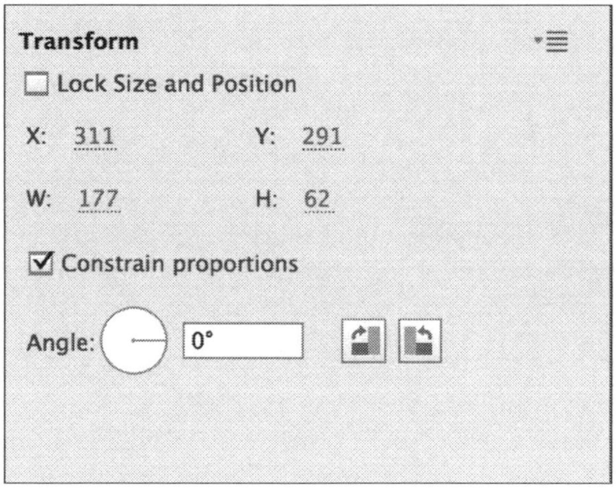

4. On the stage, use the white handles to make the Text Caption bigger.

5. Take another look at the **Properties** panel. The height and width fields of the **Options** tab should reflect the new size of the object.

If you want to give your objects a specific size, you can enter the height and the width in the **Properties** panel directly. If the **Constrain proportions** checkbox is selected, Captivate automatically calculates the new **Height** of the object when you modify the **Width** (and vice versa) so that the height/width ratio of the object does not change.

6. With the Text Caption still selected, take a look at the **X** and the **Y** values in the **Options** tab of the **Properties** panel.

7. Use your mouse to move the Text Caption around the slide.

See how the **X** and the **Y** values of the **Options** tab change as you move the Text Caption. The **X** coordinate is the distance (in pixels) between the left edge of the selected object and the left edge of the slide. The **Y** coordinate is the distance (in pixels) between the top edge of the selected object and the top of the slide. You can manually enter the **X** and the **Y** coordinates in the **Options** tab to give the selected object a pixel-precise location on the slide.

Changing the Callout and the Caption Type

You probably noticed that a Text Caption has the shape of a callout. Captivate proposes five **Callout** types for each Text Caption.

1. Use the **Filmstrip** panel to go to slide 5 of the `encoderDemo_800.cptx` file.

2. Select the Text Caption that starts with **The Adobe Media Encoder contains...**.

3. Resize this Text Caption so the entire text nicely fits on two lines.

4. Take a look at the **Caption Type** section of the **Style** tab of the **Properties** panel.

5. Open the **Caption type** drop-down list and choose the **Business Yellow** menu item under the **Caption Type** field.

6. Choose the second **Callout** type, as shown in the following screenshot:

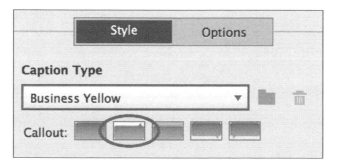

Captivate applies the new callout to the Text Caption.

Character and paragraph formatting

To finalize the look and feel of this Text Caption, you will use some more formatting options from the **Style** tab of the **Properties** panel. The steps are as follows:

1. While you're still on slide 5, make sure that the **The Adobe Media Encoder contains...** option is still selected.

2. In the **Character** section of the **Style** tab, change the font **Family** to **Verdana**.

3. Change the font **Size** to **19** points (you can type the desired size if it is not part of the options proposed in the drop-down list).

4. Finally, align the text **Center** and **Middle**.

5. Don't hesitate to resize the Text Caption if necessary.

Make sure the Text Caption looks like the following screenshot before moving on:

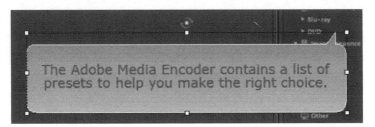

6. Save the file when done.

In *Chapter 7, Working with Styles, Master Slides, Themes, and Templates*, you will learn how to use styles and the master slides to quickly apply this formatting to the other Text Captions of the project.

This exercise concludes your first exploration of the Text Caption object. Before moving on to the next object, let's summarize what you learned about Text Captions:

- The Text Caption object is used to display text to the learner

- The Demo recording mode automatically adds Text Captions to the slides

- Changing the size or the position of an object with the mouse also changes the corresponding values in the **Options** tab of the **Properties** panel and vice versa

- Apply a **Caption Type** to the object to quickly format it

- Captivate provides five **Callout** types for each **Caption Type**

- Most of the formatting properties of Text Captions can be found in the **Style** tab of the **Properties** panel

There is still some work to be done on the other Text captions of your projects which you'll complete later in this book, for now, let's explore another object.

The Highlight Box object

The second object you will focus on is the **Highlight Box**. As its name implies, a Highlight Box is used to highlight a specific area of the screen. A Highlight Box is a rectangle that appears and disappears from the screen according to its position on the **Timeline** panel.

When using the Demo recording mode during the capture, Captivate adds one Highlight Box for each mouse click.

1. In the `Chapter03/EncoderDemo_800.cptx` project, use the **Filmstrip** panel to return to the first slide.

Slide 1 should contain four objects: two Text Captions, a Mouse, and a small blue Highlight Box below the mouse pointer.

Click the Adobe Media Encoder CS6 application

This Highlight Box has been automatically added by Captivate during filming.

2. Click on the Highlight Box to make it the active object.

Selecting the Highlight Box

Because the Highlight Box is so close to the Mouse object, you may end up selecting the Mouse instead of the Highlight Box. Remember that you can use the **Timeline** panel to select the desired object.

Selecting the Highlight Box updates the **Properties** panel. At the top of the **Style** tab, notice the **Fill** and the **Stroke** sections that provide the main formatting options of the selected Highlight Box.

- **Fill** indicates the color *inside* of the object.
- When the **Opacity** parameter is set to **0%**, the object is completely transparent. When the **Opacity** is set to **100%**, the object is completely opaque.
- The **Stroke** is the border *around* the object. You can change both the stroke **Style** and the stroke color.
- The last option is **Width**. This option lets you choose the width of the stroke. Set this option at **0** to remove the stroke from the object.

Now that you have a better idea of the available options, you can change the formatting of the selected Highlight Box:

3. Choose a dark orange as the **Fill** color.

4. Leave the **Opacity** value at **20%**.

5. Click on **Stroke**. In the color picker, choose the same orange color as the one you chose for the fill. Notice that the recently selected colors are available at the end of the color swatches.

6. Set the stroke **Width** at **2** pixels.

Make sure your **Fill** and **Stroke** sections look like the following screenshot:

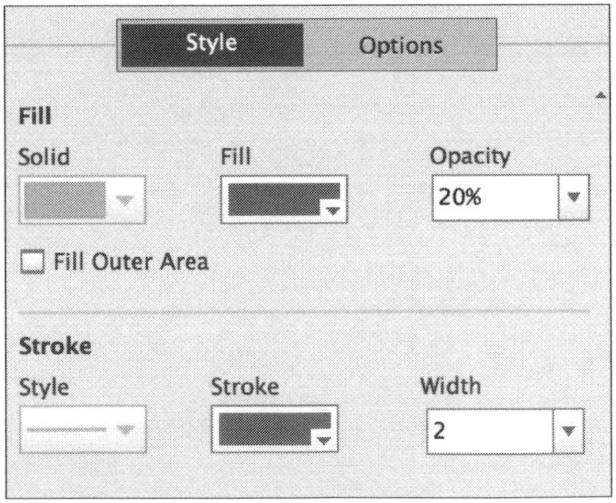

Finally, you will use the **Options** tab of the **Properties** panel to modify the size and the position of the Highlight Box.

7. Still on Slide 1 of the encoderDemo_800.cptx file, make sure the Highlight Box is the selected object.

8. Switch to the **Options** tab of the **Properties** panel.

9. For the size, change the **Width** to **24** pixels and **Height** to **19** pixels (to be able to modify the **Height** independently from the **Width**, make sure the **Constrain proportions** checkbox is deselected)

10. For the position, give the Highlight Box an **X** coordinate of **4** pixels and a **Y** coordinate of **32** pixels.

The Highlight Box should precisely cover the **Add Files (+)** icon.

11. Use the **Preview | Next 5 Slides** icon of the Big Buttons Bar to test your sequence.

Captivate generates the slides and opens the **Preview** pane. Take a close look at the Highlight box of slide 1. The timing and the formatting of the objects are of no importance at this time.

When the preview is finished, close the **Preview** pane to return to Captivate. There is one last option to experiment with.

12. Return to Slide 1 of the encoderDemo_800.cptx file and select the orange Highlight Box.

13. In the **Style** tab of the **Properties** panel, change the **Opacity** value to **70%**.

14. Select the **Fill Outer Area** checkbox situated just below the **Fill** color section.

With this option selected, the fill color of the Highlight Box is applied to the area outside of the object. The only part of the slide that will not be covered by the fill color is the inside of the Highlight Box. It is necessary to see the project in preview mode to see the **Fill Outer Area** option in action!

15. Still on slide 1 of the encoderDemo_800.cptx files, use the **Preview | Next 5 Slides** icon of the Big Buttons Bar.

When the project starts playing in the **Preview** pane, pay close attention to the way the Highlight Box behaves:

16. Return to slide 1 of the `encoderDemo_800.cptx` file and select the orange Highlight Box one last time.

17. In this particular case, you want the Highlight Box to behave normally. So, in the **Style** tab of the **Properties** panel, deselect the **Fill Outer Area** checkbox and reduce the **Opacity** value back to **20%**.

18. Save the file when done.

This last experiment concludes this discussion on Highlight Boxes. Here is a summary of what you learned:

- A Highlight Box is a rectangle used to highlight a particular spot on the slide.

- **Fill** is the inside of the Highlight Box object. The **Style** tab of the **Properties** panel lets you choose the color and the opacity of the fill.

- **Stroke** is the border around the Highlight Box object. You can choose the style, the color, and the width of the stroke in the **Properties** panel.

- Select the **Fill Outer Area** option to apply the fill color to the outside of the Highlight Box rather than to the inside.

Working with the mouse

The third object to study is the **Mouse**. Remember that during filming, only the coordinates of the mouse clicks were recorded and that the mouse movements are recreated during playback.

Understanding the mouse movements

You will start your study of the mouse object by discovering how Captivate manages the mouse movements.

1. If needed, use the **Filmstrip** panel to return to Slide 1 of the `encoderDemo_800.cptx` file.

You should see four red dots in the top-left corner of the slide. These four dots mark the starting point of the mouse.

2. Use your mouse to move the four red dots anywhere on the slide.

By moving the four red dots, you change the starting point of the mouse on slide 1 as illustrated in the following screenshot:

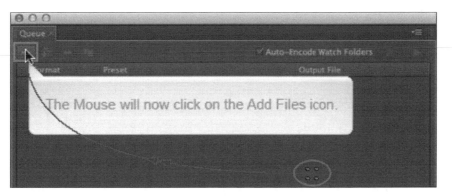

From the chosen spot, Captivate generates a curved blue line that represents the mouse movement. This curved line ends with the mouse pointer.

3. Click on the mouse pointer at the end of the curved blue line to select the Mouse object. The **Properties** panel updates.

When a Mouse object is selected, the **Properties** panel does not contain any tabs.

4. Select the **Straight Pointer Path** checkbox.

By clicking on this box, Captivate generates a straight line between the starting and ending points of the mouse movement.

5. Deselect the **Straight Pointer Path** checkbox.

6. Use the **Filmstrip** panel to select slide 2.

On the second slide, the four red dots visible on slide 1 are not visible. It means that you cannot move the starting point of the mouse on slide 2. This is because the starting point of the mouse on slide 2 corresponds to the ending point of the mouse on slide 1.

7. Use the **Filmstrip** panel to browse the remaining slides of the project.

When browsing the slides of the project, you should notice that the first slide is the only one where the starting point of the mouse movement can be moved. No other slides display the four red dots at the beginning of the curved blue line.

8. When done, return to slide 1.

9. Take the mouse pointer and move it to a random location.

10. Use the **Filmstrip** panel to select slide 2.

On slide 2, you should notice that the starting point of the curved blue line has changed and corresponds to the random location you chose on slide 1.

11. On the **Filmstrip** panel, click on slide 1 to make it the active slide.

12. Move the mouse pointer back to its original location.

13. Use the **Filmstrip** panel to go to the last slide of the project (slide 15).

On slide 15, the mouse makes a long movement. As slide 15 is the last one of the project, this movement is unnecessary. What you want to do is to completely remove the Mouse object from this slide.

14. On slide 15, right-click on the mouse pointer at the end of the blue line.

15. In the contextual menu, deselect the **Show Mouse** item. You can also use the **Modify | Mouse | Show Mouse** menu item to achieve the same result.

Note that the coordinates of the Mouse object as recorded during filming are still saved with the slide should you change your mind about the Mouse being hidden on slide 15.

16. Use the **Filmstrip** panel to go to slide 11 of the `encoderDemo_800.cptx` file.

This is the slide where you typed `400` in the **Width** field of AME. The next slide (slide 12) is where the Mouse moves to click on the **OK** button of the **Export Settings** dialog. For this particular sequence, you want to have a single action per slide. So, slide 11 should only show the typing in the **Width** field with no mouse movement. Slide 12 should show the entire Mouse movement.

17. Still on slide 11, right-click on the mouse pointer to select the Mouse object.

18. In the contextual menu, click on the **Align to Previous Slide** item.

By clicking on the **Align to Previous Slide** item, the mouse pointer on slide 11 is aligned to the mouse pointer on slide 10. Consequently, the starting and ending points of the Mouse object on slide 11 have the same coordinates and the mouse no longer moves on slide 11. Another consequence is that the starting point of the mouse on slide 12 has changed to match the location of the mouse on slide 11, effectively transporting the entire mouse movement to slide 12.

19. Go to the **Preview** icon on the Big Buttons Bar to preview the entire project.

20. In the **Preview** pane, pay close attention to the mouse movements. Make sure each click occurs at the right place.

You might see that, there is a small problem in the mouse continuity between slides 13 and 14. Because slide 14 is a Full Motion Recording that captured the mouse movement frame by frame, you cannot use the same technique to modify the mouse movement. You will address this problem in *Chapter 4, Working with Multimedia*.

21. When the preview is complete, close the **Preview** pane.

22. If needed, adjust the position of the Mouse on the slides where the click is not well positioned.

23. Save the file when done.

Formatting the mouse object

During the preview, you probably noticed a blue circle and a click sound on most mouse clicks. These two options, and a few others, can be managed in the **Properties** panel. The steps are as follows:

1. Use the **Filmstrip** panel to return to slide 1.

2. Once on slide 1, select the mouse pointer to make it the active object.

3. Take some time to inspect the properties available in the **Properties** panel, as shown in the following screenshot:

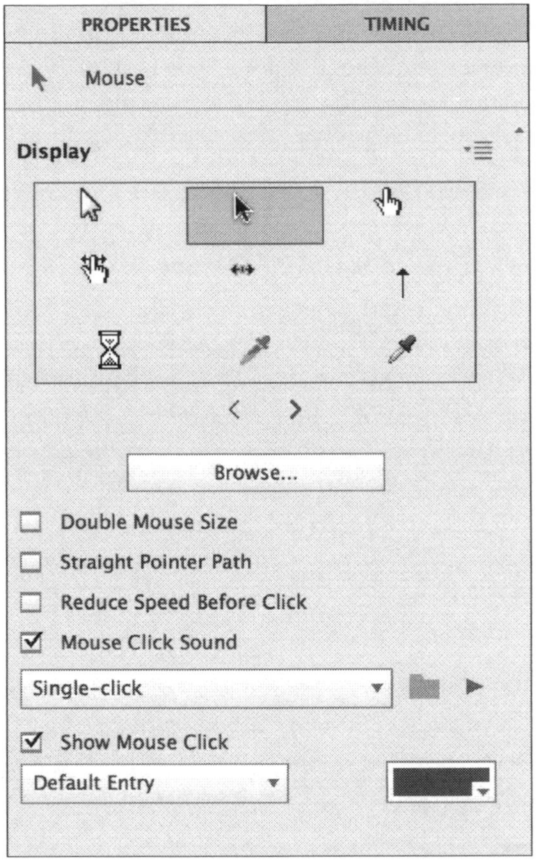

Notice the two drop-down lists that let you choose the click sound to use (single click or double click) and the shape of the visual click. You can also change the color of the visual click, if necessary.

The topmost part of the **Properties** panel lets you choose the most appropriate mouse pointer. In this example, the default pointer is perfect, so you will not change it in this project.

Choosing the right mouse pointer

My very first big eLearning project was to build an online course on SAP for a big multinational company. SAP uses custom mouse pointers that I wanted to reproduce in Captivate. A mouse pointer is a .cur file, so I clicked on the **Browse** button situated right below the collection of mouse pointers in the **Properties** panel and searched for the appropriate .cur file in the C:\Program files folder of Windows. I eventually found the .cur file I was looking for and I could import it in Captivate. If you work on a Mac, you can inspect the content of an .app file by right-clicking on the file and choose **Show package content**. You might find the .cur file you are looking for in the package. The bottom line is, your Captivate project should reproduce the behavior of the actual application as close as possible.

4. Use the **Filmstrip** panel to go to slide 2 and select the **Mouse** object.

Take a look at the **Properties** panel and notice how the **Double-click** sound has been automatically chosen by Captivate during the filming. Note that you can change it to a single click if necessary; after all, it is just a sound, not an actual click!

5. Use the **Filmstrip** panel to go to slide 8 and select the **Mouse** object.

Slide 8 is used to move the mouse pointer to the scroll bar of the **Export Settings** window before slide 9 uses a Full Motion Recording to show the scrolling movement. In the **Properties** panel, the **Mouse Click Sound** and the **Show Mouse Click** checkboxes are therefore not selected.

This concludes your first exploration of the Mouse object. Let's quickly summarize what you learned in this section:

- During the capture, only the position of the mouse at each click is recorded. A mouse movement is recreated between these positions at runtime.

- By default, the mouse movement uses a curved line, but you can make it a straight line in the **Properties** panel.

- The first slide of the project is the only slide where you can move both the starting and ending points of the mouse movement.

- To prevent the mouse from moving on a given slide, right-click on the mouse pointer and choose **Align to Previous Slide** in the contextual menu.

- Removing the Mouse from a slide does not remove its coordinates. This makes it easy to turn the Mouse back on should you change your mind.

- Moving the mouse pointer on a slide also moves the origin of the mouse movement on the next slide.

- You can add a visual click as well as a click sound in the **Properties** panel.

Working with images

The next object to discuss is the **image** object. Captivate lets you insert various types of images on any slide of the project. Once an image is inserted, you are able to modify and format the image using the Captivate image editing tools. Keep in mind though that Captivate is not an image editing application. To guarantee the best possible results, you should always prepare your images in a real image editing application (such as Adobe Photoshop or Adobe Fireworks) before inserting the image in Captivate. However, if you don't have access to these types of software applications, you can do some nice image editing right inside of Captivate.

Inserting a slide from another project

Before moving onto inserting images, you will first insert one extra slide in the **Filmstrip** panel. The steps are as follows:

1. Open the `Chapter03/videoInCaptivate.cptx` file from your exercises folder.

This project is a one-slide Captivate movie. That single slide contains four Text Captions. In order to accelerate your work, you simply copy and paste this slide into the `encoderDemo.cptx` file.

2. In the `videoInCaptivate.cptx` file, right-click on the slide thumbnail in the **Filmstrip** panel.

3. In the contextual menu, select the **Copy** item.

4. Return to the `encoderDemo_800.cptx` file.

5. In the **Filmstrip** panel, right-click on the first slide and select the **Paste** menu item.

When inserting a new slide in a Captivate project, it gets inserted after the selected slide. There is no way to insert a new slide as the first slide directly, but the **Filmstrip** panel lets you easily reorder the slides by simply dragging them up and down.

6. Use the **Filmstrip** panel to drag the new slide up so it becomes the first slide of the project.

Also, notice how the pasted slide picks up the theme applied to the current project. You will learn more about themes in *Chapter 7, Working with Styles, Master Slides, Themes, and Templates.*

Inserting an image on a slide

Now that the stage is set, let's move on to what really is the subject of this particular section: inserting pictures.

About image types

Captivate lets you insert many different image types in your projects including `.jpg`, `.gif`, and `.png` images. If you want to know more about these image formats, visit `http://www.sitepoint.com/gif-jpg-png-whats-difference/`.

1. Make sure you are still on the first slide of the `encoderDemo_800.cptx` file.

2. Use the **Media | Image** icon of on the Big Buttons Bar to insert a new image.

3. Browse to the `images/AMELogo.png` file stored in your exercises folder.

4. Click on **Open** to insert the picture.

The image is inserted in the middle of the slide. Obviously, it is way too big! Your next operation will be to resize and position this image so it integrates nicely with the other elements of the slide.

5. Make sure the image is selected on your slide.

6. Use your mouse to change the size of the image by clicking and dragging the handles. This will most likely distort the image.

You can avoid distortion by pressing and holding the *Shift* key on your keyboard while using a corner handle to resize (scale) the image.

7. In the **Style** tab of the **Properties** panel, click on the **Reset To Original Size** button to restore the image to its original aspect.

You will now use the **Options** tab of the **Properties** panel to resize this picture.

8. Switch to the **Options** tab of the **Properties** panel.

9. Make sure the **Constrain proportions** checkbox is selected and change the width of the picture to 180 pixels. Captivate calculates the new height of the image (176 pixels) so that its height/width ratio does not change.

10. Move the image to the lower left area of the slide next to the Text Captions.

Your slide should now look like the following screenshot:

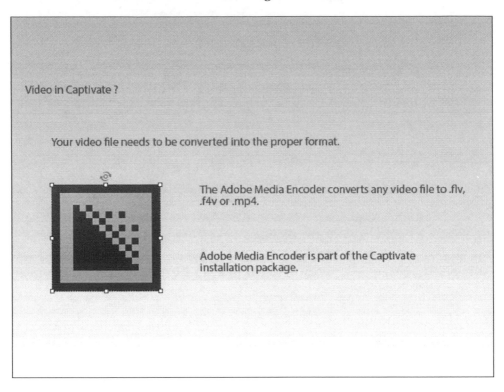

The blinking dashed green lines

While moving the image into place, you probably noticed some dashed green lines appearing and disappearing automatically on the screen. These are called the **Smart Guides**. These Smart Guides help you align objects together. If you want to turn them on or off, you can use the **View | Show Drawing/Smart Guides** menu item.

Using the image editing tools

Inserting an image in Captivate is very easy! You will now explore some of the image editing tools available in Captivate.

1. Make sure the newly imported image is selected, and take a look at the **Style** tab of the **Properties** panel.

2. Click on the **Edit Image** button.

This action opens a dialog box showing the image on the left and a set of control sliders on the right.

3. Move the sliders to see how each affects the image on the left.

4. When done, click on the **Reset All** button situated in the bottom-right corner of the dialog box.

5. Take some time to inspect the other controls available in the dialog box. Note that the image can also be flipped, resized, and cropped.

6. Click on **Cancel** to close the dialog box without saving the changes.

For the finishing touch, you use the options of the **Shadow & Reflection** section of the **Style** tab of the **Properties** panel.

7. Make sure the image is still selected.

8. In the **Style** tab of the **Properties** panel, expand the **Shadow & Reflection** section, if needed.

9. In the **Reflection** section, choose the preset you like the most.

Great! This little effect adds a whole new dimension and impact to your picture! Your students will certainly enjoy this level of detail in their visual experience.

Inserting a picture slide

Inserting images on existing slides is one of the many possibilities offered by Captivate. Another nice feature is the ability to create a brand new slide based on an image. The chosen image is used as the background picture of the new slide. You will now examine that workflow hands on:

1. Make sure you are still on the first slide of the `encoderDemo_800.cptx` file.

2. Use the **Insert | Image Slide** menu item.

3. Browse to the `images/mftc-titleBkb_fixed.png` file stored in your exercises folder and click on the **Open** button.

4. The same dialog box as in the previous exercise opens. Take some time to review the picture. Notice the **Fit to Stage** option that is selected by default.

5. When done, click on the **OK** button to proceed with the insertion of the new slide.

The new picture is inserted as a new slide. Notice that the picture has a width of 800 pixels and a height of 600 pixels, which is the exact same size as the project itself. It is not a coincidence. Remember that the images must be prepared before being inserted in Captivate. In this case, preparing the image made sure it had the right size.

6. In the **Filmstrip** panel, drag the new slide up so it is the first slide of the project.

7. Save the file when done.

Extra credit – working with characters

Characters are a collection of images that can be inserted in your Captivate projects. These images represent male and female characters in various postures. Inserting such pictures in your eLearning projects brings in a human and humorous touch.

Downloading the eLearning assets

These characters are part of the eLearning assets available with Captivate. These eLearning assets are not part of the main Captivate installation package. A separate package must be downloaded and installed to take advantage of the characters. You can find these extra installers at http://www.adobe.com/go/Cp8_win_assets_installer (for Windows) or http://www.adobe.com/go/Cp8_mac_assets_installer (for Mac). This extra credit section assumes that the eLearning assets have been installed on your system.

In this section, you will apply your new knowledge of images in Captivate on the drivingInBe.cptx file by inserting characters on top of your slides. These characters are actually .png images that can be manipulated in Captivate as any other images. The steps are as follows:

- Switch to or open the drivingInBe.cptx file.

- Use the **Media | Characters** icon of the Big Buttons Bar to open the **Characters** dialog (see the following screenshot).

- Notice the four categories in the drop-down menu; each category has various types of characters.

- Choose two characters, one male character and one female character. Insert various versions of each character in your project as you see fit.

- Use the tools provided in the **Image Edit** dialog box to edit the imported character. (The **Flip image horizontal** option of the **Image Edit** dialog box is an easy way to double the number of available postures!)

- Save the `drivingInBe.cptx` file when done.

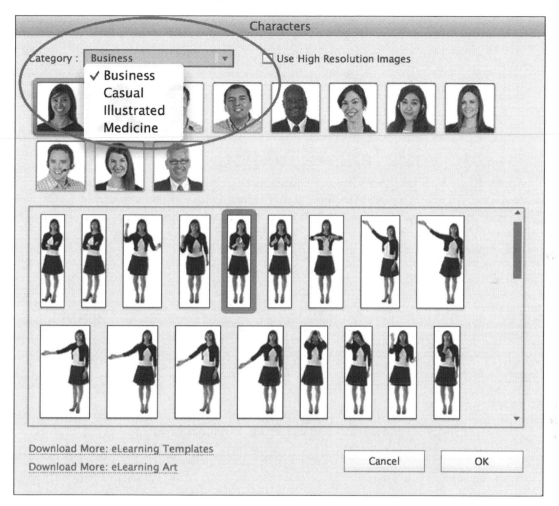

Refer to the `final/drivingInBe.cptx` file for inspiration.

This concludes your first overview of the image object. Here is a summary of what you learned in this section:

- You can easily insert many types of images in Captivate.
- Captivate provides some image editing capabilities. These are found in the **Image Edit** dialog, accessible through the **Image Edit** button situated in the **Style** tab of the **Properties** panel.
- It is best to prepare the image in another image editing application before inserting it in Captivate.

- If needed, use the **Reset To Original Size** button to change the picture back to its original state.

- Use the **Insert | Image Slide** menu item to create new slides that are based on images.

- The **Characters** are a collection of pictures that you can use in your eLearning projects.

- The installation of an extra package is required to use the characters.

Working with Text Animations

The next object you will focus on is the Text Animation object. In this exercise, you will create the front slide and the final slide of the encoder demo project and add Text Animation on both these slides using the following steps:

1. Return to the `encoderDemo_800.cptx` file.

2. Use the **Filmstrip** panel to go to the first slide of the project.

The first slide of the `encoderDemo_800.cptx` file was created in the *Inserting a picture slide* section earlier in this chapter. There are currently no objects on this slide. You will now add a Text Animation to it. The steps are as follows:

3. Click on the **Text** icon of the Big Buttons Bar and choose the **Text Animation** item in the list.

4. In the **Text Animation Properties** box, type `Adobe Media Encoder The Demonstration`.

5. Change the **Font** type to **Verdana** and the **Size** value to **52**.

6. Click on the **OK** button. The new object appears on the slide.

With the new Text Animation object selected, take some time to inspect the **Style** tab of the **Properties** panel. Most options are self-explanatory.

The new Text Animation is too wide to fit on the slide. If this happens with a regular Text Caption, you would use the white resize handles or the **Options** tab of the **Properties** panel to resize the object.

7. Make sure the Text Animation is the selected item.

8. Switch to the **Options** tab of the **Properties** panel.

As usual, the **X** and the **Y** coordinates as well as the rotation **Angle** are available in the **Options** tab. But where are the width and the height properties?

Actually, Captivate automatically calculates the size of a Text Animation object based on the text content and on the font size. So, your only options to modify the size of a Text Animation object are to modify its text content and/or its font size. In this case, you will add a line break just before the **the demonstration** part of the content.

9. Make sure the Text Animation is still selected.

10. Return to the **Style** tab of the **Properties** panel.

11. Click on the **Animation Properties** button. Alternatively, you can also **Double-click** on Text Animation.

This action reopens the **Text Animation Properties** box where you can change both the text content and the font size of your Text Animation object.

12. In the upper area of the **Text Animation Properties** box, use your mouse to place the cursor between **Encoder** and **The demonstration.**

13. Hit the *Enter* key to create a line break at the location of the cursor.

14. Click on the **OK** button to confirm the changes.

The **Text Animation Properties** box closes and the Text Animation object is updated.

15. Use your mouse to move the Text Animation to the lower-right corner of the slide.

16. In the **Style** tab of the **Properties** panel, choose an effect in the **Effect** drop-down list.

Use the **Preview** area at the top of the **Properties** panel to control the chosen effect. In the final application in *Chapter 1, Getting Started with Adobe Captivate 8*, the **Waltz** effect was used.

17. To test your new Text Animation, use the **Preview** icon of the Big Buttons Bar to preview the **Next 5 Slides**.

18. Close the **Preview** pane when done and save the file.

The first slide of the project should now look like the following screenshot:

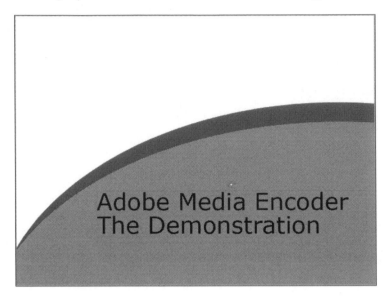

Duplicating slides

Now that the first slide of the project is finished, you will create the last slide. It will be very similar to the front slide so, instead of repeating the whole process a second time, you simply duplicate the first slide and change the content of the Text Animation.

1. In the **Filmstrip** panel, right-click on the first slide of the project and choose **Duplicate** in the contextual menu. Alternatively, you can use the *Ctrl + D* (for Windows) or *command + D* (for Mac) shortcuts.

2. In the **Filmstrip** panel, drag slide 2 to the very end of the project.

Remember that new slides get inserted *after* the currently selected slide.

3. Go to the last slide (slide 18) and select the Text Animation.

4. In the **Properties** panel, go to the **Style** tab and click on the **Animation Properties** button.

5. In the **Text Animation Properties** dialog, change the text to: Thank you for viewing this demonstration!

6. Leave the other properties unchanged and hit the **OK** button.

7. Save the file when done.

To test the new slide, use the **Filmstrip** panel to select the slide just before the last one, then use the **Preview** icon of the Big Buttons Bar to preview **From this Slide**.

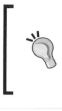

Use Text Animations with care

The Text Animation object must be used with care. It is a great effect if you use it every once in a while, but if you use it too often, it overcharges your projects, which gives an unprofessional impression. Also, it is not HTML5 compatible.

Converting a Typing object into a Text Animation object

In Captivate, a Typing object is a very special type of object. It appears only in demonstrations and is created during the initial filming of the project when text is typed in the captured application. During the filming of the Encoder Demo project, you typed some text in the **Width** field of the **Video** tab. Consequently, a Typing object was generated.

1. Still in the `encoderDemo_800.cptx` file, use the **Filmstrip** panel to go to slide 13.

2. Once on slide 13, click on the **Timeline** button at the very bottom of the screen to open the **Timeline** panel.

The **Timeline** panel contains three layers in addition to the slide itself, indicating that the slide contains three objects. One of these objects is labeled **Typing Text**. It represents the text that was typed in the **Width** field during the filming. This object was automatically generated when the slide was captured in *Chapter 2, Capturing the Slides*.

3. Click anywhere on slide 13 (but not on an object). Make sure the **Properties** panel displays the properties of the **Slide**.

4. In the **Timeline** panel, click on the **Text Typing** object to select it. Notice that the **Properties** panel is not updated and still shows the properties of the **Slide**.

The **Text Typing** object is the *only* object of Captivate that does *not* update the **Properties** panel. This unexpected behavior tells you that this object is very special indeed, and that it has no properties that you can adjust. One of the only available options is to control the typing speed by modifying the object's timing in the **Timeline** panel, but there is no solution to modify the text content, its font, its font size, or its color.

Luckily, Captivate lets you convert the Text Typing objects into Text Animations. Once converted, the Text Typing object has the same editing capabilities as any other Text Animation. Be aware, however, that a Text Animation cannot be converted back into a Typing object. Converting a Typing object into a Text Animation is a one-way definitive operation.

5. In the **Timeline** panel, right-click on the **Text Typing** object.

6. In the contextual menu, choose **Replace with Text Animation**. Remember that this operation cannot be undone:

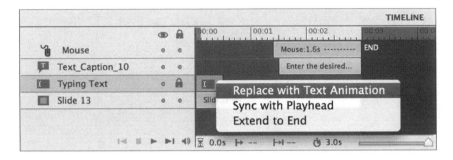

This option can be very handy in many situations, especially when you need to modify the text that was typed during the capture. Note that the effect applied to the converted Text Typing object is the **Typing Text With Sound** effect. If needed, you can use another effect, but I strongly recommend you stick to this one as it has been specifically designed to mimic the typing of a text.

> The Text Animation object has no **Fill** property. In other words, it is transparent, which causes a small problem in this case. To solve this problem, I've used a gray Highlight Box with an **Opacity** set to **100%** (to make it completely opaque). I adjusted the size of the Highlight Box so it is exactly the same size as the **Width** field. I then used the **Timeline** panel to send this Highlight Box to the bottom of the stack. Finally, I used the **Timing** panel to make the Highlight Box display for the entire duration of the slide. Look for this Highlight Box on slide 13 of the Chapter03/final/encoderDemo_800.cptx file. Can you implement it in your file as well?

This concludes the discussion on Text Animations. Let's make a quick summary of what you learned:

- The Text Animation object can be created entirely in Captivate. No need for an external application (such as Adobe Flash) to create it!

- The Text Animation object is typically used on the first and last slide of the project.

- To resize a Text Animation, change its content, add a line break into the text or change the font size.

- When text is typed during the capture, a Text Typing object is generated. Convert this object to a Text Animation for enhanced editing capabilities.

- The Text Animation object is not supported in HTML5.

Working with Smart Shapes

Smart Shapes are a predefined collection of shapes including rectangles, circles, banners, stars, arrows, and many more.

Drawing a simple Smart Shape

In this exercise, you will draw a simple rounded rectangle Smart Shape using the following steps:

1. Return to the `drivingInBe.cptx` project.
2. Use the **Filmstrip** panel to go to slide 3.

 The remaining exercises of this chapter do not account for the Character images added during the previous extra credit section.

At this moment, slide 3 should contain three objects, including one image. You will now draw a rounded rectangle that will be used as a background frame of that picture.

3. Click on the **Shapes** icon of the Big Buttons Bar and select the rounded rectangle shape in the list of available shapes.
4. Click and drag your mouse to draw a rounded rectangle shape that entirely covers the image present on slide 3. Don't hesitate to resize and move the shape if needed.

In the top-left area of the shape, you should see a yellow handle in addition to the eight white handles that surround the shape. This yellow handle is one of the features that make a Smart Shape smart. It is used to modify the shape. In the case of the rounded rectangle, this yellow handle is used to adjust the roundness of the rectangle.

5. Use the yellow handle to adjust the roundness of the rectangle to your taste.
6. When the shape is more or less into place, right-click on it and use the **Arrange | Send to back** menu item in the contextual menu.

This last step modifies the stacking order of the objects and sends the rounded rectangle behind the image. Don't worry about the exact positioning and formatting of the rounded rectangle, these elements will be adjusted later in the book.

Drawing additional Smart Shapes

In this exercise, you will discover that Captivate offers many more predefined shapes than those shown in the **Shapes** icon of the Big Buttons Bar. You will now draw a Curved Up Ribbon shape, which is a shape that is not directly accessible through the **Shapes** icon of the Big Buttons Bar. Here is how you can access it anyway:

1. In the `Chapter03/drivingInBe.cptx` project, use the **Filmstrip** panel to go to slide 2.

At this moment, slide 2 should contain only one object (in addition to the optional Character image(s) you inserted in the *Extra credit – working with characters* section). You will now draw a second object on the slide that will be used as the title container.

2. Click on the **Shapes** icon of the Big Buttons Bar to open the Smart Shape menu.

3. Click on the banner shape, as shown in the following screenshot:

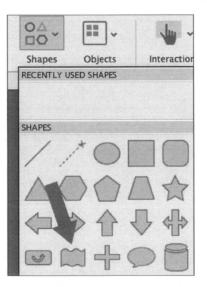

4. Click and drag your mouse to draw a banner shape in the upper area of the slide. Make the banner wide enough to accommodate the title of the slide. Don't hesitate to resize and move the shape if needed.

The banner shape that you just inserted is not exactly the shape you are looking for. Hopefully, other shapes are available in the **Properties** panel.

5. Make sure the new banner shape is selected and open the **Properties** panel (if necessary).

6. Locate the **Banner** section situated at the top of the **Style** tab.

7. Click on the little triangle situated next to the banner thumbnail to display a menu containing extra shapes.

8. Choose the **Curved Up Ribbon** shape, as shown in the following screenshot:

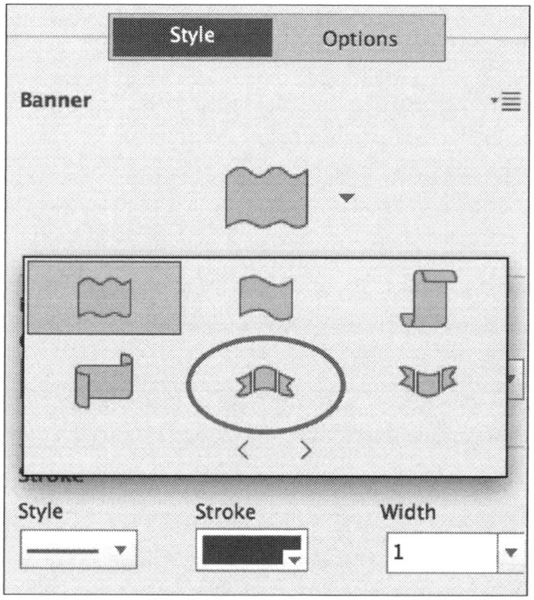

The additional shapes displayed by the **Properties** panel depend on the type of shape that is selected on the slide. In this case, you have inserted a banner shape, so the **Properties** panel shows you additional banners.

With the Curved Up Ribbon shape selected, you should see three yellow handles in addition to the eight white handles surrounding the shape.

9. Experiment with the yellow handles to see how each affects the selected shape.

When finished, make sure your slide looks like the following screenshot:

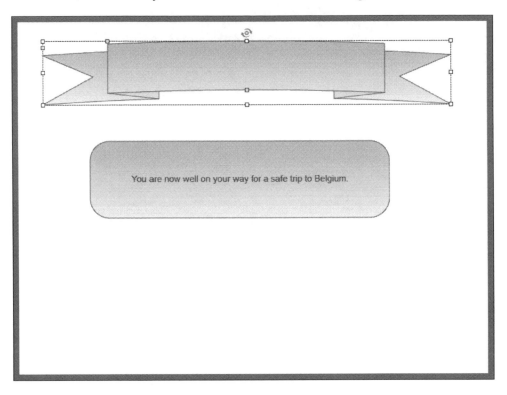

Creating and saving your own Smart Shapes

In addition to predefined shapes, Captivate allows you to draw your own Smart Shapes. Captivate 8 even introduces the possibility of saving your Smart Shapes for later use. In the following exercise, you will experiment with this feature hands-on using the following steps:

1. In the `Chapter03/drivingInBe.cptx` project, use the **Filmstrip** panel to go to slide 9.

2. Click on the **Shapes** icon of the Big Buttons Bar to open the Smart Shape menu.

3. Choose the Polygon tool in the Smart Shapes menu. It is the dotted line that ends with a star at the top of the menu.

When the Polygon tool is selected, the Mouse pointer turns into a crosshair.

4. Click anywhere on the slide where you want the first point of the Polygon to be located.

5. Click on another location to create a second point. Captivate automatically connects the two points with a dotted line.

6. Use the same technique to add the other points of the shape.

7. To close the shape, click on the first point you created. Captivate will display a small circle next to the mouse pointer to indicate that the shape can be closed.

You now have your very own custom shape on the slide. If the shape is not exactly the one you intended to create, don't worry! In the next section, you will learn how to modify the shape you just created.

Modifying a custom shape

A Smart Shape is a **vector object** similar to those you can draw with Adobe Fireworks or Adobe Illustrator. To create these shapes, designers use the Pen tool of Illustrator or Fireworks to draw Bezier points and Bezier curves. Even though Captivate is not equipped with a full -fledged pen tool, you can however access these Bezier points and modify your shape using the following steps:

1. Right-click on your shape and choose the **Edit Points** item in the contextual menu. This action reveals the points that you have defined when creating the polygon.

2. Move those points to modify the shape. You can also move the green handles to modify the curvature of the connecting lines, as shown in the following screenshot:

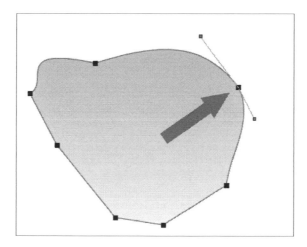

3. When you come up with the proper shape, hit the *Esc* key of your keyboard to leave the point-editing mode and select the shape.

Note that you can only move the defined points or modify their curvature, but you cannot add or remove points to and from the shape.

> **Converting predefined shapes to freeform**
>
> Another way of creating your own Smart Shapes is to start with a predefined shape and modify it using the very same technique as the one described in this section. Simply right-click on a Smart Shape and choose the **Convert to freeform** item in the contextual menu to access the Bezier points. Have fun!

Saving a custom shape

New in Captivate 8 is the ability to save your own custom shapes and add them to the list of the predefined Shapes of Captivate. In this exercise, you will save your custom shape and draw a second instance of it using the following steps:

1. On slide 9 of the `Chapter03/drivingInBe.cptx` project, make sure your custom shape is selected (with white selection handles around it).

2. Locate the **Custom** section situated at the very top of the **Style** tab in the **Properties** panel.

3. Click on the icon situated in the top-right corner of the **Custom** section and choose the **Save Shape** item, as shown in the following screenshot:

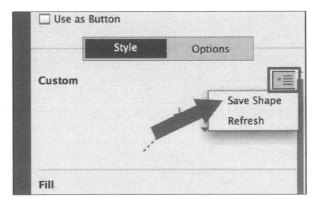

4. Type `myShape` in the **Rename Item** dialog box and click on **OK** to save your custom shape.

By saving your custom shape, you actually make it part of the collection of predefined shapes so you can reuse it in the future. Use the following steps to draw a second instance of the same shape.

5. Click on the **Shapes** icon of the Big Buttons Bar to open the Smart Shapes panel.

Note that your new shape is present in the **Recently Used Shapes** section at the top of the drop-down menu. If you did not use that shape recently, it would not be part of the Shapes menu of the Big Buttons Bar. In such a case, here is how you can draw that shape anyway.

6. Choose the Polygon tool (the dotted line that ends with a star).

7. Randomly add a few points to the slide in order to create a new custom shape. The actual shape you come up with is of no importance.

8. Make sure the new shape is selected and turn your attention to the **Custom** section at the top of the **Style** tab in the **Properties** panel.

9. Click on the little black arrow to display a list of additional shapes as described in the *Drawing additional Smart Shapes* section earlier in this chapter.

10. Choose your custom shape from the list of additional shapes.

You should now have two instances of your custom shape on the slide, effectively demonstrating how you can save and reuse the custom shapes you come up with. Now these two shapes have been added for demonstration purpose only, so your next task is to remove them from the slide.

11. Select both your custom shapes and hit the *Delete* key on your keyboard to remove them from the slide.

12. Save the file when done.

You should now be back to the original situation with only one object on the slide.

In this section of the book, you learned how to create Smart Shapes using various techniques. Before moving on to the next section, let's quickly summarize what you learned:

*   Smart Shapes are a collection of predefined shapes that can be manipulated in many ways with Captivate tools.

*   The collection of Smart Shapes includes rounded rectangles, banners triangles, and callouts, among others.

*   When a Smart Shape object is selected, special yellow handles allow you to modify the Smart Shape.

- Use the **Properties** panel to access additional shapes. The list of available additional shapes depends on the original shape you inserted on the slide.

- Use the **Polygon** tool to draw your very own custom shapes.

- Smart Shapes are vector objects similar to those you create with Adobe Illustrator or Adobe Fireworks. Use the **Edit Points** or the **Convert to Freeform** menu item to access the Bezier points and curves of your shape.

- New in Captivate 8 is the ability to save and reuse your custom shapes.

These are just a few of the amazing possibilities offered by the Smart Shapes object. In the next sections, you will explore the formatting properties of a Smart Shape and discover how Smart Shapes can be used to advantageously replace Highlight Boxes and Text Captions.

Using Smart Shapes as Highlight Boxes

A Highlight Box is a semi-transparent rectangle used to highlight a specific area of the slide in order to draw the learner's attention to that specific spot. It is a great object, but it has some limitations. First a Highlight Box can only be a rectangle. Second, the Fill Color of a Highlight Box can only be a single unique plain color; there is no way to create a gradient fill or other special effects with regular Highlight Boxes.

In this section, you will overcome these limitations by replacing the Highlight Boxes of the `encoderDemo_800.cptx` file with Smart Shapes using the following steps:

1. Return to the `Chapter03/encoderDemo_800.cptx` file.
2. Use the **Filmstrip** panel to return to slide 3 of the project.

Slide 3 marks the beginning of the screenshot-based demonstration. Remember that this slide contains four objects, including an orange Highlight Box that was automatically added to the project by the Demo automatic recording mode used during the recording.

3. Select the orange Highlight Box and hit the *Delete* key on your keyboard to delete it.
4. Click on the **Shapes** icon of the Big Buttons Bar and select the rounded rectangle tool.
5. Draw a rounded rectangle more or less where the Highlight Box was located.

You have overcome the first limitation of a Highlight Box. Any shapes of Captivate, including your own custom shapes, can be used as a Highlight Box. This gives you a myriad of new creative and pedagogical opportunities. Use them wisely.

You will now explore the formatting properties of a Smart Shape to give this particular shape the same look and feel as the Highlight Box you just deleted.

6. With the new rounded rectangle selected, turn your attention to the **Style** tab of the **Properties** panel. Open the **Properties** panel if needed.

7. Locate the three properties situated in the **Fill** section of the **Style** tab.

8. Open the **Gradient** drop-down menu and take some time to inspect the available options.

The **Fill** of a Smart Shape (in other words, inside Smart Shape) can be a **Solid Fill** (just as Highlight Boxes), a **Gradient Fill**, or an **Image Fill**. This again multiplies the creative and pedagogical opportunities:

9. When done, select the **Solid Fill** option.

10. Open the **Fill** color chooser and choose the same orange as the one you used for the Highlight Box. This color should still be listed in the recently used colors section at the end of the color chooser.

11. Locate the three properties situated in the **Stroke** section of the **Style** tab.

12. Open the **Style** dropdown and inspect the list of available options. When done, select the solid line at the very top of the drop-down menu.

13. In the **Stroke** color, choose the same orange color as the one you used for the fill of the object. This color should still be listed in the recently used colors section at the end of the color chooser.

14. Change the **Width** of the stroke to 5 pixels.

15. If necessary, adjust the size and position of the rounded rectangle.

16. Save the file when done.

At the end of this exercise, you have successfully reproduced the formatting of the former Highlight Box using a Smart Shape, as shown in the following screenshot:

The benefit of this approach is that you have access to a much wider range of shapes as compared to the unique rectangle shape of a Highlight Box object. Also, remember that the **Fill** of a Smart Shape can be a **Gradient Fill**, a **Solid Fill**, or an **Image fill** as compared to the fill of a Highlight Box that can only be a **Solid Fill**.

Highlight Box or Smart Shape?

Since the introduction of Smart Shapes in Captivate 6, I very seldom use the Highlight Box object anymore. The only benefit of using a Highlight Box is the **Fill Outer Area** option that is not available when using a Smart Shape.

Extra credit – replacing the remaining Highlight Boxes of the project.

Now you will use your new knowledge to replace the remaining Highlight Boxes of the project by Smart Shapes. It is a good time to explore the other predefined shapes offered by Captivate (remember that additional shapes can be found in the **Properties** panel). The steps are as follows:

- Go through each slide of the `encoderDemo_800.cptx` project.
- When a slide contains a Highlight Box, select and delete it.
- Use the **Shapes** icon of the Big Buttons Bar to replace the deleted Highlight Box with the most appropriate Smart Shape. It is a good opportunity to explore the other predefined shapes of Captivate. Be creative!
- Don't forget to save your file when done!

When ready, move on to the next section where you will discover yet another capability of the Smart Shape object.

Adding text inside Smart Shapes

The awesomeness of Smart Shapes does not end here! In this exercise, you will explore another amazing capability of the Smart Shape object by adding text inside a Smart Shape. This allows you to replace the Text Captions of your project by Smart Shapes.

1. Return to the `Chapter03/drivingInBe.cptx` file.
2. Use the **Filmstrip** panel to go to slide 2 of the project.

This is where you inserted the Curved Up Ribbon shape earlier in this chapter.

3. Select the Curved Up Ribbon shape and take a look at the **Style** tab of the **Properties** panel.

In the **Properties** panel, the **Style** tab should now contain four sections: the **Banner** section at the top, the **Fill** and **Stroke** sections, and a collapsible **Shadow and Reflection** section at the bottom.

4. Double-click into the Curved Up Ribbon Smart Shape. This action brings a blinking cursor inside of the shape.

5. Type Welcome inside the Smart Shape. When done, use the *Esc* key to leave text-editing mode and select the shape as an object.

6. Take another look at the **Properties** panel.

By adding text inside your Smart Shape, the **Character** and the **Margin** sections have been automatically added to the **Style** tab. These two sections are the same as those used to format the text inside a Text Caption object. It means that you have the exact same text formatting capabilities on a Smart Shape as on a Text Caption.

> **Smart Shape or Text Caption?**
>
> Since the introduction of Smart Shapes in Captivate 6, I very seldom use the Text Caption object anymore. I tend to use Smart Shapes as much as possible. I find Smart Shapes much more flexible than Text Captions and I like the much larger array of possible shapes as compared to a standard Text Caption.

In this section, you learned how Smart Shapes can be used to replace Highlight Boxes and Text Captions. Before moving on to the next section, let's quickly summarize what has been covered in this section:

*   The formatting capabilities of a Smart Shape are similar to those of a Highlight Box.

*   The **Fill** of a Smart Shape can be a **Solid Fill**, a **Gradient Fill**, or an **Image Fill**, in comparison to the **Fill** of a Highlight Box that can only be a **Solid Fill**.

*   The only option that is specific to a Highlight Box object is the **Fill Outer Area** option.

*   Text can be added inside a Smart Shape.

*   When a Smart Shape contains text, additional text formatting properties are displayed in the **Style** tab of the **Properties** panel.

*   These text formatting properties are the same as those found on a Text Caption object.

I must admit it, I love Smart Shapes! In *Chapter 6, Working with Interactive Objects*, you will discover even more capabilities of this very flexible object of Captivate, but for now, let's move on to the last topic of this chapter.

The Equation editor

The last object studied in this chapter allows you to create complicated mathematical equations and to insert them on your slides. This feature is powered by an external application called **MathMagic**. A special version of MathMagic is installed along with Captivate. In the next exercise, you will use the Equation Editor to create simple mathematical equation teaching your students how to convert a kilometer per hour speeds to miles per hour speeds. The steps are as follows:

1. Still in the `Chapter03/drivingInBe.cptx` file use the **Filmstrip** panel to go to slide 7.

2. Use the **Insert | Equation** menu item to open the **Equation Editor**.

The external **MathMagic for Captivate** application opens and a default equation is added on your slide. You may have to clear a message indicating that you are using a special version of MathMagic meant to be used with Captivate only.

3. Delete the default equation that appears in the main window of the **Equation Editor**.

MathMagic for Captivate has a lot of tools and icons representing a very large collection of mathematical symbols. In this simple exercise, you will use two of these tools identified in the following screenshot:

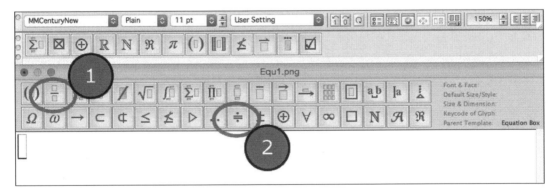

For your information, the speed in miles per hour is approximately two-thirds of the kilometers per hour equivalent. This is what you will represent by an equation. The steps are as follows:

4. Click on the icon identified as number **1** in the preceding screenshot.

5. Take the very first option proposed by this icon. This inserts a *division* symbol in the main window of the Equation Editor.

6. Type 60 Kmph in the top part of the division.

7. Type 3 in the bottom part of the division.

8. Place your cursor on the right-hand side of the division and type * 2.

9. Click on the icon identified as number **2** in the preceding screenshot.

10. Select the third tool in the third row to insert the *More or less equal to* symbol.

11. Type 40 mph on the other side of the symbol.

Make sure your equation looks like the following screenshot:

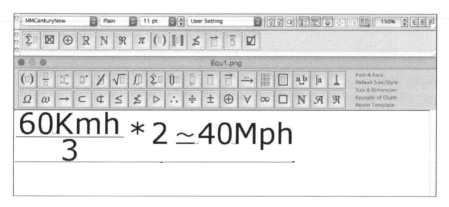

12. Select the entire equation and use the **Font** menu of **MathMagic for Captivate** to apply the **Verdana** font to the equation.

13. Use the **File | Save** menu item or use the *Ctrl + S* (Windows) or *command + S* (Mac) shortcut to save the equation. This action updates the equation on the Captivate slide.

14. Close **MathMagic for Captivate** and return to slide 7 of the drivingInBe. cptx file.

15. Move and resize the newly inserted equation so it integrates nicely with the other elements of the slide.

This exercise concludes your exploration of the standard non interactive objects scheduled for this chapter. Before moving on, let's make a quick summary of what has been discussed in this section:

- The Equation Editor feature is powered by an external application called MathMagic. When Captivate is installed, a special version of MathMagic is installed alongside Captivate.

- The Equation Editor can be used to generate complex mathematical equations using specific symbols.

- Once the external MathMagic application has generated an equation, it is inserted as a .png image on your Captivate slide.

You will explore some more objects in the coming chapters, but for now, let's wrap up this chapter by covering one last feature that will spice up your text objects.

Working with Text Effects

The Text Effects feature lets you create and apply some sophisticated visual effects to Text Captions and Smart Shapes containing text. If you are a Photoshop user, you'll be in familiar territory as Captivate's Text Effects feature shares most of its functionalities with Photoshop.

Use the following steps to experiment with Text Effects.

1. While still in the `Chapter03/drivingInBe.cptx` file, use the **Filmstrip** panel to go to slide 5 of this project.

Slide 5 should contain two Smart Shapes with text (not accounting for the Character image(s) possibly added during a previous extra credit section).

2. Select the Smart Shape that reads **Good** to make it the active object.

3. In the **Character** section of the **Style** tab of the **Properties** panel, change the font **Family** to **Verdana** and the font **Size** to **49**.

4. Still in the **Character** section of the **Properties** panel, click on the **Effects** icon (identified as (**1**) in the following screenshot).

The Text Effect menu opens. In the topmost area of the menu, eight predefined effects are ready to use (**2**). The last four effects are yours to create (**3**).

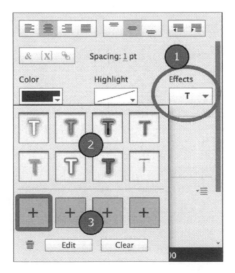

5. Click on the first empty effect.

The **Text Effects** window opens. The left-hand side of the window contains nine effects. You can easily turn these effects on and off by clicking on their respective checkboxes. The right-hand side of the window displays the options of the effect selected on the left. At this moment, no effect is applied.

6. In the left column of the **Text Effects** window, select the **Drop Shadow** checkbox.

A Drop Shadow effect is added to the selected text object. For this example, you will accept the default settings of the Drop Shadow effect.

7. In the left column of the **Text Effects** window, select the **Outer Glow** checkbox.

The **Outer Glow** effect is also applied to the Text Caption and the options of the **Outer Glow** effect are displayed in the right-hand side of the **Text Effects** window. To make your effect more attractive and visible, modify the color of the **Outer Glow** effect.

8. In the right-hand side of the **Text Effects** window, click on the **Color** option of the **Outer Glow** effect.

9. In the color picker on the right-hand side of the window, choose any bright green color. After this procedure, the **Text Effects** window should look like the following screenshot:

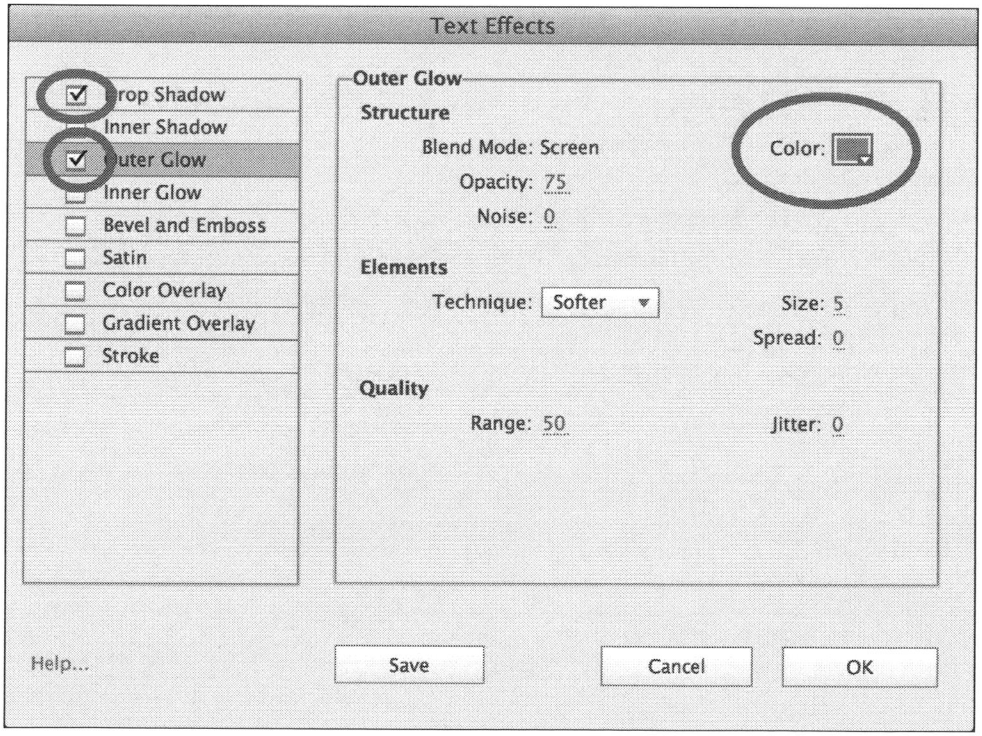

Hey! It looks like you just came up with a very nice effect. Let's save it for future use.

10. At the bottom of the **Text Effects** window, click on the **Save** button.

The **Text Effects** window closes and your effect is applied to the selected Text Caption. Because you have saved your nice effect, it will be very easy to apply it to another text object of the project.

11. While in the `drivingInBe.cptx` file, use the **Filmstrip** panel to go to slide 10.

12. Once on slide 10, select the Text Caption that reads **Good**.

13. In the **Character** section of the **Style** tab of the **Properties** panel, change the font **Family** to **Verdana** and the font **Size** to **49**.

14. While in the **Character** section of the **Properties** panel, open the **Effects** drop-down menu.

Surprise! A ninth effect is now available in the **Text Effects** icon! It is the effect that you just saved a few lines ago.

15. Click on this new effect to apply it to the selected Text Caption.

Great! You can now create some sophisticated visual effects and easily apply them to the Text Captions of your project.

16. Still in the `drivingInBe.cptx` file, use the **Filmstrip** panel to go to slide 6.

17. Once on slide 6, select the Text Caption that begins with **Belgian use…**.

18. In the **Character** section of the **Style** tab of the **Properties** panel, change the font **Family** to **Verdana** and the font **Size** to **49**. Resize the Text Caption if necessary.

19. While in the **Character** section of the **Properties** panel, open the **Effect** icon one more time.

20. Apply your new effect to the selected Text Caption.

Your new effect is applied to the **Belgian use…** Text Caption. You will now modify the color of the Outer Glow Effect. By doing so, you will come up with a new Text effect that you will save and apply to another Text Caption of the project.

21. Make sure the **Text Effects** icon is still open in the **Character** section of the **Styles** tab of the **Properties** panel.

22. Click on the **Edit** button.

The Text Effects window reopens.

23. On the left-hand side of the **Text Effects** window, click on the **Outer Glow** effect (make sure you click on the name of the effect and not on the checkbox).

24. On the right-hand side of the window, open the **Color** option of the **Outer Glow** effect.

25. In the color picker, choose any bright red color. The new **Outer Glow** color is automatically applied to the selected Text Caption.

26. At the bottom of the **Text Effect** window, click on the **Save** button to save this as a new effect.

Make sure the Text Caption looks like the following screenshot:

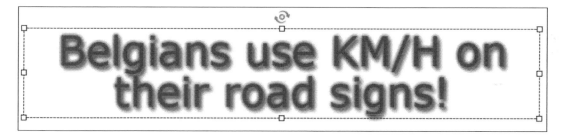

Finally, you will apply this second effect to another Text Caption of the project.

27. Use the **Filmstrip** panel to go to slide 11.

28. Once on slide 11, select the Text Caption that begins with **Belgian drive...**.

29. In the **Character** section of the **Style** tab, change the font **Family** to **Verdana** and the font **Size** to **49**. Resize the Text Caption if necessary.

30. In the **Character** section of the **Properties** panel, open the **Text Effects** icon.

31. Apply your new *red* effect to the selected Text Caption.

32. Save the `drivingInBe.cptx` file when done.

Note that such a Text Effect must be applied to the entire text content. It is not possible to select a portion of the text and apply the effect to the selected portion only.

Summary

The postproduction phase of your projects is now well in progress and you have come a long way since you entered the studio with your rushes at the beginning of this chapter.

In this chapter, you learned about the standard non interactive objects of Captivate. Although very simple to use, these objects already make the student's experience of your eLearning content much better than what it was at the beginning of this chapter. Among all the objects that you have studied, one of them stands out. The Smart Shape object lets you draw custom or predefined shapes in your project. These shapes can be used in such a wide variety of situations that they can advantageously replace the Text Captions and the Highlight Box objects.

Now let's be honest. You are not there yet! There is still a lot of work left to be done before sharing the project with your learners.

In the next chapter, you will build on your new skills and learn about other objects used to include multimedia elements into your eLearning content.

Meet the community

In this section, I want to introduce you to Lieve Weymeis. Lieve and I share our Belgian nationality, which makes us very close. I first met her in the summer of 2013 in San Jose, California, during an Adobe event. There she celebrated her ten thousandth answer on the Captivate forums with the rest of the Adobe Education team. I was fortunate enough to be part of the celebration and to have my share of the fantastic chocolate cake made for the occasion. Full respect, Lieve!

Lieve Weymeis

Lieve is civil engineer (Ir) and professional musician. After years of teaching/ research (project management / eLearning), she is now a freelance consultant/ trainer specialized in advanced Adobe Captivate. Her blog (`http://blog. lilybiri.com`) is a reference for Captivate users worldwide.

In 2009, she was invited to the Advisory Board for Captivate. As an Adobe Certified Expert, Adobe Community Professional and Adobe Education Leader, she presented about Captivate and Flipped classes, both online and live (Adobe Summits, DevLearn, Media and Learning, and so on). In the Captivate community (forums) and on social media, she has established herself as a well known and much appreciated expert.

Contact details

- **Twitter**: @Lilybiri
- **Blog**: http://blog.lilybiri.com
- **LinkedIn**: be.linkedin.com/in/lieveweymeis
- **E-mail**: info@lilybiri.com

4
Working with Multimedia

In this chapter, you will continue the post-production phase of your project by learning how you can transform your eLearning content into a great multimedia experience. *Multimedia* means that you will use various types of media, technologies, and support to transmit your message to your learner. This includes not only static text and images (already covered in the previous chapter), but also sound video and animation.

Some of this animated content can be created entirely in Captivate, while other animated content has to be developed in external applications, such as Adobe Flash or Adobe Edge Animate, and imported into Captivate when ready.

In this chapter, you will cover the following topics:

- Editing a Full Motion Recording
- Inserting Flash and HTML5 animations in the project
- Inserting video files in the project
- Adding sound effects to objects.
- Adding background music to the project
- Recording narration to the slides
- Importing external sound files into Captivate
- Editing a sound clip in Captivate
- Generating narration with the Text-to-Speech engine
- Using the **Slide Notes** panel to convert Slide Notes to Closed Captions and Text-to-Speech.
- Synchronizing the Closed Captions with the corresponding sound clip

This makes a lot of exciting things to cover, so let's get started right away by editing the Full Motion Recording captured in *Chapter 2, Capturing the Slides*.

> **Resetting your workspace to default**
>
>
> To ensure the maximum accuracy between the procedures described in this chapter and your actual experience on the computer, take some time to restart Captivate. If you are using the default interface mode, restarting Captivate will reset your workspace to default.

Editing a Full Motion Recording

In the first exercise of this chapter, you will finalize the continuity of the mouse path in the Encoder Demonstration project using the following steps:

1. Open the `Chapter04/encoderDemo_800.cptx` file of your exercises.

2. Use the **Filmstrip** panel to go to slide 15 of the project.

Remember that during the recording, you used the *Print Screen* (for Windows) or *cmd + F6* (for Mac) shortcut to manually capture slide 15. This was necessary to have a slide available to display the needed text captions. After that, you used the *F9* key (for Windows) or the *cmd + F9* shortcut (for Mac) to start a Full Motion Recording and clicked on the **Start Queue** icon.

The goal of this exercise is to have the click on the **Start Queue** icon on slide 15 and the yellowish progression bar on slide 16. To make this possible, you will modify the Full Motion Recording of slide 16 so that it begins right after the click on the **Start Cue** icon.

3. Select the Mouse object situated in the bottom-right area of slide 15.

4. Move the mouse pointer on top of the **Start Queue** icon (the green play button) of the Adobe Media Encoder.

5. With the Mouse object selected, open the **Properties** panel and select the **Mouse Click Sound** and **Show Mouse Click** checkboxes.

6. Go to **Preview | Next 5 slides** on the Big Buttons Bar to preview what you have done so far.

You should notice that the Mouse object clicks on the **Start Cue** icon twice: once on slide 15 and a second time on slide 16. To make this transition look realistic, the Full Motion Recording of slide 16 should pick up right after the click on the **Start Queue** icon and should finish right when the encoding process is finished. To do this, you need to modify the Full Motion Recording of slide 16.

7. Use the **Filmstrip** panel to go to slide 16 of the `encoderDemo_800.cptx` project.

8. Open the **Timeline** panel by clicking on the **Timeline** bar at the bottom of the screen.

9. Open the **Options** tab of the **Properties** panel and locate the **FMR Edit Options** drop-down menu.

This section of the **Properties** panel is only available on Full Motion Recording slides.

10. Open the **FMR Edit Options** drop-down menu and select the **Trim** option.

11. Leave the **Trim From** option at 0 seconds but set the **Trim To** option to 2.9 seconds.

This action is reflected on the **Timeline** panel where two vertical black bars mark the **Trim From** and **Trim To** points, respectively. Note that you can adjust the position of these markers by moving them on the **Timeline** directly.

As illustrated in the following screenshot, these two markers select a portion of 2.9 seconds at the very beginning of your Full Motion Recording. This portion is the one you want to remove:

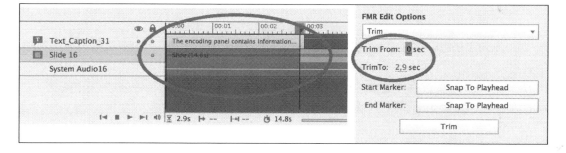

12. Click on the **Trim** button situated in the **FMR Edit Options** section of the **Properties** panel.

This last action removes the portion of the FMR identified by the **Trim From** and **Trim To** markers. The Full Motion Recording now begins exactly when the mouse clicks on the **Start Queue** icon, providing a smooth transition between the mouse movement on slide 15 and the Full Motion Recording of slide 16.

> Editing the Full Motion Recording does not edit the corresponding sound clip. Therefore, the **Chimes** sound effect captured with the System Audio feature is currently out of sync. You will address that issue later in this chapter.

You will now repeat this procedure at the end of the slide. The only difference is that you will spot the location to trim from using the **Timeline** and **Playhead**.

13. Use your mouse to move the Playhead (the vertical red line) until you see the end of the encoding process on the slide (around 8.5 seconds).

14. In the **Options** tab of the **Properties** panel, open the **FMR Edit Options** drop-down menu and choose the **Trim** item.

15. Click on the **Snap to Playhead** button associated with the **Start Marker**.

16. On the **Timeline** panel, use your mouse to move the end marker to the very end of the slide.

You should have selected the portion of the Full Motion Recording situated between 8.5 seconds and 11.9 seconds.

17. Click on the **Trim** button to remove the selected portion of video.

After these operations, the Full Motion Recording of slide 16 only shows the yellowish progress bar symbolizing the encoding of the video.

18. Use the **Filmstrip** panel to return to slide 15.

19. Click on the **Preview** icon of the Big Buttons Bar and choose the **Next 5 slides** option.

During the preview, pay close attention to the continuity of the mouse movements across Slide 15 and 16. When done, close the **Preview** pane and leave the file open for the next exercise.

Inserting external animations into the project

In this exercise, you will import animations into the project. These animations are Flash and HTML5 animations that have been created in external applications such as Adobe Flash Professional and Adobe Edge Animate.

Importing Flash animations

The first type of animation you will focus on is the Flash Animation. The external application used to generate these animations is Adobe Flash Professional and the file imported into Captivate is the compiled .swf file. If you do not have Flash Professional installed, don't worry—all the necessary animations have already been created for you.

Adobe Flash Professional file extensions

When saving a file with Adobe Flash professional, the file extension used is .fla. The .fla file contains the objects, animations, filters, and so on needed for the Flash animation to work properly. Consequently, it can be a very large file. Once the .fla file is finished, it is necessary to export it (the proper word is to *compile* it) to .swf format. The .swf file is the *compiled* version of the .fla file and is the one that can be read by the Flash Player plugin. Converting a .swf file back to .fla (an operation known as **reverse engineering**) is not possible. (Well actually, it is with specialized software, but you never get back to the *original* .fla file!)

In the next exercise, you will import a Flash animation into your Encoder Demo project. Perform the following steps to do so:

1. Return to the encoderDemo_800.cptx file.
2. Use the **Filmstrip** panel to select slide 4.

This is the slide where the mouse double-clicks on the demo_en.mov file. You will use an animation to emphasis the amazing list of file types shown in the **Enable** dropdown.

3. Insert a new rounded rectangle Smart Shape into the slide. Resize it so it covers the entire **Enable** drop-down menu.
4. With the new Smart Shape selected, open the **Properties** panel and use the **Style** tab to reduce **Opacity** of the rounded rectangle to **40%**. The other formatting properties of this object are of no importance right now.
5. Go to **Media** | **Animation** on the Big Buttons Bar to insert a new animation on the current slide.

The **Open** dialog box opens to let you locate the animation to insert.

If you do not have Adobe Flash Professional or if you do not know how to use it, don't worry! To get you started, Captivate ships with a **gallery** containing many objects that you can use in your project. The location of this gallery is as follows:

- **Windows**: C:\Program Files\Adobe\Captivate 8\Gallery
- **Mac**: /Applications/Adobe Captivate 8/Gallery

The Gallery folder is further divided into several subfolders that contain various types of objects. One of these folders is the SWF Animation folder.

6. Browse to the `SWF Animation/Arrows/Orange arrow/down.swf` file of the gallery and click on the **Open** button.

The animation is imported and appears on slide 4. Note that only `.swf` and animated `.gif` files can be inserted that way in Captivate.

7. Use the Smart Guides to place the new object, as shown in the following screenshot:

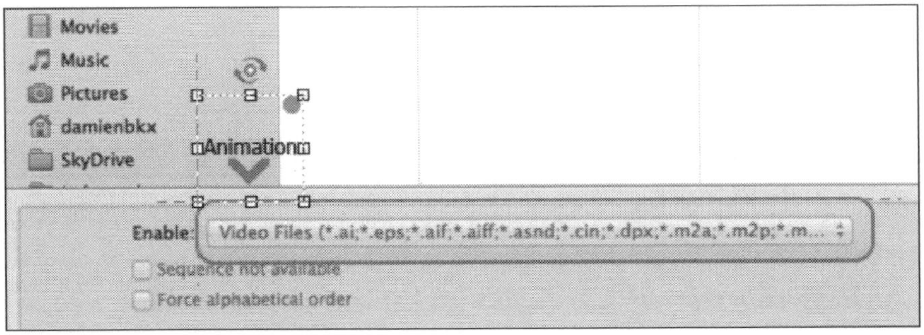

Inserting animations in the project is *that* easy! In *Chapter 5, Working with the Timeline and Other Useful Tools,* you will return to this slide and use the **Library** panel as well as the Alignment toolbar to further enhance the animations.

8. Go to **Preview | Next 5 slides** on the Big Buttons Bar to quickly have a sense of what this animation looks like.

9. Save the file when done.

During the preview, pay attention to the way the orange arrow is animated keeping in mind that the general timing of the slide is yet to be adjusted.

Such animation adds a great touch of liveliness to your slide, but it has one major limitation. Because it was made in Adobe Flash Professional, it is only supported in the Flash output of Captivate and not in the HTML5 output.

Flash animations in HTML5

When viewed in HTML5, Flash-based animations, such as the Orange Arrow that you inserted in this exercise, will gracefully degrade into a static image. The concept of graceful degradation lets you design the optimal experience (here an animated arrow). In case this optimal experience is not completely supported, it is degraded in such a way that the content is preserved (in this case, the arrow is present as an image in the HTML5 output, but is not animated). The progressive enhancement concept takes the opposite approach. It lets you design a satisfactory basic experience that you can enhance depending on the capabilities of the browser used to consume the content.

Fortunately, Captivate 8 introduces a simple mechanism that allows you to insert HTML5 animations into the project.

Importing HTML5 animations

In this exercise, you will return to the *Driving in Belgium* project to import three HTML5 animations created in Adobe Edge Animate.

Adobe Edge Animate and Adobe Flash Professional have a lot in common. Both applications let you create animations using a similar timeline-based approach. However, there are several differences between the two—the main one being the format in which the final animation is compiled. Adobe Flash Professional uses the .swf format, while Adobe Edge Animate uses HTML5, CSS, and JavaScript. This makes the animations created in Adobe Edge Animate natively compatible with any HTML5-enabled browser, including those embedded in mobile devices.

Both Adobe Flash Professional and Adobe Edge Animate are part of the Creative Cloud subscription.

If you have Adobe Edge Animate installed on your computer, the source files of the animations you will use in the next exercises are provided in the Animate/Source folder of the download associated with this book.

You will now import an HTML5 animation into your project using the following steps:

1. Open the `Chapter04/drivingInBe.cptx` file.

2. Use the **Filmstrip** panel to go to slide 13 of the project.

3. Go to **Media | HTML5** Animation on the Big Buttons Bar to start the import process.

4. Navigate to the `Animate/050-CitiesTowns.oam` file and import it into your project.

5. Hover over the newly imported object to preview it on the slide.

An `.oam` file is a special package created by Adobe Edge Animate. It works more or less like a `.zip` file. That is, the `.oam` file is a wrapper that contains all the HTML, CSS, and JavaScript resources needed to make the animation run properly.

> **Inspecting the content of an .oam file**
>
> If you want to inspect the actual content of an `.oam` file, here is a simple trick: just change the `.oam` extension to `.zip`. Then, unzip the resulting file and inspect its content. Make sure you revert the extension of the package to `.oam` before continuing with this exercise.

6. Make sure the newly imported animation is selected and turn your attention to the **Options** tab of the **Properties** panel. It may be necessary to open the **Properties** panel.

7. Make the width `600` pixels and the height `110` pixels. You may need to deselect the **Constraint Proportions** checkbox to be able to modify the height and the width independently.

8. Use your mouse to place the animation in the upper area of the slide.

9. Switch to the **Style** tab of the **Properties** panel and inspect the available properties. Most of them should be self explanatory.

10. Deselect the **Border** and the **Scrolling** checkboxes.

After these operations, your slide should look like the following screenshot:

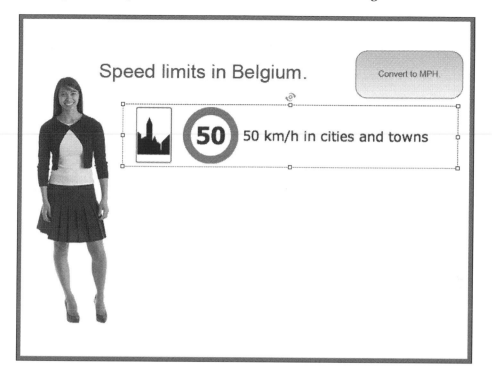

You will now use the very same procedure to import the other two HTML5 animations to the slide.

11. On the Big Buttons Bar, go to **Media | HTML5 Animation** to insert the `Animate/090-NationalRoads.oam` package onto the slide.

12. Hover over the new animation to preview it on the slide.

13. Use the **Options** tab of the **Properties** panel to give the new animation the same size as the first one (a width of `600` pixels and a height of `110` pixels).

14. Switch to the **Style** tab of the **Properties** panel and deselect the **Border** and the **Scrolling** options.

15. Place the new animation just below the first one.

16. Repeat the same set of operations with the `Animate/120-Motorways.oam` file.

Your slide should now look like the following screenshot:

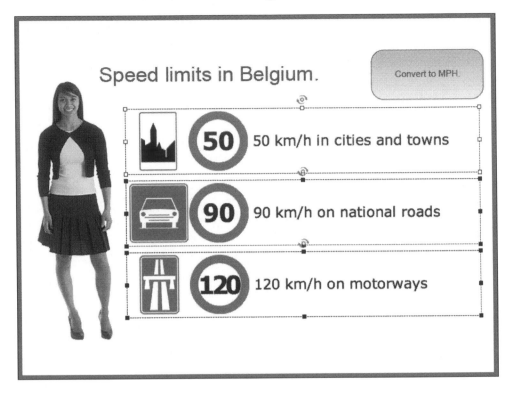

You will now preview your new HTML5 animations using the **Preview** icon of the Big Buttons Bar.

17. Go to **Preview | Next 5 slides** on the Big Buttons Bar to open the **Preview** pane.

Well, it looks like you have a problem! Your HTML5 animations are not showing in the **Preview** pane. Don't worry, there is nothing wrong with your project. The **Preview** pane shows a temporary Flash file of whatever portion of the project you want to preview. But the Edge Animate animations you just inserted are not supported in Flash, and this is why they are not showing in the **Preview** pane. To test your Edge Animate animations, it is necessary to preview the HTML5 output of the content in a web browser.

18. Close the **Preview** pane and click on the **Preview** icon of the Big Buttons Bar one more time. Choose the **HTML5 in Browser** item in the list of options.

This preview option only works for the entire project. There is currently no way to preview the HTML5 output of Next 5 slides in the browser. When the preview reaches slide 13, make sure your HTML5 animations are displayed as expected.

This concludes your overview of inserting external animations in Captivate. It is time to make a quick summary of what you have learned:

- Captivate lets you insert external .swf and .gif animations in your projects.
- These animations are typically created in Adobe Flash Professional and are not supported in HTML5.
- Captivate ships with an extensive gallery containing various types of objects that you can use in your projects.
- Edge Animate is an Adobe application used to create HTML5 animations.
- Edge Animate can package these animations in an .oam file.
- The ability to import such .oam files directly into your slide is new in Captivate 8.
- Those HTML5 animations are not supported in Flash and therefore do not appear in the Flash-based **Preview** pane of Captivate. It is necessary to test the project in a web browser to see these animations.

In the next section, you will continue your exploration of the multimedia capabilities of Captivate by inserting video files in your project.

Working with video

It's time for the next topic of this chapter: the **Video** file. Remember that Captivate was originally designed to create Adobe Flash (.swf) files that can be played back by the Adobe Flash Player plugin. In 2006, Adobe (formerly Macromedia) added video support to Flash. At that time, the Flash Player supported only a specific Flash video format: the .flv format (**flv** stands for **Flash Video**). In 2007, some limitations of the .flv format led to the development by Adobe of the .f4v Flash video format. Today, the Flash Player supports both the .flv and the .f4v video formats. Adobe Media Encoder is used to convert any kind of video to the .flv or .f4v file format.

With the arrival of HTML5, it is now possible for a web browser to play video (or audio) files natively, without the help of an external plugin such as the Flash Player. Unfortunately, the industry has not yet decided what video format/codec should be used for HTML5 video playback. As of today, it looks like two formats are emerging, the .mp4 format and the .webm format. To embrace this futuristic technology, Adobe Media Encoder and Adobe Flash now support the .mp4 video format in addition to the .flv and .f4v formats.

> For more information on Flash video, visit http://en.wikipedia.org/wiki/Flash_Video.
>
> For more information on Adobe Media Encoder, visit http://www.adobe.com/products/mediaencoder.html.

In this exercise, you will insert a new slide in the Encoder Demo project and add a video file onto it.

1. Return to the Chapter04/encoderDemo_800.cptx file.

2. Use the **Filmstrip** panel to go to slide 1.

3. Go to **Slide | Blank Slide** on the Big Buttons Bar to create a new blank slide.

The new slide is inserted as slide 2. Remember that new slides are always inserted *after* the active slide. You will now import a video file on this new slide.

4. Go to **Video | Insert Video**.

The **Insert Video** dialog opens. At the top of the **Insert Video** dialog, you have to choose either an **Event Video** or a **Multi-Slide Synchronized Video**. The following table lists some of the differences between these two options:

	Event Video	Multi-Slide Synchronized Video
Sync	Cannot be distributed over several slides	Can be distributed over several slides or not
Timeline	The Timeline of the video is independent of the Timeline of the project	The video plays in sync with the slide or slides it appears on
Playback controls	Event videos can have their own playback controls	Has no specific playback controls associated
Closed Captions	Cannot be closed captioned	Can be closed captioned

In this case, you want the video to show on slide 2 only, something that both the **Event Video** and the **Multi-Slide Synchronized Video** can do. Later in this chapter, you will add Closed Captions to the video; something that only the **Multi-Slide Synchronized Video** can do.

5. Make sure the **Multi-Slide Synchronized Video** option is the one in use.

6. Click on the **Browse** button, browse to the `videos/flv/demo_en.flv` file of your exercises folder, and click on **Open**.

7. In the lower area of the **Insert Video** dialog, select the **Modify slide duration to accommodate video** option.

8. Make sure the **Insert Video** dialog looks like the following screenshot and click on the **OK** button:

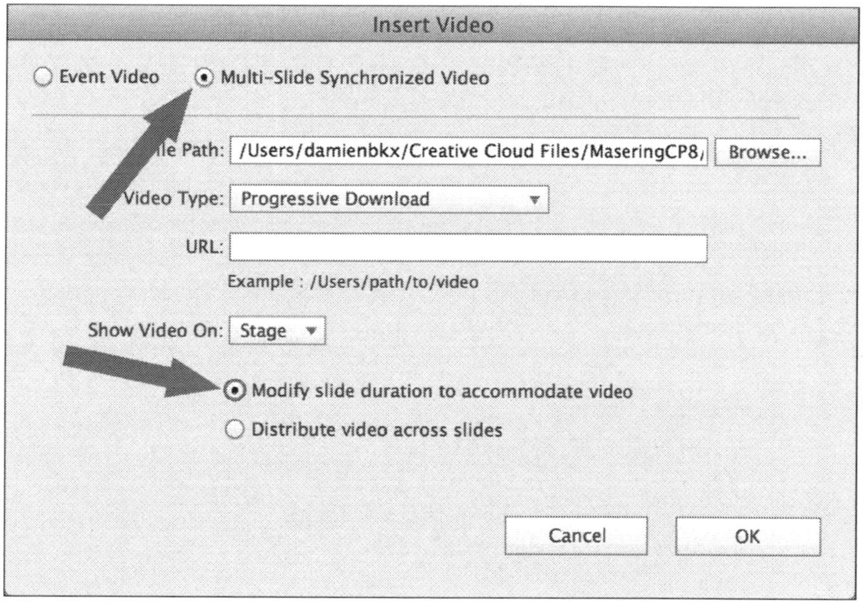

The video is inserted into the slide. Because the first frame of the video is white, it may be necessary to click on the video to reveal its boundaries.

9. Make sure the video is selected and take a look at the **Options** tab of the **Properties** panel.

Notice the message **Proportions are locked**. It means that you cannot change the width of the video independently of its height. This is done to ensure that the proportions of the video are respected when the size is changed. In this case, the size of the video was set in Adobe Media Encoder while converting the video from `.mov` to `.flv`.

10. For the position, set the **X** and the **Y** coordinates both at 200.

Take a quick look at **Timeline**; you will see that the duration of the slide matches the duration of the video file.

11. Save the file and go to **Preview | Next 5 slides** on the Big Buttons Bar.

12. When the preview is finished, close the **Preview** pane.

Let's summarize what you just learned about inserting videos in Captivate:

- There are two options available to insert videos in Captivate: **Event Video** and **Multi-Slide Synchronized Video**.

- If you want to publish your Captivate movie in Flash format, it is necessary to use the .flv, .f4v, or .mp4 video file formats.

- If you want to publish your project in HTML5, use the .mp4 video format.

- **Adobe Media Encoder (AME)** is an external application. It is part of Adobe Creative Cloud and of the default Captivate package.

- AME converts any video file to .flv, .f4v, or .mp4, so it can be used in Captivate.

Learn with the Captain!

For more about video in Captivate as well as great tips and tricks about the use of video in eLearning, I recommend two webinars by my friend Josh Cavalier (Captain Captivate). Interactive video in Captivate can be found at http://lodestone.adobeconnect.com/p9difbur5bj/ and Interactive video in Captivate (part 2) at http://lodestone.adobeconnect.com/p3s68qq8iak/.

In the next section, you will start looking into the audio support of Captivate.

Working with audio

In this section, you will discover how audio can be used in a Captivate project. You can add sound at three different levels:

- **Object level**: The sound associated with an object plays when the object appears on the screen. This is a great place to add small sound effects (whooshes, clings, bangs, tones, and so on.) to the project.

- **Project level**: Most of the time, the project-level audio clip is used to add background music to the entire project.

- **Slide level**: The audio clip plays in sync with the slide. Most of the time, this option is used to add voice-over narration.

You will now cover these three options in more detail. The one that will capture most of your attention is slide-level audio. Slide-level audio can either be recorded (with Captivate or with an external audio application) or generated by the Text-to-Speech engine of Captivate. Closed Captions can also be added to the slide-level audio.

Adding audio to the objects

Sound can be added on each and every object in Captivate. The audio clip associated with an object plays when the object appears on the stage.

While object-level audio is the preferred place to add sound effects to the project, nothing prevents you from adding narration or any other type of audio content at object level. It may be used to read aloud descriptive text or to pronounce a difficult word. This book only shows the typical use case, but don't hesitate to be creative in how you actually use this feature.

In this exercise, you will add a sound effect on the AME logo in the Encoder Demonstration project:

1. Use the **Filmstrip** panel to go to slide 3 of the `Chapter04/encoderDemo_800.cptx` file.

2. Select the AME logo to make it the active object. The **Properties** panel is updated.

3. Open the **Options** tab of the **Properties** panel and click on the **Add Audio** button. The **Object Audio** dialog shown in the following screenshot opens:

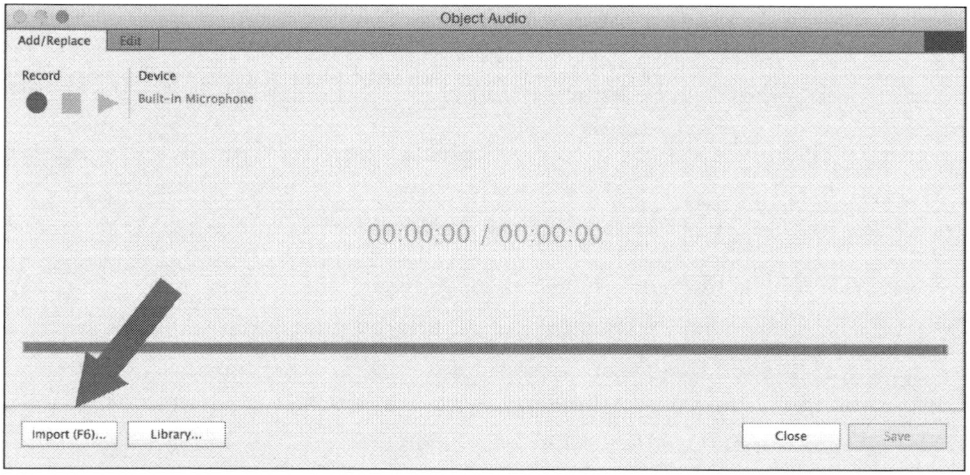

4. At the bottom of the **Object Audio** dialog, click on the **Import** button (see the arrow in the preceding screenshot). The **Import Audio** box opens.

By default, the **Import Audio** dialog displays the content of the Sound directory of the Gallery folder. Remember that a **gallery** is a collection of assets that ship with Captivate. You already used the gallery earlier in this chapter to import the animated orange arrow.

 If the **Import Audio** dialog does not show the content of the sound directory by default, remember that the gallery is located in the C:\Program Files\Adobe\Captivate 8\Gallery folder (for Windows) or in the Applications/Adobe Captivate 8/Gallery folder (for Mac).

5. At the end of the list, choose the Whoosh 2.mp3 file and click on **Open**.

The sound clip is imported into the project and the sound wave is loaded in the **Object Audio** dialog.

6. Click on the **Play** button in the top-left corner of the **Object audio** dialog to control the imported sound.

7. Click on the **Save** button at the bottom-right corner of the box.

8. Click on the **Close** button to close the **Object Audio** box.

In the **Timeline** panel, a loudspeaker icon is added to the AME logo layer indicating that an audio clip is associated with that particular object.

9. Use the **Preview** icon to preview the **Next 5 slides** and test the sound effect. Close the **Preview** pane when done.

10. In the top-right corner of the screen, click on the **Library** icon to open the **Library** panel.

Notice that the **Whoosh 2** sound clip has been added to the **Audio** section of the **Library**. It means that, if you want to use the same sound effect elsewhere in the project, there is no need to import the file a second time.

11. Don't forget to save the file when done.

Only .wav and .mp3 sound clips can be imported in Captivate. When inserting an .mp3 clip, Captivate automatically converts it to the .wav format. So you end up with two versions of the same audio clip in the **Library**: an .mp3 version and a .wav version. Internally, Captivate uses the .wav format because this uncompressed format maintains the highest possible sound quality while working with the file. You can therefore safely delete the .mp3 version from the **Library**. When you publish the movie in Flash or HTML5, Captivate converts the .wav file back to .mp3 and uses that .mp3 file in the published movie.

This concludes your overview of Object-level audio. Let's make a quick summary of what you have learned:

- In Captivate, you can associate a sound clip with any object. The sound plays when the object appears on the stage
- Usually, object-level audio is used to add sound effects to the movie
- Only sound clips in .wav or .mp3 formats can be imported into Captivate
- When an audio file is imported to the movie, it is automatically added to the **audio** section of the **Library**
- When a sound clip is added to an object, a loudspeaker icon appears in the corresponding layer of the **Timeline**

Adding background music to the entire project

In this section, you will associate an audio clip with the entire project. Usually, project-level audio is used to add **background music**, but again, nothing prevents you from adding other types of audio content at that level. To make sure that the music plays during the entire project, you will use a 15 to 30 seconds sound clip (called a sample) and make it loop for the duration of the movie.

In the next exercise, you will add background music to the Encoder Demonstration.

1. If needed, return to the Chapter04/encoderDemo_800.cptx file.
2. Go to the **Audio | Import To | Background** menu item.
3. Choose the Loop Acoustic.mp3 file from the /sound directory of the Captivate Gallery and click on **Open**.
4. The **Background Audio** dialog box opens.

The **Background Audio** dialog informs you that the duration of the `loop Acoustic.mp3` sound clip is 16 seconds, as shown in the following screenshot:

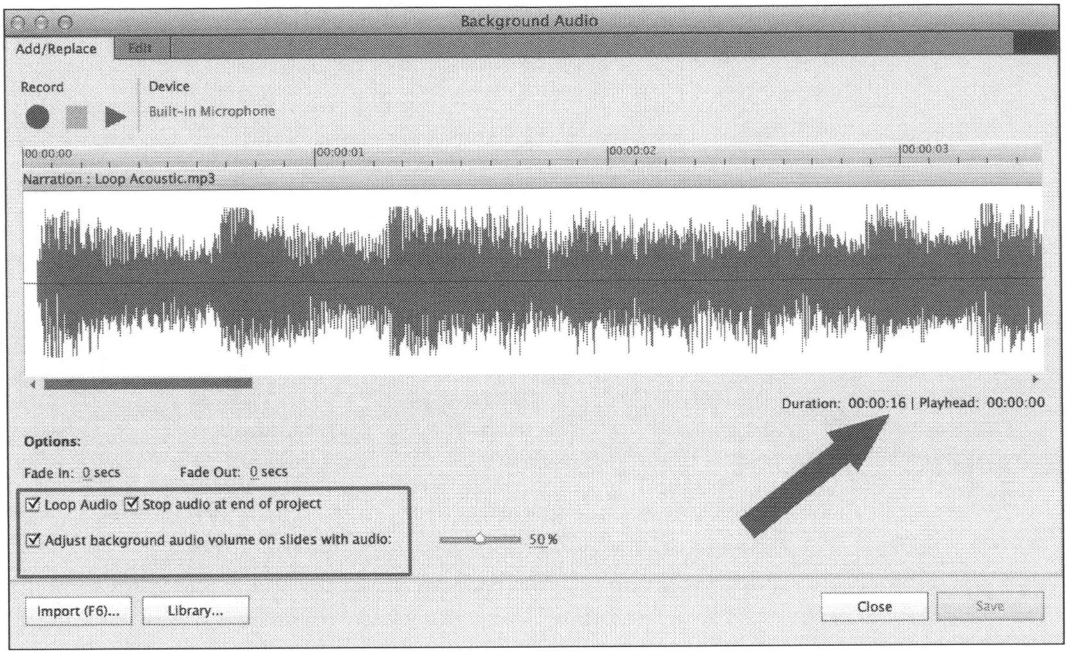

Some interesting options are situated in the lower part of the **Background Audio** dialog (see the area highlighted in the red rectangle in the lower-left area of the preceding screenshot).

- When the audio clip is finished, the **Loop Audio** option makes it start over, so the sound clip plays for the entire project.

- The **Stop audio at end of project** option should be selected at all times. If it is not selected, the background audio will keep playing even after the end of the project.

- The **Adjust background audio volume on slides with audio** option automatically lowers the volume of the background music on slides with associated slide-level audio. This option ensures that the slide audio is always louder than the background audio.

Most of the time, leaving these options to default works just fine.

5. Accept the default settings and click on **Close** to close the **Background Audio** dialog.

6. Use the **Preview** icon to preview the entire **Project**.

During the preview, you will see that the background audio volume is not reduced when the video file plays on slide 2. The volume reduction of the background audio only works when an audio file is added at the slide level, which does not include the audio track of a video file.

7. When the preview is finished, close the **Preview** pane.

8. Use the **Filmstrip** panel to go to slide 2 of the project.

9. Make sure the slide is selected, so that the **Properties** panel displays the properties of the slide.

10. In the **Options** tab of the **Properties** panel, select the **Stop Background Audio** checkbox, as shown in the following screenshot:

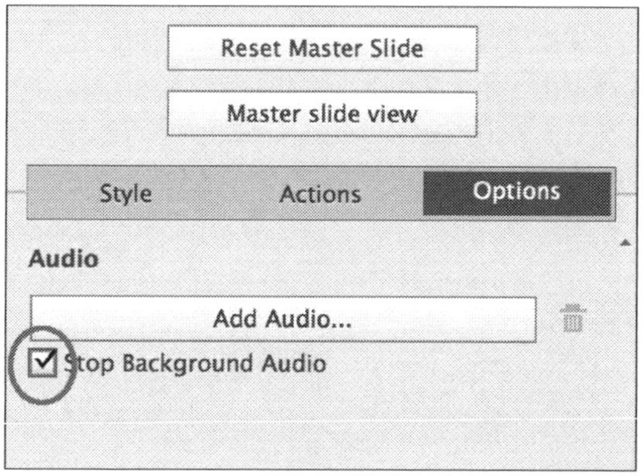

11. Use the **Preview** icon again and choose to preview the entire **Project**.

When the preview reaches the second slide of the project, the background audio should completely stop to let you see (and hear) the video file. When the project moves on to slide 3, the background music resumes and the project continues.

12. Close the **Preview** pane before continuing with this exercise.

If you need to modify the background audio or one of its associated options, go to **Audio | Edit | Background** to reopen the **Background Audio** dialog. Use the **Add/ Replace** tab of the **Background Audio** dialog to use another sound clip and the **Edit** tab to modify the current sound clip.

When to use background audio?

To be honest, I have never used background audio in a Captivate project! I find it annoying and distracting. It drives the students away from what I want them to focus on. That being said, there are probably some use cases for which background audio would be useful. If you run into one of these use cases, don't hesitate to use the feature. There is only one thing to keep in mind: *you are teaching*, so the background music you use, as well as any other features of your Captivate project, should serve the student's learning.

You will now remove the background audio that you have added to project.

13. Go to the **Audio | Remove | Background** menu item to remove the background audio.

14. Confirm you want to remove the audio clip.

15. Save the file when done.

Before moving on to the next section, this is a quick list of what you have learned about background audio:

- Audio can be added at project level. Most of the time, this feature is used to add background music to the project.

- Use the Audio menu to add, edit, and delete the background audio.

- To make sure the background music plays for the entire duration of the movie, use a short sample of music and make it loop.

- Captivate has an option to lower the volume of the background audio when a slide with an associated sound clip plays.

- Use background audio with care! It should not distract your students!

Also, remember that background audio does not need to be music. It can be, for instance, the sounds you may hear in the background in a hospital setting when learning about hospital procedures. Again, this book only shows the most typical use case and—again—it is your imagination that will ultimately define how this feature is actually used.

Adding audio to the slides

Adding audio to the slides is by far the most interesting place to use audio in Captivate. Typically, slide-level audio is where you add voice-over narration to the project.

There are three ways to add audio at slide level:

- The narration can be produced entirely within Captivate either during or after the recording
- The narration can be produced in an external application and imported into Captivate
- The Text-to-Speech engine of Captivate can generate audio clips

In this section, you will experiment with these three options one by one.

Recording narration with Captivate

The first way to insert audio at slide level is to record the needed audio clip with the tools of Captivate. To make it possible, your first concern is to carry the sound data from the microphone to Captivate by using your computer's audio interface.

 The following exercise requires a microphone. If you do not have a microphone available, just read through the steps. You'll have a chance to catch up in a subsequent exercise.

Setting up the sound system

The exact setup procedure depends on your audio equipment and on your operating system but, basically, setting up the sound system can be divided into three phases:

1. Plug the microphone into the audio input port of your computer (usually it is the red plug on your sound card).
2. Check out the audio options of your operating system:
   - For Mac, in **System Preferences**, use the **Input** tab of the **Sound** section
   - For Windows 7, use the **Manage Audio Devices** link in the **Hardware and Sound** section of the **Control panel**

3.   Check out the audio options of Captivate:

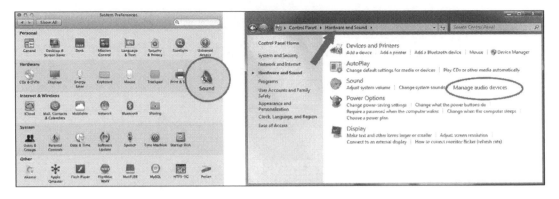

Once the audio options of the operating system are properly set up, you can safely move on to Captivate:

4.   Return to the `Chapter04/encoderDemo_800.cptx` file.

5.   Go to the **Audio | Settings** menu item to open the **Audio Settings** dialog box.

6.   Open the **Audio input Devices** drop-down list and select the audio device to which the microphone is attached.

If your computer has multiple audio input devices (such as a microphone-in and a line-in), the **Audio Input Devices** drop-down list instructs Captivate on which device it has to listen to. This is the single most important part of the procedure. If the wrong device is selected, the audio data will never reach Captivate. On the following screenshot, I instruct Captivate to listen to the audio stream coming from the built-in microphone of the computer (the actual content of the drop-down menu depends on the audio drivers installed on your system).

For the **Bitrate** option, the default should be fine. If you later decide that the default audio quality is not good enough, you can test a new recording with a higher value of **Bitrate**. Be aware that the higher the value of **Bitrate**, the bigger the file. When choosing the value of **Bitrate**, you have to find the most appropriate balance between the quality of the sound and the size of the resulting file.

7. Leave the **Bitrate** option at its default and click on the **Calibrate Input** button.

Calibrating the input is finding the right sensitivity for the microphone. If it is set too high, you'll have a saturated sound with lots of clipping, but if it is set too low, the recorded narration will be lost in the background noise. To help you out, Captivate provides an auto-calibrating feature. All you need to do is to say a few words in the microphone and let Captivate evaluate the input sensitivity to find the right value. Let's give it a try!

8. In the **Calibrate Audio Input** dialog box, click on the **Auto Calibrate** button.

9. Speak normally in your microphone until you have a message saying that the microphone has been calibrated. (If you don't know what to say, just tell a joke! Don't worry, it is not recorded!)

10. Click on the **OK** button to validate the sensitivity value and to close the **Calibrate Audio Input** dialog.

11. Close the **Audio Settings** dialog box as well.

Recording the narration

Now that both the sound system and Captivate are properly set up, it is time to concentrate on the actual recording of the voice-over narration:

1. In the `encoderDemo_800.cptx` file, use the **Filmstrip** to go to slide 3.

2. Make sure the **Properties** panel displays the properties of the **Slide**.

3. Switch to the **Option** tab of the **Properties** panel and click on the **Add Audio...** button.

The next step of the exercise is the actual recording of the sound clip. Before you press the record button, it is necessary to take some time to rehearse the narration.

The following text is the script that you will record:

Want to insert a video in Captivate? Great! Video will make your eLearning content much more engaging and fun! But before you can import a video file in Captivate, you must first convert it into a video format that the Flash player or the HTML5 browser can read! Adobe Media Encoder is an application that has been designed to convert video and audio files to the proper format for your project. The good news is that Adobe Media Encoder is part of your Captivate installation at no extra cost! Want to know how it works? Just click on the continue button.

Read those sentences out loud a few times. When you feel ready, you can move on to your first audio take!

4. Click on the red **Record Audio** button in the top-left area of the **Slide Audio** dialog. After a short countdown, read the preceding lines out loud at normal speed and with a normal voice.

5. When the recording is complete, click on the **Stop** button.

6. Control the quality of your take by clicking on the **Play** button. If you are not satisfied, start over with another take.

7. When you are satisfied with the result, click on the **Save** button and close the **Slide Audio** dialog.

If the recorded sound clip is longer than the slide, you will be prompted to extend the duration of the slide to the length of the sound clip as shown in the next screenshot. Click on **Yes** to finalize the integration of the new sound clip into the slide:

8. Click on the **Timeline** button at the bottom of the screen to open the **Timeline** panel.

In the **Timeline** panel, the new sound clip is displayed as an additional layer situated below the slide layer. If needed, you can move the sound clip on the **Timeline** to better synchronize it with the rest of the slide, but you cannot use the **Timeline** to change the duration of the sound clip.

To quickly test the slide, use the **Play** button situated at the bottom left corner of the **Timeline** panel. This button plays only the current slide without opening the **Preview** pane. This preview option does not let you test every single feature of the slide, but it is a quick and easy way to do some basic testing and synchronization.

Recording narration is not an easy task, especially if you are not used to speaking into a microphone. Here are some basic tips and tricks to help you out:

- Write down the script that needs to be recorded and rehearse it a few times before the recording.
- Keep in mind that you don't have to make it right the first time. Try as many times as needed.
- Speak slowly, especially if you have an international audience where all the students do not speak the same language.
- Have a glass of water ready to avoid the dry mouth effect. Remember that lots of student will hear the narration through a headset.
- Position the microphone within 4 to 6 inches of your mouth and slightly to the side to avoid pops and hisses on the letters S and P.
- Standing up and gesturing while speaking can help you speak more clearly and confidently, and adds more animation to your voice.
- Remove any objects that could get picked up in the audio: jewelry, a squeaky chair, and so on.

With these simple tips and tricks, a basic computer microphone and a bit of practice, you should be able to record some pretty good audio clips right away!

Whose voice should be recorded?

If you can afford it, it is best to hire a narrator, but most of the time you will be recording your own voice or the voice of a colleague or a friend. When choosing the person to read the lines, always have your students in mind. For my very first big Captivate project, I had to develop a course in English, but most of the students were not native English speakers. We met with the customer and agreed to record the voice of a non-native English speaker. (It was an employee from the next-door office who was into theater). The recorded English was not perfect, the accent was a bit strange, but it was not important because it was adapted for the audience.

Importing an external sound clip

The second solution to add audio at slide level is to import the needed audio clips into the project. When taking this approach, the audio clips are recorded and produced in a dedicated audio application.

> **Adobe Audition**
>
> Audition is the audio application from Adobe. Audition CC 2014 is available as part of a Creative Cloud subscription. Adobe Audition (formerly Cool Edit) is an awesome yet easy-to-use audio application. If Audition is available on your computer, use it to record and edit your audio clips instead of using Captivate.

In this exercise, you will import sound clips produced in Adobe Audition into the Captivate project.

1. Return to the `encoderDemo_800.cptx` file and use the **Filmstrip** panel to go to slide 3. Make sure the **Properties** panel displays the properties of the slide.

2. If you have completed the previous exercise, remove the recorded sound clip by clicking on the **Remove Audio** icon in the **Options** tab of the **Properties** panel, as shown in the following screenshot:

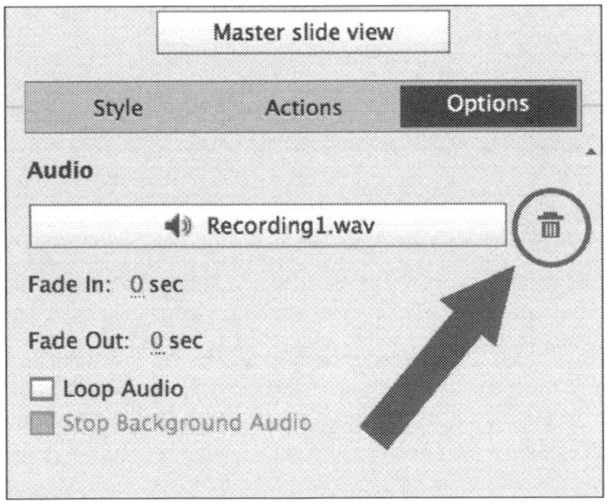

Note that this action removes the audio from the slide, but not from the **Library** of the project. You will learn more about the **Library** in *Chapter 5, Working with the Timeline and Other Useful Tools*.

3. In the **Options** tab of the **Properties** panel, click on the **Add Audio** button. The **Slide Audio** dialog box opens.

4. Click on the **Import Narration** button situated in the bottom-left corner of the dialog box.

5. Select the `audio/slide03.mp3` file situated in your exercises folder.

6. Click on **Open**. The selected file is imported into the project.

7. Click on the **Play** button to test the imported audio.

8. Save the changes by clicking on the **Save** button situated in the bottom-right corner of the **Slide Audio** dialog.

9. It is possible that the duration of the slide has to be increased to match the duration of the new audio file. Click on **Yes** if prompted to do so.

10. Close the **Slide Audio** dialog box.

11. Save the file when done.

After this procedure, the audio file appears in the **Timeline** panel as an extra layer at the very bottom of the stack.

Yes, it is that easy to import external sound clips into Captivate! If you take a look at the **Filmstrip** panel, you'll notice a loudspeaker icon next to the slide you have added audio to:

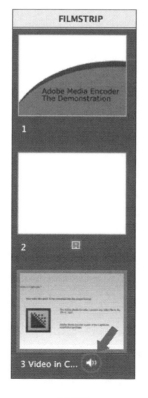

In the next chapter, you will import the remaining audio clips and learn how to use the **Timeline** panel to synchronize the audio with the other slide elements.

Using Text-to-Speech to generate narration

The third option to insert audio at slide level is to use the Text-to-Speech engine of Captivate. The idea is to type the voice-over narration in the **Slide Notes** panel and have Captivate convert it to a sound clip. To convert typed text to sound clips, Captivate uses some preinstalled voice packages called **speech agents**.

Installing the Captivate speech agents

Due to their very large size, Adobe decided to make the installation of the Text-to-Speech agents optional. Captivate 8 ships with one voice package that installs several speech agents for various languages.

The Speech agents of Captivate can be downloaded from the following locations:

- For Windows 32-bit, visit `http://www.adobe.com/go/Cp8_win32_voices_installer`
- For Windows 64-bit, visit `http://www.adobe.com/go/Cp8_win64_voices_installer`
- For Mac, visit `http://www.adobe.com/go/Cp8_mac_voices_installer`

 It is required to install the Text-to-Speech agents to go through the steps of the next exercise.

Working with the Slide Notes panel

The basic idea of Text-to-Speech is to transform a piece of typed text into a sound clip. In Captivate, you use the **Slide Notes** panel to type the text you want to convert to speech. The **Slide Notes** panel is not displayed by default, so your first task is to turn it on.

1. Open the `Chapter04/drivingInBe.cptx` file.
2. Make sure you are on the first slide of the project.
3. Go to **Window** | **Slide Notes** to turn the **Slide Notes** panel on.

By default, the **Slide Notes** panel appears at the bottom of the screen next to the **Timeline** panel.

At the far right side of the panel, the + icon is used to create a new note:

4. Click on the **+** icon to add a new note.

5. Type the following line in the new note: So, you've decided to take a trip to Belgium!

6. Click on the **+** icon to add a second note after the first one.

This part is a bit tricky! Do not hit the *Enter* key when you have typed the first note. The *Enter* key does not validate the new note, but creates a new paragraph in the note. Also, before adding a second note, make sure that your cursor is still within the first one; otherwise, the second note appears before the first one. If the second note appears before the first, you can use the **–** icon to delete the topmost note or you can drag and drop the notes to reorder them:

7. Type the following line in the second note: With the tips and tricks provided in this video, you'll soon be on your way to discover Belgium's treasures in a safely fashion.

8. Add a third note to the **Slide Notes** panel and type the following line: Type your name in the box to get started.

9. If needed, drag and drop the notes within the **Slide Notes** panel to reorder them.

When typing the text in the **Slide Notes** panel, keep in mind that a machine will soon convert it to an audio clip. This machine will not work right if the spelling is not perfect, so double-check (and even triple-check) the spellings. If the spelling is wrong, you'll get unexpected (and sometimes hilarious!) results.

10. Use the **Filmstrip** panel to browse the remaining slides of the project. Notice that the needed slide notes have already been added where appropriate.

Now that the slide notes have been correctly typed and carefully ordered, you can safely convert them to audio using the Text-to-Speech feature of Captivate.

Converting text to speech

Converting the text typed in the Slide Notes panel to speech is not difficult. All you need to do is to choose the note(s) to be converted, assign a speech agent to each note, and generate the audio file:

1. Still in the `Chapter04/drivingInBe.cptx` file, use the **Filmstrip** panel to return to slide 1 if necessary.

2. At the top of the **Slide Notes** panel, click on the **TTS** checkbox to select all three notes as shown in the following screenshot:

SLIDE NOTES	
☑	
So, you've decided to take a trip to Belgium!	
☑	
With the tips and tricks provided in this video, you'll soon be on your way to discover Belgium's treasures on a safely fashion.	
☑	
Type your name in the box to get started.	

Most of the time, you'll want to convert all the notes to speech. But, if needed, you can deselect the notes that do not need to be converted to speech.

3. Click on the Text-to-Speech button situated at the top of the **Slide Notes** panel. The **Speech Management** box opens.

The **Speech Management** box is where you assign a speech agent to each of the note(s) you selected for Text-to-Speech conversion. The number of available speech agents depends on the voice packs installed on the system (refer to the *Installing the Captivate speech agents* section for more details). Captivate also picks up third-party speech agents installed on the system.

For this exercise, you will use two speech agents: Kate and Paul. These speech agents are designed for US English text only and are included in the voice installer of Captivate.

4. In the **Speech Management** box, select all three Notes (if needed). The trick to selecting notes is to click on the caret symbol above the note and not on the note itself.

5. Open the **Speech Agent** dropdown and choose **Kate**.

For this first experience with Text-To-Speech, you will assign the same Speech Agent to every note.

6. Click on the **Generate Audio** button situated at the bottom left corner of the box. A progress bar appears on the screen as the audio is generated.

7. When the progress bar disappears, click on the **Close** button to close the **Speech Management** dialog.

8. At the bottom of the screen, switch to the **Timeline** panel.

Surprise! The **Timeline** panel now shows a sound clip layer beneath the slide layer.

9. Use the **Play** button of the **Timeline** panel to test the audio clip.

Great! The slide notes of Slide 1 have been successfully converted to speech using a speech agent named Kate. You will now repeat the same procedure on slide 3 but with another speech agent.

10. Use the **Filmstrip** panel to go to slide 3 and switch back to the **Slide Notes** panel.

11. In the **Slide Notes** panel, mark all three notes for Text-to-Speech conversion and click on the **Text-to-speech** button.

12. The **Speech Management** dialog opens.

13. Select all three notes. In the **Speech Agent** dropdown, choose **Paul** to assign this speech agent to the selected notes, as shown in the following screenshot:

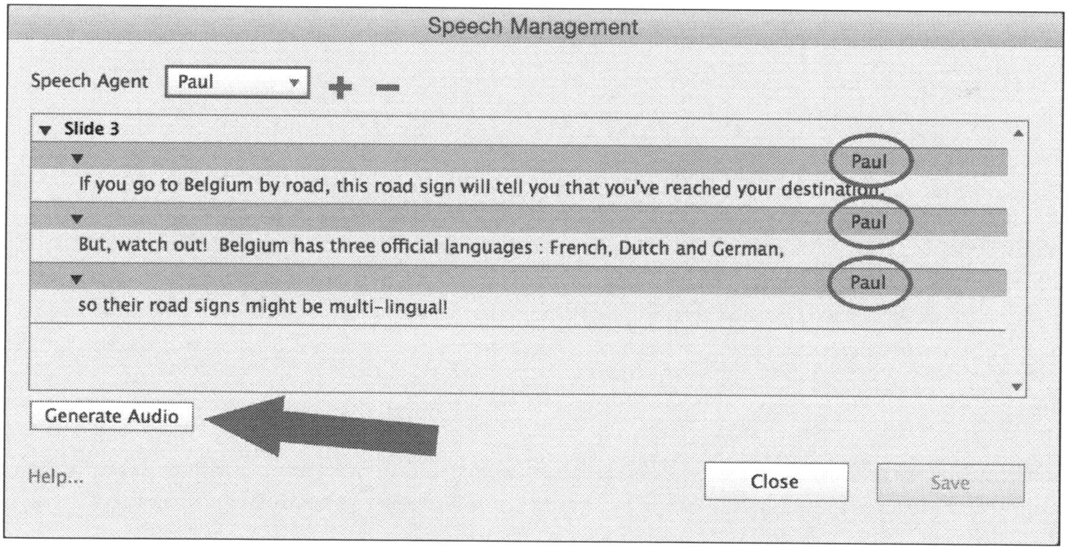

14. Click on the **Generate Audio** button (see the arrow in the preceding screenshot).

15. When the audio generation is complete, close the **Speech Management** dialog and switch to the **Timeline** panel.

Again, an audio layer containing the generated sound clip has been added to the slide. Don't hesitate to click on the play icon in the bottom-left area of the **Timeline** panel to test the new audio.

> **Text-to-Speech versus manual voice-over recording**
>
> Is Text-to-Speech better than an actual recording? A real recording takes a lot of time and, consequently, costs a lot more money. But the result is perfect and can be tailored to fit the specific needs of a particular project. Text-to-Speech is fast, easy, and cheap, but the result may sound like an old Gameboy. Another thing to consider is how easy it is to update the project if needed. Updating a Text-to-Speech audio file is dead easy. Just change the text in the Slide Notes panel and regenerate the audio. Modifying a recorded sound clip is much more difficult and costly. You may have to rent a sound studio, hire the narrator a second time, and so on. No solution is perfect, and the choice is yours.

Using the Speech Management window

To generate the remaining audio files of the project, you will use the **Speech Management** window. This feature will speed you up and make your job a little bit easier. The idea is to mark the notes for Text-to-Speech conversion throughout the entire project and generate the audio clips all at once at the end.

1. Browse the slides of the project one by one. In the **Slide Notes** panel, confirm that every note is marked for Text-to-Speech conversion.

2. When the notes of the entire project are marked, go to **Audio | Speech Management** to open the **Speech Management** window.

The window that has just opened is very similar to the one you used to generate the audio files of slides 1 and 3, except that it shows the slide notes of the entire project rather than those of the active slide only.

3. In the **Speech Management** window, select the notes of slides 1 and 3.

4. Click on the – icon to remove the selected notes.

This action does not actually delete the notes. It only clears the checkbox that marks the notes for Text-to-Speech conversion. You have to do it because the audio for slide 1 and 3 has already been successfully generated.

5. Use the Speech management window to assign a speech agent to each note. Make sure you use only **Kate** and **Paul** as these two particular agents are designed to convert US English text. Note that it is possible to assign a different Speech Agent to the different notes of the same slide.

If possible, try to match the Characters images you inserted in *Chapter 3, Working with Standard Objects*. Use Paul for the slide where the male character shows and Kate on slides when the female character shows.

6. When done, click on the **Generate Audio** button situated in the bottom-left corner of the Speech Management dialog.

Captivate generates all the needed audio files, assigns them to the correct slide, and adds them to the **Library**.

7. When done, close the **Speech management** window.

8. Review every slide of the project and make sure that all the needed audio clips are correctly generated. Use the play icon of the **Timeline** panel to test the audio.

9. Save the file when done.

You have now worked with all the options that can be used to insert audio at slide level. Here follows a quick summary of the key points that have been covered:

- There are three ways to insert audio at slide level: recording audio with Captivate, importing an audio file produced in an external application, or generating the audio clips with the Text-to-Speech engine.

- When recording audio with Captivate, ensure that the audio interface is correctly set up both in the operating system and in Captivate.

- The first time you record audio with Captivate, it is necessary to calibrate the sensitivity of your microphone. Captivate has an easy to use auto-calibrating feature.

- Audition CC 2014 is the dedicated audio application from Adobe. Use it to produce your audio clips if it is available on your system.

- The basic idea of Text-to-Speech is to convert a piece of text into an audio clip. To do so, Captivate uses speech agents.

- Captivate ships with a bunch of speech agents that are packed into an extra installer available on the Adobe website.

- Each speech agent is designed for a specific language.

- The **Slide Notes** panel is used to type the text to be converted to speech. You can choose to convert every slide note to speech or just some of them.

- A different speech agent can be assigned to the different notes of the same slide.
- The **Speech Management** window provides a quick and easy way to convert all the notes of the project to speech at once.

Editing a sound clip in Captivate

Now that you know how to insert sound in Captivate, it is time to take a look at how you can modify it. Even though Captivate is not an audio editing application, it does have some basic audio editing capabilities.

In this exercise, you will use the audio editing capabilities of Captivate to finalize the chimes sound you recorded with the System Audio feature back in *Chapter 2, Capturing the Slides*.

1. Return to the Chapter04/encoderDemo_800.cptx file.
2. Use the **Filmstrip** panel to go to slide 17.
3. Make sure the **Properties** panel shows the properties of the slide.
4. Switch to the **Options** tab of the **Properties** panel and click on the Edit Audio button (see the following screenshot). Alternatively, you can go to the **Audio | Edit | Slide** menu item to do the same thing:

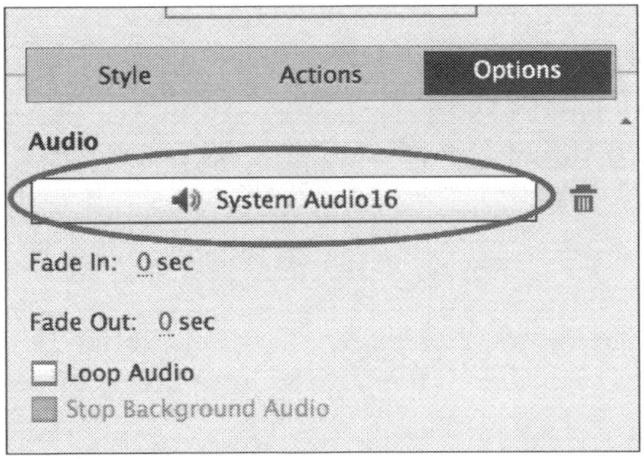

5. The **Slide Audio** dialog box opens on the **Edit** tab (see **(1)** on the next screenshot).

Locate the **Select Source** section situated in the top-left corner of the **Slide Audio** dialog (see **(2)** on the next screenshot). The audio source can be the narration, the system audio, or both the narration and the system audio. The only sound clip associated with this slide is the chimes sound that was recorded using the System Audio feature of Captivate. Therefore, the sound clip is on the system audio track.

6. Make sure the source is set to **System Audio** only.

7. Use the **Zoom** (see (3) on the next screenshot) to zoom out and have a look at the entire sound clip.

8. Click on the **Play** button to listen to the entire audio clip. Try to associate what you hear with the graphical representation of the sound as displayed in the **Slide Audio** dialog.

In an audio clip, silence takes up as much space as the sound itself. Deleting the silence at the beginning and at the end of a sound clip is an operation that should be done systematically for every sound clip, as it helps in keeping the size of the resulting movie as low as possible.

9. Use your mouse to select from the beginning of the clip up until the actual Chimes sound begins.

10. When done, hit the *Delete* key of your keyboard, or click on the trash can icon in the **Edit** section at the top of the **Slide Audio** dialog (see (4) in the next screenshot).

11. Do the same with the silence situated after the chimes sound.

12. Click on the **Play** button to test the new version of the clip.

After these operations, the **Slide Audio** dialog should look like the following screenshot:

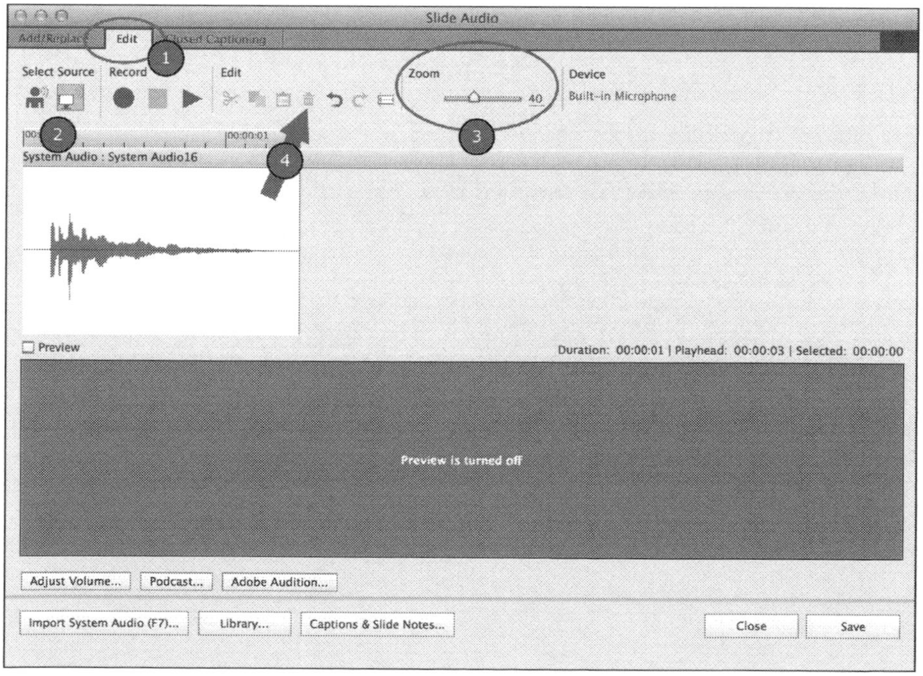

Another thing that you can do is adjust the audio volume of the sound effect. You will now use the **Adjust Volume** feature of Captivate to finalize the System Audio chimes sound of slide 17.

13. On the bottom-left corner of the **Slide Audio** dialog, click on the **Adjust Volume** button.

14. Take some time to review the options of the **Adjust Volume** box, but do not change any of them at this time.

15. In the **Audio Processing** section of the **Adjust Volume** dialog box, select the **Normalize** option and click on the **OK** button.

Normalizing an audio clip is finding the best audio level for that particular sound clip.

> **Blog post**
>
> If you want to know more about the normalization process, I've written an entire blog post on this topic, which can be found at http://www.dbr-training.eu/index.cfm/ blog/producing-high-quality-audio-content-for- captivate-part-1-normalization/.

The **Chimes** sound effect you captured with the System Audio feature of Captivate is now final.

16. Click on the **Save** button at the bottom-right corner of the **Slide Audio** dialog.

17. Click on the **Close** button to close the **Slide Audio** dialog.

In the next chapter, you will properly position this audio clip on the **Timeline** to sync it with the other slide event.

> **Round trip editing with Adobe Audition CC 2014**
>
> If Adobe Audition CC 2014 is available on your system the **Adobe Audition** button of the **Slide Audio** dialog will be enabled. Clicking on this button opens the audio clip being edited in Adobe Audition where you can use specialized and dedicated audio tools to edit your clip. When done, just save the file in Audition and it will be automatically updated in Captivate.

Using the Advanced Audio Management window

The **Advanced Audio Management** window provides a high-level overview of all the audio present in your project. In the following exercise, you will open the **Advanced Audio Management** window and take a quick look at the tools it provides using the following steps:

1. Make sure you are still in the `Chapter04/encoderDemo_800.cptx` file.

2. Go to the **Audio | Audio Management** menu item to open the **Advanced Audio Management** window.

The **Advanced Audio Management** window contains a list of all the slides of the project along with their associated audio file(s) if any.

3. In the bottom-left corner of the **Advanced Audio Management** window, select the **Show object level audio** checkbox (see (**1**) in the following screenshot).

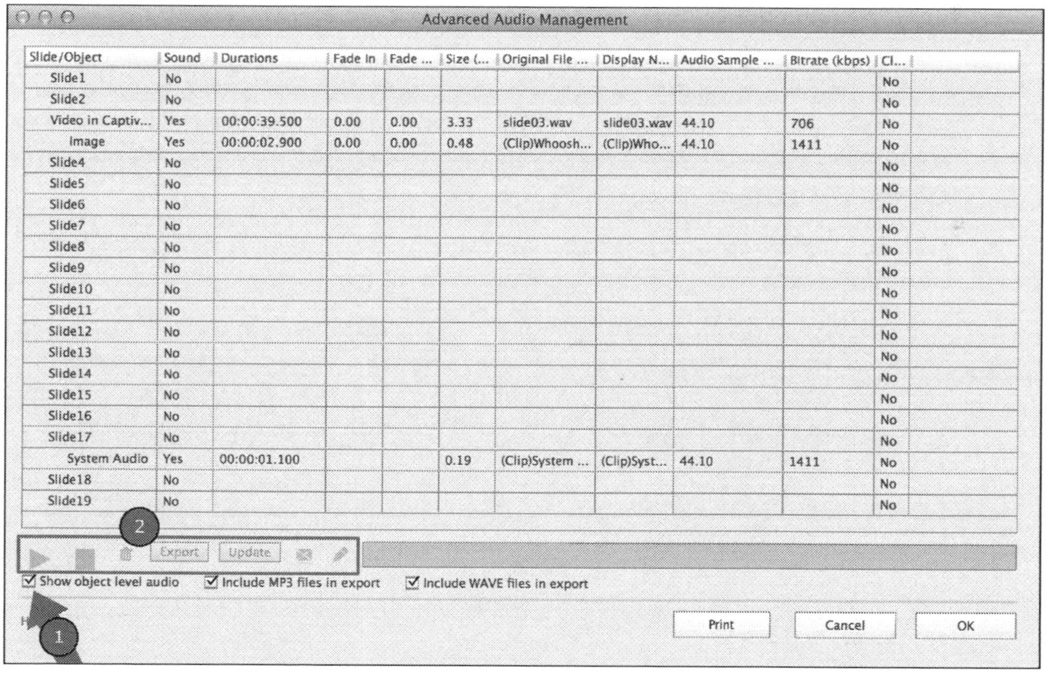

By selecting the **Show object level audio** checkbox, the list of audio files displayed in the **Advanced Audio Management** window includes the audio associated with the AME logo image of slide 3.

4. Select any of the audio files in the list.

When an audio file is selected in the **Advanced Audio Management** window, the buttons situated in the bottom part of the window are enabled (see **(2)** in the preceding screenshot). These buttons allow you to play the selected audio file, export it to a `.wav` and/or an `.mp3` file, edit the audio file, add Closed Captions, and do much more.

5. Take some time to inspect the controls of the **Advanced Audio Management** window. They should all be self explanatory.

6. Close the **Advanced Audio Management** window when done.

7. Save and close the `encoderDemo_800.cptx` file.

There really is nothing more to say about the **Advanced Audio Management** window. It is just a nice and easy way to have a general overview of all the audio used in the project.

Adding Closed Captions to the slides

Closed Captions make your eLearning content more accessible and more interesting for the learners. There are many situations where Closed Captions are useful. The main advantages are as follows:

- They make your Captivate projects accessible for hearing impaired students
- They make the project easier to understand for foreign students
- They are useful for learners that have to take the online course in an office and don't want to bother their colleagues with the voice-over narrations

So, it is a good idea to use Closed Captions each time you add voice-over narration to a slide.

In Captivate, Closed Captions are always associated with a slide-level audio clip or with a **Multi-Slide Synchronized Video** inserted by using the **Video | Insert Video** menu item. As for the Text-to-Speech narration, the text of the Closed Captions is found in the **Slide Notes** panel.

In the next exercise, you will add Closed Captions to the Encoder Demonstration.

1. Return to the `Chapter04/EncoderDemo_800.cptx` file. Use the **Filmstrip** panel to go to slide 3.

2. If needed, use the **Window | Slide Notes** menu item to reopen the **Slide Notes** panel.

Slide 3 is the first slide of the project you added narration to. There are six notes in the **Slide Notes** panel. They exactly reflect what is said in the audio file associated with the slide.

3. At the top of the **Slide Notes** panel, click on the **Audio CC** checkbox situated right next to the Text-to-Speech checkbox. This operation is shown in the following screenshot:

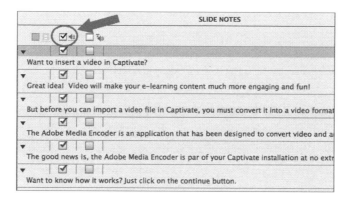

This action marks all the Slide Notes for Closed Captioning. Note that the **Audio CC** checkbox is available only if an audio file is associated with the slide. So, if you did not complete the previous exercises, you might not have the option to generate the Closed Captions!

4. In the top-right corner of the **Slide Notes** panel, click on the **Closed Captioning** button.

The **Slide Audio** box opens again, but this time it shows the **Closed Captioning** tab (**1**):

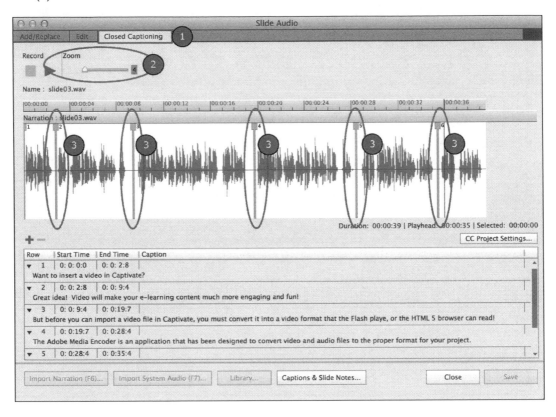

5. Use the zoom slider (**2**) to reduce the zoom level so you can see the entire sound clip.

Each of the vertical bars (**3**) represents one of the **Slide Notes** you marked for Closed Captioning.

6. Click on the **Play** button. While the audio is playing, note the current position of the yellow vertical bars as compared to the audio file.

7. If needed, adjust the position of the vertical bars and test again until all the Closed Captions are in sync with the audio.

8. When you are satisfied with the result, click on the **Save** button at the bottom right corner of the **Slide Audio** dialog.

9. Close the **Slide Audio** dialog.

Don't forget to save the file when you are done!

Viewing the Closed Captions

Now that Closed Captions have been added to slide 3 of the project, you will test it in the **Preview** pane and control the newly inserted Closed Captions.

1. Still in the `encoderDemo_800.cptx` file, use the **Filmstrip** panel to return to slide 1.

2. Use the **Preview** icon of the Big Buttons Bar to test the **Next 5 Slides**.

3. When the preview reaches the third slide (the first one with audio and Closed Captions) note that the Closed Captions do not appear.

By default, the Closed Captions do not appear in the resulting Captivate animation. It is up to the student to turn them on or leave them off while watching the project.

To let the student turn them on, you need to add a closed captioning button on the playback controls bar that appears at the bottom of the project. To add this button, you need to use the **Skin Editor**.

 In *Chapter 12, Working with Variables, Advanced Actions, and Widgets*, you will use an advanced action to have Closed Captions turned on by default.

This chapter only shows how to use the Skin Editor to add a Closed Captions toggle button to the playback controls bar. You will study the other features of the Skin Editor in *Chapter 13, Finishing Touches and Publishing*.

4. Close the **Preview** pane.

5. Use the **Project | Skin Editor** menu item to open the floating **Skin Editor** panel.

6. On the left side of the **Skin Editor**, select the **Closed Captioning** box to add a CC button on the playback controls bar.

7. Click on the **Settings** button situated right below. The **CC Project Settings** dialog box pops up.

The **CC Project Settings** dialog box lets you define the formatting of the Closed Captions.

8. Choose a sans-serif font (such as Verdana or Arial) for the **Family** field and set **Font Size** to **12**.

9. Click on the **OK** button to validate your choices and to close the **CC Projects Settings** dialog.

10. Click on the top-left corner of the floating **Skin Editor** panel to close it.

Everything is now ready to test the Closed Captions you have added to the project.

11. Make sure you are still on slide 1 of the project and go to **Preview | Next 5 slides** on the Big Buttons Bar to test the new **CC** button in the **Preview** pane.

12. When the project opens in the **Preview** pane, click on the **CC** button situated on the right side of the playback controls bar to turn the Closed Captions on.

13. When the preview reaches slide 3, you should see the associated Closed Captions displayed in sync with the audio. Keep in mind that the other elements of the slide have not been synced yet.

The Closed Captions help in making the project accessible to students with disabilities.

Closed captioning a video file

The last thing that you will do in this chapter is to add Closed Captions to the video file you imported on slide 2 of the `encoderDemo_800.cptx` project. Note that you can add Closed Captions to a video file only if it has been imported as a **Multi-Slide Synchronized Video**. The steps are as follows:

1. Still in the `Chapter04/encoderDemo_800.cptx` project, use the **Filmstrip** panel to return to slide 2. It is the slide where you imported the video file earlier in this chapter.

2. Click on the video to make it the active object.

3. Open the **Properties** panel if needed.

4. In the **Style** tab of the **Properties** panel, click on the **Edit Video Timing** button. The **Edit Video Timing** dialog opens.

The **Edit Video Timing** dialog can be used to edit the imported video file. In this exercise, it is not exactly what you want to do. You only want to add Closed Caption to the video.

5. Click on the **Closed Captioning** tab situated at the top-left corner of the **Edit Video Timing** dialog.

6. Click on the **+** icon to add a new closed caption. Type the following line: `Hi, I'm Damien. I'll be your guide during this demonstration.`

7. Click on the **+** icon a second time to add a second closed caption. Type the following line: `To get started, click on the Continue button at the bottom of your slide.`

Notice that two yellow vertical bars appear in the upper area of the **Edit Video Timing** dialog.

 Watch out! It is possible that these two bars sit on top of each other at the same location, giving the false impression that there is only one vertical bar.

8. Move these vertical bars to synchronize the Closed Captions with the video file. This is the exact same procedure as for the Closed Captions associated with the slide audio.

9. Click on the **Play** button in the top-left corner of the **Edit Video Timing** box to test the synchronization between the video and the Closed Captions. It will probably be necessary to adjust the position of the vertical bars and to retest the video a few times before the yellow bars are properly positioned.

At the end of this exercise, the **Edit Video Timing** dialog should look like the following screenshot:

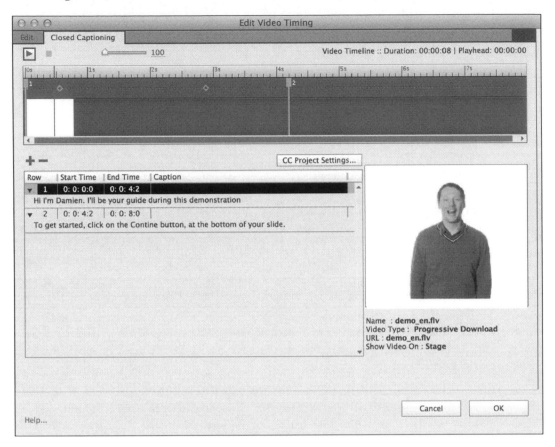

10. When done, click on **OK** to validate the changes and close the **Edit Video Timing** dialog.

11. Use the **Filmstrip** panel to return to slide 1 of the project and go to **Preview | Next 5 slides** on the Big Buttons Bar to test your new closed captions.

12. When the **Preview** pane appears, click on the **CC** icon of the playback controls bar to turn Closed Captions on. Confirm that Closed Captions have been successfully added to the video file of slide 2.

13. Save the file when finished.

Extra credit – adding Closed Captions

Closed captions can be added to every slide that has an associated audio file regardless of whether that audio file has been recorded with Captivate, imported from an external application or generated with the Text-to-Speech feature. In this section, you will add Closed Captions to the *Driving in Belgium* project. The basic steps are as follows:

- Open or return to the *Driving in Belgium* project. Use the **Filmstrip** panel to go to a slide that has an associated audio clip. These slides can be easily identified thanks to the loudspeaker icon that shows just below the slide thumbnail.

- In the **Slide Notes** panel, convert every note to Closed Captions using the **Audio CC** checkbox. It may be necessary to use the **Window | Slide Notes** menu item to turn the **Slide Notes** panel on.

- Click on the **Closed Captioning** button to open the **Slide Audio** dialog.

- Move the vertical yellow markers to synchronize the Closed Captions with the audio clip. Use the **Play** button to test the syncing between the audio and the Closed Captions.

- Repeat the procedure on each slide with associated audio.

- To test the Closed Captions, don't forget to add the **CC** button on the playback controls bar by navigating to **Project | Skin Editor**.

This exercise concludes your overview of the Closed Captioning system of Captivate. Here is a quick summary of what has been covered:

- Closed Captions are associated either with a slide-level audio clip or with a **Multi-Slide synchronized Video**.

- The text of the Closed Captions associated with a slide-level audio clip is found in the **Slide Notes** Panel.

- The text of the Closed Captions associated with a video file is found in the **Closed Captioning** tab of the **Edit Video Timing** dialog box.

- The **Slide Notes** panel is not displayed by default. Use the **Window | Slide Notes** menu item to turn it on and off.

- In the resulting animation, the closed captions are turned off by default. It is up to the student to turn them on or leave them off.

- Use the **Skin Editor** to add the CC button to the playback controls bar. The CC button is used by the student to turn the Closed Captions on or off.

Summary

In this chapter, your project has taken on a whole new dimension. With the addition of multimedia elements, your project is now much more fun and dynamic to follow and your message is more powerful than ever.

You first learned how to edit a Full Motion Recording slide before moving on to adding animations. You can import Flash animations (.swf files) if the project is to be published in Flash, or .oam packages created in Adobe Edge Animate if the project is to be published in HTML5. Remember that none of these two types of animation are supported in both the Flash and the HTML5 output.

The next media covered was the video file. Remember that it may be necessary to convert the video file to the proper format before inserting it into Captivate.

Finally, you studied the audio options of Captivate. You learned that sound can be added at object level, at slide level, or at project level. To produce the needed audio files, Captivate offers the ability to record your own clips, but you can also import audio clips produced in an external application or convert text typed in the **Slide Notes** panel to speech using one of the speech agents provided by Captivate or already present on the system.

When adding voice-over narration, it is a good idea to add Closed Captions as well. The Closed Captions greatly enhance the usability and accessibility of your Captivate movie. The same **Slide Notes** used for Text-to-Speech can also be used to generate the Closed Captions.

There is still a lot of work to do before these projects can be made available to the learners. One of the most obvious problems is the synchronization of the newly inserted audio files with the other elements of the slide. This, and many other tools, will be covered in the next chapter.

Meet the community

In this section, I want to introduce you to Allen Partridge. Allen is one of the Adobe eLearning evangelists. He is one of the main contributors to the official Captivate blog. He is also one of the favorite faces found in the countless Captivate videos that you can find on the official YouTube channel of Captivate. Allen is an awesome speaker and a wonderful teacher. His teaching background makes him an invaluable asset to the Captivate community. I had a chance to meet Allen in the summer of 2013. It was one of the highlights of my trip to California and I keep a vivid memory of that moment.

Allen Partridge

Dr. Allen Partridge is an eLearning evangelist for Adobe. In addition to his work for Adobe Systems, he continues to serve on the doctoral faculty in the Communications Media and Instructional Technology program at the Indiana University of Pennsylvania.

He has written several books and a host of articles on topics ranging from 3D game development to instructional design for new technologies. He is active in the explorations of immersive learning as well as traditional multimedia enhanced eLearning and rapid eLearning. He works closely with the eLearning Suite and Captivate teams at Adobe, providing a channel to customer needs and concerns and helping facilitate communication among team members.

Contact details

- **Blog**: http://blogs.adobe.com/captivate/
- **Twitter**: @adobeElearning
- **Facebook**: http://www.facebook.com/adobecaptivate
- **LinkedIn**: http://www.linkedin.com/in/doctorpartridge
- **YouTube**: http://www.youtube.com/adobeelearning/

5
Working with the Timeline and Other Useful Tools

A lot of things have already taken place since you entered the postproduction studio two chapters ago. But let's be honest, you're not there yet! Some of the remaining problems include the proper alignment and positioning of the objects as well as the lack of synchronization between the audio and the other elements of the slide.

In this chapter, you will primarily focus on using the **Timeline** panel to synchronize the elements you added in the previous two chapters. You will also learn about various tools and features used to manage the objects of the project and to lay them out in the physical space of the slide.

The following topics will be covered in this chapter:

- Using the library to manage the assets of the project
- Using the smart guides to easily arrange the objects
- Learning how to group and ungroup objects
- Using the Align toolbar to perfectly arrange the objects on the slides
- Using the Timeline to synchronize the various elements of the slide
- Adding custom animations to the objects

At the end of this chapter, you will better understand how the features and objects discussed in the previous two chapters come together in order to build an actual piece of eLearning content.

Preparing your work

To get the most out of this chapter, you should first reset your workspace. If you are using the default interface mode, restarting Captivate also resets your workspace to default. If you are using the advanced interface mode, use the **Window | Workspace | Reset 'Classic'** menu item to reset the classic workspace to default.

In this chapter, you will use the exercise files located in the Chapter05 folder of the download associated with this book. If you get confused by any of the step-by-step instructions, take a look at the Chapter05/final folder, which contains a copy of the exercises.

Working with the Library

The first tool you will explore in this chapter is the Library. The Library maintains a list of all the assets of the current file. These assets include the background pictures captured during the recording of the project, all the external files imported into the project (images, video, sounds, and so on), the Full Motion Recording clips, the Equations, and so on. Perform the following steps to open a project and explore its library:

1. Open or restart Captivate.
2. Open the Chapter05/encoderDemo_800.cptx file.

When using the default interface mode, a **Library** icon appears on the right side of the Big Buttons Bar just next to the **Properties** icon.

3. Click on the big **Library** icon situated at the far right side of the Big Buttons Bar. Alternatively, use the **Window | Library** menu item.

When the **Library** panel opens, it should look like the following screenshot:

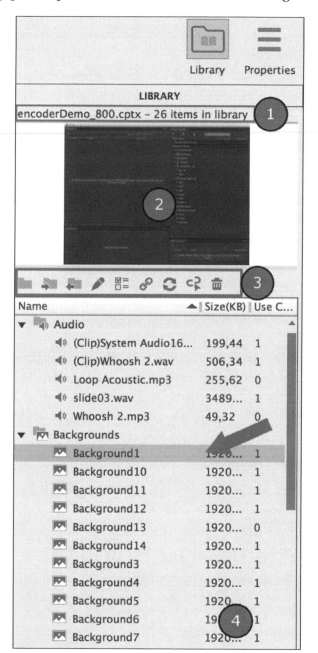

As depicted in the preceding screenshot, the Library is composed of the following elements:

- At the very top of the **Library** panel is the name of the file the library belongs to (**1**). This means that the library is associated with the currently active project only. If you switch to another project, you will also switch to another library.

- The preview area (**2**) gives a quick preview of the selected item. In the preceding screenshot, a background picture is selected (highlighted by the arrow).

- Just below the preview area, the library toolbar (**3**) displays a row of icons. These are the tools used to manage the assets present in the **Library** panel.

- The main area of the **Library** panel (**4**) lists the assets of the project organized by type.

The main area of the **Library** panel is further divided into folders representing the type of assets stored in the library.

Take some time to scroll down the **Library** panel and see the available folders. Take good note of the assets already present in the library. Can you relate them to the exercises of the previous two chapters?

4. In the `Background` folder of the library, select the `mftc-titleBkg_fixed. jpg` file. You will now explore the **Usage** dialog that will let you know where the selected image is used in the project.

5. Click on the sixth icon of the **Library** toolbar. This icon is called Usage.

6. A dialog box pops up and informs you that this particular image is used as the background of both slide 1 and slide 19.

7. Click on **OK** to close the **Usage** dialog box.

The only purpose of the **Usage** dialog box is to inform you about where the selected asset is used in the project.

Importing external assets into the library

One of the possible workflows when working with external assets is to import them all in the library of the project before inserting them on the slides. In this section, you will experiment with this workflow by importing the remaining audio files needed for this project and associating them with the corresponding slide.

1. In the `Chapter05/encoderDemo_800.cptx` file, make sure the **Library** panel is open.

2. Click on the second icon of the Library toolbar. This icon is named Import and is shown in the following screenshot:

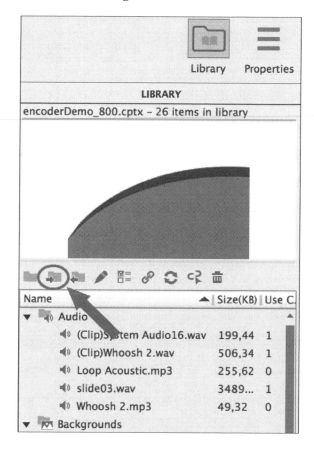

3. Browse to the audio folder of the downloaded exercises and select all the .wav audio files it contains (except the slide03.wav file that has already been imported in the previous chapter).

4. Click on the **Open** button and let Captivate import the selected audio files in the library of the project one by one.

5. When the import process is finished, you should have a message saying that 9 items have been successfully imported. Click on **OK** to acknowledge the message.

All the required audio files have been imported in the project. Your next task is to associate each of the imported files with the corresponding slide.

6. Use the **Filmstrip** panel to go to slide 4 of the Chapter05/encoderDemo_800. cptx file.

7. Drag the `slide04.wav` file from the **Audio** section of the **Library** and drop it on top of slide 4. Make sure you drop it on the slide itself and not on one of the objects present on the slide.

8. If the **Audio Import Options** dialog pops up, choose to extend the duration of the slide to match the length of the audio file.

Yes, it is that easy to import external sound clips into Captivate! If you take a look at the **Filmstrip** panel, you'll notice a loudspeaker icon next to the slides you have added audio to.

Now the rest of this exercise is easy! You will use the exact same drag and drop technique to associate the remaining audio clips with their corresponding slides. The only potential problem you have to be mindful of is to drop the audio clip on top of the slide, and not on top of one of the objects included in the slide. Use the following table to make sure you associate each audio file with the right slide.

 To avoid any problem during the drag and drop of audio files to the slides, you can drag the audio clips to the slide thumbnails in the **Filmstrip** panel as well. This makes the process go even faster and avoids the potential for associating the narration with an object rather than the slide.

Slide number	Audio clip	Slide number	Audio clip
5	slide05.wav	10	slide10.wav
6	slide06.wav	11	slide11.wav
7	slide07.wav	16	slide16.wav
8	slide08.wav	18	Slide18.wav

All the audio files have now been added to the project and associated with the correct slide. It is time to move on to the next section and discover yet another feature offered by the **Library** panel.

Reusing library items

In this section, you will learn how you can reuse the assets already present in the project library using the following steps:

1. Still in the `encoderDemo_800.cptx` file, use the **Filmstrip** panel to go to slide 5.

This is the slide on which you inserted the orange `down.swf` Flash animation in the previous chapter. When such an external file is inserted in the project, it is automatically added to the library. If you want to use the same animation again, there is no need to import it a second time. It can be taken directly from the **Library** panel and reused as many times as needed throughout the entire project. Using multiple instances of the same file helps in keeping the resulting file size as low as possible.

You will now drag and drop two more instances of this Flash animation to the slide.

2. Drag two more instances of the `down.swf` animation from the **Library** panel to the middle of the slide.

3. Drop them roughly above the rounded rectangle Smart Shape as shown in the next screenshot:

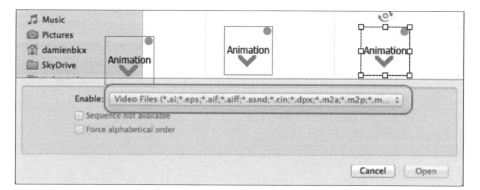

You will learn how to adjust the position of these objects later in this chapter.

Importing objects from another library

Another great feature is the ability to open the library of another file. This makes it easy to share assets between different Captivate projects. In the next exercise, you will open the library of another Captivate file in order to insert another image in the Encoder Demonstration project.

1. In the encoderDemo_800.cptx file, use the **Filmstrip** panel to go to slide 2.

2. In the **Library** panel, click on the first icon of the library toolbar. This icon is named Open Library.

3. Browse to the exercises folder and open the Chapter05/library.cptx file. The **Library** panel of this file appears as an extra floating panel.

4. If needed, enlarge the external **Library** panel. It contains a single image called inAmsterdam.jpg.

5. Drag the inAmsterdam.jpg image from the external library to the middle of slide 2.

6. Close the external library when done.

Oops, wrong image! Sorry folks, this is an image of me in Amsterdam a few hours before the AC/DC show during their 2009 Black Ice world tour! Well, even though this is not the intended picture, I've made my point: the library can be used to share assets between Captivate files. Notice that the inAmsterdam.jpg image is now present in the Images folder of the **Library** panel of the current project.

7. On slide 2, select and delete the newly inserted image.

Take another look at the **Library** panel after you deleted the image. Note that, even though it is not used in the project anymore, the image still appears in the Images folder of the library.

Deleting unused assets from the library

The unused items are the assets that are present in the project library, but are not used in the project. In order to control the size of the .cptx file, it is a good idea to remove these items from the library. In this exercise, you will use the tools of the **Library** panel to quickly identify and delete these unused items.

1. In the **Library** panel, click on the eighth icon of the **Library** toolbar. This icon is called Select Unused Items.

The unused items, including the inAmsterdam.jpg image, should be selected in the library.

2. Click on the last icon of the library toolbar (the trash can icon) to delete the selected assets.

3. Click on **Yes** to confirm the deletion.

4. Save the file when done.

That's it! Thanks to the **Library** panel, it is quick and easy to identify and delete unused assets. This will help you keep the size of your .cptx file as low as possible.

 Be careful when deleting background images because you can't get those back later if needed. To avoid problems, I always keep a backup copy of the raw material that comes out of the capture part of the process. This raw file contains the original background pictures should I need to recover some.

You will discover a few more goodies of the **Library** panel later in the book, but now let's summarize what you already know:

- The **Library** panel appears on the right-hand side of the screen, next to the **Properties** panel.

- The primary purpose of the library is to maintain a list of all the assets present in the active project. These assets include the background pictures and the Full Motion Recordings captured during the filming but also the external files imported in the project and the audio clips recorded with Captivate.

- The **Library** panel provides the necessary tools to let you manage the various assets used in the project.

- You can use the **Library** panel to insert multiple instances of the same asset in your project. This helps in keeping the project size as low as possible.

- It is possible to share assets across projects by opening the library of other .cptx files and importing the assets they contain in the current project.

- When you delete an asset from a slide, it is not deleted from the library. As a result, you may end up with a library containing many unused items.

- You can easily select and delete the unused items with the tools of the **Library** panel.

Laying out the objects on the slides

In this section, you will examine a few practical tools designed to help you quickly and easily arrange the objects on the slides of the project.

Using Smart Guides

The first of these tools are Smart Guides. These Smart Guides make it very easy to align various objects together. In this section, you will return to slide 3 of the `drivingInBe.cptx` file and precisely align the image with the rounded rectangle frame using the Smart Guides of Captivate. The steps are as follows:

1. Open the `Chapter05/drivingInBe.cptx` project and use the **Filmstrip** panel to go to slide 3.

In the previous chapter, you inserted a picture on this slide and drew a rounded rectangle Smart Shape. You will now move the image on top of the Smart Shape and use the Smart Guides to perfectly align the two objects. Your first task is to make sure that the Smart Guides are turned on.

2. Open the **View** menu.

3. Check if the **Show Drawing/Smart Guide** option at the very end of the **View** menu is enabled. If not, enable it now.

4. Move the image slowly on top of the rounded rectangle.

At some point, you should see a vertical and/or horizontal dotted green line appearing and disappearing from the screen. These are the Smart Guides. They appear automatically when alignment is possible.

5. Release the mouse when you see both a vertical and a horizontal Smart Guide (check out the following screenshot):

By releasing the mouse when both those guides are visible on the screen, you make sure that the image is perfectly centered in the rounded rectangle. Smart guides make these kinds of alignment incredibly fast and easy.

Grouping objects

Now that these two objects are correctly positioned relative to one other, you will select both the image and the rounded rectangle and group them as a single entity. The steps are as follows:

1. Click on the rounded rectangle to make it the active object.

2. Click on the image while holding the *Shift* key down. This adds the image to the current selection. You can also click and drag with your mouse to marquee-select multiple objects.

3. With both objects selected, use the **Edit | Group** menu item to group the rounded rectangle and the image together. Alternatively, you can use the *Ctrl + G* (Windows) or the *cmd + G* (Mac) shortcuts.

Now that the picture and the Smart Shape are grouped as one entity, they can be moved together without breaking their alignment.

4. Experiment with moving the picture / rounded rectangle group and confirm that both objects are moving together without breaking their alignment.

Even though these two objects have been grouped, you can still access each of these objects independently and modify the properties of just one of the group members.

5. Click on an empty area of the slide to deselect any active object. The **Properties** panel should display the properties of the slide.

6. Click once on the group to select it.

When a group is selected, the outline and the white handles surround the entire group. But, within the group, small grey dashed lines identify the members of that group.

7. While the group is selected, click on the rounded rectangle shape.

This action sub-selects the rounded rectangle shape within the group. Note that the white selection handles now surround the rounded rectangle, while the group it belongs to is identified by green handles, as shown in the following screenshot:

You can now modify the properties of the rounded rectangle within the group without affecting the other member(s) of the group or the group itself.

8. Turn your attention to the **Style** tab of the **Properties** panel.
9. In the **Fill** section, change the **Gradient Fill** value to **Solid Fill** and the **Opacity** value to **100 %**.

You will finalize the remaining properties of this object in the next chapter. In this exercise, the Smart Guides and the ability to group objects have proven their efficiency by enabling you to quickly and easily align and lay out the objects of this slide.

Using the Align toolbar

If you are looking for pixel perfect alignment and positioning, the Align toolbar is the ultimate tool. It contains the necessary icons to align, distribute, and resize the objects of your slides. By default, the Align toolbar is not displayed on the Captivate interface, so your first task is to turn it on. The steps are as follows:

1. Use the **Window | Align** menu item to turn the Align toolbar on. By default, it appears in the top-left area of the screen.

As shown in the following image, the Align toolbar contains 14 icons. During the next exercise, you will use many of these 14 icons. For ease of understanding, they will be numbered from 1 to 14, as shown in the following image:

By default, none of the icons of the Align toolbar are available. The set of available icons depends on the active selection.

2. Go to slide 2 of the `drivingInBe.cptx` file and select the curved up ribbon Smart Shape.

With one object selected on the slide, only the Center horizontally on the slide/slidelet (icon 7) and the Center vertically on the slide/slidelet (icon 8) icons are available.

3. Click on the Center horizontally on the slide/slidelet (icon 7) icon.

The curved up ribbon Smart Shape is now perfectly aligned with the horizontal center of the slide!

4. With the curved up ribbon still selected, hold the *Shift* key down while clicking on the **You are now...** Text Caption to add it to the current selection.

With two objects selected, most of the icons of the Align toolbar are available. Only the Distribute horizontally (icon 9) and the Distribute vertically (icon 10) icons are still disabled.

5. With both Smart Shapes selected, click on the Align Center (icon 2) icon.

This action moves the **You are now...** Text Caption Smart Shape below the curved up ribbon Smart Shape so that both objects are perfectly aligned.

6. Hold the *Shift* key down while clicking on either one of the two character images to add it to the current selection.

With three (or more) objects selected, all the icons of the Align toolbar are available. Make sure your slide look like the following screenshot before moving on to the next section:

Selecting multiple objects

Most of the tools of the Align toolbar require that at least two objects are selected. Selecting multiple objects is not difficult and it works in the same way in Captivate as in most other applications. However, Captivate has one important particularity when multiple objects are selected. This is what you will explore in this section.

1. Use the **Filmstrip** panel to go to slide 12 of the `drivingInBe.cptx` file.

Slide 12 contains a title, 12 images, and four rounded-rectangle Smart Shapes with text. That makes a lot of objects! These objects have been quickly placed on the slide in their approximate position. Your next task is to use the tools of the Align toolbar to perfectly align and distribute these objects on the slide.

2. Click on the topmost rounded rectangle (the one that reads **Warning signs**) to make it the active object.

3. Hold the *Shift* key down and select the three remaining rounded rectangles one by one.

Four objects are now selected and all the icons of the Align toolbar are enabled. As shown in the following screenshot, the first selected object (the topmost rounded rectangle) is surrounded by white selection handles while the remaining objects are surrounded by black selection handles:

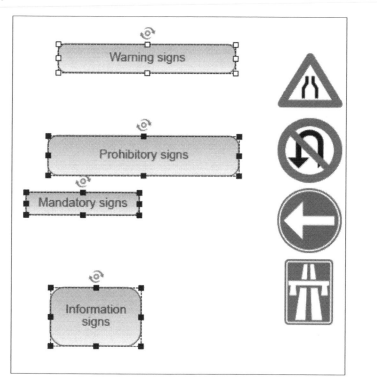

In Captivate, the first selected object is the key object of the selection. It means that the tools of the Align toolbar are calibrated based on the size and the position of that object. To make it recognizable, Captivate displays white selection handles around it and black handles around all the other objects of the selection.

4. Click on the Resize to the same size (icon 13) icon of the Align toolbar.

This operation applies the size of the key object (the object with white selection handles) to all the objects of the selection. Now that they have the same size, let's give these objects their proper position.

5. Click on the Align Left (icon 1) icon of the Align toolbar.

The left edge of the four selected objects is now perfectly aligned to the left edge of the key object.

6. Click on the Distribute vertically (icon 10) icon of the Align toolbar to space the four selected objects equally.

Now, the four rounded rectangles are now in their final position.

Extra credit – aligning and distributing the remaining objects

You now have all the knowledge you need to perfectly align the images of this slide. Here is what you need to do:

- Select the objects you want to align, paying close attention to the first one you select. Remember that the tools of the Align toolbar are calibrated based on the first selected object.

- Use the tools of the Align toolbar to move the remaining objects of the slide to their final position.

- Remember that the four rounded rectangles are already at their final position. Use them as a reference.

- Save the file when finished.

Now your slide should look like the following screenshot:

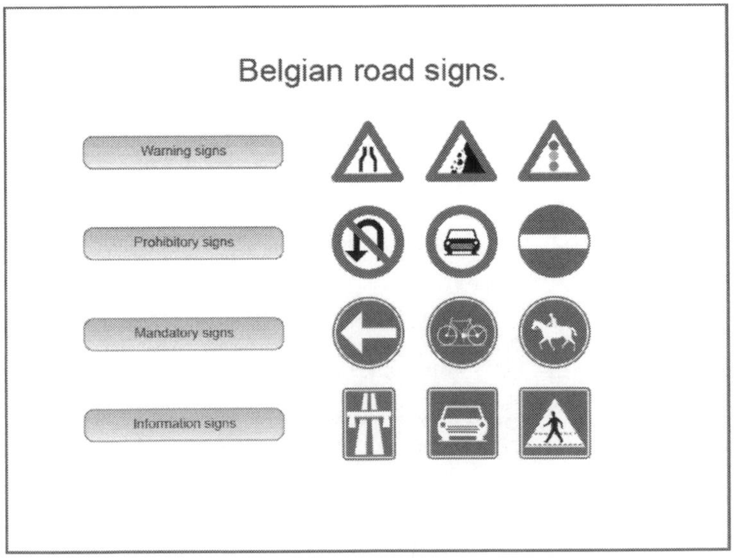

Putting it all together

The Smart Guides, the Align toolbar, and the ability to group objects are three great tools that enable you to quickly and easily align and resize the objects of the slide. But these tools are most useful when combined together. In the following exercise, you will finalize the positioning of the .swf animations you inserted on slide 5 of the encoderDemo_800.cptx file using the following steps:

1. Open or return to the Chapter05/encoderDemo_800.cptx file.

2. Use the **Filmstrip** panel to go to slide 5 of the project.

Slide 5 is where you inserted the three orange arrows animations and the rounded-rectangle Smart Shape earlier in this book. You will now properly align these objects using both the Smart Guides and the Align toolbar. When done, you will group these objects together to make sure not to break their alignment.

3. Select the rightmost orange arrow and use the Smart Guides to align its right edge to the right edge of the rounded rectangle.

This operation is shown in the following screenshot:

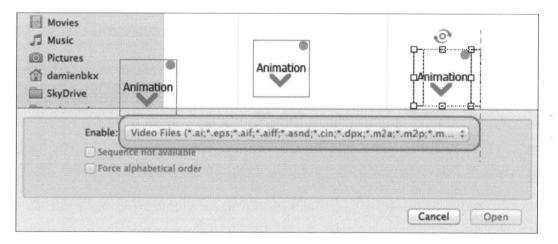

4. Click on an empty area of the slide to deselect all the objects. The **Properties** panel should display the properties of the slide.

5. Click on the leftmost orange arrow to select it. Note that white selection handles surround the selected object.

6. Keep the *Shift* key down and click on the other two orange arrows one by one to add them to the selection. After this operation, black selection handles should surround these two objects.

7. If needed use the **Window | Align** menu item to turn the Align toolbar on.

8. Click on the Align bottom (icon 6) icon of the Align toolbar.

9. Finally, click on the Distribute horizontally (icon 9) icon of the Align toolbar to space the selected objects equally.

Now that these objects are properly aligned, you will group them to make sure that their relative alignment will not be broken in the unlikely event of one of these objects being accidentally moved.

10. Hold the *Shift* key down and click on the rounded rectangle to add it to the selection. After this operation, you should have four objects selected on your slide.

11. Use the *Ctrl + G* (Windows) or the *cmd + G* (Mac) shortcut to group the selected objects.

In this exercise, you have combined the Smart Guides, the Align toolbar, and the Group feature to quickly, easily, and perfectly position the object of this slide. This concludes your exploration of the tools used to lay out objects. Before moving on to the next topic, let's summarize what we covered in this section:

- Smart Guides are dotted green lines that automatically appear and disappear as you move objects around. These guides are used to help you align objects together.

- Smart Guides can be turned on and off by using the **View | Show Drawing/Smart Guides** menu item.

- Different objects can be grouped into a single entity. When grouped, these objects can be moved all together without breaking their relative alignment.

- The Align toolbar is not part of the default interface. It is therefore necessary to explicitly turn it on by using the **Window | Align** menu item.

- There are 14 icons on the Align toolbar. The number of enabled icons depends on the number of objects selected.

- It is possible to select multiple objects in Captivate using the same techniques as in most other applications.

- The first selected object of a multiple selection is known as the key object of the selection. The tools of the Align toolbar are calibrated based on that key object.

- Captivate displays white selection handles around the key object and black selection handles around the other objects of the selection.

With a bit of practice, you will be confident with the Smart Guides and the Align toolbar!

Working with the Timeline

By default, the Timeline is initially hidden in Captivate 8. To reveal it, just click on the **Timeline** bar situated at the bottom of the interface. The primary purpose of the Timeline is to organize the sequence of events on each slide, but the **Timeline** panel can be used for other purposes as well.

Using the Timeline to select objects

Sometimes the objects are so close to each other that you might have a hard time selecting the right object. The objects can also be stacked on top of one other so that selecting an object that is not on top of the stack can be very tricky. Using the **Timeline** panel, you can make sure that the object you select is the one you actually want to select! The steps are as follows:

1. If needed, return to the Chapter05/encoderDemo_800.cptx file.
2. Click on the **Timeline** bar at the very bottom of the screen to open the **Timeline** panel.
3. Use the **Filmstrip** panel to go to slide 4 of the project.

This slide contains four objects: two Text Captions, one rounded-rectangle Smart Shape (used as a Highlight Box), and the Mouse movement. Each object corresponds to a layer in the **Timeline** panel.

4. In the **Timeline** panel, click on the layer that represents the rounded rectangle Smart Shape.

As shown in the following screenshot, eight white handles now surround the orange rounded rectangle on the stage. Selecting an object on the **Timeline** panel also selects it on the stage which, in turn, displays its properties in the **Properties** panel.

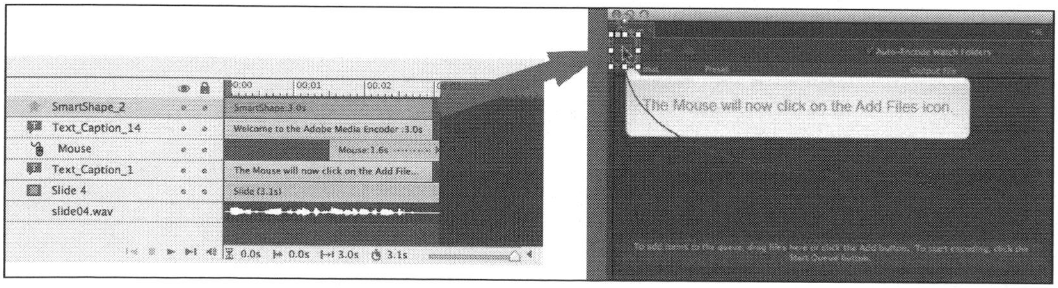

Using the Timeline to lock and unlock objects

Hiding and locking objects is another feature that will help you make the right selection. It also prevents you from accidentally modifying finished objects.

1. Make sure you are still on slide 4 of the `encoderDemo_800.cptx` file.

On slide 4, the rounded rectangle and the mouse pointer share the same area of the slide. If you try to click on one of these two objects on the stage, chances are you'll end up clicking on the other one! For this exercise, imagine that you want to select the orange rounded-rectangle Smart Shape.

2. In the **Timeline**, click on the Lock/Unlock All Items icon (see **1** in the next screenshot).

3. Click on the lock icon situated in front of the Smart Shape object (see **2** in the following screenshot):

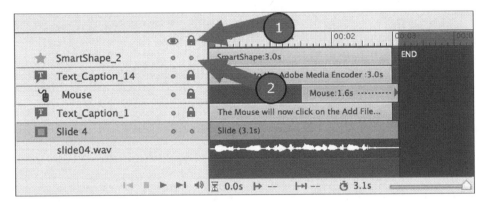

The Smart Shape is now the only object on the slide that is not locked. Consequently, it is the only one that can be selected and modified.

4. On the slide, try to select one of the Text Captions or the mouse pointer. Captivate should not let you do it!

5. However, if you try to select the Smart Shape, the application reacts normally.

6. In the **Timeline**, click on the lock icon associated with the Smart Shape.

Take a closer look at the lock icon of the Smart Shape. It is not exactly the same as the lock icons of the other objects. As shown in the following screenshot, the lock status of an object can take one of three values:

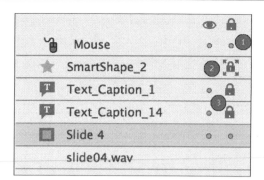

- If no icon is present (**1**), the object is completely unlocked and all its properties are accessible.

- If a lock icon with arrows is present (**2**) only the size and position of the object is locked. All the other properties (such as the Fill and the Stroke properties) are not locked and can be modified as usual.

- If a standard lock icon is displayed (**3**), then the object is completely locked and cannot even be selected.

You will now further experiment with these three lock statuses:

7. Click on the orange rounded rectangle to select it. Note that the object can be selected but the white selection handles do not appear.

8. Try to move and resize the rounded rectangle. Captivate should not let you do it.

9. Open the **Properties** panel (if needed) and turn your attention to the **Style** tab.

10. In the **Fill** section, try to raise the Opacity of the object to **30 %**.

In this case, Captivate reacts normally. This illustrates the fact that only the size and the position properties of the rounded rectangle are currently locked, while the other properties of the object can be modified normally.

11. With the rounded rectangle still selected, switch to the **Options** tab of the **Properties** panel.

In the **Transform** section, note the **Lock Size and Position** checkbox that is currently selected and the **X** and **Y** coordinates that are currently disabled.

12. Deselect the **Lock Size and Position** checkboxes.

After this operation, the **X** and **Y** properties, as well as the **Height** and the **Width** properties, are re-enabled in the **Options** tab of the **Properties** panel. Also, note that the lock icon of the rounded rectangle has disappeared from the **Timeline** — indicating that this object is no longer locked.

13. In the **Timeline** panel, click on the lock icon associated with the rounded rectangle Smart Shape three times. Note how the icon cycles through each of the three possible lock values.

14. In the **Timeline** panel, unlock both Text Captions and the Mouse.

All the objects of the slide should now be unlocked so you should be back to the original situation.

Using the Timeline to show and hide objects

In the **Timeline** panel, the Show/Hide All Items icons (the eye icons) are next to the Lock/Unlock All Items icons. These icons work in the exact same way as the Lock icons covered in the previous section. You can use them to hide objects from the slide. When the slide holds a large number of objects, it can help you select and work with the right ones keeping the others out of the way. Note that hiding an object with this tool hides it *from the Captivate interface only*, not from the final project as viewed by the students.

Using the Timeline to change the stacking order of the objects

The stacking order decides which object goes in front of or behind the other objects. In the **Timeline** panel, the topmost object is in front of any other objects. It means that, in case objects overlap, the topmost object covers the one(s) below it. The slide is always at the very bottom of the stack as it is used as the background on top of which the objects are placed. The steps are as follows:

1. Make sure you are still on slide 4 of the `Chapter04/encoderDemo_800.cptx` file.

2. If necessary, move one of the two Text Captions so both objects overlap.

In the **Timeline** panel, note that the **Welcome to the Adobe Media Encoder** Text Caption is higher in the stack than the **The Mouse will now click on the Add Files icon** Text Caption. This should be reflected on the stage in the way both Text Captions overlap.

3. In the **Timeline** panel, take the **Welcome to...** Text Caption and drag it down two levels.

The **Welcome to...** Text Caption is now below the **The mouse will now...** Text Caption.

4. Right-click on the **Welcome To...** Text Caption.

5. In the contextual menu, go to **Arrange | Bring to Front**.

This brings the **Welcome To...** Text Caption to the top of the stack, both on the stage and in the **Timeline** panel.

6. If needed, use the **Window | Align** menu item to turn the Align toolbar back on.

7. Select the **The Mouse will now...** Text Caption.

Take some time to inspect the last four icons of the Align toolbar. They are used to control the stacking order of the objects.

8. In the Align toolbar, click on the **Bring selected object to the front** icon.

This action brings the **The Mouse will now...** Text Caption back to the top of the stack, both on the stage and in the **Timeline**.

Using the Timeline to set the timing of the objects

The primary purpose of the **Timeline** is to let you control the timing of the objects on the active slide. For each object, you can choose when it appears on the stage and how long it stays visible. By carefully and precisely arranging the objects on the **Timeline**, you'll be able to achieve great visual effects very easily. The steps are as follows:

1. Make sure you are still on slide 4 of the `encoderDemo_800.cptx` file.

2. Take a look at the **Timeline** panel and note how the four objects of the slide are organized.

3. Click on an empty area of the slide to make the entire slide the active item. The **Properties** panel updates and displays the properties of the slide.

4. Switch to the **Timing** panel and change the **Slide Duration** property to `10` seconds. This change is reflected in the **Timeline** panel.

5. In the **Timeline** panel, take the right edge of the slide and drag it to the **15** seconds mark. This change is reflected in the **Slide Duration** property of the **Timing** panel.

The changes made in the **Timeline** panel are reflected in the **Timing** panel and vice versa. This gives you two methods to organize the timing of your objects.

6. Click on the **Welcome to...** Text Caption to make it the active object. The
    Timing panel updates and shows the timing properties of the Text Caption.

The **Timing** panel states that the Text Caption appears after 0 seconds and stays
visible for a specific time of 3 seconds. The **Timeline** panel is a visual representation
of this situation.

> **Adjusting the default timing of the objects**
>
> When a new object is added to the stage, its timing is set to 3 seconds
> by default. This default timing can be adjusted for each type of object
> separately. Simply go to **Edit | Preferences | Defaults** (Windows) or
> **Adobe Captivate | Preferences | Defaults** (Mac), choose an object
> from the **Select** drop-down list, and adjust the default timing of the
> selected object type.

7. Select the **The mouse will now...** Text Caption to make it the active object.

8. In the **Timeline** panel, place your mouse in the middle of the selected
    Text Caption until the mouse pointer turns to a grabbing hand.

9. Move the Text Caption to the right, so it begins at the 7 seconds mark
    on the **Timeline**.

10. While in the **Timeline** panel, place your mouse on the right edge of
    the selected Text Caption until the mouse pointer turns into a double arrow.

11. Use the mouse to extend the duration of the **The mouse will now...**
    Text Caption to the 13 seconds mark.

12. In the **Timing** panel, confirm that the selected Text Caption is set to appear
    after 7 seconds and to display for a specific time of 6 seconds.

13. In the **Timing** panel, open the **Transition** drop-down list.

In Captivate, it is possible to apply the **Fade In** and/or **Fade Out** effects on (almost)
every object. By default, the **Transition** effect lasts half a second, but you can adjust
its timing in the **Transition** section of the **Timing** panel.

14. Change the **Transition** of both Text Captions to **Fade In and Out**.

Keep these **Transitions** effects in mind when setting up the timing of your objects.
Imagine a Text Caption set to stay visible for a specific time of 3 seconds with a
default **Fade In and Fade Out** transition applied. The first half a second is used
for the Fade In effect and the last half a second is used for the Fade Out effect. It
effectively leaves only 2 seconds for the learner to read the text contained in the
Text Caption!

15. Still on slide 4, use the **Timeline** or the **Timing** panel to change the timing of the orange rounded rectangle. Make it appear at 8 seconds into the slide and stay visible for a specific time of 6 seconds.

16. Also, change the Timing of the Mouse movement so it begins at 13 seconds into the slide and lasts 2 seconds.

17. Finally, move the audio clip to the right so it begins at the 4 second mark.

The **Timeline** of slide 4 is now correct. Make sure it looks like the following screenshot (the stacking order of your objects may be different to the screenshot):

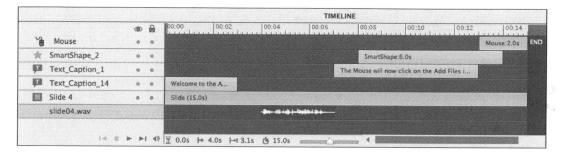

> **The strange red triangle**
>
> When moving objects on the **Timeline**, a red triangle might appear on some objects that are at the end of the **Timeline**. Read this great blog post by Kevin Siegel to find out more about this mysterious red triangle. http://iconlogic.blogs.com/weblog/2013/07/adobe-captivate-anchors-away.html.

To test the new timing of the objects, use the **Preview | Next 5 slides** menu items. If you feel that the current timing is not exactly right, don't hesitate to adjust the position of the objects on the **Timeline** to your liking. After all, you're the teacher!

Tips and tricks for great syncing

When it comes to syncing the objects of your project, the **Timeline** is your best friend. But, once again, it is a combination of many features that will help you go the extra mile and achieve great syncing. In this section, I want to share with you some of the techniques I use when syncing the projects I work on. These techniques all have one thing in common: they use many Captivate features that work hand-in-hand to produce the final effect.

Using the Sync with Playhead feature

The first technique you will learn is an entire workflow that involves the timeline and the transitions applied to the objects. You will use that workflow to sync slide 3 of the `encoderDemo_800.cptx` file. The steps are as follows:

1. Return to or open the `Chapter05/encoderDemo_800.cptx` file.

2. Use the **Filmstrip** panel to go to slide 3 of the project.

3. If needed, click on the **Timeline** bar at the bottom of the screen to open the **Timeline** panel.

Slide 3 contains four Text Captions and the Adobe Media Encoder logo. There is also an audio clip associated with the slide as indicated by the loudspeaker icon next to the slide thumbnail in the **Filmstrip** panel.

The first step of the workflow is to take care of the beginning and the ending of the slide.

4. In the **Timeline** panel, move the audio clip to the right so it begins at the 0.5 second mark.

Sound can be very intrusive, so you must use it with care. One of the things that I always do on slides with voiceover narration (such as slide 3 of the project) is to move the sound clip in the **Timeline** half a second to the right to make the audio narration begin half a second into the slide. This simple trick dramatically diminishes the intrusive and aggressive feeling that sound can induce without affecting the general rhythm of the project.

5. Scroll to the end of the **Timeline** and extend the duration of the slide to the 43 second mark.

The second step in my workflow is to modify the stacking order of the objects in the **Timeline** panel. The goal is to make it match the order in which the objects enter the slide: the first object to enter the slide at the bottom of the stack and the last one at the top. This operation is not technically required, but I think it makes the timeline much easier to work with. Keep in mind though that the stacking order on the timeline also controls how the objects overlap, so sometimes it might not be possible for the stacking order to match the timing of the slide.

6. In the **Timeline** panel, locate the layer that represents the AME logo image. It should currently be at the very top of the stack.

7. Move this layer one step down to make it match its order of entry on the slide.

In this case, the objects will appear on the stage in sync with the audio, but once on the stage they will stay visible until the end of the slide. This is a very common situation in Captivate so, to speed up the process, the next step of my workflow is to extend the duration of all the objects to the end of the slide.

8. Select all four Text Captions present on the slide. To do so, you can use either the stage or the layers of the **Timeline** panel.

9. With all four Text Captions selected, turn your attention to the **Timing** panel. It might be necessary to open the **Properties** panel before being able to access the **Timing** panel.

10. Open the **Display For** drop-down menu and choose the **Rest of Slide** item.

11. Click on the AME Logo image to select it. The **Timing** panel updates and displays the timing properties of the AME logo.

12. In the **Timing** panel, change the **Display For** property of the logo to **Rest of Slide**.

All the objects of the slide are now displayed for the entire duration of the slide. This situation should be reflected in the **Timeline** panel.

The next step of the workflow is to apply a Fade In Only transition to the objects.

13. With the AME logo image still selected, open the **Transition** drop-down menu situated in the **Timing** panel.

14. Change **Transition** to **Fade In Only** and accept the default transition time of **0.5** seconds.

15. Select all four Text Captions and repeat the process to apply the same **Fade In Only** transition to the Text Captions of the slide.

Now, let's discuss the final step of the process where you will actually sync the objects with the audio. The first Text Caption (at the bottom of the stack in the **Timeline** panel) will serve as the title of the slide and is already correctly synced.

16. Use the **Timeline** panel to select the layer that represents the **Your video files...** Text Caption.

17. Click on the play icon situated at the bottom left corner of the **Timeline** panel.

18. Listen to the audio and pause the playhead when the narration says, "You must first convert it..." (around the 13.5 seconds mark).

19. With the playhead paused at the right position, turn your attention to the **Timeline** panel and right-click on the layer that represents the **Your video file...** Text Caption.

20. In the contextual menu, click on the **Sync with Playhead** item.

This action makes the selected Text Caption appear at the current position of the playhead. Before moving on, take good note of the keyboard shortcut associated with the **Sync with Playhead** feature (*Ctrl + L* on Windows and *cmd + L* on Mac).

21. In the **Timeline** panel, click on the layer just above the currently selected one to select the next Text Caption.

22. Click on the play button at the bottom left corner of the **Timeline** panel to release the playhead.

23. Pause the playhead again when the narration says, "The Adobe Media Encoder is an application..." (around the 21 seconds mark).

24. Use the *Ctrl + L* (Windows) or the *cmd + L* (Mac) shortcuts to sync the selected Text Caption with the playhead.

25. In the **Timeline** panel, select the layer right above the selected one to select the AME logo image.

26. Use the *Ctrl + L* (Windows) or the *cmd + L* (Mac) shortcut to sync the AME logo with the playhead and make it begin at the same time as the Text Caption.

27. In the **Timeline** panel, select the layer right above the selected one to select the **Adobe Media Encoder is part...** Text Caption.

28. Click on the play button at the bottom left corner of the **Timeline** panel to release the playhead. Pause the playhead when the narration says, "The good news is, the Adobe Media Encoder..." (around the 31 seconds mark).

29. Use the *Ctrl + L* (Windows) or the *cmd + L* (Mac) shortcut to sync the selected Text Caption with the playhead.

As usual, the last step is to use the **Preview** icon of the Big Buttons Bar to test the timing of the slide.

30. Use the **Preview** icon of the Big Buttons Bar to preview the **Next 5 slides**.

Make sure that the objects are correctly synced with the audio. If needed, return to the slide and adjust the timing of the objects to your taste before testing again. Keep in mind that the formatting of this slide has not been finalized yet and that the **Continue** button is still missing. These two issues will be addressed later in the book.

At the end of this exercise, your **Timeline** panel should look like the following screenshot (the zoom of the **Timeline** has been adjusted to fit the image):

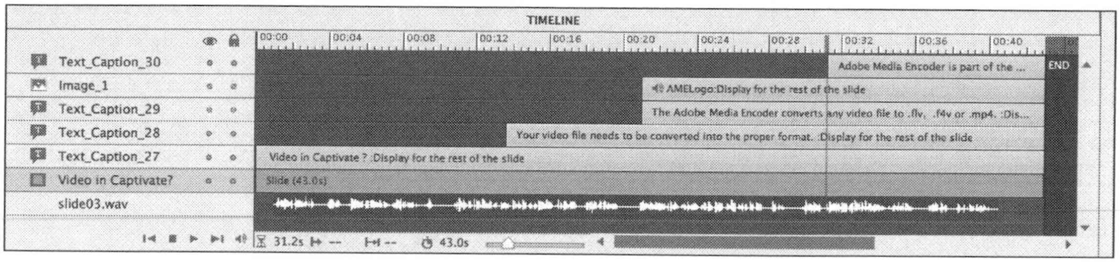

Syncing and positioning

Another technique that I use very often involves using the Align toolbar in conjunction with the **Timeline** to give the illusion that the text content of a Text Caption changes. In this section, you will experiment with this technique and have yet another example of how different Captivate features can work hand-in-hand to produce a great effect. The steps are as follows:

1. In the `Chapter05/encoderDemo_800.cptx` file, use the **Filmstrip** to go to slide 11.

Slide 11 contains two Text Captions and a mouse movement. An audio clip is also associated with this slide. Your first task is to sync the elements of the slide with the narration.

2. In the **Timeline** panel, move the audio narration to the right so it begins **0.5** seconds into the slide.

3. Select the Text Caption that reads **The chosen preset...**.

4. Use the **Timeline** panel or the **Timing** panel to make it appear after `11` seconds and stay on the stage for a specific time of `6.5` seconds.

5. Select the Text Caption that reads **Only the size...**.

6. Use the **Timeline** or the **Timing** panel to make it appear after `17.5` seconds and stay on the stage for a specific time of `5.5` seconds.

7. Select the mouse pointer and use the **Timeline** or the **Timing** panel to make it appear after `22` seconds and stay on stage for a specific time of `3` seconds.

8. If needed, use the **Timeline** panel to adjust the duration of the slide to `25` seconds.

The elements of the slide are now properly synced. The next step is to preview this new timing. After that, you will add some Captivate magic to the mix.

9. Use the **Preview** icon of the Big Buttons Bar and choose the **Next 5 Slides** item.

During the preview, pay particular attention to the two Text Captions. Although correctly synced, these objects currently offer a poor visual experience to the learner. The first thing you can do to enhance that visual experience is to add a **Fade In and Out** transition to these objects.

10. Close the **Preview** pane and return to the Captivate editing environment.

11. Still on slide 11, select both Text Captions.

12. In the **Timing** panel, open the **Transition** drop-down menu and choose the **Fade In and Out** item. Accept the default transition timing of **0.5** seconds.

13. Use the **Preview | Next 5 slides** menu item on the Big Buttons Bar to test the latest changes.

Adding a transition to these objects already makes the visual experience much better. But there is more that you can do! You will now give these two objects the very same size and the very same position, right in the center of the slide.

14. Close the **Preview** pane and select the Text Caption that reads **The chosen preset...**.

15. In the **Options** tab of the **Properties** panel, give this object a width of 300 pixels and a height of 100 pixels. It may be necessary to deselect the **Constraint proportions** checkbox to modify the height and the width independently.

16. Hold the *Shift* key down and click on the other Text Caption to add it to the selection.

Make sure that the Text Caption that reads **The chosen preset...** is surrounded by white selection handles, while the other Text Caption is surrounded by black handles.

17. If needed, use the **Window | Align** menu item to turn the Align toolbar on.

18. Click on the **Resize to the same size** (icon 13) icon of the Align toolbar.

This action applies the size of the key object (surrounded by white handles) to the other objects of the selection. In this case, both Text Captions now have the exact same size of **300** pixels in width by **100** pixels in height. Your next task is to place these two objects at the center of the slide.

19. With both Text Captions still selected, click on the **Center horizontally on the slide/slidelet** icon (icon 7) of the Align toolbar.

20. When done, click on the **Center vertically on the slide/slidelet** (icon 7) icon of the Align toolbar.

Both Text Captions are now located at the exact center of the slide.

21. Use the **Preview | Next 5 slides** icon of the Big Buttons Bar to test the latest changes.

The visual experience provided by these two Text Captions is already much better than what it was originally. However, there is one more piece to add to the puzzle in order to make it perfect!

22. In the **Timeline** panel, make sure that the objects are stacked in the order in which they appear on the slide. The first object to appear (the **The Chosen Preset...** Text Caption) at the bottom of the stack and the last object to appear (the Mouse) at the top of the stack.

23. Use the **Timeline** panel to extend the duration of the **The Chosen Preset...** Text Caption by at least 0.5 seconds.

Remember that 0.5 seconds corresponds to the duration of the Fade Out transition. By extending the duration of the **The Chosen Preset...** Text Caption by at least 0.5 seconds (make that 1 second for security), you ensure that the Fade Out effect of this Text Caption will not be seen. This is illustrated in the following screenshot:

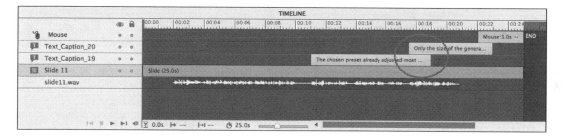

In this configuration, the **Only the size...** Text Caption will appear on top of the **The Chosen Preset...** Text Caption before it starts fading out, effectively replacing this object on the stage. Let's give this slide one more try in the **Preview** pane.

24. Use the **Preview | Next 5 slides** icons of the Big Buttons Bar to test the latest changes.

Hey! It looks like you just came up with a great effect that will dramatically enhance the visual experience of your learners. All it takes to create this experience is to cleverly combine various Captivate tools together.

Extra credit – adjusting the timing of the other slides

Now that you know the tools and techniques used to set the timing and the stacking order of the objects, browse the other slides of the encoderDemo_800.cptx and drivingInBe.cptx projects to adjust the timing of the various objects contained in the project. Refer to the Chapter05/final/encoderDemo_800.cptx and Chapter05/final/drivingInBe.cptx files of your exercise folder for examples and inspiration. Just a few tips before you get started:

- Use the **Timeline** panel whenever possible. It is the most intuitive way to adjust the timing of the objects.

- If you require precise timing, use the **Timing** panel.

- Remember the **Sync with Playhead** feature and its associated keyboard shortcut (*Ctrl + L* on windows and *cmd + L* on Mac).

- Don't hesitate to use the tools of the Align toolbar to resize and relocate the objects on the slide. Proper size/location combined with precise timing can lead to strong yet, easy to achieve, visual effects.

Not too fast and not too slow

When creating an online course with Captivate, you'll quickly discover that one of the most difficult aspects is to find the right pace. For the Text Caption object, there is an easy trick. Use the stopwatch function of your cellphone and slowly read the content of the Text Caption aloud, then round up the timing to the upper half a second. For example, if it takes you 5.7 seconds to read a Text Caption aloud, make that Text Caption stay on the stage for a specific time of 6 seconds. If your audience is multilingual, add up to 1.5 seconds to the timing so that students taking the course in a language other than their native language will be allowed extra time to read and understand your Text Captions. You can also use the **Calculate Caption Timing** preference of Captivate. When this preference is turned on, Captivate automatically calculates the length of the Text Captions based on their content.

This concludes your first overview of the timeline. Here is a quick summary of what has been covered in this section:

- The primary purpose of the timeline is to arrange the timing of the objects.

- The timeline can also be used to select the objects and to modify their stacking order.

- The **Timeline** panel is a visual representation of the properties found in the **Timing** panel. Changing the objects on the timeline updates the **Timing** panel and vice versa.

- It is possible to apply a Fade In and/or a Fade Out effect on the object using the **Transition** drop-down menu of the **Timing** panel. The default transition time is 0.5 seconds, but this can easily be changed in the **Timing** panel.

- Use the **Sync with Playhead** feature to make the selected object begin at the current location of the Playhead on the timeline.

- Achieve great special effects by cleverly combining other Captivate features with precise timing.

Adding effects to objects

Effects can be added to any objects of Captivate. This effectively reduces the need for external animations to be imported in the project as some of these animations can be created right within Captivate. In this section, you will use the built-in tools of Captivate to animate the Adobe Media encoder logo you inserted on slide 3 of the Encoder Demo project.

1. Go to the Chapter05/encoderDemo_800.cptx file.
2. Use the **Filmstrip** panel to go to slide 2.
3. Use the **Preview** icon of the Big Buttons Bar to preview the **Next 5 slides**.

When the preview reaches slide 3, pay particular attention to how the Adobe Media Encoder logo enters and leaves the stage. No particular effect should be applied. Close the **Preview** pane when finished.

4. Back in the Chapter05/encoderDemo_800.cptx file, go to slide 3 and select the Adobe Media Encoder logo.
5. Use **Window | Effects** menu item to open the **Effects** panel.

By default, the **Effects** panel appears at the bottom of the screen next to the **Timeline** panel.

The **Effects** panel also displays a timeline but, unlike the **Timeline** panel that displays the timeline of the entire slide, the **Effects** panel displays the timeline of the selected object only. In this case, the **Effects** panel displays the timeline of the Adobe Media Encoder logo (**1**):

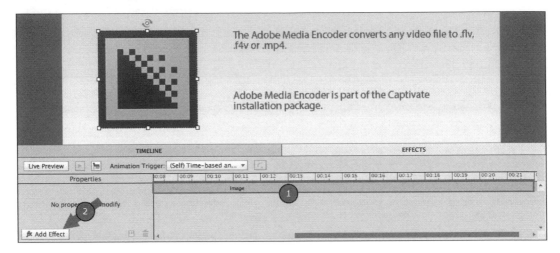

6. Click on the Add Effect icon (**2**) situated at the bottom-left corner of the **Effects** panel.

7. In the menu that pops up, navigate to **Emphasis** | **Flip** | **FlipFromCenter**.

8. In the **Effects** panel, reduce the length of the **FlipFromCenter** effect to the first half-second of the Adobe Media Encoder image timeline.

9. Save your file.

10. Use the **Preview** icon to preview the **Next 5 slides**.

Pay particular attention to the way the Adobe Media Encoder logo enters the stage. Thanks to the **Effects** panel, you have applied a nice effect to the image. This adds another great touch of design, professionalism, and dynamism to this eLearning project! Also, note that when the object is selected on the stage, a small **fx** icon appears in the top-right corner of the object indicating that an effect has been applied to the object. In Captivate 8.0.1, this effect icon also appears at the beginning of the object layer in the **Timeline** panel.

Captivate 8.0.1

Captivate 8.0.1 is a free update patch available to all Captivate 8 customers. This update fixes a lot of bugs and introduces some great enhancements to the application, the **fx** icon on the timeline being one of them. Use the **Adobe Captivate | About Adobe Captivate** (Mac) or **Help | About Adobe Captivate** (Windows) menu item to see the exact version number of your Captivate installation. If you see Captivate 8.0.1.XXX, it means the update patch has been applied. If you see Captivate 8.0.0.XXX, it means you should download and install the patch to enjoy the latest and greatest from Captivate 8.

Combining effects

In this section, you will import an image and animate it using a combination of two effects. The steps are as follows:

1. Return to the `Chapter05/drivingInBe.cptx` file.
2. Use the **Filmstrip** panel to go to slide 5.

This slide already contains two Smart Shapes with text and a Character image.

3. Use the **Media | Image** icons of the Big Buttons Bar to insert the `images/check.png` file situated in your exercises folder.
4. Use Smart Guides to position the new image on the right of the Text caption that reads **Good**.
5. Use the **Timeline** or **Timing** panel to make the image appear after `1.5` seconds and display for the rest of the slide.
6. With the image still selected, use the **Window | Effects** icons to open the **Effects** panel (if needed).
7. Use the **Add Effect** button to apply the **Entrance | Spiral In** effect to the picture. Make the effect last for the first 1.5 seconds of the object timeline.
8. Return to slide 4 and use the **Preview | Next 5 slides** icons of the Big Buttons Bar to test the latest change in the preview pane.

When the preview reaches slide 5, pay close attention to the way the green checkmark image enters the stage. Close the **Preview** pane when the preview is finished. You will now add a second effect to the same object to make it look even more engaging.

9. Return to slide 5, select the green checkmark image again, and return to the **Effects** panel.

10. Use the **Add Effect** button to add the **Emphasis | Clockwise Rotate** effect. Make it last the same 1.5 seconds as the **Spiral In** effect you added earlier.

Make sure the **Effects** panel looks like the following screenshot and use the **Preview** icon to test your sequence. When the preview is complete, close the **Preview** pane.

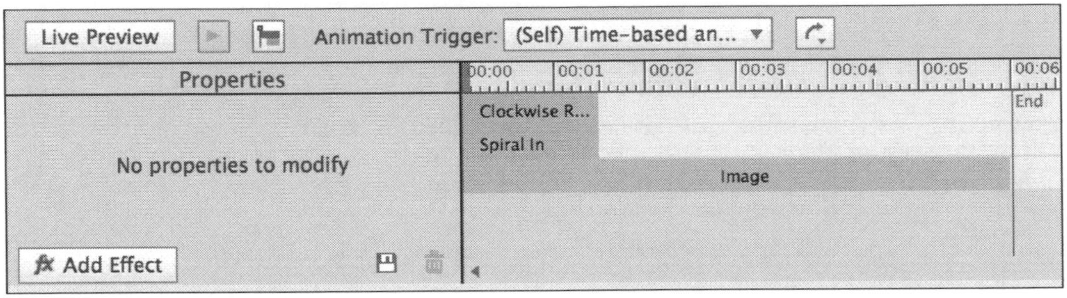

11. Still on slide 5, select the green checkmark image and copy it (*Ctrl + C* on Windows or *cmd + C* on Mac).

12. Go to slide 10 and paste (*Ctrl + V* on Windows or *cmd + V* on Mac) the image.

13. Save the file when done.

Note that the same red **fx** icon appears next to the pasted copy of the green checkmark on slide 10. When you copy/paste an object, you also copy/paste the properties of the object—including its size, position, and effects.

Extra credit – adding effects to images

Now that you have inserted an image and added effects onto it, why don't you try it on your own on another image? These are the general steps to follow:

- You will be working with the `drivingInBe.cptx` file.

- Add the `images/redCross.png` on slide 6.

- Position the red cross image in the middle of the slide, between the two Text Captions. (Remember that the Align toolbar and the Smart Guides are there to help you!)

- On the **Timeline**, make the red cross appear after 1 second and display for the rest of the slide.

- Use the **Effects** panel to add the **Spiral In** and the **Clockwise Rotate** effects.

- Make both effects last 1.5 seconds as you did for the green checkmark.

- Use the preview **Next 5 slides** feature to test your sequence.

- If everything is fine, copy-paste the red cross image on slide 11.

Finishing touches

To wrap up this section on object effects, you will inspect another slide of the project and see how the **Effects** and the **Timeline** panels can work together to produce a great visual experience.

1. Open the Chapter05/final/drivingInBe.cptx file and use the **Filmstrip** to go to slide 12.

This file represents the drivingInBe.cptx project as it should be by the end of this chapter. Don't hesitate to take some time to examine the other features of this project, especially the timing of the objects. When done, return to slide 12. It should contain five Smart Shapes with text, 12 road sign images, and one Character image.

2. Take a look at the **Timeline** panel to see how the objects of this slide are organized. Notice that the road sign images appear two-tenths of a second apart from one another.

3. Select any of the road sign images and open the **Effects** panel. The **FlipFromCenter** effect is applied to the first **0.5** seconds of each and every road sign.

4. Use the preview **Next 5 slides** feature to test the slide.

5. If necessary, adjust the timing of the objects as well as the timing of the animations to your liking.

6. Don't forget to save the file when done.

This little experiment concludes your overview of effects in Captivate. Feel free to experiment further by applying other effects to other objects. The possibilities are endless and this book only shows a few examples of what is possible.

Before wrapping up this chapter, this is a list of what you have learned about effects:

- It is possible to add effects to any object of Captivate.
- By default, the **Effects** panel is not displayed on the Captivate interface. Use the **Window | Effects** menu item to turn it on.
- In the bottom-left corner of the **Effects** panel, the Add Effect icon contains a large collection of effects to choose from.
- Effects can be combined to create sophisticated animations.

Effects in HTML5

When it comes to HTML5 compliance, each effect falls under one of these three categories:

Some effects are not at all supported in HTML5. In Captivate, these effects are identified by a small star (*) by their names.

A double star (**) identifies the effects that are partially supported in HTML5. These effects will look different in the HTML5 output compared to the Flash (.swf) output.

The remaining effects are fully supported in both the HTML5 and Flash output and can be used with no restrictions at all.

Summary

At the end of this chapter, don't hesitate to use the **Preview** | **Project** icon on the Big Buttons Bar to take a look at both projects as a whole and be amazed at the job that has already been done!

In this chapter, you have learned how to use various tools to lay out, animate, and synchronize the elements of your eLearning project. These tools include the Smart Guides, the Align toolbar, the **Effects** panel and, of course, the **Timeline**.

Used individually, these tools are great, but they are most effective when used in combination.

By syncing the elements of the slides, you have reached another milestone in the postproduction phase of your eLearning projects. However, we still have work to do. One of the most impressive capabilities of Captivate is its ability to generate highly interactive animations.

In the next chapter, you will learn how to build this interactivity, which will take your projects to an even higher level.

Meet the community

In this section, I want to introduce you to Kevin Siegel. He is an awesome technical writer and has written several Adobe Captivate courses. As an Adobe Captivate Certified Instructor, I teach a lot of Captivate classes for various customers using Kevin's courseware. Besides authoring courseware, he maintains a great blog on Captivate and eLearning that you will definitely want to bookmark.

Kevin Siegel

Kevin Siegel is the Founder and President of IconLogic, Inc. He has written more than 100 step-by-step computer training books on Adobe Captivate, Adobe RoboDemo, Adobe DreamWeaver, QuarkXPress, Adobe InDesign, Camtasia Studio, and more.

He spent 5 years in The United States Coast Guard as an award-winning photojournalist and has more than two decades of experience as a print publisher, technical writer, instructional designer, and eLearning developer. He is a certified technical trainer, has been a classroom instructor for more than 20 years, and is a frequent speaker at trade shows and conventions. He holds multiple certifications from companies such as Adobe and the CompTIA.

His company, IconLogic, offers online trainings on Captivate that are attended by students worldwide. The company also offers full development and one-on-one mentoring on Captivate and other eLearning development tools.

Contact details

- **Kevin's e-mail**: ksiegel@iconlogic.com
- **IconLogic's website**: http://www.iconlogic.com/
- **IconLogic's blog**: http://www.iconlogic.com/

6

Working with
Interactive Objects

In this chapter, you will continue the postproduction phase of your project by adding interactivity to your online courses. This will make them even more interesting, engaging, and fun to use.

This interactivity is made possible by three interactive objects (the Click Box, the Text Entry Box, and the Button) that have the ability to stop the playhead and wait for the learner to do or to type something. This introduces a whole new level of complexity to the projects, as the student shall receive feedback that depends on the action being performed. So, you will have to analyze the clicks and answers of the students and act accordingly. This concept is known as **branching**.

Captivate also provides three types of Rollover objects. Even though Rollover objects don't stop the playhead, they do provide some kind of interactivity. These objects are hidden by default and are revealed when the student rolls the mouse over a sensitive area. Finally, Captivate includes an exciting feature named the **Drag and Drop interaction**. You will discover how you can use this feature to add some advanced interactivity to your eLearning content.

Thanks to these interactive objects and features, you will be able to convert your existing demonstration into a simulation. Other important tools, such as the **Find and Replace** feature, will be unveiled along the way.

In this chapter, you will learn how to:

- Insert buttons to give students more control over the timing of the project
- Insert Rollover Captions, Rollover Images, and Rollover Slidelets for enhanced interactivity
- Convert a Smart Shape into a Rollover Smart Shape

- Convert your existing demonstration into a simulation by replacing the Mouse object by Click Boxes and Text Entry Boxes
- Use the Drag and Drop Interaction to add some sophisticated and exciting interactivity to your content

This will make for another chapter full of surprises and discoveries.

Preparing your work

To get the most out of this chapter, remember to reset your workspace. If you are using the default interface mode, restarting Captivate is enough to reset your workspace to default. If you are using the advanced interface mode, use the **Window | Workspace | Reset 'Classic'** menu item to reset the workspace to default.

In this chapter, you will use the exercise files located in the Chapter06 folder of the download associated with this book. If you get confused by any of the step-by-step instructions, take a look at the Chapter06/final folder, which contains a copy of the exercises as they will be at the end of this chapter.

Working with Buttons

The Button object is the first interactive object of Captivate you will focus on. Remember that an interactive object has the ability to stop the playhead and wait for the student to do something.

In the case of a Button, a simple click triggers an action. Despite its apparent simplicity, the Button object is an essential part of every Captivate project as it lets the student control the timing of the online course.

In this exercise, you will add a Button below the video file you inserted in *Chapter 5, Working with the Timeline and Other Useful Tools*, by performing the following steps:

1. Open the Chapter06/encoderDemo_800.cptx file.
2. Use the **Filmstrip** panel to go to slide 2.
3. Go to the **Interactions | Button** icon of the Big Buttons Bar to insert a new Button on the slide. Alternatively, you can also use the *Shift + Ctrl + B* (Windows) or the *Shift + cmd + B* (Mac) keyboard shortcut.

4. With the new Button selected, open the **Properties** panel.

When a Button is selected on the stage, the **Properties** panel shows the properties that are relevant to a Button. Take a look at the three tabs available, as shown in the following screenshot:

The **Actions** tab is displayed in addition to the usual **Style** and **Options** tabs. The **Actions** tab of the **Properties** panel only appears when an interactive object is selected.

5. In the **Style** tab of the **Properties** panel, change the Button **Caption** to Continue.

6. Take some time to inspect the other properties available in the **Style** tab of the **Properties** panel, but do not change any of them at this time.

7. Switch to the **Actions** tab of the **Properties** panel.

8. Open the **On Success** drop-down list and take some time to browse the available options. When done, choose the **Go to the next slide** option.

9. Increase the size of the Button so the new text fits comfortably in the object.

When increasing the size of the Button, think about learners taking the course on a mobile device with a touch screen. They will appreciate the bigger tap target offered by the bigger button.

10. Position the new Button in the bottom-right corner of the slide below the video (remember to select the video to reveal its boundaries).

Now that the Button has the right look and performs the right action, you need to arrange it on the **Timeline** panel. The Button is an interactive object that stops the playhead so there are a few more options than usual to take care of.

On the **Timeline** panel, the Button object is separated into two areas. As shown in the following screenshot, the separator between the two areas is a pause symbol. It represents the exact moment when the Button stops the playhead and waits for the student to click:

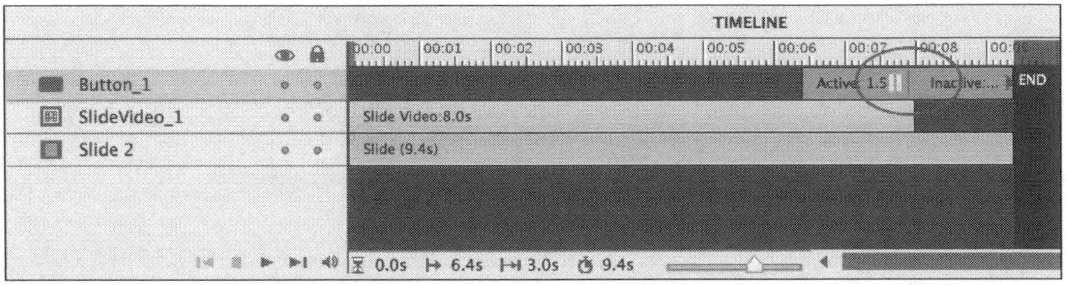

When the Button is clicked, the action set in the **On Success** drop-down menu of the **Actions** tab happens. In this case, the action is **Go to the next slide**. It means that when the learner clicks on the Button, the playhead will jump from the pause symbol directly to the first frame of the next slide. Consequently, the frames of slide 2 situated after the pause symbol of the Button will not be played.

11. Use the **Timeline** or the **Timing** panel to:
    ° Set **Appear After** to 6.5 seconds
    ° Set **Pause After** to 1.4 seconds
    ° Set **Display For** to **Rest of Slide**

12. Make sure the **Timeline** panel looks like the preceding screenshot.

13. Go to **Preview | Next 5 slides** on the Big Buttons Bar to test the new button.

The Button should appear at the end of the video file and pause the playhead more or less on the last frame of the video. When you click on the Button, the playhead jumps to the next slide and the project continues as usual.

Formatting Buttons

In this section, you will use the **Properties** panel to explore some of the properties of the Button object using the following steps:

1. Still on slide 2 of the Chapter06/encoderDemo_800.cptx file, make sure the new Button is selected.

2. Return to the **Style** tab of the **Properties** panel and open the **Text Button** drop-down menu.

This drop-down menu lists the three types of Buttons available in Captivate:

- **Text Button**: This is the default choice. It is a simple Button whose text can be customized in the **Properties** panel.

- **Transparent Button**: This is a transparent area that serves as a Button. Consider it as a sensitive area that can be added on top of a background picture.

- **Image Button**: This Button is an image (actually a set of three images) that is used as a Button. Captivate provides quite a few predesigned buttons, but you can also create your own buttons in an image-editing tool and import them in Captivate.

In this exercise, you will create a Button from an image that is on your hard disk using the **Image Button** option.

3. Choose the **Image Button** option in the drop-down menu.

4. Take some time to inspect the list of predefined buttons provided by Captivate.

5. Next to the **Image Button** dropdown, click on the folder icon. Choose the `images/buttons/mftcContinue_up.png` file of the download associated with this book.

When browsing for the image file, note that the `images/buttons` folder contains three versions of each button, as shown in the following screenshot:

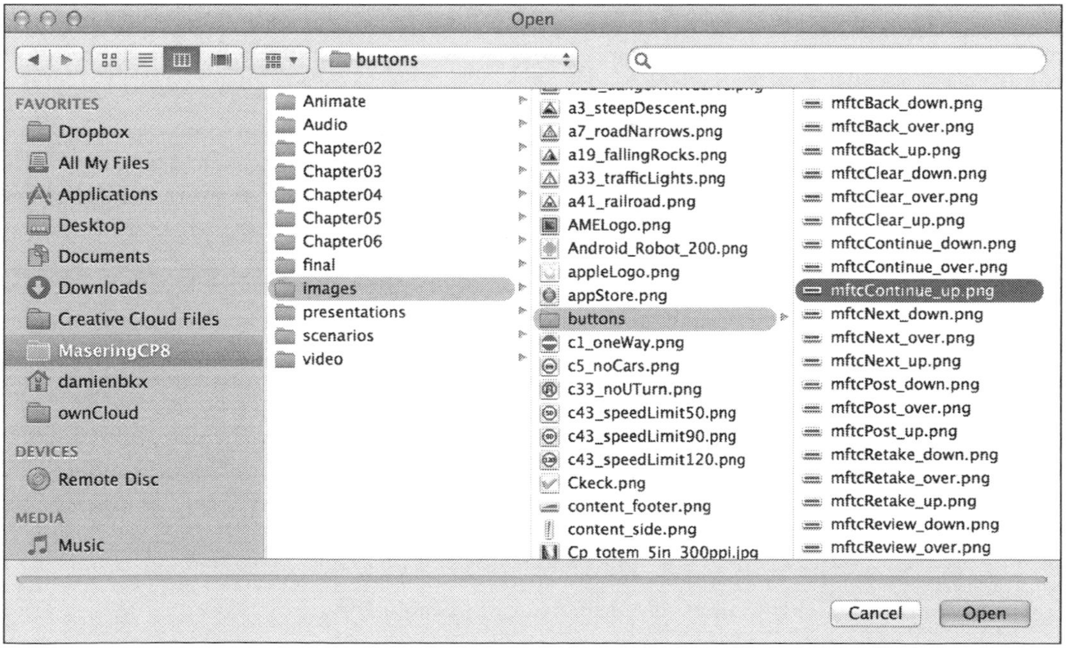

- One version ends with _up. It is the normal state of the Button.

- Another version ends with _over. It is used to change the appearance of the Button when the student rolls the mouse over the Button.

- The third version ends with _down. It is used when the student has the mouse over the Button and presses the mouse Button at the same time.

Captivate is able to recognize these three states providing that all three images are stored in the same location and that they share the very same name (with the exception of the _up, _over, and _down suffixes).

6. Save the file and go to **Preview | Next 5 slides** on the Big Buttons Bar to test the button.

7. When the Button appears on the stage, the _up image is used by default.

8. Roll your mouse over the Button without clicking to see the _over state of the Button.

9. Click and hold on the mouse button to see the _down state of the Button.

10. It is when you release the mouse button that the action specified in the **On Success** menu of the **Actions** tab of the **Properties** panel (in this case, **Go to the next slide**) is performed.

11. Close the **Preview** window and save the file when done.

This exercise concludes your first overview of the Button object of Captivate. In the next section, you will discover yet another feature of the Smart Shape object.

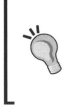

Finding the Image Buttons

When choosing **Image Button** in the **Style** tab of the **Properties** panel, Captivate offers a list of predefined Image Buttons you can choose from. The image assets pertaining to these Buttons are located at [Captivate install Path]/Gallery/buttons. This folder also includes a More subfolder that contains a few extra Image Buttons that do not appear in the **Properties** panel by default.

Using Smart Shapes as Buttons

Still not convinced by the awesomeness of Smart Shapes? This section will give you yet another argument to convince you after all!

1. Return to the Chapter06/drivingInBe.cptx file.

2. Use the **Filmstrip** to go to slide 9 of the project.

3. Use the **Shapes** icon of the Big Buttons Bar toolbar to open the Smart Shape library.

4. Select the Left Arrow shape and draw a left arrow in the left area of the slide.

5. Repeat the same set of actions to draw a Right Arrow in the right area of the slide.

6. With the Right Arrow shape selected, turn your attention to the **Style** tab of the **Properties** panel.

7. In the **Right Arrow** section, change the shape to a Right Arrow Callout. This operation is shown in the following screenshot:

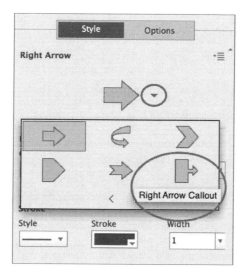

8. Repeat the same set of actions to turn the Left Arrow shape into a Left Arrow Callout shape.

9. Use the tools of the Align toolbar and the Smart Guides to give the same size to both Smart Shapes and to align them properly on the slide (it may be necessary to make the Align toolbar visible by using the **Window** | **Align** menu item).

When done, your slide should look like the following screenshot:

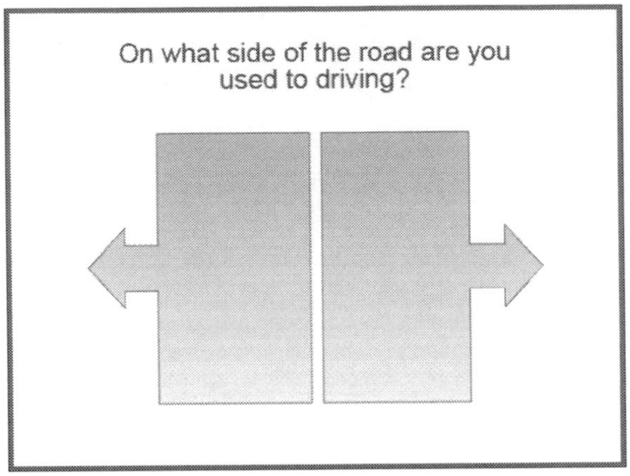

10. Double-click on the Smart Shape on the left and write `I'm used to driving on the left side of the road.`

11. Double-click on the Smart Shape on the right and write `I'm used to driving on the right side of the road.`

You now have two Smart Shapes in place on your slide. It's time to move on to the core of this exercise and turn these Smart Shapes into Buttons.

12. Take some time to inspect the **Properties** panel of these Smart Shapes.

The **Properties** panel should contain the usual **Style** and **Options** tab as for any other standard Captivate objects.

13. At the top of the **Properties** panel, select the **Use as Button** checkbox.

The **Actions** tab appears in the **Properties** panel to let you control the Button's behavior.

14. Repeat the preceding procedure for the second Smart Shape of the slide.

You will now arrange these two new Buttons on the **Timeline** panel.

15. Use the **Timeline** or the **Timing** panel to make both Buttons appear after 0 seconds and display for the **Rest of Slide**.

16. Also, make sure that the **Pause After** checkbox is selected to have both Smart Shape Buttons pause the playhead at **1.5** seconds into the slide.

17. Finally, select the Text Caption present on this slide and use the **Timing** section of the **Properties** panel to make it appear after 0 seconds and display for the **Rest of Slide**.

Make sure the **Timeline** panel of slide 9 looks like the following screenshot before continuing with this exercise:

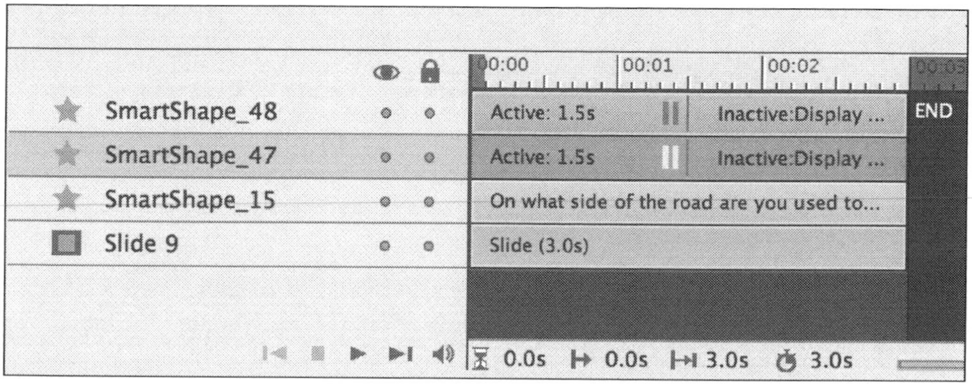

In the next chapter, you will change the formatting of these two buttons and discover yet another great new feature of Captivate 8. But for now, let's move on to the next section.

Branching with Buttons

Branching refers to providing a customized experience to learners based on their actions in the project. In this exercise, you will create two different paths in the movie. If the learner clicks on the **I'm used to driving on the right side of the road** Smart Shape, he should be redirected to slide 10 where specific feedback is provided. But if the learner clicks on the **I'm used to driving on the left side of the road** Smart Shape, she should be redirected to slide 11 where she will be shown a different feedback specific to the second answer. Use the following steps to set this branching up:

1. If needed, return to slide 9 of the `Chapter06/drivingInBe.cptx` file.
2. Select the **I'm used to driving on the right side of the road** Smart Shape.
3. In the **Actions** section of the **Properties** panel, change the **On Success** action to **Jump to slide**.
4. Select slide 10 in the dropdown that appears below.
5. Select the **I'm used to driving on the left side of the road** Smart Shape.
6. In the **Actions** section of the **Properties** panel, change the **On Success** action to **Jump to slide 11**.
7. Use the **Filmstrip** panel to go to slide 10 of the project.

8. Use the **Shapes** icon of the Big Buttons Bar to draw a rounded rectangle in the bottom right corner of the slide.

9. Double-click in the new rounded rectangle and write Continue in it. Use the *Esc* key when done to quit text edit mode and leave the shape selected.

10. At the top of the **Properties** panel, select the **Use as Button** checkbox.

11. In the **Action** tab of the **Properties** panel, change the **On Success** action of the selected Button to **Jump to slide 12**.

12. Open the **Timeline** panel (if needed) and move the new button to the end of the timeline.

The branching is now in place. You've effectively provided two different paths within your Captivate project. The chosen path depends on how the student answers the question on slide 9.

13. Save the file, return to slide 9 and use the **Preview | Next 5 slides** icon to test your sequence. Make sure you test both sides of the branching before moving on.

This concludes your first overview of the Button object. Let's make a quick listing of what has been covered in this section:

- The Button object is one of the interactive objects of Captivate.

- As such, the Button object is able to pause the playhead and wait for the student to interact with the online course.

- When an interactive object is selected, the **Properties** panel shows the **Actions** tab in addition to the **Style** and **Options** tabs.

- The **Actions** tab of the **Properties** panel is used to define what happens when the Button is clicked.

- Captivate proposes three types of Buttons: **Text Button**, **Transparent Button**, and **Image Button**.

- Because the Button stops the playhead, it is separated into two areas on the **Timeline** panel. The separator represents the exact moment when the playhead is stopped.

- Image Buttons use three different images to create the _up, _over, and _down states of the Button.

- It is possible to convert a Smart Shape into a Button. In this case, the **Properties** panel displays the **Actions** tab when the Smart Shape is selected to let you define the action to perform when the Smart Shape is being clicked.

The Button object and pedagogy

Two of the most important things to keep in mind while teaching are: to keep the students focused and to adapt your technique to each student (the latter is known as **differentiated instruction**). Basically, it means that it is the course that has to adapt to the student and not the other way around (see http://en.wikipedia.org/wiki/Differentiated_instruction for more). The Button object helps you in both these aspects. While watching a long demonstration, your students' attention will inevitably drift away from the course. Each time you add a Button, you make the students active which helps in refreshing their attention. Another benefit of the Button is that it lets each student manage the timing of the course. If you have a slide with a lot of text, it is a good idea to pause the playhead with a Button and let each student read the slide at his or her own pace.

Discovering the Rollover objects

In this section, you will discover three more objects. These objects are known as the **Rollover objects**, because they are initially hidden and show only when the user *rolls over* a specific area of the slide. This very behavior makes the Rollover objects impossible to use on touch devices such as tablets and smartphones. This is the reason why the Rollover objects are not supported in the HTML5 output of Captivate. Nevertheless, these objects are an excellent addition to any Flash-based project and are still an important part of the Captivate toolset.

Working with Rollover Captions

A **Rollover Caption** is a Text Caption that appears when the user places the mouse over a specific spot on the slide. Such a spot is known as the **Rollover Area**.

In the next exercise, you will add a Rollover Caption to the *Driving in Belgium* project by performing the following steps:

1. Return to slide 10 of the Chapter06/drinvinInBe.cptx file.

2. Select the new **Continue** button you added in the previous exercise and copy it (*Ctrl + C* on Windows or *cmd + C* on the Mac).

3. Use the **Filmstrip** panel to go to slide 14.

4. Paste the **Continue** button (*Ctrl + V* on Windows or *cmd + V* on Mac).

5. Make sure the **On Success** action of the Button is set to **Go to the next slide**.

6. In the **Timeline** panel, move the **Continue** button to the right until its pause symbol corresponds to the moment the audio narration finishes.

Slide 14 now contains two Smart Shapes with text, four images, and the **Continue** Button that pauses the playhead at around 6 seconds into the slide. The text in the top-right corner of the slide explains what you will achieve in this exercise.

7. Go to the **Objects | Rollover Caption** icon of the Big Buttons Bar to insert a new Rollover Caption. Alternately, you can use the *cmd + Shift + R* (Mac) or *Ctrl + Shift + R* (Windows) shortcut to perform the same action.

A Rollover Caption inserts two objects on the slide. The first object is a basic Text Caption. The second object is the associated Rollover Area. The Text Caption shows only *if* and *when* the student rolls the mouse over the associated Rollover Area.

8. Change the text of the Rollover Caption to `No parking is allowed at any time!`. When done, hit the *Esc* key to leave text edit mode and select the object.

9. Use the **Style** tab of the **Properties** panel to increase the font size to **28** points.

10. Resize the caption so the text comfortably fits on one line and use the Smart Guides to position it to the right of the first road sign.

11. Select the Rollover Area and position it, more or less, over the first road sign. Don't hesitate to resize the Rollover Area if necessary.

12. With the Rollover Area selected, turn your attention to the **Style** tab of the **Properties** panel.

13. In the **Fill** section, set the **Opacity** value to **0%**.

14. In the **Stroke** section set the stroke **Width** to **0**. The Rollover Area is now invisible.

15. Use the **Timeline** or the **Timing** panel to make the Rollover Area appear after 1 second and display for the **Rest of Slide**.

When done, the slide should look like the following screenshot:

16. Go to **Preview** | **Next 5 slides** on the Big Buttons Bar to test the Rollover Caption.

The Text Caption is not displayed by default. It appears only *if* and *when* you roll your mouse over the Rollover Area.

17. Close the **Preview** pane and save the file when done.

Working with Rollover Smart Shapes

In *Chapter 3*, *Working with Standard Objects*, you discovered the awesome Smart Shape object. You used it to draw a rounded rectangle around the Belgian border image. You also typed text into the Curved Up Ribbon Smart Shape and used it as a Button earlier in this chapter. You will now discover yet more goodies of this type of object by performing the following steps:

1. Return to slide 14 of the `drivingInBe.cptx` file.

2. Select either the Rollover Area or the Rollover Caption that you added in the previous section.

3. Delete the selected object.

Note that both the Rollover Area and the associated Text Captions are deleted even though only one of these two objects was selected.

4. Use the **Shapes** icon of the Big Buttons Bar to insert a left arrow Smart Shape. Place it roughly to the right of the topmost road sign to replace the Text Caption you deleted in the previous step.

5. Use the **Style** tab of the **Properties** panel to convert the new left arrow into a Left Arrow Callout.

Note that there are three yellow squares around that particular Smart Shape. Each one of these yellow squares can be used to modify the Smart Shape in a specific way.

6. Use the yellow squares and the Smart Guides to make your Smart Shape look like the one in the following screenshot:

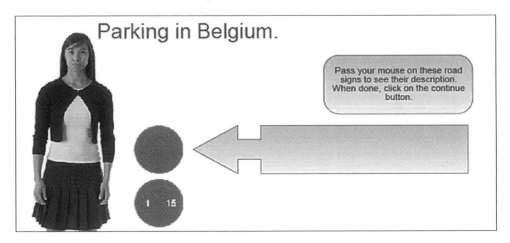

Now that the Smart Shape has the right size and the right location, you will write text into it. After that, you will duplicate it to create the remaining two Smart Shapes that are needed on this slide.

7. Double-click on the Smart Shape.

8. Type No parking is allowed at any time!. Hit the *Esc* key when done to leave text edit mode and select the shape.

9. With the Smart Shape selected, use the *Ctrl + D* (Windows) or *cmd + D* (Mac) shortcut to duplicate it. Alternatively, you can also use the **Edit | Duplicate** menu item.

10. Repeat the preceding operation to create a third copy of the Smart Shape.

11. Use the Smart Guides and/or the tools of the Align toolbar (you might need to turn it on) to position the Smart Shapes to the right of each road sign image and to align them together.

12. Change the text of the middle Smart Shape to No parking allowed between the 1st and the 15th of the month.

13. Change the text of the bottom Smart Shape to `No parking allowed between the 16th and the 31st of the month.`

So far so good, there is nothing new in this exercise. Now that the stage is set, it is time to uncover another great feature of Smart Shapes: the **Rollover Smart Shape**.

You will now associate a Rollover Area with each Smart Shape on slide 14. At runtime, the Smart Shapes will be hidden by default. They will become visible only *if* and *when* the student rolls the mouse over the corresponding Rollover Area.

14. Make sure you are still on slide 14 of the `drivingInBe.cptx` file.

15. Right-click on the topmost Smart Shape.

16. Choose the **Convert to rollover Smart Shape** item in the contextual menu.

The Smart Shape is converted into a Rollover Smart Shape and a corresponding Rollover Area appears on the slide.

17. Move and resize the Rollover Area so it roughly covers the topmost road sign.

18. Make the Rollover Area invisible. To do so, go to the **Style** tab of the **Properties** panel and reduce the fill **Opacity** to **0%** and the stroke **Width** to **0**.

19. Repeat this sequence of actions with the remaining two Smart Shapes.

20. Use the **Timeline** or the **Timing** panel to make all three Rollover Areas appear after 1 second and display for the rest of slide.

21. Use the **Preview** | **Next 5 slides** icon to test your sequence.

22. When done, close the preview pane and save the file.

The ability to convert a Smart Shape to a Rollover Smart Shape is yet another feature that makes the Smart Shape object awesome!

This concludes the overview of the Rollover Caption and Rollover Smart Shape objects. Here is a quick review of the key points discussed in this section:

- Inserting a Rollover Caption adds two objects to the Slide.

- The first object is a regular Text Caption. The second object is a corresponding Rollover Area.

- At runtime, the Text Caption appears if and when the learner rolls the mouse over the Rollover Area.

- When a Smart Shape is converted to a Rollover Smart Shape, a corresponding Rollover Area appears on the stage.

- A Rollover Smart Shape is not displayed by default. At runtime, it shows only if and when the student rolls his or her mouse over the corresponding Rollover Area.

- The Rollover objects of Captivate are not supported in the HTML5 output.

Now that you know how the Rollover Captions and Rollover Smart Shapes work, the next object is a piece of cake.

Working with Rollover Images

A **Rollover Image** is an image that shows only *if* and *when* the learner rolls the mouse over a corresponding Rollover Area.

In the next exercise, you will add three Rollover Images to the `drivingInBe.cptx` project by performing the following steps:

1. If needed, return to slide 14 of the `Chapter06/drinvinInBe.cptx` project.

2. Select the new **Continue** button and copy it (*Ctrl + C* on Windows or *cmd + C* on the Mac).

3. Use the **Filmstrip** panel to go to slide 15.

4. Paste the **Continue** button (*Ctrl + V* on Windows or *cmd + V* on the Mac).

5. In the **Timeline** panel, move the **Continue** button to the right until its pause symbol corresponds to the moment the audio narration finishes.

Slide 15 now contains five Smart Shapes with text, one image, and a button that pauses the playhead at around 9.5 seconds into the slide. The text in the top-right corner explains it all!

6. Use the **Objects | Rollover Image** icon of the Big Buttons bar to insert a new Rollover Image. Alternatively, you can use the *cmd + Shift + O* (Mac) or *Ctrl + Shift + O* (Windows) shortcut to perform the same action.

7. Browse the exercise folder for the `images/priority.png` image and click on **Open** to insert it onto the slide.

As with Rollover Captions and Rollover Smart Shapes, a Rollover Image inserts two objects on the slide: an image and its corresponding Rollover Area. At runtime, the image is displayed only *if* and *when* the learner rolls the mouse over the rollover area.

8. Use the Smart Guides and/or the tools of the Align toolbar to place the image to the right of the text that says **I have the right of the way**.

9. Move and resize the Rollover Area so it roughly covers the **I have the right of the way** Text Caption.

10. In the **Style** tab of the **Properties** panel, make the Rollover Area invisible by reducing its fill **Opacity** to **0%** and its stroke **Width** to **0**.

11. Use the **Timeline** or the **Timing** panel to make the Rollover Area appear after 5.5 seconds and display for the rest of slide.

12. Add two more Rollover Images with the same formatting and timing properties:

   ○ Use the `images/noPriority.png` file for the first one. Position it to the right of the **I do not have the right of the way** text. Move and resize the Rollover Area appropriately.

   ○ Use the `images/PriorityRight.png` image for the second one. Position it to the right of the **Those coming from the right hand side have the right of the way** text.

When done, slide 15 should look like the following screenshot:

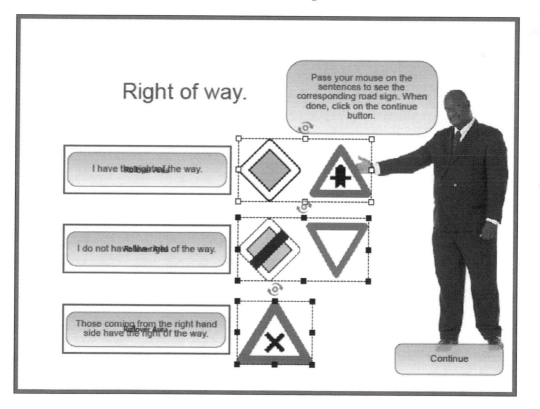

13. Save the file when done.

14. Use the **Filmstrip** panel to return to slide 14. Go to **Preview | Next 5 Sides** on the Big Buttons Bar to test your Rollover Smart Shapes and your Rollover images.

On these two slides (14 and 15), the role of the **Continue** button is critical in making the Rollover system work. It stops the playhead and lets the students go through the Rollover objects at their own pace and in the order they want. This is yet another example of the differentiated instruction concept.

Before moving on to the last rollover object, here is a quick summary of what has been covered in this section:

- The Rollover Image adds two objects to the slide: an image and its corresponding Rollover Area
- When the project is played back, the image shows only if and when the student rolls the mouse over the corresponding Rollover Area
- The Rollover Image object is not supported in the HTML5 output

Working with Rollover Slidelets

The last Rollover object of Captivate is the **Rollover Slidelet**. As with every other Rollover object of Captivate, the Rollover Slidelet adds two objects to the slide: the Slidelet itself and its corresponding Rollover Area.

Inserting and formatting a Rollover Slidelet

In this exercise, you will add a Rollover Slidelet to the *Driving in Belgium* project. Your first task will be to add one extra slide in the project before placing a Rollover Slidelet onto it using the following steps:

1. Open the `Chapter06/slidelet.cptx` file of the download associated with this book.
2. In the **Filmstrip**, click on the only slide of the project to select it.
3. Use the *Ctrl* + *C* (Windows) or *cmd* + *C* (Mac) shortcut to copy the slide.
4. Return to the `Chapter06/drinvingInBe.cptx` file and use the **Filmstrip** panel to go to slide 12.
5. Use the *Ctrl* + *V* (Windows) or *cmd* + *V* (Mac) shortcut to paste the slide.

The new slide is inserted as slide 13 of the project. With the addition of this new slide, the project now contains 16 slides in total.

If you take a closer look at the new slide 13 and at slide 14, you'll notice that they have pretty much the same content. Slide 13 is the slide on which you will add the Rollover Slidelet, which is an object that is not supported in the HTML5 output. Slide 14 contains animations imported from Edge Animate, which are not supported in the Flash output. Slide 14 will therefore be used in the HTML5 output only, and slide 13 in the Flash output only. In *Chapter 13, Finishing Touches and Publishing*, you will learn how to publish the project in Flash and in HTML5. You will also learn how to hide a slide from the publishing process. But for now, let's insert a Rollover Slidelet using the following steps.

6.   Use the **Objects | Rollover Slidelet** icon of the Big Buttons Bar to create a new Rollover Slidelet. Alternatively, you can use the *cmd + Shift + Z* (Mac) or *Ctrl + Shift + Z* (Windows) shortcut to perform the same action.

7.   Move the selected object anywhere on the slide so that it does not overlap with the object with a thick blue border.

8.   Click on the object with the thick blue border to select it.

The selected object is called the Rollover Slidelet Area. It is used as the Rollover Area of the Rollover Slidelet. You will position it on top of the **Convert Speeds to MPH** Text Caption and make it transparent.

9.   Move and resize the selected object so it roughly covers the **Convert to MPH** text.

10.   In the **Style** tab of the **Properties** panel, deselect the **Show Border** and **Show Runtime Border** checkboxes.

By deselecting the **Show Border** checkbox, you make the Rollover Slidelet Area invisible. The **Show Runtime Border** checkbox adds a border that is visible at runtime when the student rolls over the Rollover Slidelet Area.

11.   In the **Timeline** or in the **Timing** panel, make the Rollover Slidelet appear after 16 seconds and display for the rest of slide.

As expected, the **Timeline** panel shows a list of all the objects that are present on the slide. There should be 14 objects in addition to the slide itself.

12. Click on the other object of the Rollover Slidelet system to make it the active object.

The selected object is the actual Slidelet. It is the object that will appear on the slide only if and when the learner rolls the mouse over the **Convert to MPH** text.

Take another look at the **Timeline** panel and note that the objects of the slide are not listed anymore. This is because the timeline you are viewing at the moment is not the timeline of the slide, but the timeline of the Rollover Slidelet. This helps in understanding what a Rollover Slidelet really is.

A Rollover Slidelet is a slide within a slide. Consequently, objects (such as Text Captions, images, and so on) can be inserted inside the Rollover Slidelet and arranged on its timeline. At runtime, the Slidelet appears and plays its own timeline only if and when the student rolls the mouse over the corresponding Rollover Slidelet Area.

You will now give the Slidelet the correct size, position, and format. Make sure the Slidelet is selected and perform the following actions:

13. In the **Options** tab of the **Properties** panel, deselect the **Constrain proportions** checkbox.

14. Give the Slidelet a **Width** value of **630** pixels and a **Height** value of **260** pixels.

15. Go to the **Window | Align** menu item to turn the Align toolbar on if necessary.

With the Slidelet selected, take a look at the Align toolbar. Only two icons should be available. These icons are named Center Horizontally on the Slide/Slidelet and Center Vertically on the Slide/Slidelet.

16. Click on both these icons to position the Slidelet exactly at the center of the stage.

17. In the **Style** tab of the **Properties** panel, increase the Fill **Opacity** of the Slidelet to **90** %.

Your slide should now look like the following screenshot:

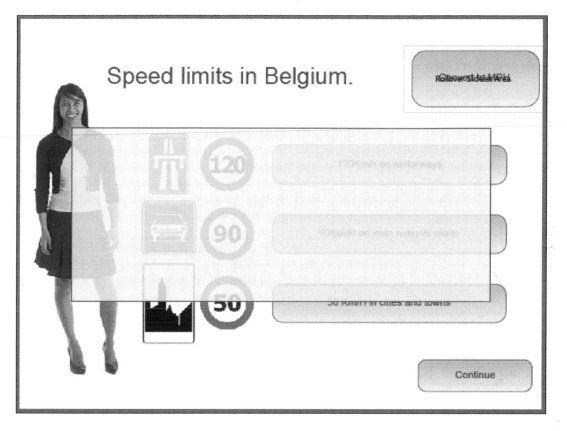

Inserting objects in a Rollover Slidelet

Now that the Rollover Slidelet is ready, you will insert three Text Captions in the Slidelet and organize them on its timeline by performing the following steps:

1. To make sure the Slidelet is the active object, take a look at the **Timeline** panel and confirm it shows the **Timeline** panel of the Slidelet, not the **Timeline** panel of the slide (no objects should appear on the **Timeline** panel).

2. Use the **Text | Text Caption** icon of the Big Buttons Bar to insert a new Text Caption in the Slidelet.

With the Slidelet selected, take some time to open the icons of the Big Buttons Bar one by one. Note that some of the objects are grayed out. It means that these objects cannot be inserted in a Slidelet. These objects are the interactive objects of Captivate, the Mouse and, of course, the Rollover Slidelet itself!

3. Type `Motorways - 120 km/H is approx. 80 MPH` in the new Text Caption and hit *Esc* to leave text edit mode and select the Text Caption.

4. In the **Style** tab of the **Properties** panel, increase the font size to **24** points.

5. Resize the Text Caption so the text comfortably fits on a single line and position it in the upper area of the Slidelet.

6. Use the same procedure to add two more Text Captions in the Slidelet:

   ° Type `National roads - 90 Km/h is approx and 60 MPH` in the second Text Caption

   ° Type `Cities and towns - 50 Km/h is approx. 30 MPH` in the third Text Caption

7. Use the tools from the Align toolbar and the Smart Guides to position the three Text Captions properly within the Slidelet.

8. In the **Timeline** or in the **Timing** panel, extend the duration of the Slidelet to 15 seconds.

9. Arrange the three Text Captions using the following properties:

   ° The topmost Caption appears after 0 seconds and displays for the rest of Slidelet

   ° The middle Caption appears after 2 seconds and displays for the rest of Slidelet

   ° The bottom Caption appears after 4 seconds and displays for the rest of Slidelet

10. Select all three Text Captions and use the **Timing** panel to apply a **Fade In Only** transition to all three Text Captions.

The **Timeline** panel of your Rollover Slidelet should now look like the following screenshot:

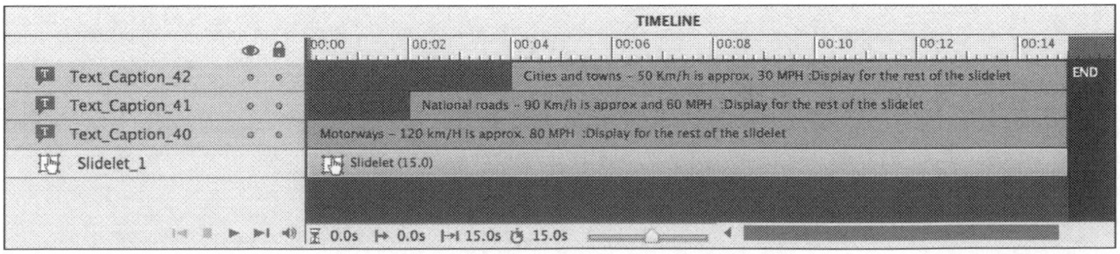

11. Save the file and use the **Preview | Next 5 Slides** icon of the Big Buttons Bar to test your sequence.

When you're finished previewing your sequence, close the **Preview** pane.

This exercise concludes your exploration of the Rollover Slidelet. Before moving on to the next topic, let's summarize what you have learned in this section:

- Like every other Rollover object, the Rollover Slidelet adds two objects to the slide: the Slidelet and a corresponding Rollover Area.

- During the playback, the Slidelet shows only if and when the student passes the mouse over the associated rollover area.

- A Rollover Slidelet is a slide within a slide. As such, it has its own timeline.

- Most standard Captivate objects can be inserted in a Rollover Slidelet.

- Some objects however cannot be inserted in a Slidelet. These are the interactive objects (Click Box, Text Entry Box, and Button), the Mouse and, of course, the Rollover Slidelet itself.

- The Rollover Slidelet is not supported in the HTML5 output.

This exercise only demonstrates part of what is possible with a Rollover Slidelet. Consult the Adobe Captivate help file at `https://helpx.adobe.com/captivate/using/rollover-slidelets.html` for more on the Rollover Slidelet.

Working with the Drag and Drop interaction

In this section, you will explore some of the amazing possibilities offered by the Drag and Drop interaction. The Drag and Drop interaction requires at least two objects. One serves as the **Drag Source** and the second one as the **Drop Target**.

- The Drag Source is the object that the user has to drag

- The Drop Target is the object onto which a Drag Source can be dropped

It does not matter what those objects are. In this example, you will use images as both the Drag Source and the Drop Target, but you could also use Text Captions, Highlight Boxes, Smart Shapes, and so on.

Of course, to make things more interesting, a single slide can contain multiple Drag Sources as well as multiple Drop Targets. Thanks to this capability, you will be able to quickly and easily create complex and fun interactions. Best of all, the Drag and Drop interaction is supported in both Flash and HTML5.

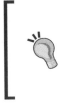

The Drag and Drop interaction in responsive projects

When Captivate 8 was released in May 2014, the Drag and Drop interaction was not supported in responsive projects. This has been fixed in the Captivate 8.0.1 update. You will learn more about responsive projects in *Chapter 9, Creating a Responsive Project.*

Using the Drag and Drop interaction wizard

For this first example, you will create a simple Drag and Drop interaction. The goal is to ask your students how many miles/hour makes 120 kilometers/hour. They will have to drag the right answer and drop it on top of the Drop Target. To create this first Drag and Drop interaction, you will use the Drag and Drop interaction wizard using the following steps:

1. Use the **Filmstrip** panel to go to slide 8 of the `Chapter06/drivingInBe.cptx` project.

As depicted in the following screenshot, this slide contains four images:

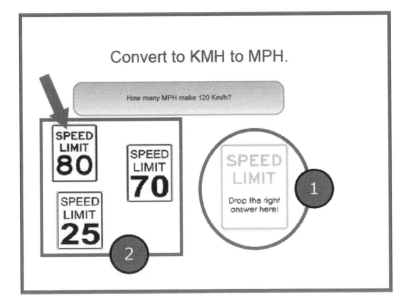

The image identified with the number **1** in the preceding screenshot is the Drop Target. The other three images, identified by the number **2**, are three Drag Sources. These three objects are draggable, but only the image identified by the arrow (the 80 miles per hour image) is the right answer to the question.

2. Use the **Interactions | Drag and Drop** icon of the Big Buttons Bar to start defining your first Drag and Drop interaction.

The Drag and Drop interaction wizard opens. It is a three step procedure that helps you quickly define a simple Drag and Drop interaction. In the first step, you have to select the Drag Sources.

3. Click one by one on all three images identified as number **2** in the preceding screenshot.

As you click, the images are surrounded by a green outline indicating a Drag Source. If you make a mistake and select the wrong object, you can always use the little red minus sign to remove the object from the selection.

4. When all three Drag Sources are selected, click on the **Next** button at the top of the screen.

In the second step of the wizard, you have to choose the objects that serve as Drop Targets. In this example, you have a single Drop Target to select.

5. Select the image identified as **1** in the preceding screenshot to make it a Drop Target.

6. Note that a blue outline is used to identify the Drop Targets.

7. Click on the **Next** button at the top of the screen.

The last step of the wizard is used to tell Captivate the answer to the question by associating the Drag Sources with the correct Drop Target. In this example, you want to associate the 80 miles per hour image (identified by an arrow in the preceding screenshot) with the Drop Target.

8. Select the 80 miles per hour image and move the small circle in the middle of the image on top of the Drop Target.

9. Make sure your slide looks like the following screenshot before you click on the **Finish** button at the top of the screen:

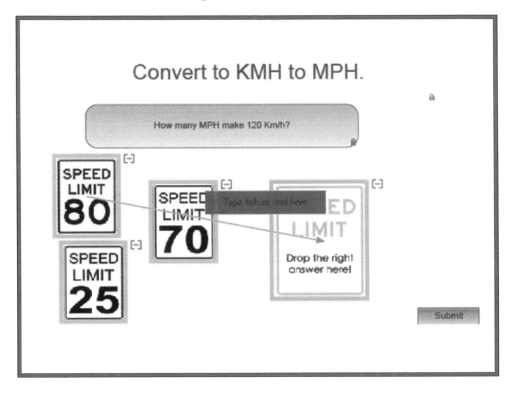

Now, let's apply the finishing touches.

10. Type `Sorry, this is not the right answer` in the red failure caption. When done, hit the *Esc* key to leave text-editing mode and select the object.

11. With the failure caption selected, use the **Style** tab of the **Properties** panel to increase the font size to 28 points and change the text color to white. When done, move and resize the Failure Caption as you see fit.

12. Save the file and use the **Preview | Next 5 Slides** icon to test your first Drag and Drop interaction.

Congratulations! You have created your first Drag and Drop interaction with Captivate! It is not yet perfect, but your students will certainly enjoy this high level of interactivity.

Using the Drag and Drop panel

The power of the Drag and Drop interaction goes way beyond this first example. In the next exercise, you will explore the **Drag and Drop** panel and fine-tune the Drag and Drop interaction you created in the previous section by performing the following steps:

1. Make sure you are still on slide 8 of the `Chapter06/drivingInBe.cptx` project.

2. Open the **Drag And Drop** panel situated on the right-hand edge of the screen next to the **Properties** and **Timing** panels. It may be necessary to click on the **Properties** icon at the right-hand side of the Big Buttons Bar to toggle this panel group on.

The **Drag and Drop** panel contains all the options pertaining to the Drag and Drop interaction. The Drag and Drop interaction wizard that you used in the previous section only gives you access to a very small subset of these options. The **Drag and Drop** panel is divided into three tabs. At the very top of the **Drag and Drop** panel, notice the trash can icon that allows you to delete the Drag and Drop interaction if needed.

3. At the top of the **Drag And Drop** panel, click on the eye icon to remove the red line and display the Drag and Drop interaction on the stage.

4. In the **Actions** tab of the **Drag and Drop** panel, select the **Infinite** checkbox to give your students unlimited attempts to give the right answer.

5. Also select the **Reset All** radio button to have the Drag Sources moved back to their original location when a wrong answer is submitted.

6. Select the Drop Target image (identified by the blue outline).

7. Switch to the **Format** tab of the **Drag And Drop** panel. Open the **Effects** drop-down menu and choose the **Zoom In** effect, as shown in the following screenshot:

8. Select all three Drag Source images.

Note that the **Format** tab of the **Drag And Drop** panel has changed and shows the options pertaining to the Drag Sources objects of the interaction.

9. Open the **Effect** drop-down and choose the **Glow** effect.

10. Save the file and use the **Preview | Next 5 Slides** icon of the Big Buttons Bar to test your updated Drag and Drop interaction.

When testing your interaction, pay close attention to the effects you applied to the Drag Sources and to the Drop target. You should see a yellow glow effect on the Drag Sources and a Zoom In Effect on the Drop Target. You will also see that, when you submit a wrong answer, the Drag Source automatically goes back to its original position.

The Drag and Drop interaction in HTML5

The Drag and Drop interaction is entirely supported in HTML5 except for one little detail. The Glow and Zoom In effects that you added on the Drag Sources and the Drop Target are not supported when the project is published in HTML5.

Using the Drag and Drop interaction for branching and navigation

In this section, you will use the Drag and Drop interaction to enable navigation between the slides of your project using the following steps. This will give you yet another use case for the Drag and Drop interaction as well as another example of the branching concept.

1. Still in the `Chapter06/drivingInBe.cptx` file, use the **Filmstrip** panel to go to slide 4.

Slide 4 contains three images along with a Smart Shape with text. To answer the question, the student has to drag the image that represents the measurement unit he uses to measure speed and drop it on top of the Drop Target image. If the student chooses the Miles per Hour image, he should be redirected to slide 6 where specific feedback is provided. But if he chooses the Kilometer per Hour image, he should be redirected to slide 5. To spice things up a little bit more, you will create this interaction entirely in the **Drag And Drop** panel without using the wizard!

2. Still on slide 4, select the Kilometer per Hour image.

3. In the topmost area of the **Properties** panel, change the name of the image to
   KPH_image and hit the *Enter* key to validate. This operation is illustrated in
   the following screenshot:

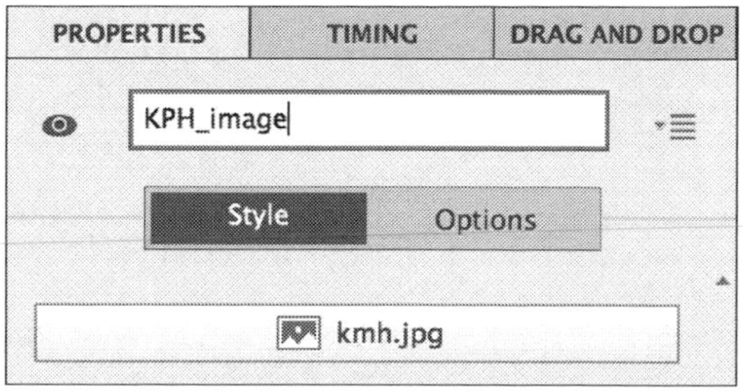

4. Select the miles per hour image and change its name to MPH_image, using the
   same procedure.

These two images will serve as the Drag Sources of your interaction. Naming these
images is not a technical requirement. It only makes the images easier to work with.

5. Select the Kilometer per Hour image and switch to the **Drag And Drop** panel
   (if the **Drag And Drop** panel is not on display, use the **Window | Drag And
   Drop** menu item to turn it on).

6. At the very top of the **Drag And Drop** panel, click on the **Create New
   Interaction** icon as shown in the following screenshot:

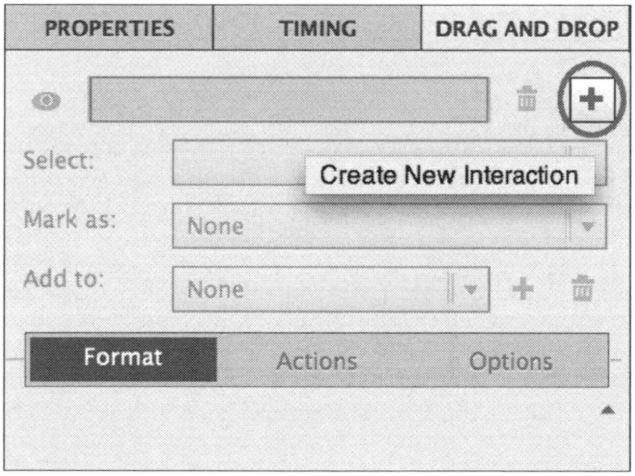

7. With the Kilometer per Hour image selected on the slide, open the **Mark As**
   drop-down menu situated at the top of the **Drag And Drop** panel to mark
   the selected image as a Drag Source.

8. Select the Miles per Hour image.

9. Once selected, mark MPH_image as another Drag Source.

Both MPH_image and KMH_image should be surrounded by a green outline identifying them as Drag Sources.

10. Select the Drop Target image and use the same technique to mark it as a Drop Target. A blue outline should appear around the selected image.

Now that the Drag Sources and the Drop Target of the interaction have been correctly identified, you will define what happens when one or other of the Drag Sources is dropped on the Drop Target.

11. With the Drop Target still selected, go to the **Style** tab of the **Drag And Drop** panel and click on the **Object Actions** button.

12. In the **Accepted Drag Sources** dialog, click on the **No Action** link associated with the KMH_image object.

13. Open the **Action** drop-down menu and choose the **Jump to slide** action. Then use the second drop-down menu to choose **Slide 5** as the destination.

14. Repeat the same sequence of actions to associate the MPH_image object with the **Jump to slide 6** action.

Note how the names of the images come in handy now! Taking the time to properly name the object of your project is a best practice that makes your life easier and saves you a lot of time.

15. Click on the **OK** button to validate and to close the **Accepted Drag Sources** dialog.

The core parameters of your Drag and drop interaction are now in place.
It is time for some fine-tuning.

16. Use the **Drag And Drop** panel to customize your interaction as you see fit. For example, you can add Glow effects on the Drag Sources and Zoom In effects on the Drop Target.

When you are finished, there is one last thing to do to completely wrap up this exercise.

17. Use the **Filmstrip** panel to go to slide 10. Select and copy (*cmd* + *C* on Mac or *Ctrl* + *C* on Windows) the **Continue** button situated at the bottom of the slide.

18. Use the **Filmstrip** panel to return to slide 5 and paste (*cmd* + *V* on Mac or *Ctrl* + *V* on Windows) the **Continue** button.

19. Open the **Timeline** panel and move the button to the right until its pause symbol corresponds to the end of the audio narration.

20. With the button still selected, turn your attention to the **Actions** tab of the **Properties** panel.

21. Change the **On Success** action of the button to **Jump to slide 9**.

With the completion of the preceding exercise, you have created another great branching experience that your student will certainly appreciate! If the student chooses the Kilometer per Hour image, he will be redirected to slide 5 where he will be provided with specific feedback before being sent to slide 9 for the second question. If the student chooses the Miles per Hour image, he will be sent to slide 6 where a sequence of three slides will teach him how to convert Miles per Hour to Kilometers per Hour.

22. While still on slide 4, use the **Preview | From this Slide** icon of the Big Buttons bar to test your Drag and Drop interaction. Make sure to test both branches.

During the preview, note that the actions set for each Drag Source object is triggered without clicking on the **Submit** button, which is therefore useless.

> **Hiding the submit button**
>
> Since there is no way to remove the **Submit** button using the options of the **Drag And Drop** panel, simply move it off the stage in the gray scrap area to remove it from the final project as seen by the students.

In *Chapter 10, Working with Quizzes*, you will create an even more sophisticated Drag and Drop interaction but, for now, let's make a quick summary of what you already know about the Drag and Drop interaction:

- To create a Drag and Drop interaction, you need at least two objects on the slide. One of them is the Drag Source, and the other one is the Drop Target.

- A Drag Source is an object that the student can drag. A Drop Target is an object on top of which a Drag Source can be dropped.

- A single slide can contain multiple Drag Sources and multiple Drop Targets.

- The Drag and Drop interaction wizard is a three step procedure that helps you create a basic Drag and Drop interaction.

- The **Drag And Drop** panel contains every option pertaining to the Drag and Drop interaction. It lets you fine-tune your interaction in many ways or even create an entire Drag and Drop interaction from scratch.

Drag and Drop extravaganza

Drag and Drop extravaganza is the title of an excellent webinar by Dr Allen Partridge, Adobe eLearning evangelist. This webinar will give you a much deeper look at the possibilities of the Drag and Drop interaction. You can access the Drag and Drop extravaganza webinar by following this link `http://www.adobe.com/cfusion/event/index.cfm?event=register_no_session&id=2252370&loc=en_us`. Note that you need a free Adobe ID to access this content.

Creating a simulation

In this section, you will convert the `encoderDemo_800.cptx` demonstration into a simulation. Remember that, when viewing a demonstration, the student is passive and only watches whatever happens on the screen. When viewing a simulation, however, the student is active and has to do things.

Technically, in Captivate, the difference between a demonstration and a simulation resides in the objects being used. The object associated with a demonstration is the Mouse object. Remember that the Mouse object lets you show the mouse on the screen and control its movements. In order to convert the demonstration to a simulation, you'll have to remove the Mouse object from the project.

Hiding the mouse is one thing, but you'll have to replace it with something else. If you think about it, there are two kinds of actions that you need to be able to simulate: clicking and typing. That's why Captivate provides two interactive objects to let you replace the mouse in a simulation. The first object is the Click Box. It is used each time you need to make the student click somewhere. The second object is the Text Entry Box. You will use it when you need the student to type something. Those two interactive objects have the ability to stop the playhead and wait for the learner to interact.

The first step in converting your demonstration to a simulation is to create the `.cptx` file of the simulation using the following procedure:

1. Return to the `encoderDemo_800.cptx` file.

2. Use the **File | Save As** menu item to create another version of this file.

3. Name the file `encoderSim_800.cptx` and save it in the `Chapter06` subfolder of your exercises.

Hiding the Mouse object

Now that the simulation file exists, the next step is to hide the Mouse object.

Hiding or removing?

When it comes to making the Mouse invisible, I use the word hide and not the word remove. This is because the coordinates of the Mouse movement are still saved with the slide even if the Mouse object is not visible. This is done to let you make the Mouse object visible again should you change your mind about hiding the Mouse. Technically, the data pertaining to the Mouse object cannot be removed from the project, hence the word *hide*.

There should be 19 slides in the project. In the **Filmstrip** panel, a mouse icon at the bottom-right corner of the slides' thumbnails identifies the slides on which the Mouse object is visible. You will now select these slides and hide the Mouse object throughout the entire project:

1. In the **Filmstrip** panel, select slide 4.

2. Hold down the *Shift* key and select slide 16. This operation selects 13 slides from slide 4 to slide 16.

3. Hold down the *cmd* (Mac) or *Ctrl* (Windows) key and click on slide 12 and slide 14 to remove them from the current selection.

Slide 12 is the Full Motion Recording slide that shows the scroll down action on the **Video** tab. Slide 14 is where a Text Animation types 300 in the **Width** field of the Adobe Media Encoder. The Mouse object does not show on these two slides, so you can safely remove them from the selection.

1. To remove the Mouse object from the selected slides, deselect the **Modify | Mouse | Show Mouse** menu item.

2. Go through the slides of the project to confirm that the Mouse object has been removed.

Your project is not yet a simulation but, with the removal of the Mouse object, it is not a demonstration anymore. The conversion is underway! Before moving on, there are a few more objects to remove/modify in the file.

Replacing the video file and the project title

One of the slides to modify is slide 2 where you will replace the video file by another one using the following steps:

1. Go to slide 2 of the project. Once there, select and remove the video file.

2. Use the **Video | Insert Video** menu item to insert a **Multi-Slide Synchronized Video**.

3. Use the `video/flv/sim_en.flv` file situated in the exercises folder.

4. At the bottom of the **Insert Video** dialog, make sure to select the **Modify slide duration to accommodate video** option and click on **OK** to validate.

5. With the video file selected, turn your attention to the **Options** tab of the **Properties** panel.

6. Position the video at **X** as `200` and **Y** as `196`.

7. Using the **Timeline** or **Timing** panel, make the video appear after 1 second.

8. In the **Timeline** panel, move the Button to the left and place its pause mark just before the end of the video.

9. Make the slide end at the same time as the button. The overall duration of the slide should be right below 6 seconds.

After this procedure, the **Timeline** panel of slide 2 should look like the following screenshot:

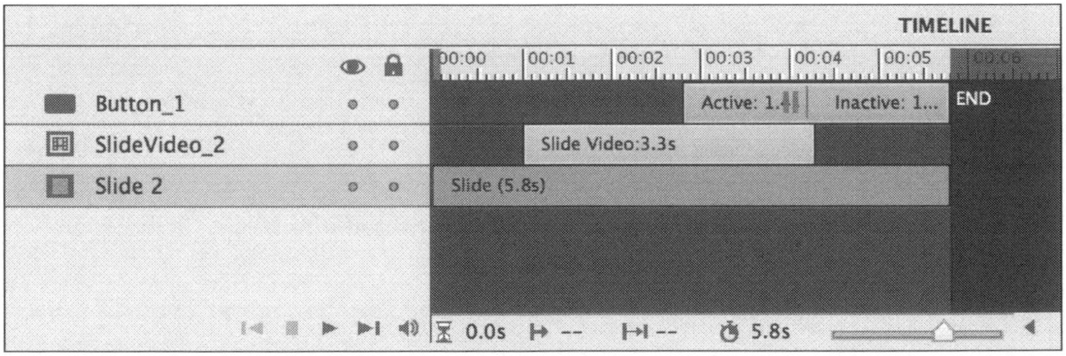

Finally, you will update the title on the first and last slide of the project.

10. Use the **Filmstrip** panel to go to slide 1.

11. Double-click on the Text Animation. The **Text Animation Properties** box opens.

12. In the box, change the word **demonstration** to `simulation` so that the sentence becomes **Adobe Media Encoder The Simulation**.

13. Use the same procedure to update the Text Animation on the last slide of the project.

14. Save the file when done.

With these updates complete, you are now well on the way to converting this demonstration into a simulation. In the next section, you will change the necessary Text Captions to give the learners precise instructions on what they have to do at each step of the simulation.

Using Find and Replace

When developing a simulation, never forget that your students will be active and will have to do things on their own. As you do not want to mislead, and possibly lose, your students, it is critical to give them precise instructions on what they have to do at each step of the simulation. For the teacher, coming up with the proper instructions is not an easy task, but it is very important for the pedagogical approach to be successful, so don't hesitate to spend the necessary time up front to come up with the proper instructions.

You will now use the Find and Replace feature to change the instructions given to the students throughout the entire project using the following steps:

1. Use the **Filmstrip** panel to go to slide 4 of the **encoderSim_800.cptx** file.

Note the message contained in the Text Caption of this slide. It says **The mouse will now click on the Add files icon**. This message was correct when in a demonstration but, in a simulation, you should change it in order to give the user the precise instruction to click on the item.

2. Browse the remaining slides of the project one by one.

Note that, on most of the remaining slides, the message contained in the Text Caption follows the same pattern as the message of slide 4. In this exercise, you will use the Find and Replace feature to change the **The mouse will now click** part of the sentence to **Click**.

3. Use the **Edit | Find and Replace** menu item to open the floating **Find And Replace** panel.

4. Type `The Mouse will now click` in the **Find** field.

5. Type `Click` (with a capital C) in the **Replace** Field.

Before moving on, take a look at the other options provided by the **Find And Replace** panel.

6. Leave these options at their default value and click on **Replace All**.

7. You should get a message saying that nine instances have been replaced. Click on **OK** to discard the confirmation box.

8. Close the **Find And Replace** panel.

9. Use the **Filmstrip** panel to browse the slides of the project.

Confirm that the text displayed in the Text Captions has changed as expected. While browsing the slides, notice that the Text Caption of slide 5 uses a slightly different pattern than the Text Captions on the other slides.

10. Use the **Filmstrip** panel to go to slide 5 and select the Text Caption.

11. Manually modify the text contained in the caption so it reads `Double-click on the demo_en.mov video file`.

At each step of the simulation, the student now has a Text Caption explaining precisely what has to be done. This is a great thing, but it is not enough! To give the student complete information about the purpose of the simulation, you should provide some extra instructions at the beginning of the project.

12. In the **Filmstrip** panel, right-click on slide 3.

13. In the contextual menu, click on the **Delete** command.

14. Read the message and click on **OK** to confirm the deletion of the slide.

You will now replace the deleted slide with another one.

15. Open the `Chapter06/instructions.cptx` file situated in your exercises folder.

This project contains a single slide that you will import into the `encoderSim_800.cptx` file using a simple copy and paste.

16. In the **Filmstrip** panel of the `instructions.cptx` file, right-click on the first (and only) slide.

17. In the contextual menu, click on **Copy**.

18. Return to the `encoderSim_800.cptx` file.

19. In the **Filmstrip** panel, right-click on slide 2.

20. In the contextual menu, click on **Paste**.

Remember that, when inserting a new slide in a project, the new slide is inserted *after* the currently selected slide.

Take some time to examine the content of the new slide. Pedagogically, it is a very important introduction slide. After reading this slide, the student will have all the required information to experience the simulation in the best possible conditions.

Let them be in charge!

The button placed on the new slide 3 has two purposes. First it pauses the playhead to let the learners read through the slide at their own pace. The second purpose of this button has to do with psychology. When doing a simulation, you confront the students with something they have to do for the first time. For some of them, this uncomfortable situation generates a lot of stress and anxiety. The button gives them time to put their thoughts together and take a deep breath before they give the go to the simulation themselves. The button gives them the illusion that they are in charge. This helps them to manage their anxiety. I have used this method successfully in many projects with great feedback from the students.

Working with Click Boxes

Your simulation is slowly taking shape but it still misses the object that will definitely make the difference in making your project interactive. This object will partially replace the Mouse object you removed earlier. This object is the Click Box.

Just like the Button object, the Click Box is an interactive object. It is used to define a sensitive area on the screen. If the learner clicks inside the Click Box, the right action is performed and the simulation moves on to the next step. If the student clicks outside the box, the wrong action is performed and the appropriate feedback should be displayed.

In this exercise, you will add the required Click Boxes to the Encoder Simulation project by performing the following steps:

1. Use the **Filmstrip** panel to go to slide 4 of the `encoderSim_800.cptx` file.
2. Open the **Timeline** panel if needed.
3. Hide the orange Smart Shape by clicking on its eye icon in the **Timeline** panel.

You need to add the Click Box at the same spot where the rounded rectangle is located. By hiding the Smart Shape, you clear the way for the Click Box to be added in the best possible conditions. Remember that, when using the eye icon as you just did, you hide the corresponding object in Captivate only, not in the resulting movie as seen by the students.

4. Use the **Interactions | Click Box** icon of the Big Buttons Bar to add the Click Box to the slide. Alternatively, you can use the *cmd* + *Shift* + *K* (Mac) or the *Ctrl* + *Shift* + *K* (Windows) shortcut to perform the same action.

Adding a Click Box adds up to four objects to the slide (it is ok if they don't all show on your screen). The first object is the Click Box itself. The three other objects are as follows:

- **Success Caption**: This Caption will show only if the student performs the right action.

- **Failure Caption**: This Caption will show only if the student does not perform the right action.

- **Hint Caption**: This Caption will show when the student rolls the mouse over the Click Box. It behaves like a Rollover Caption using the Click Box as its Rollover Area.

You will now set up the Click Box so that it behaves in the right way.

5. Move and resize the Click Box so that it covers more or less the Add file icon of the background image.

6. With the Click Box selected, turn your attention to the **Actions** tab of the **Properties** panel.

7. Confirm that the **On Success** action is set to **Go to the next slide**.

8. Deselect the **Infinite** checkbox and set the number of **Attempts** to 2. This means that you give the student two chances to perform the right action.

9. Confirm the **Last Attempt** drop-down list is set to **Continue**.

The **Continue** action simply releases the playhead, while the **Go to the next slide** action directly moves the playhead to the next slide. This setup will help you do some branching without adding any extra slides to the project.

Sizing the Click Boxes

When sizing the Click Boxes, don't hesitate to make them a bit bigger than what is actually needed. The extra space will make it easier for your students to find the Click Box and perform the right action. Don't forget that you are teaching. You want your students to concentrate on the concepts to learn, so the exact location of a mouse click is a secondary concern. This extra space will also provide a big enough tap target for students taking the course on a mobile device.

Branching with Click Boxes

Branching refers to the project reacting differently based on the actions of the learner. In this case, if the learner clicks inside of the Click Box, the right action is performed and the playhead jumps straight to the next slide where the next Click Box will again pause the playhead and wait for the learner's second action. But, if the learner clicks outside of the Click box, first the Failure Caption should be displayed and then the playhead should be released in order to play the second part of the slide's timeline. This is where you will place some feedback messages.

Working with feedback messages

There are three feedback messages associated with a Click Box: the Success, Failure, and Hint Captions. In the past, these feedback messages had the very same capabilities, options, and limitations as standard Text Captions. As of Captivate 8.0.1, these feedback messages are now based on Smart Shapes, which adds an amazing deal of extra flexibility to these objects. It is, of course, always possible to revert them back to standard Text Captions if needed.

Remember to update

Captivate 8.0.1 is Captivate 8 with the update patch released in October 2014. Make sure you are using an updated installation of Captivate to take advantage of this new feature.

In this exercise, you will first turn off the Success and Hint captions. You will then arrange the Failure Caption using the following steps.

1. Make sure the Click Box is selected and turn your attention to the **Actions** tab of the **Properties** panel.

2. In the **Display** section, deselect the **Success** and **Hint** checkboxes if necessary. Leave only the **Failure** option selected.

By deselecting the **Success** and **Hint** checkboxes, the corresponding Captions disappear from the slide. There are two objects left: the Click Box itself and the associated Failure Caption.

3. Right-click on the red Failure Caption. From this point, two things can happen:

    °   If you see the **Convert to Smart Shape** menu item in the contextual menu, it means that your failure caption is currently based on the Text Caption object. Click on the item to convert it to a Smart Shape.

    °   If you see the **Revert to Text Caption** menu item, it means that your failure caption is already based on the Smart Shape object. Just click away from the menu to close it without making any changes.

This new feature of Captivate 8.0.1 allows you to use the unique capabilities offered by the Smart Shapes for your feedback messages.

4. Right-click on the failure caption again and click on the **Replace Smart Shape** item of the contextual menu. The Smart Shapes library opens in a floating panel

5. Choose a shape of your liking to replace the default rounded rectangle. Don't forget that extra shapes are available at the top of the **Style** tab of the **Properties** panel.

6. Type `Sorry, you did not perform the right action` in the Failure Caption. When done, hit the *Esc* key to select the Failure Caption object.

7. In the **Style** tab of the **Properties** panel, change the font to **Verdana** and the font size to **16** points.

8. If needed, resize the object so the text fits comfortably in it. Then, move it to the most appropriate location.

With the Click Box and the Failure Caption at the right location, it is time to focus on the **Timeline** panel.

Using Smart Shapes for feedback messages by default

If you want your Success, Failure, and Hint Captions to use the Smart Shapes object by default, you can use the **Adobe Captivate | Preferences** (Mac) or **Edit | Preferences** (Windows) menu item to open the **Preferences** dialog. At the end of the **Defaults** category, select the **Use Smart-Shapes for SFH Captions instead of Text Captions** checkbox.

Arranging slideless branching

To finish off with this slide, you will now organize the objects on the **Timeline** panel. This will allow you to provide great feedback to your student without adding a single slide to the project! Use the following steps to set this up:

1. Open the **Timeline** panel if needed.

2. Use the eye icon of the **Timeline** panel to reveal the hidden orange Smart Shape.

3. Make the Click box appear after 3 seconds and pause the slide 1 second later.

4. Apply the same timing to the **Click on the Add files** icon Text Caption.

5. With the Text Caption selected, switch to the **Timing** panel and change the **Transition** to **Fade In Only**.

6. Insert a new rounded Rectangle on the slide. Type `The correct spot is currently highlighted`. The simulation will now continue as if you performed the right action in it.

7. Resize the new rounded rectangle and move it somewhere to the middle of the slide. Don't hesitate to use the tools of the Align toolbar if you feel it is needed.

8. In the **Timeline** or in the **Timing** panel, make the new rounded rectangle appear after 4.5 seconds and display for a specific time of 6.5 seconds. In the **Timing** panel, change **Transition** to **Fade In and Out**.

9. Select the orange rounded rectangle and give it the same timing.

10. Still in the **Timeline** panel, remove the audio narration by right-clicking on the waveform and selecting **Remove** in the contextual menu.

11. Reduce the length of the slide to 11 seconds.

At the end of this procedure, the **Timeline** panel of slide 4 should look like the following screenshot:

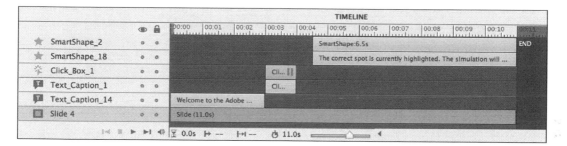

At runtime, the Click Box stops the playhead at 4 seconds into the slide and waits for the student to interact with the course. If the student performs the right action, the playhead directly jumps to slide 5 without playing the second part of slide 4. If the student performs the wrong action, the playhead is simply released and plays the orange rounded rectangle and the feedback message before moving on to slide 5. This is how you can create branching without adding any extra slides to the project.

12. Save the file and use the **Preview | Next 5 Slides** icon of the Big Buttons Bar to test your sequence.

It is necessary to test it twice. The first time, perform the right action and confirm that the playhead jumps straight to the next slide. The second time, perform the wrong action twice and confirm that the feedback messages and the Highlight Boxes are displayed before the simulation moves on to the next slide.

Extra credit – adding the remaining Click Boxes

If everything works as expected, you can use the same procedure to add a Click Box and a failure message on slides 5, 6, 7, 8, 9, 10, 13, 15, and 16. If you get stuck, use the `Chapter06/final/encoderSim_800.cptx` file as a reference. To help you out, these are the general steps of the procedure to perform on each slide:

- Hide the orange Smart Shape using the eye icon of the **Timeline** panel.

- Insert a Click Box and make it cover the same spot as the hidden Smart Shape.

- Set the Click Box so it accepts **2** attempts. It should jump to the next slide on success and continue after the last attempt.

- Make sure that the **Transition** of the Text Caption is set to **Fade In Only**.

- If needed, right-click on the Failure Caption and select the **Replace Smart Shape** menu item to choose the most appropriate Smart Shape.

- Write a failure message in the Failure Caption and adapt the formatting to your liking.

- Create a rounded rectangle with extra feedback in the same way you did on slide 4.

- Arrange the objects on the **Timeline** panel.

- Delete the un-needed objects (extra Text Captions, audio narration, and so on).

When done, don't forget to save the file and preview your project. In order to fully test the Click Boxes, it is necessary to preview the movie twice. The first time, perform the right actions and confirm that the simulation always jumps to the next slide. The second time, perform the wrong actions and confirm that the simulation displays the appropriate feedback messages.

Working with Text Entry Boxes

There is one last action to take care of on slide 14. That slide currently contains a Text Animation that automatically types the desired width of the video. In the simulation, you want the student to type this information. The interactive object that makes it possible is the Text Entry Box.

After the Button (including the Smart Shape used as a Button) and the Click Box, the Text Entry Box is the third interactive object that Captivate offers. Use the following steps to replace the Text Animation of slide 14 with a Text Entry Box:

1. Use the **Filmstrip** panel to go to slide 14 of the `encoderSim_800.cptx` file.

2. In the **Timeline** panel, use the eye icon associated with the Text Animation that writes **400** in the **Width** field to hide it from the authoring environment.

3. Use the **Text | Text Entry Box** icon of the Big Buttons Bar to insert a new Text Entry Box. Alternatively, you can use the *cmd + Shift + T* (Mac) or *Ctrl + Shift + T* (Windows) shortcut to perform the same action.

The Text Entry Box system can add up to five objects to the slide (it is ok if they don't all show on your slide):

- The Text Entry Box itself
- A Success Caption
- A Failure Caption
- A Hint Caption
- A Submit button (the Submit button is often hidden below the Success Caption)

You will now set up the Text Entry Box so it looks and behaves the way you want.

4. Move and resize the Text Entry Box object so it covers the **Width** field of the background image.

 Don't hesitate to use the Zoom feature of Captivate to help you precisely size and position the Text Entry Box.

5. With the Text Entry Box selected, turn your attention to the **Style** tab of the **Properties** panel

6. Select the **Validate User Input** checkbox.

In Captivate, the Text Entry Box object serves two very different purposes. First, it can be used to gather data from the student (when the student needs to type in their name for example). In this case, there are no right or wrong answers and the data typed in the Text Entry Box does not need to be validated. In this exercise, however, the Text Entry Box is used to mimic a typing action that occurred during the capture. There is therefore a single good answer that needs to be differentiated from the other (wrong) answers. This is why the data typed into the Text Entry Box needs to be validated.

When the **Validate User Input** checkbox is selected, the **Correct Entries** box is displayed on the screen.

7. In the **Correct Entries** box, click on the **+** sign and type 400. Do not select the **Case Sensitive** option.

Thanks to this last action, the Text Entry Box is able to tell the right answer apart from the wrong answers. You can add as many right answers as needed by clicking on the **+** sign (allowing alternative spelling of an answer to be accounted for). To remove an entry from the list, select it and click on the **–** icon.

8. With the Text Entry Box selected, deselect the **Show Text Box Frame** option situated in the **Style** tab of the **Properties** panel.

9. Switch to the **Actions** tab. In the **Display** section, deselect the **Success and Hint** checkboxes (if needed). Only leave the **Failure** checkbox selected.

10. In the **Others** section, deselect the **Show Button** option to hide the **Submit** button.

11. Switch to the **Timing** panel and set the **Transition** to **No transition** (if needed).

12. Type Sorry you did not perform the right action! in the Failure Caption. When done, hit the *Esc* key.

13. In the **Styles** tab of the **Properties** panel, change the font of the Failure Caption to **Verdana** and the font size to **16** points.

14. Move and resize the Failure Caption as you see fit.

15. Select the Text Entry Box object again.

16. In the **Action** tab of the **Properties** panel, open the **On Success** drop-down list and choose **Go to the next slide**.

17. Deselect the **Infinite Attempts** option and set the **Attempts** to **2**.

18. Make sure the **Last Attempt** dropdown is set to **Continue**.

19. Confirm that the **Shortcut** option is set to **Enter**.

The **Shortcut** option lets you choose the keyboard key (or shortcut) the student will use to submit the content of the Text Entry Box. This Shortcut option can be used as an alternative to or as a replacement for the Submit button when it is removed from the slide.

20. Switch back to the **Style** tab of the **Properties** panel.

21. In the **Character** section, set the font **Family** to **Courier New** and the **Size** to **8** (you can type it if it is not in the list). This sets the formatting properties of the text that the student will type in the Text Entry Box.

Now that the Text Entry Box looks the right way and performs the right actions, you will move to the final step of this exercise: arranging the objects on the **Timeline** panel and providing the necessary feedback.

22. Open the **Timeline** panel if needed.

23. Select the Text entry Box and use the **Timeline** or the **Timing** panel to perform the following actions:
    ° Make the object appear after 0 second
    ° Make it display for a specific time of 1 second
    ° Make it pause after 1 second

24. Select the Text Caption that reads **Enter the desired width...** and apply the same timing as for the Text Entry Box. In the **Timing** panel, change its **Transition** to **Fade In Only**.

The **Fade In Only** option is used to make sure that the Text Caption is still displayed at full opacity when the Text Entry Box pauses the playhead.

25. Insert a new rounded rectangle shape on the slide and type The simulation will now perform the right action and continue in it. Resize the Text Caption so the text fits comfortably in the object and place it somewhere in the middle of the slide.

26. In the **Timeline** or in the **Timing** panel, make the new shape appear after 1.5 seconds and display for a specific time of 5.5 seconds.

27. Use the eye icons of the **Timeline** panel to reveal the hidden Text Animation.

28. Make the Text Animation appear after 7.5 seconds and display for a specific time of 1 second.

29. Adjust the duration of the slide accordingly.

When done, make sure the **Timeline** panel looks like the following screenshot:

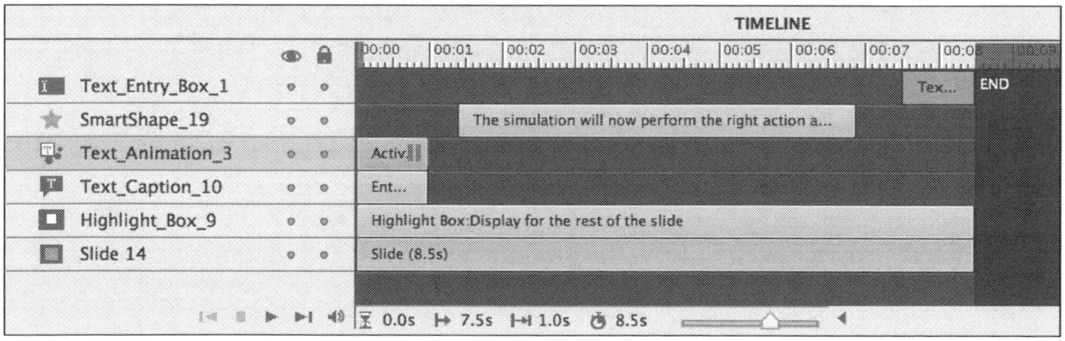

Don't forget to save the file and to test the new Text Entry Box in the **Preview** pane to make sure it works as expected.

Finishing touches

There are a few more things to do in order to completely finalize the simulation. The first fine-tuning has to do with a limitation of Captivate.

In a Captivate simulation, the Click Box object simulates a mouse click and the Text Entry Box object simulates a typing action, but there is no interactive object to simulate a drag-and-drop or a scrolling action. Because of this limitation, you will now delete slides 11 and 12 of the simulation by performing the following steps:

1. In the **Filmstrip** panel, select both slide 11 and 12.
2. Right-click on any of the selected two slides and select **Delete** from the contextual menu.
3. Click on the **OK** button to confirm the deletion of the slides.

The second thing that needs fine-tuning is the double-click action on slide 5.

4. Use the **Filmstrip** panel to return to slide 5.
5. Use the **Timeline** panel to select the Click Box object.
6. In the **Actions** tab of the **Properties** panel, select the **Double-click** checkbox.

The next fine-tuning takes place on slide 10. To better simulate the click over a link, you will turn the standard mouse pointer to a hand pointer over the Click Box.

7. Use the **Filmstrip** panel to return to slide 10.
8. Use the **Timeline** panel to select the Click Box object.
9. In the **Actions** tab of the **Properties** panel, select the **Hand Cursor** checkbox.

To convert your demonstration into this simulation, you have removed a lot of objects from the initial project. Remember that removing an object from a slide does not remove it from the project library. Before wrapping up this exercise, it is a good idea to do some housekeeping in the library.

10. Click on the **Library** icon on the right-hand side of the Big Buttons Bar to open the the project library.
11. Click on the **Select Unused Items** icon of the Library toolbar.
12. Click on the **Delete** icon of the library toolbar to remove the selected assets from the library.

The conversion of the Encoder Demonstration into its simulation counterpart is now finished. To reach this milestone, you have used many objects and features of Captivate. Let's quickly summarize them as follows:

- The main object of a demonstration is the Mouse object. The main objects of a simulation are Click Boxes and Text Entry Boxes.

- To convert a demonstration to a simulation, you must first remove the Mouse object from the demonstration and then replace it with Click Boxes and Text Entry Boxes.

- It is very important to provide specific and precise instructions to the learners at each and every step of the simulation.

- The **Find and Replace** feature is very useful to quickly modify the text contained in the Text Captions throughout the entire project.

- The three interactive objects of Captivate are the Button, the Click Box, and the Text Entry Box. These objects are able to stop the playhead and wait for the learner to interact with the movie.

- Each of these three objects also implements the branching concept.

- When using Text Entry Boxes, you can decide if the text entered by the student must be validated or not.

- If the **Validate User Input** checkbox is on, you must provide the correct answer(s) in the **Correct Entries** box.

- Failure Captions, Hint Captions, and Success Captions can be added to these interactive objects.

- In Captivate 8.0.1, these feedback messages can be based on the Smart Shapes object or on the Text Caption object.

- Captivate is not able to simulate drag-and-drop and scrolling actions in a simulation.

Summary

You are now deep into the postproduction phase of your Captivate projects. These are now very different from the original rushes. They have also become fully interactive and animated. To achieve these things, it has been necessary to add different kinds of objects to the slides and to use a lot of Captivate tools and features.

In this particular chapter, you focused on the objects that allow you to add interactivity in your Captivate projects. First, you studied the Rollover objects. You used the Rollover Caption, Rollover Images, Rollover Slidelet, and Rollover Smart Shapes to add some interactivity to the project.

You also studied three objects that have the ability to stop the playhead and wait for the students to interact with the movie. The Click Box is used to simulate a mouse click, the Text Entry Box is used to simulate the typing of a piece of text, and the Button is used to stop the playhead and let the student experience the movie in a personalized fashion. These three objects also implement the branching concept by letting you choose two different actions depending on the way the student interacts with them.

You also discovered the Drag and Drop interaction that you used to add very sophisticated interaction to the project.

In the next chapter, you will focus on the cosmetic aspect of your project. You will learn how to quickly create and apply a consistent look and feel that will further help your learner get the most out of your teaching. Let's meet in the next chapter for the final phase of postproduction.

Meet the community

In this section, I want to introduce you to Joe Ganci. He is a veteran eLearning developer and instructional designer. He has reviewed two of my Captivate books. The first time I contacted him via e-mail, he was kind enough to include a small quote in French (my native language) in his reply. We met in October 2014 during the Adobe Learning Summit in Las Vegas. He helped me while I was struggling with Adobe Presenter! Thank you Joe! Already looking forward to meet you again!

Joe Ganci

Joe Ganci is an eLearning consultant with a long track record. His design approaches and his innovative use of tools, such as Adobe Captivate, Articulate Storyline, Adobe Presenter, Articulate Studio, ZebraZapps, Interact, and others, has caused many to improve how they design and develop their eLearning and to implement new and better methods. His personal and hands-on style of consulting keeps his services constantly in demand, and he is privileged to have visited with many clients from all over the world.

He has been involved in every aspect of learning development since 1983. He holds a degree in Computer Science and is a published author, having written several books, research papers, and articles about eLearning. He is widely considered a guru for his expertise in eLearning development and conducts classes and seminars at commercial companies, government facilities, leading universities, and at many industry conferences, where he often serves as the keynote speaker. He is on a mission to improve the quality of eLearning with practical approaches that work.

Contact details

- **Web**: http://elearningjoe.com/
- **Twitter**: @elearningjoe
- **E-mail**: joe@elearningjoe.com

7
Working with Styles, Master Slides, Themes, and Templates

In this chapter, you will focus on the cosmetic aspect of the project, using Styles, Master Slides, Themes, and Templates. Your primary goal is to reach a high level of consistency in the look and feel of your eLearning content.

When developing eLearning, always keep in mind that your students will most likely experience your content while alone in front of their computer with no one around to guide them. In this chapter, you will discover that a consistent look and feel is an efficient way to get your students on task. The idea is to free them from learning how the eLearning content works and looks so that they can be fully recipient to the actual topics you want to teach them.

Captivate offers five features to help you achieve this high level of consistency. The first feature that will be discussed in this chapter is the **Swatch Manager**. You will also learn about **Styles**, **Master Slides**, **Templates**, and **Themes**.

In addition to improving your pedagogical efficiency, the use of Master Slides, Templates, Styles, Swatches, and Themes will also dramatically speed up the development of your eLearning content.

In this chapter, you will do the following:

- Explore the Swatches panel and the all-new color management features of Captivate 8.0.1
- Experiment with Styles and with the Object Styles Manager
- Experiment with the predefined Themes of Captivate

- Create a new Theme containing Styles and Master Slides
- Create a brand new Template
- Create a new Captivate project from a Template

There's a lot to cover, so let's dive right into the first topic of this chapter.

Preparing your work

To get the most out of this chapter, it is important to reset your workspace. If you are using the default interface mode, restart Captivate to reset your workspace to default. If you are using the advanced interface mode, use the **Window | Workspace | Reset 'Classic'** menu item to reset the workspace to default.

In this chapter, you will use the exercise files located in the Chapter07 folder of the download associated with this book. If you get confused by any of the step-by-step instructions, take a look at the Chapter07/final folder, which contains a copy of the exercises.

Working with the Swatch Manager

When working on an eLearning project, it is very important to precisely format the various objects present in your projects. Never forget that you are actually teaching your students something. In such a situation, most students will try to make sense out of every single formatting anomaly. Inconsistent formatting will most likely mislead and confuse your learner.

Consistent formatting in eLearning

In my first eLearning project with Captivate, I used blue Text Captions to explain things to the learners and black Text Captions when I wanted them to do something. After a short while, the learners knew that a blue Text Caption meant they just had to read through the text and a black Text Caption meant they had to do something. Learners have reported that this formatting consistency helped them structure their learning.

When it comes to color, it is very important to define a great color scheme at the beginning of the project and to stick to it throughout the development. Sometimes this color scheme will be enforced by company regulations. At other times, you'll need to strictly stick to the color scheme defined by a graphic designer. In some situations, you will be the only person involved and you'll have to define your own custom color scheme.

The Swatch Manager can help you in all the preceding situations. It is one of the newest additions to Captivate. It allows you to customize the set of colors available in your project. In this exercise, you will take your first look at Swatch Manager using the following steps:

1. Open the `Chapter07/drivingInBe.cptx` file.

2. Use the **Window | Swatch Manager** menu item to open the floating **Swatch Manager** panel.

The **Swatch Manager** panel should look similar to the following screenshot:

The main area of the **Swatch Manager** panel is covered by lots of colored squares. Each of these squares is called a **Swatch** and can be used to apply a color to various elements of the selected Captivate object. In the upper portion of the **Swatch Manager** panel, there are five buttons that are used modify the collection of Swatches available in the **Swatch Manager**: **Append, Load, Save, Reset**, and **Clear**.

Importing custom Swatches to the Swatches panel

One of the main features of the Swatch Manager panel is the ability to import and export Swatches. Thanks to this ability, you can export the Swatches created in other applications (such as Adobe Photoshop, Adobe Illustrator, or Adobe InDesign) and import them into Captivate.

In the next exercise, you will import the official brand colors of the MFTC company into the project using the following steps:

1. Click on the **Append** button of the **Swatch Manager** panel.

2. Navigate to the Chapter07/MFTC-Colors.ase file and double-click on it.

Five color Swatches are added at the end of the **Swatch Manager** panel. The imported colors are the official corporate colors of the MFTC company that you must use in your projects to comply with company policy. Note that you can also click on the **Load** button to include those swatches in **Swatch Manager**, but then the new swatches replace the default ones as opposed to being added to the existing ones.

> **Creating the .ase file**
>
> An **Adobe Swatch Exchange (ASE)** file is used to export color swatches from an Adobe Application and import them into other Adobe applications. Most Adobe applications can be used to create such an .ase file. In Captivate, use the **Save** button in the **Swatches** panel to save the current set of swatches to an .ase file. For this exercise, I have used an online service named **Adobe Color** to create the .ase file. You can find out more about Adobe Color and create your own .ase files at http://color.adobe.com.

Using custom colors

Now that the corporate colors of the MFTC company have been added to the **Swatch Manager** panel, you will use them to format the rounded rectangle Smart Shape you added on slide 3 back in *Chapter 3, Working with Standard Objects*, using the following steps:

1. In the Chapter07/drivingInBe.cptx file, use the **Filmstrip** panel to go to slide 3.

2. Select the rounded rectangle that serves as the picture frame.

Remember that the rounded rectangle and the picture are grouped. Clicking on the rounded rectangle actually selects the whole group. It is necessary to click a second time on the object to sub-select it within the group.

3. With the rounded rectangle selected, turn your attention to the **Style** tab of the **Properties** panel (it may be necessary to open the **Properties** panel).

4. Click on the **Fill** color property to open the color chooser.

As depicted in the following screenshot, the color swatches available in the color chooser of the **Fill** property (including the five custom swatches imported in the previous section) should be the very same as the swatches available in the **Swatch Manager** panel.

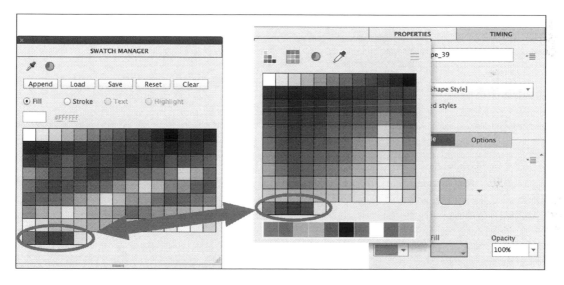

This is a new feature of the Captivate 8.0.1 update released on October 13, 2014. If your Captivate installation has not been updated, the imported swatches will not be available in the color chooser of the **Fill** property.

 In the remaining exercises of this chapter, I will refer to these colors as *Custom Color 1 to 5.*

Don't hesitate to close the **Swatch Manger** panel if you feel it is in the way.

5. Use Custom Color 1 (light brown) as the **Fill** option of the image frame.

6. Change the **Stroke** option to Custom Color 4 (dark green).

7. Increase the **Width** value to 4 pixels.

8. Save the file when done.

Confirm that the rounded rectangle shape now looks like the following screenshot:

Thanks to the **Swatch Manager** panel, you were able to import the custom colors of the MFTC brand in the project and to use them to format a Smart Shape. This is your first step toward consistent formatting. Your learner will most certainly appreciate this high level of professionalism when taking the course.

Extra credit – importing custom swatches

The custom swatches you imported in the drivingInBe.cptx file are specific to that project only. In order to ensure consistency not only within a project, but also across projects, you will now import the same set of custom swatches in the encoderDemo_800.cptx file. Here are the general steps to follow:

- Return to the encoderDemo_8000.cptx file.

- Go to **Window | Swatch Manager** to open the **Swatch Manager** panel.

- Append the swatches contained in the Chapter07/MFTC-colors.ase file to the swatches already present in the **Swatch Manager** panel.

- Close the **Swatch Manager** panel and save the Captivate project.

Before moving on to the next section, let's quickly summarize what has been covered in this one:

- The **Swatch Manager** panel has been enhanced in the Captivate 8.0.1 update released in October 2014. It is therefore necessary to install the latest Captivate update to enjoy all the goodies of the **Swatches** panel.

- The **Swatches** panel lets you customize the set of colors available in Captivate.

- One of the most interesting aspects of the **Swatches** panel is the ability to import and export an `.ase` file.

- The ASE files (`.ase`) are used to export color Swatches from one Adobe Application and import them into another Adobe Application.

- Adobe Color (`http://color.adobe.com`) is an online service that allows you to create custom color schemes and to export them as ASE files.

Working with Styles

In Captivate, the formatting properties of an object can be saved in a style enabling you to save and reapply the same properties on other objects of the same type. Captivate comes with predefined Styles, but you can of course modify these default Styles and even create your own custom Styles.

Managing Styles with the Properties panel

For the next exercise, you will return to the `encoderDemo_800.cptx` project and explore how the **Properties** panel can be used to apply and create styles:

1. Open or switch to the `Chapter07/encoderDemo_800.cptx` file.
2. Use the **Filmstrip** panel to go to slide 8.

Slide 8 contains the Text Caption that you formatted in *Chapter 3, Working with Standard Objects*. In this exercise, you will use the **Properties** panel to save the current formatting of this Text Caption as a style and to apply this style to the other Text Captions of the project.

3. Select the Text Caption that begins with **The Adobe Media Encoder contains a list**.

4. If needed, click on the **Properties** icon of the Big Buttons Bar to open the **Properties** panel.

The **Style Name** drop-down list (shown as **1** in the following screenshot) is in the topmost area of the **Properties** panel. It should tell you that the style currently applied to the selected Text Caption is the **+[Default Caption Style]** style. The **+** sign in front of the style name means that the formatting has been manually changed on top of the style. Technically, we call this a **style override**. There is no way of knowing what the formatting changes are—we just know that something has changed.

In the top-right corner of the **Properties** panel, there is another icon (marked as **2** on the above screenshot). This is the Object Options icon. It gives you access to additional options pertaining to the selected objects.

5. Click on the Object Options icon and inspect the available items.

Except for the last item (accessibility), all the other options are used to manage the style applied to the object.

Resetting a style

Resetting a style is one of the operations that can be done using the Object Options icon of the **Properties** panel.

1. With the formatted Text Caption still selected, open the Object Options icon.
2. Click on the **Reset Style** menu item.

The original **[Default Caption Style]** style is reapplied to the selected caption and the **+** sign disappears from the **Style Name** drop-down list.

3. Go to **Edit | Undo** or use the *Ctrl* + *Z* (for Windows) or *cmd* + *Z* (for Mac) shortcut to undo the last action.

Resetting a style is very practical when you want to reset the format of the selected object back to default.

Creating new Styles

Creating a new style is another operation that can be done with the Object Options icon. In this section, you will save the current formatting of the Text Caption that begins with **The Adobe Media Encoder contains a list...** as a new style using the following steps:

1. If needed, click on the Text Caption that begins with **The Adobe Media Encoder contains a list...** to make it the active object.

2. In the **Style Name** drop-down list of the **Properties** panel, confirm that the applied style is the **+[Default Caption Style]** style.

3. Click on the Object Options icon and click on the **New Style** item.

4. In the **Save New Object Style** dialog box, name the new style MFTC-Caption and click on **OK**.

Take another look at the **Style Name** drop-down menu on the **Properties** panel. It should state that the new **MFTC-Caption** style has been applied to the selected object. This style can now be applied to any other Text Caption in the project.

Applying Styles

Applying styles to existing objects is yet another operation that can be done with the **Properties** panel. In the next exercise, you will apply your new **MFTC-Caption** style to another Text Caption of this slide.

1. While still on slide 8 of the Chapter07/encoderDemo_800.cptx file, select the Text Caption that begins with **The conversion settings...**.

2. At the top of the **Properties** panel, open the **Style Name** drop-down menu.

3. Select the **MFTC-Caption** style to apply it to the selected object.

Two of the Text Captions on slide 8 should now have the **MFTC-Caption** style applied.

Modifying a Style

Modifying a style is the next action that you will perform thanks to the **Properties** panel. In this exercise, you will slightly modify the formatting of one of the Text Captions that has the **MFTC-Caption** style applied. You will then update your custom style to the new formatting and see how the other Text Caption reacts.

1. Make sure that the Text Caption that begins with **The conversion settings...** is still selected.

2. At the top of the **Properties** panel, confirm that the **MFTC-Caption** style is currently applied to the selected object.

3. In the **Style** tab of the **Properties** panel, change the font size to 20.

Because you have made a formatting change, the **+** sign appears in the **Style Name** drop-down menu. Therefore, the style currently applied to the selected Text Caption is **+MFTC-Caption**.

4. Open the Object Options icon and click on the **Save changes to Existing Style** item.

5. This action updates the **MFTC-Caption** style after the current look of the selected object. The **+** sign disappears from the **Style Name** drop-down list.

6. Select the Text Caption that begins with **The Adobe Media Encoder contains a list...**.

7. In the **Characters** section of the **Style** tab of the **Properties** panel, confirm that the new font size of 20 is applied to this Text Caption as well.

By updating the **MFTC-Caption** style, you updated the formatting of every Text Caption of the project this style is applied to.

Applying styles automatically

The style currently applied to the modified Text Captions of slide 8 is the one you want to apply to every Text Caption of the project. You could browse each slide one by one to manually apply the new style to each and every Text Caption, but there is another more automated way. The steps are as follows:

1. While still on slide 8 of the Chapter07/encoderDemo_800.cptx file, select the only remaining Text Caption that does not have the **MFTC-Caption** style applied.

2. Look at the **Style Name** drop-down menu of the **Properties** panel. Confirm that the **+[Default Capture Caption Style]** style has been applied to the selected object.

What you want to do is apply your custom **MFTC-Caption** style to all the Text Captions of the project that currently use the **[Default Capture Caption Style]** style.

3. Select any of the two Text Captions that currently use your **MFTC-Caption** style.

4. Open the Object Options icon and click on the **Apply this style to...** item.

5. In the **Apply Object Style** box, select the **[Default Capture Caption Style]** style in the drop-down list and click on **OK**.

This operation applies the **MFTC-Caption** style to every Text Caption of the project that has the **[Default Capture Caption Style]** style.

You probably expected to see the **MFTC-Caption** style being applied to the **The mouse will now click...** Text Caption, but the formatting of that Text Caption did not change. Let's try to understand why.

6. Click on the **The mouse will now click...** Text Caption to make it the active object.

7. Take a look at the **Style Name** drop-down menu at the top of the **Properties** panel. Confirm that the style applied to the selected object is the **+MFTC-Caption** style.

The truth is sometimes subtler than what your eyes tell you! The **MFTC-Caption** style has been properly applied to the Text Caption, but it is currently overridden by a manual change made to the formatting of this object when the **[Default Capture Caption Style]** style was applied.

8. Open the Object Options icon and click on the **Reset Style** item.

This action removes the style overrides, which properly applies the genuine **MFTC-Caption** style.

Automatically replacing the overrides

Before moving on to the next section, take note of the **Replace modified styles** checkbox. When this checkbox is selected, the style overrides are automatically cleared when a new style is applied to the selected object. This may sound very tempting, but it may lead to unwanted changes throughout the project, so use it with great care.

As depicted in the following screenshot, all three Text Captions of slide 8 now have the same **MFTC-Caption** style applied:

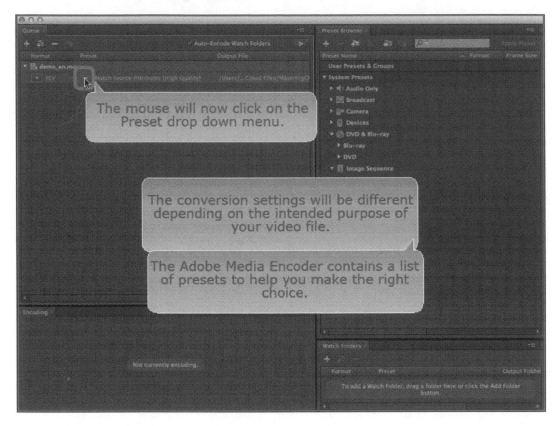

However, slide 8 is not the only one that has been affected by this change.

9. Use the **Filmstrip** panel to browse the slides of your project one by one and confirm that all the Text Captions of the project that were using the **[Default Capture Caption Style]** style are now using your custom **MFTC-Caption** style.

10. If you need to clear the style overrides, use the **Reset Style** feature. Also, don't hesitate to move and resize the Text Captions as needed.

While browsing the slides of your project, note that only some Text Captions have been affected by the style change.

11. Use the **Filmstrip** panel to go to slide 4 of the project.

There should be two Text Captions on slide 4. Neither of them are currently using your custom **MFTC-Caption** style.

12. Click on the **Welcome to the Adobe Media Encoder** Text Caption to make it the active object.

13. Take a look at the **Style Name** drop-down menu at the top of the **Properties** panel to see what style is currently applied to the selected Text Caption.

The applied style should be the **+[Default Caption Style]** style. This indicates that the current formatting of the selected object is based on the **[Default Caption Style]** style with some manual formatting added on top of it. This Text Caption still uses its default formatting because it did not have the **[Default Capture Caption Style]** style applied.

Extra credit – applying styles automatically

In this section, you will use the same procedure as in the last exercise to apply the **MFTC-Caption** style to every Text Caption currently using the **[Default Caption Style]** style. The general steps are as follows:

- Select any Text Caption of the project that is currently using the **MFTC-Caption** style.

- At the top of the **Properties** panel, open the Object Options icon and choose the **Apply this style to...** item.

- In the **Apply Object Style** window, select the **[Default Caption Style]** style and click on the **OK** button.

- Use the **Filmstrip** panel to browse the slide of the project and confirm that all Text Captions now use the **MFTC-Caption** style.

- If necessary, use the Reset Style feature to clear the style overrides.

At the end of this extra credit section, all the Text Captions should now be formatted in the same way throughout the entire project. Note that the **[Default Caption Style]** style was the style applied by default to the new Text Captions. Now that it has been replaced by your own **MFTC-Caption** style, any new Text Caption you insert in the project will automatically be associated with the **MFTC-Caption** style by default.

Extra credit – creating styles for another type of object

What is true for Text Captions also applies to other types of objects. In this section, you will create a new style for the Smart Shapes used as Highlight Boxes that you created in *Chapter 3, Working with Standard Objects*.

The general steps are as follows:

- Use the **Filmstrip** panel to return to slide 4 and select the orange Highlight Box you formatted in the previous chapter.

- Save the current formatting of the Smart Shape used as a Highlight Box as a new style named **MFTC-HighlightShape**.

- Use the Object options icon to apply the new **MFTC-HighlightShape** style to the remaining such shapes of the project (By default, these objects use the **[Default Smart Shape Style]** style).

- Browse the slides of the project and confirm that all the orange Smart Shapes now share the same style.

- If needed, use the Reset Style feature to clear the overrides.

- If needed, move and resize the Highlight Boxes so they are well-integrated into the slides.

This concludes your first explorations of the styles in Captivate. Using the styles, it has been easy and fast to format every Text Caption of the project in the very same way. This helps you achieve the high degree of formatting consistency that assists your students in the learning process and creates a more professional looking project.

Before moving on to the next topic, let's summarize what you have learned:

- Styles help you create and maintain consistent formatting throughout the entire project

- In the topmost section of the **Properties** panel, use the **Style Name** dropdown to apply a style to the selected object

- When some additional formatting is applied on an object, a **+** sign appears in front of the style name

- When you modify a style, you change the formatting of all the objects using that particular style

- The Object Options icon in the top right corner of the **Properties** panel contains the necessary options used to create, update, reset, and apply styles

Working with the Object Style Manager

So far, you have used the Object Options icon of the **Properties** panel to apply and manage styles. This icon provides quick and easy access to the main styling features of Captivate. However, behind the scenes, a much more sophisticated engine is at work!

This engine is the **Object Style Manager**. The items of the Object Options icon are just a remote control to the actual Object Style Manager. Everything made possible by these icons is also possible through the Object Style Manager, but the Object Style Manager has much more to offer.

Renaming styles

One of the extra features offered by the Object Style Manager is the ability to rename an existing style. In this section, you will experiment with this ability hands-on using the following steps:

1. Still in the `Chapter07/encoderDemo_800.cptx` project, use the **Filmstrip** panel to go to slide 3 of the project.

2. Select the **Your video file needs to be converted...** Text Caption.

3. Take a look at the **Style Name** drop-down menu of the **Properties** panel.

The style applied to the selected object should be the **[Default Caption Style]_1** style. This style was created automatically when you pasted this slide in the project back in *Chapter 3, Working with Standard Objects*. The **_1** suffix has been added to the style name in order to avoid name collision with the **[Default Caption Style]** style that already existed in the project before pasting the slide.

You will now rename that style using the following steps:

4. Go to the **Edit | Object Style Manger** menu item to open the Object Style Manager. You can also use the *Shift + F7* (for Windows) or *Shift + fn + F7* (for Mac) shortcut to do the same thing.

The Object Style Manager opens, as shown in the following screenshot:

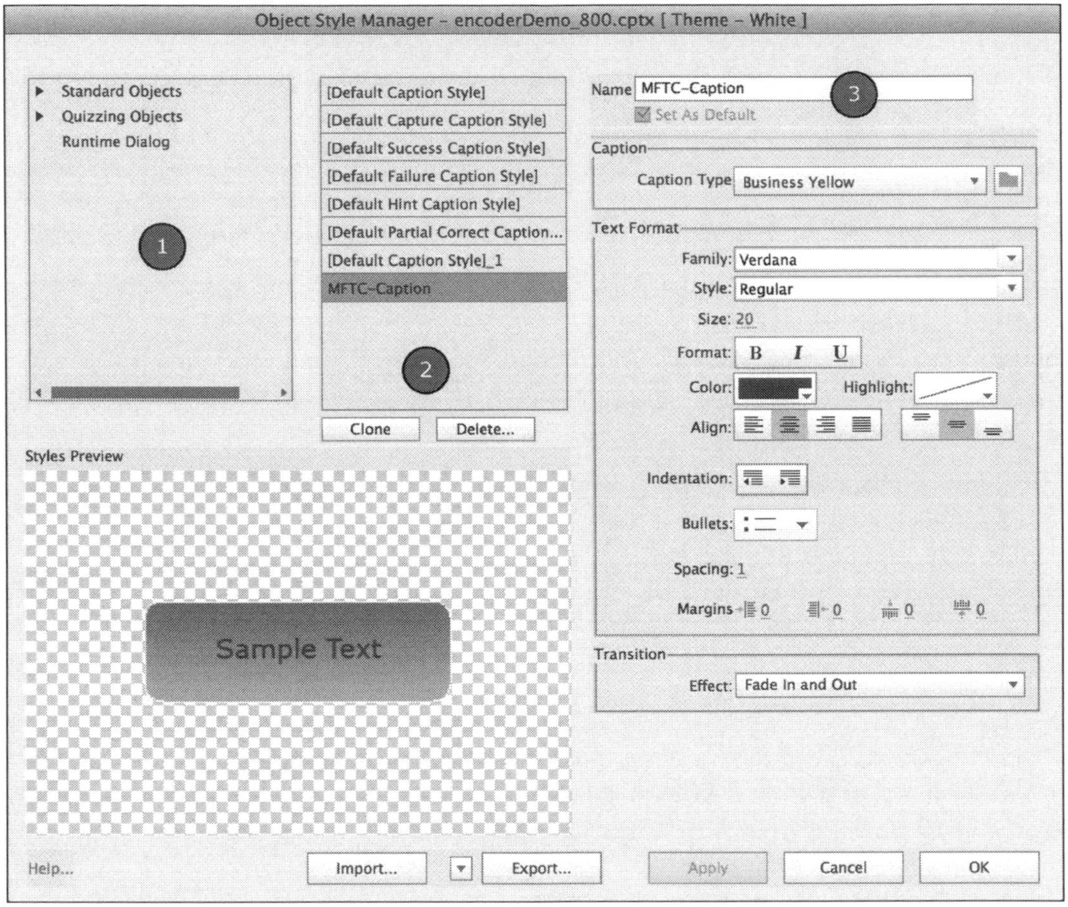

The left-hand side of the Object Style Manager (shown as **1** in the preceding screenshot) contains a list of all the object types of Captivate.

5. In the left column of the Object Style Manager, expand the **Standard Objects** section.

6. In the **Standard Objects** section, expand the **Captions** subsection and select the Text Caption object.

The middle column (shown as **2** in the preceding screenshot) shows a list of the styles that can be applied to the object type selected in the first column. In this case, the styles listed in the middle column can be applied to the Text Caption object. Among them are your custom **MFTC-Caption** style and the **[Default Caption Style]_1** style that you want to rename.

7. In the middle column, select the **[Default Caption Style]_1** style.

When a style is selected in the second column of the Object Style Manager, its properties are displayed in the third column. One of these properties is the name of the style that appears at the very top of the third column (see **3** in the preceding screenshot).

8. Change the name of the selected style to **MFTC-TransparentCaption.**

9. Click on the **OK** button at the bottom right corner of the Object Styles Manager to validate the change and close the dialog.

10. Back on slide 3, select all four Text Captions one by one.

11. In the **Style Name** dropdown of the **Properties** panel, confirm that these Text Captions all use the **MFTC-TransparentCaption** style.

This is one of the many capabilities of the Object Style Manager. In the next two sections, you will experiment with exporting and importing styles.

Exporting a style

Another one of the extra features offered by the Object Style Manager is the ability to export styles. Let's experiment with this capability hands-on:

1. Still in the `encoderDemo_800.cptx` project, use the **Edit | Object Style Manager** menu item or use the *Shift + F7* (for Windows) or the *Shift + fn + F7* (for Mac) shortcut to reopen the Object Style Manager.

2. In the left column of the Object Style Manager, select the **Standard Objects | Captions | Text Caption** object type.

3. In the middle column, select the **MFTC-Caption** style.

4. At the bottom of the **Object Style Manager**, click on the **Export** button.

5. Save the style in the `Chapter07` folder of your exercises under the name `MFTC-Caption.cps`. Acknowledge the successful export by clicking on the **OK** button.

6. Click on **OK** to close the **Object Style Manager**.

7. Save the `encoderDemo_800.cptx` file.

Exporting a style creates a `.cps` file. This file will be used to import the style in another project.

Exporting multiple styles

Clicking on the drop-down arrow situated next to the **Export** button in the Object Style Manager gives you the ability to export all the Styles of a specific object type or even all the styles of all the objects.

Importing a style

In order to use your custom **MFTC-Caption** style in another project, you will now use the Object Style Manager of another project to import the .cps file created in the previous exercise in another Captivate project using the following steps:

1. Open the Chapter07/drivingInBe.cptx file.

2. Go to **Edit | Object Style Manager** to open the Object Style Manger.

3. In the **Object Style Manager** dialog, expand the **Standard Objects** section and select the **Caption** subsection.

4. Select the **Text Caption** object.

Note that your **MFTC-Caption** style is not listed in the middle column of the Object Style Manager. This is because the styles listed in the Object Style Manager are specific to the active file only. In Captivate, each project has its own list of styles.

Adding styles globally

If you want to add styles to the Object Style Manager and make them available to every (future) project of your Captivate installation, close all open files and use the **Edit | Object Style Manager** menu item when no file is open. This allows you to open the Object Style Manager of your Captivate installation rather than the Object Style Manager of a specific project. On Windows, make sure you run Captivate as an administrator to access the Object Style Manager when no project is open.

5. At the bottom of the **Object Style Manager** dialog, click on the **Import** button.

6. Browse to the Chapter07/MFTC-Caption.cps file and click on **Open**.

7. Read the message that pops up and click on **Yes** to discard it.

8. Close the **Object Style Manager** dialog by clicking on the **OK** button.

After this operation, the **MFTC-Caption** style has been transferred to the `drivingInBe.cptx` project and you should be able to apply it to the Text Captions of this project as well.

9. In the **Filmstrip** panel, select slide 13.

10. Select the **Motorways - 120 km/H is approx. 80 MPH** Text Caption that is inside the Slidelet.

11. Use the **Style Name** drop-down list in the topmost area of the **Properties** panel to apply the **MFTC-Caption** style to the selected Text Caption.

12. Move and resize the newly formatted Text Captions appropriately. (Feel free to use the Smart Guides and the icons of the Align toolbar).

Thanks to the Object Style Manager, you have been able to transfer a style from one project to another. This workflow helps you achieve formatting consistency not only within each project, but also across different projects.

Creating a style in the Object Style Manager

To create the **MFTC-Caption** style, you used the **Create New Style** item of the Object Options icon in the topmost area of the **Properties** panel. You will now create another style from within the Object Style Manager directly, using the following steps:

1. Still in the `Chapter07/drivingInBe.cptx` file, use the *Shift + F7* (for Windows) or *Shift + fn + F7* (for Mac) shortcut to reopen the Object Style Manager.

2. In the leftmost column, expand the **Standard Objects | Smart Shapes** category.

3. In the middle column, select the **[Default Smart Shape Style]** style.

4. Click on the **Clone** button below the middle column.

Captivate duplicates the **[Default Smart Shape Style]** style and saves the clone as **[Default Smart Shape Style]1**.

5. In the rightmost column of the **Object Style Manager** dialog, rename the new style to `transparentTitle`.

6. In the **Text Format** section, change the **Family** font to **Verdana** and the **Size** to **49**.

7. In the **Fill & Stroke** section, change the value of **Opacity** to **0%** and the **Width** to **0** to make the Smart Shape transparent.

Make sure the Object Style Manager looks similar to what is shown in the following screenshot:

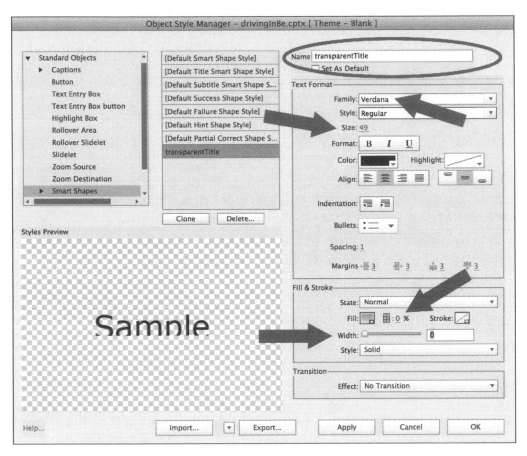

8. Leave the other options at their default settings and click on **OK** to close the Object Style Manager.

9. Use the **Filmstrip** panel to go to slide 1.

10. Select the Smart Shape containing **Drive in Belgium the safe way**.

11. Use the **Style** drop-down list of the **Properties** panel to apply the new **Transparent Title** style to the selected shape. Resize it if needed.

12. With the Smart Shape still selected, open the Object Options icon and click on the **Apply this style to** item.

13. In the box that pops up, apply the **Transparent Title** style to every Smart Shape currently using the **[Default Title Smart Shape Style]** style and click on **OK**.

14. Use the **Filmstrip** panel to browse the slides of your project one by one. If needed, use the Reset Style feature of the Object Options icon to clear the overrides.

15. Save the `drivingInBe.cptx` file when done.

This exercise concludes your overview of the Object Style Manager. Before moving on, let's summarize what you have learned:

- The items present in the Object Options icon of the **Properties** panel act as a remote control to the Object Style Manager

- The Object Style Manager provides extra tools when compared to the Object Options icon

- The leftmost column of the Object Style Manager contains a list of all the object types of Captivate

- Using the Object Style Manager, styles can be exported from a project and imported into another

- It is possible to create styles entirely in the Object Style Manager

Extra credit – exporting and importing styles

Now, you will make the **transparentTitle** style you just created available to the `encoderDemo_800.cptx` project. To do so, export it from the `drivingInBe.cptx` file to the `encoderDemo_800.cptx` file. Here are the general steps:

- In the `drivingInBe.cptx` file, open the Object Style Manager.

- Export the **transparentTitle** styles to the `Chapter07` folder of your exercises. (Remember that this style is associated with a Smart Shape.)

- Return to the `encoderDemo_800.cptx` file and use the Object Style Manager to import the style in the project.

- Save both files when done.

The Styles and the Swatch Manager are two of the tools of Captivate that help you achieve a consistent look and feel throughout your project. Although very powerful and flexible, these two tools are not the only ones available. You will now dive into Themes, a feature that was introduced in Captivate 6.

Working with Themes

A **Theme** is a file that collects all the formatting properties of a project, including (but not limited to) the Styles. Captivate installs with a handful of ready-to-use Themes right out of the box. In order to have a better idea of what a Theme is, you will start with some simple experiments using the predefined Themes of Captivate. The steps are as follows:

1. Save and close every open file in Captivate.

2. Use the **File | New Project | Blank Project** menu item.

3. In the **New Blank Project** dialog, use the **Select** drop-down menu to choose a size of **800 x 600** for the project. When done, click on the **OK** button.

Captivate creates a new blank project of the chosen size. When this new project is created, a single slide is automatically added to the **Filmstrip** panel. This new slide is already formatted and already contains several styled objects.

> **Creating a blank project from the Welcome screen**
>
> To create a new blank project, you can also use the **New** tab of the Welcome screen. In this case, you must choose the size of the new project in the bottom left corner of the Welcome screen and the **New Blank Project** dialog does not open.

Applying a Theme to an existing project

When you install Captivate, multiple predefined themes are installed along with the application. You will now apply one of these predefined themes to your new project and explore what a Theme is made of:

1. Still in your new blank project, click on the **Themes** icon of the Big Buttons Bar.

As depicted in the following screenshot, the **Themes** icon gives you access to the list of available themes. Looking at this list, you can also see that the theme currently applied to the project is the **White** theme (see the arrow in the following screenshot):

2. Click on any of the Themes present in the **Themes** icon to apply it to the current project.

3. Read the warning message about the style overrides. Click on **Yes** to acknowledge and clear the message.

The new theme is applied to the project. Take some time to look at what has changed. You should notice that, not only has the background of the slide changed, but also the formatting of the objects.

Before moving on to the next section, you will now reapply the original White theme to the project using the following steps:

4. Click on the **Themes** icon of the Big Buttons Bar to re-open the list of available themes.

5. Click on the **White** theme to reapply it to the current project.

6. Click on **Yes** to acknowledge and clear the warning message.

Now that you know how to apply themes, you will further explore this feature and discover what Themes are made of.

The elements of a Theme

A Captivate Theme is a collection of graphical elements and assets. You will now discover what Themes are made of by manipulating different Themes and explore how they affect the slides and objects of the project.

The Master Slides

The first element that makes up a Captivate Theme is a set of Master Slides. To better understand what these are, your first stop is the **Master Slide** panel.

1. Use the **Window** | **Master Slide** menu item to switch to the **Master Slide** view.

2. Enlarge the **Master Slide** panel by dragging the vertical separator between the **Master Slide** panel and the stage to the right.

The **Master Slide** panel now replaces the **Filmstrip** panel on the Captivate interface. In this view, the **Filmstrip** panel is therefore not visible.

The White Theme that is currently applied to the project contains an entire set of predefined Master Slides. Each of these Master Slides proposes a predefined layout that you can apply as is to any slide of the project. To ensure visual consistency across the Master Slides of the Theme, the first Master Slide of the panel is known as the **Main Master Slide** (shown as **1** in the following screenshot). The Main Master Slide contains the visual elements that are common to most of the (if not every) slides of the project.

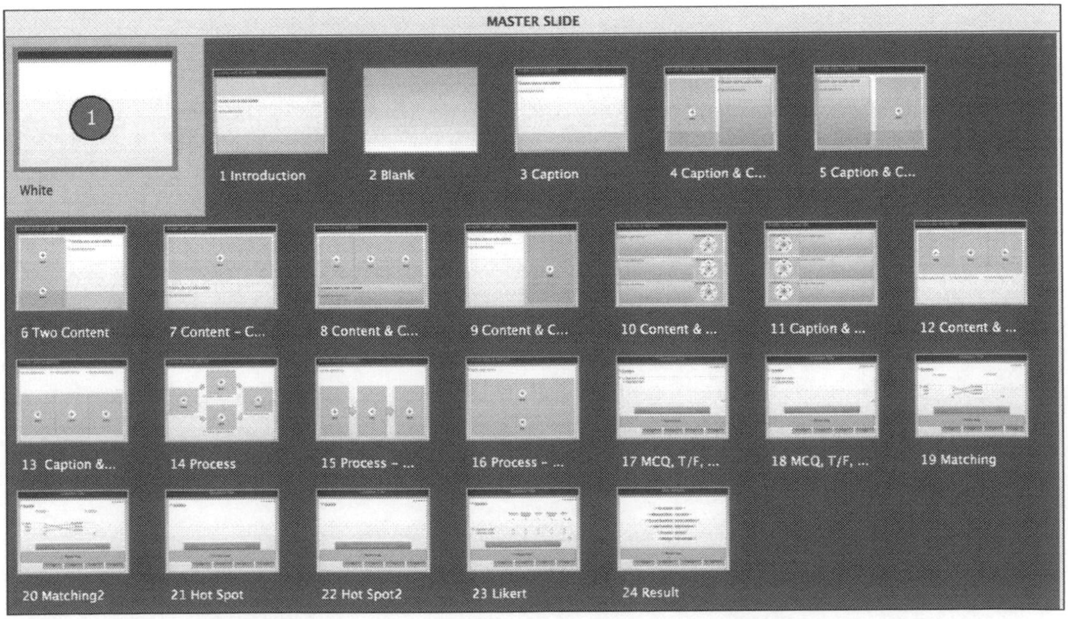

Creating slides based on Master Slides

It is possible to create new slides based on the Master Slides of the Theme using the following steps:

1. Use the **Window | Filmstrip** menu item to switch back to the **Filmstrip** view.

2. If needed, reduce the width of the **Filmstrip** panel by dragging the vertical separator between the **Filmstrip** panel and the stage to the left.

3. Use the **Insert | New Slide From | Caption** menu item to insert a new slide based on the Caption Master Slide of the Theme.

The new slide already contains several Smart Shapes and Text Captions. To be exact, the elements contained on the slides are not actual Text Captions and Smart Shapes yet. These elements are Text Caption and Smart Shapes **Placeholders**. They are used to predefine the location, size, and other formatting options of a future object.

4. Double-click on the **Double click to add title** Placeholder.

5. Type some text into the object and hit the *Esc* key.

Now that some text has been typed into the object, it is not a Placeholder anymore but an actual Smart Shape with text. The size, position, font family, font size, color, and so on of this object are inherited from the Placeholder, while the content of the Text Caption has just been typed in.

Changing the Master Slide of an existing slide

Sometimes, you may want to change the Master Slide applied to an existing slide. This is precisely what you will learn in this section.

1. Use the **Slide | Content Slide** icon of the Big Buttons Bar to insert a third slide in the project.

2. With the new slide selected, turn your attention to the **Properties** panel.

3. In the topmost section of the **Properties** panel, open the **Master Slides** drop-down menu and apply the **Caption & Content – Horizontal** Master Slide of the theme to the selected slide. This operation is depicted in the following screenshot:

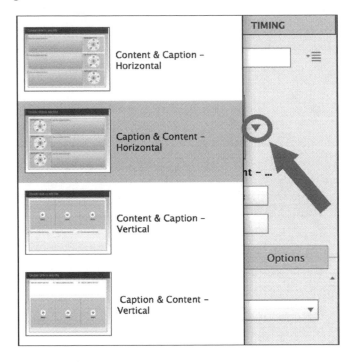

When inserting a new slide, Captivate always inserts it after the selected slide. As far as the Master Slide is concerned, Captivate uses whatever Master Slide is applied to the selected slide as the Master Slide of the new one.

After this operation, you should have three slides in your project. The third one is based on the **Caption & Content - Horizontal** Master Slide of the Theme, which also contains some Placeholders. On the left-hand side of the slide are three special Placeholder objects. These are known as Content Placeholders.

4. Roll your mouse over the icons of the Content Placeholders. Note that each icon corresponds to a Captivate Object.

5. Click on the **Image** icon of the topmost Content Placeholder, as shown in the following screenshot:

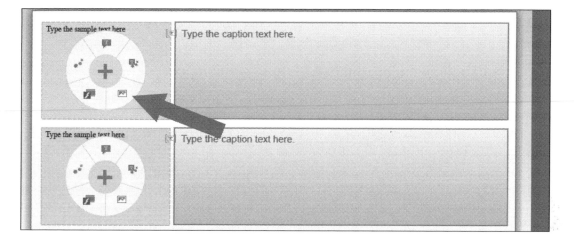

On clicking this icon, Captivate immediately opens the **Select Image from Library** dialog. From this dialog, you can choose the image to insert into the Placeholder.

6. Click on **Cancel** to close the dialog without inserting any image.
7. Take some time to experiment with the other icons of the Placeholder.

Each of these icons acts as a shortcut that inserts different kinds of content in the Placeholder. This illustrates the basic idea of Themes and Placeholders. By providing ready made slide layouts and shortcut icons right on the slides, the Themes and the Placeholders become tremendous time savers. They enable you to rapidly develop your pieces of eLearning content.

Inserting a blank slide in a themed project

In this section, you will insert a new blank slide in your project and see which Master Slide is applied by default. The steps are as follows:

1. Use the **Slide | Blank Slide** icon of the Big Buttons Bar to insert a new blank slide in the project.
2. With the new slide selected, turn your attention to the topmost section of the **Properties** panel.

Note that the **Blank** Master Slide has been automatically applied to this new slide.

3. Open the **Background** menu situated in the **Style** tab of the **Properties** panel.

4. Select the **Master Slide Background** item.

The background picture of the **Blank** Master Slide is now used as the background of the newly inserted slide. This concludes your first exploration of the Master Slides in Captivate.

Styles

The second element of a Theme is a set of object Styles. You will now experiment with Styles in the Theme using the following steps:

1. Use the **Filmstrip** panel to return to the second slide of this project.

2. Select the title (a Smart Shape with text) that you created in the previous section.

3. Take some time to inspect the **Properties** panel of the selected object. Note **Font, Color, Font Size,** and other formatting properties are currently in use.

You will now apply another Theme to the project and see how this change affects the slides and the objects.

4. Open the **Themes** icon of the Big Buttons Bar.

5. Click on the **Green** theme to apply it to the project.

6. Read the warning message and click on **Yes** to continue.

The new Theme is applied to the project.

7. Use the **Filmstrip** panel to go through the slides of the project one by one.

Note how the new Theme affects the look and feel of your project. The most obvious change is the new background picture, but a Theme is far more than that.

8. When on the second slide, select your Title Smart Shape.

9. In the **Properties** panel, note how the formatting properties of the selected object have changed.

This illustrates that, in addition to Master Slides, a Theme contains Object Styles. By applying another theme on a project, you also update the styles applied to the objects.

The third element of a Theme

In addition to Master Slides and Object Styles, a Theme contains a third element called the **Skin**. The Skin of the project will be covered in *Chapter 13, Finishing Touches and Publishing*.

You now have a much better understanding of what a Theme is. In the next section, you will create your own customized Theme and apply it to the *Driving in Belgium* project. Let's quickly summarize what you have learned in this section:

- A Theme is a collection of graphical assets and styles. It is used to quickly define the look and feel of an entire project.

- Captivate contains a dozen predefined Themes. These are available in the **Themes** icon of the Big Buttons Bar.

- A Theme is composed of three basic elements: a collection of Master Slides, the Styles to apply to the objects of the project, and the Skin of the project.

- When inserting a new slide, Captivate tries to determine the best Master Slide to apply.

- The **Properties** panel makes it possible to change the Master Slide applied to a regular slide at any time.

Creating a custom Theme

In this section, you will return to the Chapter07/drivingInBe.cptx file and create a new custom Theme. To do so, you will first apply one of the predefined Themes of Captivate to the project. You will then modify the Master Slides and the Styles of this theme to create your own custom Theme. The steps are as follows:

1. Return to the Chapter07/drivingInBe.cptx file.

2. Use the **Themes** icon of the Big Buttons Bar to apply the **Blank** theme to the project.

3. Click on **Yes** to acknowledge and clear the warning message.

By applying the **Blank** theme to the project, you modify the overall look and feel as well as the styles already present in the project. The **Blank** theme is an excellent starting point for creating your own custom theme.

4. Use the **Themes | Save Theme As** menu item to create a new Theme.

5. Save the new Theme as Chapter07/MFTC-Theme.cptm.

6. Acknowledge the successful creation of the new Theme by clicking on the **OK** button.

Note that the file extension used for themes is `.cptm`. With your new Theme saved, you can safely move on to the next step and customize the Master Slides of the Theme.

Customizing the Master Slides of the Theme

The idea behind Master Slides is quite simple. You create Master Slides with visual elements (backgrounds, logos, headers, and so on), so you can apply them to the standard slides of your project that need to share the same basic layout. If you are a PowerPoint or Keynote user, this process probably sounds very familiar. The steps are as follows:

1. Still in the `Chapter07/drivingInBe.cptx` file, use the **Window | Master Slide** menu item to return to the Master Slide view.

As shown in the following screenshot, the **Blank** Theme that you applied to the project already contains six Master Slides (shown as **1** in the following screenshot) in addition to the Main Master Slide, shown as **2** in the following screenshot. Note that the **Master Slide** panel has been enlarged to capture the screenshot:

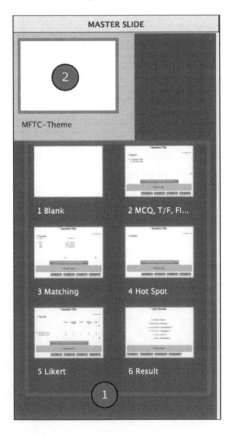

Customizing the Main Master Slide

The Main Master Slide is the first one in the **Master Slide** panel. The idea is to insert on the Main Master Slides the main graphical elements shared by most (if not all) of the other Master Slides of the project. Note that the name of the Theme (here, **MFTC-Theme**) appears below the Main Master Slide thumbnail. The steps are as follows:

1. In the **Master Slide** panel, click on the Main Master Slide to make it the active object.

2. If needed, open the **Properties** panel. Make sure it shows the properties of the Main Master Slide.

3. Use the **Media | Image** icon of the Big Buttons Bar to insert the `images/ contentSide.png` image on the main Master Slide.

4. With the image selected, turn your attention to the **Options** tab of the **Properties** panel.

5. Set both the **X** and the **Y** properties to `0` to position the image exactly in the top-left corner of the slide.

6. Use the **Media | Image** icon of the Big Buttons Bar a second time to insert the `images/contentFooter.png` image on the main Master Slide.

7. Use your mouse and the Smart Guides to position this image in the bottom-right corner of the main Master Slide.

8. Open the **Timeline** panel and completely lock these two objects using the lock icons of the **Timeline** panel.

With the addition of these two images, your project already looks much different to what it was a few minutes ago. If you take a look at the **Master Slide** panel, you should see that all the Master Slides of the Theme are now using the elements of the Main Master Slide.

The main Master Slide is also the perfect place to add legal comments such as a copyright notice. This is what you will achieve right now using the following steps:

9. Still on the Main Master Slide, use the **Text | Text Caption** icon of the Big Buttons Bar to create a new Text Caption.

10. Double-click in the new Text Caption to enter text edit mode and delete the default text.

11. In the **Character** section of the **Style** tab of the **Properties** panel, click on the **Add Symbol** icon. This operation is depicted in the following screenshot:

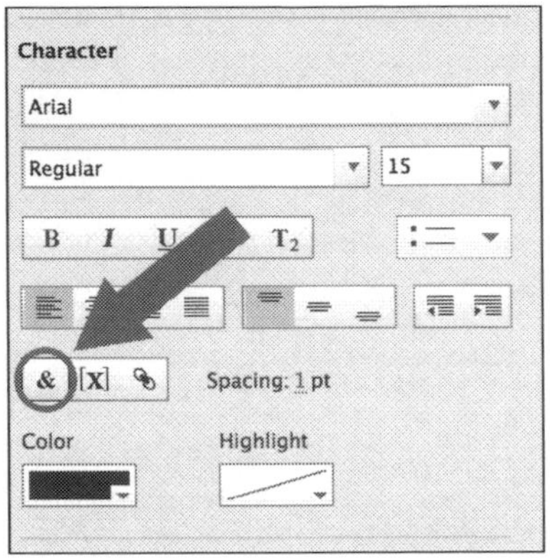

12. Click on the copyright symbol to insert it into the Text Caption.

13. Type `copyright - MFTC - 2015` after the copyright symbol. When done, hit the *Esc* key to leave Text Edit mode and select the Text Caption.

14. In the **Style** tab of the **Properties** panel, change the font to **Verdana** and the font size to 8 points (it is possible to type it if it is not in the list).

15. Move the Text Caption to the lower-right corner of the slide on top of the footer image.

16. In the **Timing** panel, make sure the **Transition** is set to **No Transition**.

17. Use the Object Options icon to create a new style after the current formatting of the copyright notice. Give that new style the name of `MFTC-copyright`.

18. Finally, use the lock icon of the **Timeline** panel to completely lock this object.

Take some time to browse the other Master Slides of the project and note that the images and the copyright notice appear on every one of them.

Adding a Master Slide to the Theme

You will now add a new Master Slide to the project. You will name it `Title` and use another image as its background using the following steps:

1. Use the **Insert | Content Master Slide** menu item to insert a new Master Slide in the project.

The new Master Slide is inserted as Master Slide number 2. Note that this new slide inherits the elements of the Main Master Slide, which is not what you want in this case.

2. Select the newly inserted Master Slide in the **Master Slide** panel and turn your attention to the **Properties** panel.

3. At the very top of the **Properties** panel, enter `Title` in the **Name** field and hit the *Enter* key to validate.

The new name appears below the Master Slide thumbnail in the **Master Slide** panel. The next step is to remove the elements that were inherited from the Main Master Slide.

4. At the top of the **Properties** panel, deselect the **Show Main Master Slide Objects** checkbox.

5. Use the **Media | Image** icon of the Big Buttons Bar to insert the `images/mftc-titleBkg_fixed.png` image.

6. Use the Lock icon of the **Timeline** panel to completely lock the new image.

The project should now contain seven Master Slides in addition to the Main Master Slide. As depicted in the following screenshot, the new **Title** Master Slide uses different background image to the other Master Slides of the project. The **Master Slide** panel has been enlarged to capture the following screenshot:

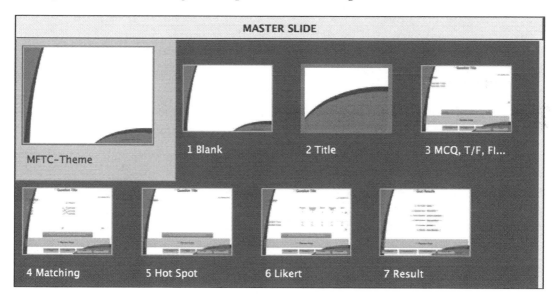

Adding Placeholders to the Master Slides

The power of Master slides goes way beyond defining common backgrounds and objects. By adding Placeholder objects, they can be used to predefine the location and styling of actual objects (such as Images, Text Captions, Smart Shapes, and so on). In this exercise, you will add a title Placeholder to the title Master Slide and customize it to the needs of your theme. The steps are as follows:

1. In the **Master Slide** panel, select the new **Title** Master Slide.

2. Use the **Insert | Placeholder Object | Title** menu item to add a Title Placeholder on the Master Slide.

3. Move and resize the Placeholder object on top of the brownish area of the background picture so it integrates nicely into the Title Master Slide.

4. With the Title Placeholder selected, turn your attention to the **Style** tab of the **Properties** panel.

The **Properties** panel of the selected Title Placeholder exposes the same properties as a Smart Shape. This is because the Title Placeholder is actually based on a Smart Shape. It means that all the features and flexibility offered by Smart Shapes are available to the Title Placeholder.

5. In the **Style** tab of the **Properties** panel, change the font to **Verdana**, select **Bold**, and align the text to the right of the Placeholder.

6. Switch to the **Timing** panel and apply a **Fade In Only** transition to the Title Placeholder.

7. Switch back to the **Properties** panel and use the Object Options icon to create a new style after the current formatting of the Title Placeholder. Give this new style the name `MFTC-mainTitle`.

At the time of design, the eLearning developer will simply double-click on the Placeholder and add the title of the project. The size, location and formatting properties of this title will be inherited from the Placeholder. This will ensure visual consistency and considerably speed up the development process.

Note that such Placeholder objects can only be inserted on Master Slides. In other words, it is not possible to insert a Placeholder object on a regular slide.

Applying the Master Slides to the Slides of the Project

In this section, you will use the Master Slides of your Theme to implement a consistent look and feel throughout the entire project. You will start by creating a new slide based on the Title Master slide using the following steps.

1. Use the **Window | Filmstrip** menu item to return to the Filmstrip view.

2. Return to the first slide of the project if needed.

3. Use the **Insert | New Slide From | Title** menu item to insert a new slide based on the **Title** Master Slide you created in the previous section.

4. In the **Filmstrip** panel, drag the new slide up to make it the first slide of the project.

5. Double-click in the title Placeholder and type `Driving in Belgium` as the title of the project.

The new title inherits its default properties (including the applied style) from the Placeholder object you created on the Master Slide. It is also important to mention that the eLearning developer is able to modify all these properties if he/she wants to. In other words, the Placeholder of the Master Slide only defines the default properties of the title, but it does not strictly enforce these properties. You will now take a look at the other slides of the project.

6. Use the **Filmstrip** panel to browse the other slides of the project one by one.

7. In the topmost area of the **Properties** panel, confirm that the **Blank** Master Slide is applied to all the other slides of the project.

Thanks to the Master Slides, all the slides of the project should now share the same general look and feel with minimal effort on your side!

Extra credit – creating the ending slide of the project

In this extra credit section, you will repeat the steps of the preceding exercise in order to create the ending slide of the project. The general steps are as follows:

*   Go to the last slide of the project.

*   Insert a new slide based on the Title Master Slide.

*   Write `Thanks for taking this online course with us` in the title Placeholder.

*   Slightly adjust the size and the position of the title if needed.

Now, you should have a total of 18 slides in your project.

Modifying a Master Slide

The Master Slides already help you achieve a high level of consistency within your project. Now they will help you maintain this consistency over time.

The design team at MFTC decided that the copyright notice should be moved to the left corner of the slide and rotated 270 degrees. Hopefully, you have cleverly placed this element on the Main Master Slide, so this change request from the design team is very easy to implement.

1. Use the **Window | Master Slide** menu item to return to the Master Slide view.

2. Select the Main Master Slide.

3. Open the **Timeline** panel to unlock the copyright notice.

4. Select the copyright notice situated at the bottom-right corner of the slide.

5. In the **Options** tab of the **Properties** panel, change the value of rotation angle to 270 degrees.

6. Move the copyright notice to the bottom-left corner of the slide so that it appears on top of the light brown area.

7. Make sure the copyright notice looks like the following screenshot and use the **Timeline** panel to lock it back.

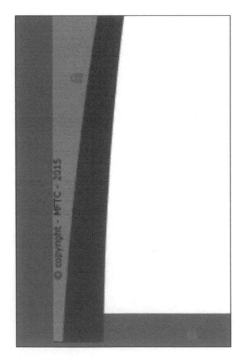

Now that the copyright notice is correctly placed in its new location, it is time to switch back to the filmstrip view and see how the standard slides react to this change.

8. Use the **Window | Filmstrip** menu item to return to the standard filmstrip view.

9. Browse the slides of the project one by one. Pay close attention to the copyright notice!

Thanks to the Main Master Slide, you have been able to implement this change request in no time! This will make for a very happy design team!

The Master Slide part of your customized Theme is complete for the moment. However, before moving on to the next section, don't forget to save the changes made to your custom Theme.

10. Use the **Themes | Save Theme** menu item to save the new Master Slide configuration in your custom `MFTC-Theme.cptm` file.

11. Save the `drivingInBe.cptx` file.

Now that the Theme is saved, let's quickly summarize what you just learned:

- To create a new Theme, apply one of the predefined Themes to your project and use the **Themes | Save Theme As** menu item

- A Theme is saved as a `.cptm` file

- The first element contained in a Theme is a set of Master Slides

- The Main Master slide is used to quickly define the general look and feel of the whole project

- By default, all the Master Slides of the project inherit the elements of the Main Master Slide

- Deselect the **Show Main Master Slide objects** checkbox to prevent the elements of the Main Master Slide from showing on a specific Master Slide.

- Use the **Insert | Content Master Slide** menu item to insert a new Master Slide in the project

- The changes made on a Master Slide are reflected on the standard slides that are based on that Master Slide

In the next section, you will define new Styles and save them in your custom Theme so that they can be easily reused in subsequent projects.

Adding Styles to the Theme

To create new styles you will return to the Object Options icon of the **Properties** panel. You will save these new styles in the Theme at the end of the exercise. Let's start by giving the proper look and feel to the standard objects of the project.

Styling the titles

In this section, you will modify the formatting of the Title Smart Shape of slide 2 using the following steps.

1. Use the **Window | Swatch Manager** menu item to open the **Swatch Manager** panel.

2. Confirm that the five custom swatches imported earlier in this chapter are still present in the **Swatch Manager** panel. If they are not, use the **Append** button of the **Swatch Manager** to reimport the `Chapter07/MFTC-Colors.ase` file. Close the **Swatch Manager** panel when done.

When you quit and launch Captivate again, the Swatches are reset to default. It may therefore be necessary to reimport your custom swatches when you need them.

3. Use the **Filmstrip** panel to return to slide 2 of the `Chapter04/drivingInBe.cptx` file.

There should be two Smart Shapes with text on slide 2, including the slide title. You will now modify the formatting of this title and save the changes in a style.

4. Select the Smart Shape that reads **Drive in Belgium the safe way**.

5. In the topmost area of the **Properties** panel, note that this object currently uses the **transparentTitle** style.

6. In the **Character** section of the **Style** tab of the **Properties** panel, reduce the font size to 36 points.

7. In the **Fill** section, apply **Solid Fill** using the **Color** of the first custom swatch (light brown) and setting **Opacity** to **100** percent.

8. Use the Object Options icon to save the current formatting of the selected shape in a new style named **MFTC-slideTitle**.

9. Return to the Object Options icon to apply the new **MFTC-slideTitle** style to all the Smart Shapes of the project that are currently using the **transparentTitle** style.

Now, all the slide titles throughout the entire project should use the same **MFTC-slideTitle** style. Your next task is to give them the very same size and the very same location using the **Options** tab of the **Properties** panel.

10. Make sure the title Smart Shape of slide 2 is still selected and turn your attention to the **Options** tab of the **Properties** panel.

11. Give the title a width of 720 pixels and a height of 80 pixels. (It may be necessary to deselect the **Constraint Proportions** checkbox to modify the Height and the Width independently).

12. For the position, give the title an **X** position of 80 and a **Y** position of 20.

Make sure that the title of slide 2 now looks like the following screenshot:

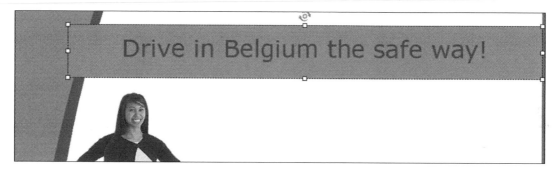

You will now apply the same sizing and positioning properties to all the slide titles throughout the entire project. Since they should all be using the same style (**MFTC-slideTitle**), this operation will be quite easy.

13. Turn your attention to the top-right corner of the **Transform** section in the **Options** tab of the **Properties** panel and click on the **Apply to All** icon.

14. Select the **Apply to all items of the same style** item.

This operation applies the properties of the **Transform** section to all the objects that are currently using the **MFTC-slideTitle** style, in other words, to all the slide titles of the project.

Placing the Master Slide objects on top

To give the slide title an even better look, you will now place the objects inherited from the Master Slide on top of the objects defined on the standard slides using the following steps:

1. Still on slide 2 of the `drivingInBe.cptx` project, click on an empty area of the slide to make it the active object.

2. In the **Style** tab of the **Properties** panel, select the **Master Slide Objects On Top** checkbox.

3. Repeat this operation on the other slides of the project that have the same type of title.

This makes the title look great, but may induce some undesirable side effects on some of the slides.

4. Use the **Filmstrip** panel to go to slide 10 of the project. Note that the title text is partially covered by the side image of the Master Slide.

5. Select the title Smart Shape to make it the active object.

6. Scroll to the very end of the **Style** tab of the **Properties** panel until you see the **Margins** section.

7. Increase the **Left** margin to 50 pixels.

This operation pushes the text of the title 50 pixels into the slide, so the elements of the Master Slide no longer cover it.

8. Rearrange the elements of slides 14, 15, and 16 so that they are not covered by the elements of the Master Slide anymore. (Don't hesitate to use the tools of the Align toolbar and the Smart Guides!).

Extra credit – styling the remaining objects

You now have all the tools you need in your hands to create the remaining styles of the project. In this extra credit section, I invite you to take some time to style the remaining objects of the project and to save the formatting you come up with in styles. Here are a few tips and ideas to get you started:

- Make the Rollover Areas of slide 16 and 17 transparent
- Change the formatting of the grey Smart Shapes that are spread into the project
- When you come up with a great formatting idea, remember to save it in a style
- Go to the **Apply this style to** feature of the Object Options icon to quickly apply the same style to multiple objects throughout the project
- Don't hesitate to move and resize some objects to make the slides look great
- Remember to use the Smart Guides and the tools of the Align toolbar to properly position the objects

And, above all, the master of all tips: have fun while designing your project. Let your creativity express itself. Remember that the learner will only enjoy the final product. They will have no clue of all the foolish ideas you might have tried to get there! So, why restrain yourself?

Saving the styles in the Theme

In order to save the newly created styles into the Theme, you simply need to save the Theme itself. By saving the Theme, you update the `MFTC-Theme.cptm` file with the updated Master Slides and styles. Use the **Themes | Save Theme** menu item to update the current Theme with the new styles.

From now on, each time you experiment with a new object in Captivate, create a style for this object and save the Theme to add the new style to the `.cptm` file. At the end of the book, your Theme will contain styles for almost every object within your project.

In the next section, you will discover Captivate templates.

Extra credit – applying the Theme to another project

The very purpose of a theme is to save the look and feel of a project so it can be applied to other projects. In this extra credit section, you will experiment with this hands-on by applying your new theme to the Encoder Demonstration project. Here are the general steps to follow:

- Open the `Chapter07/encoderDemo_800.cptx` file.

- Use the **Browse** link situated at the bottom-left corner of the **Themes** icon of the Big Buttons Bar to select your custom `MFTC-Theme.cptm` file.

- After the Theme has been applied, browse the slide of the project to apply the proper Master Slides.

- By applying the Theme, you clear the custom styles already applied to the objects of the project. That's why you need to reapply the proper styles throughout the demonstration.

- Create a new Master Slide. Make it completely blank and apply it to the slides of the screenshot-based demonstration.

- Replace objects, add buttons, and arrange the slides as needed. Don't hesitate to create new styles along the way.

- Don't forget to save the theme to update it with the new Master Slides and Styles you come up with.

- Save the project when done.

If you get confused by this exercise, don't hesitate to use the `Chapter07/final/encoderDemo_800.cptx` file as a reference. After this extra credit section, both your projects should share the very same general look and feel as described in the styling guidelines of the MFTC company.

Working with Templates

The basic idea of a Template is to create a project that can be used as a blueprint for future projects. When creating a project from a Template, a stencil copy of the Template is created that serves as the starting point for a new project. In the new project, the teacher can edit, remove, and add objects with no restrictions.

A Template can contain the same slides and objects as a regular project. The preferences applied to the Template become the default preferences of future projects that will be based on the Template. The Theme that is applied to a Template becomes the default Theme of future projects based on that Template.

In the next exercise, you will create a Template that will be used for all the demonstrations created by the developers of the MFTC company. To do so, let's pretend that the instructional and visual designers at MFTC decided the following:

- All demonstrations should have a resolution of 800 x 600 pixels
- All demonstrations should use your custom `MFTC-Theme.cptm` theme
- All demonstrations should begin with a title Slide and the title should be written in a Smart Shape using the **MFTC-MainTitle** style
- The second slide of each demonstration should state the objectives of the project
- The actual screenshot-based demonstration begins on the third slide
- When the demonstration is finished, a summary slide should emphasize the key points of what has been covered in the project
- After the summary, the ending slide should be similar to the first one with closing text

Creating a Template

To help the company enforce these rules, you will create a Template that the eLearning developers will use to create future demonstrations. This Template will not only help in producing consistent content and design across projects, but will also speed up the development process of the eLearning courses by reusing common designs, properties, and content. The steps are as follows:

1. Save and close every open project.
2. Use the **File | New Project | Project Template** menu item to start the creation of a new template. Make sure to use the **Project Template** item and not the **Project From Template** item. Alternatively, you can use the *cmd* + *T* (for Mac) or *Ctrl* + *T* (for Windows) shortcut.

3. In the **New Project Template** box, select the **800 x 600** resolution and click on **OK**.

The first rule is already enforced! All the demonstrations that will be based on this Template will use the same **800 x 600** resolution.

4. Open the **Themes** icon of the Big Buttons Bar.

5. Click on the **Browse** link situated in the bottom-left corner of the **Themes** panel.

6. Browse to the themes/MFTC-final.cptm file and apply that theme to the new Template.

Second rule enforced! All future demonstrations based on this Template will use your custom MFTC-final.cptm file.

 The MFTC-final.cptm theme is the final version of the theme you worked on in the previous section.

7. Make sure that the **Properties** panel shows the properties of the first slide of the project.

8. At the top of the **Properties** panel, use the **Master Slide** drop-down menu to apply the **Title** Master Slide of the Theme to the selected slide.

9. At the top of the **Properties** panel, also change the slide name to Intro Slide and press *Enter* to validate.

Third rule enforced! The first slide of the Template is based on the Title Master Slide of the Theme and contains a Title Smart Shape Placeholder with the **MFTC-MainTitle** style already applied.

10. Use the **Slide | Blank** menu item of the Big Buttons Bar to insert a new slide based on the **Blank** Master Slide of your Theme.

11. Use the **Properties** panel to change the name of this slide to Objectives.

12. Add a rectangle Smart Shapes to the new slide and write Objectives in it.

13. Apply the **MFTC-slideTitle** style to the new rectangle.

14. In the **Options** tab of the **Properties** panel, give the new title a width of 720 pixels and a height of 80 pixels (deselect the **Constraint Proportions** checkbox if needed).

15. Also, set **X** as 80 and **Y** as 20 to properly position the shape.

16. Click on an empty area of the slide to make it the active object.

17. In the **Properties** panel, select the **Master Slide Objects On Top** checkbox to finalize the inclusion of the title on the slide.

18. Use the Shapes icon to add a second rectangle to the slide. Write Objective 1 in it and apply the **MFTC-standardText** style.

19. Position the second Text Caption below the first one to make the slide look like the following screenshot:

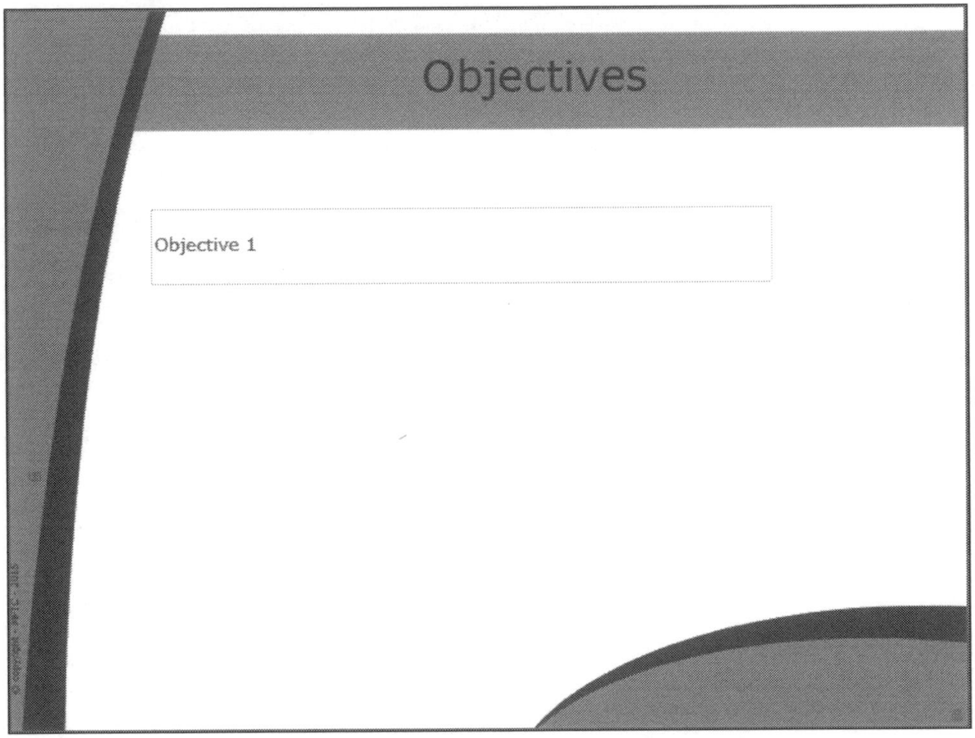

Fourth rule enforced! The second slide of the Template is ready to receive the objectives of the demonstration. The layout and styling of that content is already predefined in the Theme and in the Master Slides.

Adding Placeholder Slides

The third slide of the Template is where the actual screenshot-based demonstration should begin. When developing the Template, you do not know how long that demonstration will be and how many slides it will require. You only know that the demonstration begins on slide 3. To enforce this rule, you will now add a Placeholder Slide to the Template.

In Captivate, there are two kinds of Placeholder Slides:

- A Recording Slide Placeholder is meant to be replaced by a screenshot-based recording using the techniques covered in *Chapter 2, Capturing the Slides*.

- A Question Slide Placeholder is meant to be replaced by a Question Slide. Quizzes and Question Slides will be covered in *Chapter 10, Working with Quizzes*.

In this case, a Recording Slide Placeholder is what you need. Use the following steps to insert a Recording Slide Placeholder to the Template:

1. If needed, use the **Filmstrip** panel to go to slide 2 in the Template.

2. Use the **Insert | Placeholder Slides | Recording Slide Placeholder** menu item to add a Recording Slide Placeholder at the end of the Template.

Note that Placeholder slides can only be added to a Captivate template.

Fifth rule enforced! The Recording Slide Placeholder is added as slide 3 of the Template.

Note that the options of the **Properties** panel are all grayed out when the slide is selected. Also, note that most of the icons of the Big Buttons Bar are grayed out. This is because this Placeholder is not an actual slide. It has therefore no properties to expose in the **Properties** panel and no objects can be added on top of it.

Adding the last slides

You will now create the last two slides of the Template. Since they are very similar to the first two slides, you will copy, paste, and modify the first two slides of the project. The steps are as follows:

1. In the **Filmstrip** panel, select the first two slides of the project and use the *Ctrl + C* (for Windows) or *cmd + C* (for Mac) shortcut to copy the slides.

2. Use the **Filmstrip** panel to go to the last slide of the Template (the Placeholder slide) and use the *Ctrl + V* (Windows) or *cmd + V* (Mac) shortcut to paste the slides at the end of the Template.

3. In the **Filmstrip**, reorder the slides you have just pasted. The copy of the **Intro Slide** should be the last slide of the project.

4. When done, go to slide 4 of the Template. In the **Properties** panel and change its name to `Summary Slide`.

5. Change the text of the Title Smart Shape to `Summary` and the text of the other Smart Shape to `Summary 1`.

6. Move to the last slide of the Template and change its name to `Ending Slide`.

Sixth and seventh rules enforced! The last two slides of the Template are used to emphasize the key points learned during the demonstration and to add a nice closing slide.

Saving the Template

For the sake of this example, you can consider this Template finished. Keep in mind though that you could go much further in the development of a Captivate Template. For example, you could use the **Preferences** dialog and define the project properties in the Template itself. These would become the default preference used by future projects based on that Template. Save the Template as `Chapter07/MFTC-Demo.cptl`.

Note that the file extension used for a Captivate Template is `.cptl` and not `.cptx` as for a regular project. Next, you'll create a new project from this template.

Creating a new Captivate project from a Template

In this section, you will play the role of an eLearning developer who has to use the new Template to develop a new Captivate demonstration for the MFTC company. The steps are as follows:

1. Close every open file so that you can see the Captivate Welcome screen.
2. Switch to the **New** tab of the Welcome Screen.
3. Double-click on the **From Project Template** thumbnail.
4. Navigate to the `Chapter07/MFTC-Demo.cptl` Template file to choose it as the basis of a new project.

The new project that opens in Captivate is a stencil copy of the Template you created in the previous section. Note that the new project uses the standard `.cptx` file extension.

Before moving on, you will quickly preview the project. Use the **Preview** icon of the Big Buttons Bar to preview the entire project.

When the project appears in the **Preview** pane, note that the Smart Shape Placeholder of slide 1 does not appear in the final output. Also, note that the recording slide Placeholder is not part of the final output either. Actually, the slide count (shown at the top-left corner of the **Preview** pane) is 4 and not 5.

As long as the Placeholder objects and slides have not been replaced by actual objects and slides, they do not appear in the compiled version of the project.

5. Close the **Preview** pane to return to Captivate.

6. Use the **Filmstrip** panel to go to the first slide of the project.

7. Double-click on the Title Placeholder and type `Welcome to the Demonstration`. Hit *Esc* when done to quit text edit mode and leave the shape selected.

This action turns the Title Placeholder into an actual Smart Shape object. You must have noticed how fast it was to insert the project tile on the first slide. Rapid development is one of the key advantages of using Themes, Templates, Styles, and Placeholder.

8. With the title selected, turn your attention to the **Style** tab of the **Properties** panel.

9. Try to change the font to another one of your choice.

No warning messages appear on the screen to tell you that this property is locked by the Template and cannot be changed. In other words, the developer has the freedom to override the choices made on the Template. Remember that the Template sets the default properties of slides and objects, but it does not force the teacher/developer to use them in the final version of the project.

10. Use the **Filmstrip** panel to go to slide 3 of the project.

Slide 3 is the **Recording Slide Placeholder**. Remember that it did not show in the **Preview** pane while testing the project earlier in this section.

11. Double-click on the **Recording Slide Placeholder** slide.

Captivate switches to recording mode and displays the red recording area. All the options discussed in *Chapter 2*, *Capturing the Slides*, are available in the Recording window — except for the size of the red recording area, which is blocked by the Template at **800 x 600** pixels.

12. Click on the **Cancel** button to return to the standard Captivate interface.

13. Close the project without saving it.

This exercise concludes your overview of the Templates. Before moving on to the next chapter, let's quickly summarize what has been covered in this section:

- A Captivate Template is a blueprint used as a starting point for standard Captivate projects.

- A Template contains the very same objects and slides as a standard project.

- The Theme applied to a Template serves as the default Theme for all future projects based on that Template.

- Placeholder Slides are used to mark the location of a screen recording or the location of Question Slides in the Template.

- A Template sets the default properties and objects, but it does not strictly enforce them. In other words, a teacher/developer can override the choices made on a Template when designing the project.

- A Template file has a `.cptl` file extension.

Summary

In this chapter, you concentrated on the cosmetic aspect of the project. You discovered that it is important to create a consistent learning environment in which your learners feel comfortable enough to concentrate on learning the content and not on how the online course actually works.

In the first part of this chapter, you learned about the Swatch Manager, the Styles, and the Object Style Manager. You then used the predefined Themes of Captivate to better understand what Themes are and how they work. Next, you moved on to creating your own customized Theme. Finally, you created a Template and used that Template to create a new project.

By using the Styles, the Master Slides, the Themes, the Swatch Manager, and the Templates, you created professional-looking and consistent projects in record time with minimal effort!

With the completion of this chapter, an important part of the book comes to an end. The projects you have been working on are pretty much ready to be published.

In the next few chapters, you will learn about the more advanced features of Captivate, such as Quizzes and Advanced Actions. If all you need is to create simple projects such as the ones you just completed, feel free to jump directly to *Chapter 13, Finishing Touches and Publishing*, to learn about the publishing phase.

In the next chapter, you will quickly review the Video Demo you captured in *Chapter 2, Capturing the Slides* and generate an `.mp4` video file that can be uploaded to YouTube.

Meet the community

In this section, I want to introduce you to Richard Jenkins. He works for Adobe as an eLearning Solutions consultant. He has also authored the *Foreword* of the previous edition of this book. When I first contacted him about the *Foreword* section, he was very surprised, as he had never written a foreword before. We had a chance to meet during the Adobe Learning Summit in Las Vegas last October, but we missed each other at the closing reception! I guess I'll have to go back to Vegas next year to catch up with him!

Richard John Jenkins

Richard John Jenkins' background lies in photojournalism, film, screenwriting, neon art and design, multimedia, web publishing tools, technology training, and search engine marketing industries. During his varied career, he aligned himself with Macromedia Inc. (acquired by Adobe Systems). He was invited to join Macromedia's Systems Engineer (SE) team in 1998, focusing on the Hi-ED and K12 markets. As part of the Macromedia Education SE team, he evangelized Macromedia's products to tens of thousands of people at over 250 schools, 25 user groups, 137 companies, plus presented at dozens of public seminars, workshops, webinars, and webcast all over the U.S. and Canada. Currently, he is Adobe's eLearning Solutions consultant who supports Adobe's North American eLearning team, from where he evangelizes the eLearning solutions and technologies far and wide. In his so-called spare time, he is a fine artist who creates stylized hanging art mobiles along with abstract pastels and paintings in the Russian and German Expressionist style. When he is not creating art or working, he spends his time with his three little kids who are obsessed with computer games, endlessly walking the family dog, and stealing away a little quality time holding hands with his Starbucks-addicted wife.

Contact details

- **Blog**: http://blogs.adobe.com/captivate
- **E-mail**: Jenkins@Adobe.com

8

Producing a Video Demo

Sometimes, all you need is a good old video file that you can embed into your website or upload to YouTube. In such case a Video Demo project comes in handy. Video demos are used to create MP4 video files that the learner experiences from the beginning to the end in a linear fashion. Therefore, the advanced interactivity features of Captivate are not supported in Video Demos.

In this chapter, you will experience the entire Captivate production process using a Video Demo file as the example. First, you will return to the Video Demo you created back in *Chapter 2, Capturing the Slides*. Then, you will turn it into a professional screencast using Captivate tools. Finally, you will publish it as an .mp4 video file. If you happen to have a YouTube account, you can even upload the video file to YouTube without leaving Captivate.

In this chapter, you will:

- Tour the Video Demo interface
- Add objects in a Video Demo project
- Remove unwanted popups
- Add Transitions and Pan & Zoom effects
- Publish the Video Demo as an .mp4 file
- Publish the Video Demo to YouTube

Preparing your work

To get the most out of this chapter, it is a good idea to reset the Captivate interface to default. If you are using the default interface mode, just close and restart Captivate to reset it. If you are using the advanced interface mode, use the **Window | Workspace | Reset 'Classic'** menu item to reset Captivate to default. In this chapter, you will use the exercises stored in the Chapter08 folder of the download associated with this course. If you get confused by any of the step-by-step instructions, take a look at the Chapter08/final folder that contains a copy of the files, as they will be at the end of this chapter.

The Video Demo interface

For this chapter, you will use the Video Demo file that you created in *Chapter 2, Capturing the Slides*. Let's first open this file and take a closer look at this project:

1. Start Captivate and open the Chapter08/encoderVideo.cpvc file.

2. Use the **Preview | Project** icon of the Big Buttons Bar and take the necessary time to view the entire project.

When you click on the **Preview** icon, note that most of the previewing options are grayed out. The only thing that you can actually do is preview the entire project. Remember that a Video Demo project is aimed at producing an .mp4 video file. This content plays in one big chunk from the beginning to the end with no interactivity whatsoever. Technically, it is said that a video file offers a linear experience versus the nonlinear interactive experience of a regular project. It is therefore not based on slides, so the previewing options involving slides (Preview From this Slide, Preview Next 5 slides, and so on) are, logically, unavailable.

3. At the end of the preview, click on the **Edit** button situated at the bottom-right corner of the screen to return to the **Edit** mode.

4. Take some time to inspect the Captivate interface.

When working on a Video Demo project (with a .cpvc file extension), the Captivate interface is a bit different to what you've been used to when working on a regular project (with a .cptx file extension). All these interface changes come down to the simple fact that the published version of the project can only be an .mp4 video file.

First, note that there is no **Filmstrip** panel on the left-hand side of the screen. Since the project is not based on slides, this makes perfect sense. Also, note that the **Interactions** icon of the Big Buttons Bar is grayed out. Since video files do not support any kind of interaction, this—again—makes perfect sense.

5. Browse the other icons of the Big Buttons Bar and take note of the objects that are available in a Video Demo project.

6. Click on the **Properties** icon situated at the right end of the Big Buttons Bar.

As expected, this action opens the **Properties** panel. Just next to the **Properties** panel is the **Video Effects** panel.

7. Switch to the **Video Effects** panel and take some time to examine the available properties.

The **Video Effects** panel contains options and tools that are specific to Video Demo projects.

8. Take some time to further explore the interface. Try to spot other differences between the standard Captivate interface and the one used for Video Demo projects.

This concludes your first overview of the Video Demo projects and the associated Captivate interface. Before moving on, let's make a quick summary of what you have learned so far:

- Video Demos are used to generate linear video files in the .mp4 format.

- Video Demos use their own .cpvc file extension that is different from the .cptx extension used by standard Captivate projects.

- When working on a .cpvc project, the Captivate interface is slightly different than the standard interface of the .cptx projects. Some panels, such as the **Filmstrip** panel, are not relevant to video files and are therefore removed from the interface. Other panels, such as the **Video Effects** panel are specific to Video Demos.

The postproduction phase of a Video Demo project

Remember that the Captivate production process is made of three phases. When it comes to this particular project, the first phase (the Capture phase) has already been done in *Chapter 2, Capturing the Slides*. You will now dig into the second phase of the process.

Adding objects to a Video Demo project

First, you will take a closer look at the objects that can be added in a Video Demo project and explore how they can be used in the context of a linear video file.

Inserting images in a Video Demo project

You will create the beginning and the ending of the video using an image that you will overlay on top of the video track. Use the following steps to insert an image in the Video Demo:

1. Open the **Timeline** panel by clicking on the **Timeline** button at the bottom of the screen.

2. In the **Timeline** panel, make sure that the playhead (the vertical red line) is at the very beginning of the project. If needed, use the **Move the playhead to the beginning** icon as shown in the following screenshot:

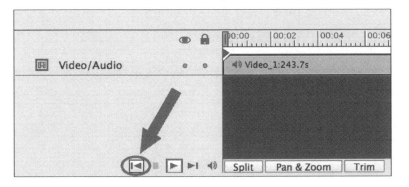

3. Use the **Media | Image** icon of the Big Buttons Bar to insert `images/mftc-titleBkg_VideoDemo.png` at the beginning of the project.

The imported image appears in the **Timeline** panel at the position of the playhead as an extra layer on top of the video file.

4. Use the **Timeline** or the **Timing** panel to extend the duration of the image to 16 seconds.

The **Properties** and **Timing** panels of the image are exactly the same as in a regular project. Inserting images in a Video Demo is very similar to inserting images in a standard Captivate project.

Extra credit – inserting the end image of the Video Demo project

In this extra credit section, you will insert the very same image at the end of the Video Demo. Because the image has already been inserted in the project, it is available in the project Library and does not need to be imported a second time. The general steps are follows:

- Move the playhead to the 3:52 seconds mark.
- Drag the `mftc-titleBkg_VideoDemo.png` file from the **Library** panel and drop it on top of the video.
- Place the image in the top-left corner of the video (**X** = 0 and **Y** = 0).
- Extend the duration of the image to the end of the Video Demo.

Now the `mftc-titleBkg_VideoDemo.png` should be displayed at the beginning and at the end of the project.

Inserting objects in a Video Demo project

A small subset of the Captivate objects is supported in a Video Demo project. Supported objects include Smart Shapes, Highlight boxes, and Text Captions, among others. Inserting and formatting these objects in a Video Demo is done in the exact same way as in a standard Captivate project. That's why this section of the book will not contain any step-by-step instructions as usual. Instead, you will apply the skills you learned in the previous chapters to insert objects in the Video Demo project.

Here are your assignments:

- Insert a rounded rectangle Smart Shape at the beginning of the project on top of the image you inserted in the previous section. Write a nice title for the Video Demo and format it in the same way as the title of the other projects you worked on in previous chapters.
- Repeat the preceding operation to add a closing comment at the end of the project.
- When you feel like an area of the screen should be highlighted, insert a Smart Shape and format is as a Highlight Box. Don't forget to use the **Timeline** panel to sync these Highlight Boxes with the rest of the Video file.
- Feel free to add other objects or Text Labels as you see fit.

Now your Video Demo should contain Images, Highlight Boxes, and other objects used to further enhance the screencast. As far as these objects are concerned, there is nothing new to learn in this section. Just take this as an opportunity to practice your new skills in a new situation. If you get confused by this assignment, don't hesitate to take a look at the `Chapter08/final/encoderDemo.cpvc` file for clarification and inspiration.

Themes in a Video Demo

You probably noticed that the **Themes** icon of the Big Buttons Bar is disabled in a Video Project. This is because themes are, unfortunately, not supported in a Video Demo project. Styles, however, are fully supported, including importing and exporting slides to and from other Captivate projects regardless of these projects being Video Demos or regular Captivate files.

Removing unwanted popups

New to Captivate 8 and specific to Video Demo projects is the ability to remove unwanted popups and tooltips that were captured during the recording. In this project, there is such a tooltip between the 1:44 and the 1:52 marks of the **Timeline** panel. You will now remove this unwanted tooltip using the following steps:

1. Still in the `Chapter08/encoderDemo.cpvc` file, use the **Timeline** panel to place the red playhead around the 1:44 mark.

2. Use the **Play / Pause** icon at the bottom left corner of the **Timeline** panel to spot the exact timing where the unwanted yellow tooltip appears and disappears.

3. When done, place the playhead when the tooltip appears on the screen.

4. Turn your attention to the **Video Effects** panel.

Remember that the **Video Effects** panel is tied to the **Properties** panel. It may therefore be necessary to open the **Properties** panel to access the **Video Effects** panel. Also, remember that the **Video Effects** panel contains options that are specific to Video Demo projects.

5. Switch to the **Popup** tab of the **Video Effects** panel.

6. Click on the **Replace** button and draw a rectangle on top of the unwanted yellow tooltip.

7. In the **Timeline** panel, extend the duration of the **Popup_Freeze_Item** so it matches the duration of the unwanted yellow tooltip on the video track.

Now, this portion of the timeline should look like the following screenshot:

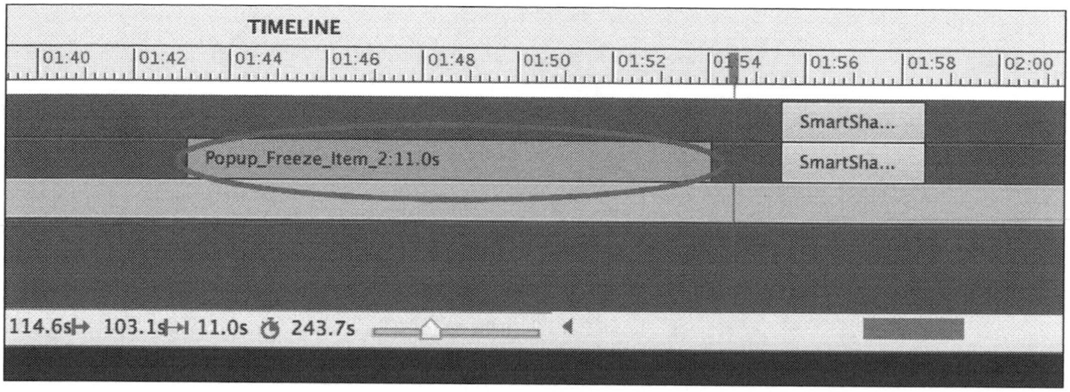

Thanks to this awesome and easy to use new feature of Captivate 8, you are now able to clean up your video captures from unwanted popups and tooltips!

Adding Pan & Zoom animation

Another very nice and easy to use feature of Video Demos is the **Pan & Zoom** animation. It allows you to zoom on a specific area of the video and to move the camera during the movie. In the next exercise, you will add two **Pan & Zoom** animations into this particular project by performing the following steps:

1. In the **Timeline** panel, move the playhead more or less to the **02:00** mark.
2. Turn your attention to the **Pan & Zoom** tab of the **Video Effects** panel.
3. In the **Pan & Zoom** panel, click on the **Add Pan & Zoom** button.

The **Pan & Zoom** panel updates and shows the available pan and zoom controls along with a thumbnail image of the current frame of the video. A blue bounding box with eight handles surrounds this thumbnail image.

4. Resize and move the blue bounding box so it covers only the **Video** tab part of the thumbnail (see **1** in the following screenshot).

5. Increase the **Speed** value of the **Pan & Zoom** animation to **1.0** sec (**2**), as shown in the following screenshot:

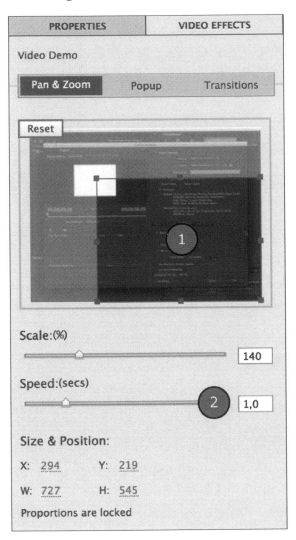

After this procedure, a **Pan & Zoom** icon appears in the **Timeline** panel. If you want to modify or delete the **Pan & Zoom** animation, just click on this icon to load the properties of this **Pan & Zoom** animation in the **Pan & Zoom** panel.

6. Because of the **Pan & Zoom** effect, it may be necessary to move and resize some of the objects you added on top of the video in the previous section.

You will now move the playhead ahead on the **Timeline** panel and add the corresponding **Zoom Out** animation.

7. In the **Timeline** panel, move the playhead more or less to the **02:49** mark.

8. Return to the **Pan & Zoom** tab of the **Video Effects** panel and click on the **Zoom Out** button to restore the view.

9. Also, increase the **Speed** value of this animation to **1.0** sec.

These actions add a second **Pan & Zoom** animation in the project as indicated by the second **Pan & Zoom** icon in the **Timeline** panel around the **02:49** mark, as shown in the following screenshot:

Adding Transitions

Another way of adding animation to a Video Demo project is to add Transitions. A **Transition** defines how the project moves from one video clip to the next.

In this case, you only have a single big video clip in your project, so the only places you can add Transitions are at the very beginning and the very end of the project. To add Transitions in the middle of a video clip, you first have to split the video into smaller sequences. You will then be able to add transitions between these sequences. Let's check it out by performing the following steps:

1. In the **Timeline** panel, move the playhead to the **00:16** mark, where the front title of the video finishes (see **1** in the following screenshot).

2. At the bottom of the **Timeline** panel, click on the **Split** button shown as (2) in the following screenshot:

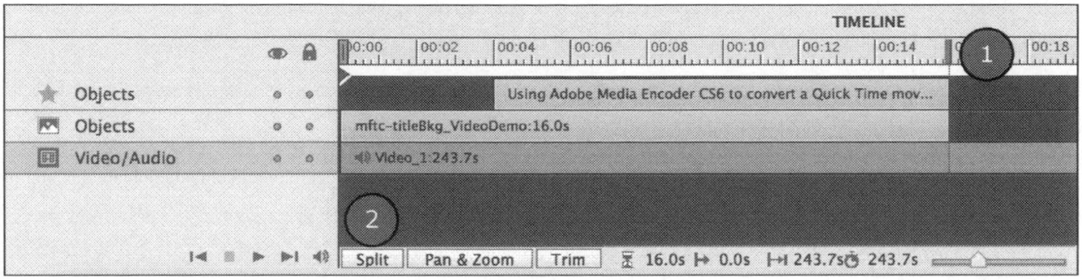

This effectively splits the video file into two separate sequences as indicated by the small diamond that appears in the **Timeline** panel at the exact location of the split. Because you now have two video clips in your project, it is possible to add a Transition between these two sequences.

3. Turn your attention to the **Transitions** tab of the **Video Effects** panel.

4. In the **Timeline** panel, click on the diamond situated between the two sequences that you have split.

5. In the **Transitions** panel, choose a Transition of your liking.

6. At the top of the **Transitions** tab, adjust the **Speed** of the Transition to your liking (**Fast**, **Medium**, or **Slow**).

7. Repeat the same sequence of actions at the end of the project (more or less at the **03:52** mark of the **Timeline** panel).

8. When done, use the **Preview | Project** icon of the Big Buttons Bar to take a look at the entire Video Demo.

During the preview, pay particular attention to the newly added **Pan & Zoom** and **Transitions**.

9. When the preview is finished, click on the **Edit** button at the bottom-right corner of the screen to return to edit mode.

10. Save the file when done.

This exercise concludes the postproduction step of the process. Your Video Demo is now ready for publication but, before that, let's summarize what has been covered in this section.

- Objects can be added on top of a Video Demo using the very same procedures and options as in a standard Captivate project.
- The only difference is that Video Demos only support a small subset of the objects available in Captivate. Interactive objects, such as Buttons and Rollover Objects, are (for instance) not supported.
- Video Demos do not support Themes, but they fully support Styles including importing and exporting styles to and from other projects.
- The **Video Effects** panel contains options that are exclusive to Video Demos.
- New in Captivate 8 is the ability to remove unwanted popups and tooltips from the video.
- The **Pan & Zoom** animations can be used to zoom on a specific part of the screen and to move the camera while playing the movie.
- Transitions can be added between two video clips. If your project is composed of a single big video track, you can split it into smaller sequences and add Transitions between these sequences.

Publishing a Video Demo project

Due to its very nature, a Video Demo project can only be published as an `.mp4` video file. In the following exercise, you will explore the available publishing options and publish the `Chapter08/encoderVideo.cpvc` project using the following steps:

1. Open or return to the `Chapter08/encoderVideo.cpvc` file.
2. Make sure the file opens in edit mode.
3. If you are not in edit mode, click on the **Edit** button at the lower-right corner of the screen. (If the **Edit** button is not displayed on the screen, it simply means that you are already in edit mode.)
4. Click on the **Publish | Publish to Computer** icon or use the **File | Publish** menu item. In both cases, the **Publish Video Demo** dialog opens.
5. In the **Publish Video Demo** dialog, make sure the **Name** of the project is `encoderVideo`.
6. Click on the **...** button and choose the `publish` folder of your exercises as the destination of the published video file.

7. Open the **Preset** dropdown. Take some time to inspect the available presets. When done, choose the **Video - Apple iPad** preset.

8. Make sure the **Publish Video Demo** dialog looks similar to what is shown in the following screenshot and click on the **Publish** button.

Publishing a Video Demo project can be quite a lengthy process, so be patient. When the process is complete, a message asks you what to do next. Notice that one of the options enables you to upload your newly created video to YouTube directly.

9. Click on the **Close** button to discard the message.

10. Use **Windows Explorer** (Windows) or **Finder** (Mac) to go to the `publish` folder of your exercises.

11. Double-click on the `encoderDemo.mp4` file to open the video in the default video player of your system.

While enjoying the final product of your hard work, remember that a Video Demo project can only be published as a video file. Also, remember that the published `.mp4` video file can only be experienced in a linear fashion and does not support any kind of interactivity.

Publishing to YouTube

Captivate includes a workflow that allows you to upload the published video file to your YouTube account without even leaving Captivate. In the next exercise, you will experiment with this workflow using the following steps:

 This exercise requires a working YouTube account. If you do not have a YouTube account, you can create one for free on the YouTube website (visit https://support.google.com/youtube/answer/161805?hl=en for details) or read through the steps of the exercise.

1. Still in the Chapter08/encoderDemo_800.cptx file, use the **File** | **Publish to YouTube** menu item to start the procedure.

Captivate directly converts your Vide Demo into an .mp4 video file without asking you to choose a preset. Since Captivate already knows that this video will be uploaded to YouTube, the proper preset is applied automatically.

2. When the publishing process is complete, enter your username and password to log on to your YouTube account.

3. Once logged in, enter the relevant project information:

   ° Enter the title of the movie in the **Title** field. This is the only required field.

   ° Enter a description in the **Description** field.

   ° Enter a list of comma-separated tags. These tags will help YouTube reference your video so that other YouTube users can find it easily.

   ° Choose the best **Category** for your video.

   ° Choose the level of **Privacy** (private or public).

4. Select the **I have read the terms & conditions** checkbox and click on the **Upload** button.

Captivate uploads the video to YouTube. When the process is complete, the **Adobe Captivate Video Publisher** window shows the direct link to our video on YouTube.

5. Click on the **Close** button to close the **Adobe Captivate Video Publisher** window.

As you can see, Captivate makes it incredibly easy to publish a Video Demo to YouTube!

For more information on YouTube's privacy settings and the difference between a public and private video, visit `https://support.google.com/youtube/answer/157177?hl=en`.

Summary

In this chapter, you went through the entire production process of a Video Demo project. Video Demos are a very special kind of project aimed at producing linear `.mp4` video files. They use their own file extension (`.cpvc`) and their own customized Captivate interface.

During the postproduction phase, you placed Captivate objects on top of the video file in order to enhance the screencast and provide the best possible experience to your learners. Inserting and formatting objects in a Video Demo works in the exact same way as in a regular Captivate project. The only difference is the type of objects available. Since a Video Demo project can only be published as a linear video file, the interactive objects of Captivate are—logically—not supported.

On one hand, Video Demos only support a small subset of the Captivate tools and objects. But on the other hand, the **Video Effects** panel contains three tools (**Pan & Zoom**, **Popup**, and **Transitions**) that are only available in Video Demo projects. The **Popup** tool is a brand new feature of Captivate 8 that allows you to remove unwanted popups and tooltips from your Captivate project.

Finally, you performed the third and last step of the production process by publishing your project as an `.mp4` video file. You even uploaded that video directly to your YouTube channel without even leaving Captivate.

Video Demos are an excellent solution when all you need is to quickly create a short screencast. In the next chapter, you will explore the all-new Responsive Projects. These projects are yet another special type of project using a slightly customized interface. They allow you to optimize your eLearning course for multiscreen delivery, placing Captivate at the cutting edge of the mLearning revolution.

Meet the community

In this section, I want to introduce you to Michael Lund, also known as CpGuru. He is an eLearning designer and a Captivate expert located in Denmark. He is one of the key members of the worldwide Captivate community and specializes in the development of Captivate Widgets. Make sure you take a look at his blog and at his awesome collection of Widgets.

Michael Lund

Michael Lund, also known as CpGuru, has been a part of the Adobe Captivate community since Version 2 and started experimenting early on with pushing Captivate to the limit and expanding its functionality with custom Flash components. He is an active participant in the Adobe Captivate forums and a community champion on http://captivate.adobe.com/.

He runs the website http://www.cpguru.com/ where he provides tips and tricks on common issues and problems with Adobe Captivate and tutorials on how to achieve more advanced things with Adobe Captivate.

The site also has a number of free and commercial Widgets for Adobe Captivate that can help you achieve more with your Adobe Captivate projects. Michael also provides freelance support and troubleshooting and develops custom Adobe Captivate Widgets if you need to achieve something special in your projects.

Contact details

- **Twitter**: @cpguru_com
- **E-mail**: support@cpguru.com
- **Website**: http://www.cpguru.com/

9

Creating a Responsive Project

In today's ultra connected world, a good portion of your students probably own multiple devices. Of course, they may want to take your eLearning course on all their devices. They might want to start the course on their desktop computer at work, continue it on their phone while commuting back home, and finish it at night on their tablet. In other situations, students might only have a mobile phone available to take the course, and sometimes the topic to teach only makes sense on a mobile device. To address these needs, you want to deliver your course on multiple screens.

As of Captivate 6, you can publish your courses in HTML5, which makes them available on mobile devices that do not support the Flash technology. Now, Captivate 8 takes it one huge step further by introducing Responsive Projects.

A **Responsive Project** is a project that you can optimize for the desktop, the tablet, and the mobile phone. It is like providing three different versions of the course in a single project.

In this chapter, you will be introduced to the key concepts and techniques used to create a responsive project in Captivate 8. While reading, keep the following two things in mind. First, everything you have learned so far can be applied to a responsive project. Second, creating a responsive project requires more experience than what a book can offer. I hope that this chapter will give you a solid understanding of the core concepts in order to jump start your own discovery of Captivate 8 Responsive Projects.

In this chapter, you will:

- Discuss the new Responsive Projects of Captivate 8
- Discuss the viewport size and the breakpoints
- Create a new Responsive Project
- Configure the breakpoints and the device height
- Explore various ways of testing a Responsive Project
- Add content to a Responsive Project
- Hide content from specific views
- Size and position your objects to make them responsive

At the end of this chapter, your first Responsive Project will be ready for publishing and you will be at the cutting edge of the mobile learning revolution.

About Responsive Projects

A Responsive Project is meant to be used on multiple devices, including tablets and smartphones that do not support the Flash technology. Therefore, it can be published only in HTML5. This means that all the restrictions of a traditional HTML5 project also apply to a Responsive Project. For example, you will not be able to add Text Animations or Rollover Objects in a Responsive Project because these features are not supported in HTML5.

Responsive design is not limited to eLearning projects made in Captivate. It is actually used by web designers and developers around the world to create websites that have the ability to automatically adapt themselves to the screen they are viewed on. To do so, they need to detect the screen width that is available to their content and adapt accordingly.

Responsive Design by Ethan Marcotte

If you want to know more about responsive design, I strongly recommend a book by Ethan Marcotte in the *A Book Apart* collection. This is the founding book of responsive design. If you have some knowledge of HTML and CSS, this is a must have resource in order to fully understand what responsive design is all about. More information on this book can be found at http://www. abookapart.com/products/responsive-web-design.

Viewport size versus screen size

At the heart of the responsive design approach is the width of the screen used by the student to consume the content. To be more exact, it is the width of the viewport that is detected—not the width of the screen. The **viewport** is the area that is actually available to the content.

On a desktop or laptop computer, the difference between the screen width and the viewport width is very easy to understand. Let's do a simple experiment to grasp that concept hands-on:

1. Open your default web browser and make sure it is in fullscreen mode.
2. Browse to `http://www.viewportsizes.com/mine`.

The main information provided by this page is the size of your viewport. Because your web browser is currently in fullscreen mode, the viewport size should be close (but not quite the same) to the resolution of your screen.

3. Use your mouse to resize your browser window and see how the viewport size evolves.

As shown in the following screenshot, the size of the viewport changes as you resize your browser window but the actual screen you use is always the same:

This viewport concept is also valid on a mobile device, even though it may be a bit subtler to grasp.

The following screenshot shows the `http://www.viewportsizes.com/mine` web page as viewed in the Safari mobile browser on an iPad mini held in landscape (left) and in portrait (right). As you can see, the viewport size changes but, once again, the actual screen used is always the same. Don't hesitate to perform these experiments on your own mobile devices and compare your results to mine.

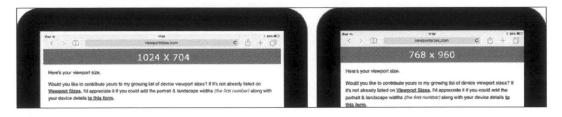

Another thing that might affect the viewport size on a mobile device is the browser used. The following screenshot shows the viewport size of the same iPad mini held in portrait mode in Safari mobile (left) and in Chrome mobile (right).

Note that the viewport size is slightly different in Chrome than in Safari. This is due to the interface elements of the browser (such as the address bar and the tabs) that use a variable portion of the screen real estate in each browser.

Understanding breakpoints

Before setting up your own Responsive Project there is one more concept to explore. To discover this second concept, you will also perform a simple experiment with your desktop or laptop computer:

1. Open the web browser of your desktop or laptop computer and maximize it to fullscreen size.

2. Browse to `http://courses.dbr-training.eu/8/goingmobile`.

This is the online version of the Responsive Project that you will build in this chapter. When viewed on a desktop or laptop computer in fullscreen mode, you should see a version of the course optimized for larger screens.

3. Use your mouse to slowly scale your browser window down. Note how the size and the position of the elements are automatically recalculated as you resize the browser window.

4. At some point, you should see that the height of the slide changes and that another layout is applied.

The point at which the layout changes is situated at a width of exactly 768 px. In other words, if the width of the browser (actually the viewport) is above 768 px, one layout is applied, but if the width of the viewport falls under 768 px, another layout is applied. You just discovered a breakpoint.

The layout that is applied after the breakpoint (in other words when the viewport width is lower than 768 px) is optimized for a tablet device held in portrait mode. Note that even though you are using a desktop or laptop computer, it is the tablet-optimized layout that is applied when the viewport width is at or under 768 px.

5. Keep scaling the browser window down and see how the position and the size of the elements of the slide are recalculated in real time as you resize the browser window.

This simple experiment should better explain what a breakpoint is and how these breakpoints work. Before moving on to the next section, let's take some time to summarize the important concepts uncovered in this section:

- The aim of responsive design is to provide an optimized viewing experience across a wide range of devices and form factors.

- To achieve this goal, responsive design uses fluid sizing and positioning techniques, responsive images, and breakpoints.

- Responsive design is not limited to eLearning courses made in Captivate, but is widely used in web and app design by thousands of designers around the world.

- A Captivate 8 Responsive Project can only be published in HTML5. The capabilities and restrictions of a standard HTML5 project also apply to a Responsive Project.

- A breakpoint defines the exact viewport width at which the layout breaks and another layout is applied.

- The breakpoints, and therefore the optimized layouts, are based on the width of the viewport and not on the detection of an actual device. This explains why the tablet-optimized layout is applied to the downsized browser window on a desktop computer.

- The viewport width and the screen width are two different things.

In the next section, you will start the creation of your very first Responsive Project.

To learn more about these concepts, there is a video course on Responsive eLearning with Captivate 8 available on *Adobe KnowHow*. The course itself is for a fee, but there is a free sample of 15 minutes that walks you through these concepts using another approach. I suggest you take some time to watch this 15-minute sample at `https://www.adobeknowhow.com/courselanding/create-responsive-elearning-adobe-captivate-8`.

Setting up a Responsive Project

It is now time to open Captivate and set up your first Responsive Project using the following steps:

1. Open Captivate or close every open file.
2. Switch to the **New** tab of the Welcome screen.
3. Double-click on the **Responsive Project** thumbnail. Alternatively, you can also use the **File | New Project | Responsive Project** menu item.

This action creates a new Responsive Project. Note that the choice to create a Responsive Project or a regular Captivate project must be done up front when creating the project. As of Captivate 8, it is not yet possible to take an existing non-responsive project and make it responsive after the fact.

The workspace of Captivate should be very similar to what you are used to, with the exception of an extra ruler that spans across the top of the screen. This ruler contains three predefined breakpoints. As shown in the following screenshot, the first breakpoint is called the **Primary** breakpoint and is situated at **1024** pixels.

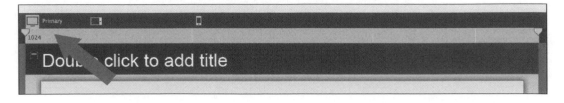

Also, note that the breakpoint ruler is green when the **Primary** breakpoint is selected. You will now discover the other two breakpoints using the following steps.

4. In the breakpoint ruler, click on the icon of a tablet to select the second breakpoint.

The stage and all the elements it contains are resized. In the breakpoint ruler at the top of the stage, the second breakpoint is now selected. It is called the **Tablet** breakpoint and is situated at **768** pixels. Note the blue color associated with the **Tablet** breakpoint.

5. In the breakpoint ruler, click on the icon of a smartphone to select the third and last breakpoint.

Once again, the stage and the elements it contains are resized. The third breakpoint is called the **Mobile** breakpoint and is situated at **360** pixels. The orange color is associated with this third breakpoint.

Adjusting the breakpoints

In some situations, the default location of these three breakpoints works just fine But, in other situations, some adjustments are needed. In this project, you want to target the regular screen of a desktop or laptop computer in the **Primary** view, an iPad mini held in portrait in the **Tablet** view, and an iPhone 4 held in portrait in the **Mobile** view. You will now adjust the breakpoints to fit these particular specifications by using the following steps:

1. Click on the **Primary** breakpoint in the breakpoints ruler to select it.
2. Use your mouse to move the breakpoint all the way to the left.

Captivate should stop at a width of **1280** pixels. It is not possible to have a stage wider than **1280** pixels in a Responsive Project. For this project, the default width of **1024** pixels is perfect, so you will now move this breakpoint back to its original location.

3. Move the **Primary** breakpoint to the right until it is placed at **1024** pixels.
4. Return to your web browser and browse to http://www.viewportsizes.com.
5. Once on the website, type iPad in the **Filter** field at the top of the page.

The portrait width of an iPad mini is **768** pixels. In Captivate, the **Tablet** breakpoint is placed at 768 pixels by default, which is perfectly fine for the needs of this project.

6. Still on the http://www.viewportsizes.com website, type iPhone in the **Filter** field at the top of the page.

The portrait width of an iPhone 4 is **320** pixels. In Captivate, the **Mobile** breakpoint is placed at 360 pixels by default. You will now move it to 320 pixels so that it matches the portrait width of an iPhone 4.

7. Return to Captivate and select the **Mobile** breakpoint.

8. Move the **Mobile** breakpoint to the right until it is placed at exactly 320 pixels.

Note that the minimum width of the stage in the **Mobile** breakpoint is 320 pixels. In other words, the stage cannot be narrower than 320 pixels in a Responsive Project.

The viewport size of your device

Before moving on to the next section, take some time to inspect the `http://viewportsizes.com` site a little further. For example, type the name of the devices you own and compare their characteristics to the breakpoints of the current project. Will the project fit on your devices? How do you need to change the breakpoints so the project perfectly fits your devices?

The breakpoints are now in place. But these breakpoints only take care of the width of the stage. In the next section, you will adjust the height of the stage in each breakpoint.

Adjusting the slide height

Captivate slides have a fixed height. This is the primary difference between a Captivate project and a regular responsive website whose page height is infinite. In this section, you will adjust the height of the stage in all three breakpoints. The steps are as follows:

1. Still in Captivate, click on the desktop icon situated on the left side of the breakpoint switcher to return to the **Primary** view.

2. On the far right of the breakpoint ruler, select the **View Device Height** checkbox.

As shown in the following screenshot, a yellow border now surrounds the stage in the **Primary** view, and the slide height is displayed in the top left corner of the stage:

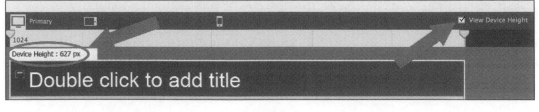

For the **Primary** view, a slide height of 627 pixels is perfect. It matches the viewport size of an iPad held in landscape and provides a big enough area on a desktop or laptop computer.

3. Click on the **Tablet** breakpoint to select it.

4. Return to `http://www.viewportsizes.com/` and type `iPad` in the filter field at the top of the page. According to the site, the height of an iPad is **1024** pixels.

5. Use your mouse to drag the yellow rectangle situated at the bottom of the stage down until the stage height is around **950** pixels.

 It may be needed to reduce the zoom magnification to perform this action in good conditions.

After this operation, the stage should look like the following screenshot (the zoom magnification has been reduced to 50 percent in the screenshot):

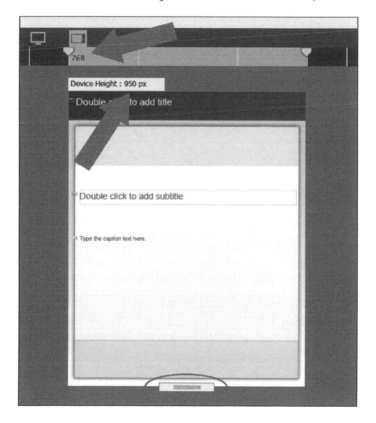

With a height of 950 pixels, the Captivate slide can fit on an iPad screen and still account for the screen real estate consumed by the interface elements of the browser such as the address bar and the tabs.

6.   Still in the **Tablet** view, make sure the slide is the selected object and open the **Properties** panel.

7.   Note that, at the end of the **Properties** panel, the **Slide Height** property is currently unavailable.

8.   Click on the chain icon (Unlink from Device height) next to the **Slide Height** property.

By default, the slide height is linked to the device height. By clicking on the chain icon you have broken the link between the slide height and the device (or viewport) height. This allows you to modify the height of the Captivate slide without modifying the height of the device.

9.   Use the **Properties** panel to change the **Slide Height** to **1024** pixels.

On the stage, note that the slide is now a little bit higher than the yellow rectangle. This means that this particular slide will generate a vertical scrollbar on the tablet device held in portrait. Scrolling is something you want to avoid as much as possible, so you will now enable the link between the device height and the **Slide Height**.

10.   In the **Properties** panel, click on the chain icon next to the **Slide Height** property to enable the link.

The slide height is automatically readjusted to the device height of 950 pixels.

11.   Use the breakpoint ruler to select the **Mobile** breakpoint.

By default, the device height in the **Mobile** breakpoint is set to **415** pixels. According to the http://www.viewportsizes.com/ website, the screen of an iPhone 4 has a height of 480 pixels. A slide height of 415 pixels is perfect to accommodate the slide itself plus the interface elements of the mobile browser.

Applying a responsive theme

To finish up with the setup phase of your first Responsive Project, you will now apply a responsive theme to the project and examine the various components of the theme. Perform the following steps to apply a responsive theme to the project.

1.   Still in the same Responsive Project, click on the **Themes** icon of the Big Buttons Bar to open the themes gallery.

2.   Click on the **Browse** link situated in the bottom left corner of the themes gallery.

3. Apply the `Themes/MFTC-Responsive.cptm` theme to the current project.

4. Click on **Yes** to acknowledge and clear the warning message.

Responsive themes are very similar to the regular themes that were covered in *Chapter 7, Working with Styles, Master Slides, Themes, and Templates*. The only difference is that they contain three versions of each Master Slide and of each Style to account for the three different views of a Responsive Project. Let's explore these differences hands-on using the following steps:

5. Use the breakpoint switcher to return to the **Primary** breakpoint.

6. Use the **Window | Master Slide** menu item to return to the Master Slide view.

7. Use the **Master Slide** panel on the left-hand side of the screen to select the **Title** Master Slide.

8. Use the breakpoint switcher to switch to the **Tablet** and **Mobile** views. Notice how the layout of the **Title Slide** evolves as the stage is resized.

This Master Slide has been optimized for all three views right in the theme. When this responsive theme is applied to a project, all three versions of the Master Slide are imported into the project.

9. Repeat this same experiment with the other Master Slides of the theme. Note how each of them is optimized for all three breakpoints.

10. When done, use the **Window | Filmstrip** menu item to return to the Filmstrip view.

11. Double-click in the title placeholder and type `Title of the slide`. When done, hit the *Esc* key to leave text edit mode and keep the object selected.

12. Use the **Style Name** drop-down menu at the top of the **Properties** panel to apply the **MFTC-MainTitle** style to the selected object.

13. While in the **Primary** view, take a look at the font size in the **Style** tab of the **Properties** panel.

14. Switch to the **Tablet** view and control the font size of the title in the **Properties** panel.

15. Switch to the **Mobile** view and control once again the font size of the title in the **Properties** panel.

You should have noticed that the font size is different in each breakpoint. This is because the **MFTC-MainTitle** style has been optimized for all three views. You will now take another look at this optimized style in the Object Style Manager.

16. Use the **Edit | Object Style Manager** menu item to open the **Object Style Manager**.

17. From the leftmost column of the **Object Style Manager**, expand the **Standard Objects | Smart Shapes | Title** section.

18. In the middle column, select the **MFTC-MainTitle** style.

The rightmost column of the **Object Style Manager** now shows the formatting properties of the **MFTC-MainTitle** style. As shown in the following screenshot, the **Break Points** drop-down menu allows you to choose which view-optimized version of the style is displayed:

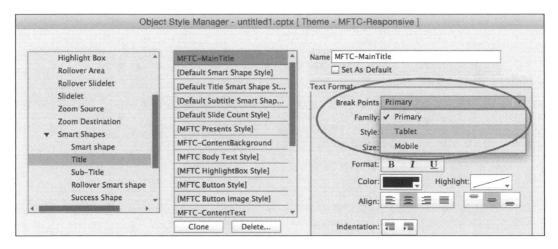

These simple experiments show you that three versions of each Master Slide and three versions of each Style are part of the responsive theme applied to the project.

19. At the bottom-right corner of the **Object Style Manager**, click on the **Cancel** button to close the dialog box.

20. Save the file as `Chapter09/responsiveTest.cptx`.

Your first Responsive Project is now ready to be developed. In the next section, you will learn how such a project can be previewed and tested. Now, let's quickly summarize what has been covered in this section:

- In Captivate, a Responsive Project contains three breakpoints called the **Primary** breakpoint, the **Tablet** breakpoint, and the **Mobile** breakpoint.

- The breakpoint ruler at the top of the screen allows you to move these breakpoints, but it is not possible to add or remove breakpoints.

- The **Primary** breakpoint cannot be wider than **1280** px. The **Mobile** breakpoint cannot be narrower than **320** px.

- When the **Show Device Height** checkbox is selected, a yellow rectangle encloses the slide and the device height is shown in the top-left corner of the slide. This yellow rectangle represents the screen of the device and can be used to modify the device height if necessary.

- By default, the Device Height is linked to the Slide Height, but it is possible to decouple these two properties in the **Properties** panel. This allows you to create slides that are higher than the screen, which generates a vertical scrollbar at runtime.

- Use the http://www.viewportsizes.com website to check the size of various mobile devices.

- A responsive theme can be applied to a Responsive Project.

- Responsive themes are very similar to standard themes, except that they contain three versions of each Master Slide and three versions of each style.

Testing a Responsive Project

To effectively test a Responsive Project, you must be able to test it across all three breakpoints. You must also be able to test the interactions using a touchscreen rather than a mouse. This makes testing a Responsive Project a huge challenge. Captivate 8 is packed with many innovative features that will effectively enable you to test your Responsive Projects in a wide variety of situations. This is what you will review in this section.

Testing in the authoring environment

The first and most simple way to test your project is to use the play icon situated in the bottom-left corner of the **Timeline** panel. This feature allows you to test the current slide right in the authoring environment of Captivate without opening any preview window or external browser. This **Preview** option is great for testing the synchronization of the objects or to quickly preview a single slide. However, it is not able to render all the animated and interactive features of Captivate.

This option works in the exact same way in Responsive Projects as in regular projects. The only difference is the ability to choose a breakpoint and to test the slide in the active breakpoint.

Testing in a browser

The second option is to test the project in a web browser. Using this option, all the animated and interactive features of Captivate are fully supported. This option is also available for regular Captivate projects, but it works differently in Responsive Projects. Let's experiment with this feature and discover the differences between the way it works in regular projects and in Responsive Projects using the following steps:

1. Open Captivate if necessary.

2. Use the **File | Open** menu item to open the `final/goingMobile.cptx` file of the download associated with this book.

The file you just opened is the final version of the project you'll work with in this chapter. You will use this final version to experiment with the preview options available for Responsive Projects.

3. Click on the **Preview** icon of the Big Buttons Bar and take some time to examine the available options. Note the similarities and differences as compared to a regular project.

4. Click on the **Preview | Next 5 slides** icon of the Big Buttons Bar.

A Responsive Project can only be published in HTML5, so the next 5 slides are converted to HTML5 and played in the default web browser. In a regular Captivate project, this **Preview** option would open the **Preview** pane and play a precompiled Flash version of the content.

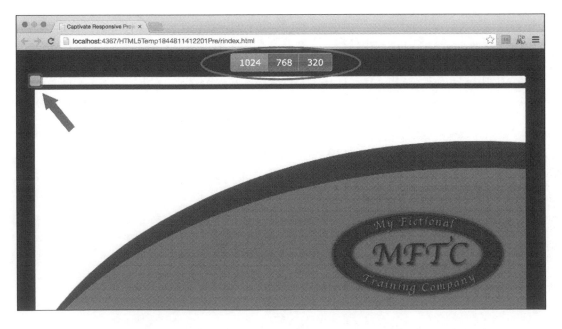

As shown in the preceding screenshot, there are three buttons above the preview that represent the three breakpoints. Just below the buttons is a slider (see the arrow in the preceding screenshot) that allows you to modify the width of the stage during the preview. This slider makes it easy to test the responsiveness of your projects in between the breakpoints.

1. In the web browser, click on the **768** button to test the **Tablet** breakpoint.

2. Also, click on the **320** button to test the **Mobile** breakpoint.

3. Use your mouse to slowly move the scrubber all the way to the left.

> As you do so, note how the objects of the slide are automatically resized and relocated as the width of the stage increases. Also, note how the project jumps from one breakpoint to the other when the width of the stage matches the position of a breakpoint. Finally, note the number in the middle of the slide that represents the current width of the stage as you resize it with the slider.

4. Close the web browser and return to Captivate. Keep the project open for the next sections.

This preview option is excellent to test the project as you develop it. That being said, using this option, you preview the project on your desktop or laptop computer using a physical keyboard and a mouse to interact with the course. This is a much different experience than what your mobile students will have when interacting with your course using their fingers and the virtual keyboard of their touch devices. This is why you need to test your responsive projects on actual devices before publishing them.

Testing with Adobe Edge Inspect

To preview your project on an actual mobile device, Captivate 8 has been integrated with **Adobe Edge Inspect**. Adobe Edge Inspect (formerly Adobe Shadow) is a system that allows you to quickly preview your HTML5 applications on mobile devices without the need to upload these applications to a web server.

Installing Adobe Edge Inspect

Before you can test your Responsive Project on your devices using Edge Inspect, it is necessary to install all the components of the Edge Inspect system on your computer and on your devices.

The Adobe Edge Inspect system is made up of the following components:

- **The Adobe Edge Inspect helper application**: This application is available on Windows and Mac OS. It can be downloaded using the Creative Cloud desktop application or directly from the Adobe website at `https://creative.adobe.com/products/inspect`.

- **Google Chrome**: At the time of this writing, Edge Inspect only works with the Google Chrome web browser. If you're already using Chrome, you're good to go. If not, you must install Google Chrome to use Edge Inspect. Chrome can be downloaded from `http://www.google.com/chrome/`.

- **The Google Chrome browser extension**: Edge Inspect requires the installation of a free Google Chrome extension. The Edge Inspect Chrome extension can be downloaded from `http://www.adobe.com/go/inspect_chrome_app`.

- **The Edge Inspect mobile application**: You must install the free Edge Inspect mobile application on each of your mobile devices. There is a version for iOS (`http://www.adobe.com/go/inspect_ios_app`), Android (`http://www.adobe.com/go/inspect_android_app`), and Kindle Fire (`http://www.adobe.com/go/inspect_amazon_android_app`).

Make sure you install all the components of the Edge Inspect ecosystem before moving on to the next section.

Installing Edge Inspect

More information on installing Adobe Edge Inspect can be found at `https://forums.adobe.com/docs/DOC-2535`. If you are a Windows user, a step-by-step tutorial can be found at `http://www.techrepublic.com/blog/web-designer/test-your-website-on-mobile-devices-with-adobe-edge-inspect-cc/`.

Testing a Captivate project on your mobile devices

In this section, you will use Adobe Edge Inspect to test your Responsive Project on your actual devices. Before starting with this section, make sure that you meet the following requirements:

- All the components on the Edge Inspect system are properly installed as described in the previous section

- Your computer and all the devices you want to use for the test are connected to the same Wi-Fi network

If the preceding requirements are met, use the following steps to test the project on your mobile devices (the first step is to make Edge Inspect ready):

1. Start the Edge Inspect helper application. You should have installed this application in the previous section.

2. If you are working on a Mac, an Edge Inspect icon should appear in the top-right corner of the screen. If you are working on Windows, the same icon should appear in the notification area at the bottom-right corner of the screen.

3. Launch the Chrome web browser with the Edge Inspect extension installed. Confirm that a colored Edge Inspect icon is displayed in the top-right corner of the Chrome browser.

The next step is to connect your mobile device(s) to the Edge Inspect Chrome extension.

4. Open the Adobe Edge Inspect application installed on one of your mobile devices.

5. Tap on the name of your computer when it appears in the list.

6. Type the pass code that appears on your mobile device in the Edge Inspect chrome extension.

7. Repeat the three previous steps on each mobile device you want to test your course on.

Adobe Edge Inspect and the Creative Cloud

Adobe Edge Inspect is available as part of the Creative Cloud. Free Creative Cloud members can connect one device at a time to the Edge inspect system. Paid Creative Cloud members can connect an unlimited number of devices to Edge Inspect. More information on Adobe Edge Inspect can be found at `https://creative.adobe.com/products/inspect`.

After these operations, the Edge Inspect Chrome extension should list all the connected devices as shown in the following screenshot:

Now that your devices are connected to the Edge Inspect system, the last step takes place in Captivate.

8. Open Captivate and return to the `final/goingMobile.cptx` file.

9. Use the **Preview | In Adobe Edge Inspect** icon of the Big Buttons Bar.

The entire project is rendered in the Chrome web browser. Thanks to the Adobe Edge Inspect system running in the background, whatever web page you see in Chrome (in this case, your Captivate course) is also displayed on your connected mobile devices.

10. Take some time to go through the entire project on your mobile devices and see how using tap actions and a virtual keyboard changes the student's experience.

Make sure all the interactions still make sense on a mobile device and that the buttons and other interactive elements offer a big enough tap target for the finger of the student. You may find out that a project that works fine on each breakpoint when viewed on a desktop or laptop computer actually needs some extra work when viewed on an actual mobile device.

After completing this section, you know how to test your Responsive Project extensively both on your computer and on your mobile devices. Before moving on to the next part of this chapter, here is a quick summary of what has been covered in this section:

- Captivate offers three ways to test your Responsive Projects. You can test them in the authoring environment, in a web browser, or right on your mobile devices.

- Testing in the authoring environment works in the exact same way as with a regular Captivate project.

- Unlike regular projects, all the preview options situated in the **Preview** icon of the Big Buttons Bar open the default web browser. This is because a Responsive Project can only be published in HTML5.

- When testing in a web browser, you can modify the width of the stage by using either the buttons that represent the breakpoints or the slider situated at the top of the preview area.

- Testing in the web browser is great, but it does not allow you to experience the course using an actual touch device.

- Adobe Edge Inspect allows you to test your Captivate courses on your mobile devices without uploading them to a web server. It is necessary to install all the components of the Edge Inspect system to be able to test the course using Edge Inspect.

Adding content in a Responsive Project

Now that you know how to test and preview your Responsive Project, it is time to explore how such a project can be developed. Hopefully, the tools and concepts you have already learned while working with regular projects also apply to the Responsive Projects of Captivate 8. There are just a few specifics to add on top of what you already know. This is what you will focus on in this section.

First, let's get ready using the following steps:

1. Return to Captivate and close every open file without saving the changes.
2. Open the `Chapter09/goingMobile.cptx` file.

This is the same file as the one you used in the previous section, but at an earlier stage of its development.

Understanding the view hierarchy

At the heart of each Responsive Project are the three breakpoints that define the three optimized views. When it comes to adding content there is a hierarchy between these three views. Captivate uses the **desktop-first** approach. It means that a smaller view always inherits whatever happens on a parent view. You will now experiment with this concept hands-on using the following steps:

1. Still in the `Chapter09/goingMobile.cptx` file, use the **Filmstrip** to go to slide 16.

2. Make sure you are currently viewing the **Primary** view. If not, use the breakpoint switcher to go to the **Primary** view.

3. Double-click on the **Title** placeholder and type `The responsive website`. When done, hit the *Esc* key to quit text edit mode and leave the title selected.

4. Use the breakpoint switcher to switch to the **Tablet** and **Mobile** views. Confirm that the title you typed in the **Primary** view also appears on the **Tablet** and **Mobile** views.

5. Return to the **Primary** view.

6. Select the title and delete it.

7. Check the **Tablet** and **Mobile** views and confirm that the title has been deleted in all three views.

This first experiment clearly shows you that whatever you type in the **Primary** view is copied over to the **Tablet** and **Mobile** views. In other words, the child (**Tablet**) view and the grandchild (**Mobile**) view inherit the content of the parent (**Primary**) view. You will now conduct a second experiment and add some content to the **Tablet** view directly.

8. Still on slide 16 of the same project, use the breakpoint switcher to go to the **Tablet** view.

9. Double-click in the **Title** placeholder and type `The responsive website`. When done, hit the *Esc* key to quit the text edit mode and leave the title selected.

10. Use the breakpoint switcher to switch to the **Mobile** view and confirm that the title you typed in the **Tablet** view also appears in the **Mobile** view.

11. When done, return to the **Primary** view and confirm that the title typed in the **Tablet** view does not appear. The original empty placeholder object should still be displayed.

12. While in the **Primary** view, double-click on the **Title** placeholder and type
    `How does a responsive website work?.`

13. When done, hit the *Esc* key to quit the text edit mode and leave the
    title selected.

This second experiment shows you that whatever you type in the child (**Tablet**)
view is inherited by the grandchild (**Mobile**) view, but does not affect the parent
(**Primary**) view. This allows you to display slightly different text content in all three
views if necessary.

It also illustrates the desktop-first approach used by Captivate. The proper way to
use this system is to add the text content in the **Primary** view whenever possible, so
the content is inherited by the other two views. You can then modify the text content
on the other two views, if necessary, without affecting the parent (**Primary**) view.

Extra credit – adding text content in a Responsive Project

Let's add some more text on slide 16 of the project. You will do this in the **Primary**
view so that the text is typed in all three views. When done, you will control the
Tablet and **Mobile** views and make the necessary changes if needed. The general
steps are follows:

- Make sure you are in the **Primary** view.

- Double-click on the Text Caption placeholder and type `Uses CSS3 Media`
  `Queries to apply different sets of rules to each view.` Feel free to
  resize the Text Caption so the text comfortably fits in the object.

- Add three more Text Captions containing the following text:
    - `Applied layout depends on the available width`
    - `The whole page is downloaded before the layout is`
      `applied`
    - `Students use a browser to access the content`

- Use the tools of the Align toolbar to properly align and position the objects.

- Control the **Tablet** and **Mobile** views and make the necessary changes.
  These changes may include modifying the text content, but also moving
  and resizing the Text Captions as required by the stage size.

At the end of this extra credit section, your slide should look like the following screenshots:

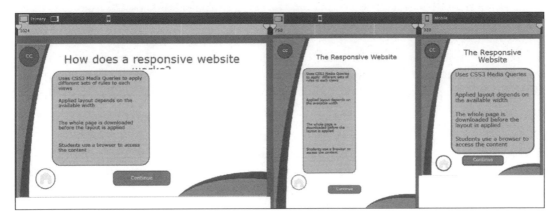

Relinking views

In the previous section, you learned that there is a hierarchy between the views of a Responsive Project and that Captivate has adopted the desktop-first approach. In this section, you will further experiment with this concept and learn how the views can be unlinked and relinked using the following steps:

1. Make sure you are still on slide 16 of the Chapter09/goingMobile.cptx file.

2. If needed, use the breakpoint switcher to return to the **Primary** view.

3. Use the **Media | Image** icon of the Big Buttons Bar to insert the images/ MediaQueries.png image onto the slide.

4. Move and resize the image so the slide looks like the next screenshot.

Note that part of the image is situated off the stage. This is perfectly fine; just keep in mind that the student will only see the portion of the image that is actually on the stage.

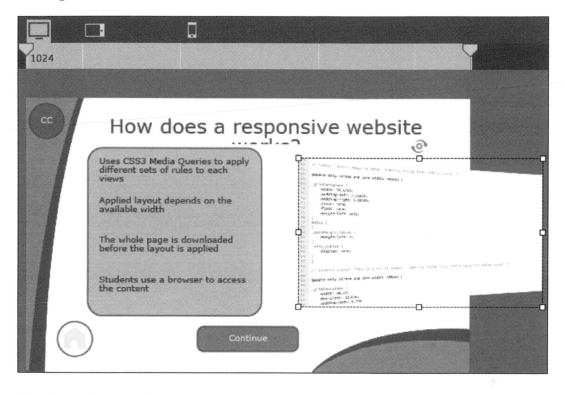

Thanks to the views being linked to one another, the size and position of the image, as defined in the **Primary** view, should be applied to the **Tablet** and **Mobile** view. Let's check this out!

5. With the image selected, click on the **Properties** icon of the Big Buttons Bar to open the **Properties** panel (if needed).

Note that the click on the **Properties** icon has actually opened three panels. The usual **Properties** and **Timing** panels are both displayed, but there is also the **Position** panel that is only present in Responsive Projects.

6. Switch to the **Position** panel (if needed) and inspect the available properties.

Note that the properties pertaining to the size and to the position of the object in the **Primary** view are surrounded by a green outline. This green color is the same as the one used in the breakpoint switcher when the **Primary** view is selected.

7. Switch to the **Tablet** view and confirm that the image is displayed with the same size and at the same location as in the **Primary** view.

8. Remember that the color used in the breakpoint switcher when the **Tablet** view is selected is blue.

Note that the size and position properties of the selected image are still surrounded by the same green outline as in the **Primary** view. This is to emphasis the fact that these properties are currently inherited from the **Primary** view and are not defined at the **Tablet** view level.

9. Switch to the **Mobile** view and confirm that the image is displayed with the same size and at the same location as in the **Primary** and **Tablet** views.

10. Remember that the color used in the breakpoint switcher when the **Mobile** view is selected is orange.

In the **Position** panel, the size and position properties of the selected image are, once again, surrounded by the same green outline because they are inherited from the **Primary** view through the **Tablet** view.

11. Return to the **Tablet** view.

12. Use your mouse to enlarge and relocate the picture so it nicely fits into the **Tablet** view.

13. While doing so, keep a close eye on the properties displayed in the **Position** panel.

Did you notice that the **Properties** displayed in the **Position** panel are now surrounded by a blue outline? This is because these properties are now set at the **Tablet** view level and are no longer inherited from the **Primary** view. By modifying the size and the position of the image in the **Tablet** view, you have broken the link between the **Primary** and the **Tablet** view.

14. Switch to the **Mobile** view and take a look at the properties displayed in the **Position** panel when the image is selected.

These properties are surrounded by a blue outline indicating that they are inherited from the **Tablet** view. The link that exists between the **Tablet** and the **Mobile** view has not yet been broken.

15. Move and resize the image in the **Mobile** view. Don't try to make it fit in this small screen; just move and resize it randomly.

Note that the properties of the **Position** panel are now surrounded by the orange color of the **Mobile** view. The link between the **Tablet** and the **Mobile** view has been broken.

As of Captivate 8, this was the end of the story. But in October 2014, Adobe released an important update for Captivate. This update makes the story a little longer.

Updating Captivate

The update released in October 2014 is completely free of charge. I strongly recommend that every Captivate user update their installation. Visit https://www.adobe.com/support/captivate/downloads.html for more about updating Captivate. The last part of the current exercise requires an updated Captivate installation.

The October 2014 update brings an important number of new features into Captivate. One of them is the ability to relink the views of a responsive project. In your case, you will imagine that you want to apply the current size and position of the **Tablet** view to all three views.

16. Return to the **Tablet** view and make sure the image is selected. In the **Position** panel, the size and position properties are surrounded by a blue outline.

17. Right-click on the image and choose the **Apply position properties to the all views** menu item.

After this operation, the size and the position of the image is the same in all three views. Also, notice that the properties of the **Position** panel are now surrounded by the green color of the **Primary** view. This clearly indicates that the link between the views has been restored.

18. Arrange the size and the position of the image in the **Primary** and **Tablet** views as you see fit.

At the end of this exercise, the image should look fine both in **Primary** and **Tablet** views. In the **Mobile** view, however, the limited screen real estate makes it impossible to place the image correctly.

Extra credit – relinking text content

Now that you have a better understanding of the relationship that unites the three views of a responsive project, you will restore the link of the title Smart Shape so that the text content is the same as in the **Tablet** view in all the views. The general steps are as follows:

- Switch to the **Tablet** view.
- Right-click on the Title Smart Shape.
- Choose the **Apply Text to all views** menu item.

This action applies the text content of the **Tablet** view to all three views without modifying the position and size properties. Note that the options of the contextual menu are not exactly the same as when you right-click on an image.

Excluding content from views

In this section, you will explore how to exclude content from a view without affecting the other views of the project. In the next exercise, you will make sure that the image you imported on slide 16 in the previous section does not appear in the **Mobile** view, using the following steps:

1. Return to slide 16 of the `Chapter09/goingMobile.cptx` file if needed.
2. Switch to the **Mobile** view and select the image.
3. Delete the selected image while in the **Mobile** view.
4. Switch to the **Tablet** and **Primary** view and confirm that the image has also disappeared from these two views.

This little experiment tells you that an object (in this case an image) is inserted on a slide, not in a specific view. That is, inserting an object inserts it in all three views and removing an object removes it from all three views as well. In this case, you want the image to be excluded from the **Mobile** view without affecting the **Primary** and **Tablet** views, so deleting the image is not the way to go.

5. Use the **Edit | Undo** menu item as many times as needed until the image reappears. You can also use the *cmd* + *Z* (Mac) or *Ctrl* + *Z* (Windows) shortcut to perform the same action.

6. Back in the **Mobile** view, select the image and move it off the stage as shown in the following screenshot:

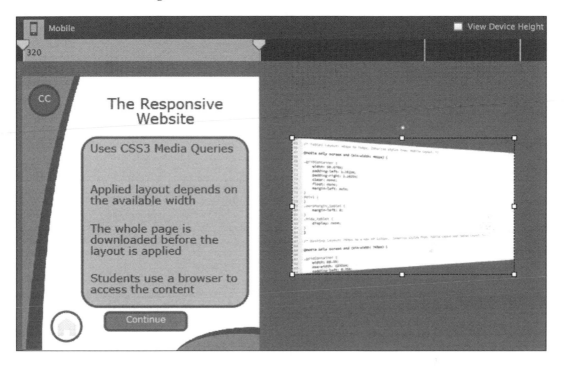

This action removes the image from the **Mobile** view without affecting the **Primary** and **Tablet** views.

Excluding content from other views

Sometimes, the objects of your Responsive Project are specific to one view and do not appear in any of the other two views. In this section you will run into one such situation and discover how Captivate 8 handles it, using the following steps:

1. Still in the Chapter09/goingMobile.cptx file, use the **Filmstrip** panel to go to slide 8. Make sure you are in the **Primary** view.

2. Use the **Shapes** icon of the Big Buttons Bar to draw a right pointing arrow on the stage.

3. Use the **Properties** panel to apply the **MFTC HighlightBox Style** style to the new arrow.

4. While in the **Primary** view, size, and position the arrow so the slide looks like the following screenshot:

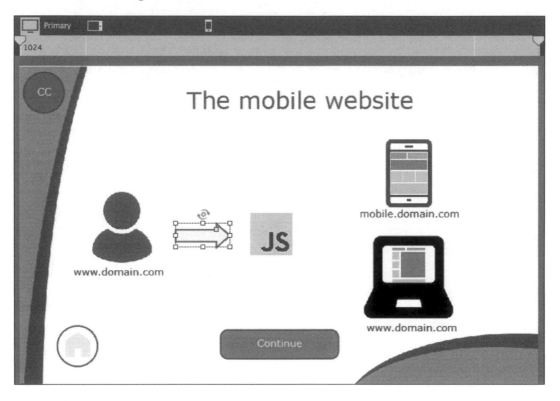

You will now switch to the **Tablet** view and modify the arrow accordingly.

5. Switch to the **Tablet** view and keep the arrow selected.

6. If needed, click the **Properties** icon of the Big Buttons Bar and switch to the **Position** panel

The objects of the slide have already been rearranged in the **Tablet** view. When it comes to the new arrow, its size and position properties are currently inherited from the **Primary** view as confirmed by the green outline surrounding the properties exposed in the **Position** panel.

7. Move the arrow and place it in between the image of the user and the square **JS** image.

8. Slightly enlarge the arrow so that it fits nicely on the slide. Make sure the arrow looks like the following screenshot before continuing:

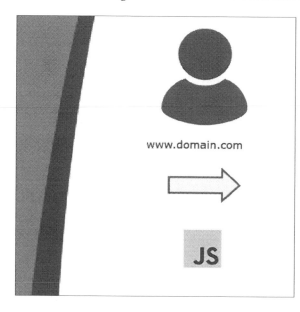

By moving and resizing the arrow in the **Tablet** view, the properties exposed in the **Position** panel are not inherited from the **Primary** view anymore. These are therefore surrounded by a blue outline.

9. Return to the **Primary** view and confirm that the changes made to the arrow while in the **Tablet** view do not affect the primary view.

10. Return to the **Tablet** view.

11. With the arrow selected, turn your attention to the **Options** tab of the **Properties** panel.

12. Apply a rotation of **90** degrees to the arrow. After this operation, the arrow should be pointing down.

13. Return to the **Primary** view.

(Bad) Surprise! While the size and the position of the arrow is specific to each view, the rotation you applied while in the **Tablet** view has been applied to the object in the **Primary** view as well. This tells you that the rotation property is not specific to a view but is applied to the object across all the views, which causes you a problem in this case.

To solve this problem, you need three arrows (one for each view), so that you will be able to apply a different rotation on each arrow.

14. Return to the **Tablet** view and select the arrow.

15. Right-click on the arrow and chose the **Exclude from Other Views** item in the contextual menu.

16. Switch to the **Primary** view, then to the **Mobile** view, and confirm that the arrow has been moved to the scrap area in both these views. When done, return to the **Tablet** view.

17. At the top of the **Properties** panel, change the name of the arrow to `Arrow1_tablet`.

In this exercise, you'll need three arrows in every view. That makes a lot of arrows! Properly naming them will help you spot them on the **Timeline** panel when it is time to sync these objects with the other elements of the slide.

18. Return to the **Primary** view.

19. Use the **Shapes** icon of the Big Buttons Bar to draw a new right pointing arrow on the stage.

20. Use the **Properties** panel to apply the **MFTC HighlightBox Style** style to the new arrow.

21. Size and position the arrow so it replaces the arrow you inserted earlier in this exercise.

22. At the top of the **Properties** panel, change the name of the arrow to `Arrow1_primary`.

23. Right-click on the new arrow and choose the **Exclude from Other Views** menu item. This moves the arrow in the scrap area in both the **Tablet** and **Mobile** views.

24. Switch to the **Mobile** view and repeat the preceding operations to add a third version of this arrow optimized for the **Mobile** view. Name it `Arrow1_mobile` in the **Properties** panel.

At the end of this exercise, the three views of slide 16 should look like the following screenshots:

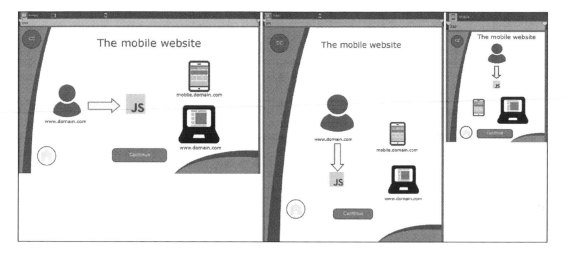

Extra credit – creating the remaining arrows

Let's use the exact same procedure to create two more arrows on each of the three views (that makes six arrows in total). Don't forget to exclude the arrows from the other views and to properly name them. The general steps are as follows:

- Go to the **Primary** view and draw the second arrow.
- Apply the style and give the arrow the proper size and position.
- Exclude it from the other views.
- Give it a name in the **Properties** panel.
- Repeat the preceding steps in the other views.

At the end of this section, there should be nine arrows on slide 16: three in each of the three views and the rest in the scrap area.

This exercise concludes this section on inserting objects in a responsive project. Before moving on to the next section, let's make a quick summary of what has been covered:

- To insert objects in a responsive project, you can use the same icons and tools as in a regular project.
- Objects are added to the entire slide, not to a specific view. Objects are removed from the entire slide, not from a specific view.
- Most of the properties of the objects (including the size, the position and the text formatting properties) are specific to a view.

- The properties applied in a parent view are inherited by the child view. The properties set on the **Primary** view are inherited by the **Tablet** and **Mobile** views. The properties applied to the **Tablet** view are inherited by the **Mobile** view.

- When modifying an inherited property in the **Tablet** or in the **Mobile** view, you break the link between the current view and the parent view.

- As of Captivate 8.0.1, it is possible to re-establish the broken link by right-clicking on an object and choosing the **Apply to all views** menu item.

- Some properties (such as the rotation) are always applied to an object across all the views.

- Moving an object to the scrap area effectively removes it from the current view.

- To make an object visible in one view only, right-click on the object and choose the **Exclude from Other Views** menu item.

So far, you have learned how to insert objects and how to arrange them at the breakpoints. In the next section, you will learn how to make these objects responsive in between the breakpoints.

Sizing and positioning content in a Responsive Project

When defining the position of the breakpoints earlier in this chapter, you had to choose the devices that you wanted to design for. In this case, you decided to place the breakpoints according to the viewport width of an iPad mini held in portrait mode and of an iPhone 4 also in portrait mode. This is probably sufficient for the vast majority of the situations, but there will be students who will take the course on different devices than those anticipated.

In this section, you will concentrate on the responsiveness of the course in between the breakpoints. If a student has a screen width that does not quite exactly match the position of the breakpoints, the course will look fine anyway.

Making images responsive

A responsive object has the ability to adapt its size and position to the screen on which it is viewed. To make this adaptation possible, it is necessary to employ slightly different sizing techniques than those used in a regular project.

First, you will try to identify the potential problem, using the following steps:

1. Close every open file and return to the Captivate 8 Welcome screen.
2. Open the `Chapter09/goingMobile_2.cptx` file.

This file contains the same project as in the previous section, but at a more advanced stage of development, as slide 8 and slide 16 have been synchronized with an imported audio file.

3. Use the **Filmstrip** to go to slide 16.
4. Take some time to reinspect the layout of this slide in the **Primary**, **Tablet**, and **Mobile** views.

While doing so, note that the image is bigger in the **Tablet** view than in the **Primary** view. Also, remember that the image does not appear in the **Mobile** view (it has been moved to the scrap area).

5. Use the **Preview | Next 5 slides** on the Big Buttons Bar to test the project in the default browser.
6. When in the browser, use the buttons at the top of the preview to control the image in all three breakpoints.

Normally, you should not detect any problems. When the screen width exactly matches the position of a breakpoint, the slide appears exactly as it does in Captivate.

7. Still in the preview, click on the **1024** button to see the **Primary** view.
8. Use your mouse to slowly move the width slider situated between the buttons and the preview to the right.

As you do so, take a close look at how the elements of the slide behave in between the breakpoints. As shown in the following screenshot, the size of the image is fixed and only changes when a breakpoint is reached:

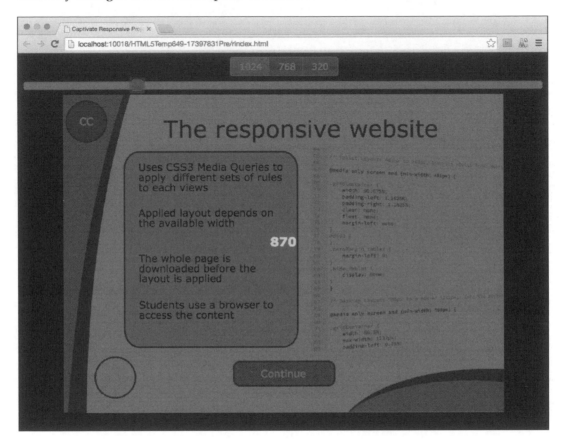

You will now make the image responsive using the following steps:

9. Return to Captivate. Make sure you are on slide 16 in the **Primary** view.

10. Select the image and turn your attention to the **Position** panel. It may be necessary to click on the **Properties** icon of the Big Buttons Bar to access the **Position** panel.

Note that the size of the image as exposed in the **Position** panel is expressed in pixels. A size expressed in pixels is known as an absolute size. It means that the size will always be the same regardless of the situation. This explains why the image is currently not responsive and always has the same size.

11. Open the **Height** drop-down menu and choose the % item.

12. Also open the **Width** drop-down menu and choose the same % item

The **Position** panel should now look like the following screenshot:

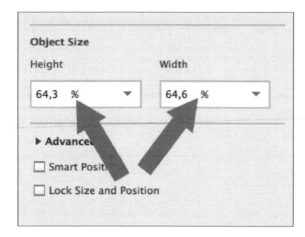

The values in the preceding image mean that the **Height** of the image in the **Primary** view will always be 64.3 percent of the height of the slide. The **Width** of the image will always be 64.6 percent of the width of the slide. With these settings, the actual size of the image will be automatically recalculated as the size of the slide changes.

13. Switch to the **Tablet** view.

14. In the **Position** panel, change both the height and the width of the image to %.

15. Return to the **Primary** view.

16. Use the **Preview | Next 5 slides** on the Big Buttons Bar to test these changes in the default web browser.

17. When in the browser, use your mouse to slowly move the width slider to the right. Observe the behavior of the image as you do so.

Unlike the previous attempt, the image is now automatically resized as you change the width of the stage. A percent size is known as a relative size. It means that it is calculated as a fraction of another dimension.

This behavior reveals another problem: the image gets distorted when being resized. It looks like only the width of the image changes, while the height is always the same, even though both the **Height** and the **Width** are using percent values in Captivate.

This behavior is easily explained. In Captivate, a slide always has a fixed height, even in a responsive project. Because the height of the slide is fixed, 64.3 percent of the height is also a fixed value! In conclusion, the image always has the same height because the slide always has the same height regardless of the value being expressed in pixels or in percent.

To make the image fully responsive, you must find a way to resize the image according to the viewport width, while maintaining the height/width ratio of the image.

18. Return to Captivate. Make sure you are on slide 16 in the **Primary** view.

19. Select the image and turn your attention to the **Position** panel.

20. Open the **Height** drop-down menu and change the value to **Auto**.

21. Repeat this action in the **Tablet** view.

22. Return to the **Primary** view and go to **Preview | Next 5 slides** on the Big Buttons Bar to test the change in the web browser.

23. When in the browser, use your mouse to slowly move the width slider to the right.

24. Keep the browser open for the next section

The **Auto** value you chose for the **Height** ensures that the width/height ratio of the image never changes. Because the width of the image is expressed as a percentage of the width of the slide, the width of the image is automatically recalculated as the width of the slide changes which, in turn, changes the height of the image.

Congratulations! You just made this image fully responsive!

Creating responsive text

In the previous section, you discovered the difference between absolute sizing (using pixels) and relative sizing (using percent). In this section, you will extend that knowledge to create responsive Text Captions.

Still in the web browser, keep experimenting with the slider at the top of the preview but, this time, concentrate on the Text Captions situated on the left side of the slide.

As shown in the following screenshot, the font size of some of these Text Captions changes as the slide is being resized while the font size is fixed in other Text Captions. In some extreme situations, the text content might even be cut out!

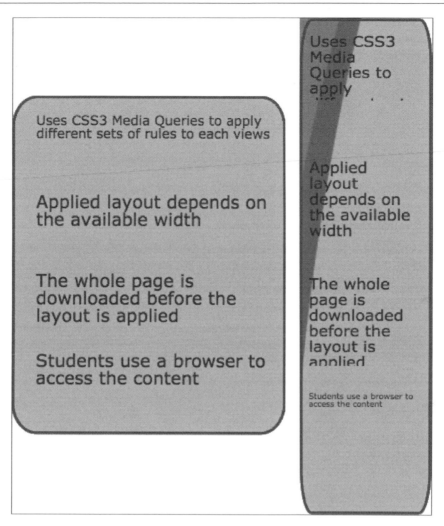

You will now return to Captivate and examine the sizing properties of these Text
Captions using the following steps.

1. Return to Captivate and make sure you are on slide 16 of the project in the
   Primary view.

2. Select the Text Caption that reads **Uses CSS3 Media Queries...**.

3. Turn your attention to the **Position** panel at the right edge of the screen.

Note that the **Width** of the selected object is expressed in percent and that the **Height** is set to **Auto**. This means that the selected Caption is fully responsive.

4. Select the Text Caption that reads **Applied layout depends…**.

5. Examine the properties exposed in the **Position** panel.

Note that both the **Height** and the **Width** are expressed in percent. This means that this object is only partially responsive. Its width is responsive and depends on the width of the viewport. Because the height of a Captivate slide is fixed, its height is always the same. This explains why the font size of the text written in this object never changes.

6. In the **Position** panel, change the **Height** of the selected Text Caption to Auto both in the **Primary** and the **Tablet** view.

7. When done, return to the **Primary** view and use the **Preview | Next 5 slides** icon of the Big Buttons Bar to test the change in the default web browser.

8. Use the slider to resize the slide and confirm that the font size of the second Text Caption changes accordingly.

When the width of a Text Caption is expressed as a percentage and its height is set to **Auto**, the Text Caption is fully responsive. The font size therefore changes so that the text is never cut out when the object is resized.

9. Return to Captivate and make all four Text Captions responsive by setting their **Height** value to **Auto** in all three views.

10. When done, return to the **Primary** view and use the **Preview | Next 5 slides** icon one last time to test these changes in the default web browser.

11. Confirm that the font size of these four Text Captions is now fluid and that the text content is no longer cut out when you scrub the slider.

Once again, it is the combination of a relative width (expressed in percent) and a height set to **Auto** that has made these objects fully responsive.

Before moving on to the next topic, let's make a quick summary of what has been covered in the previous two sections:

*   A responsive object has the ability to adapt its size and its position depending on the available slide real estate.

*   An object has an absolute size when its dimensions are expressed in pixels. In such cases, the object is not responsive and its size never changes.

*   A size expressed in percent is said to be a relative size. It is calculated as a fraction of another dimension (usually, the height or the width of the slide).

- The height of a Captivate slide is fixed. The height of an object is therefore also fixed regardless of it being expressed in pixels or in percent.
- Set the height to **Auto** to maintain the aspect ratio of an object.
- When the width of an object is expressed in percent and the height is set to **Auto**, the object is fully responsive. If this object is a Text Caption (or a Smart Shape containing text) even the font size is responsive.

Pixel and percent positioning

In the previous section, you discovered how to make the size of the objects responsive. In this section, you will discover how to make the position of the objects responsive. The basic idea is very similar to what was covered in the previous section. You can express the position of the objects either in pixels (absolute positioning) or in percent (relative positioning).

In the following exercise, you will experiment with this concept and discover how Captivate implements it using the following steps:

1. Return to the `Chapter09/goingMobile_2.cptx` file.
2. Use the **Filmstrip** panel to go to slide 16 and make sure you are in the **Primary** view.
3. Use the **Preview | Next 5 slides** icon of the Big Buttons bar to test this slide in the web browser.

This time, you will concentrate on the home button situated in the bottom-left corner of the slide. This button is made up of two objects (a Smart Shape and an image) situated on top of each other. As shown in the following screenshot, the overlay position of these two objects is not maintained when you modify the width of the viewport using the slider at the top of the preview. This problem is particularly visible in the **Tablet** view:

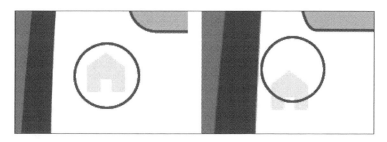

4. Close the web browser and return to Captivate.

5. While in the **Primary** view, select the circle Smart Shape that is on top of the home image.

6. Turn your attention to the **Position** panel situated on the right edge of the screen.

Note that the size of this object is expressed in pixels. This means that the circle button will always have the same size within the **Primary** view.

When it comes to the position of the object, the **Position** panel exposes four properties: **Top**, **Bottom**, **Left**, and **Right**. At this moment, only the **Bottom** and the **Left** properties are available.

7. Open the **Top** drop-down menu and choose the % menu item. This action sets the **Top** property of the selected object and disables the **Bottom** property.

8. Open the **Right** drop-down menu and choose the % menu item. This action sets the **Right** property of the selected object and disables the **Left** property.

This little experiment tells you that there can only be two position properties active at the same time. For the vertical property, you can use either **Top** or **Bottom**, but not both at the same time. For the horizontal property, use either **Left** or **Right** but do not use both at the same time.

9. Open the **Bottom** drop-down menu again and take some time to examine the available menu items.

10. Choose the **px** item. This sets the **Bottom** property of the circle to **35 px** and disables the **Top** property.

11. Open the **Left** drop-down menu and take some time to examine the available menu items. When done, choose the **px** item to set the **Left** property to **74 px** and to disable the **Right** property.

With these settings applied, the bottom edge of the circle is currently located at 35 pixels from the bottom edge of the slide and the left edge of the circle is currently located at 74 pixels from the left edge of the slide.

12. Switch to the **Tablet** view and repeat the preceding operations to apply a pixel value to both the **Bottom** and the **Left** property of the circle.

13. If necessary, click on the **Timeline** button at the bottom of the screen to open the **Timeline** panel.

14. Use the **Timeline** panel to select the home image situated behind the circle.

15. In the **Position** panel, make sure that the **Left** and the **Bottom** properties are enabled and using % values.

16. Return to the **Primary** view and confirm that the home image is using % values for the **Bottom** and **Left** properties.

As depicted in the following screenshot, the left edge of the Home image and the left edge of the slide will always be at a distance of **8.7** % of the total width of the slide. The same reasoning is valid for the **Bottom** property. The distance between the bottom edge of the image and the bottom edge of the slide will always be equivalent to **8.6** % of the total height of the slide.

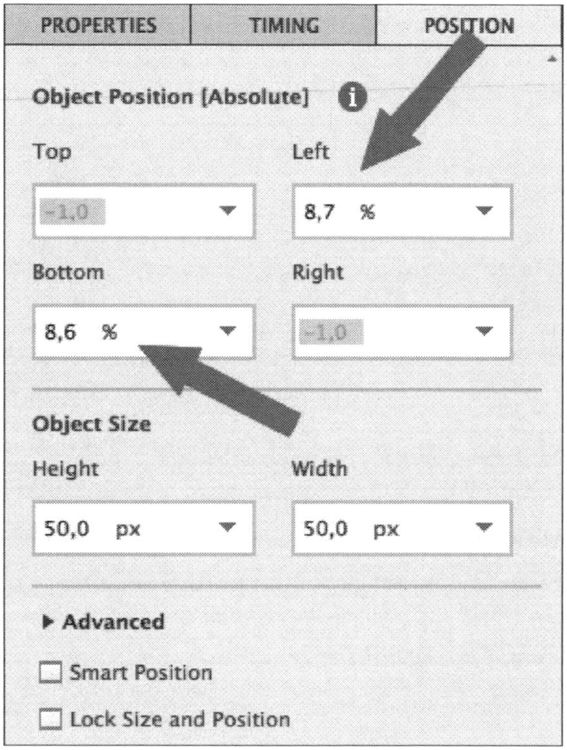

17. Use the **Preview | Next 5 slides** icon to test these settings in the web browser.

As you reduce the width of the slide with the slider, you should immediately notice that the distance between the left edge of the slide and the left edge of the circle does not change within a view. This is because this object uses absolute positioning expressed in pixels.

The story is a little bit different for the home image. Because its **Left** property uses a percentage, the actual distance between the left edge of the image and the left edge of the slide is constantly recalculated and is reduced as the width of the slide is reduced.

18. Close the browser and return to Captivate.

19. Select the circle Smart Shape while in the **Primary** view.

20. Use the **Position** panel to change its **Left** and **Bottom** properties to a percentage.

21. Repeat this operation in the **Tablet** view.

22. Return to the **Primary** view and use the **Preview | Next 5 slides** icon to test these changes in the web browser.

As expected, the position of both the circle Smart Shape and the home image are now re-calculated as the width of the slide is reduced. Unfortunately, you will see that the overlay position of these two objects is still not perfectly maintained. This is particularly visible at the very end of the **Tablet** breakpoint, just before jumping to the **Mobile** breakpoint.

Using Percent Relative positioning

To make sure that the relative position of overlaid objects is maintained at all times, Captivate proposes a third measurement unit to express the position of the objects. In this exercise, you will discover this third unit hands-on, using the following steps.

1. Close the web browser and return to Captivate.

2. Make sure you are on slide 16 of the same project in the **Primary** view.

3. Select the circle Smart Shape and return to the **Position** panel.

4. Open the **Bottom** property and choose the % **Relative** item.

5. Open the **Left** property and inspect the available items.

Note that the % **Relative** unit is not available for the **Left** property. The % **Relative** unit is only available for the vertical properties of an object. The vertical properties are the **Top**, **Bottom**, and **Height** properties.

6. Click on the % item of the **Left** property to keep it selected.

7. Use the **Timeline** to select the home image that is behind the circle Smart Shape.

8. In the **Position** panel, change the **Bottom** property of the image to % **Relative**.

9. Switch to the **Tablet** view and repeat these operations for both the circle Smart Shape and the home image.

10. When done, return to the **Primary** view, save the file and use the **Preview | Next 5 slides** icon of the Big Buttons Bar to test the changes in the web browser.

The relative position of these two objects should now be maintained across the entire width of the slide as you move the slider.

Before moving on to the final section of this chapter, let's make a quick summary of what has been covered in this section:

- In a Responsive Project, the **Position** panel exposes four properties to define the position of an object. These are the **Top**, **Bottom**, **Left**, and **Right** properties.

- You can only set one vertical (**Top** or **Bottom**) and one horizontal (**Left** or **Right**) property at a time.

- Each of these four properties can be expressed either in pixels or in percent.

- If expressed in pixels, the position of the object is said to be an absolute position. When absolutely positioned, the object will never move even if the slide is resized.

- If expressed in percent, the actual position of the object on the slide is calculated as a fraction of the available viewport width and/or height.

- To maintain the relative position of overlaid objects, you must use the % **Relative** measurement unit.

- The % **Relative** unit is only available for the vertical properties (**Height**, **Top**, and **Bottom**).

In the next section, you will learn how to use the Smart Positioning system to position objects relative to each other.

Using Smart Position

The **Top**, **Bottom**, **Left**, and **Right** properties of the **Position** panel represent the distance between the selected object and the top, bottom, right and left edges of the slide. In other words, the positioning techniques that you learned in the previous two sections allow you to place the objects relative to the slide itself.

Smart Position allows you to position the objects relative to one another. You will now discover this new positioning technique hands-on using the following steps:

1. Return to the Chapter09/goingMobile_2.cptx file.

2. Use the **Filmstrip** panel to go to slide 7 and make sure you are in the **Primary** view.

3. Take some time to examine how the objects are laid out in the Primary view. When done, switch to the **Tablet** view then to the **Mobile** view and examine the positioning of the objects in those two views as well.

4. Return to the **Primary** view when done.

As you can see, the objects present on this slide are correctly positioned in all three views. It means that, at the breakpoints, this slide looks perfectly fine. Once again, it is the responsive behavior of these objects in between the breakpoints that is of interest.

5. Use the **Preview | Next 5 slides** icon of the Big Buttons Bar to test the slide in the web browser.

6. When in the browser, use the slider at the top of the preview to reduce the width of the stage.

As depicted in the following screenshot (taken at a slider position of 810 pixels), the initial alignment of the objects is not maintained in between the breakpoints.

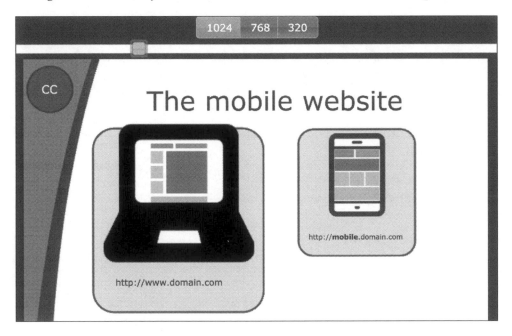

You will now turn Smart Position on and further examine how these objects are positioned.

7. Close the web browser and return to Captivate.

8. Select the image of a laptop computer in the left area of the slide and turn your attention to the **Position** panel.

9. In the **Advanced** section of the **Position** panel, select the **Smart Position** checkbox.

This action reveals two pink lines on the stage. These lines originate from the top and left edges of the selected image and end with an anchor that attaches the lines to the top and the left edges of the slide. This tells you that the selected image is positioned relative to the slide. In the **Position** panel, the **Top** and **Left** properties of the selected object are enabled.

10. Select the image of a smartphone situated in the right area of the screen.

As depicted in the following screenshot, the Smart Position lines tell you that this object is positioned relative to its surrounding box, not to the absolute edges of the slide.

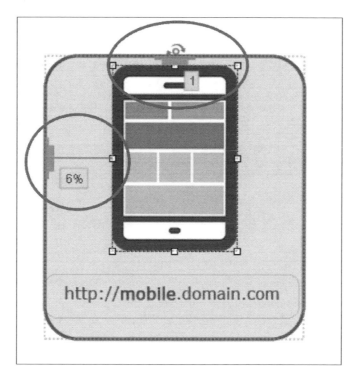

This means that the smartphone image will always be separated from the top edge of its surrounding box by a distance equivalent to one percent of the total height of the slide. Its left edge will also be separated from the left edge of its surrounding box by a distance equivalent to **6 %** of the total width of the slide. Thanks to this positioning system, the image of the smartphone will move along with its surrounding box when the slide is resized.

In the **Position** panel, the **Top** and **Left** properties of this image are enabled, but the values are not the same as those shown on the slide. This is because the values exposed in the **Position** panel are always calculated based on the slide and not based on the surrounding objects.

You will now change the Smart Position of the laptop computer image so it is calculated relative to its surrounding box, rather than relative to the slide.

11. Select the laptop computer image situated in the left area of the slide.

12. Grab the Smart Position anchor situated at the top of the slide and move it down until you see a docking line appearing across the top of the surrounding box.

This action is depicted in the following screenshot:

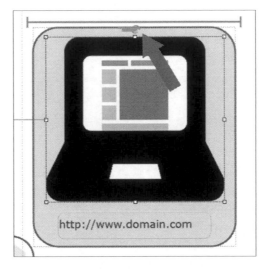

13. Repeat the same action with the left anchor point. Drag it to the right until you see a vertical docking line spanning across the height of the box surrounding the image.

14. Use the **Preview | Next 5 slides** icon of the Big Buttons Bar to test this slide in the web browser.

15. When in the web browser, use the slider to reduce the width of the stage and confirm that the laptop computer image stays in its surrounding box as you reduce the slide width.

Note that you changed the Smart Position of the laptop computer image in the **Primary** view only. When testing in the browser, you might therefore identify other problems with this image in the other views.

16. Return to Captivate and select the rounded rectangle Smart Shape that is behind the laptop computer image.

17. Press the down arrow of your keyboard several times to move the selected object down.

Note that the image of the laptop computer moves along with the Smart Shape. This is another consequence of the Smart Position system. The image of the laptop computer moves along with the Smart Shape so that the distance between these objects does not change.

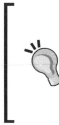

Moving objects with the keyboard

Using the keyboard arrows, you can move the selected object one pixel at a time in any direction. To move these objects 10 pixels at a time, add the *Shift* key to the mix. For example, the pressing the Right Arrow moves the selected object 1 pixel to the right, while pressing the *Shift + Right Arrow* combination moves the object 10 pixels to the right.

Extra credit – smart positioning the other objects

You will now apply the same technique to the other objects of the slide. Your goal is to maintain the position of the objects as defined in each three views across the entire width of the slider when previewing the project. These are the general steps to follow:

- Make sure **Smart Position** is turned on in the **Position** panel.
- Select an object on the stage and check the pink lines and their associated anchor points to determine how the selected object is positioned.
- If you decide that the pink lines do not make sense grab the associated anchor points and attach them to other objects.
- Repeat this operation on each object and in each view.
- Don't forget to test the project in the web browser and to move the slider at the top of the browser window to make sure the alignment of the objects is maintained at all times.

For example, you might want to position the rounded rectangle on the right relative to the rounded rectangle on the left. You might also want to position these rounded rectangles relative to the bottom of the title, and so on.

If you need more explanation, look for the final version of this project in the `final/` `goingMobile.cptx` file of the download associated with this book.

Before wrapping up this chapter, let's take a moment to summarize what you learned in this section:

- Smart Position allows you to position the objects relative to one another rather than relative to the slide.

- Smart Position is always there, but it is necessary to turn it on in the **Position** panel to make it visible on the slide.

- When visible Smart Position reveals two pink lines and their associated anchor point. One pink line is used for the vertical position (**Top** or **Bottom**) and the second one for the horizontal position (**Left** or **Right**).

- Grab an anchor point with your mouse and anchor it on another object to change the positioning scheme of the selected object.

- When linked by Smart Position, objects move together as the stage is resized in a responsive context.

- Smart Position properties are view-specific. Don't forget to repeat the process in all three views.

Summary

After reading this chapter, you should be familiar with the tools and techniques used to create a responsive eLearning project. Remember that the basic idea of a responsive project is to let you optimize the way the project looks on mobile devices. To do so, Captivate creates three breakpoints in the Responsive Projects. These breakpoints are used to define three views.

The **Primary** view is typically applied to desktop and laptop computers, as well as to tablets when held in landscape. The **Tablet** view is typically applied to tablets held in portrait. And finally, the **Mobile** view is applied to the smaller screen of a smartphone.

At runtime, the project is able to automatically decide which view to apply based on the width of the screen it is viewed on.

When creating a Responsive Project, keep in mind that the basic objects and tools are the same as in regular projects. However, there are some differences that make creating a responsive project a bit tricky to develop and test. When adding objects, remember that there is a hierarchy between the views. What you add in the **Primary** view is inherited by the **Tablet** and the **Mobile** view, but not the other way around. Captivate has adopted the desktop-first approach. When positioning and sizing the objects, remember to use percent values to make the object responsive. Smart positioning allows you to position objects relative to one another rather than relative to the slide.

When it comes to testing a responsive project, Captivate will almost always use your default web browser. This is because a responsive project can only be published in HTML5. It is also possible to use Adobe Edge Inspect to test your projects on actual touch devices without uploading them to a web server.

With a bit of practice and a lot of testing along the way, you'll soon be an expert at creating responsive eLearning content that your students will enjoy on all their devices.

In the next chapter, you will take an in-depth look at Quizzes—one of the most powerful features of Captivate.

Meet the community

In this section, I would like to introduce you to Josh Cavalier. He had a secret identity in the Captivate community, which for years had been a well-guarded secret. But now, we all know that Captain Captivate, the superhero of the Captivate community, was in fact Josh Cavalier! Even though he has recently announced his retirement as Captain Captivate, he will still be around and active in the community using his real name

> *"I may have retired the cape, but Captain Captivate will always live on. I absolutely love where Adobe is taking Adobe Captivate, and I enjoy every opportunity to train eLearning developers on the tool."*

You definitely want to take a look at his website, and especially at the Webinar section, where you'll be able to access some great Captivate and eLearning content for free!

Josh Cavalier

Josh Cavalier, who founded Lodestone in 1999, is in charge of Lodestone's eLearning consulting services and leads the overall direction and operations of Lodestone's eLearning team. He brings 20 years of eLearning development experience, technology implementation, and vision to his clients. Prior to Lodestone, he was an art director for Handshaw, a leading eLearning services company. He was one of the key resources leading the effort for streamlining Handshaw's eLearning development process and transition from CD ROM delivery to the web. He holds a Bachelor's degree in Fine Arts from Rochester Institute of Technology.

Contact details

- **Website:** http://www.lodestone.com/
- **Twitter:** @joshcav

10
Working with Quizzes

Assessing students' knowledge has always been one of the primary concerns of anyone involved in teaching. When it comes to eLearning, addressing the assessment issue is both a pedagogical and technical challenge.

On the pedagogical side, one of the factors that characterize the eLearning experience is the fact that learners sit alone in front of their computers with no one around to assist them. As teachers, we have to leave "lighthouses" along the learner's path in order to make sure that the lonely learner does not get lost and confused. Constant assessment helps keep the learners on track. By giving them many opportunities to test and validate their new knowledge, the learners can immediately identify the areas of the course that deserve more attention and can build new knowledge on solid ground.

On the technical side, Captivate contains a powerful quizzing engine that lets you insert different kinds of **Question Slides** into your projects. At the end of the quiz, Captivate can also send a detailed report to a **Learning Management System** (**LMS**). It is a server that is able to host eLearning content and track the learner's progress through the online courses it hosts.

In this chapter, you will:

- Insert various kinds of Question Slides into your Captivate projects using several different techniques
- Explore how some of the objects of Captivate can be added to the quiz
- Create a Question Pool and insert random Question Slides in the project
- Create a Pretest
- Explore and set Quiz Preferences

- Provide feedback to the students by using the branching capabilities of the Question Slides and the quiz

- Set up reporting to an LMS server

- Discuss the SCORM, AICC, and Tin Can standards used to communicate the quiz results to the LMS server

> **Preparing your work**
>
> To get the most out of this chapter, take some time to reset the Captivate interface to default. If you are using the default interface mode, just close and restart Captivate and you're good to go. If you use the advanced interface mode, use the **Window | Workspace | Reset 'Classic'** menu item and reset Captivate to default. In this chapter, you will use the exercises stored in the Chapter10 folder of the download associated with this course. If you get confused by any of the instructions, take a look at the Chapter10/final folder that contains a copy of the files.

Introducing the quiz

During the first part of this chapter, you will insert a quiz at the end of the *Driving in Belgium* project. On the pedagogical side, it is very important to introduce the quiz to the students and to explicitly explain what is going to happen. You will now insert two more slides into the *Driving In Belgium* project using the following steps:

1. Open Captivate.

2. Open the Chapter10/drivingInBe.cptx file.

3. Use the **Filmstrip** panel to go to slide 17.

Slide 17 is the last slide of the actual course as it stands. You want your quiz to be inserted in between slide 17 and the final slide of the project.

4. Use the **Slides | Content Slide** icon of the Big Buttons Bar to insert a new slide in the project. Remember that a new slide is always inserted after the currently selected slide.

5. In the **Properties** panel, apply the **Title** Master Slide to the new slide.

6. Double-click on the Title placeholder and type Driving in Belgium [Enter] The Quiz.

It is easy to insert new slides when a theme is applied to the project. Since the visual part is all taken care of by the Master Slides included in the theme, you can safely concentrate on the content to deliver. You will now insert a second slide after slide 18. This second slide has already been created for you in another project. All you need to do is to copy and paste it in this project using the following steps:

7. Open the `Chapter10/DIB_QuizIntro.cptx` project.

8. In the **Filmstrip** panel, select the one and only slide of the `dib_quizIntro.cptx` file.

9. Press *Ctrl + C* (for Windows) or *cmd + C* (for Mac) to place the slide in the clipboard.

10. Return to slide 18 of the `drivingInBe.cptx` file.

11. Use the *Ctrl + V* (for Windows) or *cmd + V* (for Mac) shortcut to paste the slide.

 Note how the imported slide picks up the theme already applied to the project.

12. Select the title of slide 19 (the Smart Shape that reads **The Quiz**).

13. In the **Properties** panel, use the **Style Name** dropdown to apply the **MFTC-slideTitle** style to the selected object.

14. Click on an empty area of the slide. Confirm that the properties of the slide itself are now displayed in the **Properties** panel.

15. In the **Style** tab of the **Properties** panel, select the **Master Slide Objects On Top** checkbox.

This action places the slide title behind the decorative elements of the Master Slide.

16. Select the Smart Shape button at the bottom of the slide.

17. In the **Properties** panel, apply the **MFTC-ShapeButton** style to the selected object.

18. Use the **Filmstrip** to return to slide 17.

19. Use the **Preview | Next 5 slides** icon of the Big Buttons Bar to test your new slides in the preview pane.

This gives you the chance to experience the new slides in a manner that is close to what your students will experience while taking the test.

20. When the preview is finished, close the **Preview** pane.

21. Close the `dib_quizIntro.cptx` project.

22. Finally, save the `Chapter10/drivingInBe.cptx` file.

At the end of this procedure, there should be 20 slides in the project.

Creating Question Slides

In Captivate, a Question Slide is a very special kind of slide. When inserting the first Question Slide in a project, you automatically create a quiz. There are many options that you can set, either for each specific Question Slide, or for the entire quiz.

Captivate supports eight types of Question Slides. In this section, you will insert and explore each of these question types one by one.

One quiz per project

Although very powerful, the Captivate quiz engine has some limitations. While it is possible to insert regular slides in between the Question Slides, all the Question Slides of a project always belong to the same quiz. In other words, there can only be a single quiz in each project. There are certain workarounds to this limitation, some of which are described in the great blog post by *Lieve Weymeis* at `http://blog.lilybiri.com/creating-customized-question-slides-using-adv`.

Inserting the first Question Slide

To get started, you will now insert the first Question Slide in your project using the following steps:

1. Return to the `Chapter10/drinvingInBe.cptx` project.

2. Use the **Filmstrip** panel to go to slide 19.

3. Click on the **Slides | Question Slide** icon of the Big Buttons Bar. The **Insert Questions** dialog box opens.

The **Insert Questions** dialog box provides a list of all the types of Question Slides available in Captivate. For this first example, you will add a single **Multiple Choice** question to the project.

4. In the **Insert Questions** dialog, select the **Multiple Choice** checkbox.

5. Open the **Graded** drop-down list associated with the **Multiple Choice** checkbox.

The drop-down list provides three options:

- **Graded**: This type of question has right and wrong answers. For example, "Is Belgium a multilingual country?" is a question that has a right or a wrong answer (true/false), so it is a Graded question (by the way, the answer is true!).

- **Survey**: This type of question is used to gather the learner's opinion about something. As such, it has no right or wrong answer. For example, "Would you recommend this eLearning course to your friends?" is a survey question (yes/no).

- **Pretest**: This type of question is not part of the quiz and the answer is not reported to the server. A pretest is used to assess the student's knowledge before taking the course. It is possible to add branching based on the outcome of the pretest. For example, the student who passes the pretest can skip the course if he wants to, but the student who fails the pretest has to take the course to gain the required knowledge.

Here, you want to add a single Graded Multiple Choice question.

6. Select **Graded** in the drop-down list.

7. Make sure that the **Insert Questions** dialog looks like the following screenshot:

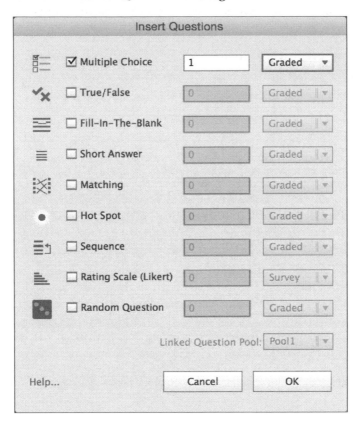

8. Click on the **OK** button to generate the Question Slide and to close the **Insert Questions** dialog.

Take a look at the **Filmstrip** panel. It now contains 22 slides. This means that the operation you just completed has added *two* slides to the project.

- As expected, the Multiple Choice question has been inserted after the slide that was selected. In this case, the Multiple Choice question is slide 20.

- Since the new slide is the first Question Slide of the project, Captivate has also generated the **Quiz Results** slide as slide 21.

The **Quiz Results** slide contains a lot of automatically generated elements.

9. Use the **Filmstrip** panel to go to slide 20.

10. Inspect the various elements that have been automatically added to the Multiple Choice question slide.

Most of these elements are self-explanatory. The only element that probably requires an explanation is the **Review Area** section. This area is used to display feedback messages to the student at the end of the quiz. The content of these messages depends on the outcome of the quiz.

The **Quiz Results** slide is generated by default when a new quiz is created (or, in other words, when the first Question Slide is added to the project). It is possible to turn this slide off if you want to.

11. Use the **Quiz | Quiz Preferences** menu item to open the Quiz Preferences dialog box.

12. On the left-hand side of the **Preferences** dialog, click on the **Settings** category of the **Quiz** section.

Watch out! There is another **Settings** category in the **Recording** section. Make sure you use the one in the **Quiz** section, as shown in the following screenshot:

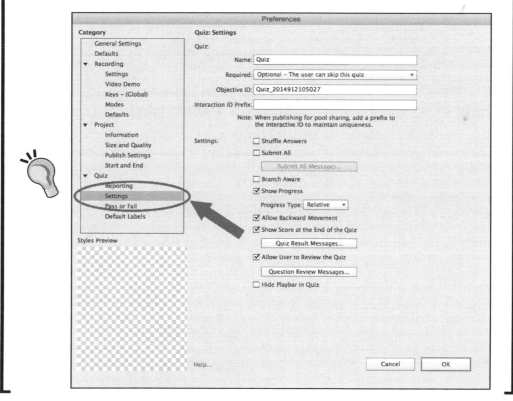

13. Deselect the **Show Score at the End of the Quiz** checkbox.

14. Click on the **OK** button to apply the changes and close the **Preferences** dialog.

When the operation is completed, take another look at **Filmstrip**. Note that slide 21 is grayed out and that an eye icon appears under its thumbnail. This means that the slide is hidden. In other words, it is still in the project, but it is not displayed to the student.

15. On the **Filmstrip** panel, click on the eye icon below slide 21.

This action turns the visibility of slide 21 back on. It is equivalent to returning to the **Preferences** dialog to turn the **Show Score at the End of Quiz** checkbox back on.

Turning the visibility of slides on and off

Turning the visibility of slides on and off is not limited to the **Quiz Results** slide. You can actually use this handy feature on any slide of the project. Simply right-click on a slide in the **Filmstrip** panel and choose **Hide Slide** in the contextual menu. This might be useful if a slide has been updated, but you want to retain a record of the original slide. It can also be used on multilingual projects to hide or show the slides pertaining to a particular language version.

Using the Multiple Choice question

The basic principle of a Multiple Choice question is to provide multiple possible answers to a given question. The student has to choose the correct answer from a predefined list.

In the following exercise, you will configure the Multiple Choice question you added in the previous section using the following steps:

1. Return to the `Chapter10/drivingInBe.cptx` project.

2. Use the **Filmstrip** panel to go to slide 20.

Slide 20 is the first Question Slide of the project. As you can see, lots of objects have been automatically generated on this slide.

Watch out! It is possible that some objects sit on top of other objects. For example, move the orange *Incomplete Caption* to reveal the *Incorrect Caption* and the *Correct Caption*!

The purpose of most of the generated objects should be obvious, but some of them require more explanation, as follows:

- The **Review Area** is related to the **Review Quiz** button situated on the **Quiz Results** slide (currently, slide 21). If the learner clicks on that button at the end of the quiz, he/she are allowed to review the quiz. In such a case, **Review Area** is used to display an appropriate feedback message to the student.

- The student uses the four buttons at the bottom of the slide (**Clear, Back, Skip**, and **Submit**) to interact with the quiz. It is possible to control the visibility of each of these buttons either for the entire quiz or for each specific Question Slide.

- The **Progress Indicator** at the bottom-right corner of the slide title can also be customized in the **Preferences** dialog.

- During the quiz, the feedback messages situated in the lower area of the slide are all turned off by default. They are automatically revealed depending on the student's answer to the question. It is therefore not a problem if they overlap.

Every element of the Question Slide can be customized. If necessary, you can even insert extra objects (such as Images, Animations, or Text Captions) using the same techniques as those used for a standard slide.

Understanding the basic question properties

Text Captions are used to display the question and the list of possible answers. Your next task is to customize these Text Captions using the following steps:

1. Double-click on the Text Caption that reads **Type the question here** to select it in edit mode. When done, triple-click on the same object to select its content.

2. Type What are the three official languages of Belgium? and hit the *Esc* key.

3. Double-click on the first possible answer to select it in edit mode, then triple-click on the same object to select its entire content. Type French as the first possible answer.

4. Use the same technique to write English as the second possible answer.

To make this question more interesting, you need to add other answers to the list.

5. Open the **Quiz** panel situated in the panel group on the right edge of the screen. You may need to click on the **Properties** icon of the Big Buttons Bar to open the panel group.

6. In the topmost section of the **Quiz** panel, change the value of the **Answers** field to 5. Captivate generates three more answers on the Question Slide.

7. Type German, Dutch, and Spanish in the newly generated answers as shown on the following screenshot:

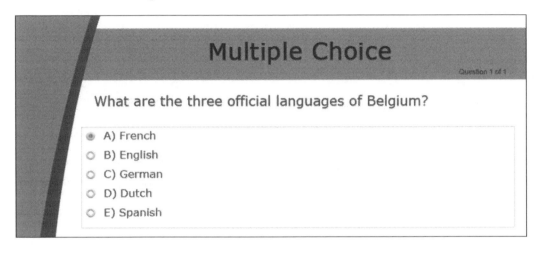

Currently, the Question Slide only accepts one of the answers from the list as the correct answer, but Belgium is a complicated country with three official languages! Fortunately, Captivate has an option that allows the Multiple Choice question to accept multiple correct answers.

8. Select the **Multiple Answers** checkbox situated in the topmost section of the **Quiz** panel.

On the Question Slide, this action changes the radio buttons associated with each of the possible answers to checkboxes. You will now tell Captivate what the right answers are.

9. On the Question Slide, select all three correct answers (**French, German,** and **Dutch**).

Working with Partial Scoring

In this case, the question is either entirely right (if the user selects all three correct answers) or entirely wrong (in every other case). **Partial Scoring** allows you to make this question partially correct if the student selects some of the right answers but not all. This advanced option is currently available on Multiple Choices questions only. You will now turn Partial Scoring on using the following steps:

1. Select the **Partial Score** checkbox from the topmost section of the **Quiz** panel.

Note that, by selecting the **Partial Score** checkbox, the **Points** and **Penalty** options of the **Quiz** panel are disabled. When Partial Scoring is turned on, each possible answer of the Multiple Choice question is assigned a specific score.

2. Select the first possible answer of the Question Slide (**French**) and return to the **Properties** panel.

3. Switch to the **Options** tab of the **Properties** panel and change the **Points** of this answer to 5.

4. Select the second possible answer (**English**) and confirm it is worth **0 Points**.

5. Repeat the same procedure with the remaining possible answers. The **Dutch** and **German** answers should each grant 5 points to the student, while the **Spanish** answer is worth 0 points.

Now that Captivate is able to tell the right from the wrong answers, you can fine-tune some additional options of this Question Slide.

6. Return to the **Quiz** panel and select the **Shuffle Answers** checkbox.

The **Shuffle Answers** checkbox instructs Captivate to display the possible answers in a random order each time a student takes the quiz.

7. In the **Captions** section of the **Quiz** panel, deselect the **Incomplete** checkbox. This removes the yellow feedback message from the Question Slide.

8. Also, deselect the **Back** and the **Next** checkboxes to remove the corresponding buttons from the slide.

Make sure your Multiple Choice question looks like the following screenshot before continuing:

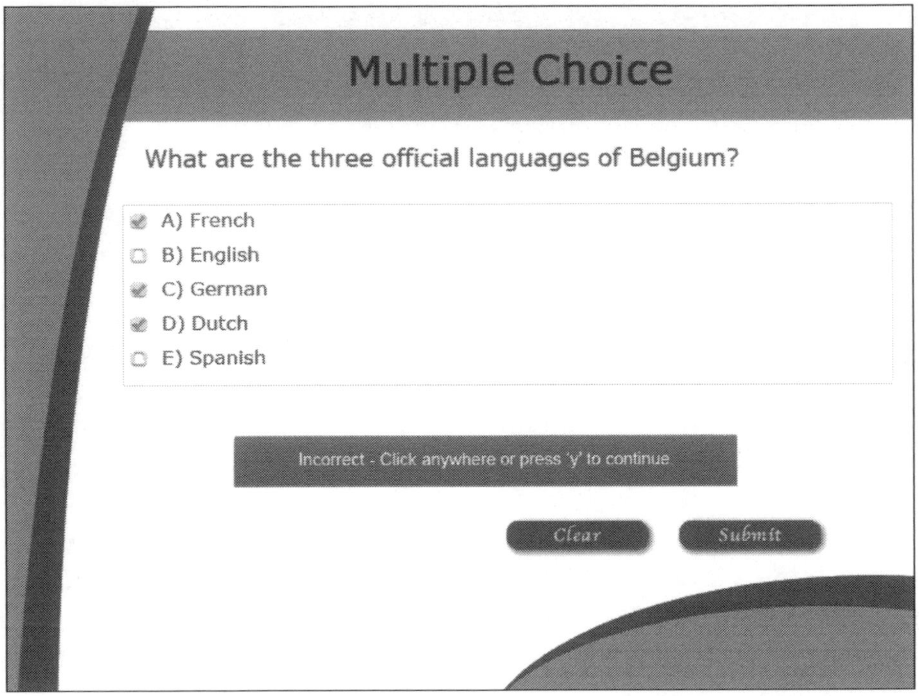

Branching with Question Slides

The last thing to do with this Question Slide is to decide how Captivate should react when the learner submits an answer. Remember that Captivate can react differently when the right or the wrong answer is submitted. This concept is known as branching. Use the following steps to implement branching on this Question Slide:

1. Scroll down the **Quiz** panel until you see the **Action** section.
2. Make sure the **On Success** action is set to **Continue**.
3. Also, confirm that the **Attempts** option is set to **1**.
4. Open the **Last Attempt** drop-down list and inspect the available options.
5. Select the **Jump to slide** action and choose **4 Slide 4** in the **Slide** drop-down list that appears just below.

Slide 4 explains the multilingual status of Belgium. If the student does not answer this Multiple Choice question right, redirect him/her to that slide in order to explain that particular topic once more.

6. Use the **Filmstrip** panel to return to slide 4 of the project.

7. Select the **Continue** button situated in the bottom center of the slide.

8. In the **Action** tab of the **Properties** panel, change the **On Success** action to **Return To Quiz**.

If a quiz is in progress, this action redirects the student to the current Question Slide in the quiz. If no quiz is in progress, this action has no special effect and the **Continue** action is assumed.

9. When done, use the **Filmstrip** panel to return to slide 20 of the project.

Finalizing the Question Slide

You're almost done! There are just a few final things to do in order to complete this first Question Slide:

1. Take some time to inspect the remaining options available in the **Quiz** panel, but do not change any of them at this time.

Pay particular attention to the following:

- You can still change the question **Type** to **Graded** or **Survey**

- You can set a **Time Limit** to answer that particular question

You will now take care of the two feedback messages.

2. If necessary, move the red incorrect feedback message to reveal the green correct message that is underneath.

3. Change the text of the green feedback message to Great answer! Click anywhere to continue.

4. Change the text of the red feedback message to Sorry, your answer is not correct! The Official languages of Belgium are French, Dutch, and German. Belgian road signs might be in one or more of these languages. Click anywhere to continue.

Using Smart Shapes as feedback messages

By default, the feedback messages present on a question slide are based on the Text Caption object. In other words, the capabilities and limitations of a standard Text Caption also apply to these two feedback messages. Captivate 8.0.1 has a new feature: the possibility to turn these feedback messages to Smart Shapes. Using Smart Shapes instead of Text Captions gives you access to all the capabilities of the Smart Shapes object, including a whole collection of shapes, and access to extra properties such as the Opacity, Gradient fills, and more.

You will now turn the current feedback messages into rounded rectangle Smart Shapes using the following steps:

> It is necessary to use an updated version of Captivate to go through this exercise. Make sure you're using Captivate 8.0.1 (or more) and not the original Captivate 8.0.0.

1. Right-click on the red failure caption and choose the **Convert To Smart-shape** menu item.

2. Choose the Rounded Rectangle in the Smart Shape gallery. Note that you could choose any other Smart Shape as compared to the unique rectangle shape of a regular Text Caption.

3. With the failure Smart Shape selected, use the **Properties** panel to apply the **MFTC-negativeFeedback** style to the failure message.

4. Repeat the preceding operations on the green Correct Caption. Turn it into a Rounded Rectangle Smart Shape and apply the **MFTC-positiveFeedback** style to it.

5. Move and resize these two feedback messages as you see fit. Remember that these messages will never be displayed at the same time, so it is not a problem if they overlap.

This concludes your exploration of the Multiple Choice question type. As you can see, there is a multitude of options available to help you fine-tune your assessments. The final version of your Multiple Choice question slide should look like the following screenshot:

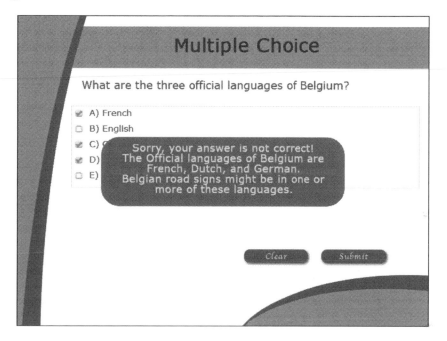

Importing Question Slides from a GIFT file

General Import Format Technology (GIFT) is a text file that allows you to use a simple text editor to write various types of questions. This text file can then be imported into GIFT-compliant eLearning applications and systems, making it easy to share question banks across these systems.

Captivate offers the ability to import a GIFT file into your projects. Thanks to this feature, you can import questions into Captivate that were originally created in another GIFT-compliant application. Note that Captivate can import a GIFT file created in another system, but it cannot export the Question Slides of a quiz into a GIFT file.

> The GIFT format was developed by Moodle, a popular open source LMS. To learn more about the GIFT format, refer to the page on the official Moodle website (https://docs.moodle.org/28/en/GIFT_format).

In the following exercise, you will take a look at such a file and import it into the *Driving In Belgium* project using the following steps:

1. Open the `Chapter10/DIB-gift.txt` file in a text editor such as Text Edit (for Mac) or Notepad (for Windows).

2. Take some time to read through this text file, making sure you don't change any of its content.

Even without knowing anything about the GIFT format, reading it is easy. This particular file contains three questions. The first one is a **Matching** question, the second a **Short Answer** question, and the last one is a **True/False** question.

3. Return to the `Chapter10/drivingInBe.cptx` project and use the **Filmstrip** panel to return to slide 20.

4. Use the **Quiz | Import GIFT Format File** menu item to import these three questions into Captivate.

5. Select the `Chapter10/DIB-gift.txt` file and click on **Open** to begin the importation process.

Captivate parses the GIFT file and creates three additional Question Slides in the project. These new slides are added after the selected one as slides 21, 22, and 23.

 The GIFT file you just imported is a Moodle question bank that has been exported with the built-in export feature of Moodle. Some manual edits have been necessary to import it into Captivate without errors. To learn more about creating question banks with Moodle, visit `https://docs.moodle.org/28/en/Question_bank`. To learn more about exporting Moodle questions to a GIFT file, visit `https://docs.moodle.org/28/en/Export_questions`.

Working with Matching questions

The first question that has been imported from the GIFT file is a **Matching** question. The basic idea is to provide two columns of elements. The student has to match an element of the first column with one or more element(s) in the second column. In the next exercise, you will take a look at the imported Matching question and modify some of its properties using the following steps:

1. In the `Chapter10/drivingInBe.cptx` project, use the **Filmstrip** panel to go to slide 21.

2. Take some time to inspect this slide and to compare it with the content of the GIFT file.

To make the question more interesting (and the answer more difficult to find), you will provide a different number of items in both columns.

3. In the topmost area of the **Quiz** panel, increase the number of items of **Column 2** to **5**.

4. Select the **Shuffle Column 1** checkbox.

The **Shuffle Column 1** checkbox instructs Captivate to display the options of the first column in a random order each time a student takes the quiz.

You will now change the text of the two extra items in **Column 2**.

5. Type 30 km/h and Unlimited in the two extra items in **Column 2**.

6. Return to the **Quiz** panel.

7. In the topmost section, change the **Points** to **15**.

8. Select the **Motorway** item in the first column of the Matching question.

9. Open the drop-down list that appears in front of the **Motorway** item.

This drop-down list is used to tell Captivate the right answer. In this case, this operation is useless as the right answer is part of the information that has been imported from the GIFT file. Note that several items in the first column could match a single item in the second column. This can be used to create very interesting and complex matching questions.

10. Click on an empty area of the slide to deselect the currently selected object and close the associated drop-down menu.

11. In the **Captions** section of the **Quiz** panel, deselect the **Incomplete** Caption to remove the yellow feedback message.

12. Also, deselect the **Back** and **Next** checkboxes to remove the corresponding buttons from the slide.

13. Leave all the other options of the **Quiz Properties** panel with their current values.

Before moving on to the next question type, feel free to move and resize the objects of this slide according to taste. Remember that, when it comes to aligning and resizing objects, some great tools are available on the Align toolbar. Make sure your slide looks like the following screenshot when done:

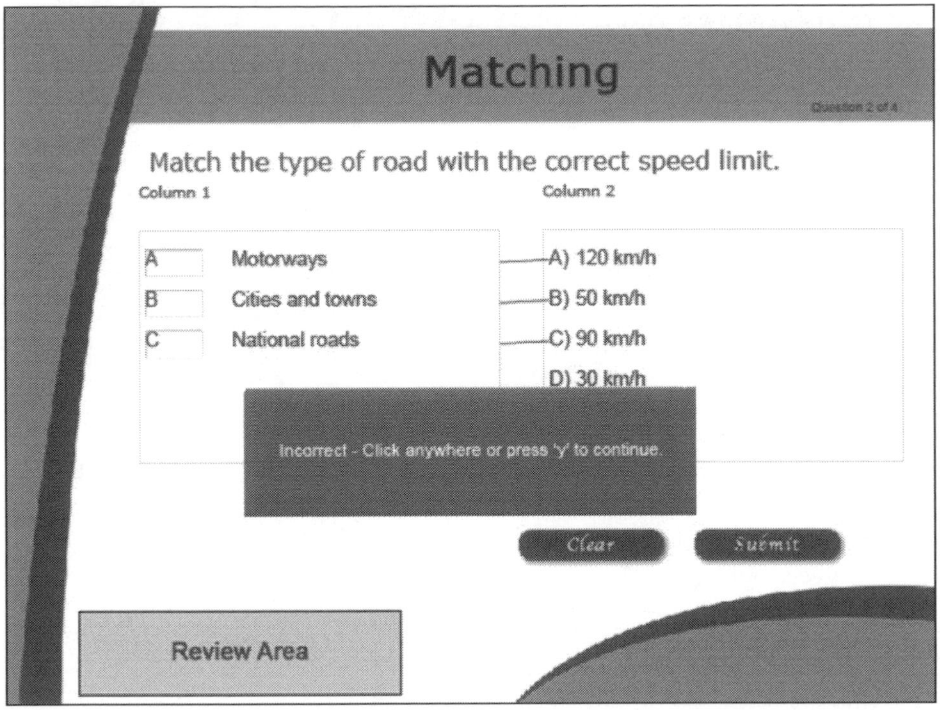

Working with Short Answer questions

The second question inserted from the GIFT file is a Short Answer question. In a Short Answer question, the student must type in a few words or a short sentence as the answer. Captivate then matches the supplied answer against a predefined list of correct answers. Let's take a look at the Short Answer question using the following steps:

1. In `Chapter10/drivingInBe.cptx`, use the **Filmstrip** panel to go to slide 22.

2. Take some time to inspect this slide and to compare it with the content of the GIFT file.

3. Select the big Answer Area situated in the middle of the slide. When selected, the **Correct Entries** box is displayed.

4. Compare the content of the **Correct Entries** box to the content of the GIFT file.

The **Correct Entries** box contains the list of entries that the answer provided by the student will be matched against. Note that you can add more correct answers by clicking on the + icon situated at the top-right corner of the **Correct Entries** box.

Coming up with the right question

As a teacher, coming up with the right question is always a challenge. This is especially true with the Short Answer question type. You need to find a question whose answer is obvious enough for a computer to correct, complicated enough to have some pedagogical value, and flexible enough to allow the students to type the same answer in different ways.

The main properties of this question are now in place. It's time for some fine-tuning.

5. In the topmost section of the **Quiz** panel, change the **Points** value to **5** and the **Penalty** value to **1**.

The **Penalty** value removes one point from the student's score if the wrong answer is given.

6. In the **Captions** section of the **Quiz** panel, deselect the **Incomplete** Caption. This removes the yellow feedback message and reveals the failure caption that was underneath.

7. Deselect the **Back** and **Next** checkboxes to remove the corresponding buttons from the slide.

8. Leave all the other options of the **Quiz Properties** panel with their current settings.

9. Don't hesitate to rearrange the elements of the slide as you see fit, keeping in mind that the success and failure captions are never displayed at the same time. Therefore, it is not a problem if they overlap.

That's it for the Short Answer question. Make sure your slide looks more or less like the following screenshot and save the file before moving on:

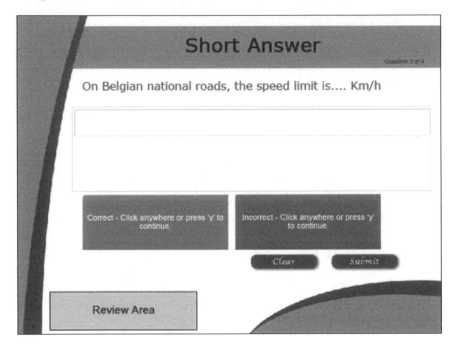

Working with True/False questions

The third question imported from the GIFT file is a **True/False** question. A True/ False question is actually a Multiple Choice question with only two possible answers. By default, these two answers are *true* and *false*, but you can change these defaults to anything you like (such as yes/no, man/woman, and so on) as long as there are no more than two different answers. Perform the following steps to explore and modify the imported True/False question type:

1. In the `drivingInBe.cptx` file, use the **Filmstrip** panel to go to slide 23.

The GIFT file format does not allow you to change the default answers of a True/False question. In this case, these default values (**True** and **False**) do not make sense. Your first task is to adjust the possible answers so that the question actually makes sense.

2. Change the text of the **True** answer to `On the Left Side`.
3. Change the text of the **False** answer to `On the Right Side`.

This illustrates that the possible answers of a True/False question can actually be something other than *true* and *false*. The important point here is to ask a question that has no more than two possible answers, whatever these answers are.

4. Make sure that **On the Right Side** is selected as the correct answer.

5. In the **Quiz** panel, change the **Points** value to 5.

As usual, you will now fine-tune the other properties of this question slide.

6. In the **Quiz** panel, deselect the **Incomplete** Caption to remove the yellow feedback message.

7. Deselect the **Back** and **Next** checkboxes to remove the corresponding buttons from the slide.

8. Leave all the other options of the **Quiz** panel at their current settings.

9. Rearrange the elements of the slide as you see fit and customize the success and failure feedback messages at will.

When done, your slide should look like the following screenshot:

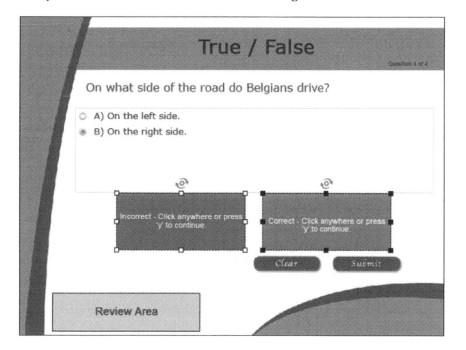

Adding the remaining Question Slides

To speed you up and let you focus on the Question Slides specifics, the remaining Question Slides of this project have already been created for you. They are stored in the Chapter10/additionalQuestions.cptx file. In this section, you will simply copy and paste the questions in the additionalQuestions.cptx file into the drivingInBe.cptx file:

1. Open the Chapter10/additionalQuestions.cptx project.

2. Use the **Filmstrip** panel of the additionalQuestions.cptx file to select the first slide of this project.

3. Press the *Shift* key and select slide 4 in the **Filmstrip** panel.

This action selects from slide 1 to slide 4. In other words, you have selected all but the last slide of the additionalQuestions.cptx file. The last slide of this project is the automatic **Quiz Result** slide of the quiz.

4. Use the *Ctrl + C* (for Windows) or *cmd + C* (for Mac) shortcut to copy the selected slides to the clipboard.

5. Return to slide 23 of the drivingInBe.cptx file.

6. Use the *Ctrl + V* (for Windows) or *cmd + V* (for Mac) shortcut to paste the slides.

Four Question Slides are added to the project after slide 23. At the end of this exercise, there should be 29 slides in the drivingInBe.cptx file.

7. Save the drivingInBe.cptx file.

8. Close the additionalQuestions.cptx file.

The stage is set for you to explore the remaining question types available in Captivate.

Working with Fill-In-The-Blank questions

The next question type is the **Fill-In-The-Blank** question. The idea is to remove one or more words from a given sentence. The student has to *fill in the blank(s)* either by typing the missing words or by choosing them from a drop-down list. Perform the following steps to explore the Fill-in-The-Blank question:

1. Use the **Filmstrip** panel to go to slide 24 of the Chapter10/drivingInBe.cptx project.

2. Click on an empty area of the slide to make sure that the slide is the currently selected element.

3. In the **Properties** panel, click on the **Reset Master Slide** button.

This action reapplies the Master slide onto the imported question slide. This is done to make sure that the styles defined in the theme and the elements defined in the Master Slide are properly applied.

Note the **On Belgian motorways, the speed limit is 120 km/h** sentence that has been typed for you. This sentence is the one from which some words will be taken out. In this case, you will delete the word **motorways** and replace it with a drop-down list of possible answers the students will have to choose from.

4. Select the word **motorways**.
5. At the top of the **Quiz** panel, click on the **Mark Blank** button.

Note that a dashed line now underlines the selected word. This is how Captivate marks the words that are taken out of the original sentence. You will now tell Captivate that you want to replace this word with a drop-down list.

6. Click on the underlined word until the **Correct Entries** box appears on the screen.
7. In the bottom-left corner of the box, change **User Input** to **Dropdown List** (**1** in the following screenshot).
8. Click on the **+** icon (**2** in the following screenshot) three times to add three additional entries in the list. There should now be four possible answers in the list.
9. Type `national roads`, `cities and towns`, and `railroad` as possible entries in the list.
10. Show Captivate the right answer by selecting the **motorways** option (note that you can mark multiple entries as correct).
11. Select the **Shuffle Answers** checkbox.

The **Shuffle Answers** checkbox instructs Captivate to display the options of the drop-down list in a random order each time a student takes the quiz.

Make sure your list looks like the following screenshot before moving on:

The other properties of this Question Slide have already been taken care of for you. Feel free to arrange the object contained on the slide as you see fit.

Spacing the answer

Captivate uses the width of the redacted words to generate the drop-down menu. If one of the items of the drop down is wider than the redacted word, it might not be completely visible in the drop-down menu. The workaround is to manually add some extra spaces in the **Correct Entries** dialog just after the redacted word.

That's it for the Fill-In-The-Blank question. Of course, it is possible to mark more than one blank in the same sentence. In such cases, Captivate awards points only if the whole sentence is correct. This question type does not support partial scoring and is, therefore, completely right or completely wrong!

Working with Hotspot questions

The idea of the Hotspot question is to display an image on the slide and let the student choose the right spot(s) on this image. In this example, you will display road signs and ask the student to choose the sign that corresponds to a given situation, using the following steps:

1. Return to the `drivingInBe.cptx` file and use the **Filmstrip** panel to go to slide 25.

2. Click on the **Reset Master Slide** button situated in the topmost section of the **Properties** panel to reapply the Master Slide to the imported question.

Slide 25 has been imported from the `additionalQuestions.cptx` file. An image containing various Belgian road signs has been added in the middle of the slide. There is also a single rectangular Hotspot on top of the image. The student will be asked to click on the road sign(s) that give(s) the right of way.

In this example, two of the signs present on the image are used to give the right of the way. Your next task is to add one more Hotspot to the slide and to position the Hotspots above the right answers.

3. In the topmost section of the **Quiz** panel, change the number of **Answers** to 2.

This action generates a second Hotspot on the Question Slide.

4. Position the first Hotspot on top of the first road sign and the second Hotspot on top of the last road sign. It may be necessary to resize the Hotspots.

5. Select one of the two Hotspots. In the **Style** tab of the **Properties** panel, change the stroke **Width** to 0 to turn off the border of the selected Hotspot.

6. At the top of the **Properties** panel, click on the **Object Option** icon and choose the **Create New Style** item in the list.

7. Save the current formatting of the selected hotspot as MFTC-transparentHotSpot.

8. Apply the new **MFTC-transparentHotspot** style to the second hotspot.

Take some time to take a closer look at the **Quiz** panel to check out the available properties for a Hotspot question. Don't hesitate to arrange them as you see fit.

9. Arrange the elements of this slide as you see fit.

At the end of this section, the Hotspot Question Slide should look similar to the following screenshot:

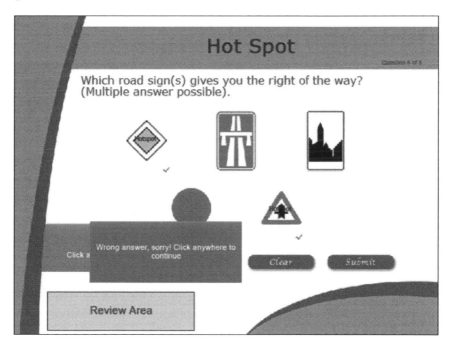

That's it for the Hotspot question! As you can see, there is nothing really difficult about this question type, just another great assessment tool in your teacher's toolset.

Working with Sequence questions

The idea of the **Sequence** question is to provide the student with a set of steps that have to be arranged in the correct order. Perform the following steps to use the Sequence question:

1. In the `Chapter10/drivingInBe.cptx` project, use the **Filmstrip** panel to go to slide 26.

2. In the upper section of the **Properties** panel, click on the **Reset Master Slide** button to reapply the Master Slide to the currently selected question.

3. In the top section of the **Quiz** panel, change the number of **Answers** to 5.

This action generates three additional steps. There should now be five steps in the sequence.

4. Change the text of the five steps as follows: `Get a nice parking slot.`, `Turn off the engine.`, `Get out of the car.`, `Make sure the doors are locked.`, and `Visit Belgium!`.

In this case, there is no need to show Captivate the right answer. Captivate will simply display these steps in a random order each time a student takes the quiz. The right answer is the order in which you typed the sentences on the slide.

5. In the **Quiz** panel, make sure the **Points** option is set to **10**. Also, add a **Penalty** value of **2** points.

These options instruct Captivate to add 10 points to the student's score in case the answer is right and to subtract 2 points from the score when the answer is wrong.

6. As usual, feel free to arrange the objects of this Question Slide as you see fit.

This concludes your overview of the Sequence question. Make sure it looks like the following screenshot before continuing:

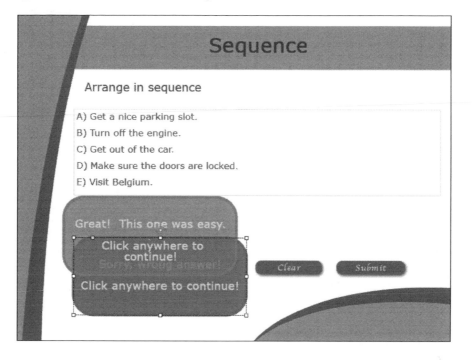

There is one last question type to go through before you can give your quiz a first test run in the **Preview** pane.

Creating surveys with Likert questions

This one is a bit special. It is the only question type that cannot be Graded. The **Rating Scale (Likert)** question is used to gather feedback and opinions, so there is no right or wrong answer for this type of question. The idea is to display statements on the screen and have the students specify their level of agreement with these statements using a rating scale.

> **Reporting Likert questions to an LMS**
>
> It is the LMS that determines what level of information may be extracted from the course. Some LMS support a very detailed set of information, while other LMS only support basic information about the course and the quiz. Although Captivate sends a comprehensive report to the LMS, all the items of the Likert question might not be available for data analysis on the server. Check the documentation of your LMS to find out what exactly is supported. There is more on LMS and reporting in the *Reporting scores to an LMS* section later in this chapter.

In the following exercise, you will configure a Likert question using the following steps:

1. Go to slide 27 of the `Chapter10/drivingInBe.cptx` project.

2. In the **Quiz** panel, change the number of **Answers** to 3.

3. Open the **Rating Scale** drop-down list to reduce the scale to **3** items.

These actions create two extra statements and their corresponding objects on the slide. The **Rating Scale** option has left only three *levels of agreement* for each statement. This option is for the entire slide. It is not possible to set this option separately for each statement.

4. Change the text of the three statements as follows: `I learned interesting things in this online course.`, `eLearning is a great learning solution`, and `I would recommend this course to a friend.`

5. Change the label of the three columns to `Disagree`, `Neutral`, and `Agree`.

6. Feel free to move and resize the objects of this slide as you see fit.

This question is a Survey question, so there is no right or wrong answer. Consequently, there are no green and red feedback messages available.

You will provide some feedback to the student by importing a regular slide in the middle of the quiz, right after the Survey question.

7. Open the `Chapter10/surveyFeedback.cptx` project of the downloaded exercise files.

This file contains a single slide that will be used as the feedback message for the survey.

8. Copy and paste the single slide of the `surveyFeedback.cptx` file as slide 28 of the `drivingInBe.cptx` file.

This extra slide is situated after the Likert question but before the **Quiz Results** slide. This illustrates the possibility to add a regular slide in the middle of the quiz.

> This extra slide also features another use of the **Characters** feature. On this slide, transparent Text Captions have been carefully positioned right above the images of the actors. To give the illusion of text being written on the images, I have used two different cursive fonts and applied **Rotation** to both Text Captions.

9. Take some time to inspect the objects of this slide, their timing on the **Timeline**, and their properties in the **Properties** panel.

In this exercise, you have created a **Rating Scale (Likert)** Survey question and added an extra slide in the middle of the quiz to provide some feedback to the student.

Previewing the quiz

You now have one example of each possible question type in the project. It is now time to experience the quiz hands-on! Since you did not change any of the Quiz Preferences yet, you will live through the default quiz experience. Perform the following steps to preview the quiz:

1. Use the **Filmstrip** panel to return to slide 18.
2. Use the **Preview | From this slide** icon of the Big Buttons Bar to preview the project from slide 18 to the end.
3. Go through the entire quiz as a learner would.
4. When you reach the **Quiz Results** slide, click on the **Review Quiz** button.

The **Review Quiz** button takes you back to the first slide of the quiz. Use the Forward button of the Playback Controls bar to go through each Question Slide. Note how Captivate shows the right, wrong, incomplete, and expected answers.

When you get back to the **Quiz Results** slide, take some time to inspect the information it contains. Pay particular attention to the message written at the end of the slide (**Sorry you failed** or **Congratulations, you passed**). It is a general feedback message that depends on the outcome of the quiz. Obviously, you have to set a passing score in order to let Captivate know when to display one message or the other.

5. Click on the **Continue** button to move on to the last slide of the project.
6. When done, close the **Preview** pane to return to Captivate and save the file.

Remember that you did not change any of the Quiz Preferences yet. In the *Quiz preferences* section in this chapter, you will review the options that allow you to customize the quiz. But, before that, you will take a deeper look at the Pretest feature.

Creating a Pretest

So far, you have created Graded and Survey questions. In this section, you will explore the Pretest questions. Pretest questions are exactly the same as Survey or Graded questions, but a few features make them special:

- First, Pretest questions are not part of the quiz. Their result is not accounted for when generating the **Quiz Results** slide.

- Second, Pretest questions are not part of the interaction report that is sent to an LMS (more on reporting to an LMS in the *Reporting scores to an LMS* section later in this chapter).

In the following exercise, you will insert a Pretest in the `encoderDemo_800.cptx` file using the following steps:

1. Open the `Chapter10/encoderDemo_800.cptx` project and use the **Filmstrip** panel to go to slide 2.

Creating a Pretest question is a similar process to creating a standard Graded or Survey question, so the Pretest has already been created for you in the `Chapter10/pretest.cptx` file.

2. Open the `Chapter10/pretest.cptx` project.

3. Use the **Filmstrip** panel to select slides 1, 2, 3, and 4 of the `pretest.cptx` file.

4. Copy the selected slides and return to the `encoderDemo_800.cptx` file.

5. In the **Filmstrip** panel of the `encoderDemo_800.cptx` file, right-click on slide 2 and paste the slides.

The four slides of the Pretest are inserted after slide 2. Slide 3 is a standard slide used to introduce the Pretest to the student. The actual Pretest is made up of the next three slides. Slide 7 is automatically generated as the **Quiz Results** slide.

6. Use the **Filmstrip** panel to go to slide 3 of the project.

7. Select the slide title and use the **Properties** panel to apply the **MFTC-SlideTitle** style to the selected object.

8. Click on an empty area of the slide to make it the selected element.

9. In the **Properties** panel, select the **Master Slide Objects On Top** checkbox.

10. Select the **OK Let's go!** button situated at the bottom of the slide.

11. Use the **Properties** panel to apply the **MFTC-shapeButton** style to the selected object.

12. Use the **Filmstrip** panel to go to slide 4.

13. Click on the **Reset Master Slide** button in the topmost area of the **Properties** panel.

14. Repeat the previous step on slide 5 and slide 6.

In order to better understand the Pretest feature, you will now test this project in the **Preview** pane to experience it hands-on.

15. Use the **Preview | Project** icon of the Big Buttons Bar icon to preview the entire project.

While in the **Preview** pane, there are some major changes to note. First, the Playback Controls Bar at the bottom of the project holds fewer controls than before. When a Pretest is inserted into a project, Captivate automatically disables most of the Playback Controls to prevent the student from skipping the Pretest.

After taking the entire quiz, the **Quiz Results** slide is displayed. Regardless of the answers you provided during the Pretest, your score will always be **0** and the **Total Questions** count will also always be **0**. Remember that the Pretest questions are *not* part of the actual quiz!

16. Close the **Preview** pane when the preview is finished.

17. In the **Filmstrip** panel, right-click on the **Quiz Results** slide (slide 7) and click on **Hide Slide** in the Contextual menu.

Since the Pretest is not part of the quiz, the **Quiz Results** slide of this project is useless and can be safely hidden.

In *Chapter 12, Working with Variables, Advanced Actions, and Widgets*, you will use an Advanced Action to redirect the student to a different slide depending on the outcome of the Pretest.

At the end of this section, you have inserted one question of each type and explored the Pretest feature of Captivate. It is time to make a quick summary of what has been covered:

- There are eight types of Question Slides available in Captivate.

- Each question can either be a Graded, Survey, or Pretest question. The only exception to this is the Rating Scale (Likert) question that can only be a Survey question.

- A Graded question has right and wrong answers. A Survey question is used to gather feedback and opinions from the students. As such, it does not have right or wrong answers. A Pretest question is not part of the quiz and is used to assess the student's knowledge before taking the online course.

- Use the **Slides | Question Slide** icon of the Big Buttons Bar to insert Question Slides into the project.

- The GIFT file format can be used to import questions into Captivate questions which have been created in external third party systems. Captivate cannot export the questions of a Quiz to a GIFT file. It can only import a GIFT file created externally.

- When inserting the first Question Slide, Captivate automatically generates the **Quiz Results** slide. This slide can be hidden in the Quiz Preferences or in the **Filmstrip** panel, but it cannot be deleted from the project.

- The **Quiz** panel is used to set up the options specific to each type of Question Slides.

- Each Graded question can weight a different amount of **Points** when the student answers the question correctly. If the answer is not correct, it is possible to remove some points from the student's score by applying a **Penalty** value.

- Partial Scoring is available for Multiple Choice questions only.

- By default, the feedback messages contained on a question slide are based on the Text Caption object. New in Captivate 8.0.1 is the ability to convert these messages to Smart Shape, which gives you access to a much wider range of shapes and options.

- When a Pretest is inserted into a project, Captivate automatically turns off most of the Playback Controls to prevent the students from skipping the quiz.

In the next section, you will concentrate on Quiz Preferences.

Exploring the Quiz Preferences

Now that you have a better idea of how a quiz works by default, you will return to the **Preferences** dialog to take a deeper look at the available options, using the following steps:

1. Return to the `Chapter10/drivingInBe.cptx` file.

2. Use the **Quiz | Quiz Preferences** menu item to open the **Preferences** dialog.

By default, the **Preferences** dialog opens on the **Reporting** section. This section will be discussed later in this chapter.

3. On the left-hand side of the **Preferences** dialog, click on the **Settings** category of the **Quiz** section, as shown in the following screenshot:

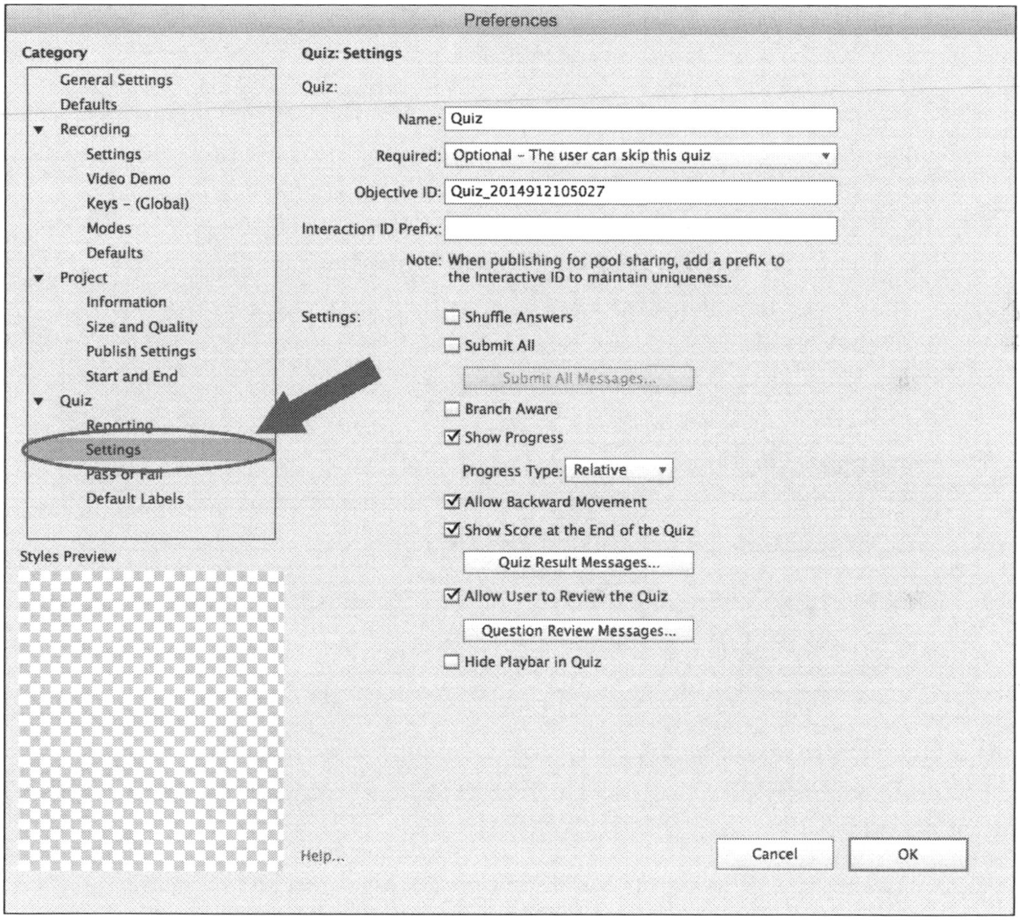

Take some time to review the options of this page.

4. Deselect the **Show Progress** checkbox. This removes the progress indicator situated in the top-right corner of the Question Slides.

The progress indicator is used to provide the students with an indication of their progress in the quiz. The Captivate default progress indicator shows the relative progress (**Question 1 of 3**) or the absolute progress (**Question 1**) to the student.

A customized progress indicator

Lieve Weymeis, also known as *Lilybiri*, is the queen of Advanced Actions. She has found a way to create a customized progress indicator using Advanced Actions and Variables. See her blog post at `http://blog.lilybiri.com/customized-progress-indicator`. Advanced Actions and Variables will be covered in *Chapter 12, Working with Variables, Advanced Actions, and Widgets*.

5. Deselect the **Allow Backward Movement** checkbox.

6. Click on **Yes** to remove the (now not needed) **Back** buttons from the Question Slides.

7. Make sure the **Show Score at the End of Quiz** checkbox is selected.

8. Click on the **Quiz Results Messages...** button. The **Quiz Results Messages** dialog opens.

The **Quiz Results Messages** dialog is where you can customize the information that appears in the **Quiz Results** slide, at the very end of the quiz.

9. Deselect the **Correct Questions** and **Total Questions** checkboxes.

10. Also, deselect the **Quiz Attempts** checkbox.

These actions remove the corresponding messages from the **Quiz Results** slide.

11. If needed, customize the **Pass Message** and **Fail Message**.

These are the messages that are displayed in the **Review Area** of the **Quiz Results** slide at the end of the quiz.

12. Click on the **OK** button to validate your changes and close the box.

13. Deselect the **Allow User to Review the Quiz** checkbox.

This action removes the **Review Quiz** button from the **Quiz Results** slide and the **Review Area** from each of the Question Slides.

14. Select the **Hide Playbar in Quiz** checkbox.

This option hides the Playback Controls during the quiz. This is done to ensure that students cannot use the Playback Controls to go back and forth in the quiz or to skip the quiz.

Note the **Submit All** checkbox. When selected, the answers to the questions are all submitted together at the end of the quiz. This allows the students to travel back and forth in the quiz and change their answers to the questions before submitting them all at once at the end.

15. Click on the **OK** button to validate the changes and close the **Preferences** dialog.

16. Use the **Filmstrip** panel to go to slide 29.

Slide 29 is the **Quiz Results** slide. Note that it contains less information than before and that the **Review Quiz** button has been removed. This matches the checkboxes configuration you created in the **Preferences** dialog.

Setting the passing score of a quiz

When the student reaches the **Quiz Results** slide, Captivate displays a message that depends on the outcome of the quiz. To display this message, Captivate must be informed of what the passing score of the quiz is. If the student reaches that passing score, Captivate displays the **Pass Message**; otherwise, the **Fail Message** is displayed.

In this section, you will set the passing score of the quiz and add some branching.

First, you will import two more slides into the project and place them after the quiz. One will congratulate the student who passes the quiz, and the other one will ask the students who fails to take the test again later. Use the following steps to import these slides:

1. Open the `Chapter10/quizFeedback.cptx` project.

2. Use the **Filmstrip** panel to select both the slides of this file and copy them.

3. Return to slide 29 of the `drivingInBe.cptx` file and paste the slides.

4. Use the **Filmstrip** panel to go to slide 30.

5. Apply the **MFTC-slideTitle** style to the slide title and the **MFTC-ShapeButton** style to the **Continue** button.

6. With the slide being the active object, go to the **Properties** panel to select **the Master Slide Objects On Top** checkbox.

7. Repeat the above operations on slide 31.

8. On slide 31, apply **MFTC-transparentTextShape** to the second Smart Shape with text situated in the middle of the slide.

After this procedure, the `drivingInBe.cptx` file should contain 32 slides, as shown in the following screenshot:

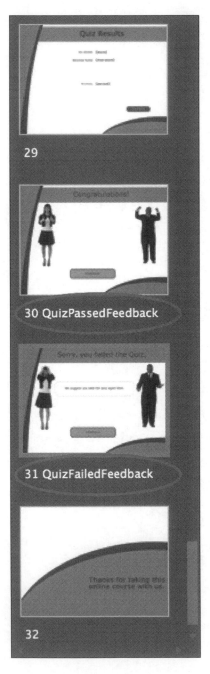

The stage is set! You will now return to the **Preferences** dialog to set the passing score of the quiz and arrange branching.

9. Make sure you are *not* on slide 30 or 31 of the `drivingInBe.cptx` file.

10. Use the **Quiz | Quiz Preferences** menu item to return to the **Preferences** dialog.

11. Click on the **Pass or Fail** category situated in the **Quiz** section of the **Preferences** dialog.

The main **Pass or Fail** option is situated at the top of the dialog box. Note that there are two ways to set the passing score for a quiz: as a *percentage* or as a certain amount of *points* to reach. The total amount of points is the sum of the points set for all the Question Slides of the quiz (excluding the points of the Pretest slides, if any).

12. In the **Pass/Fail Options** section, set the passing score to 50 percent.

You will now configure the actions that have to take place when the student passes or fails the test.

13. In the **If Passing Grade** section, set the **Action** drop-down list to **Jump to slide**. Then, select **30 Quiz Passed Feedback** from the **Slide** drop-down list.

14. In the **If Failing Grade** section, allow the user one attempt and set the **Action** drop-down list to **Jump to slide**. Then, select **31 Quiz Failed Feedback** from the **Slide** drop-down list.

Setting the pass and fail options and adding some branching on the quiz is that easy! Before moving on to the next step, take a quick look at the **Default Labels** preferences pane.

15. Click on the **Default Labels** category situated on the left-hand side of the **Preferences** dialog.

The **Default Labels** preferences are used to change the default text and the default formatting of the various elements of a Question Slide. It is best to change these options before the first Question Slide is added to the project (or—even better—in a Template). In this case, it is too late!

16. Click on the **OK** button to validate the changes and close the **Preferences** dialog.

There is one more little thing to do in order to finalize the branching system of the quiz.

17. Use the **Filmstrip** panel to go to slide 30.

18. Select the **Continue** button at the bottom center of the slide.

19. In the **Action** tab of the **Properties** panel, set the **on Success** action to **Jump to slide** and choose **slide 32** in the **Slide** drop-down list.

20. Use the **Preview | Project** icon of the Big Buttons Bar to test the entire project.

21. When done, close the **Preview** pane and save the file.

Your quiz is now up and running. In the next section, you will add some spice to the mix by creating a Question Pool. Now, let's make a quick summary of what you have just learned:

- By default, each Question Slide contains four buttons and a **Review Area**.

- By default, Captivate generates a **Quiz Results** slide and displays it at the end of the quiz.

- By default, the **Quiz Results** slide contains the **Review Quiz** button that allows the student to return to each Question Slide and get feedback on the submitted answer.

- You can allow the students to go backward in the quiz, but a submitted answer cannot be changed for another answer.

- The **Submit All** checkbox allows the students to change their answers until they submit all their answers together at the end of the quiz.

- The **Preferences** dialog contains many options to let you fine-tune the student's experience. Some of these options are used to turn the objects of all the Question Slides on or off.

- You can use the **Preferences** dialog to set the passing score of the quiz and to add any branching that depends on the outcome of the quiz.

Working with Question Pools

A **Question Pool** is a repository of Question Slides. The idea is to let Captivate randomly choose questions in the pool in order to create a unique quiz for each student. You can have as many Question Pools as you want in a Captivate project, and each pool can contain an unlimited number of Question Slides.

Creating a Question Pool

In this example, you will create a single Question Pool, add six Question Slides to it, and instruct Captivate to randomly choose one question from the pool and insert it into the quiz.

Use the following steps to create a Question Pool:

1. Make sure you are still in the `Chapter10/drivingInBe.cptx` project.

2. Use the **Quiz | Question Pool Manager** menu item to open the **Question Pool Manager** dialog.

The **Question Pool Manager** dialog is divided into two main areas:

- On the upper-left side of the box, there is a list of all the Question Pools of the project. Just above the list of pools, the **+** and **–** icons (see **1** in the following screenshot) are used to add or remove Question Pools.

- The right-hand side of the box shows the list of the Question Slides associated with the pool selected on the left-hand side. The **+** and **–** icons (see **2** in the following screenshot) are used to add new Question Slides into the selected pool or to remove existing Question Slides from the selected pool:

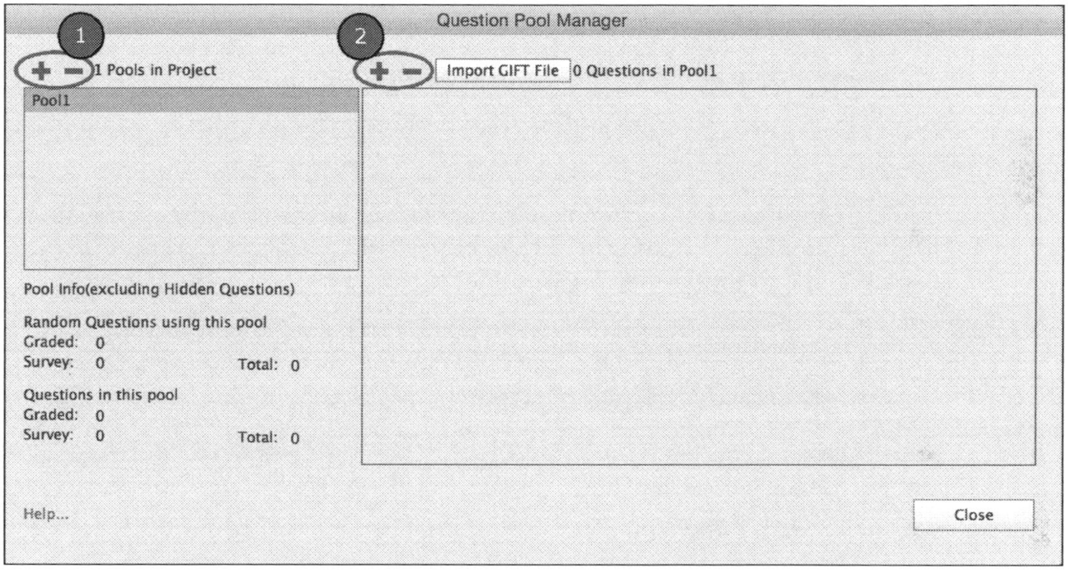

Note that the first Question Pool named **Pool1** was automatically created by Captivate when you opened the **Question Pool Manager** dialog. The **Import GIFT file** button lets you import questions from a GIFT file directly into the selected Question Pool. You will now rename this Question Pool using the following steps:

3. On the left-hand side of the **Question Pool Manager** dialog, double-click on the **Pool1** entry of the list of pools.

4. Name the pool DIB_pool1 and press the *Enter* key.

5. Click on the **Close** button to close the **Question Pool Manager** dialog.

Now that you have a Question Pool available, you will add questions to it.

Inserting questions in a Question Pool

You could have used the **Question Pool Manager** dialog to create new Question Slides directly into the pool, but you will use another technique. Instead of creating new Question Slides to fill the Question Pool, you will move some of the existing Question Slides of the quiz into the new pool using the following steps:

1. Use the **Filmstrip** panel to go to slide 21. Hold the *Shift* key down and click on slide 26.

This operation selects six slides from slide 21 to slide 26.

2. In the **Filmstrip** panel, right-click on one of the selected slides.
3. In the contextual menu, click on the **Move Questions to | DIB_Pool1** item.

This operation removes the selected slides from the **Filmstrip** and moves them into the Question Pool.

4. Open the **Question Pool** panel that appears right next to the **Timeline** panel at the bottom of the screen. (If the **Question Pool** panel is not present on the screen, use the **Window | Question Pool** menu item to turn it on).

Six Question Slides should be displayed in the **Question Pool** panel indicating that they have been moved into **DIB_pool1** correctly. Another way of accessing the same information is by using the **Question Pool Manager** dialog.

5. Use the **Quiz | Question Pool Manager** to open the **Question Pool Manager** dialog once again.
6. Make sure that the **DIB_pool1** Question Pool is selected on the left-hand side of the dialog and take a look at the right-hand side.

When **DIB_pool1** is selected, the right-hand side of the **Question Pool Manager** dialog lists the six Question Slides included in the pool.

7. Click on the **Close** button to close the **Question Pool Manager** dialog.

The Question Pool is now ready for action! The next step is to randomly pick questions from the pool and add them to the main quiz.

> **Share Question Pools with other projects**
>
> You may have noticed the **Import Question Pools** menu item under the **Quiz** menu. Using this feature, you can easily import a Question Pool from another project into this project.

Inserting random Question Slides in the main project

Remember that the idea of a Question Pool is to have a repository of questions available in order to generate random quizzes. In this section, you will randomly pick one question from the **DIB_pool1** Question Pool and insert it into the quiz using the following steps:

1. Use the **Filmstrip** panel to go to slide 20 of the `drivingInBe.cptx` file.

Slide 20 is the Multiple Choice question you created earlier in this chapter. It is the first question of the quiz.

2. Use the **Quiz | Random Question Slide** menu item to insert a random question into the main project.

The quiz currently starts with the same Multiple Choice question of slide 20 for each student. The second question is randomly picked from the Question Pool at runtime. Finally, the quiz ends in the same way for every student, with the survey on slide 22.

3. Use the **Filmstrip** panel to go to slide 21.
4. Take a look at the **Quiz** panel.

The **Quiz** panel of a **Random Question** slide only contains a fraction of the options available in the **Quiz** panel of a regular Question Slide. Two options are available: the **Points** and **Penalty** properties.

5. If needed, open the **Question Pool** panel situated right next to the **Timeline** panel at the bottom of the screen.
6. Select any Question Slide in the **DIB_pool1** Question Pool.
7. When the selected question is loaded in the main area of the Captivate interface, take a look at the **Quiz** panel.

Again, the **Quiz** panel contains fewer options than the **Quiz** panel of a regular Question Slide. Two of the missing options are the **Points** and **Penalty** properties.

When combining the options of the **Quiz** panel of the random Question Slide in the main project with the options of the **Quiz** panel of a Question Slide within a Question Pool, you more or less obtain the **Quiz** panel of a regular Question Slide.

8. Return to slide 21 of the main **Filmstrip** panel. In the topmost section of the **Quiz** panel, make sure that the **Points** property is set to 10 and the **Penalty** property is set to 1.

Now that you have a random question in the quiz, you will give your random quiz a try.

9.   Use the **Preview | Project** icon on the Big Buttons Bar to test the entire project in the **Preview** pane.

When you reach the quiz, pay close attention to the second question. Try to answer the questions correctly so that the **Quiz Passed Feedback** slide is displayed when the quiz is over.

10. When you are done, close the **Preview** pane.

11. Use the **Preview | Project** icon to test the entire project a second time.

When you reach the quiz for the second time, note that the second question is not the same as it was at the first attempt. Give wrong answers so that you fail the quiz.

12. Make sure that the **Quiz Fail Feedback** slide is displayed at the end of the quiz.

Your random quiz is now up and running. It is time to make a quick summary of what you have just learned:

*   A Question Pool is a repository of Question Slides from which Captivate randomly picks questions at runtime.

*   A Captivate project can include as many Question Pools as needed. A Question Pool can contain as many Question Slides as needed.

*   The **Quiz | Import** Question Pool menu item can be used to import a Question Pool of another project into the current project.

*   Use the **Quiz | Question Pool Manager** menu item to create new Question Pools and to add Question Slides in the available pools.

*   GIFT files can be imported directly into a Question Pool.

*   If the project already contains Question Slides, they can be moved to a Question Pool at any time. Questions in a Question Pool can also be moved back to the main project using the same technique.

*   A quiz can be made up of a mix of regular Questions Slides and random questions from different Question Pools.

*   The **Quiz** panel of a Random Question slide contains only a fraction of the options available for a regular Question Slide. The remaining options are associated with each Question Slide in the **Question Pool** panel.

Great! You now have a pretty good idea of what a Captivate quiz is, and of the myriad of options available. In the next section, you will quickly return to the Master Slide panel to examine how the look and feel of the Question Slides is achieved.

Styling the elements of the Question Slides

In this section, you will return to the Master Slide view and take a quick look at the Master Slides that define the look and feel of the Quiz, using the following steps

1. Make sure you are still in the `Chapter10/drivingInBe.cptx` file.

2. Use the **Window | Master Slide** menu item to return to the Master slide view.

On the left-hand side of the screen, the **Master Slide** panel contains eight Master Slides. Some of them control the look and feel of the Question Slides and of the **Quiz Results** slide.

3. In the **Master Slide** panel, right-click on the **MCQ, T/F, FIB, Sequence** Master Slide and try to delete it.

Captivate informs you that at least one quiz Master Slide of each type must be present in the project. The selected Master Slide therefore cannot be deleted. This particular Master Slide is used to control the look and feel of the Multiple Choice, True/False, Fill-In-The-Blank, and Sequence Question Slides of the project.

4. Take a quick look at the other Master Slides present in the **Master Slides** panel.

The **Matching** Master Slide is used by the Matching questions, the **Hot Spot** Master Slide is used by the Hot Spot questions and the **Likert** Master Slide is used by the Likert questions. Finally, the **Result** Master Slide controls the look and feel of the Quiz Result slide. These Master slides cannot be deleted from the theme.

5. Use the **Window | Filmstrip** menu item to return to the main filmstrip.

6. Use the **Filmstrip** panel to select slide 20 (the Multiple Choice question at the beginning of the Quiz).

7. With the slide selected, take a look at the **Properties** panel.

As shown in the following screenshot, Captivate has automatically applied the **MCQ, T/F, FIB, Sequence** Master Slide to slide 20. Actually, when inserting a Question Slide into the project, Captivate automatically applies the proper Master Slide to the new question depending on the type of question being inserted.

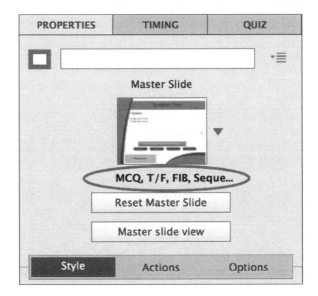

You will now try to apply a different Master Slide to this question slide.

8. In the **Properties** panel, click on the arrow next to the **Master Slide** thumbnail.

Even though there are eight Master Slides present in the theme, only that one Master Slide can be applied to the selected question slide.

Before moving on to the next section, let's quickly summarize what has been covered in this section:

- When a Question Slide is added to the project, Captivate automatically applies the proper Master Slide based on the type of the question being inserted.
- In the Theme, there are five Master Slides that are used to control the look and feel of the Question Slides and of the Quiz Result slide.
- These Master Slides cannot be removed from the Theme. Every single Captivate Theme must contain at least these five Master Slides.
- The position and formatting of the object as defined on these Master Slides are inherited by the Question Slides of the main project.

Reporting scores to an LMS

The Captivate help files give the following definition for an LMS:

> *"You can use a learning management system (LMS) to distribute a computer-based tutorial created using Adobe Captivate over the Internet. A learning management system is used to provide, track, and manage web-based training."*

An LMS offers many services to both teachers and students involved in eLearning activities. The following list states some of them:

- An LMS is a website that is able to host your eLearning courses.

- An LMS maintains a list of teachers and students. Thanks to this listing, an LMS can be used to enroll students in online courses and to define one or more teacher(s) for each course.

- An LMS is able to enforce the pedagogical decisions of the teacher. For example, the LMS can be programmed to give access to the next part of the course only if the current activity has been completed. Some LMS can also enforce branching by automatically providing an additional activity for those students who have failed a quiz and so on.

- An LMS is able to communicate with your Captivate-powered content (and vice versa). This gives you access to many pieces of information such as the number of students that have taken the course, the time it took to complete an activity, the results of the quizzes, and even a detailed report of every interaction performed by each student while taking the course.

- There are many other services that an LMS has to offer.

There are many LMS available and there are a myriad of companies, schools, and universities that have deployed an LMS to deliver, track, and manage their web-based training. Some LMS are commercially licensed and can be quite expensive, but there are also several open source LMS platforms that are free to use and easy to deploy on a web server.

Moodle

Moodle is one of the most popular and powerful open source LMS solutions. Personally, I have used Moodle for many eLearning projects, and it has never let me down. However, Moodle has a fairly steep learning curve. Packt Publishing has published an impressive array of titles on Moodle, providing the necessary documentation to get you started. More information on Moodle is available at `http://www.moodle.org`. More information about Packt books on Moodle is available at `https://www.packtpub.com/all/?search=moodle`.

For a list of the most popular LMS, check out the references on `http://en.wikipedia.org/wiki/List_of_learning_management_systems`.

Understanding SCORM, AICC, and Tin Can

Each LMS has its pros and cons and each contains a unique set of features. However, every LMS must be able to host eLearning content created by a myriad of different authoring tools (Adobe Captivate being one of the many eLearning authoring tools available).

It is important to keep in mind that you can create courses using a myriad of tools but, at the same time, it is critical to ensure that these courses can communicate with various LMS. This is where SCORM, AICC, and Tin Can come into play.

These are three internationally accepted standards used to make the communication between your eLearning content and your LMS possible. When choosing an LMS for your organization, make sure that the chosen solution is compliant with SCORM, AICC, or Tin Can. Captivate is SCORM, AICC, and Tin Can compliant, so Captivate courses can be integrated in virtually every LMS available on the market. Let's now discuss these three standards in more detail:

- **SCORM** stands for **Sharable Content Object Reference Model**. SCORM is maintained by the **Advanced Distributed Learning (ADL)** (`http://www.adlnet.org/`) project of the US Department of Defense. SCORM is a **reference model**. It means that it aggregates standards created by other organizations. The goal is to build a single standard based on the work done by other organizations that are active in the eLearning field. See the Wikipedia page on SCORM at `http://en.wikipedia.org/wiki/SCORM`.

- **AICC** stands for **Aviation Industry Computer-based Training Committee**. The initial idea was to provide a unique training and testing environment for the aviation industry in order to ensure the same training and testing standard for all the airline companies in the world. For more information, see the AICC page on Wikipedia at `http://en.wikipedia.org/wiki/Aviation_Industry_Computer-Based_Training_Committee` or the official AICC website at `http://www.aicc.org/`.

- **Tin Can** is the newest standard. The Tin Can API, now officially known as **Experience API (xAPI)**, is an eLearning software specification that allows learning content and learning systems to speak to each other in a manner that records and tracks all types of learning experiences. Learning experiences are recorded in a **Learning Record Store (LRS)**. LRS can exist within traditional LMSes or on their own. You can find out more about the Tin Can API at `http://tincanapi.com/`.

Now that you have a better idea of what a LMS is and know about the standards in use, you can enable reporting in your Captivate project.

 On December 11, 2014, AICC announced that it would be dissolved and the AICC standard no longer maintained. All the work of AICC has been transferred to ADL, which oversees both the SCORM and the Tin Can standards. See the official announcement on `http://www.aicc.org` or on the AICC Twitter feed at `https://twitter.com/aicc`.

Enabling reporting in Captivate

To have Captivate publish an LMS-ready package, you have to set options at different locations throughout the project.

In the next exercise, you will make your quiz ready to be integrated in a SCORM-compliant LMS. You will first inspect the options available at the interaction level before moving on to project-level reporting options.

Reporting options at the interaction level

Each "scorable" object of Captivate is automatically assigned with a unique **Interaction ID**. This Interaction ID is what makes data tracking by the LMS possible. Perform the following steps to view and change the Interaction IDs:

1. Use the **Filmstrip** panel to go to slide 20 of the `drivingInBelgium.cptx` file.
2. Scroll down the **Quiz** panel until you see the **Reporting** section.
3. In the **Reporting** section of the **Quiz** panel, make sure the **Report Answer** checkbox is selected.

This checkbox enables you to choose which interactions are reported to the LMS. Also, note that Captivate has automatically assigned a random **Interaction ID** to this question Slide. Most of the time, this default random **Interaction ID** is enough, but you can assign this question a unique **Interaction ID** on your own if you want to. The **Reporting** section of the **Quiz** panel should now look like the following screenshot:

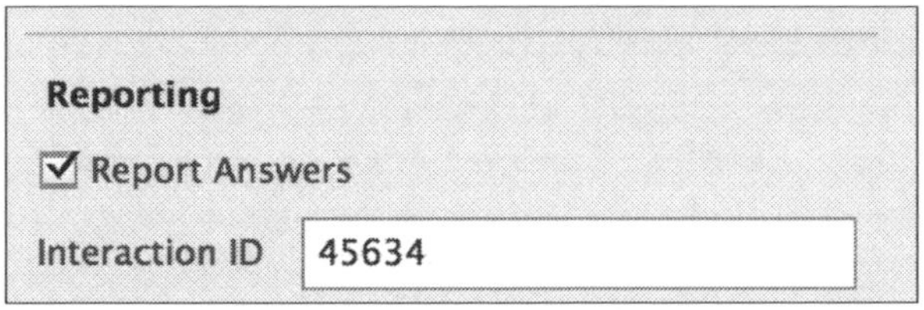

Reporting

☑ Report Answers

Interaction ID   45634

Note that there can be no spaces or special characters in the **Interaction ID**. If you type your own **Interaction** ID with a prohibited character, Captivate turns the spaces and special characters typed in the **Interaction ID** field into underscores.

Reporting the random Question Slides

In this section, you will take a closer look at the reporting options of a random question slide using the following steps:

1. Still in the `Chapter10/DrivingInBe.cptx` file, use the **Filmstrip** panel to go to slide 21 of the project. Slide 21 is the random Question Slide of the quiz.

2. In the **Reporting** section of the **Quiz** panel, make sure the **Report Answer** checkbox is selected.

Note that only the Report Answer checkbox is available when a Random Question Slide is selected. The Interaction ID must be defined for each individual question in the Question Pool.

3. Return to the **Question Pool** panel situated right next to the **Timeline** panel at the bottom of the screen. If the **Question Pool** panel is not available, use the **Window | Question Pool** menu item to turn it on.

4. Select any of the Question Slides available in the Question Pool.

5. In the **Reporting** section of the **Quiz** panel, note that only the **Interaction ID** field is available.

For the purpose of this exercise, the default **Interaction IDs** are perfect. Don't hesitate to modify them if you need to. Just keep in mind that these **Interaction IDs** must be unique.

The decision to report the answer to the LMS is taken at the random Question Slide level in the main **Filmstrip**. This allows you to reuse the same question in different Captivate projects and decide—in each project—whether this particular question should be reported or not. The **Interaction ID** is defined at Question Slide level in the Question Pool. This means that the **Interaction ID** will accompany the question slide wherever it is used.

Using a Drag and Drop interaction as a Question Slide

The Question Slides that make up a quiz are not the only interactions that can be reported to an LMS. There are a bunch of other objects that also have this capability. One such feature is the Drag and Drop interaction. This interaction has built-in reporting capabilities that are very similar to those of a regular Question Slide.

In this section, you will import a new slide into the project, define a Drag and Drop interaction, and make this interaction part of the quiz by configuring its reporting options:

1. Open the `Chapter10/dragAndDrop.cptx` file.

2. In the **Filmstrip** panel, select the first and only slide of this project.

3. Use the *cmd + C* (for Mac) or *Ctrl + C* (for Windows) shortcut to copy the selected slide.

4. Return to the `Chapter10/drivingInBe.cptx` file and use the **Filmstrip** panel to go to slide 21.

5. Use the *cmd + V* (for Mac) or *Ctrl + V* (for Windows) shortcut to paste the selected slide as slide 22 of the `drivingInBe.cptx` file.

6. Select the slide title and use the **Properties** panel to apply the **MFTC-slideTitle** style.

7. Click on an empty area of the slide to make it the selected object.

8. Select the **Master Slide Objects On Top** checkbox situated in the topmost section of the **Properties** panel.

The newly inserted slide contains a lot of objects. The Text Caption at the top of the slide explains what the student will have to do. As far as Drag and Drop is concerned, each road sign image is a Drag Source, and the four black and white images at the bottom part of the slide are the Drop Targets.

9. Use the **Insert | Launch Drag and Drop Interaction Wizard** menu item to start defining your Drag and Drop interaction.

The first step of the **Drag And Drop Interaction Wizard** consists of selecting the Drag Sources of the interaction. In this case, there are twelve Drag Sources to select.

10. Select the three prohibitory sign images (the red circles) by clicking on them one by one while holding the *Shift* key down.

11. At the top of the screen, click on the **+** icon situated next to the **Add To Type** drop-down menu.

12. In the **Add new type** box, type `prohibitorySgn` and click on **OK**.

Grouping the Drag Sources into types will help you map these Drag Sources with their corresponding Drop Targets in the third and last step of the wizard. This process is depicted in the following screenshot:

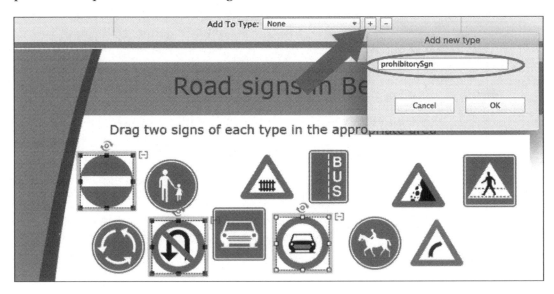

13. Repeat this process with other types of road signs. Refer to the following table for precise instructions:

What to select	Tip	Name of type
Mandatory signs	The blue circles	`mandatorySgn`
Warning signs	The red triangles	`warningSgn`
Information signs	The blue rectangle	`informationSgn`

After this part of the process, you should have defined the 12 Drag Sources of your slide.

14. Click on the **Next** button situated in the top-right area of the screen to go to the second step of the wizard.

The second step of the wizard is where you define the Drop Targets of the interaction.

15. Click one by one on all four black and white images in the lower part of the slide to identify them as drop targets.

16. These images are surrounded with a blue outline indicating the Drop Targets of the interaction.

17. Click on the **Next** button situated in the top-right area of the screen to go to the third and last step of the wizard.

The third step of the wizard is where you map the Drag Sources with their corresponding Drop Targets.

18. Select the little circle situated in the middle of any one of the warning signs (any red triangle). Drop that little icon on the warning sign to the Drop Target.

19. Thanks to the Drag Source types you created in the first step of the wizard, all three warning signs are automatically mapped to that Drop Target.

20. Repeat the same operation with the remaining three types of road signs.

At the end of this process, your slide should look like the following screenshot:

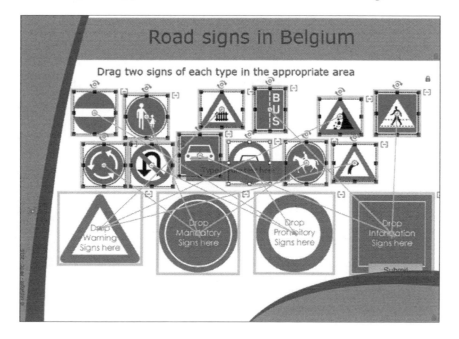

21. Click on **Finish** to close the **Drag and Drop interaction Wizard**.

Apart from the larger number of objects involved, the process of creating this Drag and Drop interaction is very similar to the process you used to define the other Drag and Drop interactions, which you created earlier in this book. But the wizard can only take you that far and—in this case—you need to go a bit further.

In the next part of this exercise, you will use the **Drag and Drop** panel to further change the settings of this Drag and Drop interaction.

22. Open the **Drag and Drop** panel situated on the right edge of the interface, next to the **Properties** and **Library** panels. (If the **Drag and Drop** panel is not present, use the **Window | Drag and Drop** menu item to turn it on.)

23. Click on the **Correct Answers** button situated in the **Options** tab of the **Drag and Drop** panel.

The **Correct Answers** dialog contains various options to let you decide what the correct answer to the Drag and Drop interaction is. It currently shows your four Drop Targets and their associated Drag Sources in a list. In this case, you want the student to drag two road signs of each type to the corresponding Drop Target.

24. In the **Count** column of the list, double-click on **3** to change the number to **2**.

This is how you tell Captivate that dropping two road signs of each type on the corresponding Drop Target is enough for the answer to be correct.

25. Leave the other options of the **Correct Answers** dialog with their current values.

26. Make sure the **Correct Answers** dialog looks like the following screenshot and click on **OK** to validate:

After all these steps, the main options of your Drag and Drop interaction are now in place. The next step is to make it part of the quiz.

27. Select the **Include in Quiz** checkbox situated in the **Reporting** section at the end of the **Actions** tab of the **Drag and Drop** panel.

This action reveals more options. These are very similar to the **Reporting** options found in the **Quiz** panel when a regular Question Slide is selected. It is therefore very easy to include the Drag and Drop interaction in the quiz, and to report the results to the LMS.

28. If needed, select the **Report Answer** checkbox to have this interaction reported to the LMS.

Your quiz now contains one Multiple Choice question, one Random Question, and a graded Drag and Drop interaction.

Feel free to further customize this Drag and Drop interaction with the techniques you learned in *Chapter 6, Working with Interactive Objects*. For example, you could use the **Drag and Drop** panel to add either a Glow or Zoom In effect on the Drag Sources and Drop Targets. You can also apply the **MFTC-questionSubmit** style to the **Submit** button of the interaction, reposition this button, turn the **Reset** button on and apply the **MFTC-questionClear** style, and so on. There are a bunch of actions you can perform to finalize this Drag and Drop interaction. Don't forget to save the file before moving on to the next section.

Using the other scorable objects

In addition to regular Question Slides and the Drag and Drop interaction, some other objects in Captivate can also be scored. In this section, you will return to the Encoder Simulation you created in *Chapter 6, Working with Interactive Objects*, and explore how Click Boxes, Buttons, and Text Entry boxes can also be added to the quiz.

1. Open the Chapter10/encoderSim_800.cptx file. Use the **Filmstrip** panel to go to slide 2.
2. Select the **Continue** button in the lower area of the slide.

With the button selected, take a look at the **Actions** tab of the **Properties** panel and note that it contains a **Reporting** section.

3. Select the **Include in Quiz** checkbox.
4. Take a look at the available options. Note that these are the same as for a regular question slide.
5. When done, deselect the **Include in Quiz** checkbox.

This little experiment demonstrates the possibility of including the interaction defined by a button (or by a Smart Shape used as a button) in the quiz and in the report sent by Captivate to the LMS.

6. Use the **Filmstrip** panel to go to slide 4. Use the **Timeline** panel to select the Click Box (it may be necessary to select it from the **Timeline** panel).

7. Note the **Reporting** section situated at the end of the **Action** tab of the **Properties** panel.

8. Take some time to look at the available options, but make sure you put them back to their current value when done.

9. Use the **Filmstrip** panel to go to slide 12.

10. Select the Text Entry Box and take a look at the **Reporting** section situated at the end of the **Actions** tab in the **Properties** panel.

Each of these three interactive objects can be added to the quiz by selecting the **Include in Quiz** checkbox. Once included in the quiz, these objects have the very same reporting capabilities as a regular Question Slide and their points value is added to the points value of the quiz.

When selecting the **Include In Quiz** checkbox and not the **Report Answer** checkbox, you include an interactive object in the quiz without reporting the interaction to the LMS. Captivate then uses these objects to generate the **Quiz Results** slide but does not report these interactions to the LMS.

11. Close the `encoderSim_800.cptx` file without saving the changes.

In this section, you have explored the scorable objects of Captivate and learned that the reporting capabilities are not limited to Question Slides.

The Advanced Interaction dialog

Use the **Project | Advanced Interaction** menu item to open the **Advanced Interaction** dialog. This floating panel provides a list of all the scorable objects of the project in addition to a great summary view of their current settings.

In the next section, you will explore project-level reporting options.

Setting up project-level reporting options

Now that you have decided on which interaction is to be included in the quiz and reported to the LMS, it's time to focus on project-level reporting options. This is where you will configure the settings that will report the data to the LMS.

Before putting in all this effort, it is important to check what level of information your LMS can receive and what is the standard (SCORM, AICC, or Tin Can) that your LMS uses. In this exercise, you will report the data to Moodle. A quick look in the Moodle documentation (`http://docs.moodle.org/28/en/SCORM_FAQ`) tells you that Moodle is SCORM 1.2-compliant.

Perform the following steps to create a SCORM 1.2 package that can be integrated into Moodle:

1. If needed, return to the `Chapter10/drivingInBe.cptx` file.
2. Use the **Quiz | Quiz Preferences** menu item to open the **Preferences** dialog.
3. In the left-hand side of the **Preferences** dialog, make sure that you are on the **Reporting** category.
4. At the top of the page, select the **Enable reporting for this project** checkbox.

When I conduct a Captivate class, I often refer to this checkbox as being the *main circuit breaker* of the reporting system.

5. Open the **LMS** drop-down menu.

The LMS drop-down lists some of the most popular LMS and lets you quickly apply specific settings that are optimized for each LMS.

6. Choose **Moodle** as the LMS.

This action automatically adjusts most of the options of **Reporting Preferences** to values that a Moodle LMS expects. If your LMS is not listed, you would use the **Other Standard LMSs** item.

7. Open the **Standard** drop-down list.

The **Standard** drop-down menu is probably the single most important option of this **Preferences** page. It allows you to choose the reporting standard used to report the scoring and tracking data to the LMS. By choosing **Moodle** as the LMS in the previous step, this option has been automatically set to **SCORM 1.2**.

8. Make sure you choose the **SCORM 1.2** option in the drop-down list.

You will now decide how Captivate will report the status of the course. If there is a quiz in the project, you probably want the status to be either *pass* or *fail*. If the project does not contain a quiz and you just want to track the completion status of the project, choose *complete* or *incomplete*. Knowing your LMS and how it receives and deals with the information is important when making these decisions. In this case, Moodle can accept both representations of the status, but it might not be true for every LMS.

9. In the **Status Representation** section, select the **Incomplete |
    Passed/Failed** option.

You will now instruct Captivate that you want to consider this piece of eLearning content as complete when the student has passed the quiz.

10. In the **Success/Completion Criteria** section, choose the **Slide views
     and/or quiz** option.

11. Deselect the **Slide Views** checkbox, but leave the **Quiz is Passed**
     checkbox selected.

Finally, you need to decide what data you want to see reported to the LMS. Basically, you can choose to report only the final score of the student or to report the final score plus some details about each interaction. In this case, you want to report the score of the student as a percentage as well as the interaction data.

12. In the **Data To Report** section, choose to report **Quiz Score** as **Percentage**.

13. Make sure the **Interaction Data** checkbox is selected.

At the end of this procedure, make sure your **Preferences** dialog looks like the following screenshot:

Since you are using the SCORM standard, there is one extra step to go through. This extra step is the creation of the SCORM manifest file.

Enabling reporting in a "quizless" project

These reporting options are not limited to projects containing a quiz. Reporting can be used to track only the completion status of a project. Some LMS are able to reveal the next activity of a course when and only when they receive the *complete* status report from the current activity.

Creating a SCORM manifest file

A SCORM manifest is an .xml file named imsmanifest.xml. This manifest file is an essential component of any SCORM package. It is used to describe the course to the SCORM-compliant LMS. Without this file, the LMS is unable to integrate Captivate projects in a course or gather the tracking data sent by the project.

If this sounds too technical for you, don't worry! Captivate can generate that manifest file for you by using the following procedure:

1. Still in the **Reporting** category of the **Preferences** dialog, click on the **Configure** button situated next to the **SCORM 1.2** standard at the top of the box.

The first section of the **Manifest** dialog is the **Course** section. The **Course** section is used to enter the metadata of the project. This metadata is used by the LMS to display the course information to the student and to enhance the integration of the project into the LMS.

2. In the **Course** section of the **Manifest** dialog, enter the following information:
    - **Identifier**: DrivingInBe101
    - **Title**: Driving in Belgium
    - **Description**: Enter any meaningful description in this field

The second part of the **Manifest** dialog is named **SCO**.

SCO stands for **Shareable Content Object**. This concept is at the heart of the SCORM standard. In the SCORM specification, a course can be composed of many activities. Each of these activities must have a unique SCO identifier. Using a SCORM Packager application (such as the *Multi SCO Packager* or *Reload*), it is possible to integrate a Captivate project in a larger SCORM-compliant course containing lots of other content made by lots of other applications. This is why it is important to specify the SCO identity of your Captivate project. By default, Captivate generates a random SCO that is based on the name of the project.

3. Enter DrivingInBe101 in the SCO **Identifier** field.

4. Enter `Driving in Belgium` in the SCO **Title** field.

The **Manifest** dialog should now look like the following screenshot:

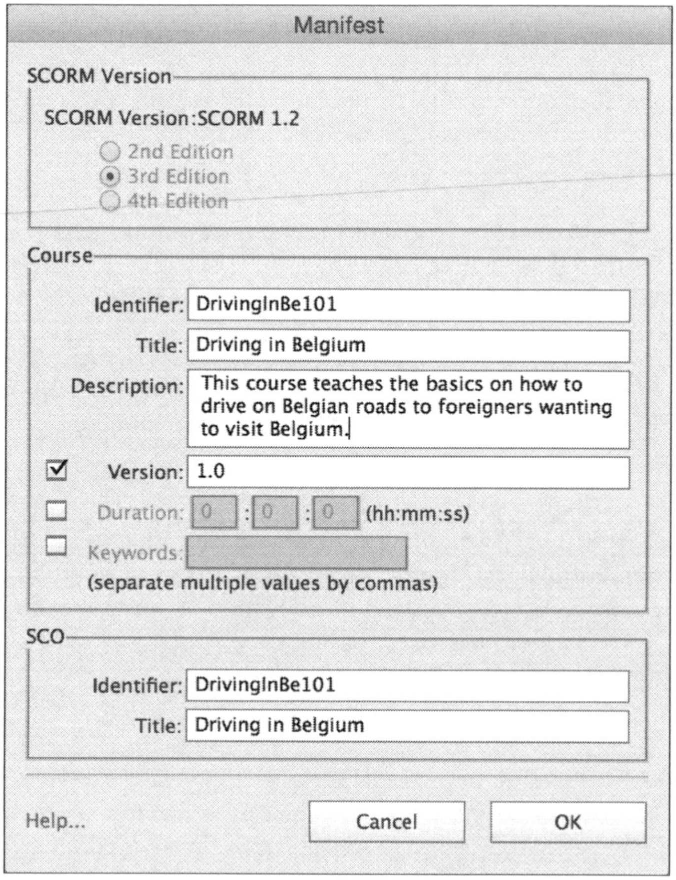

5. Click on **OK** to validate the changes and close the dialog box.
6. Click on the **OK** button of the **Preferences** dialog.
7. Make sure you save the file when done.

The project is now ready to be published as a SCORM package. This step is covered in *Chapter 13, Finishing Touches and Publishing*.

Summary

With the addition of Question Slides and quizzes, your project is no longer a simple demonstration or simulation. It is a highly interactive eLearning package that is able to integrate nicely in virtually every LMS in the market. On the pedagogical side, you discovered the eLearning answer to the assessment challenge, which is one of the primary concerns of any teacher. On the technical side, you discovered the SCORM, AICC, and Tin Can standards that make communication between the eLearning content and the LMS possible.

In this chapter, you learned about each of the eight question types of Captivate. You created a Question Pool before exploring the **Quiz Preferences** and the myriad options available. In the second part of this chapter, you learned how the quiz results and other interactions can be reported to an LMS.

In the next chapter, you will dig into some more advanced stuff and discover how Captivate can be used with other Adobe and third party tools.

Meet the community

In this section, I'll introduce you to two individuals from the same family. Together with two other members of the family, they own and manage Infosemantics, an Australian-based company specialized in eLearning development and Captivate widgets.

Rod Ward

The director of Infosemantics, Rod, is a Technical Author, Information Designer, and eLearning Developer with over a decade of industry experience. Based in Perth since 1986, he has worked for companies large and small across Australia. Rod's specialties are the design and development of eLearning courses using sound instructional design principles and Adobe's suite of eLearning software tools. Rod is also the author of three e-books about Adobe Captivate, two about troubleshooting issues, and one about using Advanced Actions.

Tristan Ward

Tristan is a Flash, ActionScript, and HTML5 expert. He builds many of the Flash Animations and interactivity add-ins included in Infosemantics' Captivate eLearning courses. Tristan is deservedly famous throughout the Adobe Captivate world for his *Widget King* blog, which contains many articles about creating AS3 Widgets using his WidgetFactory API, now the leading platform for creating AS3 Widgets for Captivate. He's also our go-to guy for video editing.

Contact details

- **Website**: `http://www.infosemantics.com.au/`
- **Twitter**: Rod `@Infosemantics` and Tristan `@WidgetFactory`
- **Tristan's blog**: `http://www.infosemantics.com.au/widgetking/`

11
Using Captivate with Other Applications

In this chapter, you will explore how Captivate can be used with other applications. These external applications include Adobe products such as Adobe Flash Professional, Adobe Audition, and Adobe Photoshop, but Captivate can also integrate with third-party applications such as Microsoft Word and Microsoft PowerPoint.

There are many benefits in using Captivate with these external applications. If your company already has a significant amount of training material made using PowerPoint, you'll be able to recycle this existing material and build on what already exists. By integrating Microsoft Word in the workflow, you can export the Text Captions and the Slide Notes to a Microsoft Word document and send it out to a translation service where the translators won't need any knowledge of Captivate to help you localize your eLearning content. By exporting the Captivate project to Flash Professional, you will be able to leverage the full power of the Flash platform in your Captivate Project.

In this chapter, you will:

- Create a new Captivate project from a PowerPoint presentation
- Add a PowerPoint slide in the middle of an existing Captivate project
- Explore the round-trip editing workflow between Captivate and PowerPoint
- Localize a Captivate project by exporting the Text Captions and Slide Notes to Microsoft Word, and reimport them back into Captivate once translated
- Import a Photoshop document into Captivate
- Explore the round-trip operations with Adobe Audition
- Export the Captivate Project to Flash Professional
- Export the project to an XML file

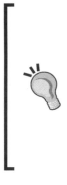

Preparing your work

At the beginning of this chapter, it is a good idea to take some time to reset the Captivate interface to default. If you are using the default interface mode, just close and restart Captivate and you're good to go. If you use the advanced interface mode, use the **Window | Workspace | Reset 'Classic'** menu item to reset Captivate to default. In this chapter, you will use the exercises stored in the Chapter11 folder of this book's companion files. If you get confused by any of the step-by-step instructions, take a look at the Chapter11/final folder, which contains a copy of the files.

Integrating Captivate with PowerPoint

In this section, you will discover the tight integration that unites Microsoft PowerPoint and Adobe Captivate. This integration includes many features such as creating a new Captivate project from a Microsoft PowerPoint presentation or including slides from a presentation in an existing Captivate project.

Captivate shares these features with another software product from Adobe called **Adobe Presenter**. Adobe Presenter is a Microsoft PowerPoint plugin. In PowerPoint 2007 and later versions, Presenter installs an extra ribbon at the top of the PowerPoint interface. Presenter can be used to publish a PowerPoint presentation to Flash and/or HTML5 using a technique that is similar to what is used in Captivate. Presenter also includes the ability to add narration and subtitles to a PowerPoint presentation and includes pretty much the same quiz engine as the one used in Captivate. One of the best features of Presenter is Adobe Presenter Video Express, which allows you to create stunning professional screencasts. The Adobe Presenter PowerPoint plugin is only available on Windows. Adobe Presenter Video Express is available on both Mac and Windows. Visit http://www.adobe.com/products/presenter.html for more information.

Converting an existing presentation to Captivate

In this first exercise, you will convert an existing PowerPoint presentation into a new Captivate project. You will use a simple workflow that allows you to open a PowerPoint file from the Welcome screen. But first, let's take a look at the original PowerPoint presentation.

Viewing the presentation in PowerPoint

If PowerPoint is available on your system, take a look at the presentation before converting it into a Captivate project. Perform the following steps to view the presentation in PowerPoint:

1. Open Microsoft PowerPoint.

2. When in PowerPoint, open the `presentations/AdobeCaptivate.ppt` presentation situated in the exercises files.

3. Use the **Slide Show | View Slide Show** menu item or hit the *F5* shortcut key to start the slideshow.

While viewing the presentation, focus your attention on the following:

- The presentation has 11 slides.

- There is a transition between all the slides of the presentation

- On the first and last slide, the text is animated using an effect that has no equivalent in the Captivate **Effects** panel

- The presentation is mainly composed of text and images, and most of it is animated

- Some of the effects used to animate the objects of PowerPoint have an equivalent in Captivate, but some do not

- Sometimes a mouse click is needed to go to the next step of the presentation, but sometimes not

- Some of the presentation slides include Slide Notes

- Slide 10 includes two links to the Adobe website

Spelling errors and typos have been intentionally left over in the presentation. Don't correct them; they will be used to demonstrate the round-tripping workflow between Captivate and PowerPoint.

4. Close PowerPoint without saving the changes made to the presentation.

You will now convert this presentation into a Captivate project and see how the PowerPoint features listed above are carried over (or not) into Captivate.

Creating a Captivate project from a PowerPoint presentation

In this section, you will convert the file you have viewed in PowerPoint into a Captivate project.

.ppt or .pptx?

Captivate can import both .ppt and .pptx files. However, when importing a .pptx file, it must first be converted to .ppt before being imported into Captivate. The conversion from .pptx to .ppt requires opening the file in PowerPoint. Consequently, PowerPoint must be installed on your computer when importing a .pptx file into Captivate. When importing a .ppt file, that conversion is not needed and PowerPoint is therefore not mandatory. That's the reason why I chose to use the .ppt files in this book instead of the newer .pptx file format. The .pptx files are available in the exercise folder for you to experiment with if desired.

Before starting with this exercise, make sure the PowerPoint presentation is closed. Perform the following steps to convert the PowerPoint presentation into a Captivate project:

1. Return to Captivate and close any open file. The exercise begins on the Captivate Welcome screen.

2. Switch to the **New** tab of the Welcome screen if needed.

3. Double-click on the **From PowerPoint** thumbnail, as shown in the following screenshot. (Alternatively, you can use the **File | New Project | Project From MS PowerPoint** menu item to do the same operation).

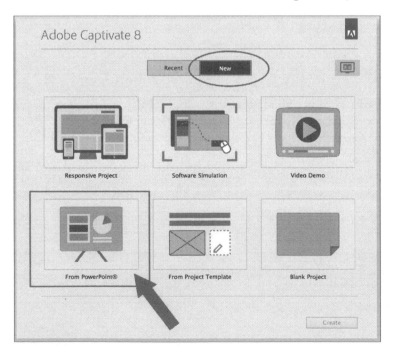

4. Browse to the `presentations/AdobeCaptivate.ppt` file in the exercises folder and click on **Open**.

Captivate converts the PowerPoint slides into Captivate slides one by one. Depending on the presentation to convert and on the capabilities of your computer, this operation can be quite lengthy, so be patient. When the conversion is finished, Captivate opens the **Convert PowerPoint Presentations** dialog box.

5. At the top of the dialog box, change the **Name** of the project to `AdobeCaptivateIntro`.

6. Open the **Preset Sizes** dropdown and change the size of the project to **800 x 600**.

Captivate lets you choose which PowerPoint slides to import into the project. Use the **Clear All** and **Select All** buttons to quickly select or deselect the entire set of slides. In this case, you want to import the entire PowerPoint presentation into Captivate, so make sure all the PowerPoint slides are selected before moving on.

7. At the end of the dialog box, set the **Advance Slide** option to **On mouse click**.

8. Make sure the **Linked** checkbox is selected.

It is very important to get these last two options right! The **Advance Slide** option lets you decide how Captivate advances from one slide to the next. On choosing **On mouse click**, Captivate generates a Click Box on top of every imported slide. This Click Box stops the Playhead and waits for the student to click anywhere on the slide to continue to the next step of the project.

The **Linked** checkbox is even more important. Captivate proposes two ways to insert a PowerPoint presentation in a project:

- When **Linked** is not selected, you create an **embedded** presentation. It means that a copy of the original PowerPoint presentation is entirely integrated into the `.cptx` file. This copy is completely independent from the original `.ppt` (or `.pptx`) file.

- When the **Linked** checkbox is selected, the PowerPoint presentation is also embedded into Captivate, but Captivate maintains a link between the copy of the PowerPoint file that is embedded in the `.cptx` file and the original PowerPoint file. This link can be used to update the Captivate file when a change is made to the PowerPoint presentation.

Make sure the **Convert PowerPoint Presentations** dialog looks like the following screenshot before moving on:

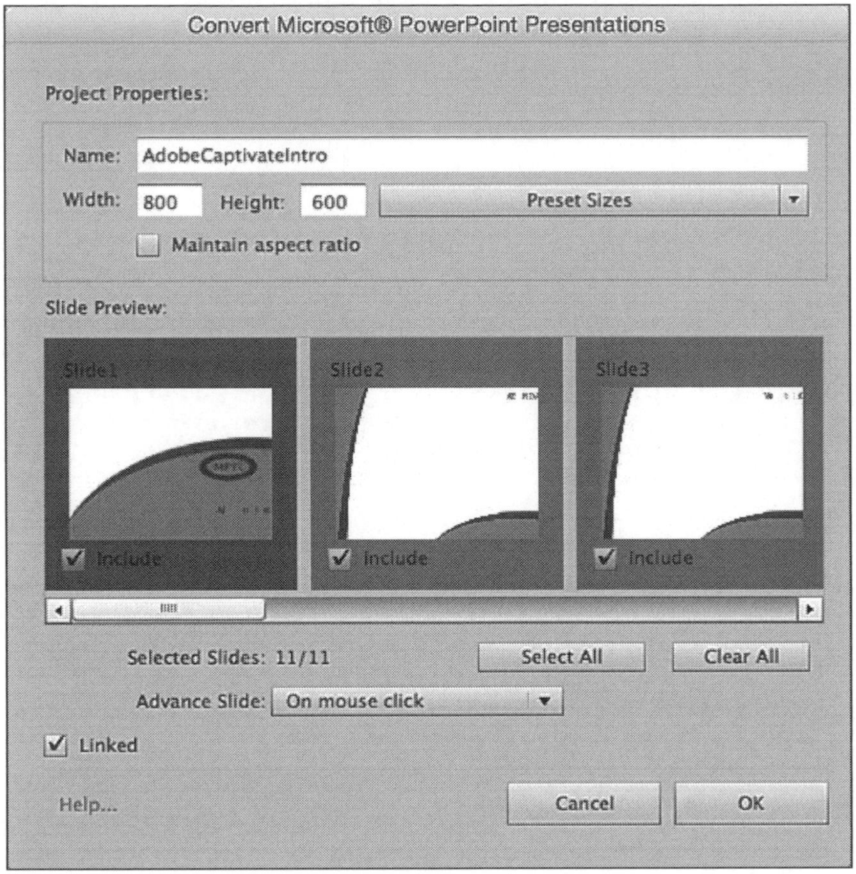

9. Click on the **OK** button.

10. Take some time to read the message that appears on the screen. Click on **Yes** to acknowledge the message and clear the message box.

This message tells you that the size of the imported presentation is not the same as the size of the Captivate file it is imported in. However, Captivate does a good job of converting the size while maintaining good quality, so you can safely acknowledge the message and move on with the exercise.

Captivate creates a new project from the original PowerPoint presentation. Depending on the presentation to convert and on the capabilities of your computer, this process can be quite lengthy, so be patient. When the importation is finished, an 11-slide project is loaded into Captivate. In the **Filmstrip** panel, notice that each slide has a name that is derived from the slide title as entered in PowerPoint.

You will now test the entire project to see how well (or how badly) Captivate handles the conversion from PowerPoint.

11. Save the file as `Chapter11/AdobeCaptivateIntro.cptx`.

12. Use the **Preview | Project** icon of the Big Buttons Bar to test the entire project in the **Preview** pane.

Now test the entire project. You will observe the following things:

- Captivate does a pretty good job of converting a PowerPoint presentation into a Captivate project

- Most animations are carried over from PowerPoint, even if the corresponding effect does not exist in Captivate

- The transitions are correctly imported and played back

- The links on slide 9 are functional

The conversion of the PowerPoint presentation to a Captivate project is now complete.

13. Close the **Preview** pane when done.

What you just experienced in the **Preview** pane is close to how the students will experience the project. You will now take a closer look at the Captivate editing environment to discover other properties from the original presentation that are carried over in Captivate.

14. If needed, use the **Filmstrip** to return to the first slide of the project.

15. Use the **Window | Slide Notes** menu item to open the **Slide Notes** panel. Remember that, by default, this panel appears at the bottom of the screen, next to the **Timeline**.

The Slide Notes typed in Microsoft PowerPoint have been imported in the **Slide Notes** panel of Captivate. Remember that these Slide Notes can be converted to Speech and to Closed Captions. The fact that Captivate imports this data from PowerPoint is a great productivity feature and a huge timesaver.

 The Slides Notes added to the original PowerPoint file after it has been converted into a Captivate project is not synced with the Captivate file.

16. Use the **Filmstrip** to go to slide 2.

17. At the bottom of the screen, open the **Timeline** panel.

In PowerPoint, this slide holds quite a few pieces of text arranged in a bulleted list. You would expect the Captivate version of that slide to contain a lot of Text Captions. Unfortunately, the PowerPoint to Captivate conversion does not go that far. In Captivate, each PowerPoint slide is considered as a single animated object. The individual components of this animation do not show in the **Timeline** panel.

Consequently, modifying the content or the layout of the project must be done in PowerPoint, not in Captivate. In the next section, you will learn how you can modify the project in PowerPoint and import the edits into Captivate through a process called Round Tripping.

Round Tripping between Captivate and PowerPoint

Round Tripping is the process by which you can invoke PowerPoint from within Captivate, edit the presentation in PowerPoint, and import the modifications back into Captivate. If you are working on Windows, PowerPoint can even be displayed within the Captivate interface, so you won't even have to leave the Captivate environment. If you are working on a Mac, you'll be redirected to the actual PowerPoint application.

 The following exercise requires both PowerPoint and Captivate to be installed on your computer. On Windows, Office 2003 (SP3) or higher is required. On Mac, Office 2004 and up will do.

In the next exercise, you will modify a slide in PowerPoint and return to Captivate using the following steps:

1. In the `Chapter11/AdobeCaptivateIntro.cptx` file, use the **Filmstrip** panel to go to slide 4.

2. Right-click anywhere on the slide and choose **Edit With Microsoft PowerPoint | Edit Presentation**, as shown in the following screenshot.

If you get a message saying that Captivate is unable to open the PowerPoint presentation because of a permission problem, return to PowerPoint to make sure the presentation is closed before starting this procedure in Captivate.

What follows depends on the operating system you are working on. On Windows, PowerPoint opens within the Captivate interface, allowing you to edit the presentation using all the tools and features of PowerPoint without even leaving Captivate. On Mac, PowerPoint automatically opens in its own separate window and loads the presentation you want to edit.

Pay close attention to the remaining steps of this exercise. The round-tripping experience on Windows is very different from the one on the Mac.

3. (Mac only) When PowerPoint is open, go to slide 4 of the PowerPoint presentation.

4. On slide 4, change **October 204** to October 2004.

5. (Mac only) Use the **File | Save** menu item of PowerPoint to save the presentation.

6. (Mac only) Return to Captivate. A message asks if you want to import the updated presentation. Click on **Yes** and let Captivate make the necessary changes in the project.

7. (Mac only) Close the PowerPoint application manually.
8. (Windows only) Click on the **Save** button situated in the upper-left corner of the interface. PowerPoint closes and the Captivate project is automatically updated.
9. Save the Captivate file when done.
10. For both Mac and Windows users, use the **Preview | Project** icon of the Big Buttons Bar to preview the entire project in the **Preview** pane.

When the preview reaches slide 4, pay close attention to the text in the main textbox. The modification made in PowerPoint should be reflected in the Captivate project.

Updating a linked PowerPoint presentation

In the next exercise, you will open PowerPoint and modify the presentation in the PowerPoint application. This is very different from what you did in the previous exercise where the workflow was triggered from within Captivate. You will then return to Captivate and update the project accordingly. The steps are as follows:

1. Return to PowerPoint and open the `presentations/AdobeCaptivate.ppt` file.
2. Go to slide 3 of the presentation and change **SCROM** to SCORM in the main textbox.
3. Save the presentation and close PowerPoint.
4. Return to Captivate.

Since you selected the **Linked** checkbox when converting the PowerPoint presentation, Captivate is able to pick up the change made in the PowerPoint file and should display the same message as in the previous screenshot. If the message is not displayed automatically, the **Library** panel offers a way to manually update the Captivate Project so it reflects the changes made in the PowerPoint presentation.

5. If the message shown in the previous screenshot is displayed on your screen, click on **No** to close the message without updating the Captivate project.

6. Open the **Library** panel situated next to the **Properties** panel on the right-hand side of the screen.

7. In the **Presentations** section of the **Library**, locate the **AdobeCaptivate** presentation.

Notice the red dot in the **Status** column, as shown in the following screenshot. It indicates that the linked PowerPoint presentation and the Captivate project are out of sync.

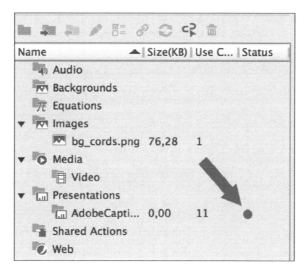

8. In the **Library** panel, click on the red dot associated with the **AdobeCaptivate** presentation.

This refreshes the linked presentation and puts the Captivate project and the PowerPoint presentation back in sync. At the end of the process, the **Status** color should turn back to green.

There are a few more operations that can be performed in a PowerPoint presentation from the **Library** panel.

9. In the **Library** panel of Captivate, right-click on the **Adobe Captivate** presentation.

10. In the contextual menu, click on the **Change To "Embedded"** menu item.

11. Click on **OK** to clear the acknowledgement message.

After this operation, the link between the copy of the PowerPoint file that is embedded in Captivate and the external PowerPoint presentation is broken. The changes made to the external PowerPoint file will no longer be picked up by Captivate.

12. In the **Presentations** folder of the **Library**, right-click on the **AdobeCaptivate** presentation again.

13. In the contextual menu, click on the **Change To "Linked"** menu item.

14. Browse to the `/Chapter11` folder of the exercises files and save the PowerPoint file as `Chapter11/AdobeCaptivate_linked.ppt`.

15. Again, click on the **OK** button to clear the message.

16. Save the Captivate project when done.

This operation saves a new copy of the embedded PowerPoint presentation as a new PowerPoint file and creates a link between this new file and the Captivate Project. It is not possible to recreate the link to the original PowerPoint file. Instead, you create a new PowerPoint file and link that new file to the Captivate project.

Inserting a PowerPoint slide in a Captivate project

In the previous two sections, you learned how to convert an entire PowerPoint presentation into a new Captivate project. But sometimes, only a few PowerPoint slides must be inserted in the middle of an existing Captivate project.

In the next exercise, you will insert a single PowerPoint slide in the middle of the Encoder Demonstration project using the following steps.

1. Open the `chapter11/endoderDemo_800.cptx` file situated in the exercises folder.

2. Use the **Filmstrip** panel to go to slide 23 of the project.

Slide 23 should be the last slide of the screenshot-based demonstration and the second to last in the project.

3. Click on the **Slides | PowerPoint Slide** icon of the Big Buttons Bar.

4. In the box that opens, make sure that **Slide 23** is selected, as shown in the following screenshot:

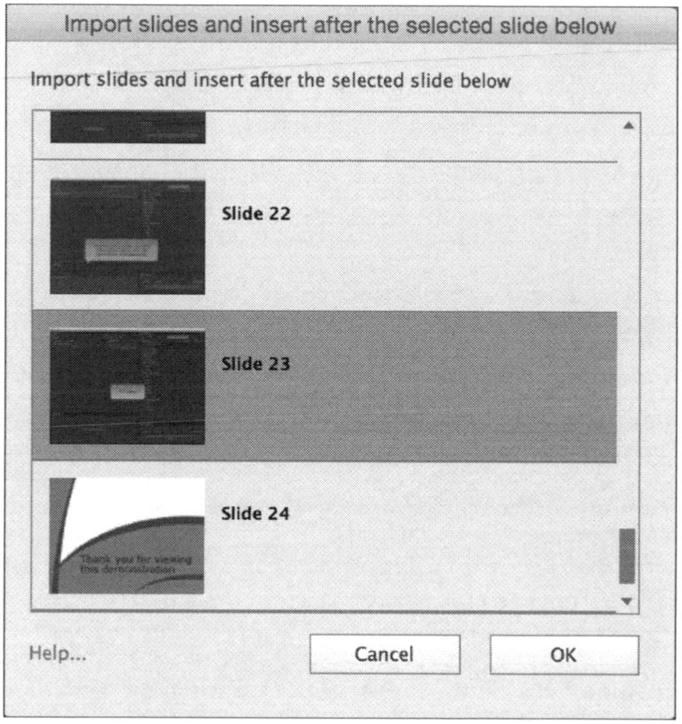

The imported PowerPoint slide(s) will be inserted after the slide selected in this dialog box.

5. Click on the **OK** button and browse to the presentations/mediaEncoder. ppt PowerPoint file situated in the exercises folder. Click on the **Open** button.

6. In the **Convert PowerPoint Presentations** dialog, open the **Advance Slide** dropdown and select the **Automatically** option.

This time, you do not want Captivate to generate an extra clickbox on top of the slide as you did when converting a PowerPoint file earlier in this chapter.

7. Leave the other options with their current value and click on the **OK** button.

8. Take some time to read the message and click on **Yes** to acknowledge and clear it.

The PowerPoint slide is inserted as slide 24 of the Encoder Demonstration project. You will now insert a native Captivate object on top of the imported PowerPoint slide

9. Open the **Timeline** panel and extend the duration of the slide to 13 seconds.

10. With the new slide as the selected object, use the **Properties** panel to apply the **Blank** Master Slide of the Theme to the imported slide.

11. Use the **Shapes** icon of the Big Buttons Bar to draw a rounded rectangle at the bottom of the slide.

12. Double-click in the rounded rectangle and write Continue into the shape.

13. Hit the *Esc* key to quit text edit mode and leave the shape selected.

14. At the top of the **Properties** panel, select the **Use as Button** checkbox.

15. Use the **Style** drop-down menu to apply the **MFTC-ShapeButton** style to the new button.

16. In the **Action** tab of the **Properties** panel, make sure that the **On Success** action of the new button is set to **Go to the next slide**.

17. Move and resize the button so it integrates nicely with the rest of the slide.

18. In the **Timeline** panel, move the button to the very end of the slide **Timeline**.

19. Save the file when done.

20. Use the **Preview | Project** icon of the Big Button Bar to test the entire project.

In this exercise, you have inserted a PowerPoint slide in the middle of an existing Captivate project. This presentation is available in the **Library** of the project and can be edited using the same Round Tripping workflow discussed earlier in this chapter.

This exercise also demonstrates the ability to add standard Captivate objects on top of the imported PowerPoint slides.

Controlling the user experience

Importing the PowerPoint slides with the **Advance Automatically** feature and adding your own buttons on top of the imported slides allows you to better control the user experience of the imported projects. Lots of Captivate developers adopt the workflow described in this exercise rather than letting Captivate create a clickbox on top of every single PowerPoint slide as you did in the first exercise of this chapter when choosing **Advance On a Mouse Click**.

This concludes your overview of the integration between Microsoft PowerPoint and Adobe Captivate. Before moving on, it is time to summarize the key points of what has been covered:

- It is possible to convert an entire PowerPoint presentation into a Captivate project.

- Captivate can import both a `.ppt` and a `.pptx` file. A `.ppt` file can be imported in Captivate even if PowerPoint is not installed on the computer. When importing a `.pptx` file, PowerPoint must be installed on the system along with Captivate.

- When converting PowerPoint to Captivate, most animation, effects, and transitions are carried over, even if they are not natively supported by Captivate.

- Each PowerPoint slide is imported as a single animation. It is not possible to access each individual object of the original PowerPoint slide in Captivate.

- An imported presentation cannot be updated in Captivate. To update a presentation, it is necessary to use PowerPoint.

- An imported PowerPoint presentation is either an Embedded presentation or a Linked presentation. An Embedded presentation is entirely integrated into the Captivate project. A Linked presentation is also integrated in the Captivate project, but maintains a link with the original PowerPoint presentation. This link can be used to keep the PowerPoint presentation and the Captivate project in sync.

- Round Tripping is a concept that enables you to invoke PowerPoint from within Captivate, update the presentation in PowerPoint, and import the changes back into Captivate.

- The actual round-tripping experience depends on the operating system in use (Mac or Windows).

- It is possible to insert only a few PowerPoint slides in the middle of an existing Captivate project.

- All the Captivate objects can be inserted on top of the imported PowerPoint slide(s).

In the next section, you will use a workflow that involves Captivate and Microsoft Word to localize a Captivate project.

Importing PowerPoint versus animating native Captivate objects

In the early versions of Captivate, the **Effects** panel did not exist. As it was impossible to animate objects directly in Captivate, it was very common to create slides in PowerPoint and insert them into Captivate. Since the introduction of the **Effects** panel in Captivate 5, any native Captivate object can be animated in ways that are very similar to what is found in PowerPoint. In my opinion, the PowerPoint integration is a great tool to recycle existing content made in PowerPoint, or to involve non-Captivate developers in the production process. That being said, I think that new content should be developed entirely in Captivate whenever possible because it offers far more flexibility and does not require constant back and forth between two heavy applications.

Localizing a Captivate project using Microsoft Word

In this section, you will create the French version of the Encoder Demonstration (but don't worry if you don't know French!). There are three basic steps to produce the French version of the project:

- Recapture the screenshots of the demonstration using the French version of the Adobe Media Encoder application

- Translate the Text Captions and the Slide Notes

- Localize the other assets (such as the video file or additional imported images)

In the following exercise, you will concentrate on the second step of this process and see how Microsoft Word can help you translate the Text Captions and the Slide Notes of your Captivate project using the following steps:

1. Open the `Chapter11/encoderDemo_800_fr.cptx` file.

2. Use the **Filmstrip** panel to go to slide 4 of the project.

Notice that the background of slide 4 is a screenshot of the French version of Adobe Media Encoder. The same is true for the other screenshot-based slides of the project. For the purpose of this exercise, the **Pretest** has been removed from the French project. Apart from these (not so) small details, this project is the very same project as the English one you created in previous chapters.

To get the French screenshots into the English project, I've followed these simple steps:

- Install a French version of Adobe Media Encoder on the computer (actually in a virtual machine) and use it to re-record the same screenshots as the ones you recorded in *Chapter 2*, *Capturing the Slides*.

- Open the English version of the project and use the **Save As** menu item to save it as encoderDemo_800_fr.cptx.

- Use the **File | Import | External Library...** menu item and import the **Library** of the French project into the English project.

- Insert the **Backgrounds** of the external **Library** to the corresponding English slides and use the **Merge With Background** feature to override the old English background with the new French background.

After this simple procedure, the file you just opened is ready for the second step of the process, that is, the translation of the Text Captions and the Slide Notes in Microsoft Word using the following steps.

 The following exercise requires Microsoft Word to be installed on the computer along with Captivate.

3. Make sure you are still in the Chapter11/encoderDemo_800_fr.cptx file.

4. Use the **File | Export | Project Captions and Closed Captions...** menu item to export the Text Captions and the Slide Notes to a Word document.

5. Save the file as Chapter11/encoderDemo_800_frCaptions.doc.

When the export is complete, Captivate displays a message that asks whether you want to see the generated Word document.

6. Click on **Yes** to open Microsoft Word and view the generated document.

The generated Word document should look like the following screenshot:

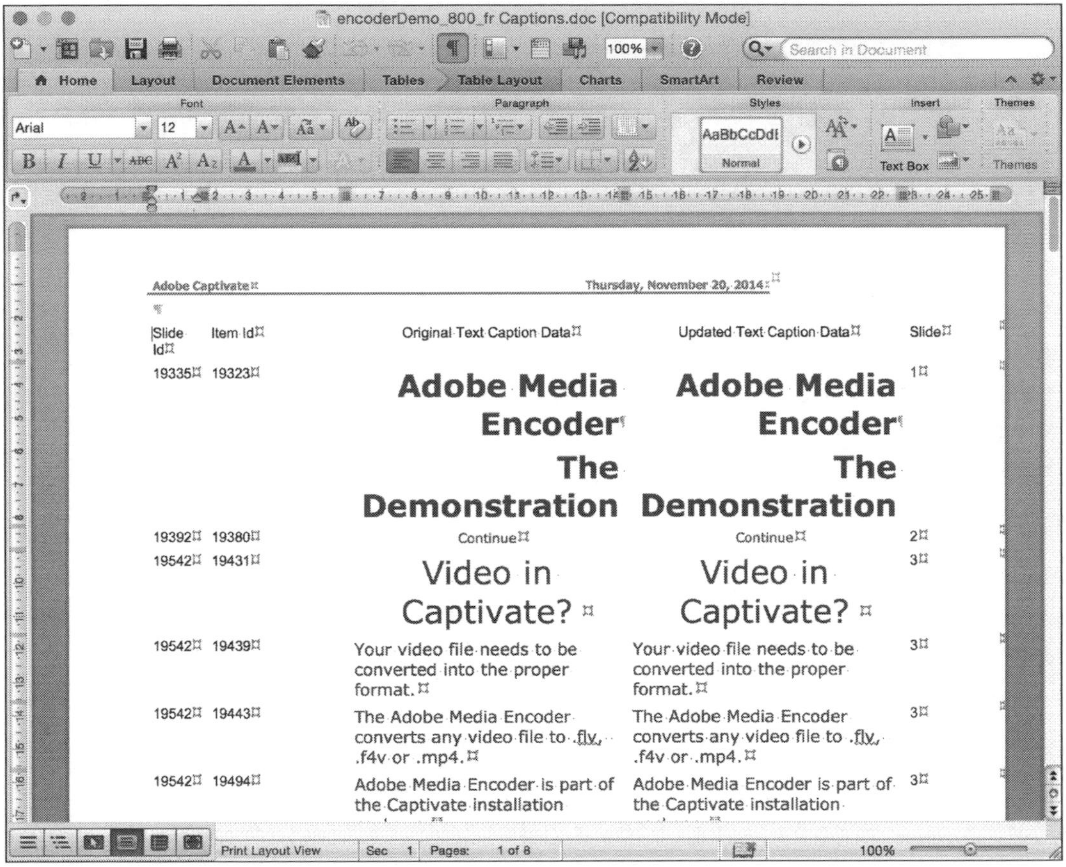

The generated Word document is a five-column table. The first two columns hold the **Slide ID** and **Item ID**. Do not change anything in the first two columns. When the translated text is imported back into the project, these two pieces of information will be used by Captivate to uniquely identify the object into which the text needs to be imported.

The third column is the original text as written in the source language. The fourth column is where the translator will do his job. The translated text should be entered in the fourth column of the table.

The last column is the slide number on which the object is found.

7. Change the text in the fourth column of the Word document.

If you don't know French, don't worry. For the sake of this exercise, you can translate the first few captions in any language you want (or just update the text in any way!). After completing this task, save and close the Word document.

You will now import the updated Text Captions and Slide Notes back into the Captivate project.

8. Return to Captivate in the `encoderDemo_800_fr.cptx` file.
9. Use the **File | Import | Project Captions and Closed Captions....** menu item.
10. Import the updated `Chapter11/encoderDemo_800_frCaptions.doc` file.

Captivate imports the Word document, reads the data it contains, and updates the Text Captions, the Slide Notes, and the Closed Captions of the project. This process can be quite lengthy, so be patient. When the import process is complete, use the **Filmstrip** panel to browse through the slides of the project, and see the updated Text Captions and Slide Notes.

11. Don't forget to save the `encoderDemo_800_fr.cptx` file when done.

This simple workflow is only one step in the translation of an eLearning project into a foreign language. At this point of the exercise, the screenshots, the Text Captions, the Smart Shapes with text, the Slide Notes, and the Closed Captions have been updated. However, the localization work is not over. The video file on slide 2 needs to be updated, and all the narration must be re-recorded in French and imported into the project.

These remaining actions are beyond the scope of this book, but all the techniques needed to complete them have been discussed in previous chapters.

Importing a Photoshop file into Captivate

Photoshop is one of the most famous and widely used Adobe applications. It is an amazing image-editing tool aimed at the professional designer. Many design companies around the world use Photoshop as one of their primary tools to develop the look and feel of the projects they work on.

Therefore it is common to have a designer make use of Photoshop to create the look and feel of a Captivate project. This is why the Captivate engineering team came up with a specific feature to import a Photoshop file into Captivate.

In Photoshop, each piece of the image is stored on a separate **layer**. At the bottom of the layer stack is the background layer. The other layers are arranged on top of the background in a way that is similar to that found in the Captivate **Timeline**.

The **Import from Photoshop** feature is able to retain the layers and layers comps of the original Photoshop file during the importation process, creating a separate image for each of the layers contained in the Photoshop document. You will see the benefit of this approach during the next exercise.

The following screenshot is the Photoshop file, as seen in Photoshop CC 2014. The Photoshop **Layers** panel has been enlarged for better viewing.

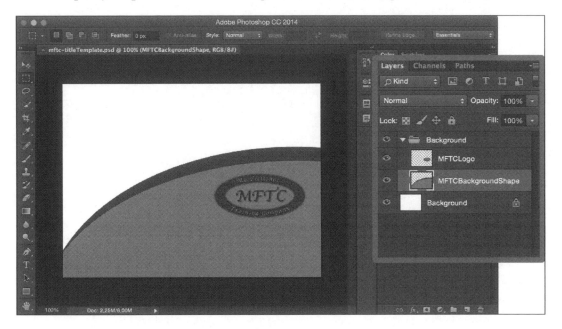

The image in the preceding screenshot has three layers, as highlighted by the red outline:

- At the bottom of the stack, the **Background** layer is a white rectangle that covers the whole image.
- Then, there is the **MFTCBackgroundShape** layer. It is the brownish area that covers the bottom right portion of the image.
- At the top of the stack, the **MFTCLogo** layer contains the MFTC company logo.

You will now import this Photoshop document into the Driving in Belgium project in order to create a new version of the introduction slide.

> **Examine the file in Photoshop**
>
> If you do have Photoshop available on your system, don't hesitate to open the `images/mftc-titleTemplate.psd` file in Photoshop and further examine its content. Just make sure you don't make any changes to the file.

For the sake of clarity, close every open project before starting the following exercise:

1. Open the `Chapter11/drivingInBe.cptx` file.

2. When the project is open, use the **Window | Master Slide** menu item to switch to Master Slide view.

3. Use the **Master Slide** panel on the left-hand side of the screen to select the **Title** Master Slide (the third Master Slide of the panel).

4. Use the **Insert | Content Master Slide** menu item to insert a new Master Slide in the project. This new Master slide is inserted after the selected Master Slide.

5. With the new Master Slide selected, use the **Properties** panel to change the name of the Master Slide to `Title Photoshop` and hit *Enter* to validate.

6. Still in the **Properties** panel, deselect the **Show Master Slide Objects** checkbox.

The new Master Slide should now be completely blank. Next, you will insert the Photoshop file described on the previous page on this new Master slide.

7. On the new Master Slide, use the **File | Import | Photoshop File** menu item to start the procedure.

8. Import the `Images/mftc-titleTemplate.psd` Photoshop file situated in the exercises folder. (Note that the file extension of a Photoshop file is `.psd`, which stands for PhotoShop Document.)

Captivate opens the **Import "mftcTitleTemplate.psd"** dialog box.

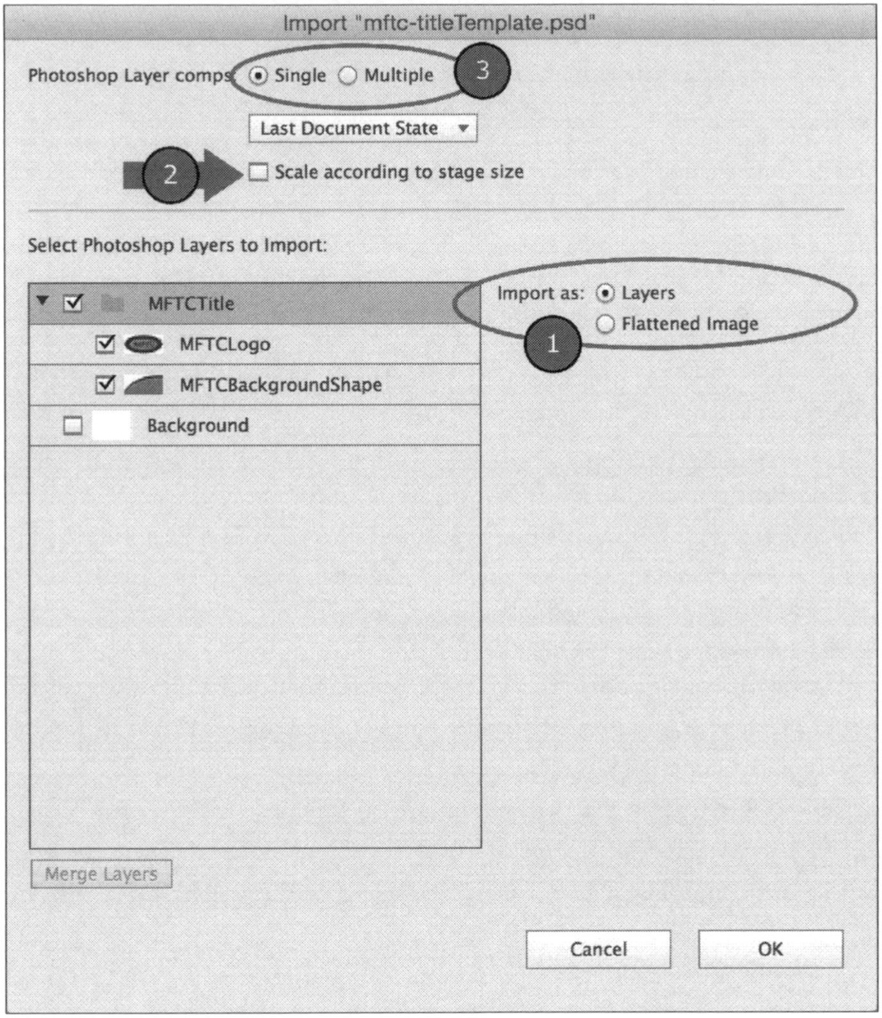

First of all, note that you can import all the **Layers** of the original Photoshop file or import a **Flattened Image** (1). A **Flattened Image** is an image where all the layers have been combined into one single image.

Notice also the **Scale according to stage size** checkbox (2). If selected, the Photoshop image is automatically enlarged or reduced to fit the size of the Captivate project.

Photoshop users should notice the **Photoshop Layer comps** option at the top of the dialog (**3**).

9. Make sure that **Import as Layers** (**1**) is selected.

10. In the main area of the dialog, deselect the **Background** layer (you do not want to import that blank rectangle).

11. Click on the **OK** button to import the remaining two Photoshop layers into Captivate.

12. When the importation is complete, click on the **Timeline** button at the bottom of the screen to open the **Timeline** panel.

This is where the import from Photoshop feature shows its awesomeness. Two images have been imported on the new Master Slide. This means that *a separate image has been created for each of the imported layers.*

13. Select the MFTC logo.

14. At the top of the **Timing** panel, apply a **Fade In Only** transition to the logo.

This illustrates that these two images can be treated as two entirely separate objects in Captivate. Transitions, effects, and other treatments can be applied to each image separately. On regular slides, you can even arrange each component of the imported Photoshop file on the Timeline. This capability is not available on Master Slides though.

15. Use the Master Slide panel to return to the **Title** Master Slide.

16. While on the **Title** Master Slide, use the **Insert | Placeholder Objects | Title** menu item and insert a Title Smart Shape placeholder on the Master Slide.

17. Use the **Properties** panel to apply the **MFTC-MainTitle** style to the newly inserted placeholder.

18. Arrange the objects of the Master Slide as you see fit. The goal is to come up with the greatest title slide ever created in the entire universe!

Inserting a Photoshop file into Captivate is that easy. The last step of the process is to actually use this new Master Slide in the Project.

19. Use the **Window | Filmstrip** menu item and return to the main project.

20. Use the **Filmstrip** panel on the left-hand side of the screen to select the very first slide of the project.

21. Use the **Properties** panel to make this slide use the new **Title Photoshop** Master Slide. This process is shown in the following screenshot:

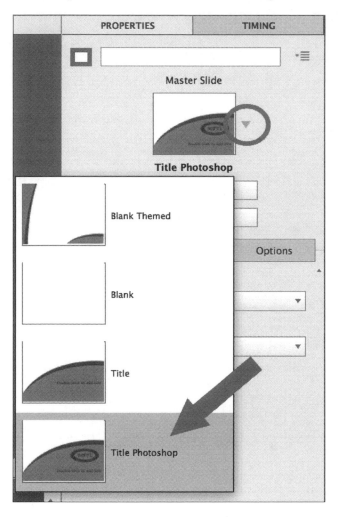

In the next section, you will examine the round-tripping workflow between Captivate and Photoshop.

Round Tripping between Captivate and Photoshop

Now that the Photoshop file has been imported into the Captivate project, let's pretend you want to modify the Photoshop file a little bit. The Round Trip editing workflow that exists between Captivate and Photoshop allows you to do it without reimporting the whole Photoshop document again. Let's examine this workflow hands-on using the following steps.

 The following exercise requires Photoshop to be installed on your system along with Captivate. If Photoshop is not available on your computer, just read through the steps to have an idea of the workflow. You can also download a 30-days trial version of Adobe Photoshop on the Adobe website at https://creative.adobe.com/products/download/photoshop.

1. In the Chapter11/drivingInBe.cptx file, click on the **Library** icon of the Big Buttons Bar to open the **Library** panel.

2. Scroll down the **Library** panel until you see the **MFTC-titleTemplate.psd** folder.

3. Use the disclose triangle to toggle the folder open, if necessary.

In the **Library** panel, the imported Photoshop file is seen as a folder and each of the imported layers is seen as an image within that folder. This is shown in the following screenshot:

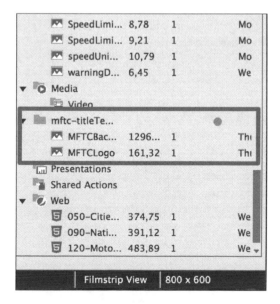

4. Right-click on the **MFTC-titleTemplate.psd** folder or on any of the images it contains and select the **Edit PSD Source File** item from the contextual menu.

This action opens the .psd file in Photoshop. Note that all the layers of the .psd document are available in Photoshop, not only the one you right-clicked on in Captivate. From here, you can use all the Photoshop tools to modify your image.

5. Feel free to modify the image using the Photoshop tools.

6. When done, save and close the Photoshop file.

7. Captivate automatically updates the components of the .psd document.

This simple procedure illustrates the tight integration that exists between Captivate and Photoshop. If you have Photoshop available on your system, this Round Trip editing workflow will greatly enhance your authoring experience.

In the next section, you will explore the integration between Captivate and Adobe Audition but before that, let's quickly summarize what has been covered in this section:

- Photoshop is a professional image-editing application developed by Adobe.
- Photoshop uses a layer-based system to create complex compositions.
- Captivate contains a specific tool to import Photoshop files into the project.
- You can import a flattened image into Captivate or maintain the layers found in the Photoshop file during the importation.
- If the Photoshop layers are maintained, each layer is imported as a separate image in Captivate. This allows you to arrange these images on the **Timeline** and apply different effects to the different parts of the imported image.
- You can edit the original .psd file using the round-trip editing workflow between Captivate and Photoshop.
- In the **Library** panel, the Photoshop document is a folder.

Editing audio with Adobe Audition

Adobe Audition (formerly CoolEdit) is the Creative Cloud audio editing and mixing application. It allows you to manipulate your audio clips in ways that are impossible in Captivate. Thanks to Audition, you can apply effects and filters to your audio clips and create sophisticated multitrack sessions. Audition is also particularly good at sound restoration—so if you have a background noise, a pop, or a hiss to remove, Audition is the way to go!

The following exercise requires that Audition CC 2014 is installed on your computer alongside Captivate. The free 30-day trial of Audition will do. If you don't have access to Audition, you will not be able to complete this exercise. If so, just read through the steps to have an idea of the workflow.

If Audition is installed on your computer alongside Captivate, you can take advantage of some special workflows that unite the two applications. You will now discover these workflows hands-on using the following steps.

1. Return to the `Chapter11/encoderDemo_800.cptx` file.

2. Use the **Filmstrip** panel to go to slide 8 of the project.

3. Select the Adobe Media Encoder logo image.

The AME logo that you imported earlier on this slide is associated with an audio clip. This can be seen on the **Timeline** panel, as shown in the following screenshot:

Remember that this audio clip plays when the object appears on the stage. Also, remember that an effect is applied to this object as indicated by be the small **fx** symbol that appears both in the **Timeline** panel (new in Captivate 8.0.1) and next to the object, when selected.

4. With the AME logo selected, turn your attention to the **Options** tab of the **Properties** panel.

5. In the **Audio** section, click on the **(Clip)Whoosh 2.wav** button to open the **Object Audio** dialog.

The **Object Audio** dialog was covered in *Chapter 4, Working with Multimedia*. It allows you to change and modify the audio clip using Captivate tools. But sometimes, the Captivate audio editing tools are not enough. If Adobe Audition is installed on the same computer as Captivate, an Adobe Audition button will become available at the bottom of the **Object Audio** window.

6. Click on the **Adobe Audition** button in the bottom area of the **Object Audio** window.

Adobe Audition opens and loads the audio clip. The following screenshot shows the **(Clip)Whoosh 2.wav** as seen in Adobe Audition CC 2014:

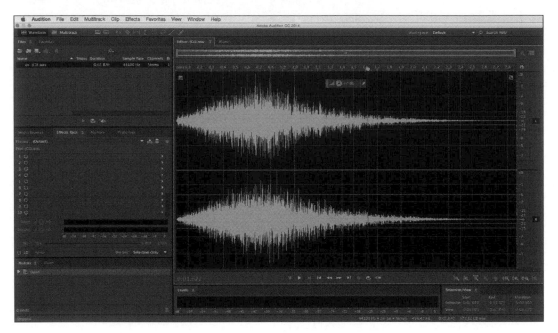

7. Edit the audio clip in Adobe Audition using all the tools, filters and presets you want to. When done, save and close the file in Audition and return to Captivate.

Captivate should automatically pick up the changes and update the audio clip.

8. Click on the **Save** button in the bottom-right corner of the **Object Audio** dialog and close the **Object Audio** dialog.

Thanks to this simple workflow, Adobe Audition is only one click away when working in Captivate. Your students will certainly enjoy the crystal clear noise-free audio clips that you will produce for them. Note that this workflow also works with audio clips associated with a slide or with the background audio associated with the entire project.

You will now return to the **Library** panel of Captivate and explore yet another way to invoke Audition from within Captivate.

9. Make sure you are still on slide 8 of the `Chapter11/`
    `encoderDemo_800.cptx` file.

10. Open the **Timeline** panel if needed.

11. When in the **Timeline** panel, right-click on the sound clip associated with the slide.

12. Choose the **Find in Library** menu item.

This action opens the **Library** panel and automatically selects the audio clip you right-clicked on. (in this case, the **slide03.wav** audio clip—remember that when you inserted the audio clip in the project, the slides of the pretest were not yet present. The current slide 8 used to be slide 3)

13. Right-click on the **slide03.wav** item of the **Library**.

14. Choose **Edit With...** in the contextual menu.

15. Browse to the Adobe Audition executable file. On Mac, look for the `/Applications/Adobe Audition CC 2014/ Adobe Audition CC 2014.app` file. On Windows, look for the `C:\Program Files\Adobe\Adobe Audition CC 2014\Audition.exe` file.

16. The selected audio clip opens in Adobe Audition. You can now use the Audition tool filters and presets to edit this audio clip in ways not available in Captivate. When done, save and close the audio file.

17. Captivate should automatically pick up the changes and load a new version of the audio clip.

This simple exercise concludes the overview of the integration between Adobe Captivate and Adobe Audition. In the next section, you will export your Captivate project to Flash Professional. Now, let's make a quick summary of what has been covered in this section:

- Adobe Audition is the Creative Cloud professional audio editing application.

- If Captivate and Audition are both installed on the same computer, the **Adobe Audition** button of the Audio Edit dialog box will light up.

- This button allows you to open Audition from within Captivate. You can then use the advanced tools of Audition to manipulate your audio file in many ways not possible in Captivate.

- When you save the file in Audition, Captivate automatically picks up the changes and adapts your eLearning project accordingly.

- Right-click on an element of the **Library** and choose the **Edit With...** menu item to open it in an external application.

Exporting to Flash Professional

Adobe Flash Professional and Captivate have a lot in common. Both applications are used primarily to generate the .swf files that can be played back by the free Flash Player plugin.

That being said, the Flash technology has a lot more to offer than what is actually used by Captivate. Adobe Flash Professional is the ultimate Flash authoring tool. By using Adobe Flash Professional, a Flash developer is able to leverage the full power of the Flash technology. It is possible to export a Captivate project to Flash Professional so that a Flash developer is able to tweak the Captivate projects in many ways that are not possible in Captivate.

In the next exercise, you will export the Captivate project to Flash Professional CS6, CC, or CC 2014.

 Parts of the following exercise require Flash Professional CS6, CC, or CC 2014 to be installed on the computer, along with Captivate.

The steps to export the Captivate project to Flash Professional CS6 or CC are as follows:

1. Open or return to the Chapter11/encoderDemo_800.cptx Captivate file.

2. Depending on the version of Flash available on your system, use the **File | Export | To Flash CS6** or **File | Export | To Flash CC** menu item (if you have Flash CC 2014, use the Flash CC export).

3. In the **Export To Flash Options** dialog box, change the **Location** to the Chapter11 folder of the exercise files.

4. Make sure the **Publish to Folder** checkbox is selected.

5. Take some time to explore the remaining options of the dialog, but leave them all at their current settings.

6. Click on the **Export** button, as shown in the following screenshot:

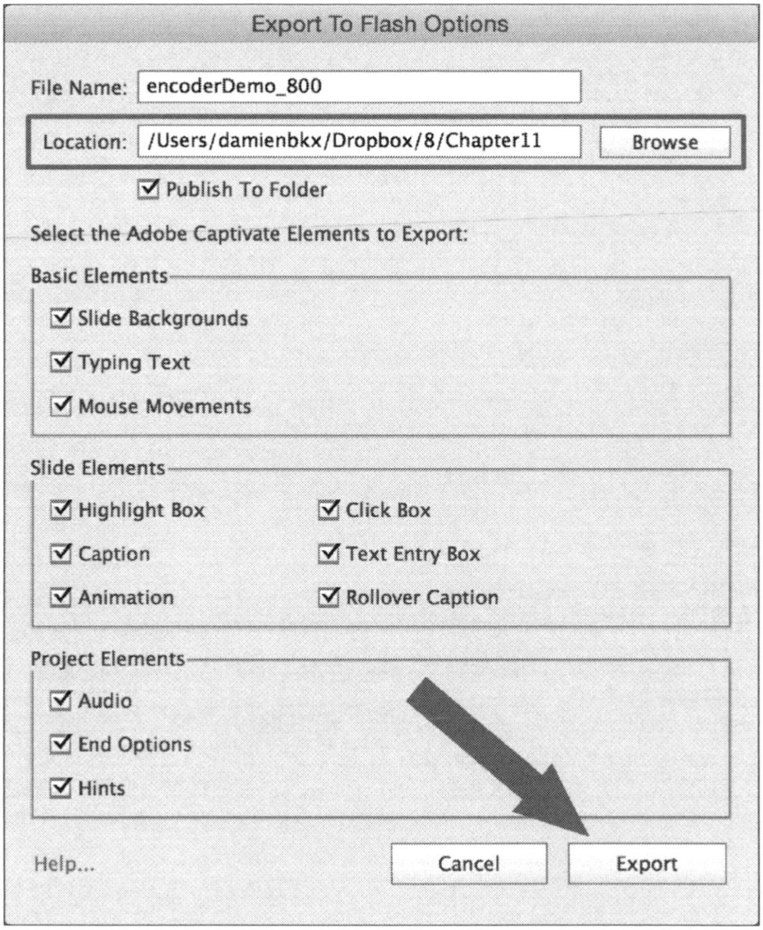

Captivate generates the slides and exports the project as a Flash file with a
.fla extension.

7. Use the Finder (for Mac) or Windows Explorer (for Windows) to navigate to
the Chapter11/encoderDemo_800 folder of the exercises.

8. If Flash Professional CC or CS6 is available on your system, double-click on
the encoderDemo_800.fla file to open it in Flash Professional.

When in Flash Professional, the Flash developer has access to the underlying code of your Captivate project, as shown in the following screenshot:

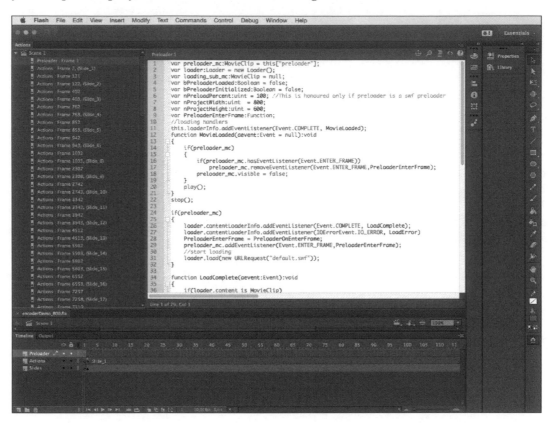

Learning how to leverage all that power in Flash Professional is way beyond the scope of this book, but give the generated .fla file to a trained Flash developer and he will know what to do with it!

This discussion concludes the overview of the Export To Flash feature. Let's quickly summarize what has been covered in this section:

- Both Adobe Flash Professional and Adobe Captivate are used to generate Flash content.
- Captivate only uses a small portion of the power of Flash.

- It is possible to export the Captivate project to Flash, in order to leverage the full power of the Flash technology.

- Exporting the Captivate project to Flash generates a `.fla` file that can be opened by the Adobe Flash Professional application. When the project is finished, it is necessary to use Flash Professional to compile it into a `.swf` file. The `.swf` file is the one that the Flash player is able to read.

Exporting the project to XML

In this section, you will export the project as an XML file. Exporting the Captivate project to `.xml` gives you access to a much wider range of properties and content than the Export to Microsoft Word feature you used earlier in this chapter. According to the official Adobe Captivate blog, the exported XML file contains the following:

Text Captions, Text Animations, Rollover Captions, Default text and correct entries in Text Entry Box, Success/Failure/Hint Captions and button text for all interactive objects, Text Buttons, Slide Notes, Text and Rollover Captions in Rollover Slidelets, Quiz Buttons and Feedback captions, Project Info, Project Start and End options, text messages for password and Expiry Messages.

 See the original post at `http://blogs.adobe.com/ captivate/2009/05/quick_editing_of_text_ using_xm_1.html`.

Here are the steps to export your project to an XML file:

1. Return to the `chapter11/encoderDemo_800.cptx` file.
2. Use the **File | Export | To XML** menu item.
3. Export the project as `chapter11/encoderDemo_800.xml` in the exercises folder.

When the export is finished, Captivate asks whether you want to open the resulting XML file.

4. Click on **No** to close the message box and return to Captivate.

The resulting XML can be opened and updated with any XML editor. When the editing is done, use the **File | Import | From XML...** menu item to import the updated data back into Captivate.

Summary

In this chapter, you have learnt some of the workflows that integrate Captivate with other applications. Some of these applications, such as Photoshop, Audition, and Flash, are part of the Adobe product line and others, such as Microsoft Word and Microsoft PowerPoint, are third-party applications.

By using the PowerPoint workflows, you are able to recycle existing content made in PowerPoint. When it comes to localization, you can export the Text Captions and the Slide Notes to a Microsoft Word document, send it to a translation service, and import it back into Captivate. There is no need for the translators to know anything about Captivate to make this workflow work. When importing a Photoshop file into Captivate, you can decide to maintain the layers of the original Photoshop file, which gives you a great deal of flexibility to further customize the imported images using the tools and effects of Captivate. Exporting to Audition allows you to tweak your audio files in many ways and exporting the project to Flash gives you access to the full power of the Flash platform.

When used correctly, these workflows are huge time savers that help you streamline the production process of your eLearning content.

Your projects are almost finished now. In the next chapter, you will discover some of the most powerful and advanced features of Captivate. Thanks to the Variables and the Advanced Actions, you will be able to add an even higher degree of interactivity and customization to your projects. You will also learn about the Widgets and the Smart Learning Interactions used to extend the capabilities of Captivate.

Meet the community

In this section, I want to introduce you to Jim Leichliter. Jim is a software developer that specializes in the development of Captivate Widgets. He has always been very supportive and has agreed to feature my books on his home page. This collaboration of ours makes me better understand the amazing power of a community such as the one Jim and I are fortunate enough to be part of.

Jim Leichliter

Jim Leichliter of CaptivateDev.com is a software developer with 14 years of experience and has a love for eLearning. Not only does he build Captivate Widgets, but he also helps clients integrate Captivate with third-party systems to create mashups, interactive games, and reporting solutions.

Contact details

- **Blog**: http://CaptivateDev.com
- **Twitter**: @CaptivatePro
- **E-mail**: Jim@CaptivateDev.com

12

Working with Variables, Advanced Actions, and Widgets

In this chapter, you will take advantage of the scripting capabilities of Flash and HTML5. The Flash technology includes a programming language named **ActionScript**. This language is one of the most powerful tools included in the Flash platform. It can be used to implement virtually anything Flash is capable of (and that means a lot of things indeed!). When publishing a Captivate project to Flash, a lot of ActionScript code is generated behind the scenes. It is the Flash Player that executes this ActionScript at runtime. If you decide to publish your projects in HTML5, Captivate generates a lot of JavaScript code instead. It is the browser that executes this JavaScript code at runtime.

Captivate exposes part of this technology to the eLearning developer. Now, let's be honest, you won't actually be writing real ActionScript or JavaScript in Captivate (being an ActionScript or JavaScript developer is a full-time job that requires proper training and real programming skills), but you will be able to create some small scripts anyway—using buttons, drop-down lists, and dialog boxes. In Captivate, these small scripts are named **Advanced Actions**.

Thanks to Advanced Actions, you will be able to dramatically enhance the eLearning experience of the students. For example, you can perform the following actions:

- Dynamically generate text in Text Captions based on student input
- Show and hide objects in response to system or user events
- Trigger a sequence of actions instead of a single action when a Click Box or a Button is clicked, and so on

Most of the time, Advanced Actions need to store and read data in the memory of the computer, so you need a robust system to manage this data. This task is handled by **variables**. Basically, a variable is a named space in the memory of the computer in which you can store pieces of data. When referencing the name of a variable, you can access the data it holds and use this data in Advanced Actions.

Individuals with advanced programming skills can also create **Widgets** and **Smart Learning Interactions**. These are used to extend the original toolset of Captivate. They are written in ActionScript and/or JavaScript. The tools used to develop Widgets include Adobe Flash Professional and Flash Builder. Many pre-made Widgets and Smart Learning Interactions are included in Captivate by default. You can also find more Widgets and Interactions on the Web.

In this chapter, you will:

- Learn about and use System Variables
- Store student input in a User Variable
- Use variables to generate text dynamically
- Create and use a Geolocation variable
- Create Standard and Conditional Advanced Actions
- Insert and customize a Smart Learning Interaction

Preparing your work

Before getting started with this new chapter, take some time to reset the Captivate interface to default. If you are using the default interface mode, just close and restart Captivate. If you use the advanced interface mode, use the **Window** | **Workspace** | **Reset 'Classic'** menu item to reset Captivate to default. In this chapter, you will use the exercises stored in the Chapter12 folder of this book's companion files. If you get confused by any of the instructions, take a look at the Chapter12/final folder, which contains a copy of the files, as they will be at the end of this chapter.

Working with variables

Every single programming language in the world makes use of variables to store and retrieve data to and from the memory of the computer. ActionScript and JavaScript are no exception! In Captivate, it is enough to know that a variable is a named space in the memory of the computer in which data can be read or written.

To make a long story short, a variable is made up of two things:

- **Name**: This name must comply with strict naming rules and conventions. In ActionScript, for instance, the name of a variable cannot contain any spaces or special characters (such as, @, é, è, ç, à, #, ?, /, and so on). When writing a script, the programmer uses the name of the variable to access the data it holds.

- **Value**: This is the piece of data that the variable contains. This value can change (vary) during the execution of the script or each time the script is executed, hence the name, variable.

For example, `v_firstName = "Damien"` defines a variable:

- `v_firstName`: This is the name of the variable
- `Damien`: This is the value of the variable

The Next time the script is executed, you might have `v_firstName = "Bill"` or `v_firstName = "Linda"`, depending on the first name of the student who is taking the course.

In most programming languages, when a variable is created (the proper word is declared), the programmer must specify the type of data that the variable will hold (data types include text string, integer, date, Boolean, and so on), but Captivate has decided to keep things simple so that you don't have to worry about data types in your Captivate scripts.

System and User Variables

In Captivate, there are two kinds of variables available:

- **System Variables**: These are automatically created by Captivate. You can use them in your scripts to retrieve information about the movie, the system, or even to control various aspects of the movie.

- **User Variables**: These are your own custom variables that you create for your own specific use.

Exploring System Variables

Enough talking for now! Let's go back to Captivate to start your hands-on exploration of variables by performing the following steps:

1. Open the `Chapter12/drivingInBe.cptx` file.
2. Use the **Project | Variables** menu item to open the **Variables** dialog box.

3. Open the **Type** drop-down list and choose **System** (see **1** in the following screenshot):

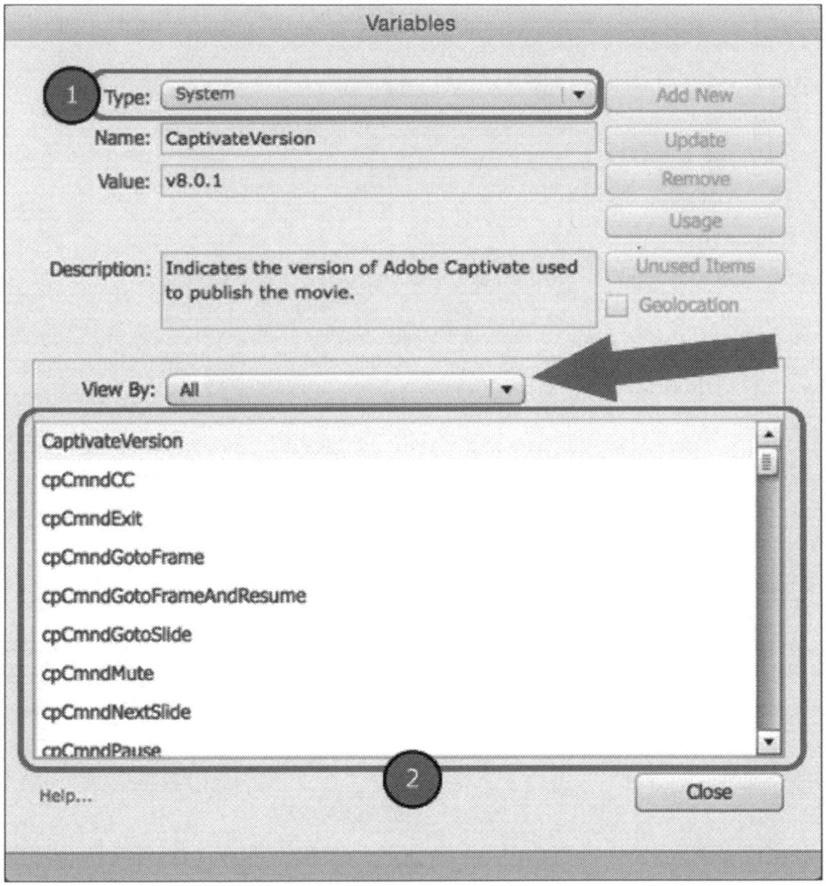

When selecting **System** in the **Type** dropdown, the list of the available System Variables appears in the main area (marked as **2** in the preceding screenshot) of the **Variables** dialog. You can also see the **View By** dropdown (see the arrow in the preceding screenshot) that allows you to filter the variables by their category.

4. Open the **View By** dropdown, and take some time to examine the available options. When done, select the **Movie Information** category.

The variables not pertaining to the **Movie Information** category are filtered out of the **Variables** dialog.

5. Select the **CaptivateVersion** variable.

The upper area of the **Variables** dialog now displays the information of the **CaptivateVersion** variable. The **CaptivateVersion** variable gives you access to the current version number of Captivate.

6. Take some time to review the other System Variables available.

7. When done, click on **Close** to close the **Variables** dialog.

Now that you have a better idea of the available System Variables, you can use some of them to dynamically generate the content of some Text Captions.

Generating text dynamically

You can include variables in your Text Captions and in various other places where text is supported. To be more exact, you can use the names of the Variables to specify the pieces of data you want to print on the screen. At runtime, the Flash Player (if the project is published in Flash) or the web browser (if the project is published in HTML5) replaces the name of the variable with the current value of the variable.

In the next exercise, you will create a small note on the last slide of the project containing the version of Captivate used to create the project, using the following steps:

1. Still in the `Chapter12/drivinginBe.cptx` file, use the **Filmstrip** panel to go to the last slide of the project (slide 28).

2. Insert a new Text Caption on the last slide. Type `This project is powered by Captivate` in the Text Caption.

3. Apply the **MFTC-Copyright** style to the Text Caption and move it to the bottom-left corner of the slide.

4. In the **Timing** or in the **Timeline** panel, make the Text Caption appear after 0 seconds and display for the rest of the slide.

So far, so good! This is just about inserting and formatting a new Text Caption. Now what you want is to automatically insert the version number of Captivate at the end of the Text Caption.

5. Double-click on the new Text Caption and place your cursor at the end of the text, after the word **Captivate**.

6. Add a space in the Text Caption after the word **Captivate**.

7. In the **Properties** panel, go to the **Character** section on the **Style** tab and click on the **Insert Variable** icon, as shown in the following screenshot:

This action opens the **Insert Variable** dialog. You will use this dialog box to choose the variable whose value is to be inserted in the Text Caption.

8. In the **Insert Variable** dialog, change **Variable Type** from **User** to **System** if necessary.

9. In the **View By** drop-down list, choose the **Movie Information** category.

10. Open the **Variables** dropdown, and choose the **CaptivateVersion** variable from the list of available variables.

11. Click on **OK** to add the variable to the end of the Text Caption.

Thanks to this sequence of actions, you have added the **CaptivateVersion** system variable to the end of the new Text Caption. Actually, it is the name of the variable that has been added to the Text Caption. The Text Caption now reads **This project is powered by Captivate $$CaptivateVersion$$**. At runtime, the **$$CaptivateVersion$$** part of the sentence will be automatically replaced by the value of the **CaptivateVersion** variable.

You will now test the new Text Caption in the **Preview** pane.

12. Use the **Filmstrip** panel to return to slide 27.

13. Use the **Preview | From This Slide** icon of the Big Buttons Bar to preview your sequence in the **Preview** pane.

14. When the last slide appears in the **Preview** pane, pay close attention to the newly added Text Caption.

15. Close the **Preview** pane when done, and save the file.

Normally, the Text Caption should read something like this: **This project is powered by Captivate 8.0.1!**

This first experience with Variables teaches you what **Dynamic Text** is. It is a piece of text that is generated on the fly at runtime.

Extra credit – generating a Quiz Results slide for the Pretest

In this section, you will create a **Quiz Results** slide for the Pretest you added to the Encoder Demonstration project. To do this, you will use the **cpQuizInfoPretestScorePercentage** System Variable. This System Variable gives you access to the result of the Pretest expressed as a percentage.

The general steps of this exercise are as follows:

- Open both the `encoderDemo_800.cptx` and `pretestFeedback.cptx` files situated in the `Chapter12` folder.

- Copy the two slides of the `pretestFeedback.cptx` file and paste them as slides 8 and 9 of the `encoderDemo_800.cptx` project. Don't forget to select the **Master Slide Objects On Top** checkbox to finalize the integration of the new slides in the project.

- On slides 8 and 9, replace the **XXX** part of the Text Captions with the **cpQuizInfoPretestScorePercentage** System Variable.

- Set the actions of the Buttons of the two new slides to implement proper branching:
    ○ On slide 8, the **Skip** button jumps to the last slide of the project
    ○ On slide 8, the **Take it anyway** button jumps to slide 10
    ○ On slide 9, the **Let's go** button jumps to slide 10

- Preview the project several times to ensure that every Text Caption shows the right information and that every button takes the student to the right slide.

At the end of this section, the branching associated with the Pretest is not completely finished just yet. You will address this issue using a Conditional Advanced Action in the *Using a Conditional Action to implement branching with the Pretest* section later in this chapter. Don't forget to save and close the files when done!

Using User Variables

What is true for System Variables is also true for User Variables. In the next exercise, you will create a User Variable to store the first name of the student taking the course. To capture the value of that variable, you will ask the student to type his first name in a Text Entry Box that you will associate with the User Variable.

Creating a User Variable

First of all, you will create your own User Variable using the following steps:

1. Return to the `Chapter12/drivingInBe.cptx` file.
2. Use the **Project | Variables** menu item to open the **Variables** dialog box.
3. Make sure that **User** is selected in the **Type** dropdown.

Note that Captivate has already generated two User Variables. These variables expose the name and ID of the student when the course is hosted on an LMS.

4. Click on the **Add New** button to create a new variable.
5. Type `v_name` in the **Name** field.

This will be the name of your new variable. Remember that the name of a variable must comply with a strict set of rules and conventions, which are as follows:

- A variable name cannot contain a space
- A variable name cannot contain any special characters

In addition to these rules, some names are reserved by ActionScript and JavaScript and cannot be used as the names of our user-defined variables.

 See the Captivate Help page at `http://help.adobe.com/en_US/captivate/cp/using/WSDF6E7000-1121-4808-B61B-CCAB6A554AD3.html` for a complete list of ActionScript-reserved names.

6. Leave the **Value** field empty.
7. Optionally, add a meaningful **Description** to the new variable.
8. Click on **Save** to create the variable and close the **Variables** dialog.

Now that the variable exists, you will add a Text Entry Box on the second slide of the project to capture the value to be stored in it.

Capturing values with Text Entry Boxes

First of all, you must insert a new Text Entry Box on slide 2 of the *Driving In Belgium* project using the following steps:

1. Use the **Filmstrip** panel to go to slide 2 of the `drivingInBe.cptx` project.

2. Use the **Text | Text Entry Box** icon of the Big Buttons Bar to create a new Text Entry Box.

As covered in *Chapter 6, Working with Interactive Objects*, Captivate inserts up to five objects that make up the Text Entry Box system (three feedback Captions, one **Submit** button, and the Text Entry Box itself). In the case of this particular Text Entry Box, you do not need all these objects, so your first task is to disable the objects you do not need.

3. Make sure the Text Entry Box is the selected object.

4. If needed, click on the **Properties** icon of the Big Buttons Bar to open the **Properties** panel.

5. In the **Style** tab of the **Properties** panel, make sure that the **Validate User Input** checkbox is not selected.

This time, you want to use a Text Entry Box to gather a piece of data (in this case, the name of the learner). There are therefore no right and wrong answers, so there is no need to validate what the user types in the Text Entry Box against a list of predefined correct answers. This is very different from what you did in *Chapter 6, Working with Interactive Objects*, where there was only one possible correct answer that the learner had to fill in correctly.

Instead, you will associate this Text Entry Box with the custom v_name variable you created in the previous section.

6. Still in the **Style** tab of the **Properties** panel, open the **Variable** drop-down list.

7. Select the **v_name** variable from the list of available variables.

Your Text Entry Box is now associated with the **v_name** variable. It means that whatever the student types in the Text Entry Box at runtime will become the value of the **v_name** variable.

8. In the **Action** section of the **Properties** panel, change the **On Success** action to **Go to the next slide**.

9. Move and resize the Text Entry Box and the associated **Submit** button so it fits nicely on the stage.

10. Use the **Properties** panel to apply the **MFTC-SubmitButton** style to the **Submit** button.

11. In the **Character** section of the **Style** tab of the **Properties** panel, adjust the formatting to your taste. The choices you make here apply to the text that the student will type in the box.

12. Move the Text Entry Box to the end of the **Timeline** panel.

The Text Entry Box is now ready to capture the first name of the student and to store that value in the **v_name** variable.

Using user-defined variables to dynamically generate text

The last step of this exercise is to use the **v_name** variable and its associated value to dynamically generate the content of a Text Caption using the following steps:

1. Use the **Filmstrip** panel to go to slide 3 of the `drivingInBe.cptx` project.

2. Double-click in the **Welcome** Text Caption and place your cursor at the end of the word.

3. Use the spacebar to add a space after the word **Welcome**.

4. In the **Character** section of the **Style** tab of the **Properties** panel, click on the **Insert Variable** icon.

5. In the **Insert Variable** dialog, choose to insert the **v_name** User variable.

6. Change the **Maximum length** value to 30 characters to accommodate longer first names.

7. When the **Insert Variable** dialog looks similar to the following screenshot, click on the **OK** button:

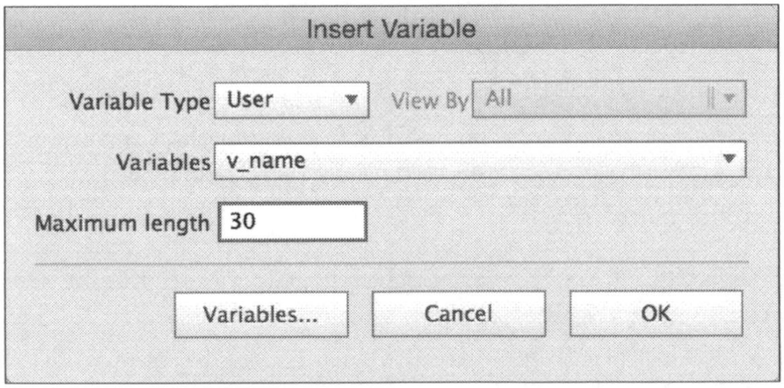

This action inserts the **v_name** variable in the new Text Caption and encloses it in double dollar ($$) signs. The full text of the Caption is now **Welcome $$v_name$$**. Remember that, at runtime, the **$$v_name$$** part of the sentence will be automatically replaced by the first name of the student as typed in the Text Entry Box of the previous slide.

8. When done, save the file and use the **Preview | Project** icon of the Big Buttons Bar to preview the whole Project.

On the second slide, type your first name in the Text Entry Box and click on the **Submit** button. On slide 3, your name should be displayed in the Text Caption.

9. Close the **Preview** pane, and save the file when done.

This exercise concludes your first exploration of System and User Variables. Before moving on to creating more variables and using them in Advanced Actions, let's make a quick summary of what you have learned so far:

- A variable is a named space in the memory of the computer. When referencing the name of a variable, you can access the data that the variable holds.

- There are two types of variables in Captivate. System Variables are automatically created by Captivate. User Variables are yours to create.

- It is possible to add variables in Text Captions. This creates dynamic text in the project.

- A dynamic text is a text that is generated on the fly at runtime. The Flash Player or the JavaScript engine of the browser simply retrieves the current value of a given variable to generate the content of a Text Caption.

- A Text Entry box can be associated with a User Variable. The value typed by the student in the Text Entry Box at runtime becomes the value of the associated variable. Once captured and stored in a variable, that piece of data can be used in any script or in any Text Caption.

Working with Advanced Actions

An Advanced Action is a small script that is executed at runtime by the Flash Player or by the JavaScript engine of the web browser. These Advanced Actions can be used to manipulate the data contained in Variables, the objects of Captivate or even the project itself.

In Captivate, there are three families of Advanced Actions:

- **Standard Actions**: These actions are simple procedures that are always executed in the same way.

- **Conditional Actions**: These actions are a bit more complex. They can evaluate if a given condition is true or false and act accordingly. Consequently, they do not always perform the same set of actions each time they are executed.

- **Shared Actions**: These actions are designed to be reused throughout a given project or even shared across projects.

In the next exercise, you will create a couple of Standard Actions to get a sense of what they can achieve.

Using Standard Actions

A Standard Action is the simplest form of Advanced Action that can be created in Captivate. A Standard Action is simply a list of instructions that the Flash Player or the JavaScript engine of the browser executes one by one, and in order, in response to an event.

Automatically turning on Closed Captions with Advanced Actions

Your first Advanced Action will manipulate one of the many System Variables of Captivate to automatically turn the Closed Captions on when the course starts.

First, you will use the following steps to find out the name of the variable to manipulate:

1. Still in the `drivingInBe.cptx` file, use the **Projects | Variables** menu item to open the **Variables** dialog.

2. Make sure the **Type** drop-down list is set to display the System Variables.

3. In the **View By** dropdown, choose the **Movie Control** category.

4. Select the first variable of the list named **cpCmndCC**.

The description says it all! This variable is a Boolean variable. It means that it can only have two values: 1 or 0. When the value of the variable is set to 1, the Closed Captions are turned on, but if it is set to 0, the Closed Captions do not appear. So basically, what you have to write is an Advanced Action that assigns the value 1 to the **cpCmndCC** System Variable.

5. Close the **Variables** dialog.

6. Use the **Project | Advanced Actions** menu item to open the **Advanced Actions** dialog.

7. In the top-left corner of the dialog, type `displayCC` in the **Action Name** field.

Note that the name of the action must comply with the same strict rules as the name of the variables (no spaces and no special characters).

8. In the **Actions** area of the dialog, double-click on the first line of the table.

This adds a first step to the Advanced Action. In the first column, a yellow warning sign indicates that the action is invalid in its current state. In the second column is a drop-down menu containing a list of possible actions.

9. Open the **Select Action...** dropdown and take some time to inspect the list of possible actions.

10. When done, choose the **Assign** action from the list.

11. Open the **Select Variable** dropdown and take some time to inspect the available Variables.

The **Select Variable** drop-down list proposes a list of Variables whose value can be changed. (For instance, the **CaptivateVersion** variable you used earlier is not listed, because you cannot change the value of this variable. It is a read-only variable).

12. At the very top of the list, select the **cpCmndCC** variable.

13. Open the second **Variable** drop-down list and choose **Literal**.

14. Type `1` in the field that appears and press *Enter*.

The whole sentence becomes **Assign cpCmndCC with 1**. In plain English, it translates to, turn the Closed Captions on. Note that the yellow warning sign in front of the action changes into a green checkmark. This is an indication that Captivate understands the first instruction of your Advanced Action, which is very good news!

15. Double-click on the second line of the table to add a second step into the action.

16. In the **Select Action...** dropdown, choose the **Continue** action. This ensures that the project will continue playing normally after the Closed Captions have been turned on.

The warning sign at the beginning of the second line of the table immediately turns to a green checkmark, because the **Continue** action does not require any kind of extra parameter to work.

Make sure the **Advanced Actions** dialog looks like the following screenshot before continuing with this exercise:

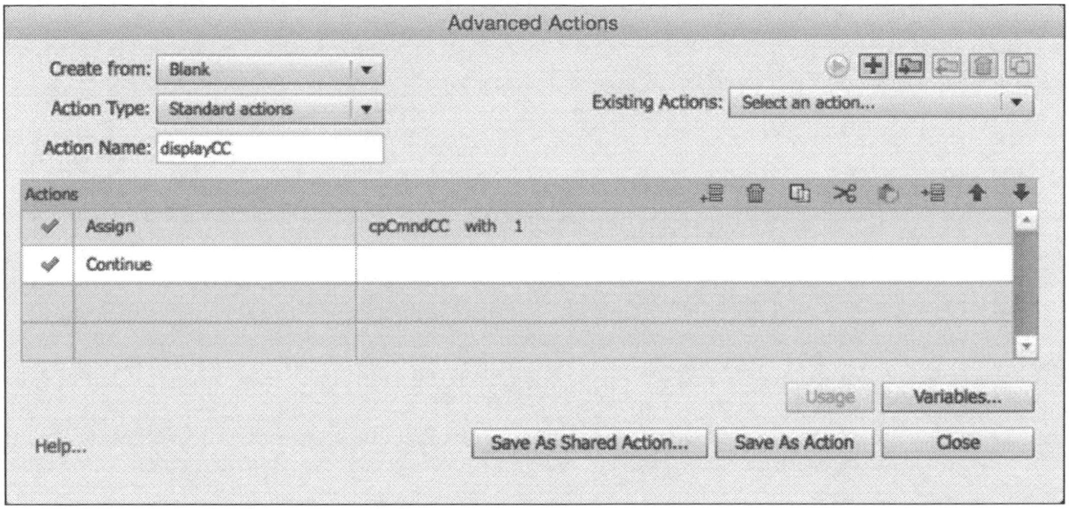

17. Click on the **Save As Action** button at the bottom of the dialog to save the Advanced Action.

18. Acknowledge the successful saving of the Advanced Action and **Close** the **Advanced Action** dialog.

Your Advanced Action is now ready, but one last piece of the puzzle is still missing. You need to tell Captivate when you want your action to be executed. In other words, you need to bind the action to the event that will trigger the action.

In Captivate there are lots of events you can bind actions to. Some of them are system events (for example, the start of a movie, the beginning of a slide, and so on), and some of them are student-driven events (typically, a click on a button). In this case, you will ask Captivate to execute the action when the playhead enters the second slide of the project. This is an example of a system event.

19. Use the **Filmstrip** panel to go to slide number 2. Make sure that the **Properties** panel shows the properties of the slide.

20. In the **Actions** tab of the **Properties** panel, open the **On Enter** drop-down list.

21. Take some time to inspect the possible actions and choose the **Execute Advanced Actions** item.

22. Make sure that the **displayCC** action appears in the **Script** dropdown as shown in the following screenshot:

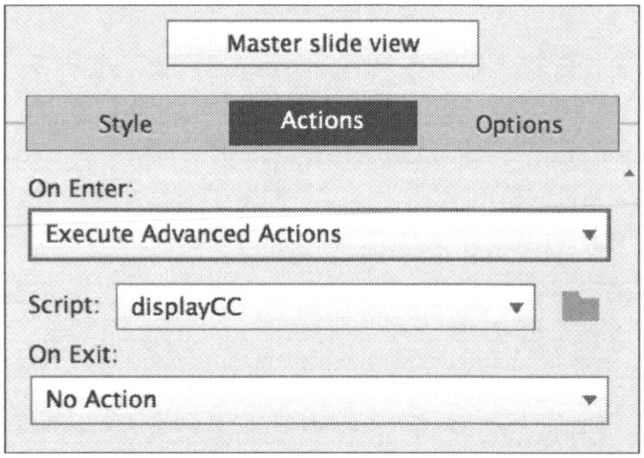

Master slide view

Style	Actions	Options

On Enter:

Execute Advanced Actions ▼

Script: | displayCC ▼ |

On Exit:

No Action ▼

23. Save the file and use the **Preview** | **Project** icon of the Big Buttons Bar to test the project.

In the **Preview** pane, Closed Captions should automatically be turned on when the preview reaches slide 2.

This first example illustrates how an Advanced Action can be used to manipulate a System Variable and how to bind an action to an event. By automatically turning on Closed Captions, you enhance the overall experience of your beloved students.

Don't forget that other System Variables can be manipulated in the same way, allowing you to do things such as muting or unmuting the sound, setting the audio volume, jumping to a slide, hiding or showing the Playback Controls, and more.

Extra credit – turning Closed Captions off

The last slide of the project with associated audio (and consequently with associated Closed Captions) is slide number 17, so it is safe to turn Closed Captions off at the end of slide 17. In this section, you will build a second Advanced Action that turns Closed Captions off by assigning the value 0 to the **cpCmndCC** System Variable. Captivate should execute this second Advanced Action when the student clicks on the **Continue** button of slide 17.

The main steps are as follows:

- Use the **Project | Advanced Actions** menu item to open the **Advanced Actions** dialog.

- Create a second Advanced Action named `hideCC` that assigns the value 0 to the **cpCmndCC** System Variable and then goes to the next slide.

- Save the script as an Advanced Action.

- On slide 17, in the **Actions** tab of the **Properties** panel of the **Continue** button, bind the **hideCC** Advanced Action to the **On Success** event.

- Save the file and preview the entire project. In the **Preview** pane, make sure that Closed Captions are turned on at the beginning of slide 2 and are turned off at the end of slide 17.

This second example illustrates how an Advanced Action can be bound to a student-driven event (the click on a button) instead of a system event.

Using Conditional Actions

The second kind of Advanced Action available is the Conditional Action. A Conditional Action is a bit more complex than a Standard Action in that it is able to evaluate if a condition is true or false and act accordingly.

To illustrate this capability, you will add a new slide in the project after slide 12. On that new slide, you will display a feedback message to the students that is specific to the way they answered the two preceding questions.

Remember that you asked the students two questions in the first part of the movie (the measurement unit they use to measure speed and if they drive on the right or on the left side of the road). If you aggregate the answers of those two questions, you can face three different situations:

Situation	Speed units	Side of road	Score	Meaning
1	Km/h	Right	2	Ok to drive in Belgium
2	MPH	Left	0	Change all your habits to drive in Belgium
3	MPH	Right	1	Change some driving habits to drive in Belgium
	Km/h	Left		

To keep track of the answers, you will assign a score to each question: a score of 1 if the student does the same thing as in Belgium, and a score of 0 if the student's habits are different from the Belgian way of driving.

Your Conditional Action will display a feedback message that depends on the score of the student.

Creating the necessary variables

You will begin this exercise by creating yet another user-defined variable using the steps below. You will use it to store the score of the student as he progresses into the project and answers the questions.

1. Return to the `Chapter12/drivingInBe.cptx` project.
2. Use the **Project | Variables** menu item to return to the **Variables** dialog.
3. Click on the **Add New** button to create a new variable.
4. In the **Name** field, type `v_num_studentScore`.

V_num_studentScore will be the name of the new variable. The `num_` prefix states that this variable will hold numeric data.

5. In the **Value** field, give this variable an initial value of `0`.

The action of giving an initial value to a variable is named initialization. In programmers jargon, what you are doing in the **Variables** dialog translates to "declaring the **v_num_studentScore** variable and initializing it to 0".

6. Optionally, type a description in the **Description** field.
7. Click on the **Save** button to save the new variable.

Make sure the **Variables** dialog looks like the following screenshot:

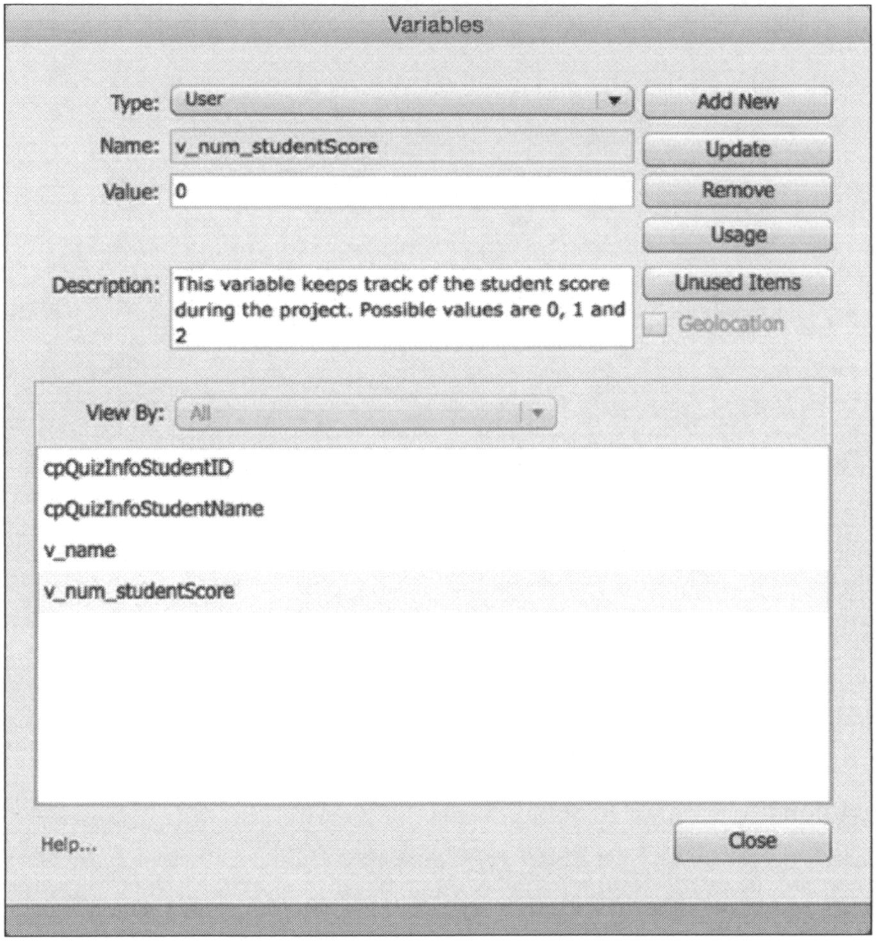

8. Click on the **Close** button to close the **Variables** dialog.

9. Don't forget to save the file when done.

Thanks to this new variable, you now have a mechanism in place to track the student's score throughout the entire project.

Naming variables

You already know that the name of a variable must comply with strict naming rules (no space, no special characters, and so on). That being said, any name that complies with these rules is not necessarily right. When naming variables, it is important to stick to conventions in addition to complying with rules, especially when working in a team. If no naming convention exists among the developers of a team, everyone ends up with his own naming rules and habits. In this case, it is nearly impossible to keep track of the variables and to maintain the projects over time. In this exercise, you used the num_ prefix to remember that this particular variable stores numerical values. This is one of the possible naming conventions, but any other convention will do! The bottom line is that complying with the technical rules is not enough!

Assigning a score to each possible answer

At the beginning of the project, each student has a score of zero. Technically, you have translated this situation by initializing your **v_num_studentScore** variable to 0. Now the score of each student will evolve depending on the answers given in the project.

There are two places where the score of the student can change:

- When entering slide 6, the score has to increase by one point. Slide 6 is the feedback slide where the student chooses the Km/h answer to the first question.

- When entering slide 11, the score also has to be incremented by one. Slide 11 is the feedback slide where the student answers "On the right side" to the second question.

In programmers jargon, increasing the value of a variable is called incrementing a variable by a value. In this case, you will increment the value of the **v_num_studentScore** variable by one when entering slide 6 and slide 11, using the following steps:

1. Use the **Filmstrip** panel to go to slide 6 of the project.

2. Open the **Properties** panel if needed and make sure it shows the properties of the Slide.

3. In the **Actions** tab of the **Properties** panel, open the **On Enter** dropdown.

4. Select the **Increment** action from the list.

5. In the **Increment** drop-down menu, make sure that the **v_num_studentScore** variable is selected.

6. Type 1 In the **By** field.

The whole action should read: increment the **v_num_studentScore** variable by 1 when entering slide 6. This is shown in the following screenshot:

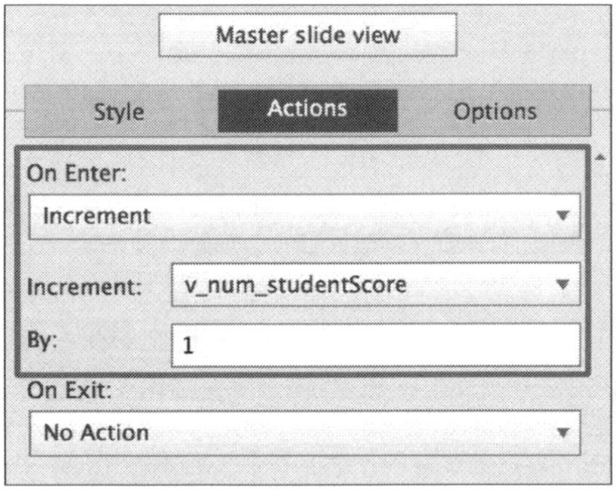

7. Repeat the same sequence of actions when entering slide 11 of the project.

Depending on the student's answers to the questions, the **v_num_studentScore** variable can now have three different values:

- If the student chooses Miles per Hour and drives on the left side of the road, the **v_num_studentScore** variable is never incremented and stays at its initial value of **0**

- If the students chooses Kilometers per Hour and drives on the right side of the road, the **v_num_studentScore** variable is incremented twice, so its final value is **2**

- In the in-between situation, the **v_num_studentScore** variable is incremented only once, so its final value is **1**

In the next step of the exercise, you will insert a new slide in the project and prepare three feedback messages for the three situations described previously.

Giving names to objects

First of all, you will insert a new slide in the project and prepare three standard Text Captions on it using the following steps:

1. Use the **Filmstrip** panel to go to slide 12 of the `drivingInBe.cptx` file.

2. Open the `Chapter12/DIB_feedback.cptx` file.

3. Copy the only slide of the `DIB_feedback.cptx` file and paste it as `slide 13` of the `drivingInBe.cptx` file.

The slide you just copied contains three Text Captions that are situated on top of each other in the center of the slide. In the **Timeline** panel, these three Text Captions are set to appear on stage at the very same time and to stay visible for 3 seconds. A button stops the playhead 1.5 seconds into the slide and waits for the click of the learner to jump to the next slide.

At runtime, only one of these Text Captions will be displayed to the student. The chosen Text Caption depends on the student's score as described in the preceding table. To make this possible, all three Text Captions must be initially hidden from the stage. An Advanced Action is used to check the score of the student and turn on the visibility of the right Text Caption.

In this exercise, you will prepare this system by assigning a name to each Text Caption and by turning their visibility off.

4. Go to slide 13, and use the **Timeline** panel to select the topmost Text Caption.

This first Text Caption is shown when the **v_num_studentScore** variable has a value of **0**.

5. Make sure the **Properties** panel shows the properties of the selected Text Caption.

6. At the top of the **Properties** panel, change the **Name** of the Text Caption to `TC_feedback_0`.

This name will make it much easier for you to pinpoint this particular object while writing the Conditional Action in the next section. The second thing to do is to instruct Captivate to hide this Text Caption by default.

7. Still in the **Properties** panel of this Text Caption, click on the eye icon next to the name of the object you just typed in.

A red line appears in the eye icon indicating that this object will not be displayed to the student by default. Your **Properties** panel should now look like the following screenshot:

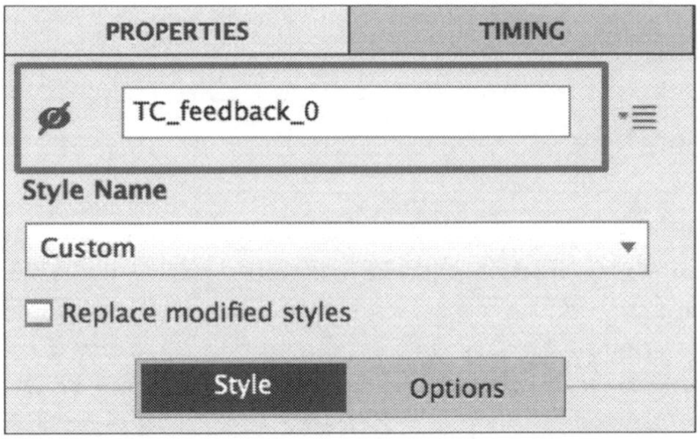

PROPERTIES	TIMING

TC_feedback_0

Style Name

Custom ▾

☐ Replace modified styles

Style	Options

Note that this action does not hide the object from the stage in the editing environment of Captivate, but it does hide it from your students. To hide the object from the stage in Captivate, it is necessary to turn off the associated eye icon in the **Timeline** panel.

8. In the **Timeline** panel, close the eye icon associated with the **TC_feedback_0** Text Caption.

9. Use the **Timeline** panel to select the middle Text Caption.

10. In the **Properties** panel, change the **Name** of that Text Caption to **TC_feedback_1**, and click on the eye icon.

11. In the **Timeline** panel, close the eye icon associated with the **TC_feedback_1** Text Caption.

12. Select the last Text Caption. Change its name to TC_feedback_2, and click on the eye icon to turn its visibility off. Also, hide it from the stage by closing the associated eye icon in the **Timeline** panel.

In this exercise, you have changed the names of three Text Captions. These names must comply with the same naming rules as the variables (no spaces and no special characters). Remember that observing technical requirements is not enough! It is much better if you also comply with some kind of naming convention. In this exercise, the TC_ prefix stands for Text Caption and the rest is the name of the object.

At the end of this exercise, the **Timeline** panel of slide 13 should look like the following screenshot:

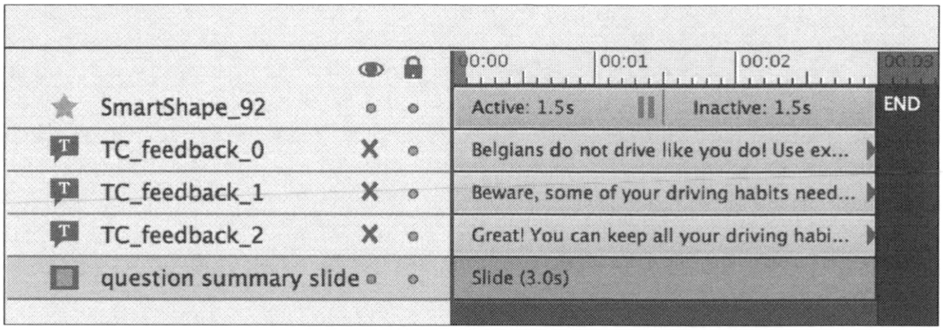

		👁	🔒	0:00	00:01	00:02	00:03
⭐	SmartShape_92	◦	◦	Active: 1.5s	⏸	Inactive: 1.5s	END
💬	TC_feedback_0	✗	◦	Belgians do not drive like you do! Use ex... ▸			
💬	TC_feedback_1	✗	◦	Beware, some of your driving habits need... ▸			
💬	TC_feedback_2	✗	◦	Great! You can keep all your driving habi... ▸			
◻	question summary slide	◦	◦	Slide (3.0s)			

Let's make one last experiment before moving on to the next step.

13. Use the **Filmstrip** panel to go to slide 12.

14. Once on slide 12, use the **Preview** | **Next 5 slides** icon of the Big Buttons Bar to preview the sequence in the **Preview** pane.

15. When the preview reaches slide 13, confirm that no Text Caption appears in the **Preview** pane.

16. When done, close the **Preview** pane, and save the file.

The stage is set! The feedback messages are ready, and you have a variable with three possible values to test against. The last piece of the puzzle is to create a Conditional Action that will evaluate the value of the **v_num_studentScore** variable and decide which of the three feedback messages on slide 13 will be revealed to the student.

Conditionally showing and hiding objects

In this section, you will create the Conditional Advanced Action that will combine all the pieces of the puzzle together. When it will be done, you will bind this action to the **On Enter** event of slide 13. Use the following steps to create your Conditional Advanced Action:

1. Still in the `drivingInBe.cptx` file, use the **Project** | **Advanced Actions** menu item to open the **Advanced Actions** dialog.

2. In the top-left corner of the **Advanced Actions** dialog, open the **Action Type** dropdown, and select **Conditional Actions** from the list.

The **Advanced Actions** dialog updates and shows the interface that you will use to create the Conditional Advanced Action.

3. Still in the top-left corner of the dialog box, type `showScoreFeedback` in the **Action Name** field.

Remember that the name of an action cannot contain any spaces or special characters.

It is now time to dig into the real stuff and create the Conditional Advanced Action. You will start by coding the first-case scenario, when the **v_num_studentScore** variable has a value of **0**.

4. At the top of the box, double-click on the blue **Untitled** button, and change the text to score `0`.

This step is optional and has no technical influence on how this action is executed. By adding a title to the branches of a Conditional Action, you just make your job a little bit easier when debugging and maintaining this action in the future.

5. In the **If** part of the Text Caption dialog box, double-click on the first line of the table to add the first condition.
6. Open the **variable** dropdown and select the **variable** option from the list. Then, open the list again to select the **v_num_studentScore** variable.
7. Open the **Select comparison operator** dropdown, and choose the **is equal to** option from the list of available operators.
8. Open the last dropdown and choose **literal** from the list. Then type `0` in the field that appears.

The whole expression should now read **v_num_studentScore is equal to 0** and a green checkmark should appear in the first column of the table, as shown in the following screenshot:

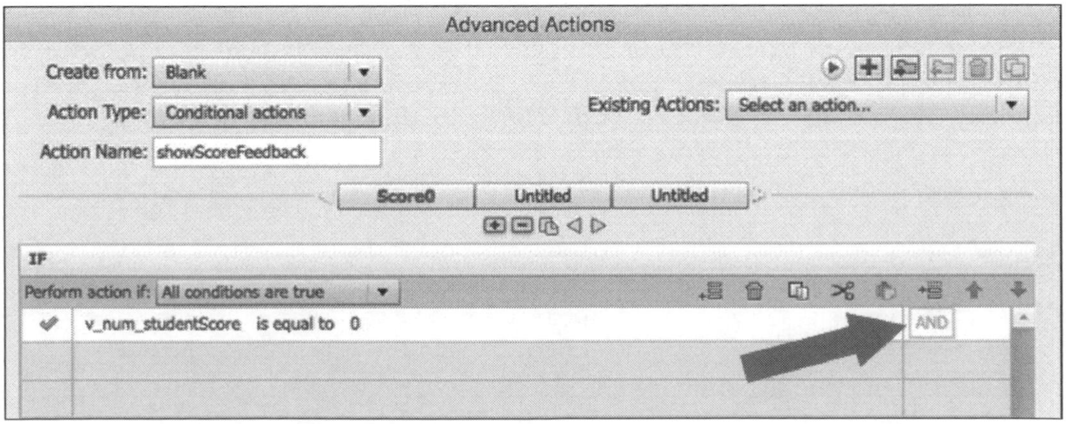

Note the **AND** word at the end of the table row (see the arrow in the preceding screenshot). It tells you that you can add more conditions that will be united by an **AND** operator. In other words, every individual condition should be true for the entire condition to be true.

9. Open the **Perform action if** dropdown, and choose the **Any of the conditions true** option from the list.

Note that the **AND** keyword switches to **OR**. In this case, the entire condition is true if any one of the individual conditions is true.

10. Open the **Perform** actions if dropdown again and choose the **Custom** option from the list.

In this situation, it is up to the developer to choose between **AND** and **OR** at the end of every single condition. This allows you to create very complex conditions. In this exercise, you only have a single condition, so the choice between **AND** and **OR** is not important.

11. Open the **Perform action if** dropdown one last time, and choose the **All conditions are true** option to return to the default setting.

12. In the **Actions** area of the dialog, double-click on the first row of the table to add a first action.

13. Open the **Select Action** dropdown and choose **Show** from the list of available actions.

14. Open the **Select Item** dropdown and choose the **TC_feedback_0** item from the list.

15. Add a **Continue** action in the second row of the **Actions** area.

Make sure there is a green checkmark in front of both actions before continuing. Note how the name you added to the Text Caption in the previous section comes in handy now. Make sure the **Advanced Actions** dialog looks like the following screenshot before continuing:

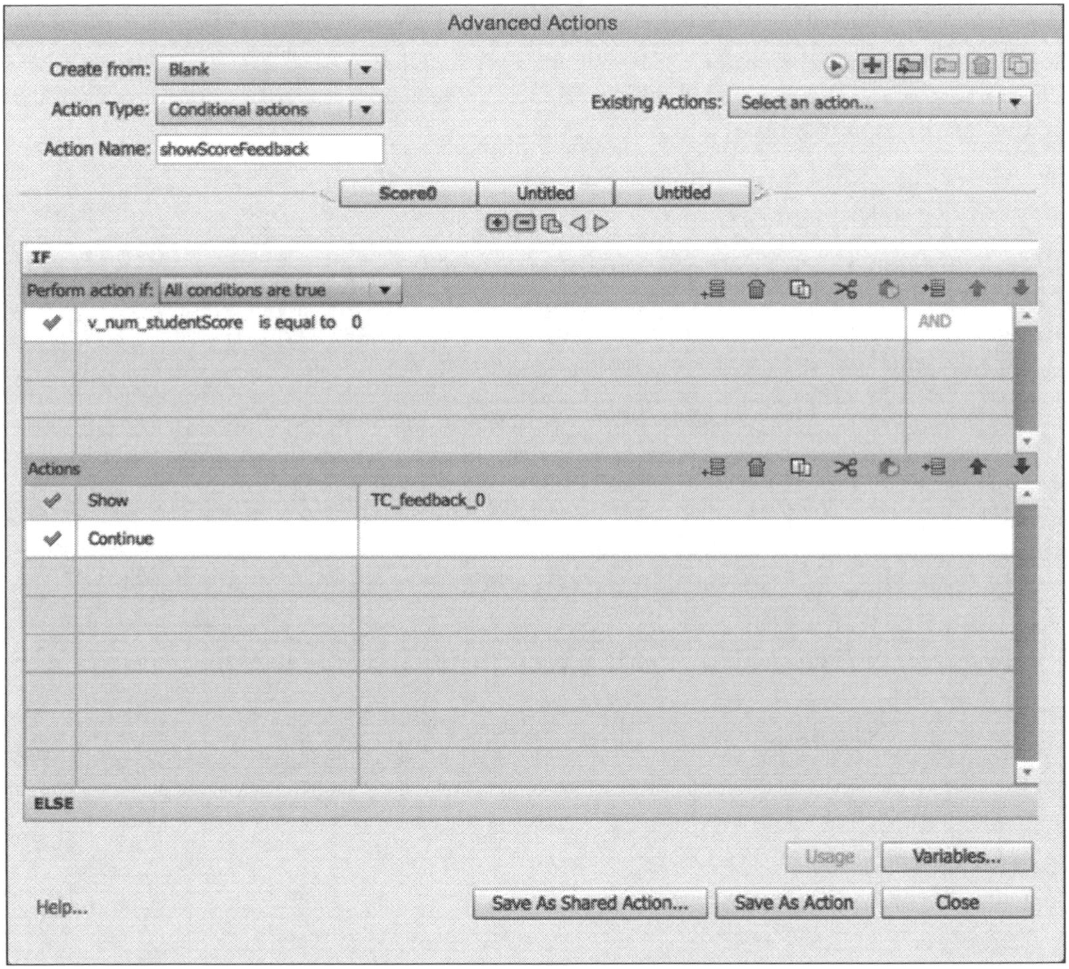

So far, you have coded the first of three scenarios. You will now add a second branch to this Conditional Advanced Action to cope with the second scenario.

16. At the top of the Conditional action, double-click on the first **Untitled** button. Rename this button Score 1.

This opens a second **If... Else** table in the **Advanced Actions** dialog. In Captivate, such a table is called a **decision**. By default, a Conditional Advanced Action contains three decisions; hence the three buttons at the top of the interface.

17. In the **IF** part of the second decision, double-click on the first line of the table to add a first condition.

18. Open the first dropdown and choose **variable** from the list. Open the same dropdown again and choose the **v_num_studentScore** variable from the list of available variables.

19. In the second drop-down list, choose the **is equal to** operator.

20. Open the last dropdown, choose **literal** from the list, and type 1 in the field that appears.

The condition should now read **v_num_studentScore is equal to_1** with a green checkmark in the first column. With the condition in place, you can now turn your attention to the bottom part of the dialog where you must define the corresponding action.

21. Double-click on the first line of the **Actions** area.

22. Open the **Select action** dropdown and choose the **Show** action from the list.

23. Open the **Select Item** dropdown and choose the **TC_feedback1** item from the list. In the second row of the table, set the second action to **Continue**.

The Conditional Action now accommodates two of the three possible scenarios. To code the last scenario, you will simply add a third decision to the mix.

24. Double-click on the third (**Untitled**) decision and rename it Score 2.

25. In the **IF** panel of the third decision, use the same techniques as discussed in the previous steps of this exercise to code the condition. It should read **v_num_studentScore is equal to 2**.

26. In the **Action** panel, set the first action to **Show** TC_feedback_2 and the second action to **Continue**.

27. Make sure the **Advanced Actions** panel looks like the following screenshot. Note the three decisions at the top of the dialog:

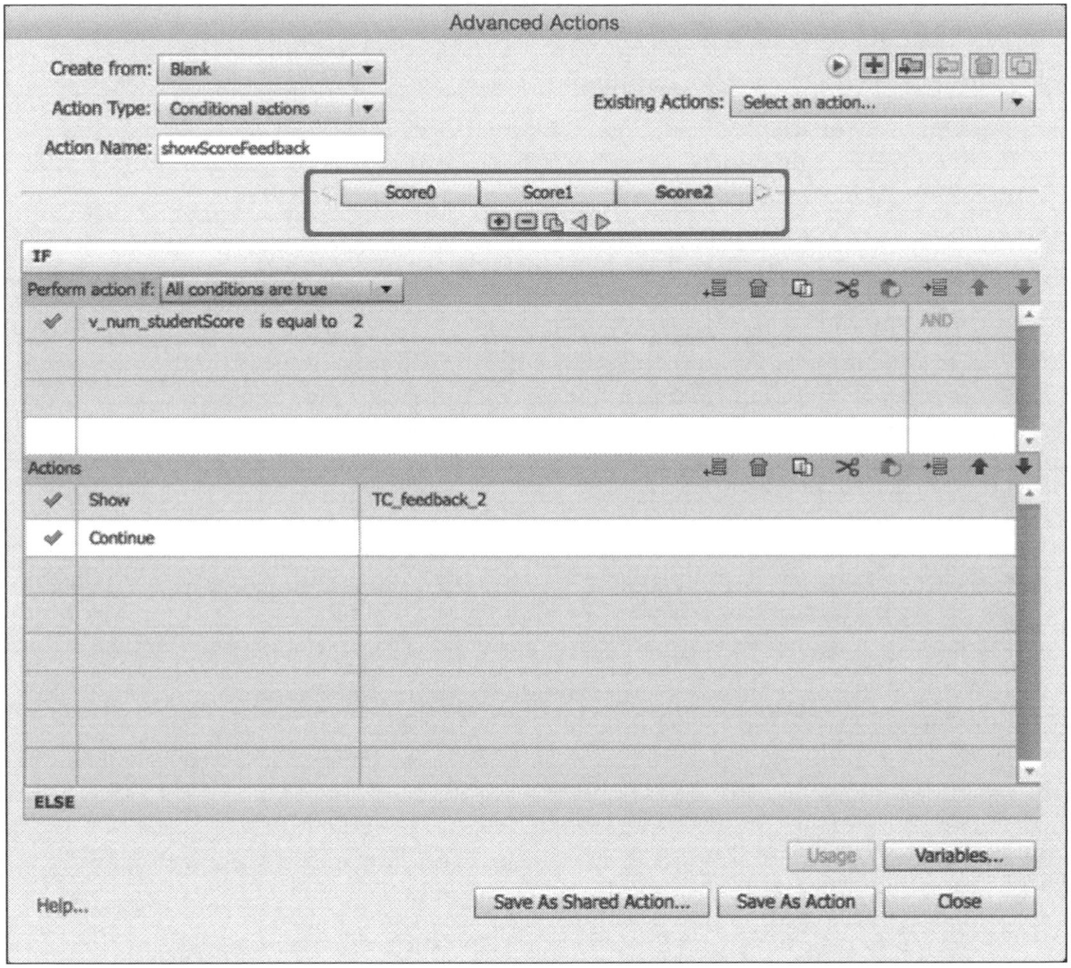

28. At the bottom of the **Advanced Actions** dialog, click on the **Save As Action** button.

29. Acknowledge the successful save of the script, and click on the **Close** button to close the **Advanced Actions** dialog.

The Conditional Advanced Action is now correctly coded, but there is one last step that is missing. Remember that an action must be triggered by an event. In this case, you want the action to run when entering slide 13.

30. Use the **Filmstrip** panel to go to slide 13.

31. In the **Actions** tab of the **Properties** panel of slide 13, open the **On Enter** dropdown.

32. Choose **Execute Advanced Actions** from the drop-down list.

33. Choose the **showScoreFeedback** action in the **Script** dropdown.

34. Use the **Filmstrip** panel to go to slide 11 and select the **Continue** button.

35. In the **Action** tab of the **Properties** panel, change the **On Success** dropdown to **Jump to slide**. Choose to jump to slide 13 from the **Slide** dropdown.

For the testing phase, you have to preview the entire project three times in order to test each of the three possible situations. Each time a test is run, you will answer differently to the question and see if the right feedback message shows up on slide 13.

36. Use the **Preview | Project** icon of the Big Buttons Bar to preview the entire project. When the preview reaches slide 13, pay close attention to the message that is displayed.

37. Repeat this operation twice more. Make sure that you answer differently to the first two questions each time.

Normally, all three tests should run fine. The message displayed on slide 13 depends on the value of the **v_num_studentScore** variable, which itself depends on the answers of the student.

Using a Conditional Action to implement branching with the Pretest

In this section, you will return to the Encoder Demonstration project to finalize the insertion of the Pretest, using the following steps:

1. If needed, open the `Chapter12/encoderDemo_800.cptx` project.

The Pretest is composed of three question slides. These question slides are slides 4, 5, and 6 of the project. Slide 7 is the automatically generated **Quiz Results** slide. Remember that, because the Pretest questions are not actually part of the Quiz, the **Quiz Results** slide displays a score of **0** regardless of the outcome of the Pretest. That's why you decided to hide slide 7 and to replace it with slides 8 and 9. Earlier in this chapter, you used the **cpQuizInfoPretestScorePercentage** System Variable to display the student's score on these two slides.

In this exercise, you will instruct Captivate to display slide 8 if the student passes the Pretest and slide 9 if the student fails the Pretest.

2. Use the **Filmstrip** panel to go to slide 6 of the project.

Slide 6 is the last question slide of the Pretest. Since slide 6 is a Question Slide, the Quiz panel is available on the right hand side of the screen.

3. If needed, click on the **Properties** button of the Big Buttons Bar to access the **Quiz** panel of slide 6.

4. In the **Actions** section of the **Quiz** panel, click on the **Edit Pretest Action** button.

This opens the **Advanced Actions** dialog box. A Conditional Advanced Action named **CPPretestAction** automatically loads into the dialog box.

> If the **CPPretest** action does not load automatically, just make sure that the **Action Type** drop-down menu is set to **Conditional Actions** and choose **CPPretestAction** in the **Existing Actions** dropdown. This is shown in the next screenshot.

Captivate automatically generated **CPPretestAction** when you inserted the first Pretest Question Slide in the project. This action is automatically triggered at the end of the Pretest. Note that it uses the **cpQuizInfoPretestScorePercentage** System Variable and compares it to 50. The action is set to **Go to Next Slide** by default, as shown in the following screenshot:

5. Double-click on the **Go to Next Slide** action. Then, open the **Select Action** dropdown, and choose the **Jump to slide** action.

6. Open the **Select Slide** dropdown, and choose to jump to slide 8, **Pretest Success**.

The first part of the branching is finished! Captivate knows that it has to display slide 8 if the value of cpQuizInfoPretestScorePercentage is greater than or equal to 50 or, in other words, if the student has passed the Pretest. If the student receives a grade less than 50, he fails and Captivate must jump to slide 9.

7. At the bottom of the **Advanced Actions** dialog, click on **ELSE** (see the red rectangle in the preceding screenshot).

Note that the default action of the **ELSE** clause is also the **Go to Next Slide** action. In this case, you have to change it to jump to slide 9.

8. Double-click on the **Go to Next Slide** action. Then, open the **Select Action** dropdown and choose the **Jump to slide** action from the list.

9. Open the **Select Slide** dropdown, and choose to jump to slide **9 Pretest fail**.

10. Click on the **Update Action** button at the bottom of the **Advanced Actions** dialog to save the changes made to the **CPPretestAction** script.

11. Acknowledge the successful update of the script and close the **Advanced Actions** dialog.

Now that you have modified **CPPretestAction**, Captivate knows what to do when the student passes or fails the Pretest. To make sure everything works as expected, make sure you test it out.

12. Use the **Preview | Project** icon of the Big Button Bar to test the entire project in the **Preview** pane.

Make sure to test the project twice. The first time you should fail the Pretest and confirm that Captivate shows slide 9. The second time, make sure you pass the Pretest so that Captivate displays slide 8 and gives you the opportunity to skip the demonstration.

Using Shared Actions

A Shared Action is an Advanced Action (standard or conditional) that can be reused multiple times in a single project or shared across multiple projects.

In *Chapter 6, Working with Interactive Objects*, you used the rollover objects of Captivate on slide 17 (Rollover Captions and Rollover Smart Shapes) and 18 (Rollover Image) of the `drivingInBe.cptx` project. These objects are great, but they are only supported in the Flash output of the project. In the next exercise you will return to the `drivingInBe.cptx` project and make it mobile-compliant by replacing the rollover objects you used on slide 17 and 18 with buttons that the student will use to toggle the visibility of objects on and off. The first step of this process is to import the necessary slides into the project.

Importing the necessary slides

To speed you up and let you concentrate on the Shared Action part of the process, the necessary slides have already been created for you. You will now delete the slides containing the Rollover Objects not supported in HTML5 and replace them with new slides, using the following steps:

1. Return to the `Chapter12/drivingInBe.cptx` file.
2. Use the **Filmstrip** to select slides 17 and 18.
3. Right-click on any of the selected slides and choose **Delete** in the contextual menu. Confirm the deletion of the two slides in the warning message.

You will now replace the deleted slides with new ones that are supported in HTML5.

4. Open the `Chapter12/Rollover_touch.cptx` file.
5. Use the **Filmstrip** panel to select both slides of the `Rollover_touch.cptx` project.
6. Copy the selected slides (*Ctrl* + *C* on Windows or *cmd* + *C* on the Mac).
7. Return to the `drivingInBe.cptx` file and use the **Filmstrip** panel to select slide 16 of the project.
8. Use the *Ctrl* + *V* (Windows) or *cmd* + *V* (Mac) shortcut to paste the slides.

The pasted slides provide the same information as the slides you deleted. The only difference is in the objects being used. Actual images and Smart Shapes replace the Rollover Images and Rollover Smart Shapes of the deleted slides, while transparent Smart Shapes used as buttons replace the associated Rollover Areas.

Creating the necessary variables and naming the objects

The next step in converting the rollover objects into HTML5-compliant interactions is to create the necessary variables and to name the objects. Remember that naming the objects is not technically required, but it will make your life much easier later in the process when using your Shared Action. Use the following steps to create the variables and name the objects:

1. Still in the `Chapter12/drivingInBe.cptx` project, use the **Filmstrip** panel to go to slide 16.
2. Select the **No parking is allowed at any time** Smart Shape.
3. At the top of the **Properties** panel, note the red line across the eye icon indicating that this Smart Shape will not be visible to the learners.
4. Next to the eye icon, change the name of this object to `shape_noParking` and press *Enter* to validate the name.

You will now create a new User Variable that you will use to track the visibility status of this object. This new variable will have a value of **0** when the **shape_ noParking** object is invisible and a value of **1** when the object is visible. Use the following steps to create the variable.

5. Use the **Project | Variables** menu item to open the **Variables** dialog box.
6. At the top of the **Variables** dialog, click on the **Add New** button.
7. Type `v_shapeNoParking_visible` as the variable name.
8. Type `0` as the initial value of the variable.
9. Optionally, type a meaningful description in the **Description** field.
10. Click on the **Save** button to save the new variable.

Make sure that the **Variables** dialog looks like the following screenshot before moving on:

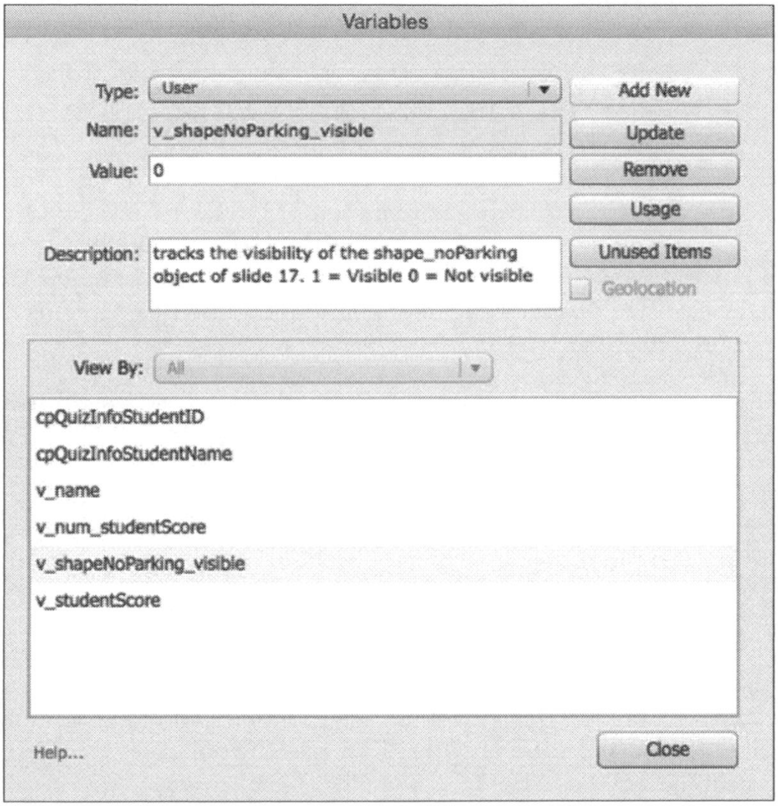

Variables		
Type: User		Add New
Name: v_shapeNoParking_visible		Update
Value: 0		Remove
		Usage
Description: tracks the visibility of the shape_noParking object of slide 17. 1 = Visible 0 = Not visible		Unused Items
		☐ Geolocation

View By: All

cpQuizInfoStudentID
cpQuizInfoStudentName
v_name
v_num_studentScore
v_shapeNoParking_visible
v_studentScore

Help...   Close

Extra credit – creating the remaining variables

Now you will repeat the procedure from the previous section with the remaining objects. There are five more objects to name and five more variables to create. The general steps go as follows:

- Select the object to name.
- Give it a name in the **Properties** panel and hit *Enter* to validate the new name.
- Make sure the object is invisible in the output (there is a red line on the eye icon).
- Go to the **Variables** dialog and create the associated user variable. Don't forget to give it an initial value of 0.

Refer to the following table to name the objects and create the variables:

Slide	Object	Name	Variable
17	No parking allowed between the 1st and the 15th of the month	shape_noP1stHalf	v_shapeNoP1stHalf_visible
17	No parking allowed between the 16th and the 31st of the month	shape_noP2ndHalf	v_shapeNoP2ndHalf_visible
18	Right of way image	img_priority	v_imgPriority_visible
18	No right of way image	img_noPriority	v_imgNoPriority_visible
18	Right priority image	img_priorityRight	v_imgRightPriority_visible

After this section, all the elements are in place for the creation of the Shared action.

Creating the Shared Action

If you think about it, you have three objects on slide 17 and three objects on slide 18 on which you want to apply a similar behavior (toggling the visibility of the objects on and off when clicking on the associated transparent Smart Shape). Prior to Captivate 7, when there were no Shared Actions available, you had to create six entirely different Advanced Actions to achieve that result. Thanks to the Shared Actions, you only need to create a single Advanced Action that you will reuse multiple times.

In this exercise, you will use the following steps to create a Conditional Advanced Action that checks the value of the **v_shapeNoParking_visible** variable and turns the corresponding object on or off accordingly:

1. Still in the Chapter12/drivingInBe.cptx file, use the **Project | Advanced Actions** menu item to open the **Advanced Actions** dialog.
2. Open the **Action Type** drop-down menu and choose the **Conditional actions** item.
3. Type toggleVisibility in the **Action Name** field.
4. Double-click in the first line of the **IF** part to add a first condition to the action.
5. Open the **Variables** dropdown and click on the **variable** item.
6. Choose the **v_shapeNoParking_visible** variable from the list.

7. Open the **Select comparison operator** list and choose the **is equal to** item.

8. Open the **variable** dropdown situated on the right hand side of the comparison operator and choose the **literal** item.

9. Type 1 in the field that appears and validate with the *Enter* key.

The condition of the Advanced Action is now complete. The sentence should read if the **v_shapeNoParking_visible** variable has a value of **1** (or in plain English, if the **No parking** Smart Shape is visible). If this condition evaluates to true, you must hide the **shape_noParking** object and toggle the value of the **v_shapeNoParking_visible** variable back to **0**. You will now code these actions using the following steps.

10. Double-click in the first line of the **Actions** area of the dialog to add a first action.

11. Open the **Select Action** dropdown and choose the **Hide** action from the list.

12. Choose the **shape_noParking** object in the second drop-down menu.

13. Double-click on the second line on the action to add a second action in the **Then** part of the dialog.

14. Open the **Select Action** dropdown and choose the **Toggle** action in the list.

15. Choose the **v_shapeNoParking_visible** variable in the second drop-down menu.

Make sure the **Advanced Actions** dialog looks like the following screenshot:

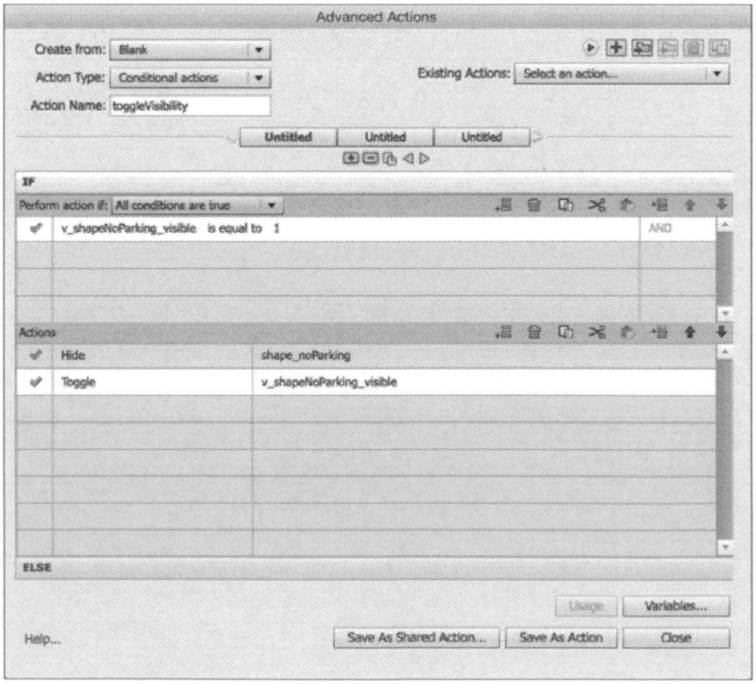

You will now open the **Else** pane and tell Captivate what should happen when the condition is not met (when the object is not visible). In this case, you want to show the object and toggle the value of the associated variable to 1.

16. Click on the **Else** label situated at the bottom of the dialog.

17. Double-click in the first line of the **Else** panel to add a first action.

18. Open the **Select Action** dropdown and choose the **Show** action from the list.

19. Choose the **shape_noParking** object in the second dropdown menu.

20. Double-click on the second line on the action to add a second action in the **Else** part of the dialog.

21. Open the **Select Action** dropdown and choose the **Toggle** action from the list.

22. Choose the **v_shapeNoParking_visible** variable in the second drop-down menu.

The Advanced Action is now finished. Basically, it checks the current value of a variable to see if the corresponding object is currently visible or not. If the object is visible, the action hides it and updates the variable accordingly. If the object is not visible, the action shows it and also updates the associated variable.

Saving the Shared Action

So far, creating the Shared Action is no different from creating a regular action. You will now save the Action developed in the previous section as a Shared Action using the following steps:

1. Still in the **Advanced Actions** dialog of the `drivingInBe.cptx` file, click on the **Save As Shared Action** button at the bottom of the dialog.

This action opens the **Save As Shared Action** box. In this box, you will be able to define the parameters of the Shared Action. Remember that a Shared Action is meant to be reused multiple times in the project (or even across projects). The parameters of the Shared Action are the elements of the Action that differ each time the action is executed. In this case, you need two parameters: the variable to update and the object to show or hide. You will now create those two parameters using the following steps.

2. Select the checkbox associated with the **v_shapeNoParking_visible** parameter.

3. Type `Associated Variable` in the associated **Parameter Description** field.

4. Type `Object to Show or Hide` in the **Parameter Description** field associated with the **shape_noParking** object.

Make sure the **Save As Shared Action** box looks like the following screenshot before continuing:

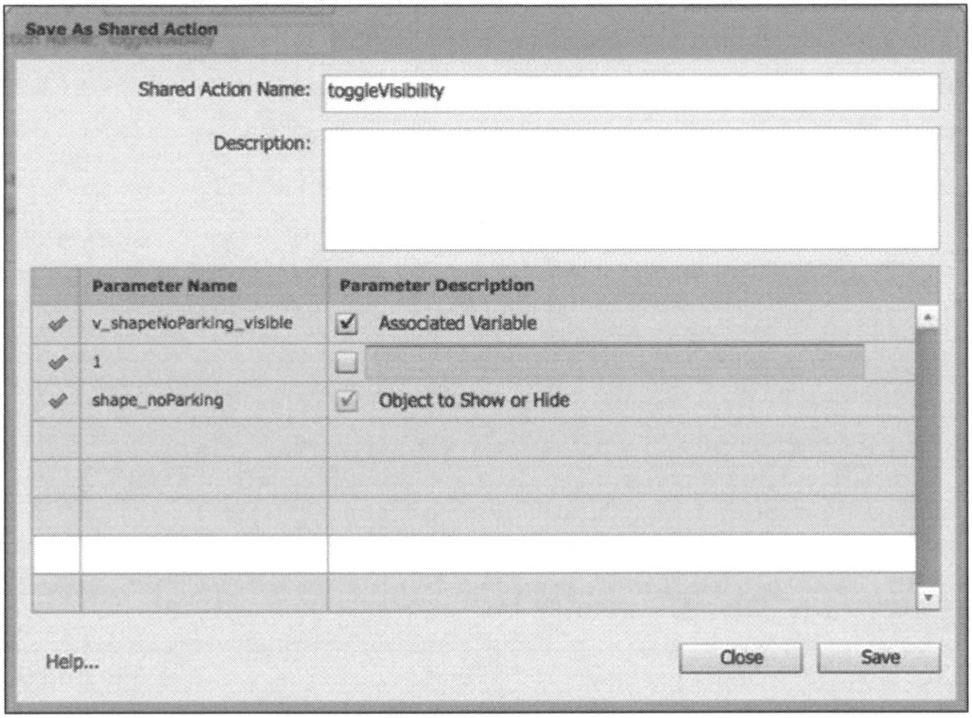

Save As Shared Action		

Shared Action Name: toggleVisibility

Description:

Parameter Name		Parameter Description
✔	v_shapeNoParking_visible	☑ Associated Variable
✔	1	☐
✔	shape_noParking	☑ Object to Show or Hide

Help...   Close   Save

5. When done, click on the **Save** button of the **Save As Shared Action** dialog.

6. Clear the information message and **Close** the **Advanced Actions** dialog.

The Shared Action is now completely defined and saved in the project. The next step is to bind this action to an event. In this case, the event is a click on the transparent button associated with each object.

Using and reusing the Shared Action

The last step of the process is to use and reuse your shared action. As with any other action, you do so by binding this action to an event. Only this time, you bind the same Shared Action to many different events and set different action parameters each time. You will test it out on the **No Parking** Smart Shape using the following steps:

1. Still in the `drivingInBe.cptx` file, use the **Filmstrip** panel to go to slide 17.

2. Select the rounded rectangle Smart Shape situated on top of the topmost road sign.

The selected rounded rectangle is a Smart Shape used as a button. You will use it as a replacement for the Rollover Area that used to be associated with the **No Parking** Rollover Smart Shape in the old version of the slide. When the learner clicks on this button, the **shape_noParking** object must either show or hide depending on the current value of the v_noParking_visible variable.

3. In the **Actions** tab of the **Properties** panel, open the **On Success** drop-down list.

4. Choose the **Execute Shared Action** item.

5. Make sure the **toggleVisibility** action is selected in the drop-down list that appears just below.

6. Click on the little **{P}** icon situated next to the name of the action. This opens the **Shared Action Parameters** dialog.

7. Choose **v_shapeNoParking_visible** as the value of the **Associated Variable** parameter.

8. Choose **shape_noParking** as the value of the **Object to Show Or Hide** parameter.

These actions are illustrated in the following screenshot:

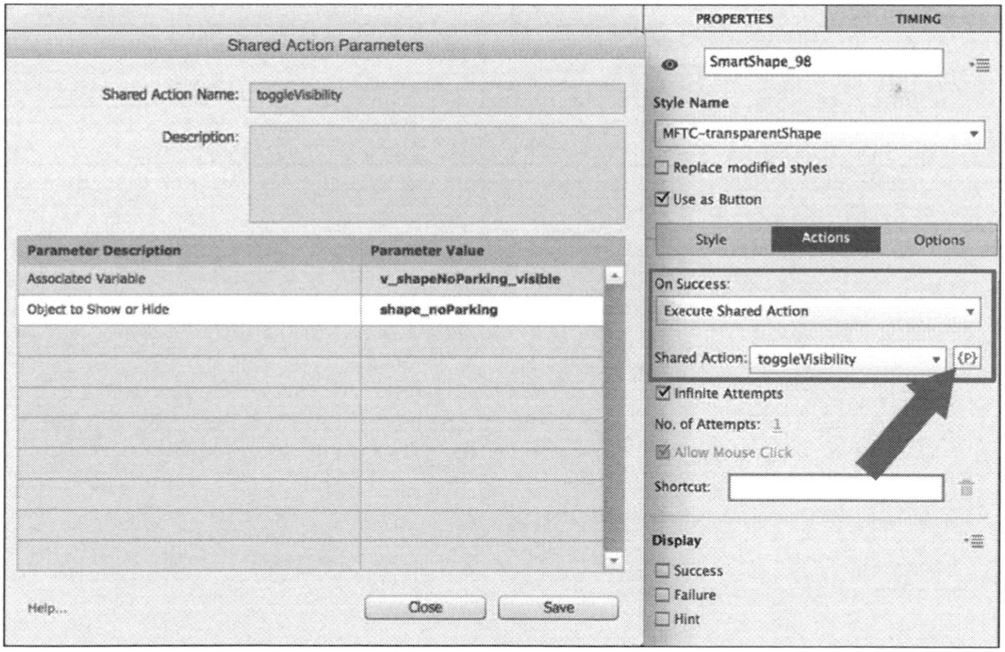

9. Click on the **Save** button of the **Shared Action Parameters** dialog to finalize the process.

Extra credit – reusing the Shared Action

All you need to do now is to bind the same Shared Action to the **On Success** event of the other transparent Smart Shape on slides 17 and 18. With each click, the Shared Action will be executed using different parameters each time. The steps are as follows:

- Select a transparent Smart Shape associated with an object to show or hide.

- In the **Actions** tab of the **Properties** panel, bind the **toggleVisibility** Shared Action to the **On Success** event of the selected button.

- Click on the {P} icon and choose the parameters pertaining to the selected button.

- When done, use the **Project | Next 5 slides** icon of the Big Buttons Bar to test your sequence.

Refer to the following table to choose the right parameters for the Shared Action:

Slide	Object	Associated Variable	Object to Show / Hide
17	No parking allowed between the 1st and the 15th of the month.	v_shapeNoP1stHalf_visible	shape_noP1stHalf
17	No parking allowed between the 16th and the 31st of the month.	v_shapeNoP2ndHalf_visible	shape_noP2ndHalf
18	Right of way image	v_imgPriority_visible	img_priority
18	No right of way image	v_imgNoPriority_visible	img_noPriority
18	Right priority image	v_imgRightPriority_visible	img_priorityRight

Shared Advanced Actions are a very powerful feature of Captivate.

If you want to know more about it, feel free to consult the official Captivate Help page on Shared Actions at http://helpx.adobe. com/captivate/using/shared-actions.html. There are also lots of video tutorials on Advanced Actions on the Captivate YouTube channel. For example, check out the video on how to create Shared Advanced Actions that can be reused across projects at http://www.youtube.com/watch?v=AWC0uPMpY5w.

Your first exploration of the Advanced Actions of Captivate is now complete. It is time to make a quick summary of what has been covered before moving on to the next section:

- There are three kinds of Advanced Actions in Captivate: Standard Actions, Conditional Actions, and Shared Actions.

- A Standard Action is a simple list of instructions executed one by one and in order at runtime.

- A Conditional Action checks if a condition is met before executing an action.

- A Shared Action is an Advanced Action that can be reused multiple times in a project or even across multiple projects.

- When creating a Conditional Action, you can create as many decisions as needed. Each decision is executed one by one by Captivate regardless of the outcome of any preceding decision.

- The Advanced Actions can be used to manipulate system or user-defined variables to manipulate the objects of the project or to manipulate the project itself.

- It is possible to give a name to any objects of the Captivate project. This makes it easier to manipulate these objects with Advanced Actions or to use them as parameters of Shared Advanced Actions.

- It is necessary to bind an action to an event in order to instruct Captivate about when an action should be executed.

- There are two kinds of events in Captivate, system events and student-driven events.

- System events are triggered automatically by the project. Examples of system events are the beginning or the end of a slide, the start of the project, and so on.

- Student-driven events are triggered by an action performed by the student. The typical student-driven event is a click on a button, but it could also be a click on a Click Box, the answer to a Question Slide, and so on.

- When inserting a Pretest in a project, Captivate automatically creates the **CPPretestAction** Conditional Advanced Action. This Advanced Action is automatically executed at the end of the Pretest. You can use it to implement branching based on the outcome of the Pretest.

Variables and Advanced Actions are one of the most advanced topics found in Captivate. You've only scratched the surface of this powerful feature in this book. With time and experience, you'll be able to take full advantage of this most powerful tool.

For more on Advanced Actions, make sure you subscribe to the Blog of Lieve Weymeis aka Lilybiri at `http://blog.lilybiri.com/`. She is a world-class specialist in Advanced Actions, and her blog is second to none when it comes to Variables, Advanced Actions, and other advanced tips and tricks with Captivate.

Geolocation in Adobe Captivate

What makes mobile learning so exciting and promising is the unique capabilities of mobile devices. One such capability is called **Geolocation**, which is the ability to detect where the learner is located while using his mobile device. Many apps take advantage of this ability to provide different content based on the user's location. For example, you can ask your mobile device to look for a restaurant within a 5 miles radius of your current location.

Captivate 8 introduces a way to leverage that power in your eLearning course. You can now access the location of the learner and provide content based on where the learner is located.

Take the Driving in Belgium project, for example. Its target audience is foreigners who want to visit Belgium. In other words, this project is not aimed at Belgian residents. In the next exercise, you will use the new Geolocation capabilities of Captivate 8 to detect the location of the learner taking the course. If you detect that the learner is in Belgium, you should display a warning message and give the learner the opportunity to skip the course. In every other situation the course needs to take place normally.

Inserting an extra slide

First you will insert a new slide in the project. To speed you up, this slide has already been created in another project. All you need to do is to copy and paste it, using the following steps:

1. Still in the `drivingInBe.cptx` project, use the **Filmstrip** to return to the first slide of the project.

2. Open the `Chapter12/DIB_Geolocation.cptx` file.

3. In the **Filmstrip** panel, select and copy the first and only slide of the project.

4. Return to the `drivingInBe.cptx` file and paste the slide as slide 2 of the `drivingInBe.cptx` project.

5. Select the **No I will skip it** button.

6. In the **Actions** tab of the **Properties** panel, change the action of the button to **Jump to slide**.

7. Select the last slide of the project (**Slide 30**) in the **Slide** dropdown that appears just below.

This new slide should be displayed to Belgian learners only. In the next section, you will learn how you can access the location of the learner taking the course.

Detecting the location of the learner

Captivate 8 includes a new System Variable that returns the latitude and longitude coordinates of the learner. Use the following steps to inspect this new variable and understand how it works.

1. Still in the `drivingInBe.cptx` project, use the **Project | Variables** menu item to open the **Variables** dialog.

2. At the top of the **Variables** dialog, change the **Type** to **System**.

3. Open the **View By** drop-down list

4. Scroll to the end of the list and choose the **Mobile** item.

5. Select the **cpInfoGeolocation** variable.

The **cpInfoGeolocation** System Variable is new to Captivate 8. As explained in the **Description**, it returns the geometric coordinates of the learner taking the course. It actually returns the latitude and longitude coordinates of the learner. This ability is based on the Geolocation capabilities of the device used when taking the course.

Note that desktop and laptop computers can also be Geolocalized based on the network they are connected to and on their IP address, so Geolocation is not specific to mobile devices. That being said, the accuracy of the Geolocation data largely depends on the device used.

Geolocation and privacy

Many users decide to block their Geolocation data for privacy reasons. This means that you may not have access to this data even if the learner is using a Geolocation-aware device. You must respect this decision of the learner and always provide a default scenario that does not depend on the learner's location.

Creating a custom Geolocation variable

Now that you have a way to detect the user's location, you will create a new User Variable in which you will store the Geolocation coordinates of Belgium. At runtime, you will compare the **cpInfoGeolocation** variable to your custom Belgium variable. If you detect that the learner is in Belgium, you will display the slide that you inserted in the project earlier in this section. Use the following steps to create a custom Belgium variable:

1. Still in the **Variables** dialog of the `drivingInBe.cptx` file, use the **Type** dropdown to return to the **User** Variables.

2. Click on the **Add New** button to create a new User Variable.

3. Type `v_locationBelgium` in the **Name** field.

4. Select the **Geolocation** checkbox situated below the **Unused Items** button.

By selecting this checkbox, you tell Captivate that you want to create a custom Geolocation variable. The difference between a Geolocation variable and a standard variable is in the way you express the value of the variable. When defining a standard variable you simply type its initial value in the **Value** field of the **Variable** dialog box. When defining a Geolocation variable you must supply the **Latitude**, **Longitude**, and **Accuracy** values, as shown in the following screenshot:

The **Latitude** and **Longitude** values are used to define a precise spot on Earth. The value of **Accuracy** is measured in meters. It defines the radius of a circle whose center is the precise spot defined by the **Latitude** and **Longitude** coordinates. If the location of the learner as returned by the **cpInfoGeolocation** system variable is within that circle, the leaner is considered to be at the custom location.

 The remaining steps of the exercise require that you have installed the Captivate 8.0.1 update and that you are connected to the Internet.

5. Click on the **Choose From Map** icon. This icon is a new feature of the Captivate 8.0.1 update.

The box that opens is based on Google Maps, which explains why you must be connected to the Internet to make it work. Note that a circle and two points are present on top of the Google Map.

6. Type `Belgium` in the search field situated in the top part of the window.

7. Then adjust the position of the two points so that the circle more or less covers Belgium on the map.

8. When done, click on the **Submit** button situated just below the **Search** field.

Note that the **Latitude**, **Longitude**, and **Accuracy** components of the Geolocation variable have been automatically filled in. The center of the circle is used to define the **Latitude** and **Longitude** components, and the radius of the circle is used for the **Accuracy** component of the variable.

9. Click on the **Save** button to save the new variable and close the **Variables** dialog.

In the next section, you will use this new variable to check if the learner is in Belgium or not, and act accordingly.

Altering the content based on the learner's location

The **cpInfoGeolocation** variable gives you access to the location of the learner and your custom **v_locationBelgium** variable defines what area of the world you want to consider as Belgium. In this section, you will create a conditional Advanced Action that will compare these two variables and decide if slide 2 should be displayed to the learner or skipped, using the following steps:

1. Use **Project | Advanced Actions** to open the **Advanced Actions** dialog.

2. Change the **Action Type** to **Conditional actions**.

3. Type checkBeLocation as the name of the action.

4. In the **IF** part of the action, check if the **cpInfoGeolocation** variable is equal to the **v_locationBelgium** variable.

5. In the **Actions** part of the dialog box, double-click on the first line and choose the **Continue** action.

6. Click on the **Else** label situated at the bottom of the dialog box.

7. Double-click on the first line of the **Else** panel and choose the **Go to Next Slide** action.

8. Click on the **Save As Action** button situated at the end of the dialog box.

9. Acknowledge the successful creation of the script and close the Advanced Action dialog.

The last piece of the puzzle is to decide when the action needs to be performed. In this case, you will bind this action to a system event using the following steps.

10. Use the **Filmstrip** panel to go to slide 2, if necessary.

11. In the **Actions** tab of the **Properties** panel, open the **On Enter** drop-down list.

12. Choose the **Execute Advanced Action** item from the list.

13. Select the **checkBeLocation** action in the **Script** drop-down menu.

The advanced action is executed when the playhead enters slide 2. If the Geolocation of the learner is within the circle defined by the **v_locationBelgium** variable, the playhead continues normally. In any other situation, the playhead jumps directly to the next slide and skips slide 2.

14. Return to the first slide of the project and use the **Preview | In Browser** icon to test your project.

If you happen to be in Belgium, you should see slide 2. In any other case, Captivate should skip it and continue with the project normally.

This exercise illustrates how you can use the new Geolocation capabilities of Captivate to modify the content that is supplied to the learner, based on their location.

Blog post

Allen Partridge, Adobe eLearning evangelist, has written an excellent blog post that illustrates another use case for these Geolocation capabilities. See this blog post and download the sample files at the following address `http://blogs.adobe.com/captivate/2014/06/ location-aware-learning-example-with-complete-source- files-for-the-australia-zoo-app.html`.

In the next section, you will learn about Advanced Learning Interactions. Now let's take some time to summarize what has been covered in this section.

- Captivate 8 introduced Geolocation capabilities, that is, the ability to detect the learner's location and act accordingly.

- The new **cpInfoGeolocation** System Variable exposes the learner's location when taking the course. This ability depends on the device used by the learner and on its privacy settings.

- Select the **Geolocation** checkbox in the **Variables** dialog to create custom user variables that define a location. These variables define a circle on the globe. If the user is inside the circle, Captivate considers that the user is at the custom-defined location.

- The center of this circle is a point defined by latitude and longitude coordinates. The radius of the circle is defined by the Accuracy parameter expressed in meters.

- The Captivate 8.0.1 update provides a map to make it easy to define custom locations.

Working with Smart Learning Interactions

Smart Learning Interactions are complex interactive objects with built-in logic and behavior. Captivate contains a bunch of Smart Learning Interactions by default, but it is also possible to download more Interactions from the Internet. When inserted on a Captivate slide, Smart Learning Interactions can be used as is, or customized in various ways. The best part is that Smart Learning Interactions are entirely compatible with both Flash and HTML5. In the next few sections, you will explore a few of these Smart Learning Interactions.

Working with the Accordion Interaction

In the next exercise, you will add one more slide to the *Driving in Belgium* project and insert the **Accordion** Smart Learning Interaction, using the following steps:

1. If needed, return to the `Chapter12/drivingInBe.cptx` file.

2. Use the **Filmstrip** panel to go to the second slide of the project.

3. Use the **Slides | Blank Slide** icon of the Big Buttons Bar to insert a new slide based on the Blank Master Slide of the Theme.

The new slide is inserted as slide 3 of the project.

4. Draw a rounded rectangle Smart Shape in the bottom center area of the new slide.

5. Write `Continue` in the rounded rectangle.

6. With the Rounded Rectangle selected, turn your attention to the **Properties** panel.

7. At the top of the **Properties** panel, select the **Use as Button** checkbox.

8. In the **Actions** tab of the **Properties** panel, make sure the **On Success** action is set to **Go to the next slide**.

9. Use the **Properties** panel to apply the **MFTC-ShapeButton** style.

The stage is set! Your next task is to insert a Smart Learning Interaction on this new slide.

10. Use the **Interactions | Learning Interaction** icon of the Big Buttons Bar to open the **Select Interaction** dialog.

The **Select Interaction** dialog shows a list of all the Interactions available in Captivate.

11. Take some time to inspect the available Interactions. When done, select the **Accordion** Interaction (the first one on the list) and click on the **Insert** button to insert it onto slide 3. This is shown in the following screenshot:

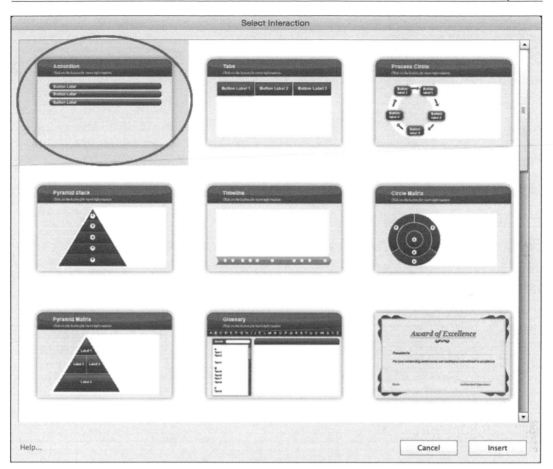

This action inserts the **Accordion** Smart Interaction onto slide 3 and opens the **Configure Interaction** dialog box. You will use it to customize both the content and the look and feel of the Accordion.

12. Use the left-hand side column of the **Configure Interaction** dialog to choose a Theme of your liking. (In the example in the Chapter12/final folder under, I chose **Theme 7**.)

13. Double-click in the Interaction title in the header area and type a nice Interaction title.

14. Repeat the same operation to customize the subtitle of the Interaction.

That's it for the look and feel of the Interaction. You will now customize the content of the Accordion.

15. In the main area of the **Widget Properties** dialog, double-click on the first button of the Accordion, and change its title to Description.

16. Double-click on the content area of the first Accordion, and type a short description of the project.

17. Change the **Button Label 2** title to Target Audience and the **Button Label 3** title to Length of the project.

18. Double-click on the **Button Label 4** title and click on the Minus button to delete it from the Accordion.

You should now have three panels left in the Accordion Interaction, as shown in the following screenshot:

19. Add appropriate descriptive text in each of the three panels.

20. Don't hesitate to explore the other options available and to further customize your Accordion Interaction. When done, click on the **OK** button.

21. Move and resize the Accordion so that it integrates nicely into the slide.

22. Use the **Preview | Next 5 slides** icon of the Big Buttons Bar to test your sequence.

Your exploration of the Accordion Interaction is now finished. If you want to further customize your Interaction, all you need to do is to double-click on the Interaction to reopen the **Widget Properties** dialog.

Working with the Web Object Interaction

The next Interaction you will work with is the Web Object Interaction. It allows you to embed an actual web browser right within your eLearning project. The students can therefore consult a preselected web page right in the middle of their online course! Let's check it out by performing the following steps:

1. Still in the `Chapter12/drivingInBe.cptx` project, use the **Filmstrip** panel to go to slide 20 of the project.

Slide 20 should be the last slide before the Quiz. You will add an extra slide just after slide 20. This slide displays a webpage containing extra information about travelling to Belgium.

2. Use the **Slides | Blank Slide** icon of the Big Buttons Bar to insert a new slide based on the Blank Master Slide of the Theme.

3. Add a Rounded Rectangle Smart Shape to the slide. Use it as a button that directs the learner to the next slide. Apply the **MFTC-ShapeButton** style and position the new button in the bottom center area of the slide. Type `Continue` as the button label.

Now that the slide is ready, let's proceed with the insertion of the Web Object Interaction in the middle of this slide.

4. Use the **Interactions | Learning Interaction** icon of the Big Buttons Bar to open the **Select Interaction** dialog.

5. Scroll to the end of the list to select the **Web Object** Interaction. When done, click on the **Insert** button.

As with the Accordion Interaction, the **Configure interaction** dialog opens. The options available in the dialog box here are much different. The fact that the **Configure interaction** dialog opens is common to all Interactions, but since each Interaction has its own set of options, the actual content of the dialog is down to each Interaction. In this case, all you need to do is to enter the URL of the web page you want to display and configure a few extra options.

6. Enter `http://wikitravel.org/en/Belgium` in the **Address** field.

7. Optionally, click on the **Preview** button to see what the Interaction looks like once inserted on the slide (an Internet connection is required).

8. Take some time to examine the other options of the **Configure interaction** dialog and adjust them at will. Ensure the **Display In Slide** option is selected, as shown in the following screenshot:

Configure interaction

Website

Address: http://wikitravel.org/en/Belgium

Preview

☑ Auto Load

⦿ Display in slide

☐ Border   ☐ Scrolling   ☑ "Loading..." Animation

◯ Display in a new browser window

Window Size   Browser Controls

Default ▾   All Browser Controls ▾

Width   Height

400 ⏶⏷   400 ⏶⏷

Help...   Cancel   OK

9. Click on the **OK** button to insert the Web Object Interaction onto the slide with the selected options.

10. Move and resize the Interaction as needed, and save the file.

Since an Internet connection is required for this Interaction to work, it is necessary to test the project in a web browser to make the Web Object Interaction function correctly.

11. Click on the **Preview | In Browser** icon of the Big Buttons Bar to test your project. Alternatively, you can use the *F12* (Windows) or *cmd + F12* (Mac) shortcuts.

If the Interaction does not work as expected in your web browser, make sure you are using the latest available version of both your browser and the Flash Player. If it still doesn't work, try using another browser for this test.

When on slide 21, confirm that the webpage defined in the **Configure Interaction** dialog correctly shows in the middle of the slide.

Extra credit – working with the Award of Excellence Interaction

Now, you will add one last Interaction to the project. The **Award of Excellence** Interaction delivers a certificate to the students who have passed the quiz.

The general steps are as follows:

- Go to slide 30 of the `Chapter12/drivingInBe.cptx` project.
- Use the **Interactions | Learning Interaction** icon of the Big Buttons Bar to insert the **Award of Excellence** Interaction.
- Choose one of the predefined Themes, and configure the Interaction as you see fit. Most options should be self-explanatory.
- Move and resize the Interaction as you see fit.
- Test the project. Make sure you pass the Quiz to see your newly inserted Award of Excellence Interaction!

This exercise concludes your exploration of the Smart Learning Interactions Captivate. Keep in mind that you have only used a few Interactions in this book. There are a lot more pedagogical and fun opportunities to discover in the other Smart Learning Interactions. Don't hesitate to spend some time experimenting with these Interactions. There are some great tutorials and videos available on the Internet if you want to get more examples and insights on these features.

More on Smart Learning Interactions

Some interesting links to get you started with the Smart Learning Interactions on Adobe TV are available at `http://tv.adobe. com/watch/new-in-adobe-captivate-6/smart-learning-interactions/`.

One of the sneak peeks revealed just before the release of Captivate 6 is available at `http://blogs.adobe.com/captivate/2012/06/adobe-captivate-6-sneak-peek-4-interactions-actors. html`.

A YouTube video on the new Interactions of Captivate 7 is available at `http://www.youtube.com/watch?v=zqp4mkpqzT0`.

Summary

Thanks to Advanced Actions and Variables, you have been able to add a whole new level of interactivity to your projects. The good news is that you have only briefly approached the tip of the iceberg in this book. The possibilities are virtually endless, and your imagination is the ultimate limit to what can be achieved.

To implement Advanced Actions and Variables, Captivate takes advantage of the scripting capabilities included in both the Flash and the HTML5 technologies. Advanced Actions and Variables can be used to create dynamic Text Captions, to turn the visibility of objects on and off, to control the movie, to access information about the movie, and much more.

Flash developers and ActionScript programmers can also contribute to Captivate by creating extra Widgets and Smart Learning Interactions. These Widgets are extra features that can be added to your Captivate projects. If you are an ActionScript or HTML5 developer, don't hesitate to write your own Widgets and Interactions. If you come up with a great one, make sure you make it available to the community. The best Widgets are yet to be written.

With the completion of this chapter, your projects can now be considered as final. Going back to the Captivate production workflow described at the very beginning of the book, you have now completed the second part of the process: the postproduction phase. As anticipated, this has been the most time-consuming and feature-rich phase of the whole process.

In the next chapter, you will finally make your work available to your learners by performing the final part of the process: the publishing step will allow you to publish your projects in various formats.

Meet the community

Rick Zanotti is a legend in the eLearning community. Everyone knows him and he knows everyone! This is probably due to his numerous video podcasts that he makes with a very wide number of eLearning influences from all over the world. I strongly recommend you subscribe to his Vimeo channels to get the latest and greatest from the best minds of our industry.

Rick Zanotti

Rick Zanotti is the president of RELATE, a well-known multimedia and eLearning development firm. Rick has a long career in Information Systems and over 20 years of experience in eLearning and media design. He's been a Systems Analyst, Instructional Designer, programmer, web developer, and voice talent. He runs a number of technical and industry-specific Internet broadcasts on the RELATECASTS channel. Rick was on the advisory board for RoboDemo/Adobe Captivate for 10 years.

Contact details

- **Website**: http://www.relate.com/
- **Twitter**: @rickzanotti
- **Facebook**: rickzanotti
- **Google+**: rickzanotti
- **Shows**: Video netcasts
- **eLearnChat**: http://vimeo.com/channels/elearnchat
- **SchreckTeck**: http://vimeo.com/channels/schreckteck
- **RELATE**: http://vimeo.com/channels/relate

13
Finishing Touches and Publishing

With all the work that you did in previous chapters, your time in the post-production studio is almost over. There are just a couple of things left to be done before the project can finally be published.

Most of these final changes are options and features that you will set for the entire project. They include checking the spelling, entering the project metadata, choosing how the project starts and ends, and so on. The most important of these final changes is probably the creation of a skin in the Skin Editor. A Skin allows you to customize the Playback Controls bar and create the project's Table of Contents, among other things.

In the second part of this chapter, you will focus on the third and last step of the Captivate production process: publishing the project. Publishing is the process by which you make your Captivate projects available to the outside world. Most of the time, you'll publish your movies in the Adobe Flash format or in the HTML5 format, so that any student can enjoy the content of your online course across devices. However, Captivate can also publish the movie in many other formats, which you will also learn about.

In this chapter, you will perform the following actions:

- Check the spelling of the entire project
- Set the Start and End preferences of the movie
- Enter the project metadata to enhance the accessibility of the project
- Export the properties of a project and import them back into another project
- Customize the project Skin
- Add a Table of Contents

- Show and hide slides
- Publish the project in various formats
- Publish a SCORM package
- Use the Multi-SCORM Packager
- Convert your HTML5 project into a native application using the PhoneGap Build service

At the end of this chapter, your work as an eLearning developer will be finished and your content will be ready to be pushed online.

> **Preparing your work**
>
> Before getting started with this chapter, take some time to reset the Captivate interface to default. If you are using the default interface mode, just close and restart Captivate. If you use the advanced interface mode, use the **Window | Workspace | Reset 'Classic'** menu item to reset Captivate to default. In this chapter, you will use the exercises stored in the Chapter13 folder of this book's companion files. If you get confused by any of the step-by-step instructions, take a look at the Chapter13/final folder, which contains a copy of the files as they will be at the end of this chapter. When publishing the projects, you will use the publish folder of the exercises. The publish/final folder contains the published versions of the files situated in the Chapter13/final folder.

Finishing touches

With the completion of *Chapter 12, Working with Variables, Advanced Actions, and Widgets*, your projects are complete. There are, however, a few more things to do before the projects can be published. In this section, you will focus on these small finishing touches.

Checking the spelling

Checking the spelling is probably one of the most fundamental finishing touches. After all, you are a teacher and teachers know how to write with no mistakes. The Captivate Spell Checker works like any other Spell Checker found in any other text-authoring application.

In Captivate, the Spell Checker has the ability to check the text typed in various locations throughout the project. This includes the text typed in Text Captions, Smart Shapes, Slide Notes, Text Animations, Buttons, and the Table of Contents.

Before using the Spell Checker feature, take a quick look at the options using the following steps:

1. Open the `Chapter13/encoderDemo_800.cptx` project.

2. Open the **Preferences** dialog of Captivate by using the **Edit | Preferences** menu item (for Windows) or the **Adobe Captivate | Preferences** menu item (for Mac).

3. On the left-hand side of the **Preferences** dialog, click on the **General Settings** category.

4. Click on the **Spelling Preferences...** button to open the **Spelling Options** dialog, as shown in the following screenshot:

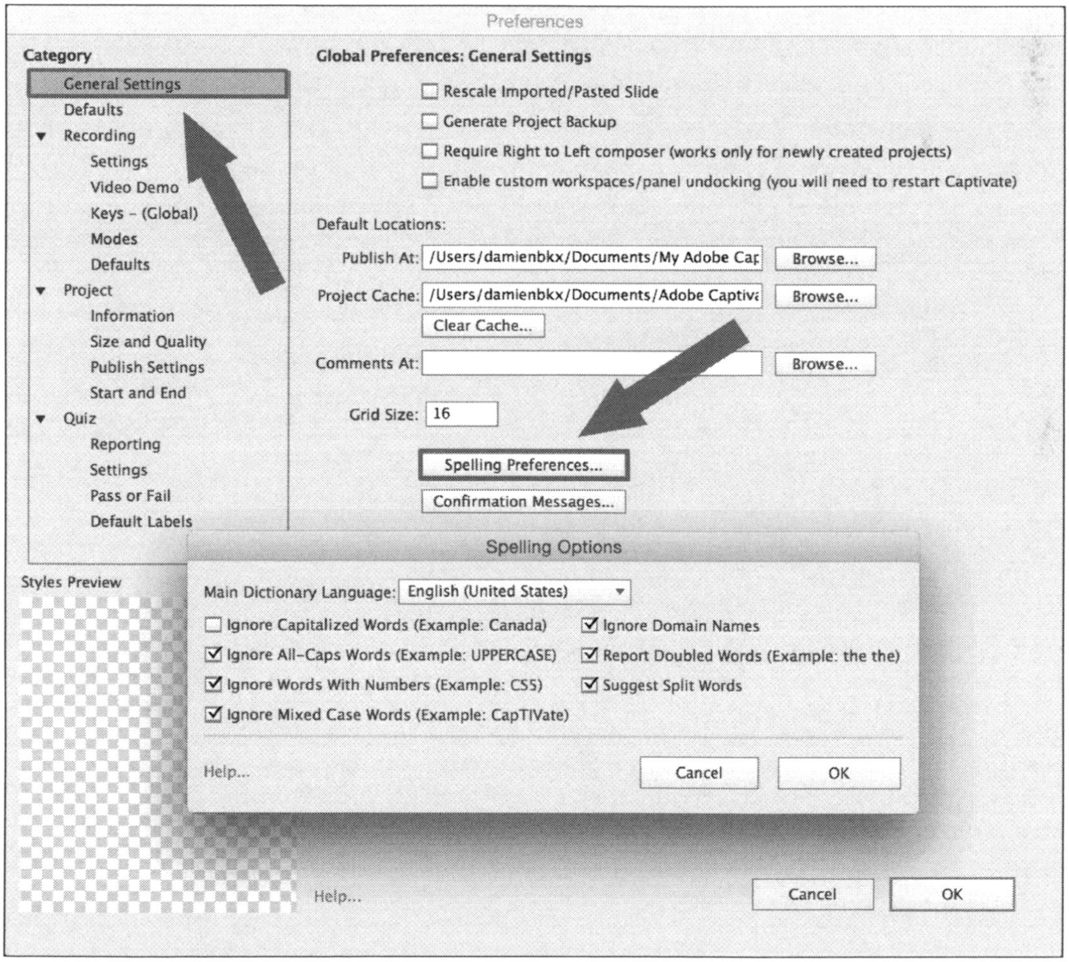

The main option of this box is **Main Dictionary Language**. By default, most the checkboxes of the **Spelling Options** dialog box are selected.

5. Open the **Main Dictionary Language** drop-down list and take some time to inspect the available languages. Is yours in the list?

6. For this exercise, make sure you choose **English (United States)** as the **Main Dictionary Language**.

7. Take some time to inspect the other dialog box options. They should be pretty much self-explanatory. Make sure they are all selected before moving on.

8. Click on the **OK** button to close the **Spelling Options** dialog, and then click on **OK** to validate the changes and close the **Preferences** dialog.

Now that you have a better idea of the available Spell Checker options, you will use this feature to check the spelling of the Encoder Demonstration.

9. Use the **Project | Check Spelling...** menu item (or press the *F7* shortcut key) to launch the Spell Checker.

Some spelling errors have been left behind in this project. Each time a spelling mistake is found, the Spell Checker stops and proposes replacement words. Let the Spell Checker go through the whole project and handle each spelling mistake; they are detected using the dialog shown in the following screenshot:

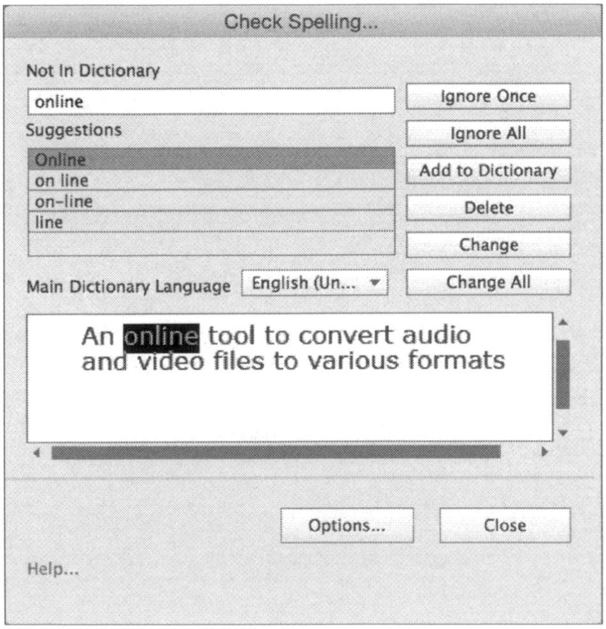

There are two important buttons at the end of the **Check Spelling** window.

10. Click on the **Options...** button at the end of the **Check Spelling...** dialog.

The same **Spelling Options** dialog you accessed through the **Preferences** dialog opens.

11. Leave all **Spelling Options** to their current settings and click on **OK** to close the **Spelling Options** dialog.
12. Click on the **Help...** link in the bottom-left corner of the **Check Spelling...** dialog.

This **Help...** link can be found in the bottom-left corner of several dialog boxes throughout Captivate. It opens the default browser and displays the **Adobe Captivate Help** page that explains the options of the current dialog box. The **Help...** link is an easy and fast way to access specific help content.

13. Take some time to review the help page. When done, close your browser and return to Captivate.

When the spell-check is over, a box informs you that the check is complete and that a certain number of corrections have been made (in my case, four errors were corrected).

14. Click on the **OK** button to discard the information box.
15. Make sure you save the file before moving on.

With the spell-check completed, the final phase of the post-production process is now underway. Checking the spelling in Captivate is as easy as checking the spelling in any other text-authoring application. Just remember that it is an essential part of any professional eLearning project.

Here is a quick summary of what has been covered in this section:

- Captivate contains a Spell Checker that works in the same way as any other Spell Checker found in virtually every text-authoring application.
- The Spell Checker of Captivate has the ability to check the spelling of all the text typed throughout the application. This includes the text typed in Text Captions, Slide Notes, Text Animations, Buttons, and the Table of Contents.
- The **Spelling Options** can be accessed through the **Preferences** dialog or directly from the **Check Spelling** dialog.
- The **Help...** link found in the bottom-left corner of many dialog boxes opens the default browser and displays the help page specifically dedicated to that dialog box. It is a quick and easy way to access specific help content.
- Checking the spelling is an essential part of any professional eLearning project.

Exploring the Start and End preferences

Another final touch you will focus on will let you decide how the movie should start and how it should end. This is very important to fine-tune a student's experience and to optimize the performance of the project when viewed over the Internet.

In the following exercise, you will explore the available Start and End preferences using the following steps:

1. If needed, return to the `Chapter13/encoderDemo_800.cptx` file.

2. Use the **Edit | Preferences** (for Windows) menu item or the **Adobe Captivate | Preferences** menu item (for Mac) to open the **Preferences** dialog.

3. On the left-hand side of the **Preferences** dialog, select the **Start and End** category situated in the **Project** section.

The preferences pertaining to the **Project** section of the **Preferences** dialog are specific to the current project only. Your screen should now display the dialog shown in the following screenshot:

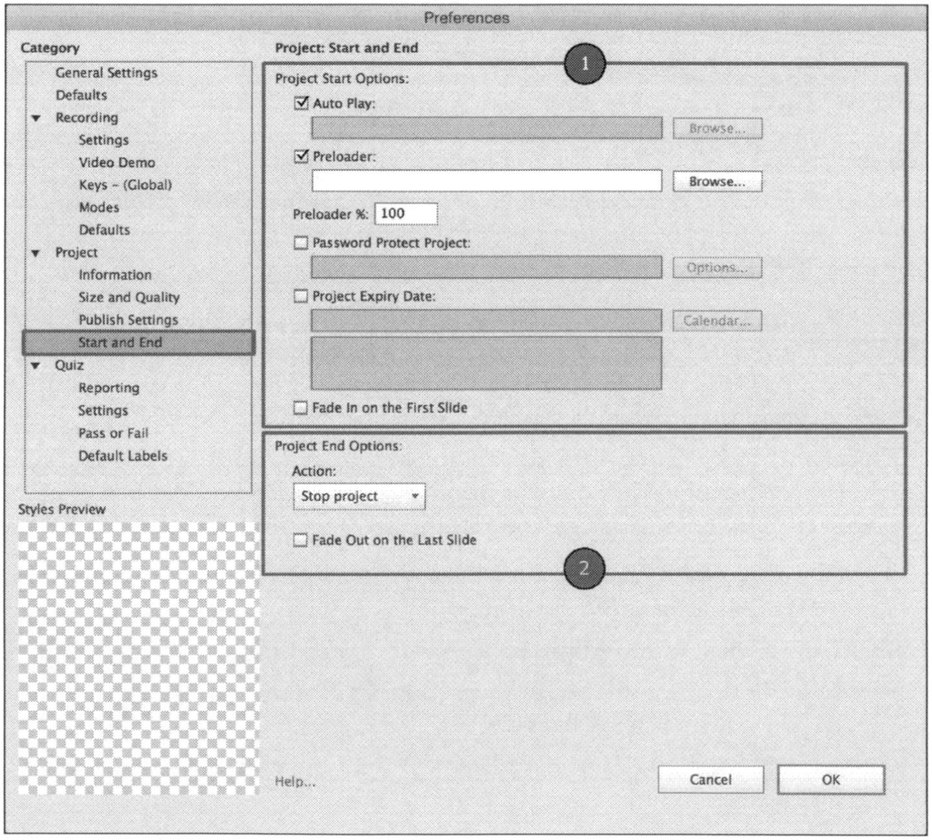

The **Start and End** preference page is divided into two sections. The **Project Start Options** section, shown as (**1**) in the previous screenshot, is in the top-half of the page. At the end of the page, you have the **Project End Options** section, shown as (**2**) in the previous screenshot.

The following options are available under the **Project Start** section:

- **Auto Play**: If this option is selected, the project will start playing as soon as it finishes loading. If it is not selected, the student has to click on the **Play** button to view the project. In that case, you can use the **Browse** button to choose a static image that is displayed until the student clicks on the **Play** button (such an image is often called a poster image).

- **Preloader**: The **Preloader** checkbox is an image or a Flash Animation (.swf) that is displayed while the movie is loading. If **Preloader** is selected and no preloader file is supplied, Captivate uses its default preloader; you can also create your own custom preloader or choose one from the gallery.

- **Preloader %**: To me, this is the most important option of this **Preferences** pane. It represents the percentage of the file that has to be downloaded before the movie starts playing. If set to 50 percent, it means that the movie will start playing when 50 percent of the entire file is downloaded. The remaining 50 percent will be loaded while the beginning of the movie is being played. Use this option when the project is large and contains lots of audio or video. It reduces waiting time for the student, which provides a much smoother learning experience.

> Kevin Siegel gives you more details about the **Preloader** and **Preloader %** options. Here is an interesting blog post from the Iconlogic's blog: http://iconlogic.blogs.com/weblog/2014/05/adobe-captivate-preloaders.html.

- **Password Protect Project**: This option is self-explanatory. Share the password only with those individuals who should be granted access to the project. Use this option if the project contains confidential information or if you want to share a beta release of the project with a limited team of reviewers.

- **Project Expiry Date**: Use this option to set an expiry date for the project. The project will not be accessible if a student wants to access it after the expiry date.

- **Fade In on First Slide**: This option is turned on by default and provides a smoother transition when the student enters the course.

The following options are available under the **Project End Options** section:

- **Action**: The **Action** drop-down list is used to select an action that is fired when the project is complete. By default, the **Stop project** action is selected.

- **Fade Out on Last Slide**: This option is turned on by default.

Now that you have had an in-depth overview of the available options, you can set the **Start and End** preferences of this particular project.

4. Set the **Preloader** % option to 50.

This particular movie contains a lot of sound, and sound takes a lot of time to download. With the **Preloader** % option set to 50, the time spent by a student waiting for the movie to download is divided by two.

5. Leave the remaining options with their default settings and click on **OK**.

6. Don't forget to save the file when done.

This concludes your overview of the **Start and End** preferences. Let's create a quick list of what you have learned so far:

- In the **Preferences** dialog, the pages pertaining to the **Project** section are specific to the current project only

- In the **Start and End** category, Captivate exposes options and features to let you decide how the project should start and what happens when it has finished playing

- Use these options to enhance the user experience, enforce some basic security, and optimize the loading time of the movie

Using the project metadata and accessibility

Metadata is data about data. In the Captivate files you are creating, the main data consists of the slides and all the objects and features that make up the project. Metadata is information such as the slide count, the author of the project, the description of the project, the resolution, and so on. All this information is data about data or, to use the proper word, metadata.

Some of this metadata (such as the slide count, the resolution, the length, and so on) is automatically generated by Captivate, while other metadata has to be manually entered.

Metadata is essential if you want to create accessible projects. An accessible project is a project that can be accessed by people with disabilities. There are many things that you can do in a Captivate project to make it accessible. One of those things is to take the time to enter the metadata. This metadata is used by assistive devices of those with disabilities (devices such as Braille readers, screen readers, Text-To-Speech utilities, and so on) to provide the best possible learning experience to these students.

> **Section 508**
>
> Many countries around the world have adopted some kind of accessibility standards, rules, and even laws. Most of the time, these standards are based on the **Web Accessibility Initiative (WAI)**, a document developed by the **World Wide Web Consortium (W3C)** (visit www.w3.org/WAI for more information). In U.S. legislation, these standards are implemented as an amendment to the U.S. Rehabilitation Act of 1973. This amendment is commonly known as Section 508. When a project is 508-compliant, it simply means that it complies with the accessibility requirements of this legal document.

In the following exercise, you will take the first step toward making this project accessible by using the **Project Info** dialog to enter the metadata of the project, using the following steps:

1. Return to the `Chapter13/encoderDemo_800.cptx` file.

2. Use the **Edit | Preferences** (for Windows) or **Adobe Captivate | Preferences** (for Mac) menu item to open the **Preferences** dialog.

3. On the left-hand side of the **Preferences** dialog, click on the **Information** category situated in the **Project** section.

The upper section of the **Project Information** preferences is used to manually enter the missing metadata, while the bottom section displays the automatically generated metadata. These display the estimated **Time**, the **Resolution**, the number of **Slides**, and the number of **Hidden Slides**.

4. Type `My Fictional Training Company-MFTC` in the **Company** field.

5. Type `2015-MFTC` in the **Copyright** field.

6. Enter `Adobe Media Encoder - Demonstration` in the **Project Name** field.

7. Type `This project shows the students how to use the Adobe Media Encoder to convert a Quick Time movie into Flash Video` in the **Description** field.

8. Fill the remaining fields (**Author**, **Email**, and **Website**) with your own name, e-mail address, and website URL. Note that none of these fields are mandatory. If you do not have a website, just leave the field blank.

Your screen should now look like the following screenshot:

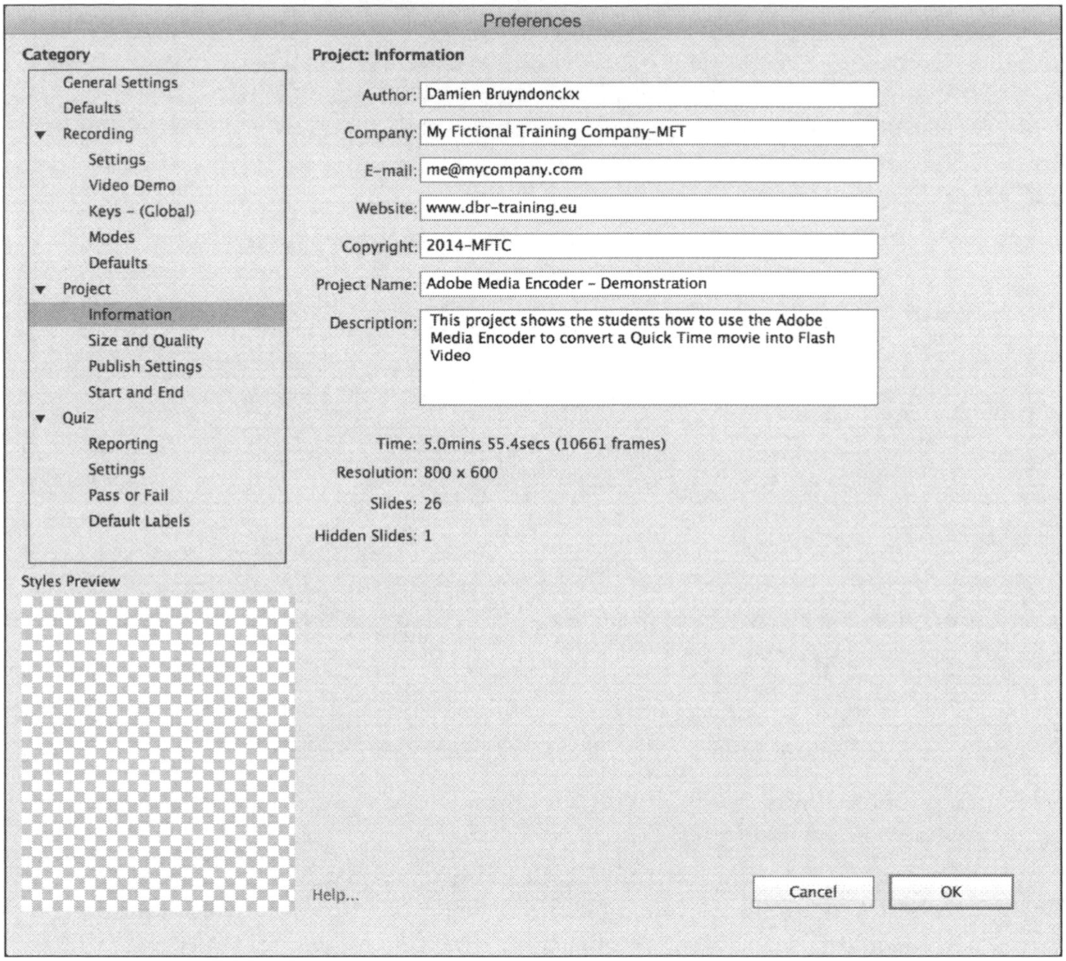

9. Click on the **OK** button when done to close the **Preferences** dialog.

Back in the main Captivate interface, the **Project Info** panel gives you easy access to some of this metadata.

10. Use the **Window | Project** info menu item to open the **Project Info** panel.

11. The **Project Info** panel opens and displays the automatically generated metadata.

The **Project Info** panel only displays some of the metadata. It cannot be used to create new metadata or modify the existing metadata.

> **Testing the size of the published project before publishing**
>
> The Captivate 8.0.1 update has introduced an interesting feature in the **Project** panel. This feature allows you to control the size of the published project without actually publishing it. Use the **Check** links associated with the **Size (HTML)** and **Size (Swf)** labels to test the size of the published projects.

By entering the project metadata, you have taken the first important step toward making the project 508-compliant. This is a very good point, but there is a lot more that can be done throughout Captivate to further enhance the accessibility of the project. For example, you can add accessibility text to each individual slide using the **Properties** panel. There are some great blog posts on this subject as well as some very interesting pages in the official Captivate documentation:

- The accessibility page from the official Captivate documentation is available at `http://help.adobe.com/en_US/captivate/cp/using/WSc1b83f70210cd1011d7107e311c7efcf707-8000.html`

- The Captivate Accessibility overview page on the Adobe website is available at `http://www.adobe.com/accessibility/products/captivate/overview.html`

This concludes our little discussion on project accessibility and metadata. Here is a quick summary of what has been covered:

- Metadata is data about data.

- Metadata is essential to make projects accessible.

- Captivate automatically generates some of the metadata, while other metadata has to be entered manually.

- An accessible project is a project that can be accessed in good conditions by people with disabilities. These particular students use some specific input and output devices (such as Braille readers, text-to-speech utilities, and so on). These devices work better if you take the time to enter some extra metadata in your projects.

- The accessibility guidelines and standards are commonly known as Section 508, in reference to an amendment to the U.S. Rehabilitation Act of 1973.

- For some institutions, creating projects that comply with Section 508 is required by law. Check with your legal department.

- Use the **Project Information** preferences to manually enter the project metadata.

Exploring other project preferences

There are some more project preferences available in Captivate that are good to explore before publishing. Most of the time, the default settings for these particular options work just fine, so you won't modify any of these options in the Encoder Demonstration project.

In the following exercises, you will simply take a look at these preferences and briefly discuss some of them:

1. Return to the `Chapter13/encoderDemo_800.cptx` file.

2. Use the **Edit | Preferences** menu item (for Windows) or the **Adobe Captivate | Preferences** menu item (for Mac) to open the **Preferences** dialog.

3. Open the **Size and Quality** category situated in the **Project** section.

This particular **Preferences** page provides options to control how the Captivate project is converted into Flash or HTML5 upon publication. If you want more information about any one of these options, don't hesitate to click on the **Help...** link in the bottom-left corner of the **Preferences** dialog.

4. Click on the **Publish Settings** category situated in the **Project** section in the left column of the **Preferences** dialog.

This **Preferences** page displays additional options about how the project will be converted to Flash or HTML5. Once again, the default options work just fine for the vast majority of the project. We will briefly discuss some of these options:

- **Frames Per Second**: Use this option if you want to embed your Captivate project in another Flash project that has a different frame rate to 30 frames per second, or if you want to insert a video in your project that was created with a different FPS value. Otherwise, leave this option with its default value of 30 fps.

- **Publish Adobe Connect metadata**: This option adds some metadata to the project, thus producing a slightly larger file. This metadata is designed to facilitate the integration of the Captivate project in Adobe Connect. If you do not have access to an Adobe Connect server, there is no point in turning this option on.

> See this great blog post by Michael Lund (also known as the Captivate Guru) about how the Adobe Connect metadata affects the size of the resulting file: `http://www.cpguru.com/2008/12/30/reducing-the-file-size-of-your-captivate-projects/`.

- **Enable Accessibility**: This option also adds extra information to the Captivate project, but it also makes the project 508-compliant. If this option is not selected, the accessibility options set throughout the project are useless.

- **Externalize Resources**: When publishing to Flash, Captivate produces a single SWF file containing the whole project by default. Consequently, this file can be very large and hard to download for the students. Externalizing resources tells Captivate to generate many smaller SWF files that reference each other. This option may help in optimizing the download time of a large project, but it makes it more difficult to push the Captivate project online once published. Note that some assets (such as the inserted video files) are always externalized. Also, note that, when publishing to HTML5, all the resources are always externalized.

Other options on the **Preferences** page should be self explanatory. Don't hesitate to click on the **Help...** link if you need more information.

5. Click on the **Cancel** button to close the **Preferences** dialog and discard the changes you've made along the way.

This concludes the tour of project preferences. You will now export the preferences of this project and import them into another project.

Exporting project preferences

Remember that the options pertaining to the **Project** section of the **Preferences** dialog are specific to the current project only.

If you want to apply the very same set of **Preferences** to another project, Captivate lets you export the preferences of the current project and reimport them into another project. In the following exercise, you will export the preferences of the Encoder Demonstration and apply them to the Encoder simulation:

1. Return to the `Chapter13/encoderDemo_800.cptx` file.
2. Use the **File | Export | Preferences...** menu item to export the preferences of the demonstration.
3. Save the preferences file as `Chapter13/encoderDemo_800_Preferences. cpr`. It should be the default name proposed by Captivate.
4. Click on **OK** to acknowledge the information box telling you that the export has been successful.

Note that the file extension of such a preference file is `.cpr`. You will now open the simulation and import the preferences of the demonstration. At the end of this process, both files will share the exact same project preferences.

5. Open the `Chapter13/encoderSim_800.cptx` file.

This is the simulation you created back in *Chapter 6, Working with Interactive Objects*. The only difference is that I've applied to this project the Theme that you developed in *Chapter 7, Working with Styles, Master Slides, Themes, and Templates*.

6. Use the **File | Import | Preferences** menu item to import a preference file in the project.

7. Browse to the `encoderDemo_800_Preferences.cpr` file that you created earlier in this exercise and click on **Open**.

After a short while, an information box should appear on the screen telling you that the preferences were successfully imported.

8. Click on **OK** to discard the information box.

9. Use the **Edit | Preferences** (for Windows) menu item or **Adobe Captivate | Preferences** (for Mac) menu item to open the **Preferences** dialog of the `encoderSim_800.cptx` file.

10. Open the **Information** category situated in the **Project** section of the **Preferences** dialog.

The same metadata you entered in the Encoder Demonstration should have been applied to the simulation.

11. Change the **Project Name** field to `Adobe Media Encoder - Simulation`.

12. Change the project's **Description** field to `This project guides the student in using the Adobe Media Encoder to convert a QuickTime movie into Flash Video`.

13. Leave the other metadata with current values, click on **OK** to validate the changes, and close the **Preferences** dialog.

14. Use the **File | Save All** menu item to save both the Encoder Demonstration and the Encoder simulation in one action.

Here is a quick summary of what you have learned about the remaining project preferences:

- Most of the time, the default settings of the **SWF Size and Quality** and **Publish Settings** pages of the **Preferences** dialog work just fine.

- These settings help you control the size of the published Flash or HTML5 application and optimize the download time of the project. On the other hand, they can be quite technical and require some knowledge of Flash and HTML to be used with full efficiency.

- It is possible to export the preferences of one project and import them back into another project.

> **The Preferences and the templates**
>
> 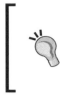 Templates offer another convenient way to share preferences and metadata across projects. Remember that the preferences defined on a template become the default preferences of all the future projects based on this template.

Customizing the project Skin

The Skin of a project is a collection of elements that are, for the most part, displayed around the slides. It means that the elements of the Skin are not part of the actual eLearning content. Learners use them to interact with the Captivate content, which enhances the overall user experience. A Skin is made up of the following three elements:

- **The Playback Controls bar**: This is the most visible element of the Skin. It contains the necessary buttons and switches used by the student to control the playback of the course. It also contains a progress bar that tracks the student's progress in the Captivate project.

- **The Borders**: The Skin Editor lets you create Borders around your projects. You can turn each of the four Borders on and/or off and choose their width, color, and texture.

- **The Table of Contents**: This is the last element of a Skin. By default, it is turned off, but it is very easy to turn it on and generate a Table of Contents for the project.

By default, Captivate contains a handful of predefined Skins that you can apply as is to your projects for rapid development. However, you also have the option of customizing any of the existing Skins and saving it with your own unique Skin name.

Also, remember that the Skin is the third element of a Theme. The other two elements are the Styles and the Master Slides. This has already been covered in *Chapter 7, Working with Styles, Master Slides, Themes, and Templates*.

In this section, each of the three elements of the Skin will be discussed one by one. While doing so, you will slowly create a unique Skin design that you will save and apply to other projects. Some more features of Captivate will be uncovered along the way.

Customizing the Playback Controls bar

The first and most visible element of the Skin is the Playback Controls bar. By default, it appears below the project and contains the necessary buttons and switches to let the student control the playback of the project.

In the following exercise, you will explore the available options and create a customized Playback Controls bar for your projects:

1. Return to the `Chapter13/encoderSim_800.cptx` file.

2. Use the **Project | Skin Editor** menu item to open the **Skin Editor** floating pane.

The **Skin Editor** floating pane should look similar to what is shown in the following screenshot:

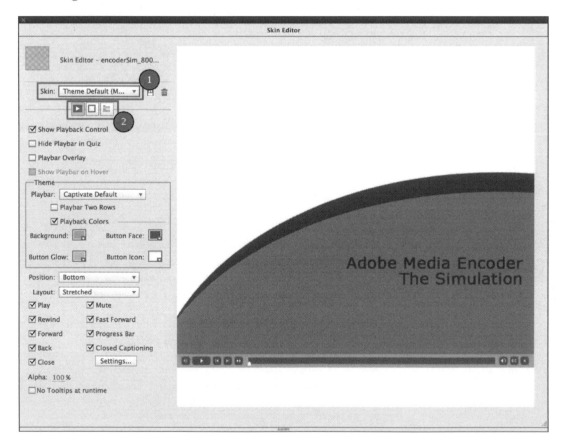

The **Skin Editor** floating pane is divided into two main areas. On the left-hand side, are the switches, boxes, and buttons you will use to customize the various elements of the Skin. On the right-hand side, there is a live preview of the first slide of the project. This area of the **Skin Editor** is automatically updated as you turn the options of the left area on and off.

In the upper-left area of the **Skin Editor** floating pane, notice two important controls. The **Skin** drop-down list (marked as (**1**) on the previous screenshot) is used to choose and apply one of the predefined Captivate Skins to the project. Then, there are three icons (marked as (**2**) in the preceding screenshot). Each of them represents one of the elements of the Skin: the Playback Control, the Borders, and the Table of Contents.

3. Open the **Skin** drop-down list and choose any Skin you want.

4. The chosen Skin is applied to the project and the preview area of the **Skin Editor** is updated.

5. Open the **Skin** drop-down list again and reapply the **Theme Default** Skin to the project.

The **Theme Default** Skin is the one that is stored in the Theme applied to the project. As you can see, the colors of the Theme Default skin are yet to be defined after the look and feel of the project.

6. Click on the **Background Color** feature in the **Theme** section of the left bar.

7. Click on the eye dropper icon situated in the top-right corner of the color chooser.

8. Take a close look at your mouse pointer. It should look like an eyedropper. With this pointer active, click anywhere on the brown background where the **Adobe Media Encoder – The Demonstration** title is located.

The eyedropper tool takes the color of the pixel you click on and applies it to the **Background Color** property of the Playback Controls bar. This tool is an incredibly fast and easy way to make two different elements share the same color.

9. Customize the other colors of the Playback Controls bar to your taste.

 Remember that the Swatches Manager offers the ability to import a custom set of color swatches into the project. Don't hesitate to use this ability to choose the colors of the Playback Controls and give them the same look and feel as the rest of the project.

You will now remove the Playback Controls bar and see how the Skin updates.

10. Deselect the **Show Playback Control** checkbox.

When the preview updates, notice that the Playback Controls are no longer displayed and that a border appears at the bottom of the project where the Playback Controls bar used to be. This is shown in the following screenshot:

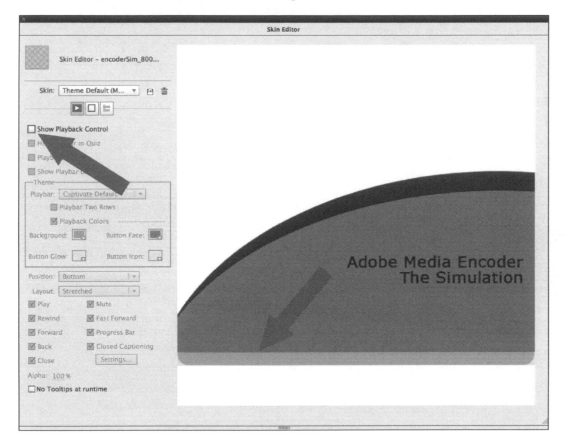

This is very interesting and deserves further investigation.

By default, when a Playback Controls bar is applied, a bottom border that has the same width as the Playback Controls bar is also automatically applied to the project. The idea is to put the Playback Controls bar on top of that bottom border so that it does not overlap with the content. This is a very good thing and it works just fine most of the time. That being said, this system increases the overall height of the project. If you remember the discussion we had in *Chapter 2, Capturing the Slides*, about the resolution of the movie, this can be quite a problem in some situations.

You will now set the Skin so that the Playback Controls are displayed without adding a single pixel to the height of the movie.

11. Select the **Show Playback Control** checkbox to turn the Playback Controls back on.

12. Select the **Playbar Overlay** checkbox below **Show Playback Control**.

In the preview area of the **Skin Editor**, you should see that the Playback Controls bar now overlaps with the slide. Now, let's turn off the border.

13. Click on the **Borders** icon. It is the second of the three icons situated just below the **Skin** drop-down list.

14. Deselect the **Show Border** checkbox.

This is how you can accommodate Playback Controls without adding a single pixel to the height of the movie. The benefit is that the height of the project, as defined in *Chapter 2, Capturing the Slides*, is now respected. The disadvantage is that the Playback Controls could now sit on top of some important information displayed at the bottom of the slides.

15. Close the **Skin Editor** floating pane.

16. Use the **Preview | Next 5 Slides** icon of the Big Buttons Bar to test the new Playback Controls configuration.

17. When the preview is over, close the **Preview** pane.

In this example, you want the Playback Controls to be situated outside of the actual eLearning content. You will now return to the **Skin Editor** floating pane to revert your latest changes before further exploring the other available options.

18. Use the **Project | Skin Editor** menu item to reopen the floating **Skin Editor** pane.

19. Deselect the **Playbar Overlay** checkbox.

20. Deselect the **Rewind, Forward, Back, Close,** and **Fast Forward** checkboxes.

21. Make sure the **Play, Mute, Progress Bar,** and **Closed Captioning** checkboxes are selected.

After this operation, the Playback Controls bar should contain only three buttons along with the Progress bar. You will now change the settings for the Closed Caption.

22. Click on the **Settings** button below the **Closed Captioning** checkbox.

23. In the **CC Project Settings** dialog, choose the **Verdana** font family and change the font's **Size** value to 14 and the value of the number of **Lines** to 2.

24. Click on the **OK** button to close the **CC Project Settings** dialog.

25. Take some time to inspect the remaining options of the Playback Controls bar. Make sure you do not change any of them before moving on to the next step.

With the completion of this exercise, you can consider the Playback Controls bar as final. Let's give it a try by using the **Preview** pane.

26. Close the floating **Skin Editor** pane.

27. Use the **Preview | Project** icon of the Big Buttons Bar to preview the entire project.

When the course starts to play, take a look at the Playback Controls bar situated below the project. It contains three buttons and the progress bar as specified in the **Skin Editor** floating pane during the preceding exercise. Don't hesitate to click on the **CC** button to have a look at the changes you made in the **CC Project Settings** dialog.

28. Close the **Preview** pane.

In the next section, you will discover the second element of a Captivate Skin: Borders.

Working with Borders

Borders are the second main element of a Captivate Skin. As discussed in the *Customizing the Playback Controls* section, adding a Playback Controls bar automatically adds a corresponding bottom border so that the Playback Controls do not overlap with the slide elements.

In the following exercise, you will further experiment with the Borders and discover some more properties:

1. While still in the encoderSim_800.cptx file, use the **Project | Skin Editor** menu item to return to the **Skin Editor** floating pane.

2. Click on the **Borders** icon situated right below the **Skin** drop-down list.

3. Select the **Show Borders** checkbox to turn the borders back on.

In the **Borders** tab of the **Skin Editor** floating pane, note that Bottom Borders is currently turned on, as shown in the following screenshot:

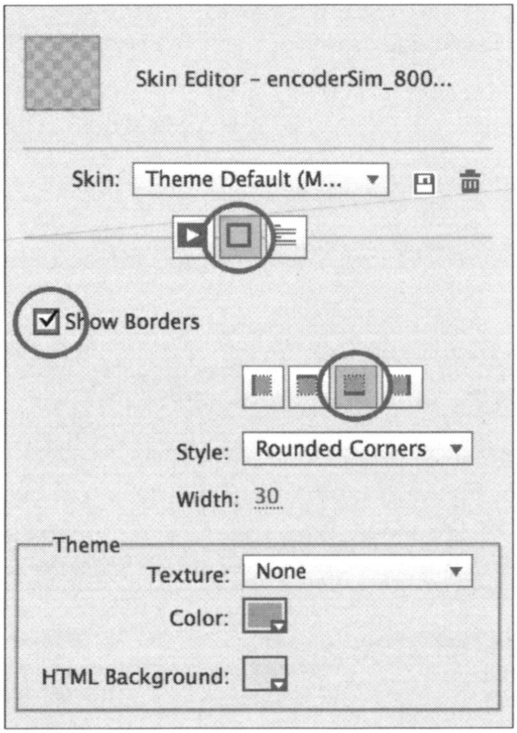

The bottom border is currently situated below the Playback Controls bar, which explains why you don't see it even if it is turned on. You will now turn all four borders on and explore the available formatting options.

4. Click on the left border, right border, and top border icons to turn the corresponding borders on.

5. In the **Style** drop-down list, choose the **Square Edge** style.

6. Click on the **Color** chooser. Use the eyedropper tool situated in the top-right corner of the color chooser to give your border the same light brown color as the background of the slide.

7. Open the **Texture** drop-down list and choose any texture you want.

8. Change the **Width** option of the borders to 80.

The previous steps illustrate the available Border options. You will now arrange these options to fit the particular needs of the Encoder simulation.

Let's start with the most obvious change to be made: turning off this awful texture! (I do not like textures. They make the project look like my grandmother's kitchen!)

9. Open the **Texture** drop-down list again and choose **None** at the very top of the list.

This action turns the **Texture** feature off. With the **Texture** option turned off, the brownish border reappears.

10. Turn the top, left, and right borders off. Leave only the bottom border on.

11. Reduce the **Width** option of the border to 30 pixels.

12. Close the floating **Skin Editor** pane and save the file.

With the completion of the preceding exercises, the first two elements of the Skin (Playback Controls and Borders) are now in place. In the next section, you will focus on the third and last element of the Skin: the Table of Contents.

Adding a Table of Contents

The Table of Contents is the third and last element of the Skin. By default, the Table of Contents is turned off.

In the following exercise, you will turn the Table of Contents on and explore the available options:

1. While still in the `Chapter13/encoderSim_800.cptx` file, use the **Project | Table of Contents...** menu item to open the **Skin Editor** floating pane on the **Table of Contents** page.

2. Click on the **Show TOC** checkbox to turn the Table of Contents on.

By default, the Table of Contents appears on the left-hand side of the project and lists every single slide. At this moment, the slides are named **Slide 1**, **Slide 2**, and so on. In the next section of this exercise, you will experiment with two ways of changing the names of the slides in the Table of Contents.

The first way is to change the name of the slide directly in the **Skin Editor** floating pane using the following steps:

3. Double-click on the **Slide 1** title below the **Show TOC** checkbox.
4. Change the name of the slide to Introduction and press the *Enter* key.

After a short while, the preview area displays the updated Table of Contents.

The second way of changing the slide name involves closing the **Skin Editor** floating pane and using the **Properties** panel of each slide to specify a slide label.

5. Close the floating **Skin Editor** panel.
6. Use the **Filmstrip** panel to select slide 2. Make sure the **Properties** panel shows the properties of the slide and not the properties of any of the slide elements.
7. At the top of the **Properties** panel, type Video Slide in the **Label** field.
8. Press *Enter* to validate the change.

When done, take another look at the **Filmstrip** panel. The slide label should be displayed below the corresponding thumbnail.

9. Use the same technique to enter a label for the other slides of the project.
   - For **Slide 3**, change the label to Simulation Instructions
   - For **Slide 4**, change the label to Beginning of the Simulation.
   - For **Slide 17**, change the label to Ending slide.
   - Leave the **Label** field of the other slides empty.

10. Use the **Project | Table of Content** menu item to reopen the **Skin Editor** floating pane on the **Table of Contents** page.

11. Click on the **Reset TOC** icon situated below the list of TOC entries, as shown in the following screenshot:

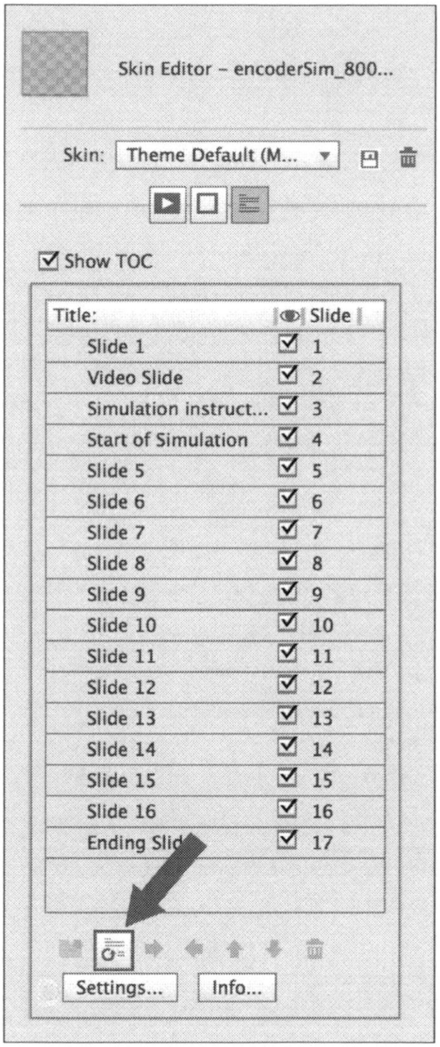

When clicking on this icon, Captivate inspects the slides of the project and regenerates the entries of the Table of Contents. Note that the slide label, if any, is used as the title of the corresponding TOC entry.

Also, note that there is no label for slide 1 now. This tells you that manually changing the name of the slide in the TOC editor does *not* add a corresponding label to the slide.

About slide labels

In the current exercise, you are using slide labels to generate the entries of the Table of Contents, but adding labels to slides serves many other purposes as well. First of all, it makes the project easier to use and maintain, but the main benefit of the slide label is probably the enhanced accessibility it provides. The slide label provides yet more metadata used by the assistive devices of those with disabilities and is mandatory to make the eLearning project 508-compliant.

You will now re-enter a name for slide 1 and hide the unnecessary slides from the Table of Contents.

12. In the **Skin Editor** floating pane, double-click on the **Slide 1** title in the list of TOC entries. Retype Introduction and press the *Enter* key.

13. Uncheck the visibility checkbox for slides 5 through 16.

In the preview area of the **Skin Editor** floating pane, the corresponding slides disappear from the Table of Contents. At this point, there should be only 5 slides mentioned in the Table of Contents.

You will now finalize the look and feel of the Table of Contents.

14. Click on the **Info...** button situated at the bottom of the **Skin Editor** floating pane, just below the list of TOC entries. The **TOC Information** dialog opens.

15. In the **TOC Information** dialog, click on the **Project Information** button.

This last action copies the available project metadata to the corresponding fields of the **TOC Information** box.

16. Type Adobe Media Encoder - Simulation in the **Title** field of the **TOC Information** dialog.

17. At the bottom of the **TOC Information** dialog, change the font to **Verdana**. Also, change the font color to one of the colors defined in your theme.

18. Click on the **OK** button to validate your choices and close the **TOC Information** dialog.

At this point, the Table of Contents is almost ready. One of the remaining problems is the extra space the Table of Contents requires to display properly. To address this problem, you will ask Captivate to position the Table of Contents on top of the slide and to provide a way to toggle its visibility on and off.

19. Click on the **Settings...** button situated at the bottom of the **Skin Editor** floating pane, below the list of TOC entries.

20. At the top of the **TOC Settings** dialog, change the **Style** option to **Overlay**.

21. In the **Color** section, click on the **Background** color and use the dropper tool to apply the same brownish color as the one used on the slide itself.

22. Use the same technique to customize the other colors of the Table of Contents to your taste.

23. Change the **Alpha** value to **65** % to create a semitransparent Table of Contents.

24. Take some time to explore the other available options and feel free to modify them at will. When done, your screen should look similar to what is shown in the following screenshot:

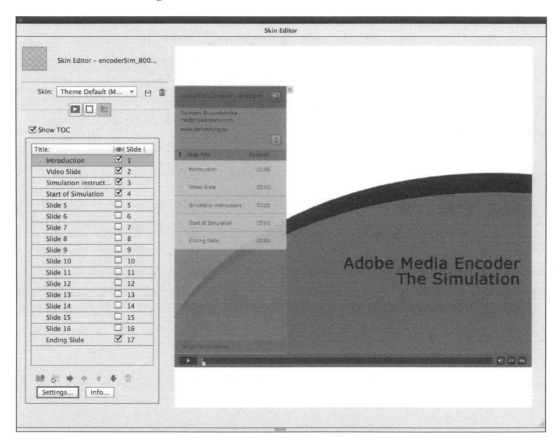

25. When you are happy with your Table of Contents, click on **OK** to validate your choices and close the **TOC Settings** dialog.

26. Close the **Skin Editor** floating pane and save the file.

Your Table of Contents is now ready. It is time to give it a try in the **Preview** pane.

27. Use the **Preview | Project** icon of the Big Buttons Bar to preview the entire project.

28. When the **Preview** pane opens, click on the small double-arrow in the top-left corner of the slide to reveal the Table of Contents.

29. Click on the same icon to turn off the Table of Contents.

Notice the new **TOC** button at the right edge of the Playback Controls bar.

30. Click on the **TOC** icon situated at the right edge of the Playback Controls bar to reveal the Table of Contents.

31. Click on the **TOC** icon again to turn off the visibility of the Table of Contents.

32. Close the **Preview** pane and save the file.

With the addition of the Table of Contents, the Skin of your project is now final. It looks so great (no kidding!) that you want to apply it to other projects you are working on.

Applying the same Skin to other projects

To create the Skin of the Encoder simulation, you started from the **Theme Default** Skin and you customized it. In this section, you will make the current Skin the **Theme Default** Skin, save the Theme, and apply it to other projects using the following steps:

1. While still in the `encoderSim_800.cptx` file, use the **Project | Skin Editor** menu item to reopen the floating **Skin Editor** pane.

The **Skin** dropdown indicates that the **Theme Default (Modified)** Skin is currently in use.

2. Click on the **Save As** icon next to the **Skin** drop-down list.

3. In the **Save As** box that pops up, leave the **Theme Default** name as it is and click on **OK**.

4. Confirm that you want to replace the existing **Theme Default** Skin with a new one.

5. Close the **Skin Editor** floating pane.

The new Skin is now saved as the Default Skin of the applied Theme. You will now save the Theme in a new file and apply that theme to the Encoder Demonstration.

6. Use the **Theme | Save Theme As** menu item to save the current theme as a new file.

7. Save the Theme in your exercise folder as `themes/mftc_theme_final_800.cptm`.

8. Switch to (or open) the `Chapter13/encoderDemo_800.cptx` file.

9. When in the demonstration project, click on the **Themes** icon of the Big Buttons Bar to open the Themes picker.

10. Click on the **Browse** link situated at the bottom left corner of the Themes selector.

11. Apply the `themes/mftc_theme_final_800.cptm` theme that you created earlier in this exercise to the current project.

12. Click on **Yes** to confirm that you want to apply the new theme to the demonstration.

13. Go through the slides of your project as some styles and Master Slides must be reapplied after applying the theme to the project

Both your demonstration and your simulation now share the very same theme. It means that they share the same set of Styles, the same Master Slides, and the very same Skin.

14. Use the **Project | Skin** menu item to open the **Skin Editor** of the `Chapter13/encoderDemo_800.cptx` file.

On the **Playback Controls** page of the **Skin Editor** floating pane, note that some of the checkboxes are not available. This is due to the presence of a pretest in this project. When a pretest is present in the project, most of the controls of the Playback Controls Bar cannot be turned on. That being said, all the other properties of the Playback Controls bar (such as colors) are derived from the theme and are the same as in the simulation file.

15. Click on the **TOC** icon situated below the **Skin** drop-down menu to jump to the **TOC** page of the Skin.

16. Click on the **Show TOC** checkbox to turn the TOC on.

By default, the Table of Contents is not activated. When turned on, note that the TOC has the exact same look and feel as in the Simulation project.

17. Deselect the **Show TOC** checkbox to turn the TOC off.

18. Close the floating **Skin Editor** panel.

19. Save the file when done.

Applying this Skin to future projects

If you want to apply this Skin by default to future projects, one of the possible approaches is to apply the theme that contains the Skin to a Captivate Template (a .cptl file). All Captivate Projects made from that template would therefore inherit the Skin applied to that template.

Here is a quick summary of what has been covered in the Skin Editor section of this chapter:

- A Skin is a collection of three elements: Playback Controls, Borders, and a Table of Contents.
- By default, adding a Playback Controls bar to the project automatically adds a corresponding border. The idea is to place the Playback Controls on top of the border to avoid overlapping between the Playback Controls bar and the project.
- You can customize the Playback Controls bar in many ways using the Skin Editor panel.
- You can also turn the Borders on and off, change their width, their color, or their texture.
- By default, the Table of Contents is turned off.
- It is possible to add labels to the slides. Slide labels serve many purposes. For example, they make it easier for the developer to work with the project, they provide enhanced accessibility, and they are used to automatically generate the TOC.
- The **Skin Editor** floating pane provides many options to fine-tune the Table of Contents.
- Captivate contains default predefined Skins for rapid development.
- When you modify one of the predefined Skins, you actually create a new Skin that can be saved and reapplied to another project.
- The Skin of a project is one of the elements of the applied Theme. All the projects that have the same Theme inherit the same Skin.

Now that all *finishing touches* have been taken care of, you will move on to the final phase of the general Captivate production workflow and make your eLearning content available to the outside world.

Publishing a Captivate project

So far, you have been working with .cptx files, which is the default native file type of Captivate. The .cptx file format is great for creating and designing projects, but it has two major disadvantages:

- It can become very large. Consequently, it is difficult for you to upload the file to a website and for the student to download and view it.

- Opening a .cptx file requires that Captivate is installed on the computer system.

Publishing a Captivate movie is converting (the proper word is *compiling*) the .cptx file into a format that can be easily deployed on a web server (or on a LMS), downloaded and viewed by the students.

The primary format used to publish your projects is the .swf format. **SWF** (pronounced *swiff*) stands for **Shockwave Flash**. It is the file format used by the free Adobe Flash player plugin installed on more than 98 percent of computers connected to the Internet. It has two advantages over the .cptx file:

- A .swf file is usually much lighter than its .cptx counterpart making it much easier to upload and download across the Internet.

- Any browser equipped with the free Adobe Flash plugin is able to open and play the .swf file. This makes it incredibly easy to deploy the courses made by Captivate.

That being said, the .swf format has some major disadvantages on its own:

- It requires the Adobe Flash Player plugin to be installed. If, for whatever reason, the plugin is not available, the .swf file cannot be played back.

- It cannot be modified. To modify a .swf file, you need to reopen the corresponding .cptx file, modify it in Captivate, and publish another version of the .swf file.

- The Flash Player plugin is no longer available on mobile devices. Consequently, a .swf file cannot be played back on a smartphone or on a tablet device.

To overcome those limitations, other publishing formats are available in Captivate. The most popular alternative to the .swf format is the HTML5 format. When published in HTML5, the project can be played back in any modern browser without the need for an extra plugin. HTML5-enabled projects can also be played back on mobile devices such as iOS and Android devices. Remember also that the new Responsive Projects introduced by Captivate 8 can only be published in HTML5.

HTML5 also has its caveats. HTML5 cannot reproduce every single feature, animation and interaction that Flash has made us accustomed to. That's why certain features (such as Rollover Objects and Text Animations) are not supported when you publish your file in HTML5.

 For a complete list of unsupported features in HTML5, visit `http://helpx.adobe.com/captivate/using/publish-projects-html5-files.html`.

In the next section, you will explore the various publishing options available in Captivate.

Publishing to Flash

In the history of Captivate, Flash has always been the primary publishing option. Even though HTML5 publishing is now taking the lead, publishing to Flash is still an important Captivate feature.

In the following exercise, you will publish the Encoder Demonstration project to Flash using the default options:

1. Return to the `Chapter13/encoderDemo_800.cptx` file.
2. Click on the **Publish | Publish to Computer** icon of the Big Buttons Bar. Alternatively, you can also use the **File | Publish** menu item.
3. In the **Publish** dialog, change the value of **Project Title** to `encoderDemo_800_flash`.
4. Click on the folder icon situated next to the **Location** field.
5. Select the `/publish` folder of your exercises as the publish location.
6. Make sure the **Publish to Folder** checkbox is selected.
7. Check whether the selected **Output Format** option is **SWF**.

The **Publish** dialog should now look like the following screenshot:

```
┌──────────────────────────────────────────────────────────────────┐
│                    Publish To My Computer                          │
│                                                                    │
│   Publish as:   [ HTML5 / SWF   ▼ ]                                │
│                                                                    │
│   Project Title: [ encoderDemo_800_flash              ]            │
│                                                                    │
│   Location:   [ /Users/damienbkx/Dropbox/8/publish    ]  [📁]      │
│               ☐ Zip Files    ☑ Publish To Folder                   │
│                                                                    │
│                                                                    │
│   Output Format:  [ SWF ]  [ HTML5 ]    ☑ Force re-publish on all slides │
│                                                                    │
│                   ☐ Full Screen         ☐ Scalable HTML content    │
│                                                                    │
│                   ☐ Export PDF          ☐ Seamless Tabbing(IE only)│
│                                                                    │
│   Flash Player:  [ Flash Player 10   ▼ ]                           │
│                                                                    │
│   [ More ]                              [ Close ]   [ Publish ]     │
└──────────────────────────────────────────────────────────────────┘
```

Take a quick look at the remaining options, but leave them all with their current values.

8. Click on the **Publish** button at the bottom-right corner of the **Publish** dialog box.

When Captivate has finished publishing the movie, an information box appears on the screen asking whether you want to view the output.

9. Click on **No** to discard the information box and return to Captivate.

You will now use Finder (for Mac) or Windows Explorer (for Windows) to take a look at the files Captivate has generated.

10. Use Finder (for Mac) or Windows Explorer (for Windows) to browse to the /publish folder of your exercises.

Because you selected the **Publish to Folder** checkbox in the **Publish** dialog, Captivate has automatically created the encoderDemo_800_flash subfolder in the /publish folder.

11. Open the encoderDemo_800_flash subfolder to inspect its content.

There should be five files stored in this location:

- `encoderDemo_800_flash.swf`: This is the main Flash file containing the compiled version of the `.cptx` project

- `encoderDemo_800_flash.html`: This file is an HTML page used to wrap the Flash file

- `standard.js`: This is a JavaScript file used to make the Flash player work well within the HTML page

- `demo_en.flv`: This is the video file used on slide 2 of the movie

- `captivate.css`: This file provides the necessary style rules to ensure the proper formatting of the HTML page

If you want to embed the compiled Captivate movie in an existing HTML page, only the `.swf` file (plus, in this case, the `.flv` video) is needed. The HTML editor (such as Adobe Dreamweaver) will recreate the necessary HTML, JavaScript, and CSS files.

Captivate and Dreamweaver

Adobe Dreamweaver CC 2014 is the HTML editor of the Creative Cloud and the industry-leading solution for authoring professional web pages. Inserting a Captivate file in a Dreamweaver page is dead easy! First, move or copy the main Flash file (`.swf`) as well as the required support files (in this case, the `.flv` video file), if any, somewhere in the root folder of the Dreamweaver site. When done, use the **Files** panel of Dreamweaver to drag and drop the main `.swf` file onto the HTML page. That's it! More information on Dreamweaver can be found at `http://www.adobe.com/products/dreamweaver.html`.

You will now test the compiled project in a web browser. This is an important test as it closely recreates the conditions in which the students will experience the movie once it is uploaded to a web server.

12. Double-click on the `encoderDemo_800_flash.html` file to open it in a web browser.

13. Enjoy the final version of the demonstration you have created!

Now that you have experienced the workflow of publishing the project to Flash with the default options, you will explore some additional publishing options.

Using the Scalable HTML content option

Back in *Chapter 2*, *Capturing the Slides*, there was a discussion on choosing the right size for the project. One of the solutions was to use the **Scalable HTML content** option of Captivate. Thanks to this option, the eLearning content is automatically resized to fit the screen on which it is viewed. Let's experiment with this option hands-on, using the following steps:

1. Return to the `Chapter13/encoderDemo_800.cptx` file.

2. Click on the **Publish | Publish to Computer** icon of the Big Buttons Bar to reopen the **Publish** dialog. The publishing options you defined in the previous section should have been maintained.

3. Change the **Project Title** value to `encoderDemo_800_flashScalable`.

4. Ensure that the publish **Location** still is the `/publish` folder of the exercise, that the **Publish to Folder** checkbox is still selected, and that the selected **Output Format** is **SWF**.

5. Select the **Scalable HTML content** checkbox in the lower-right area of the **Publish** dialog.

6. Leave the remaining options with their current values and click on the **Publish** button at the bottom-right corner of the **Publish** dialog box.

When Captivate has finished publishing the movie, an information box appears on the screen asking whether you want to view the output.

7. Click on **Yes** to discard the information box and open the published movie in the default web browser.

During the playback, use your mouse to resize your browser window and note how the movie is resized and always fits the available space without being distorted.

 The Scalable HTML Content option also works when the project is published in HTML5.

Publishing to HTML5

One of the main goals of HTML5 is to provide a plugin-free paradigm. It means that the interactivity and strong visual experience brought to the Internet by plugins (such as Adobe Flash) should be supported natively by browsers and their underlying technologies (mainly HTML, CSS, and JavaScript) without the need for an extra third-party plugin.

Since plugins are no longer necessary to deliver rich interactive content, any modern browser should be capable of rendering the interactive eLearning courses created by Captivate. This includes the browsers installed on mobile devices, such as tablets and smartphones.

This is an enormous change not only for the industry but also for Captivate users and eLearning developers. Thanks to HTML5, your students are able to enjoy your eLearning content across all their devices. By introducing the Responsive Projects, Captivate 8 takes it one huge step further. A Responsive Project is one of the few Captivate features that work in HTML5 only with no Flash equivalent. This fact demonstrates that HTML5 publishing is now taking the lead over the original Flash-based publishing. It also clearly shows that the future of Captivate and of eLearning is HTML5.

Using the HTML5 Tracker panel

Because HTML5 and Flash are two different technologies, everything possible in Flash is not always possible in HTML5. Consequently, some features of Captivate that are supported in Flash are not supported in HTML5. When planning a project, it is necessary to decide up front the format (Flash or HTML5) in which the project will be published and only use the objects supported by the chosen publication format.

In the following exercise, you will use the **HTML5 Tracker** to better understand what features of the Encoder Demonstration are (un)supported in HTML5:

1. Return to the `encoderDemo_800.cptx` file.
2. Use the **Window | HTML5 Tracker** menu item to open the **HTML5 Tracker** floating panel.

The **HTML5 Tracker** floating panel informs you that some of the features used in this project are not supported in HTML5, as shown in the following screenshot:

On slide 12, the orange arrow animations you inserted back in *Chapter 4, Working with Multimedia* are not supported in HTML5. This does not mean that you cannot publish this project in HTML5; it just means that the orange arrow animation will not behave in the same way as in the Flash output. In the case of such an animation, there is nothing to worry about. It will simply be replaced by a static image when published in HTML5. In other words, the arrow will be there but it won't be animated.

3. Close the **HTML5 Tracker** panel.

> A comprehensive list of all the objects and features that are not supported in the HTML5 output is available on the official Captivate site at `http://helpx.adobe.com/captivate/using/publish-projects-html5-files.html`. Make sure you read that page before publishing your projects in HTML5.

In the next exercise, you will publish the Encoder Demonstration in the HTML5 publishing format.

Publishing the project in HTML5

The process of publishing the project in HTML5 is very similar to the process of publishing the project to Flash. Perform the following steps to publish the project in HTML5:

1. Return to the `encoderDemo_800.cptx` file.

2. Use the **Publish | Publish to Computer** menu item of the Big Buttons Bar to reopen the **Publish** dialog.

3. Change the **Project Title** value to `encoderDemo_800_HTML5`.

4. Ensure that the publish location is still the `/publish` folder of your exercises.

5. In the **Output Format Option** section, select the **HTML5** button and deselect the **SWF** button.

6. Deselect the **Scalable HTML content** checkbox.

7. Leave the other options with their current values and click on the **Publish** button.

Captivate informs you that some features used in this project are not supported in HTML5. This is something you already anticipated while looking at the **HTML5 Tracker** panel.

8. Click on **Yes** to discard the message and start the publication to HTML5.

The process of publishing to HTML5 is much longer than the publication to Flash. One of the reasons is that Captivate needs to open the Adobe Media Encoder to convert the .flv video used on slide 2 and the Full Motion Recordings of slide 19 and 24 to the .mp4 format.

When the publish process is complete, a second message appears asking if you want to view the output.

9. Click on **No** to discard the message and return to the standard Captivate interface.

You will now use Windows Explorer (for Windows) or Finder (for Mac) to take a closer look at the generated files.

10. Use Windows Explorer (for Windows) or Finder (for Mac) to go to the publish/encoderDemo_800_HTML5 folder of the exercises.

You should find a bunch of files and folders in the encoderDemo_800_HTML5 folder:

- index.html: This file is the main HTML file. This is the file that loads in the web browser to play the course.
- /ar: This folder contains the required audio assets in .mp3 format.
- /dr: This folder contains the required images. Note that the mouse pointers, the slide backgrounds, as well as all the Text Captions are exported as .png images.
- /vr: This folder contains the required video files in .mp4 format.
- /assets: This folder contains the necessary CSS and JavaScript files.

You will now test this version of the project in a web browser.

11. Double-click on the index.html file to open it in the default web browser.

When testing the HTML5 version of the project in a web browser, note that the Animations of slide 12 have been replaced by static images, as anticipated in the **HTML5 Tracker** panel. Apart from this detail, Captivate does a pretty good job in converting the demonstration to HTML5.

Publishing to Flash and HTML5

When in the **Publish** dialog, it is possible to select both the **SWF** and the **HTML5 Output Formats** at the same time. When publishing in both formats, Captivate generates the assets of both the Flash and HTML5 applications in the same folder. It also generates one extra file called `multiscreen.html`. This file is used to detect the device used to visit the course. If a desktop/laptop is detected, it redirects the student to the Flash version of the course. However, if a mobile device is detected, it redirects the student to the HTML5 version. Don't hesitate to test it out by selecting both the **SWF** and the **HTML5 Output Formats** before publishing the project.

Publishing a Responsive Project

The process of publishing a responsive project is very similar to the process of publishing a standard project to HTML5. However, there are a few interesting options that can be fine-tuned before publication, because a Responsive Project is designed to be consumed on a mobile device right from the start.

Using Mobile Palette

One of the things that characterize the mobile experience (versus the desktop/laptop experience) is the touch screen. Owners of tablets and smartphones use their fingers to interact with their devices by performing various multi-touch gestures. These gestures include swipes, taps, double taps, pinches, and so on. New in Captivate 8 is the ability to leverage the power of those mobile gestures in your projects. This is what you will examine right now, using the following steps:

1. Open the `Chapter13/goingMobile.cptx` project. It is the Responsive Project you created in *Chapter 9, Creating a Responsive Project*.

2. Use the **Window | Mobile Palette** menu item to open the **Mobile Palette** panel.

As shown in the following screenshots, the **Mobile Palette** allows you to enable mobile **Gestures** and **Geolocation** services for that project.

Note that you can enable or disable gestures as a whole. There is currently no way to enable some gestures while leaving others disabled.

3. Make sure the **Gestures Configuration** checkbox is selected for that project.

Since this project does not use any **Geolocation** capabilities, there is no need to select the **Geolocation** option.

4. Deselect the **Geolocation** checkbox if needed.
5. Click on **OK** to validate the changes and to close the **Mobile Palette** panel.

This new option of Captivate 8 is yet another mobile-only option that has no equivalent in Flash. Note that these options are not limited to a Responsive Project. You can use **Gestures and Geolocation** on any standard project as well.

Publishing a Responsive Project

The actual publication process is the same as for a standard project published in HTML5. Let's check it out using the following steps:

1. In the `Chapter13/goingMobile.cptx` file, use the **Publish | Publish for Devices** menu item on the Big Buttons Bar to reopen the **Publish** dialog.

At the top of the **Publish** dialog, note that the **Publish as** option is set to **HTML5** without any options to turn it off or choose another publishing format.

2. If needed, change the **Project Title** to `Going Mobile`.

3. Use the folder icon to choose the `/publish` folder of your exercise as the publish location.

4. Make sure the **Zip Files** checkbox is deselected.

The **Publish** dialog should now look like the following screenshot:

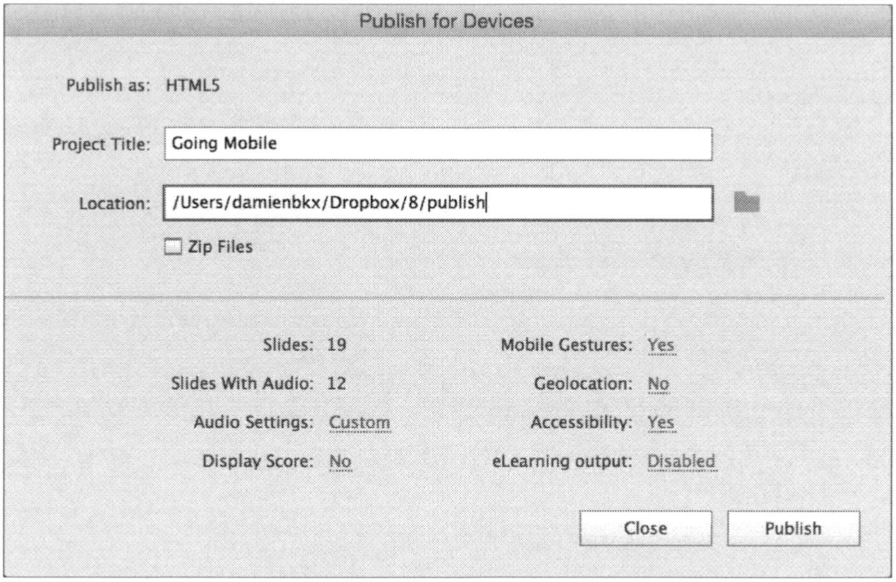

Note that the bottom part of the dialog box displays information about the project being published. Also, note that you can use the blue links to access various panels and preferences should you need to perform some last-minute changes before publishing.

5. Click on the **Publish** button in the bottom-right corner of the dialog box.

When the publish process is complete, a second message appears asking whether you want to view the output.

6. Click on **Yes** to discard the message and view the published project in a web browser.

That's it! Apart from the fact that a Responsive Project can only be published in HTML5, the process is actually the same as for a standard project published in HTML5. Before moving on to the next section, take some time to inspect the published files on your computer. They should be situated in the `/publish/Going Mobile` folder of your exercises.

Publishing an eLearning-enabled project

As a Captivate user, publishing an eLearning-enabled project is not very different from publishing a normal project in Flash or HTML5. However, behind the scenes, Captivate generates a whole bunch of files to enable SCORM, AICC, or Tin Can reporting. In this section, you will publish your SCORM-enabled *Driving in Belgium* project.

Hiding and showing slides

The Driving In Belgium project must be published in both the Flash and the HTML5 output formats, but the Rollover Slidelet you used on slide 17 is not supported in HTML5. That's why you have created two versions of this slide: one version to be used in the Flash project (slide 17) and a second version to be used in the HTML5 project (slide 18). In this section, you will get the project ready to publish in the HTML5 format:

1. Open or switch to the `Chapter13/drivingInBe.cptx` file.
2. Use the **Filmstrip** panel to go to slide 17 of the project.
3. In the **Filmstrip** panel, right-click on slide 17.
4. Choose the **Hide Slide** item in the contextual menu.

Slide 17 is now hidden, which means that it won't be displayed to the students even if it is still an integral part of the project.

5. Use the **Filmstrip** to select slide 18 of the project.

Slide 18 contains the same information as slide 17, but uses objects and features that are supported in HTML5.

Publishing the SCORM package in HTML5

In this section, you will publish the SCORM-enabled project in HTML5 using the following steps:

1. In the `Chapter13/drivingInBe.cptx` file, use the **Publish | Publish to Computer** menu item on the Big Buttons Bar to open the **Publish** dialog.

2. Change the **Project Title** value to `drivingInBe_HTML5_Scorm`.

3. Ensure that the publish **Location** is the `/publish` folder of your exercises.

Note that the **Zip Files** option has been automatically selected by Captivate. This is because this particular project has been configured to enable reporting to a SCORM-compliant LMS. You should leave this checkbox selected when publishing an eLearning-enabled project. After being published, you simply have to upload that single `.zip` file to the LMS as is. A SCORM-compliant LMS is able to unzip the package and properly deploy the files it contains.

4. In the **Output Format** section, make sure the **HTML5** option is the only one selected.

5. Click on the **More** button in the bottom-left corner of the **Publish** dialog.

Take good note of the information revealed by the **More** button. Note that the **eLearning Output** is set to `SCORM 1.2` as configured in *Chapter 10, Working with Quizzes*.

6. Click on the **Publish** button in the bottom right corner of the **Publish** dialog.

A dialog box should warn you that negative scoring is not supported in SCORM 1.2. This means that some of the scoring properties that have been set for your quizzes will not be enforced by the LMS because they are not supported in SCORM 1.2. These unsupported scoring options include negative scoring, penalties, and partial scoring.

7. Click on **Yes** to acknowledge the message and move on with publishing the project anyway. Also, clear the message telling you that some features are not supported in HTML5.

8. Acknowledge the **Publish Complete** message by clicking on the **OK** button.

You will now take a look at the generated `.zip` file.

9. Use Finder (for Mac) or Windows Explorer (for Windows) to navigate to the `/publish` folder of the exercises files.

You should find the `drivingInBe_HTML5_scorm.zip` file in this folder.

10. Unzip the file to take a closer look at its content.

This is where the magic takes place! In the unzipped version of the file, you should find the same files as when you published a regular non-SCORM project in HTML5. However, because you decided to produce a SCORM-compliant package, Captivate has generated lots of extra files. These extra files are used to enable communication between the LMS and the eLearning content produced by Captivate.

The most important of these extra files is `imsmanifest.xml`. This file is the SCORM manifest file. It must be stored in the root of the SCORM package. Feel free to open this file in your favorite text editor to take a look at its content (but make sure you do not modify it). The manifest file describes the course structure to the LMS using a SCORM-compliant XML format.

Note that the extra files that Captivate generates depend on the standard being used (SCORM, AICC, or Tin Can) and of the chosen version of SCORM.

Test your SCORM packages for free

If you do not have a SCORM or Tin Can-compliant LMS available, you can still test the SCORM and Tin Can features of your Captivate project by setting up a free account with SCORM Cloud at `https://cloud.scorm.com/sc/guest/SignUpForm`. SCORM Cloud is a web-based LMS. Their free service can be used as a great testing platform, but if you want to use SCORM Cloud to host your real online courses, you'll have to upgrade to a paid subscription plan. There is a great blog post about creating an LMS-ready file in Captivate and uploading it to SCORM Cloud available at `http://blogs.adobe.com/captivate/2011/11/demystifying-captivate%E2%80%93lms-integration.html`.

Extra credit – publishing the Flash version of the SCORM package

In this section, you will publish the Flash version of your eLearning-enabled project as a SCORM package. The general steps are as follows:

- Unhide slide 17 and hide slide 18 to make the project ready for Flash publishing.

- Use the **Publish | Publish to Computer** icon of the Big Buttons Bar to open the **Publish** dialog.

- Make sure the **Output Format** option is set to **SWF** and the **Location** is the /publish folder of the exercises.

- Change the name of the project to `drivingInBe_swf_scorm`.

- Publish the file.

Captivate should generate the `drivingInBe_swf_scorm.zip` file in the `/publish` folder. Don't hesitate to unzip that file and inspect its content.

Working with the Multi SCO packager

In *Chapter 10, Working with Quizzes,* you discovered that the concept of a **Sharable Content Object (SCO)** is at the heart of the SCORM specification. As far as SCORM is concerned, the eLearning-enabled content you published in the previous section are both considered as SCOs. Each of these SCOs contains its own manifest file. One of the key pieces of information contained in the `imsmanifest.xml` file is the unique SCO identifier of this particular package as entered in the **Manifest** dialog box of Captivate.

One of the most interesting aspects of SCORM is the ability to take different SCOs, arrange them in a course, and publish them as a single SCORM package. This is precisely what the MultiSco packager enables you to do.

In the next exercise, you will create one more SCO and use the MultiSco packager to package multiple SCOs into a single package.

Creating the SCOs

Captivate is not the only eLearning authoring tool that can produce valid SCORM packages. You can therefore use the MultiSco packager to include in a single course content developed by different authoring tools.

Creating a SCORM package from the Video Demo project

A Video Demo is a project using the `.cpvc` file extension. As discussed earlier in *Chapter 8, Producing a Video Demo,* this project can only be published as an `.mp4` video file. The publishing options available for a Video Demo project do not allow for the creation of a SCORM package. But, there is a trick! In the next exercise, you will import a `.cpvc` Video Demo project inside a standard Captivate project and publish it as a SCORM package, using the following steps:

1. Return to Captivate and close every open file.

2. Use the **File | New Project | Blank Project** menu item to create a new (blank) Captivate project.

3. In the **New Blank Project** dialog, select the predefined size of **800 x 600** and click on **OK**.

Captivate creates a new project that is 800 pixels in width and 600 pixels in height. The next step is to insert the Video Demo CPVC project inside this new project.

4. Use the **Insert | CPVC Slide** menu item to insert the Video Demo into the current project.

5. Browse to the `Chapter13/encoderVideo.cpvc` file and click on **Open**.

6. In the **Filmstrip** panel, right-click on slide 1 and delete it.

7. Save the file as `Chapter13/EncoderVideo.cptx`.

By using the **Insert | CPCV Slide** menu item, you have inserted the Video Demo as a new slide in a regular project. As far as Captivate is concerned, this project is a standard project that uses the `.cptx` file extension. The Video Demo project can therefore be published as a SCORM package.

8. Use the **Quiz | Quiz Preferences** menu item to open the **Preferences** dialog on the **Quiz Reporting** page.

9. At the top of the page, select the **Enable reporting for this project** checkbox.

10. Open the **LMS** drop-down menu and choose **Moodle** as the LMS.

11. Click on the **Configure** button to create a SCORM manifest.

12. Enter the following values in the **Manifest** dialog:

Field	Content
Course Identifier	`encoderVideo`
Course Title	`The Adobe Media Encoder Video Demo`
Course Description	`This video shows the student how to convert a Quick Time movie into Flash Video`
SCO Identifier	`encoderVideo` ·
SCO Title	`The Adobe Media Encoder Video Demo`

13. Click on **OK** to validate and close the **Manifest** dialog.

There is no quiz in this particular file, but it does not mean that you have nothing to track! In a project without a quiz, SCORM can be used to track the completion status of the project by the students.

14. In the **Status Representation** section, make sure that the **Incomplete ---> Complete** option is selected.

15. In the **Success/Completion Criteria** section, select the **Slide Views** checkbox and deselect the **Quiz** checkbox.

16. Since there is no quiz in this project, deselect the **Interaction Data** checkbox situated in the **Data To Report** section.

17. Click on **OK** to validate and close the **Quiz Preferences** dialog.

Now that Quiz Reporting Preferences have been correctly entered, the last step is to publish this project as a SCORM package.

18. Use the **Publish | Publish to Computer** icon of the Big Buttons Bar to open the **Publish** dialog.

19. If needed, change the **Project Title** to encoderVideo.

20. Use the /publish folder of the exercise as the publish location.

21. Select **SWF** in the **Output Format**.

22. Make sure that the **Zip Files** option is selected.

23. Leave all the other options with their default values and click on **Publish**.

24. When the publication process is finished, use Finder (for Mac) or Windows Explorer (for Windows) to browse to the /publish folder of your exercises.

You should see another SCORM package named encoderVideo.zip. This ZIP file contains all the assets that are necessary to integrate the Video Demo project into a SCORM 1.2-compliant LMS such as Moodle.

Creating a single-course package from multiple SCOs

The publish folder of your exercises should now contain three separate SCORM packages: drivingInBe_HTML5_Scorm.zip, drivingInBe_swf_Scorm.zip, and encoderVideo.zip. Each of these packages has a unique SCO identifier defined in the imsManifest.xml file situated inside each package.

Using the MultiSco packager, you will now combine these SCOs into a single SCORM course. At the end of this procedure, you will have a single .zip file containing all three modules. This single .zip file can be uploaded as is into a SCORM-compliant LMS such as Moodle.

Perform the following steps to create the SCORM package:

1. Return to Captivate and use the **File | New Project | Multi-SCORM Packager** menu item to open the **multiscoPackager** AIR application.

The **multiscoPackager** application is an external AIR application that is part of your Captivate installation. As shown in the following screenshot, **multiscoPackager** proposes three course templates, the leftmost template being the simplest one:

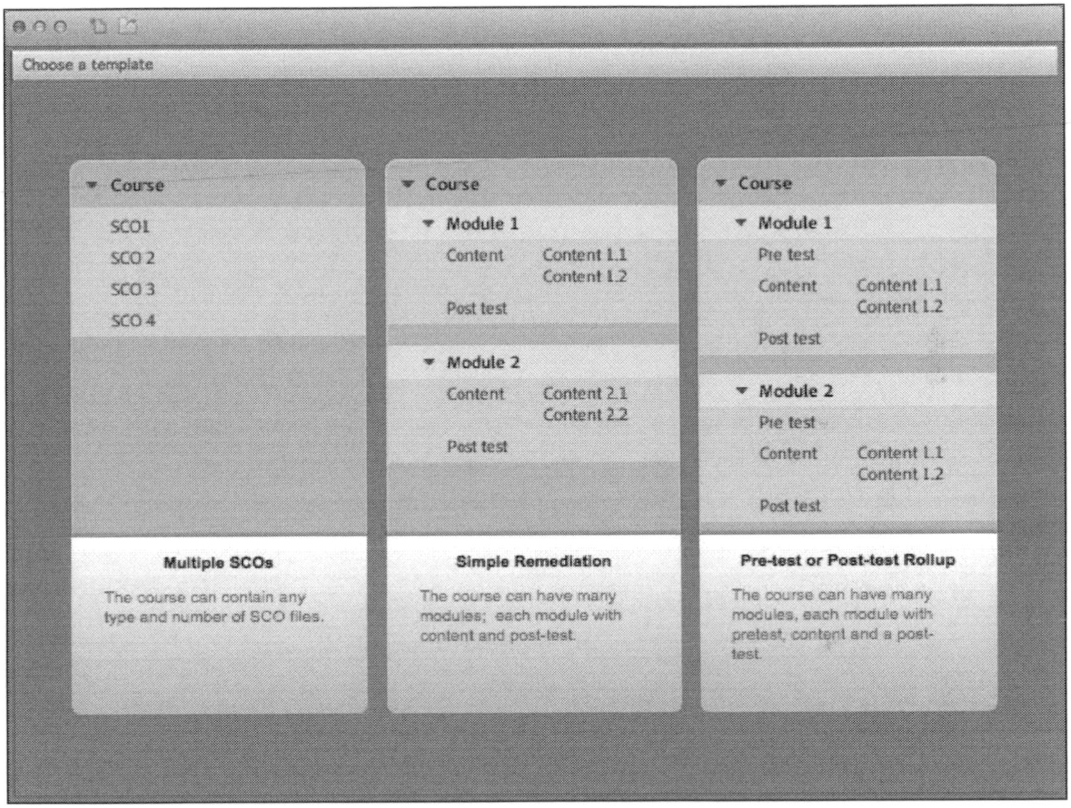

In *Chapter 10, Working with Quizzes*, you learned that Moodle is SCORM 1.2-compliant. It means that you need to generate a SCORM 1.2-compliant package if you want to upload your course to Moodle. In the **multiscoPackager** application, only the simplest template is SCORM 1.2-compliant.

2. Click on the first (leftmost) template named **Multiple SCOs**.
3. Enter the following information in the Course Manifest Details dialog:
    ◦ Select **1.2** in the **Version** drop-down menu under **SCORM Version**.
    ◦ Type `mftc_bestOfSeries` in the **Identifier** field.
    ◦ Type `The best of MFTC` in the **Title** field.

- ° Type Experience the best courses of the MFTC company in this sample Course package in the **Description** field.
- ° Type 1 in the **Version** field.

4. Click on **OK** to validate the changes and close the **Course Manifest Details** dialog.

The information you just typed in the **Course Manifest Details** dialog box will be merged with the manifest files of each individual SCO contained in this course in order to create a single SCORM manifest for the entire course. The next step is to add multiple SCOs into the course.

5. Click on the **+** icon situated in the top-right corner of the **multiscoPackager** application (identified by the tooltip).

6. Browse to the publish folder of your exercise and select the drivingInBe_ HTML5_scorm.zip package. Click on **Open** to add the package to the course.

7. Repeat the same operation to add the drivingInBe_swf_scorm.zip and encoderVideo.zip packages of your publish folder to the course.

You can add as many SCORM packages as needed into the course. Note the arrow icons at the bottom-right corner of the **multiscoPackager** application. They allow you to reorder or delete the SCOs inside the course.

Now that every SCO has been added to the course, the last step is to publish the course as a single SCORM package that contains all three SCOs.

8. Click on the **Publish Course** icon in the top-left corner of the **multiscoPackager** application.

9. In the **Publish SCO package** dialog, use the **Publish Folder** field to choose the /publish folder of the exercises as the output folder of the package.

10. Click on the **Publish** button. When the process is complete, click on **OK** to acknowledge the successful creation of the SCORM package.

11. Close the **multiscoPackager** application.

12. Use Finder (for Mac) or Windows Explorer (for Windows) to browse to the /publish folder of your exercises.

You should see the new mfct_bestOfSeries.zip package that has been created by the MultiSco packager application. This package contains the three modules that you added in the MultiSco packager in the previous section. Feel free to unzip the package to check its content. You should be able to locate a single imsManifest.xml file as well as the assets pertaining to each of the three modules you added to the course.

When using the Multi SCORM Packager, remember the following points:

- Each individual component needs to be published as a SCORM package that contains a valid `imsManifest.xml` file. Such a package is called a **Sharable Content Object (SCO)**.

- A single SCO can be used in many different courses' packages.

- A single course can contain an unlimited number of SCOs.

- The generated course package can be uploaded as a single unit to a SCORM-compliant LMS.

- There are different versions of SCORM. Make sure you create course packages that are compliant with whatever SCORM version your LMS supports.

- The Multi SCORM Packager of Captivate proposes three course templates to choose from. Make sure the chosen template can be used with the version of SCORM that you are targeting.

This concludes your exploration of the Multi SCORM Packager of Captivate.

 For more information on the Multi-SCORM Packager, refer to the article on the Adobe website at `http://helpx.adobe.com/captivate/using/multi-scorm-packager.html`.

Publishing to PDF

Another publishing option available in Captivate is to publish the project as an Adobe PDF document. This process is tied to the Flash publishing process covered previously. When converting to PDF, Captivate first converts the project to Flash and then embeds the resulting `.swf` file inside a PDF document. To read the Flash file embedded in the PDF document, the free Adobe Acrobat Reader simply relies on the Flash player plugin that is installed on the student's computer. This is why this option does not work on a mobile device, even if the Adobe Reader app is installed.

Publishing the Captivate project to PDF is a great way to make the eLearning course available offline. The students can, for example, download the PDF file from a website and take the course on a train or an airplane where no Internet connection is available. However, be aware that, if the course is viewed offline or outside an LMS, quiz scores and the course completion status cannot be tracked.

Now, let's publish the Encoder Demonstration to PDF:

1. Return to the `Chapter13/encoderDemo_800.cptx` file if needed.
2. Click on the **Publish | Publish to Computer** icon of the Big Buttons Bar.
3. In the central area, change **Project Title** to `encoderDemo_800_pdf`.
4. Make sure the **Location** field still points to the `/publish` folder of the exercises.
5. Choose **SWF** as the only **Output Format**.
6. Make sure the **Publish to Folder** checkbox is selected.
7. In the bottom-left area of the **Publish** dialog, select the **Export PDF** checkbox.
8. Click on the **Publish** button situated in the lower-right corner of the **Publish** dialog.

When the publishing process is complete, a message tells you that Acrobat 9 or higher is required to read the generated PDF file.

9. Click on **OK** to acknowledge the message. A second information box opens.
10. Click on **No** to discard the second message and close the **Publish** dialog.
11. Use Finder (for Mac) or Windows Explorer (for Windows) to browse to the `/publish/encoderDemo_800_pdf` folder of the exercises.

There should be six files in the `encoderDemo_800_pdf` folder. Actually, publishing to PDF is an extra option of the standard publishing to Flash feature.

12. Delete everything but the PDF file from the `encoderDemo_800_pdf` folder.
13. Double-click on the `encoderDemo_800_pdf.pdf` file to open it in Adobe Acrobat.
14. Note that the file opens normally in Adobe Acrobat. This proves that all the necessary files and assets have been correctly embedded into the PDF file.

In the next section, you will explore another option of Captivate: publishing the project as a standalone application.

Publishing as a standalone application

When publishing as a standalone application, Captivate generates an `.exe` file for playback on Windows or an `.app` file for playback on Mac. The `.exe` (for Windows) or `.app` (for Mac) files contain the compiled `.swf` file plus a light version of the Flash player.

The advantages and disadvantages of a standalone application are similar to those of a PDF file. That is, the file can be viewed offline on a train, an airplane, or elsewhere, but the features requiring an Internet connection will not work.

Publishing standalone in Captivate 8

Publishing as a standalone application is an old feature of Captivate: it was already present in Captivate 1! For some reason, it has been removed from the original Captivate 8 release. It has been reintroduced in the Captivate 8.0.1 update again by popular demand. The exercise of this section therefore requires an updated Captivate 8 installation.

In the following exercise, you will publish the Captivate file as a standalone application for Mac or Windows using the following steps:

1. If needed, return to the `Chapter13/encoderDemo_800.cptx` file.
2. Click on the **Publish | Publish to Computer** icon of the Big Buttons Bar.
3. At the top of the **Publish** dialog, open the **Publish As** drop-down menu.
4. Choose the **Executable** menu item.
5. Open the **Publish Type** drop-down menu.
6. If you are on Windows, choose **Windows Executable (*.exe)**. If you are using Mac, choose **MAC Executable (*.app)**.
7. If needed, change **Project Title** to `encoderDemo_800`.
8. Make sure that the `/publish` folder of the exercises is still the current publish **Location**.

Take some time to inspect the other options of the **Publish** dialog. One of them allows you to choose a custom icon for the generated `.exe` (for Windows) or `.app` (for Mac) files.

9. Leave the other options with their current values and click on the **Publish** button.

When the publish process is complete, an information box asks whether you want to see the generated output.

10. Click on **No** to clear the information message and to close the **Publish** dialog.

Now that the standalone application has been generated, you will use Finder (for Mac) or Windows Explorer (for Windows) to take a look at the /publish folder and test the newly created applications.

11. Use Finder (for Mac) or Windows Explorer (for Windows) to browse to the /publish folder of the exercises.

12. Double-click on encoderDemo_800.exe (for Windows) or encoderDemo_800.app (for Mac) to open the generated application.

The Captivate movie opens as a standalone application in its own window. Notice that no browser is necessary to play the movie.

This publish format is particularly useful when you want to burn the movie on a CD-ROM. When generating a Windows executable (.exe), Captivate can even generate an autorun.ini file so that the project automatically plays when the CD-ROM is inserted in the computer.

Publishing as an .mp4 video file

When publishing a project as a video, Captivate generates an .mp4 file and proposes various video presets for the conversion. Actually, Captivate first generates a .swf file and then converts it into an .mp4 video file.

After the conversion, the video file can be played on any media player that is capable of reading the .mp4 format. It is an ideal solution if you want to upload the resulting movie to YouTube or if you want to make it available to non-Flash devices. On the other hand, the generated .mp4 video file permits only a linear experience, that is, no interaction or branching is possible. The student experiences the video from the beginning to the end in a linear fashion, as is the case while watching a motion picture in a movie theatre or on TV. Consequently, converting a Captivate project to a video file is well suited for a demonstration but does not work well with simulations.

In the following exercise, you will convert the Encoder Demonstration into an .mp4 video using the following steps:

1. If needed, return to the Chapter13/encoderDemo_800.cptx file.
2. Click on the **Publish | Publish to Computer** icon of the Big Buttons Bar.
3. Open the **Publish As** drop-down menu and choose the **Video** item.
4. If needed, change **Project Title** to encoderDemo_800.
5. Ensure that the **Location** field still points to the /publish folder of the exercises.

6. Open the **Select Preset** drop-down list. Take some time to inspect the available options and choose **YouTube Widescreen HD**.

7. Click on the **Publish** button in the bottom-right corner of the **Publish** dialog.

Publishing to a video file is quite a lengthy process, so be patient. First, you will see that Captivate converts the project into a `.swf` file. When that first conversion is over, Captivate opens a second box named **Adobe Captivate Video Publisher** and converts the `.swf` file to an `.mp4` video. At the end of the whole process, the **Adobe Captivate Video Publisher** dialog can publish the generated video to YouTube or just open it.

8. Close the **Adobe Captivate Video Publisher** window.

9. As usual, use Finder (for Mac) or Windows Explorer (for Windows) to take a look at the `/publish` folder of your exercises.

10. Double-click on the `encoderDemo_800.mp4` file. The video opens in the appropriate media player.

The generated video file can be uploaded to YouTube, DailyMotion, or any other video-hosting service. You can also host the video on your own internal video-streaming server (such as a Flash Media server) if you have one available.

Publishing to YouTube

Captivate includes a workflow that allows you to publish your Captivate movie to a video file and upload it to your YouTube account without even leaving Captivate.

In the following exercise, you will convert your Captivate file to a video and upload it to YouTube.

 This exercise requires a YouTube account. If you do not have a YouTube account, you can create one for free on the YouTube website or read through the steps of the exercise.

Perform the following steps to upload the video to YouTube:

1. Return to the `Chapter13/encoderDemo_800.cptx` file.

2. Use **File | Publish to YouTube** to start the process.

When using that menu item, Captivate generates the slides as if you were publishing the movie in the Flash format. When that first conversion is complete, Captivate opens the **Adobe Captivate Video Publisher** window and converts the `.swf` file to `.mp4`. So far, the process is exactly the same as the one used in the previous section. At the end of the process, however, Captivate opens another window.

3. Enter your username and password to log on to your YouTube Account.

4. Select the **I've read Adobe Privacy Policy** checkbox and click on **Login**.

5. Once logged in, enter the relevant project information.

    ° Enter the title of the movie in the **Title** field. This is the only required field.

    ° Enter a description in the **Description** field. By default, the description entered in the **Project Info** preferences pane (if any) is used.

    ° Enter a list of comma-separated tags. These tags will help YouTube reference your video so that other YouTube users can find it easily.

    ° Choose the best **Category** for your video.

    ° Choose the level of **Privacy** (private or public).

6. Select the **I have read the terms & conditions** checkbox and click on the **Upload** button.

Captivate uploads the video to YouTube. When the process is complete, the **Adobe Captivate Video Publisher** window shows the direct link to our video on YouTube.

7. Click on the **Close** button to close the **Adobe Captivate Video Publisher** window.

As you can see, Captivate makes it incredibly easy to publish a project to YouTube!

 For more information on YouTube's privacy settings and the difference between a public and private video, visit `https://support.google.com/youtube/answer/157177?hl=en`.

Publishing to Microsoft Word

Another important publishing option to cover is the publication of the Captivate movie as a Microsoft Word document. There are four formats available: Handout, Lesson, Step by Step guide, and Storyboard.

 This publication option requires that both Adobe Captivate and Microsoft Word are installed on the same system. If you do not have Microsoft Word installed on your computer, just read through the steps of this exercise to understand the workflow.

Use the following steps to publish your Captivate movie as a Microsoft Word file using the Handout template:

1. Return to the `Chapter13/encoderDemo_800.cptx` file.
2. Use the **File | Print** menu item to open the **Print** dialog box.
3. In the left-hand side column, change the **Project Title** to `encoderDemo_800_handout`.
4. Make sure the **Folder** field still points to the `/publish` folder of the exercises.
5. In the **Export Range** section, make sure that **All** is selected. You could publish a smaller selection of slides if needed.

That's it for the usual options. Before clicking on the **Publish** button, you have a few more options available in the right column of the **Print** dialog.

6. Open the **Type** drop-down list. Inspect the available options and choose the **Handouts** type.
7. In the **Handout Layout Options** section, leave the **Use table in the output** option selected.
8. Open the **Slides Per Page** dropdown and choose to have two slides on each page of the Word document.
9. Select the **Caption Text**, **Slide Notes**, and **Include mouse Path** checkboxes.
10. Take some time to inspect the remaining options, but leave them all with their current values.
11. When ready, click on the **Publish** button.

Captivate generates the Word document according to the options defined in the **Publish** dialog. When done, an information box appears asking whether you want to view the generated file.

12. Click on **No** to discard the information box and close the **Print** dialog.

13. Use Finder (for Mac) or Windows Explorer (for Windows) to browse to the publish folder of your exercises.

14. Double-click on the newly created `encoderDemo_800_handout.doc` file.

The file opens in Microsoft Word. Take some time to inspect the generated Word document. Can you find the effect of each of the boxes you selected in the **Print** dialog?

Extra credit – publishing to Word

In this section, you will test the remaining Microsoft Word publishing options by generating a Lesson, Step by Step guide, and Storyboard. The steps are as follows:

- Use the **File | Print** menu item to open the **Print** dialog box.

- Give the project a meaningful Project Title.

- In the right area of the **Print** dialog, change the **Type** to **Lesson**, **Step by Step**, or **Storyboard**.

- Experiment with other options as well. Each **Type** has a specific set of options available, which are (for the most part) self-explanatory.

- When ready, click on the **Publish** button.

- Use Finder (for Mac) or Windows Explorer (for Windows) to browse to the `/publish` folder and test your files in Microsoft Word.

Publishing for devices

When publishing an HTML5 application, you rely on the web browser installed on the computer (or device) of the student to render the course. That is, if the course is viewed on a tablet, your student needs to open the web browser installed on the tablet to see the course.

When using the **Publish for Devices (app)** feature of Captivate 8.0.1, you can generate a native mobile application from your eLearning content. This means that your course will be distributed by an app store (such as the Apple App Store for iOS or the Google Play Store for Android) and will be installed as another app on the device of your learners.

The Adobe Captivate App Packager

Prior to Captivate 8.0.1 (including in the original Captivate 8 release), this feature was available in the external Adobe Captivate App Packager application. As of Captivate 8.0.1, the App Packager application is no longer supported. Instead, it is now fully integrated in Captivate.

To convert your course into a native application, Captivate relies on the Adobe **PhoneGap Build** service. This online service can convert any HTML5/CSS/JavaScript web application into a native mobile application. PhoneGap build supports many mobile platforms including iOS, Android, and Windows Phone.

More information on the Adobe PhoneGap build service can be found at https://build.phonegap.com/.

When using this option, Captivate first publishes the project in HTML5 and then uploads the HTML5 application to the PhoneGap Build service where it is compiled into a native iOS and/or Android application. Because this system relies on HTML5, all the capabilities and limitations of regular HTML5 projects also apply to the projects published as apps.

The following exercise requires a PhoneGap Build account. You can register with the PhoneGap Build service for free at https://build.phonegap.com/ If you already have an Adobe ID, you can use it to log in to the free PhoneGap build service. Also, if you are a Creative Cloud subscriber, the premium PhoneGap Build plan is included in your Creative Cloud subscription.

You will now experiment with this service hands-on using the following steps:

1. Make sure you are still in the `encoderDemo_800.cptx` project.
2. Use the **Publish | Publish for Devices (App)** icon of the big Buttons Bar.
3. Log in to your PhoneGap Build account using your Adobe ID credentials.
4. Open the **App** drop-down menu, inspect its content and choose the **Create New** item.
5. Type `encoder Demo` in the **Name** field.
6. Type `1` in the **Version** field.
7. Type `encoderDemo` in the **Package** field.

8. Ensure that the **Publish for Devices (app)** dialog looks like the following screenshot and click on the **Next** button:

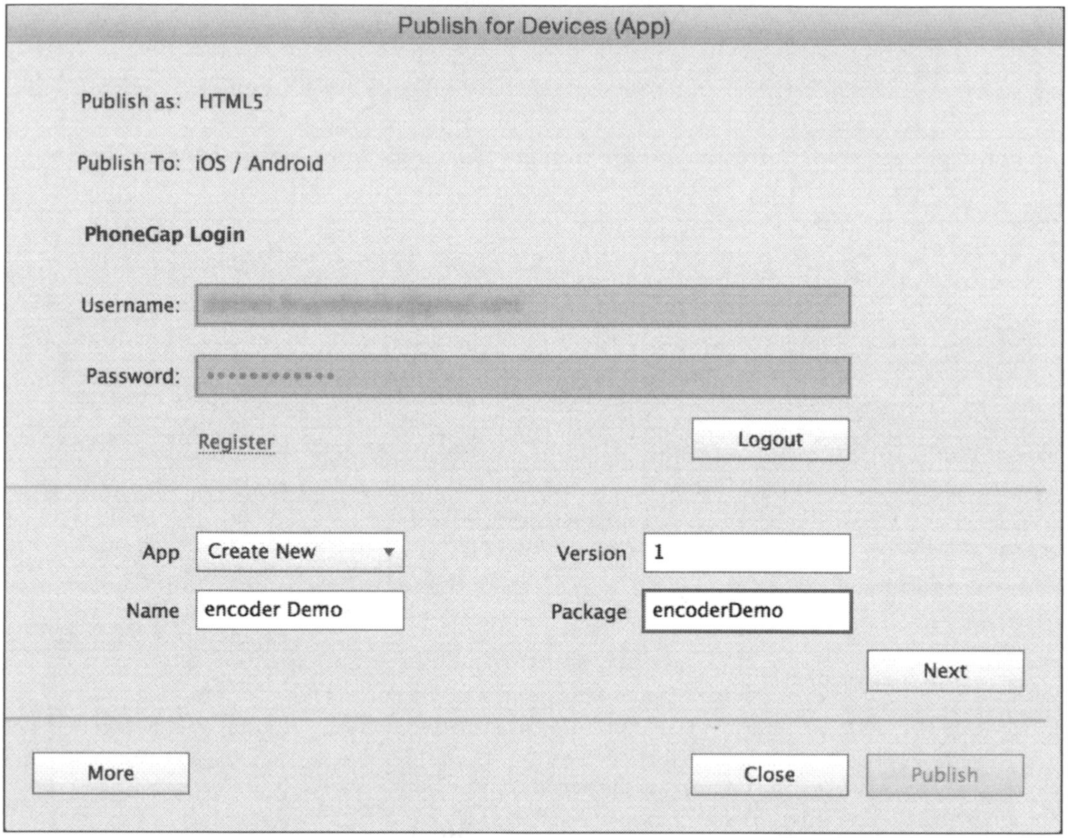

The second part of the process, after you click on the **Next** button, is where you decide for which platforms (iOS and/or Android) you want to compile your HTML5 application. Note that, if you want to compile your eLearning course as an iOS application, you need to be registered as an Apple developer and pay the annual Apple Developer fee. This will give you access to the Apple Developer website where you will be able to access your Apple signing certificate.

More information on the Apple Developer program can be found at `https://developer.apple.com/programs/`.

This certificate is needed to sign and certify the applications you want to submit to the Apple App Store. Without that certificate, PhoneGap Build cannot compile your eLearning content into an iOS application.

 Once you have the necessary certificate, you need to enter it in your PhoneGap Build profile. Use the following documentation to upload your signing certificate into your PhoneGap Build account: `http://docs.build.phonegap.com/en_US/3.3.0/signing_signing-ios.md.html`.

9. If you have an Apple Developer Account, select the iOS checkbox and choose the **Title** and **Certificate** values for your application. If you do not have an Apple Developer Account, deselect the iOS checkbox.

10. Leave the **Android** checkbox selected.

Android also requires a certificate, but this certificate is not mandatory to compile the application for testing purposes. You can therefore move on with this exercise even if you don't have the necessary Android certificates.

11. Click on the **Publish** button.

Captivate begins the process by publishing the content in HTML5. When that step is finished, Captivate uploads the published HTML5 application to the PhoneGap Build service where it will be compiled into a native Android (and/or iOS) application.

When the upload to PhoneGap is complete, Captivate displays a message asking you if you want to download the native mobile application.

12. Click on **Download** to open your web browser on the PhoneGap Build website.

13. Click on the Android link (see the arrow in the following screenshot) or scan the QR code with your mobile device to download your native Android application:

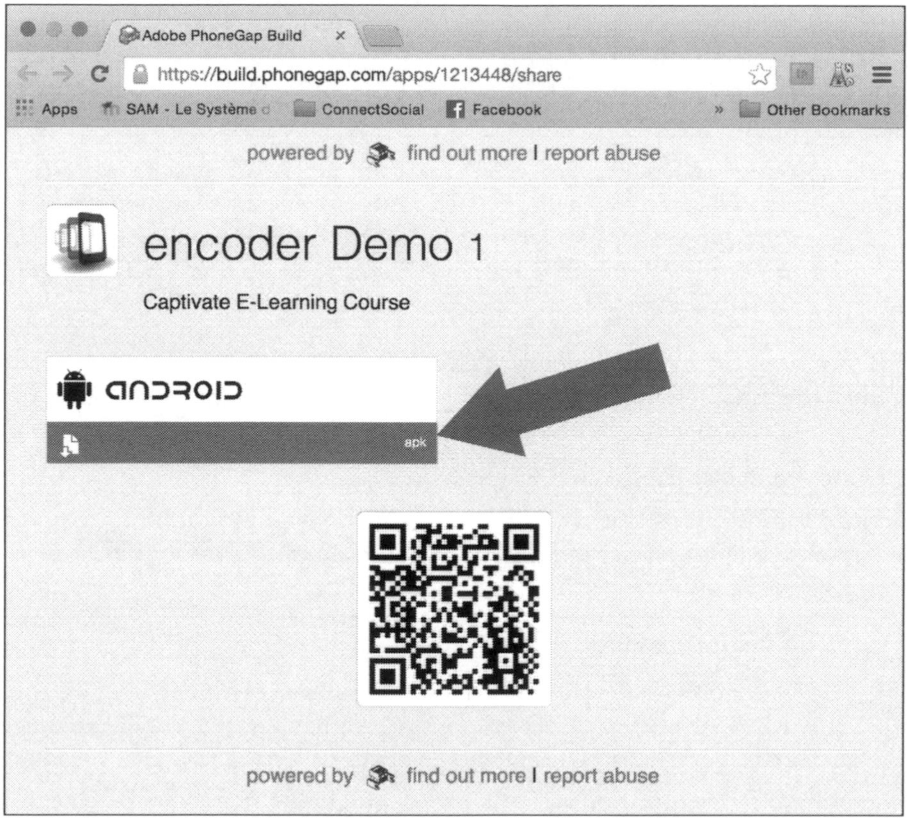

[Another demonstration of this feature can be found on YouTube at `https://www.youtube.com/watch?v=3bl_O_gP92Q`.]

This last exercise concludes your overview of the publishing options of Captivate. So let's have a quick summary of what has been covered so far:

- Publishing is the third and last step of the Captivate Workflow. The goal is to make the content available to the learners in a variety of formats.
- The main publishing formats of Captivate are the Flash (SWF) format and the HTML5 format.

- When publishing in Flash, Captivate generates a `.swf` file that can be played back by the free Adobe Flash Player plugin.

- The generated `.swf` file can be embedded in a PDF document for offline viewing. This option requires Adobe Reader 9 or later versions.

- A project published in HTML5 can be played back on virtually any mobile device, including iOS and Android devices.

- Not every feature of Captivate is supported in HTML5. Use the **HTML5 Tracker** panel to find out which slides/objects of your project are not supported.

- It is possible to hide and show slides. A hidden slide is not part of the published project, even though it is sill in the `.cptx` file.

- Captivate 8 introduced the **Mobile Palette**, which allows you to enable Gestures and Geolocation services

- When publishing as a standalone application, Captivate produces either an `.exe` file for playback on Windows or an `.app` file for playback on a Mac.

- Captivate can produce an `.mp4` video that can be optimized for YouTube and for playback on a mobile device.

- When publishing as a PDF file or standalone application, the published project can no longer connect to the Internet. Consequently, some features that require an Internet connection (such as communicating with an LMS) do not work.

- When the project is published as a video file, it can only be experienced as a linear video that plays from the beginning to the end. Consequently, interactivity and branching are not supported.

- As of Captivate 8.0.1, it is possible to publish your eLearning content as native Android and/or iOS applications. This capability relies on the PhoneGap Build service from Adobe.

- When creating an iOS application, it is necessary to be registered as an Apple developer and to possess the necessary signing certificates.

- Use the **File | Print** menu item to publish your files as Microsoft Word documents.

Summary

At the end of this chapter, you can proudly turn off the lights and leave the post-production studio. You have gone through the three major steps of the production process—uncovering lots of Captivate features, tools, and objects along the way!

In this particular chapter, you first focused on the final fine-tuning you can apply to the project before the actual publishing phase. You have checked the spelling, decided how the movie should start and end, added metadata to the project, and created a unique Skin, among other things. Now that all these final changes have been taken care of, the movie is finally ready for publication.

In the second part of this chapter, you concentrated on the **Publish** dialog box where you gained experience of the main publishing features of Captivate. Publishing is the process by which the movie is made available to the outside world.

Publishing to Flash is the first (and historic) publishing option of Captivate. When published in HTML5, the project can be played back on any device equipped with a modern web browser. This includes a vast majority of mobile devices.

Other publishing formats of Captivate include publishing as a standalone application, publishing as an .mp4 video file, and publishing as a Microsoft Word document. The .mp4 video files produced by Captivate can easily be uploaded to YouTube without even leaving the application.

Congratulations on achieving this important milestone! With the completion of this chapter comes the end of the book. I hope you have enjoyed reading these pages, and that you have acquired the knowledge you needed to create the next generation of eLearning content with Adobe Captivate.

As for me, I would like to thank you for reading my book. I'm already looking forward to your feedback or to meeting you in person during an eLearning or Captivate event somewhere in the world.

Until then, have fun with Adobe Captivate!

Meet the community

Kirsten Rourke is an amazing technical trainer with a real passion for education and technology. I met her in October 2014 during the Adobe Learning Summit and I was amazed by her session on Captivate and Edge Animate. If you ever have a chance to attend one of her courses or one of her sessions, go for it! You won't be disappointed!

Kirsten Rourke

Kirsten Rourke has worked as a full time technical trainer and instructional designer since 2000. She uses her previous career skills in occupational therapy and her theater background to help transform people's relationship to technology training. She works remotely with an eLearning development firm in LA, teaches Adobe eLearning and Design software classes across the US, and manages a local (Central MA) Adobe User Group that covers both Adobe Creative Cloud and eLearning products.

In her roles as a ACP/ACI (Adobe Community Professional/Adobe Certified Instructor) she also does public speaking on eLearning development, Captivate, and Creative Cloud products at seminars like the Adobe Learning Summit (co-hosted with DevLearn). She also teaches storyboarding and Captivate speed techniques in live webinars and in-person sessions. In her spare time she co-hosts a weekly video interview podcast "eMediaChat" and organizes seminars and photowalks.

Contact details

- **Website**: http://www.kirstenrourke.com
- **Twitter**: @rourketraining
- **Podcast**: http://vimeo.com/channels/emediachat
- **Facebook**: https://www.facebook.com/groups/CMAAUG/

Index

Symbols

.mp4 video file
  Captivate project, publishing as 582, 583
.oam file
  content, inspecting 130
.ppt file 442
.pptx file 442

A

Accordion Interaction
  working with 522-524
ActionScript 475
Adobe Audition
  about 148, 464
  used, for editing audio 464-467
Adobe Audition CC 2014
  used, for round trip editing 158
Adobe Captivate. *See* **Captivate**
Adobe Color
  about 264
  URL 264, 267
Adobe Dreamweaver CC 2014
  about 563
  URL 563
Adobe Edge Inspect
  about 341
  and Creative Cloud 343
  Captivate project, testing on mobile
      device 342-345
  Edge Inspect mobile application 342
  Google Chrome 342
  Google Chrome browser extension 342
  helper application 342
  installing 341, 342

  used, for testing Responsive Project 341-345
Adobe Edge Inspect helper application
  URL 342
Adobe Flash Professional
  Captivate project, exporting to 468-470
  file extensions 127
Adobe Media Encoder (AME)
  about 34, 136
  URL 134
Adobe PhoneGap Build service
  about 587
  URL 587, 589
Adobe Presenter 440
Adobe Presenter Video Express
  URL 440
Adobe Swatch Exchange (ASE) 264
Advanced Actions
  about 475, 485
  Conditional Action 486, 490
  Shared Action 486, 506
  Standard Action, using 486
Advanced Audio Management window
  using 159, 160
Advanced Distributed Learning (ADL)
  URL 422
advanced interface mode 10
Align toolbar
  multiple objects, selecting 184-186
  using 183, 184
Apple Developer program
  URL 589
audio
  adding, at object level 136
  adding, at project level 136
  adding, at slide level 136
  adding, to objects 137-139

adding, to slides 142
editing, with Adobe Audition 464-467
external sound clip, importing 148-150
narration, recording with Captivate 143
Text-to-Speech, using to generate
    narration 150
working with 136
automatic panning 61-63
Aviation Industry Computer-based Training
    Committee (AICC)
about 422, 423
URL 423

B

background music
adding, to project 139-142
using 142
Big Buttons Bar (BBB) 7
branching
about 20, 211
Buttons, using 219, 220
Drag and Drop interaction, using 238-241
breakpoints
about 330-332
adjusting 333, 334
Buttons
formatting 214-216
Image Buttons, searching 216
Smart Shapes, using as 216-219
used, for branching 219-221
working with 212-214

C

Captivate
about 2
and Photoshop, Round Tripping 463, 464
and PowerPoint, Round Tripping 446-448
benefits 439
controlling, during shooting session 45, 46
documentation, URL 541
existing presentation, converting to 440
Geolocation 516
Help page, URL 482
in TCS 4
integrating, with PowerPoint 440-453
interface 6

objects 76
obtaining 2
panning feature, using 32
perpetual license 2
Photoshop file, importing 457-462
pre-work 72
reporting, enabling 423
sound clip, editing 156-158
subscription 3
subscription model, URL 3
Text Effects 116
updating 351
URL 566
used, for recording narration 143
Captivate 8
standalone application, publishing 581
Captivate 8.0.1 205
Captivate capture engine
FMR mode 43-45
implications 42
working 41, 42
Captivate interface
about 6-9
advanced interface mode, using 10-12
Big Buttons Bar (BBB) 7
custom workspaces, deleting 15, 16
custom workspaces, renaming 15, 16
Menu bar 7
new workspace, creating 14, 15
normal interface mode 16, 17
panels, working with 12, 13
summarizing 9
workspace, creating 13
Captivate perpetual license
about 2
URL 2, 3
Captivate project
application, resetting 37
application to record, preparing 34, 35
camera tricks 51
creating, from PowerPoint
    presentation 441-446
eLearning-enabled project, publishing 571
exporting, to Adobe Flash
    Professional 468-470
exporting, to XML 471
localizing, with Microsoft Word 454-457

movie, recording 37
Multi SCO packager, working with 574
other versions, recording 51-53
PowerPoint slide, inserting 450-454
publishing 560
publishing, as .mp4 video file 582
publishing, as standalone application 580
publishing, to Flash 561-563
publishing, to HTML5 564
publishing, to Microsoft Word 585, 586
publishing, to PDF 579, 580
publishing, to YouTube 583, 584
recording 34
Responsive Project, publishing 568, 569
rushes, previewing 41
Scalable HTML content option, using 564
scenario, rehearsing 36
second rushes, reviewing 54, 55
URL 471
Captivate project, publishing to HTML5
about 565
HTML5 Tracker panel, using 565, 566
steps 566-568
Click Boxes
branching with 249
Failure Caption 248
Hint Caption 248
remaining Click Boxes, adding 252
sizing 248
Success Caption 248
working with 247, 248
Click Boxes, branching
about 249
feedback messages, working with 249, 250
slideless branching, arranging 250, 251
Closed Captions
adding, to slides 160-163, 167
adding, to video file 164-166
viewing 163, 164
Conditional Action
necessary variables, creating 491-493
objects, displaying 497-503
objects, hiding 497-503
objects, naming 495-497
score, assigning 493, 494

used, for branching
    implementation 503-505
using 490
content, Responsive Project
adding 345
excluding, from other views 353-356
excluding, from views 352, 353
percent, positioning 365-367
percent relative positioning 368
pixel, positioning 365-368
positioning 358
remaining arrows, creating 357, 358
responsive image, creating 359-362
responsive text, creating 362-365
sizing 358
Smart Position, using 369-372
view hierarchy 346
Creative Cloud
and Adobe Edge Inspect 343
customized progress indicator
URL 410
custom swatches
importing, to panel 264
custom Theme
creating 289
Master Slides of Theme, customizing 290

D

decision 501
demonstration 17, 26
desktop-first approach 346
differentiated instruction
about 221
URL 221
Drag and Drop interaction
in HTML 238
used, for branching 238
used, for navigation 238
wizard, using 234-236
working with 233, 234
Drag and Drop panel
using 237, 238
Drag Source 233
Driving in Belgium application 21, 22
Drop Target 233

E

Edge Inspect mobile application
URL 342
effects
adding, to images 206, 207
adding, to objects 203, 204
combining 205, 206
in HTML5 208
eLearning assets
URL, for download 96
eLearning-enabled project
publishing 571
SCORM package Flash version,
publishing 573
SCORM package, publishing in
HTML5 572, 573
slides, displaying 571
slides, hiding 571
elements, Question Slides
styling 419, 420
embedded presentation 443
Encoder demonstration 17-19
Encoder simulation 20, 21
Encoder Video Demo 24-26
Equation editor
using 114, 115
Experience API (xAPI) 423
external animations
Flash animations, importing 126-128
HTML5 animations, importing 129-133
inserting, into project 126

F

Fill-In-The-Blank questions
working with 398-400
Find and Replace feature 211
finishing touches
about 532
accessibility 538-541
project metadata, using 538-541
project preferences, exploring 542, 543
project preferences, exporting 543, 544
project Skin, customizing 545
same Skin, applying to other
projects 557-559

spelling, checking 532-535
Start and End preferences,
exploring 536-538
Flash
Captivate project, publishing to 561-563
Flash animations
importing 126-128
in HTML5 129
Flash Video (flv)
about 133
URL 134
Flattened Image 460
Full Motion Recording (FMR)
editing 124-126
mode, limitations 45
mode 43-45

G

gallery 138
General Import Format Technology. *See*
GIFT file
Geolocation, Adobe Captivate
about 516
content based, altering 520, 521
custom Geolocation variable,
creating 518, 519
extra slide, inserting 516
learner location, detecting 517
GIFT file
about 392
Question Slides, importing 391
URL 391
Going Mobile responsive application
about 22-24
URL 24
Google Chrome
URL 342

H

Highlight Box
about 83
replacing 112
Smart Shapes, using as 110-112
Hotspot questions
working with 400, 401

HTML5
    animations, importing 129-133
    Captivate project, publishing to 565
    URL 561

I

images
    characters, working with 96-98
    editing tools, using 94
    end images, inserting, in Video Demo
        project 315
    inserting, in Video Demo project 314
    inserting, on slide 93, 94
    picture slide, inserting 95, 96
    slide, inserting from another project 92
    types 93
    working with 92
Import from Photoshop feature 458
Interaction ID 423

L

Learning Management System. *See* **LMS**
Learning Record Store (LRS) 423
library
    external assets, importing 174-176
    items, reusing 177
    objects, importing from another library 178
    unused assets, deleting 178, 179
    working with 172-174
Library panel
    working with 172-174
Likert questions
    reporting, to LMS 404
    used, for creating surveys 403
Lilybiri
    URL 516
LMS
    about 421
    AICC 422
    scores, reporting 421
    SCORM 422
    Tin Can 422
    URL 422

M

Mac
    shortcuts 40
Macromedia Captivate 1
Main Master Slide 284
manual panning 61-63
Master Slides
    about 284
    applying, to slides 295
    based slides, creating 285
    blank slide, inserting in themed project 287
    changing, of existing slide 285-287
    modifying 296, 297
    Placeholders, adding 294
Master Slides, Theme
    customizing 290
    ending slide, creating 295
    Main Master Slide, customizing 291, 292
Matching question
    working with 392, 393
MathMagic 114
metadata 538
Microsoft Word
    Captivate project, publishing to 585
    used, for localizing Captivate
        project 454-457
Modal floating panel 19
Moodle
    about 422
    URL 422, 431
mouse
    formatting 89-91
    movements 86-89
    right pointer, selecting 91
    working with 86
movie recording
    about 37
    assistive devices access, enabling 38
    sequence, recording 38-40
Multiple Choice question
    basic question properties 385, 386
    Partial Scoring, working with 387
    Smart Shapes, using as feedback
        messages 390
    using 384, 385

Multi SCO packager
SCORM package, creating from Video Demo project 574-576
URL 579
used, for creating single-course package 576-578
using, considerations 579
working with 574

N

narration
generating, with Text-to-Speech engine 150
recording 145-147
recording, with Captivate 143
sound system, setting up 143-145
voice, recording 147

O

objects
Align toolbar, using 183
default timing, adjusting 194
displaying, with Timeline 192
effects, adding 203, 204
grouping 181, 182
hiding, with Timeline 192
importing, from another library 178
inserting, in Video Demo project 315, 316
laying out, on slides 180
locking, with Timeline 190-192
positioning 199-201
remaining objects, aligning 186
remaining objects, distributing 186
selecting, with Timeline 189
slide timing, adjusting 202
Smart Guides, using 180, 181
stacking order, changing with Timeline 192, 193
summarizing 187, 188
syncing 199-201
syncing, tips 195
Sync with Playhead feature, using 196-198
timing, setting with Timeline 193-195
unlocking, with Timeline 190-192
objects, Captivate
Equation editor 114
Highlight Box 83

images 92
mouse 86
Smart Shapes 103
Text Animations 98
Text Caption 76
Object Style Manager
about 275
style, creating 279-281
style, exporting 277-281
style, importing 278-281
styles, renaming 275-277
working with 275

P

Partial Scoring
about 387
working with 387
PDF
Captivate project, publishing to 579, 580
Photoshop
about 457
and Captivate, Round Tripping 463, 464
file, examining 459
importing, into Captivate 457-462
postproduction phase, Video Demo project
about 313
objects, adding 314
Pan & Zoom animation, adding 317-319
Transition, adding 319-321
unwanted popups, removing 316, 317
PowerPoint
and Captivate, Round Tripping 446-448
Captivate, integrating with 440-453
importing, versus animating native Captivate objects 454
presentation, Captivate project creating 441
presentation, viewing 441
slide, inserting in Captivate project 450-453
presentation, updating 448-450
Pretest questions
creating 406-408
Progress Indicator 385
project
rescaling 67
project Skin
Borders 545

Borders, working with 550-552
customizing 545
Playback Controls bar, customizing 546-550
Playback Controls bar element 545
Table of Contents 545
Table of Contents, adding 552-557
Properties panel
used, for managing styles 267
working with 72-75
Publish for Devices (app) feature
using 586-591
publishing process 531

Q

Question Pools
creating 414, 415
questions, inserting 416
random Question Slides, inserting 417, 418
working with 414
Question Slides
about 377
branching with 388, 389
creating 380
elements, styling 419, 420
Fill-In-The-Blank questions,
    working with 398, 399
finalizing 389
first Question Slide, inserting 380-384
Hotspot questions, working with 400, 401
importing, from GIFT file 391, 392
Likert questions, used for creating
    surveys 403-405
Matching questions, working with 392, 393
Multiple Choice question, using 384
remaining Question Slides, adding 398
Sequence questions, working with 402, 403
Short Answer questions,
    working with 394-396
True/False questions,
    working with 396, 397
URL 380
visibility, turning off 384
visibility, turning on 384
quiz
about 378
inserting 378, 379

preferences 408
previewing 405
quiz preferences
about 409, 410
options 408
passing score, setting 411-414

R

Rating Scale (Likert) question 403
recording preferences
automatic recording modes,
    exploring 47-49
exploring 47
recording settings, exploring 50
Video Demo preferences pane 50
reporting, Captivate
enabling 423
options, at interaction level 423
project-level reporting options,
    setting up 431-433
random Question Slides 424
SCORM manifest file, creating 434, 435
reporting options, at interaction level
about 423
Drag and Drop interaction, using as
    Question Slide 425-429
random Question Slides, reporting 424
scorable objects, using 429, 430
responsive capture 63-66
responsive design
URL 328
Responsive Project
about 327, 328
breakpoints 330, 331
breakpoints, adjusting 333, 334
content, adding 345
content, positioning 358
content, sizing 358
Mobile Palette, using 568, 569
previewing 18
publishing, steps 568-571
responsive theme, applying 336-338
setting up 332, 333
slide height, adjusting 334-336
testing 339
testing, in authoring environment 339

testing, in browser 340, 341
testing, with Adobe Edge Inspect 341
using 33
viewport size, versus screen size 329, 330
reverse engineering 127
Rollover Area 221
Rollover Caption
working with 221-223
Rollover Image
working with 226-228
Rollover objects
discovering 221
Rollover Captions, working with 221-223
Rollover Images, working with 226-228
Rollover Slidelets, working with 228
Rollover Smart Shapes, working
with 223-226
Rollover Slidelet
formatting 228-230
inserting 228-230
objects, inserting 231-233
URL 233
working with 228
Rollover Smart Shapes
working with 223-226
Rotation 405
Round Tripping
about 446
between Captivate, and Photoshop 463, 464
between Captivate,
and PowerPoint 446-448
rushes
about 29
previewing 41

S

sample applications
Driving in Belgium application 21
Encoder demonstration 17
Encoder simulation 20
Encoder Video Demo 24-26
exploring 17
Going Mobile responsive application 22-24
sample apps scenario 27
Scalable HTML Content feature
using 33

SCORM
about 422
manifest file, creating 434, 435
URL 422
SCORM packages
creating, from Video Demo project 574, 575
publishing, in HTML5 572, 573
testing, URL 573
screen sizes
URL 34
Sequence questions
working with 402, 403
Sharable Content
Object (SCO) 434, 574, 579
Sharable Content Object Reference Model.
See **SCORM**
Shared Action
about 506
creating 509-511
objects, naming 507
reusing 512-515
saving 511, 512
slides, importing 506, 507
URL 514
using 512, 513
variables, creating 507-509
Shared Advanced Actions
URL 514
Short Answer questions
working with 394, 395
simulation
about 20, 26
Click Boxes, working with 247, 248
creating 242
Find and Replace, using 245, 246
Mouse object, hiding 243
project title, replacing 244
summarizing 256, 257
Text Entry Boxes, working with 252-255
video file, replacing 244, 245
Skin 289
Skin Editor 163
slide capture project
application, downsizing 31
Captivate panning feature, using 32
guidelines 33, 34
issue, describing 30, 31

resizing, after initial shooting 31
responsive project, using 33
right resolution, selecting 30
Scalable HTML Content feature, using 33
slide labels 555
Slide Notes panel
working with 150, 151
slides
audio, adding 143
Closed Captions, adding to 160-163
Smart Guides
about 94
using 180, 181
Smart Learning Interactions
Accordion Interaction,
working with 522-524
Award of Excellence Interaction, working
with 527
reference links 527
Web Object Interaction,
working with 525-527
working with 521
Smart Position
applying, to other objects 373, 374
using 369-373
Smart Shapes
creating 106
custom shape, modifying 107, 108
custom shape, saving 108, 109
drawing 103-105
Highlight Box, replacing 112
saving 106
text, adding inside 112, 113
using, as Buttons 216-219
using, as Highlight Box 110-112
working with 103
sound clip, Captivate
editing 156-158
speech agents
about 150
URL, for download 150
standalone application
Captivate project, publishing as 580-582
Standard Action
used, for automatically turning off Closed
Captions 489

used, for automatically turning on Closed
Captions 486-489
using 486
style override 268
styles
adding, to Theme 298
applying 269
applying automatically 270-273
creating, for another object type 273, 274
managing, with Properties panel 267, 268
modifying 270
new Styles, creating 269
Object style Manager, working with 275
remaining objects, styling 300
resetting 268
working with 267
submit button
hiding 241
Swatch 263
Swatch Manager
about 261
custom colors, using 264-266
custom swatches, importing 266, 267
custom swatches, importing to panel 264
working with 262, 263
System Audio
URL 56
used, for recording 55-58
System Variables
about 477
exploring 477-479

T

Technical Communication Suite (TCS)
about 4
Captivate 4
URL 4
Template
creating 302-304
last slides, adding 305
Placeholder Slides, adding 304, 305
saving 306
used, for creating Captivate
project 306-308
working with 302

text
converting, to speech 152-154
Text Animations
slides, duplicating 100, 101
Typing object, converting into 101, 102
working with 98, 99
Text Caption
Callout, changing 81
caption type, changing 81
character, formatting 82
content, modifying 76, 77
formatting 80
paragraph, formatting 82
text captions, creating 78, 79
text captions, moving 80, 81
text captions, resizing 80
using 76
Text Effects
working with 116-119
Text Entry Boxes
used, for capturing values 483, 484
Text-to-Speech engine
Captivate speech agents, installing 150
Slide Notes panel, working with 150, 151
Speech Management window,
using 154, 155
using 150
versus manual voice-over recording 154
Theme
about 282
applying, to existing project 282
applying, to project 301
elements 284
Master Slide, adding 292, 293
Master Slides panel 284
styles 288, 289
styles, saving 301
working with 282
Timeline, using
for setting object timing 193-195
for displaying objects 192
for hiding objects 192
for locking objects 190, 191
for object selection 189
for stacking order modification 192
for unlocking objects 190, 191
working with 189

Tin Can
about 422, 423
URL 423
Title Smart Shape
Master Slide objects,
placing on top 299, 300
styling 298, 299
Transition
about 319
adding 319-321
True/False questions
working with 396
typical production workflow
about 4
editing phase 5
preproduction phase 4
publishing phase 5
slide, capturing 5
Typing object
converting, into Text Animation 101, 102

U

User Variables
about 477
creating 482
user-defined variables, using 484, 485
using 482
values, capturing with Text Entry
Boxes 483

V

variables
components, name 477
components, value 477
naming 493
Quiz Results slide for Pretest,
generating 481
System Variables 477
text, generating dynamically 479-481
User Variables 477
working with 476, 477
vector object 107
video
working with 133-136
Video Demo project
about 311

end images, inserting 315
images, inserting 314
interface 312, 313
objects, adding 314
objects, inserting 315, 316
postproduction phase 313
publishing 321, 322
publishing, to YouTube 323
recording mode 58-60
themes 316
view hierarchy
about 346, 347
desktop-first approach 346
text content, adding in
  Responsive Project 347
text content, relinking 352
views, relinking 348-351
viewport size
URL 329-339
versus screen size 329, 330

W

Web Accessibility Initiative (WAI) 539
Web Object Interaction
working with 525, 526

workspace
about 13
creating 13-15
custom workspaces, deleting 15
custom workspaces, renaming 15
in normal mode 16, 17
preparing 172, 212
World Wide Web Consortium (W3C)
URL 539

X

XML
Captivate project, exporting to 471

Y

YouTube
Captivate project, publishing to 583, 584
URL 323, 324, 590
Video Demo project, publishing 323

[PACKT] Thank you for buying
PUBLISHING
Mastering Adobe Captivate 8

About Packt Publishing

Packt, pronounced 'packed', published its first book, *Mastering phpMyAdmin for Effective MySQL Management*, in April 2004, and subsequently continued to specialize in publishing highly focused books on specific technologies and solutions.

Our books and publications share the experiences of your fellow IT professionals in adapting and customizing today's systems, applications, and frameworks. Our solution-based books give you the knowledge and power to customize the software and technologies you're using to get the job done. Packt books are more specific and less general than the IT books you have seen in the past. Our unique business model allows us to bring you more focused information, giving you more of what you need to know, and less of what you don't.

Packt is a modern yet unique publishing company that focuses on producing quality, cutting-edge books for communities of developers, administrators, and newbies alike. For more information, please visit our website at www.packtpub.com.

Writing for Packt

We welcome all inquiries from people who are interested in authoring. Book proposals should be sent to author@packtpub.com. If your book idea is still at an early stage and you would like to discuss it first before writing a formal book proposal, then please contact us; one of our commissioning editors will get in touch with you.

We're not just looking for published authors; if you have strong technical skills but no writing experience, our experienced editors can help you develop a writing career, or simply get some additional reward for your expertise.

Adobe Captivate 7 for Mobile Learning

ISBN: 978-1-84969-955-6   Paperback: 136 pages

Create mobile-friendly and interactive m-learning content with Adobe Captivate 7

1. Explore the various ways to bring your eLearning content to mobile platforms.

2. Create a high definition screencast and upload it to YouTube.

3. Create mobile-friendly and interactive software demonstrations and SCORM-compliant quizzes.

Mastering Adobe Premiere Pro CS6 HOTSHOT

ISBN: 978-1-84969-478-0   Paperback: 284 pages

Take your video editing skills to new and exciting levels with eight fantastic projects

1. Discover new workflows and the exciting new features of Premiere Pro CS6.

2. Take your video editing skills to exciting new levels with clear, concise instructions (and supplied footage).

3. Explore powerful time-saving features that other users don't even know about!

4. Work on actual real-world video editing projects such as short films, interviews, multi-cam, special effects, and the creation of video montages.

Please check **www.PacktPub.com** for information on our titles

Learning Adobe Edge Animate

ISBN: 978-1-84969-242-7   Paperback: 368 pages

Create engaging motion and rich interactivity with Adobe Edge Animate

1. Master the Edge Animate interface and unleash your creativity through standard HTML, CSS, and JavaScript.

2. Packed with an abundance of information regarding the Edge Animate application and related toolsets.

3. Robust motion and interactivity through web standards.

Fast Track to Adobe Captivate 6 [Video]

ISBN: 978-1-84969-953-2   Duration: 02:15 hours

Get to grips with the basics of using Adobe Captivate 6 to create your own interactive e-learning and m-learning content right away

1. Engage learners by inserting aesthetically-pleasing interactive content into your course with out-of-the-box interactions such as an animated rollover, process circle, and timeline using Adobe Captivate 6.

2. Quickly convert PowerPoint slides including objects, animations, and multimedia into rich interactive presentations using an improved conversion library.

Made in the USA
San Bernardino, CA
03 February 2017